Lingua Tersancta, Or, a Most Sure and Compleat Allegorick Dictionary to the Holy Language of the Spirit
by William Freke

Address:
HardPress
8345 NW 66TH ST #2561
MIAMI FL 33166-2626
USA
Email: info@hardpress.net

tinued Providence evidenced hereby, both to receive juſt and ſolid Comfort under their ſeveral Afflictions, and withal, with the greater Vigor to fly to thee their only Safety and Deliverer.

And thus mayſt thou at length crown us as with the Deſcent of thy *New Jeruſalem* among us, and whereby both thou and thy Chriſt may again at length vouchſafe as to inhabit among us ; and while theſe mine Inſtructions, as a little Mite out of thine holy Treaſury, even as in the Spirit of *Elijah*, renew and inflame to us the decay'd and loſt Zeal of thy Servants, confounding the petty Cavils and Prejudices, as well of *Turks*, *Jews* as Infidels, againſt thy holy Jeſus, and eſtabliſhing as for ever and ever as well our own Chriſtian Peace, amidſt all our ſeveral Schiſms, Diviſions and Animoſities, as amongſt all Men ſuch a Brotherly Love as may correſpond to thine holy Will and Commandments.

To Thee, and beſides whom nothing is, much leſs may pretend to either of Glory or Power, but at thy Pleaſure, be all Honour and Glory both now and for ever more.

TO

To the READER.

AS the Subject I am delivering is for the most part new and surprizing, so it seems not a Design likely to be unacceptable, that I as in the Entrance thereof, give the Reader a little Account of my self and the Author therein.

And if any shall conceive that I do this by way of Pride, I shall only retort to him by this single Question, As where is his Charity? But if any thing Personal in me may be of Instruction to the Reader, in that I am sure I cannot miscarry, while I am delivering it thus, no more than in accommodating him with the same Matter in Precepts only.

For my Birth and Temporal Station, I conceive it avails but little to relate thereof; but for the Frame of my Mind 'thas been always this, I always follow'd what I thought most Virtuous, True and Good, with a Courage undaunted, from my Infancy to this very Hour; and if I may be happy by this Skill to bless Mankind, this alone is the Clue I can prescribe whereby Almighty God has led me to it.

To be singular, exploded of all, wondred at by all, is no Novelty to me; the Iron Link of Sincerity which I have hitherto held, and I hope in God shall to my last Day, has made all this Treatment familiar to me, but not without Uneasiness enough, all may guess: for who would choose so to think and so to act, as to be always separate and sequestred from others, and as a Bird in the Wilderness?

And yet to let all Men see that God suffers no such Conditions for his and Pieties sake to any Man in vain, the Converse you see I have thus lost with Men, I have got again from God himself, and from above: In Truth I may say, by this my Skill has he comforted me, or else surely of all Men I both had been and were the most miserable.

My Friends also, I bless his Divine Majesty, as by a singular Virtue and Charity, he has all along inspired with a kind Tenderness to me notwithstanding; they, to do them most of them Justice, as conscious of the like possible Virtue in themselves, have as even against Hope allowed me not only all common Regards in this State, but truly a good Friendship withal.

A

The common Topick of the Improbability of my Designs, and Courses in the Ballance of Human Reasoning, has not had the Effect to suppress their kinder Engagements to me from Blood and Relation; no, on the contrary, as if led by an Invincibility of Virtue, they have continued their Affections to me, and that tho but upon the bare Possibility of my virtual Correspondence thereto.

Besides, that Natural Obstinacy of Temper that Virtue and Religion necessarily inspires Men with, how often has it been offensive in me? Not to mention the continual Irregularities and Offensiveness of my Studies and Actions, quite excentrick to the common Rules of Prudence of the World, and of Consequence most ungrateful to all such Friends as seek or study our Good.

I were to be wicked indeed, not to suppose my self to have acted to the best in all I have done; but alas what is that to the matter? Is it not too often the Fault of most good Men to offend by Positiveness and Dogmaticalness? and in that can I say, I have been spotless in my Methods?

The brightest Truths without their Veils, are they not intolerable? and tho we are sure we are in the right, will either Religion or Gratitude permit us to appear with other than the greatest Modesty to our Friends in such Truths, and till such time as we are in a Capacity to impart to such our Friends our own full Convictions also?

Nor has this been all neither, have I been able to flatter or use Arts of Dissimulation to rectify such unhappy Conditions where they have happened? No, on the contrary, an unlucky Fire of Disposition, and that could never correct it self by a Repentance inconsistent with Virtue, has hurried me on as further and further in such Circumstances, and as if it were possible to render me unworthy of all Regard and Esteem with them.

But on the contrary, these my Friends, as if good only for Goodness sake, and tho above all likely Recompence from me, yet how have they acted as towards me hereon? why truly they have had a Patience and Charity towards me, as if they would see every Ember of glowing Virtue extinguished in me e'er they would desert me; and since they have, what other Acknowledgment can I make thereof than such a Memorial as this, and which I must needs owe to the very Virtue it self in them, if not the Persons?

The Fulsom Idolatry of Dedications for it, indeed is an Incense I cannot offer; the Majesty Divine must and cannot but have all the ultimate States and Posts of my Honours and Regards: but he the Fountain of Virtue loves Virtue, and he it is, who tho he may restrain me in Gratitude, yet withal admits me not to receive Benefits, and yet remain only in an ungrateful Insensibility.

Be ye then as standing Monumental Exemplary Bulwarks to a poor and helpless distressed Sincerity; and as the Woman who anointed our Saviour to his Funeral, was to have a Memorial therefore lasting as the Gospel, so may all Men learn from hence from you, that to encourage Virtue in all Forms, and even against all Hopes, is withal of it self the greatest Virtue, I may call it the Mother Virtue, and that gives Life to such nobler further Seeds of Virtue as else would needs perish in their Conceptions.

To

To be brief, I come, as hal'd by Duty and in Chains, and like Jonas in an ungrateful Meſſage, to publiſh my Skill, oppreſt with Labours, a Spectacle for Singularity, and a By-Word for the Mocker; but I am ſincere, at leaſt I think my ſelf ſo: I pretend to no more than I think I can anſwer; and you alſo, however my Performances may anſwer, muſt at leaſt be acknowledged by all, to have acquitted your ſelves to the utmoſt; and while the Praiſe of Prefaces, that too commonly like Frankincenſe amidſt dead Corpſes, is made to divert the Stenches that would be otherwiſe intolerable to you, becomes but as a Debt, and that as in Duty neither to God nor Man I ought to deny you.

But I'le divert my Reader in theſe Matters no longer, I'le only acquaint him with a ſingle Advice concerning the enſuing Volume, and conclude.

When on Peruſal of this Dictionary, a vaſt and mighty Latitude in the ſeveral Symbols thereof preſent unto him, I would not have him diſmayed or diſcouraged thereat, and as if little Certainty therefore were to be expected thereon: For Inſtance, in the Symbol of God, the very firſt that preſents, is there not of the greateſt Variety imaginable therein?

And thus is it not ſometimes literal and abſolute of the true God, ſometimes Allegorick and correſpondent to a leſſer Power in the falſe Gods? and ſo is it not ſometimes Allegorick of Husbands, Prieſts, Kings, Governments, &c. yea and ſometimes of the very Devil?

To aſſiſt in this Variety and Latitude therefore, I thought it neceſſary here to acquaint my Reader, that conſiſts the whole end of my Grammar: and as to ſhew the ſame Rules over and over again herein, I thought would be tedious, and render my Dictionary too voluminous; ſo I concluded my beſt Courſe would be to model all ſuch Obſervations into one common Rule of Grammar apart, and which on Examination might facilitate to the Reader theſe and all the like Difficulties whatever.

　　　　　　　　　　　　　　　　　　　　　　　　　Farewel.

Lingua Tersancta.

CHAP. I.
Of SPIRITS.

GOD.
(1)

C Hrift. Vid. *Religion:*
Holy Ghoft, or a white Pigeon feeing, gives of Devotion with focial Succefs.

See defcend on you, your felf act as a publick Preacher, as Chrift did.

Falfe one, as a Devil feen, has fhewn of Riches.

Heathen or Popifh feen, fhew and have fhewn good or bad, as their Offices.

Leffer Gods have fhewn of the leffer Priefts. *Vid. Saints* in *Dead.*

Seen fighting, have fhewn National Wars.

Sad or difconfolate, has fhewn of miferable Iffue.

Glad or profperous, has given all the Good of their Office.

In foreign Habit, has fhewn Good or Ill thence.

Difarm'd, or flinging away their Arms, fhews you helplefs.

Abfent on confulting, or pufhing you away, great Mifery to you.

Strike him in the Forehead with a Stone, to a Souldier die fo.

Sort. *Saturn* fupping with, fhew'd to one Imprifonment.

Neptune feen kind, gave one good by Fifhing.

Bacchus feen aiding, gave one good by others drinking.

Jupiter feen fend his Chariot to *Vefpafian,* fhew'd him after Emperor.

B

GOD. Falfe,

2

GOD Falſe. *Jupiter* ſeen ſend a young Woman to *Hannibal*, his Ca
(1)   tainſhip.

Shaking Hands with, to *Jul. Cæſar* Death.

Waſhing one as the Sun anointed him, the Gibb

· True in circumſtance proper, as Bleſſing on Prayer ; or appea
ing between the Cherubims or in his Temple, is ſt
literal of him, or elſe is allegorick.

In Majeſty to ſome, has ſhewn of the King or High Prie
to a Wife, her Husband's calling her to accour

Sarah call'd *Abraham* Lord. ⎰ Scripture Allego
Have I not ſaid ye are Gods ? ⎱ Gods.
Satan the God of this World. ⎰

Accompanying him not ſpeaking, Death.

Acting to many, what the King or Government ſhall do.

Advice. Vid. *ſpeak* infrà.

Angry. Vid. *ſpeak* infrà.

Beating you, Death : Who can bear Infinity ?

Whipping *A.* his Sickneſs ; but departing ſmiling on'
with his Recovery.

Calling out to him. Vid. *Prayer* in *Religion*.

Doing things ſeen, if poſſible, they are done.

If impoſſible, it ſhews of ſomewhat unexpected.

Entring a Houſe with him, threats Death or great Sickneſ
And not return, evade great Danger of Death nea

Hearing him, gives Secrets, and an obedient holy Life.

Houſe. Vid. *Enter* ſuprà.

Join Right Hands with him, die.

Made one ſeem your ſelf, to the Rich Power.
to the Poor Riches.

Godlike in Veſture, the ſame in repute only.

Praying. Vid. *Religion*.

Receiving from him, is perfect Health, *& è contra.*
impure things, is Diſeaſes and Woe.

Seeing him, to ſome Death or grievous Sickneſs.
to ſome, gives the beginning of true Wiſdor
and Learning.
to ſome it diſcovers Secrets, and changes Lit
for the better.

Speaking heard, ſhews all Truth ; but if to others, beſt.
To ſome, Good from their King, Prince or Prieſ
To him ſhews the beginning of Prophecy.

Bleſſing you, unleſs literal, may ſhew you kind to you
Miniſter.

Condemn'd of him, has ſhewn the like of the King or State

Curſing God, threats with extremeſt Miſery.

Forgiven by him, pardon'd by the King or State.

Lamenting heard has ſhewn of publick Ills, and a wicke
Prince.

GOD Tru

GOD True. Pitying you, threats you extremest Miseries juslty.
(1)
Promising kindly, shews of greatest publick Blessings
answerable.

Threatning you, shews of some exceeding great Ill.
Unknown Words from him, Death, as your *Mene Tekel:*
But Threats or Hopes forgot, not to be.

's Voice hear in general, live well, and understand Secrets.
Unknown. Vid. *Threats* suprà.

Impostures are either in circumstance unproper, or thro
Voices unknown heard from Heaven.

Stretching out his Hand to you gives you Aid, Joy and
Success.

Trusting in him, gives assur'd Deliverance, as is the Ill.

Taking from us is horrible, as receiving of him is excellent.
Unpleasant seen to you, ill.

's Ways or Fences seeing, has shewn of hearing of some
of his Judgments.

Worshipping him in general shews greatest Joy.
　　Vid. also *Religion.*

Changing his Worship, to a King, Tyranny.
　　　　　　　　to a Noble, Rebellion.
　　　　　　　　to a common Person, Perjury.
　　　　　　　　to a Wife, Adultery.

Despising him, shews of greatest Misery or Good.
God seen sacrifice to God, greatest Heresy and Change.
Vows and Offerings making, shews of Love and Di-
lection.

Spirits seen generally shew of Cheats from their Uncertainty ; and as
(2)　neither Angels nor Devils, but Spirit in the Church or in
circumstance proper, and as in the Scriptures, does often
shew of the Holy Ghost.

Shap'd, and so also is the Course of such Tricks.
like an old Man, in doting Courses.
like a Woman, in false Opinions.
like *J. S.* an Atheist, in Atheism.
like *R.* a Diviner, in Divination.

Sort. *B*'s Spirit *A.* cry'd out on, as carrying her away, she remov'd, fearing his Cheats in Love.

In comely Aspect and white, a Cheat too, but giving Conso-
lation.

Deform'd and black, Deceit, with Temptation to Sin.
　　Vid. *Angel* and *Devil* infrà.

's Child see Command, the Hopes of Delusions.
Invisible Spirit, a most secret Cheat not to be trac'd.
　　Vid. *Hear* in *Sense.*

Ill one hindred *A.* in ringing a Bell, a Cheat frustrated his
publick Dealings.

To a Minister, profitless Labours with his Parishioners.

Spirits. Sort. Ill one stop'd *A.* as going down stairs, a Cheat baulks
(2) his Designs from Action.

—— in a good Work, a Hypocrite interrupted him in't.

Acts in general. Vid. *Witchcraft* infra.

Become one, that is, be deem'd a Cheat.

Catches your Hand, Imputation of a Cheat stops your Actions.

Conjure many troubling you, forswear being a Cheat.

Adjure one, act with a Piety commanding according.

Conjuring Book reading, teasing men up to fatal Quarrels.

A Spirit appearing, the Quarrel issuing on't.

Abjure. Vid. *Words* in *Discourse.*

Discoursing one, discovers Secrets and Masters Cheats.

Encompassed by you, reputed all over a Cheat.

Free shake hands with one, allow your self to be cheated.

Frighted by one, in terror of a subtle Cheat.

Heard in the dark, foreshew'd of Caterwauling Night-tricks.

Lying with. Vid. *Bodily Action.*

Seeing them only, shews of a bold Courage and clear Conscience, as daring Cheats.

Teas'd by a Spirit, under continual Solicitations of Cheating, *&c.*

to rise from Bed, to cease quiet Repose
therefore, *&c.*

Like a Man's Finger punching you by
frequent rational Items.

Walk with one, Design in a self-deluding Course.

Angel. A Spirit shews of a Cheat at large, so an Angel of a private
(3) Cheat temporal for the sake of a Divine Message ; and as
a Devil, the like by reason of Despair. The Difference is
this : A Message from the Spirit, if in circumstance, is
more august and general, and as from an Angel, is more
particular. And as thus the Dispensation of the Prophets
was by Angels, and whilst that of Christ was by the Spirit :
So also a peculiar Purity or Sacrifice is met in us by an
Angel ; but a general or universal one only by God himself, and his Spirit.

Like a Boy, embrace Command, as to inherit Divine Messages.

Child, still good ; but bearded, as observ'd, never seen.

Man where regular as in its nature, an active Course.

Woman see, that is, command an Angelick Science.

seen to *Hannibal,* shew'd of his War to answer
his Father's Vow.

One seen purely and no more, to some good News.

Before them such good News approaching.

To some shews of happy Messages and Attorneys.

To some, Messages from God, as in circumstance.

Vid. *Vision* & *Apparition.*

Angel.

Angel. Many feen in a Room with you, good.

(3) But with deform'd Figures among 'em, has fhewn Treafon. Afcend and defcend from Heaven by a Ladder, *Jacob*'s Divine Converfe to himfelf and Pofterity.

Fly o'er your Houfe, gives you of all Joy and Comfort near.

An half-Angel ftands in *A*'s way, a pretended Divine Meffage offer'd to obftruct him.

Become one your felf, fortunates you in Meffages Divine and Human.

Cloth'd in yellow feen, fhew'd of a Plague Infection. V. *Great* inf.

Encouraging you, fome Divine prefum'd Meffage heartning you.

Defcending from Heaven cloth'd yellow, a Plague Infection menacing.

Free with one, that is, frequent in Divine Monitions.

Great *A.* call'd by thrice, anfwer'd, he could not come ; efcaping a Plague Infection.

Leading you, fills you with Grace.

Leaving you fhews you ceafe to act as a Divine Mcffenger.

Speaking to one, gives them Wifdom, and partakes them in Divine Meffages.

to St. *Paul* one faid, *God has given thee all have fail'd with thee*, Acts 27. That is, his Apoftlefhip was their Delverance.

Stops you in fome Work, and the like does your Divine Meffage Prefumption.

Travail with one, that is, your felf defign, as if you were fuch a Meffenger from God.

Genius or Guardian is a Divine Energy more peculiar to our private (4) Being or Felicity, and as Angel fhews of a Meffage more at large.

Seen, fhews of a Divine fatal Notice imparted us according.

Defcend from Heaven and call one, fhew'd him of his Death near.

Good on embracing, fhews of fome exceeding Good approaching.

Shewing me Funeral Tickets chang'd to blank Paper, fhew'd me of a neareft fick Friend recovering.

Ill feen depart, fhews of fome great Ill removing.

Forcing you, threats you mentally conftrain'd to an unhappy Courfe.

Cherubims feen are better than Angels, as fhewing of the immediate (5) Prefence of God.

Looking not well, threat you conform not well to the Divine Prefence.

Over your Chamber-door, forbidding your leaving that Managery.

a Church-door, the fame as, &c.

Apparitions fhew of Cheats, as do Spirits, but with more Inftability.

(6) feen to Lovers, threat them with Falfhood.

Apparitions.

Apparitions.   Viſions ſeen in a Dream are of danger to all.
(6)   They ſhew Acts on moſt apparent Self-deluſions.
                 A Woman meeting ſ. ſaid ſhe was an Apparition ; that is,
                   a Scheme offering him fair, would prove a Deluſion in
                   the end.
Devil ſeen, to moſt ſhews of Courſes to deſpair, and to the Sick Death.
(7)   to ſome, wicked Lords.
               to ſome, Thieves, Enemies, and Bailiffs.
               to ſome, Melancholy, Anger, Tumult, and Sickneſs.
    Shape. Fair and Godlike ſeen, he has ſhewn Riches.
            Naked, ſhews of Miſery, with Diſtreſs and Want.
            Great, powerful.
            Black and hideous, Deſpair, with wicked Horror.
            With Horns and Claws, beaſtly and cruel in Torments.
            Like a Man.   Vid. *Aſſaulted* infra.
                        Friendly a Courſe once menacing, Deſpair be-
                          coming profitable.
                        And Wife, a prejudice Conſpiracy Deſpair.
                   Boys ſee, command the Hopes or Inheritance of Con-
                     ſpirators or Deſpair.
                   A Woman, a Science or Church-Conſpiracy.
                   To him Girls would kill *A*'s Friend, that is, little Opinions
                     would curb *A*'s Freedom with him, as wicked.
          Aſſaulted by a Man-Devil, State Proſecutions menacing.
                   Woman Devil, Eccleſiaſtick, *&c.*
    Become Wood ſee, find your Fear of Deſpair become contemptible.
    Carrying one, to ill Men the Croſs.
                   to great Men, Danger of wild Beaſts.
          Carried away, by one has ſhewn of Temptation and Treachery.
                   To others it has ſhewn Ruin and Death near.
    Coming into his Chamber, and gathering, yelling about his Bed,
        Spira's Deſpair.
    Deſtroying a Platform of his, avoiding Death menacing.
    Fighting with one, threats greateſt Troubles of Mind, and Deſpair.
                   Beating him ſhews of overcoming Enemies.
                   Many ſeen together has ſhewn of Conteſts among ill Men.
    Flinging down part of your Houſe ſeen, one of your Family dies.
                   Threatning the whole, the Maſter himſelf near Death.
    Following you, Conſpiracy or Deſpair beſetting you.
    Haling him in hideous Shapes, K. *Richard* the 3*d*'s Fate the Eve
        e'er ſlain in Battel.
    Holding one's Hand ſeen, ſhew'd him his Servants leaving his Ser-
        vice in Diſtraction.
          Leaving your Palm, a Conſpiracy to rob you ceaſing.
    Howling hear, be ſenſible of diſmal Iſſues of Deſpair.
    Interrupting you ſeen, threats you ſome grievous Curſe.
    Looking out of your Chamber Window ſee, find of Conſpiracies
        againſt your Manageries.

                                                    Devil.

Devil. Many. Vid. *Fight* supra.

(7) Marrying one, threats with Horror and Death.

  Poffefs'd by one, gives you Benefit from your Prince, with long Life.

     To the Sick, Death with Horrour.

  Pofture. His Back toward you gives you advantage o'er fuch Defpair, &c.

  Putting on your Cloths feen, threats you with Defpair and Death.

  Speaking to you, threats you in Deceit, Temptation and Treachery,

    to fome, threats of their Death and Ruin near.

    Threatning to fome, Confpiracies and great Troubles of Mind.

      to others Dangers from Princes and Magiftrates.

  Standing before you fee, perceive of your Obftructions by Defpair and horrid Events.

  Teafing. Vid. *Vex* in *Paffion.*

  Vanifhes after fighting you, the Caufe of your Defpair ceafes,

  Walking Weft fee, find your Confpirator acts to his own detriment.

  Wreftling him, contending in Confpiracies and Defpair.

Heaven. Vid. *Air* poftea.

(8) Paradife feeing, promifes you Wifdom and Piety nigh to flourifh.

  Living in it fhews Celibacy.

  Being in it to fome, has fhewn of being of the College of Priefts.

  A Man feen let down thence, fhew'd of a good King and happy Kingdom ; but chain'd, a Tyrant, &c.

Hell feeing threats with Grief and Sadnefs,

(9) to fome it has fhewn of the King's Treafures.

  to fome it has fhewn greateft Hopes and Pleafures difappointed.

  Living, their Wickednefs.

  To the Judg, Injuftice.

  To the Wife, Adultery.

  To the Enterprizer, Error and Defpair.

  Suffering there, threats the Difcovery of fuch Wickednefs.

  Hearing Groans there, prefents with Admonitions to Repentance.

  Rifing thence with a Sword one feen, threated of a Tyrant.

    But he will end miferably.

  Defcend there and not return, Death, Gallies or Banifhment.

    To fome Mifery, Idlenefs, and Sicknefs.

    To the Retired and Students, Difcovery of Secrets,

    To the miferable, Privacy and Infenfibility.

    To the Superftitious, continued Ignorance.

  And return again, to the Rich Misfortune.

    to the Poor and Weak, Good.

Elyfian Fields fhew of Mifery and Temporal Delufion of Joy.

                  Ghoft,

Ghoſt.   Sort. Conquer'd Perſons ſeen, promiſes you the like Victory.
(10)   Known's ſeen, has foreſhewn of happy News from foreign Parts.

Neighbours alive eſcape from, avoid his Cheats againſt you.

Old man's threats you ; that is, you fear prejudice by ſome doting Methods.

Vid. alſo *Dead* poſtea.

Female tempts you to lie with her, ſome Cheat Opinion offers.

Embracing fondly, deſigning in Error to a Self-cheat.

Vaniſhing on refuſal ; that is, you avoid it on better Examination.

Your Wife coming in its place, rectified it, proving agreeable to your Art, &c.

Avoid in a Houſe ; that is, ſhun a Cheat in Oeconomy or Converſe.

Calling a Man off a Player's Stage ſeen to a Woman, loſe her Sweetheart by a Cheat.

Fighting, Controverſy in Cheats.

Frighted by one, the Terror of a Cheat approaching.

Paſs by one to the Eaſt in a broad Way, thro care eſcape Death.

A. ſees her little Ghoſt follow *B*'s great Ghoſt, *A.* a Child died ſoon after *B.*

Fairies ſeen, to ſome has ſhewn of reading Romances.
(11)   to ſome has ſhewn of Whores and Night Vagaries.

to all, as Enchantment, they beguile with vain Expectations.

Enchantment fearing, threats with Terrors of Deluſions.
(12)   Seeing ſhews of things preſenting, beguiling, Expectation and Sadneſs.

Hindring ſhews of baulking, beguiles and impoſes on you.

Being in, ſhews of Intanglement in vain Hopes, Secrets and Sorrows.

Haunted things ſeen, threat with Methods and Pleaſures prepar'd that vaniſh.

By the Dead, vex'd with People from home.

Spirits, vex'd with vain Imaginations and Diſappointments.

Vid. *Dead* & *Company.*

Abjure.   Vid. *Diſcourſe.*

Houſe being in ; that is, in an Oeconomy or Converſe not real or true.

In every Room, in every Relation or Subſiſtance anſwerable.

Witchcraft purſuing you, perverſe Troubles vexing you.
(13)   Perſecuting you, the ſame, but to worſe iſſue.

Prevailing, to ſome has ſhewn of Luſt or ill Fortune overpowering.

Witchcraft.

Witchcraft. Removed, such Obstructions cured.

(13) Hagrid, Vid. *Nightman* in *Sleep.*

Witch seen long invulnerable, shew'd of long incurable Vexations.

Drag'd to a Justice, shew'd of Happiness in a contrary course, or a thorough Cure near.

Stand in your Court, threats a Scandal, as bad obstruct Approaches to you.

Kill'd by your Prayers, threats of removing such ill Fortune to your Desires.

That you thought did you ill, shews of your contriving to evade such hurt.

White-Witch, shews as the other, but with a Veil of appearing Goodness.

's Imps wait to kill, that is, strive to prevent the Efforts of a most perverse Fortune.

Divination in general, shews of Divination.

(14) Diviners consulting, threat you greatest Cares and Troubles.

not answering you the worse and more durable. Vid. *Dreams* infra.

Aruspex being, foreshews a Man's being a Butcher, or a Murderer.

To others it has shewn mining and searching the Earth.

Auspicium foreshews all sorts of hunting and Prediction.

To others, great Cares, Foresights and Journies.

Astrology shews of Divine Prediction with Deceit.

To a Tradesman, Idleness in Art with Contempt.

To a Gentleman the same with Pleasure.

Chiromancy shews to the Poor being Bayliffs.

To the Rich it gives taking of Thieves.

To others it has shewn of teaching to write, &c.

Dream Interpreters, shew of mistaking Blunderers.

Interpreted by Persons credible in your Dream its self, that's true.

Vid. *Bodily Action,* in *Sleep.*

Perceive your self dreaming, have your Wits about you.

Dreams in general shew of Contention and Reproof from far.

Interpreting, threats with a dangerous Issue in great things.

Twice of the same thing, Vid. 2 in Numbers.

Gipsies, Vid. *Person* in *Grammar.*

Magick shews of Religion and vain Divination.

Prediction consulting, threats with all sorts of Trouble.

Not answering you, the Trouble the worse.

Divination

Divination. Metapoſcopy threats with Slavery, and Enquiry of Guilt.
(14)　　 Phyſiognomy foreſhews the Study of Natural Philoſophy
　　　　　　　and Phyſick.
　　　　　　To others it ſhews of Love and Anatomy, and
　　　　　　　Painting ones ſelf.
　　　　　　To others it threats with Deceit, Divination and
　　　　　　　Infamy.
　　Prophet, Vid. *Religion.*
　　Second Sight Perſons ſeen, threat of Fatal Events occurring.
　　　　　　　　Out of your Window as to your
　　　　　　　　Family Managery.
Glory or Rays. See Chriſt in, diſcover the practick Methods to conſum-
(15)　　　mate Chriſtianity, all conſuming and irreſiſtible.
　　　　A Woman in, that is the ſame in Scheme or Science
　　　　　only.
　　　　　　In Bed with Kiſs, be moſt happy in ſuch
　　　　　　　Scheme Hopes.
　　　　Perſon with ſpeak to, that is, your ſelf tranſact in
　　　　　ſuch State.
　　　　　　Stands in your way, ſuch methods obſtruct
　　　　　　　your proceeds, as, &c.
　　　　　　　At a Room Door, you muſt
　　　　　　　not quit ſuch a method
　　　　　　　of Converſe, &c.
　　Vid. *Crown of Fire* in *Fire.*

CHAP. II.

Of Death Literal.

P*Erſons.* Brothers and Siſters dead, ſeen to many, has ſhewn long Life.
　(1)　Conſumptive dead haunted by, threats you with Symptoms
　　　of ſuch like Conſumption approaching.
　　Emperor purſuing one, ſhew'd him of Robbers threatning him.
　　Schoolmaſter dead having for a Boy, ſhew'd of his dying e'er
　　taught.
　　Apoſtles and Prophets dead bringing one a Crown, ſhew'd him
　　Martyrdom.
　　St. *Chriſtopher* often call'd and not coming, ſhew'd one drown-
　　ing.
　　Self ſeeming dead at home, and in Apparel proper, may
　　ſhew Death, elſe not.
　　Friend, or another ſeen dead, alſo muſt be ſo, and in Circum-
　　ſtance according.

Acts. Brought a Crown to one by the Apoſtles and Prophets, ſhew'd
(2)   him Martyrdom.

Buying Victuals of them, to the Sick threats with loſs of Stomach.

Carrying away your Goods, Money, Apparel or Victuals, to many Death.

unneceſſary things to Life, threats with wanting Health to uſe them.

about a dead Body ſeen, that is, find your ſelf ſtrug-
ling for Life.

Company, *A.* with her Child ſeem'd in Company with *B.* dead,
and her Child as mortally hurt by lying in near.

Dying again ſeen if Parents, Death to a Grandſon of the
Name, *&c.*

Eating with them threats Death or extreme Poverty.

to others Sickneſs, reſtraining from eating.

But with a dead Father, has ſhewn of being wiſely temperate for Health.

Examining *A*'s Works about him, not yet finiſh'd, ſhew'd *A.* died
e'er he ended them.

Fetching another way threatning, ſhew'd of their Death menac'd ſo threatned.

Following the Dead if in ill Circumſtance, threats Death.

Follow'd in a Dance by a Dead Man at a Wedding, ſhew'd of
Miſery, and Death attending their new Joy in't.

Forcing *A.* away to a place unknown, threated him of a violent Death.

Giving them ſomething, to many Death.

Given a ſleepy Potion by ones dead Father, Death.

Winding Sheet by one dead, he in danger of their
like Death.

Going to a Place unknown with them, and not returning, Death.

Hal'd to a place unknown with them, threats with violent Ilneſs.

Overcome by them on it, Death.

Forcing your ſelf back on it, Recovery.

Held by the Dead, prevented by Death.

Haunted by the Dead, Approaches of their like Death near.

on every ſide do what you can.

's Houſe, Vid. *The Grammar.*

Chamber be in with them, that is, in a Managery will
never be finiſh'd.

Join'd to them, to the Sick Death.

Kiſſing you, threats you deadly Infirmities, but with long Life.

with putrid Matter on their Lips, the Infirmity the
worſe.

Leave a Room to them entring, ceaſe a courſe, as fearing Death.

Lying down with the Dead, to the Sick threats Death without
Hopes of Recovery.

Acts. Lying down with the Dead with Hopes of Recovery, of a little
(2)   Sickneſs.

         with one only thought dead, gives Recovery, with
              Difficulty.

             Dead ſeeming alive die, tho in Hopes
               of Life.

Making your Beds ſeeing, threats Sickneſs to your Relations, ge-
    nerally your Gueſts.

Offer'd Coffee by a dead Coffee-man, ſhew'd *A.* forbearing drinking it as unwholeſome.

Overlooking your Actions, ſee threats Death hindring them finiſh-
    ing.

       unleſs in Place unknown, and then delay for a while,
        only for Sickneſs.

Poſſeſs the Dead's Houſe, you Maſter if ſick, recover.

            he Maſter, you ſurely die.

Purſued by them, threats you with Terrors of their like Death.

Putting your Clothes on and off again ſeen, threats you with
Death in them.

Race on a White Horſe with them, die.

Removing a dead Body to a Place unknown, Sickneſs.

            and not returning on't, Death.

Ride, carrying the Dead behind you, die.

Sleeping with them, to ſome gives an eaſy Death.

Snatching Money, Clothes or Victuals from us, threats us Sick-
       neſs or Death.

       Silver or Jewels from us, threats us the Death of a
        Son or Wife.

       Away his own things as when alive, ſhews they'l
        prove uſeleſs.

       Something wanting ſeen of what ſnatch'd, ſhew'd
        of recovering hardly.

       Books from one lying in Bed in a Students Gown,
        Deſpair of Life ſtops his Study.

Speaking 's Father, threatning the Emperor *Caracalla* Death,
foreſhew'd his Murder.

       Drown'd Man advis'd *A.* againſt his Voyage, by it he
        eſcap'd drowning.

       Threatning ſeen, has ſhewn of ſome Miſchief ac-
        cording irretrievable.

          Conſumptive dead ſee threat you, a
           Conſumption threats you.

          Be Friends again, all is well.

A's firſt Wife as angry at his 2*d* Match, threatned to
fetch away his 2*d* Wife, and ſhe died on it.

Touching you, threats you Infirmity, but withal gives you long
    Life.

       The Back of your Hand, ſtops your Work a while only.

                             Acts.

A.'s. Unfeen heard call you, threats your Death near.

(2)   Walking in A. B. *Laud*'s Chamber, Cardinal *Woolfey* feen, and calling my Lord thrice, A. B. *Laud*'s Death.

Death. Affaulting you, threats you danger of Death according.

(3)   Leaving a green Bow behind him, efcape Death by fuch.
Shooting at Mankind feen, fhew'd of a great Mortality near.
Wreftling with, fhews of Sicknefs, or fuing of Heirs.
Flying from them feen, to the Sick Recovery.
Vid. *Sceleton* infrà.
Watch hear in your Chamber in a private Managery, gradually hazard your Death.

A. can't fleep in fear of hearing him, he proves reftlefly active to prevent fuch hurt.

Try to kill him by force, that is, to prevent fuch Ill, oddly not wifely.

Rattles before Death A. is told of, that is, he acts fo as to be as near Death.

Kill'd as drown'd, if in Circumftance proper, may fhew of drowning indeed, or elfe is Allegory.

By another alfo has been oft in Literal, where in Circumftances, &c.

Beafts 's Bitch A. faw die in puppying, fhe whelped dangeroufly, and had no more Puppies after, but recovered then.

Carcafe. Carrion eating Creatures feen, threat with Death to Malefactors, &c.

(4)   Putrid Lips of the Dead kiffing, fhew'd A. of recovering in worft State.

Sceleton dancing with, has threated of Death,

Entring A's Chamber a little vanifhes, the Death menace of his Managery goes off.

Purfued by Death, threatning your Hopes, &c.

Vid. *Death* fuprà.

Wake e'er you come up to one lying before you, be vigorous in a courfe, but not to Death.

Bones of dead Men my Court Walls feen made of, fhew'd me of Reforters to me dying.

Death's Head A. faw lie on his Pillar, he avoided Death menac'd by Neglects.

Of Ivory, a projected Death of noblefs.

Corps A. feeing in his beft Chamber Bed, fhew'd of his burying fuch a likely Gueft.

Carry, Vid. *Dead Perfon* fuprà.

Meet another dragging one by her Coach fide, try to hinder fuch ones Fate that's rich.

Going back on't, he recovers, but ftanding ftill he dies.

Have one at her Bridal Houfe, to a Wife deadly Sicknefs, near by her own fault.

                                                    Carcafe.

Carcaſe. Hand only ſeen dead, ſhew'd of a Maid Servant removing, a
  (4)   deadly ſick.

Funeral. Wait on *A*'s Corps, to keep it in a literal Dream, be near a
  (5)   occaſion of that Perſon's Death.

Standing back in Eaſt, *A*. ſeeing 3 Corps carried on in
    Street in a Weſt Village, ſhew'd his Recovery o
    Sickneſs.

Unknown paſſing by *A*. in Mourning to the left, ſhew'd *A*. o
    a Friend dying.

Paſſing-Bell *A*. then ſick hearing for himſelf, ſhew'd him hi
    Death.

Hear for a Neighbour, by your charitable Car
    prevent his Death.

Vid. *Clav. Secret*, that is my *Grammar*.

Coffin black ſeen to ſome, Death, or danger of Death, as, &c
    Is ſet down by your Bed ſide, a conſtant Terror c
    Death invades you in your Manageries.

See unknown 4 ſtand with a Coffin in your Cham
    ber, avoid a rational Overture of Death.

Seen in your Chamber tho, removes the Terror
    of Death thence.

A. left a dead Gentleman in a Coffin in an un-
    known Chamber, he recovered to ſcorn Gen
    teel Aids to Health.

Carrying by you ſeen, ſhews of ſome ill Conduct
    menacing your Death.

On your left Shoulder, threats you c
    Fatal Melancholy.

Set by your Bedſide in an unknown Houſe, re-
    move and lay by the cauſeleſs fears of Death.

Unknown would take meaſure of *A*. for one, and
    he was menac'd Death by chance after.

Sitting in a Room to look on one, ſhew'd *A*. o
    examining about Mens Deaths.

Pall *A*. could not hold to ſnack, her Infirmity prov'd not fa-
    tal, but irrecoverable.

Graves and Church-yards ſeen in general, threat with fatal
    Melancholies.

Open yours, and come out on't, retrieve your ſelf nea
    miraculouſly from Death.

Mourning, Vid. *Apparel*.

Tickets in *A*'s Hand, ſhew'd him chang'd to blank Paper by
    his good Genius, ſhew'd him his ſick Friend recover'd.

Sermon, Vid. *Religion*.

Hag mourning treading upon, triumphing o'er the Terror
    of Death.

Winding-Sheet, Vid. *Shroud* infra.

Funerals. Joint-Stools dancing before him, A. went from his own
(5)   Home into his own Church-yard, that is, A. died.

Bier rise from near a Grave and run away, narrowly escape
     Death.

In a Church Porch overgrown with Ivy, after a
     tedious Sickness.

Bearers seeing that would carry him off, shew'd A. of es-
     caping Death narrowly.

Shroud cloth'd in, A. went from his Home into his Church-
     yard, he died.

See with a Coffin in your Chamber, avoid Death
     narrowly.

Or Flannel tied at Head, A. seeing brought him by one
     thought like the Dead, shew'd him near Death,
     but escaping.

Searchers seen in Place unknown to view you, shews you
     narrowly escape Death.

Cake Funeral seeing, threats of Death, Circumstances me-
     nacing also.

Emballment eating, learning from G O D's fatal Predictions on
     the Wicked.

Impolluted by the Carcase not abominable, as were
     their Lives.

Tomb. Gravestone, yours turn back, alter your threatning Doom of Death.
(6.)   What wrote on it forgot, a Fate of Death not
     to be.

Tomb like an House seen, has shewn the Masters Death.

Dwelling in one, threats Death.

Opened, Death to one in Family.

Stars seen fall on it, some great Man dies.

Worshipping it, shews of burying some Ancestors.

Adorn'd with Flowers seen, threats with an unjust and untime-
     ly Death.

Your own seen so, shews of your own
     Death, or some near a Kin, with
     short Fame.

Burning with Flame, gives a more exceeding Glory of the de-
     ceased, &c.

Without Flame, threats great Sickness or Infamy to one
     in Family.

C H A P.

CHAP III.
Of Death Allegorical.

PErſons ſorts. (1) Biſhop purſuing you, ſome wicked Awe attending you.

Brother dead, travel with deſign, wherein you are aided by your Rival.

Children, Vid. C. ⎫
Daughter, Vid. D. ⎬ in *Grammar.*

Enemies flattering you, ſhews of Deceit.
Threatning you, ſhews of Hindrance.

Father, Vid. F. in *Grammar.*

Friend talking to, gives you Proſperity and long Life.

Grandmother in Law threatning, ſhew'd of Popery terrifying.

Kings, Vid. K. in *Government.*

Lord, Vid. L. in *Grammar.*

Lover, Vid. L. in *Grammar.*

Maſter beating him to an Apothecary, ſhew'd his Pou Froſt-broke.

Parents and Friends ſeen, is better than Enemies.

Queen in Bed with, negligent in a Command belongs not to you.

Relations ſeen, promiſe long Life.

Robbers known ſit by, that is, be in an erroneous fix'd courſe, to certain Loſs.

Servant attending you, ceaſe the occaſion of ſuch Service.
To others, ſhews of the like Good or Service unknown done you.

Note. Generally th Dead ſhew us of Wicked neſs or Privation, whe thus in Allegory, and ſo t be conſtrued according.

By Name in general, Vid. *G O D*'s ſuprà.

Alexander the Great ſeen, gives of Succeſs in great things.

Apelles, ſhews of Projects moſt excellent and rare.

Caligula teaching, ſhew'd *Seneca* of taking *Nero* like him to Pupil.

Domitian purſuing A. ſhew'd of Houſe-Robbers threatning him.

Eſculapius ſeen, draw all the Humors to a place, threated an Impoſtume then.

Gemini, or *Caſtor* and *Pollux* ſeen, ſhew of Good and Aid.

Helena ſeen, threats ill, as was her Lot.

Hercules's Statue ſeen aiding, to the Honeſt Good.
to the Wicked Ill.

Perſons,

Perfons. *Hercules* feen inviting *Alexander*, forefhewed his hard, but
(1)   fure Victory of *Tyre*.

's Works finifhing to a Woman, forefhew'd her being
burnt, as was he at laft.

Saints in general, Vid. *G O D* fuprà.

Images, Vid. *Popifh* in *Religion*
Many, Vid. *Many* in *Company*.

Chrift, Vid. *Religion.*

Solomon by a River *A.* feeing the Queen of *Sheba* approach, *A.* himfelf proves as admir'd for Riches
and Honour.

Prophets, Vid. *Religion.*

Virgin *Mary* difcourfing, gives Joy and Profperity.
To the Sick it gives Recovery,
as thro a Piety greater than
in a Motherly Scheme only.

Little and mean, *A.* meeting with a Chrift
in her Arms, fhew'd of his meeting Papifts.

St. *Peter* huffing, and a Captain threatning fighting, he
yielded, whilft I with *Mofes* walk'd off out of my Brother's Back-fide into his Field : Meeknefs or Rafhnefs
deferted, fupported my Courage to rely on *G O D*
before him.

Patriarchs, *&c.* feen, fhew us fomewhat of their Faith
renewed.

A Play of *Abraham*, *A.* faw acted; he was near
for Religion, parted from's Friends alfo, as
was *Abraham.*

Tutelar feen difarmed to a Papift, threats him utmoft
Mifery.

Leonard breaking off his Chains, gave a Prifoner
liberty.

They particularly aid or hurt, as is their Jurif-
diction.

Correcting a Prince, baulk'd him in his Defign
againft a protected Place.

Of a Country, the fame to that Country.

Actions fhew to us ftill of fome Religious matters.

Contending, threats of Wars between Kingdoms.

Difarm'd, threats of Mifery without Aid.

Dref's'd fine and going to a Place feen, gives
you a Good according.

Receiving from them, promifes the good of
their Power and Virtue.

Sad or nafty feen, threats your Impiety, fcanda-
lizing you as to their Imitation.

In a Foreign Habit feen, gives you a good or
ill thence according.

C

Perfons.

Perfons. Common Dead feen, fhew of Rogues and wicked People, as, &c.
(1)   *Note.* In this feems founded the whole Idolatry
of the Heathen World, Almighty GOD in this his
holy Language reprefenting all extraordinary Courfes
and Virtues, by fuch feveral and known Perfons, as whether dead or alive have been eminent and particular
Examples therein, and withal of his Fatherly Care and
Tendernefs thereon, meeting us conftantly with his Divine Monitions and Predictions accordingly, and where-
ever Circumftance of Place or Action prefented meet
therefore; Men hereon miftaking fondly the Language
for the Speaker, and the Creature for the Creator, inftead
of adoring the one and invifible Lord : therefore what
have they done, but worfhip'd his Hieroglyphick and
Allegory Pictures in his ftead; and fo, as I may fay,
have built Temples to nothing, and where the fupreme
GOD was only their real Director and Affiftant, and
to whom be all Honour and Glory both now and for
evermore ?

Vid. *Perfons* in the *Grammar.*

Seem dead your felf if not with other dead, is good, and generally
(2)   changes Manners for the beft.

In what Place, in that thing, &c.

In Heaven in Defpair, as to Riches
and Preferment.

Manner, Vid. *Dying* infrà.

Seeming dead is eafier than dying, it gives
Accomplifhment.

And reviving again, to the
Contender gives Victory.

To fome, Retirement and Freedom of Care.

To fome, Riches and the Princes Favour.

To the Single, Marriage.

Servant, Lofs of Service.

If in Truft, Lofs of Credit.

Sick, Health.

Well, Change for the beft.

Author, Works furviving him.

Doubtful, Quiet and Eafe.

Parent, a hopeful Progeny.

Suiter for Land or Inheritance, good, elfe ill.

Tradefman and Merchant, Lofs of Bufinefs.

Papift, fometimes Monkery.

Offender, Exile.

Degrees. Dead feeming fhews of Change, &c.
as 'tis.

Reviving e'er buried, Defpair in
full Hopes.

Seem dead your felf. Degrees, dead, and laid out to fome Dreffing,
(2) for Nuptials.

Funeral having, gives Riches to
deferve one.

A Bifhop and Mourners at-
tending, the nobler.

Buried being, as much Riches as
Earth on you.

In another's Garden, thro
your Expectance on
their Eftate.

As dead, to fome imprifon'd or
flander'd for Roguery.

As alive, fhews of unjuft Slanders.

Tomb having, fhews of leaving an
Inheritance.

of Brafs, compofing
Works to furvive
Ages.

Manner. Vid. *Dying* infra.

Death at home, and in Apparel proper,
fhews of Death indeed.

in a ftrange Place, Change as to
fuch Circumftances.

at home and in Apparel improper,
change manner of living there.

without Affection or Apparel, and
naturally, change Manners.

with ill Affection, change to ill.

with Apparel without Affection,
become a Prieft.

with Apparel and bad Affection,
Servitude or Exile.

Violent with ill Affection, Goal or Gallies.

with no Affection, compell'd to
gainful Service.

Others, fhews them chang'd to us, or they become Rogues,
as, &c.

Reviv'd Friend feen tho, fhews he loves you
again.

Vid. *Actions of Dead* infra in general:

Vid. *Dying* infra.

Acquaintance feen, fhews of fomewhat wanting,
as is the Perfon.

To others it fhews Deceit, and vain feeking of
Aid.

Brother feen, fhews of Rival Intereft, Fears vanifhing, or an Enemy dying.

C 2 *Seeming*

Seeming dead others.
(2)

Creditor seen dying, gives an end of Heavines[s]

Daughter so, shews of some Debt paid.

Debtor seen dead, shews of your bad Payme[nt] near an end.

Father seen dead, is ill tho dead, it threats los[s] a Friendship as great.

Fellow-rower burying, shew'd of the Ships Pr[ofit] lost.

Friend dead, shews of Separation and Trav[el] or his ceasing to love you.

   To some, be happy not to need his Aid

   To some it has foreshewn his being dru[nk] when wanted.

Master of the Forepart of a Ship seen dea[d] threated the Forepart lost.

Minister that married you seeming dead, threa[ts] you in want of some Bargain lasting such Match.

   His dead Wife, tho seen reviv'd, shew'd unexpectedly equitably made good.

Neighbour seen dead, shews he ceases to be Neig[h] bourly.

   's Ghost haunting you, troubling you wi[th] his Roguery on't.

Reviv'd seen, he becomes neighbourly again.

Vid. *Tradesman* infra.

Strangers seeming so, shew of some Aid une[x] pectedly wanting.

   Alive seeming so, shews you some way de ceiv'd without remedy.

Trader-fellow seen sick, shew'd *A.* himself wan[t] ing Business.

   Dying, shew'd *A.* leaving h[is] Trade on it.

   Buried on't, shew'd him leavi[ng] the Parish upon't.

Uncle, *A.* told his was dead, shew'd him of Guardian Awe gone off.

Wife, yours seen dead, shews you of some Con tract destroy'd.

Dead acting in general, shew of underhand and unexpected Designs issuing
(3)

   In your Business with you, shew 'twill never b[e] finish'd.

   To some it shews their Executors will so do

Travel with thy dead Brother, Act wherein thy Rival will assist thee.

Vid. *Company.*

Vid. *Grammar.*

Dead acting.
(3)

Aiding us seen, shews us unexpected Aid.

Angry. Vid. *Speak & Threaten* infra.

Apparel. Vid. *Put on* infra, & *Clothes* infra.

Appearing for Persons alive, threats us with Rogues and Cheats, what is not for what is.

Belly. Vid. *Parts* infra.

Bring. Vid. *Give* infra,

Business. Vid. *Act in general* supra.

Calling you. Vid. *Call* in *Discourse*.

Carrying away things as in circumstance, Loss by some conceal'd Knavery.

Vid. *Force & Remove* infra.

Clothes, Dressing. Vid. *Apparel & Put on* infra.

     Ill cloth'd seen, generally hurts the Dreamer, as if alive, by ill Repute.

     Seen put on yours, threats you dying in them.

     Cloth'd warm and in riding Habit, *A.* seeing her dead Mother, shew'd her in Riding and Warmth to be her Life.

Company. Vid. *Company.*

Vid. *Converse* infra.

Consecrations to the Dead, neither good to give nor take.

     Taking them, enriching you with knavish Profits.

     Hence says our Saviour, *Let the Dead bury their Dead,* and whose Parables are all built on this Language,

Conversing many dead, beset with many Rogueries.

     Two dead, imperfect Error or false imagin'd Roguery.

     To some, transact with their Executors.

     A dead Friend, gives you long Life and Happiness.

     A. seem'd in *London* with her dead Father, Grandmother, and faithful Maid, her kind Husband proves a Supply of all such Defects to her.

     Vid. *Speak* infra.

     Vid. *Chap. Discourse.*

Covering the Dead, shews of concealing others Rogueries.

Deform'd seen, threats the Dreamer of some other answerable.

     Vid. *Clothes* supra.

Dressing. Vid. *Clothes* supra,

Design. Vid. *Act* supra.

Discourse. Vid. *Converse* supra, & *Speak* infra.

Dying again, if Parent, &c. to some Gain by such Parent's Friend.

     to others, lose a Friendship again as good and great,

Dead

Dead aĉting. Eating Victuals they provide, unexpectedly eating ſuch.
(3)
       gave *A.* ſhew'd of *A*'s Gain by their
        Aid or Advice before when alive.
   Vid. *Invitation* in *Company.*
Eating, *A.* ſat down with one dead at a Tavern, but eat
      not ; he by Abſence near miſs'd
      a good Entertainment.
    with *W. F.* like *F. F.* that is, thro
    F. F's means.
Fighting ſeen, to many has ſhewn of negative Diſputes.
    with one alive, ſhew'd of Diſputes about
    Abſence and Preſence.
Following the Dead, imitating them in their Lives.
Gentle ſeen good, ſhewing you paſs the preſent time luckily.
Giving them, to ſome Loſs.
   us, ſhews of our imitating their Lives, Toils or
    Actions, and if what's good, to good.
    to ſome, Benefit from the Ground.
Grieving. Vid. *Part* infrâ.
Held by them, fruſtrate by Knavery, as is the Perſon.
Haunting us. Vid. *Inchantment* in *Spirit.*
   To Murderers it ſhews avoiding its Avengement
   they fear.
   To ſome, teas'd by Cheats, or vex'd by Men
   not at home.
   Haunted by his dead Father, teas'd by a cheating
   Benefactor.
Have. Vid. *Poſſeſs* infrâ.
Helping us, villanous Courſes aſſiſting us.
's Houſe be in. Vid. *Grammar.*
   Vid. *Poſſeſs'd & Living* infrâ.
Jealous of his dead Son, *A.* ſaw *B. A.* was in circumſtance
   to renew in another the like Jealouſy.
Inviting. Vid. *Invitation* in *Company.*
Kiſs them. Vid. *Bodily Aĉtion.*
Lend them ſuch Keys, that is, your Care accordingly ceaſes.
Like. Vid. *Reſemble* infrâ.
Lying with the Dead. Vid. *Bodily Aĉtion,*
   carnally with a dead Woman, being lov'd and main-
   tain'd by ſome great Lady.
   down as dead among the Dead, ſhews of being wic-
    ked among the Dead.
    If known, wicked as they, when alive.
   In Bed with them, negligent, as were they
   when alive as to Health, &c.
   You riſing from them, you diſcover and avoid
   ſuch Roguery.
   They riſing from you, you are hindred of ſome
   ſuch ill Purpoſe.

          Dead

Dead acting. Living with the Dead. Vid. *Grammar.*
(3)
    As alone live among them ; that is, be singularly honest among Rogues.

Living seeing their dead Children, having full Command of their Roguery.

Making a Feast, to some a Profit by Inheritance or Woodsale.

Marrying seen, shews of the Destruction of Contracts.

Meeting and opposing them, shews of resisting of Rogueries.
    Give them way, consent to their Admission.

Merry a dead Prince seen, shew'd of vain Hopes to follow.
    the Dead seen is good in Death-Menaces.

Pain. Vid. *Part* infra.

Part of him in Pain, threats Sin or Sickness to the Dreamer or his Friend, as is the Member.

Belly of the Dead A. burying Ornaments in, shew'd him of Good News, but in evil Riches.

Possessing a Place seen, shew'd of its being transfer'd in Trust to Heirs.
    Vid. *House* & *Living* supra.

    Vid. *Grammar.*

Prayer for them shews of Requests not to be granted.

Receiving from them. Vid. *Give* & *Make* supra.

Removing a dead Body, to some hiding, a Scandal or Roguery.
    Vid. *Carry* supra.

Resembled by Persons alive, shews of a wicked Life according.

Reviving seen, threats the Dreamer or some other with Sin and Repentance.

    To some unexpected things come in hope.

    To some, Miscarriage in plain Designs and sure Hopes.

    To some, Victory, when of themselves, and seeming dead before.

    To some, unexpected Trouble and Charge.

Of your dead Friend, Aid unexpected in his like Course approaches you.

    Predecessor, threats you some Right in Succession in question.

    Father, to a Servant shew'd her Master like to stay from his Journy design'd.

    One known seen, shews you lose that Wish while you live.

    Daughter dead seen, shew'd A. of his Debt paid return'd as bad Money.

    Vid. *Hanging* in *Posture.*

    A dead Coffee-man, an old Tittle Tattle set again on foot.

    An Acquaintance seen in his time, you miss some Hope, as is the Person.

Dead

Dead acting, Reviving of a dead Wife ſeen, ſhew'd of as great and
(3) lasting a Charge renew'd.

Many ſeen, ſhews of horrible Confuſion.

Of Beaſts. Vid. *Death.*

Dying again on revival, undoing all what before.

A. ſaw his dead Wife, he buried a
Child left by her.

Robbing you, threats you Loſs irretrievable by Knavery or
Miſtake.

Sad, ill cloth'd, or deform'd ſeen, threats you with ſuch
like Ills.

Seeing them in general, Conſiderations and Diſcourſes
will preſent, as were their Tempers when alive.

Sell. Vid. *Buy* ſupra.

Shewing them ſomewhat. Vid. *Shew* in *Action.*

Having a Power or Privilege you
dare not boaſt of, cowardly.

Sleeping ſeen, to ſome has ſhewn an idle Life among
Debauchees.

Speaking. Vid. *Converſe* ſupra.

to us, if known, ſhews we ſay the ſame to their
Succeſſors.

unknown, the ſame good or ill is unknown done you.

Talk with your dead Father-in-law, be ſufficient a-
gainſt ſelf-ended Commanders.

a dead Miniſter, have Courage againſt
the Rogueries of Miniſters.

A. ſeem'd welcom'd by the Dead at their once home,
their Executors made A. ſo.

Chriſt offer'd A. one thing of two, as accepted it befel
him.

A dead Judg ask'd A. if he wanted him, he was near
tempted to judg ill for Gain.

A's firſt Wife dead ſeem'd angry at his 2d Match, and
threaten'd to fetch away his 2d Wife, ſhe died.

Call. Vid. *Call* in *Diſcourſe.*

Taking, &c. Vid. *Carry* & *Snatch* ſupra.

Threatning. Vid. *Speak* ſupra.

Travelling. Vid. *Going* & *Haling* ſupra.

with thy dead Brother, act aſſiſted by thy Rival.

Turn ones ſelf to a dead Man, play the Knave.

Tying A's Feet ſeen, ſhew'd of Knaveries obſtructing his
Actions.

Victuals. Vid. *Eat* ſupra.

Writings of theirs A. going to fetch, ſhew'd of his ſearching of Books for God's ſpiritual Diſpenſations on ill
Mens Deaths.

Dying

ying in general shews of the approach of what is shewn by the Dead,
(4)   and as dead, shews of the same in perfection.
        Vid. *Seeming dead* supra.
        If to shew, of real Death. Vid. *Grammar.*
        Natural dying, shews of Changes falling of course on
        neglect.
        Violent Death &c. con.
Seeing a Crow, promises you exceeding old Age.
        the King, threats you Damage, as your greatest Safeguard
        failing.
        a Woman, but restor'd again, shew'd of an exploded
        Opinion recover'd.
        his Saddle Horse, shew'd A. of keeping a Coach not to
        need him.
        a rich Man, shew'd of a Hog kill'd.
        your Friend in an old unknown House, shews of his ad-
        vancing to a happier Oeconomy.
Seeming inevitably, shews the same as being kill'd or dead.
With loss of Blood, with loss of Money.
Of a Fever, shew'd of a Change of Life for Grief.
    Flux, shews of committing ill.
    Dropsy, shews you drown'd in Business.
    Age, threats you with Poverty and Impotence.
kill'd in general.   Vid. *Shoot* & *Fight* in *War.*
(5)   Vid. *Condemn'd* in *Law.*
        Shews a Delivery of Care by a thorough Dispatch.
            To others, change of State for good or ill, as
               in circumstance.
            Of the State, taken for granted, and as
               Killing shews it in Action.
Drown'd in Water, to a Maid a great Belly.
            to other, Confusion in dark Thoughts and
               Cares.
    the Sea, join'd to an Whore.
    Overpower'd by Waves, troubled beyond Courage.
           near by a Torrent pressing into a Room,
           and so your Truth by common Vogue:
           by a Flood in a Field, Bodily Humours
           near destroying you.
Smother'd by unknown fearing, find wrong Reasons like to baffle
    your Proceeds.
Stifled in an iron Engine, confounded in some resolute Pro-
    ject.
        near in your Bed, that is, near confounded by your
        Wife's Methods.
Snakestung in her Father's Garden, to a Maid married off with a
    Portion to leave him.
In publick, to Servants and private Men publick Power.

                                   Kill'd

Kill'd in publick. In a Town, Promiſes, Place or Office there.
(5) In the Dirt, threats with Confuſion thro Error and Diſgrace.
By Juſtice, ſhews the Good or Ill the greater.
Vid. Law.
Strangled, ſhews of Anguiſh and change of Place, giving a new Air.
Buried quick, to the Sick Health.
to Youth Heat and Luſt.
Crucified, to the Poor and Voyagers good.
to the Rich ill.
to Servants Liberty.
to the Single Weddings.
to others change of Place.
By Beaſts, gives to Servants Liberty, as if ſaid, Be for the future free of paſſionate Wills.
Torn by them only, abus'd by Scandal.
till the Blood come, had to Juſtice by it.
By an Elephant, Death.
By your ſelf, the Good or Ill is according from your ſelf.
Diſſect your own Body ſeeming dead, the ſame confirm'd.
To others, Death by ones Gluttony, or one like ones ſelf.
A. eat a Neck of Mutton, and then rip'd up his Belly to kill himſelf, he bred up a Duck, and after loſt him.
By another a raſh man, loſe the Privileges of good Converſation thro Raſhneſs.
To others, the good or ill by them.
A Souldier, become deſperate to Change of Fortune, as to be ſuch.
An Enemy, loſt utterly in ſome Benefit by ſuch an ill Courſe.
By another by the Blow of a Hammer, oppreſt to Idleneſs.
Like to be, but prevented, ſhew'd of a great Danger eſcap'd.
Kill a Man unknown your ſelf, aſſures your Buſineſs, and that you are
(6) Maſter in your Methods, and as is ſaid, you are not to be thought ignorant.
to a Phyſician, promiſes exquiſite Skill.
Like to be hang'd for it, the better.
Vid. alſo Behead in Head in Body.
Mumble him. Vid. Fight.
Your Father (an horrible Sign) deſtroy your own Safeguard of Being.
A Man unknown, and be reputed in a damnable State for't, deſtroy a pious Courſe.
An Enemy, rid you of ſuch an ill Courſe, or obtain ſome Suit.
Ki

ill Your Wife, and sell her Flesh at Shambles, prostitute her for
(6)   Gain.

               at a Papist's House destroying her, imposing Methods
               in Oeconomy.

A Shoomaker, furnish you in Leather Ware, not to want his Aid.
Another's Child, reap the Benefit of his Expectation.

              seen dead, shews the same taken for granted.

A Throng, dismiss many useless Methods and Cares.

A Witch by saying your Prayers, have your Wishes o'er all your
    perverse Fortunes.

A Deer, become Master of a smaller Trade Profit, as, &c.

lain Persons shew of reasonable Courses compass'd to your Will.
(7)   You to marry his Heir on't, that is, command the
             Good of the contrary Course.

       Vid. *Seeming dead* supra in *Dead.*

Husband, hers near seen by Girls, trifling Opinions near
    destroying his Freedom.

Wife seen, shews of your Contract someway destroy'd.

Mother-in-law seen, shews of your Slavery near an end.

Spaniard trying to kill, Aim to remove Jealousies by
    loose Persons.

Many seen, shew of Business dispatch'd, and Courses over.

At the Eye, destroy'd in reasonable Prospects and Designs.

          No Blood seen on it, with a clever conceal'd
          Malice.

Poison'd with Wormwood, drunk with Tyranny.

Smother'd your eldest Son seen, your Estate Expecta-
    tion stifled.

Her sucking Child seen to a Nurse, shew'd of such a
    Nurse Child remov'd.

Beasts.   Vid. *Butcher* in *Trade.*

   They shew of some Powers or Persons extinct.

Monsters seen shew of unnatural Inclinations vanquish'd.

A Deer seen by a Lion, shew'd of a Hazard Profit made
    certain by a stout Effort.

Duck seen reviv'd, shew'd of a pretence Service thought
    lost, recover'd.

   Horse.   Vid. *H.* in *Beasts.*

Beasts of Prey seen, shew of some greedy Designs against you
        vanquish'd.

          A Wolf, one suing you so at Law.

Snakes shew of subtle erroneous Insinuations powerless
    against you.

        Stinging her mortally, marrying a Man courts her.

Hornet seen, shews of some Designer against your Ho-
    nour baffled.

   Lice seen gives Delivery from Care and Heaviness.

        by another, thro their Aid.

                            Slain

Slain Beaſts. Weeſel in a Chimney-Corner ſeen, ſhew'd of a gre
(7)   Fewel Waſte prevented.

       Four Sheep coming up to you deſtroy, ſhun a good Coun
         cil of Profit offering.

       Four Rabbits coming up to you kill, the ſame of a ſecre
         Courſe of Profit offering.

Carcaſe. Carrion eating your ſelf, threats you with Poverty and Sad
(8)   neſs, and as if drove thereto.

       Fiſh dead ſeen, ſhew of vain Hopes.

       Hogsfleſh dying of it ſelf ſeen, ſhew'd of near but profitleſ
         Husbandry.

       Eagles feeing, promiſes well to Servants, and leaving ſharp
         Maſters.

       Oxen ſeen, threats of ſome great Plague.

       Rats ſeen, ſhews you of Servants ſick or leaving your Ser
         vice.

       Fat Ox *A.* ſeem'd to have in Houſe, that is, he had ſome a
         live to ſell, which 'twould be ill Husbandry to keep longer
         by him.

Bones. Skeleton fine of a Man hang'd *A.* got in his Chamber,
         he grew rich by ill Actions.

       and Tombs being among, ſhew'd *A.* of Gain by dead
         Friends.

       Marrowbone found in a Church-yard, thought a Beaſt's,
         but proving a Man's, *A.* eat, a flattering Defrauder
         of Executors.

       Vid. alſo *Bones* in *Body Human.*

Corps in general.   Vid. *Dead Perſon ſupra.*

         To be buried.   Vid. *Buried ſupra.*

       Unknown ſeen, ſhew'd of a Buſineſs to be done with-
         out diſpute. ————

       Abhorring, avoiding ſomewhat abominable.

       In Funeral Proceſs.   Vid. *Funeral* infra.

Hanging up ſeen, ſhew'd of an abominable Error in ſuſ-
         pence.

         Half rotten, that is, near forgot, and out of
         regard.

Diſſected ſeen, ſo many Pieces, ſo many Rogueries.

         Bankrupts with relation to Eſtate ſquandred.

         Cut to pieces in a Converſe, ill publick Converſe
         remov'd.

         His Neck ſlit with a Knife, his whole Force
         defeated.

Hiding or removing ſuch in aid to another, cloaking his
         Roguery.

Funeral feeing in general, ſhews an end of Miſery and Vexation.
(9)   Publick in a City, with Council attending, ſhew'd of a
       great Debt paid off.

                                  Funeral

uneral of your Wife seen, shews of some Contract destroy'd.
(9) Self seen, gives you Honour, but short-liv'd, as, &c.
Having, the same.

Meet your Corps coming, be unexpectedly in circumstance contrary.

Of a Woman in general, shews of some Opinion brought to certainty, or a Scheme put to practice.

with a Bottle for Harvest, shew'd A. bringing in his first Harvest.

a Noble *Dutch* Woman, finish an ingenious Industry to be beyond Scheme only.

Procession follow a dead Corps not in Mourning, pursue a Roguery.

of a Benefactor Relation, attain to some good according.

follow'd her Brother's Corps in his native Place to Church in a Coffin with a Woman, A. not in Mourning ; A. heard how such Brother married to his Ruin.

Passing Bell heard for his Daughter, shew'd A. of his Beggarliness near an end.

Coffin colour'd A. seeing for his Funeral in his Hall, shew'd of his atchieving a new good way of Livelihood.

Grave A. seeing dug at his Seat Door, shew'd him of a Debt charg'd on him.

too short seeming, that is, less than expected.

dug in his Passage, shew'd of his paying a Debt e'er he could well transact his Business.

Passing by one in a Field, shew'd A. of attaining to have a House of his own, and where to claim Burial.

Sermon making, shew'd of claiming a dormant Right.

Bearers often shew Usurers.

Bier A. ceas'd from lying under its Clothes, he ceas'd from acting wickedly.

Buried in general shews the same as dead.

See your Brother or Enemy, shews you of some Strife come to an end.

Seem your self, gives you as much Wealth as Earth on you.

in another's Garden, out of their Estate.

Vid. *Seeming dead* supra.

Alive, threats with Imprisonment and Captivity.

In a stinking Tomb, shew'd A. of marrying disgracefully.

Tomb. Shrine of a dead King's Whore reſpecting, ſhew'd *A.* of receivi
(10)   bad Money.

Sort noble, ſhew'd of a Book of excellent Wiſdom.

to others, illuſtrates the Worth of themſelves
their Anceſtors.

In general it ſhews of Actions worthy ſuch Mon
ment.

Iſle, Tomb the more glorious.

with three Rooms, the more exceedingly gl
rious.

Ruin'd ſeen, to ſome has ſhewn Baniſhment, and as if F
mily State over to you.

Perſons. Fathers, *A* ſeeing her's with a ſtinking Hole in
ſhew'd of his being ſpoke of infamouſ
after his Death.

A's Mother buried in't, ſhe married again a
his Death, as ill.

Anceſtors ſeen fine, promiſes you a laſting Fame.

Reverſion giving, promiſes of the lil
Good again in delay.

Thunder touching it, Glory.

Hurting it, Infamy.

Open'd, his Life examin'd after his Death.

Statues ſeen thereon, his or ſome Deſcel
dant's great Fame.

A Reſurrection ſeen there, ſhews of or
of his Family becoming glorious.

Another's ſeeing, threats you a Priſon.

Child of one year's old Marble Tomb ſeen, ſhew'd
a rich Book of one year's Labour.

Full of Serpents, ſhews your Anceſtors have bee
wicked.

Cankers, naſty Idlers.

Glowworms, famous and of Authority in th
Commonwealth.

Owls, contemptible Perſons.

Mice, Thieves.

Lizards, harmleſs Folks.

Dragons, noble Tyrants.

Actions. Earthquake making yours, the Prince's Edict raiſin
you.

Get Treaſure there, find learned Books and grea
Secrets.

Having one, to Servants Liberty, to others Land.

a foreign one, that is, die, dwell or marr
there.

Earthquake. Vid. *E.* ſupra.

Hiding in one, ſhews of acting wickedly.

Tout

Tomb. Actions. Make one, that is, marry and have Children, or do
(10)   many good Acts.

              A fair Foundation of one seen, the promi-
                 sing beginning of Books, &c.
           Many, do many fine things.
        Trees seen growing, thence promise of your Family's
        Restore.

CHAP. IV.

Of the Sun and Stars.

S *UN* in Scripture shew'd of the Empire, and darken'd, a fatal
  (1)   Change in it.
          So in other cases too in circumstance proper.
In private Vision, shews mostly of dispatch of Business.
    To many, the true Notion of Difficulties, confound-
      ing them.
    To most, clear Reasoning in opposition to Candles
      little Arts.
    To the Sick, Health, chiefly if in the Eyes.
    To the Prisoner, Liberty.
⊙ ☽ and Stars, to *Joseph* Father, Mother and Brethren:
    seeming greater, shew Prosperity.
             lesser, threat Decay.
Anointing one, shew'd his being hang'd and quarter'd.
Apparell'd as a Carter seen, good to Carters, Carriers and Wan-
                derers.
                to the sick, dangerous.
Become one, that is, a Judg or Mayor.
Catching at him thrice, foreshew'd to one a Kingdom.
Chamber. Vid. *Enter* infra.
Clothes. Vid. *Apparel* supra.
Colour clear shews Assuredness with great Persons, who will
    effect your Business.
    Clouded and hot, &c.
    Obscure and troubled, still bad, but to the Secret and
      Hider.
          To Princes and great Persons, Danger.
Dark seen, threats with Sickness or sore Eyes.
        To the secret or doubtful, good.
Bright shining, gives present Relief in Necessities.
Eclipsed seen, to some ill News.
         to some, the Death of a Son or Father.
Bloody in revenge, gives Success.

                               Sun.

Sun.
(1)

Colour Bloody. To others it threats capital Punishment to one in Family.

Black, threats with Destruction to the whole Family.

Conjunction. Vid. *Eclipse* supra in *Colour*.

Course. Rifing or fetting clear, good to all but the Secret.

Changing his Courfe threats, and fo the Nation her Government.

Rife with the Sun and run with the ☾, forefhew'd one the Gibbet.

☉ high feen, fhew'd one of rifing early and making the Day longer.

Rifing in the Eaft, eafes Sicknefs, and returns Travellers.

to the Secret, Difcovery.

to Travellers, the Way good.

to fome it gives a juft Prince.

to fore Eyes and Blindnefs, Relief.

to others, good Actions or getting of Children.

North, helps Poverty.

Weft fhews of vain Hopes, but to the Miferable gives Relief.

to the Secret, Difcovery.

to bad Eyes and the Sick, Health.

to Travellers, Return, and loft Hopes good.

Elfe to all very bad and Hindrance.

Out of her Womb *Auguftus*'s Mother.

Setting in the Eaft, fpoils Bufinefs.

Weft, fhews of Time fhort.

To a Woman it gives a Son.

Not fetting at all, fhews of Chriftian Reconciliations. The Day alters.

Darkned feen, the Peril of a King.

Vid. *Colour* fupra.

Difappearing, conceals Villanies.

To others it threats Death or Sicknefs.

To the Secret, generally good.

Eclipfed. Vid. *Colour* fupra.

Entring a Chamber, exceeding Good or Ill, as, &c.

Its Gifts, Children, and to a King a Son.

His Beams only entring a Houfe, Profperity, tho not great.

Your Bed, may threat you a Fever.

Better than if the Sun himfelf.

Falling out of Heaven feen, fhews of fome Empire altering or King dying.

Sun Falling on a House, threats it in danger of Fire.
(1)   to others, Danger of the Judg's Sentence.
Following him seeming dead, threats with Hanging.
Giving or taking any thing, Loss or Danger.
Handling, to a King gives a Captive Prince.
            to a Noble, Rebellion.
            to others, Freedom of Care.
House seen in, to some Fire, or other great Evil.
            to some, a Son shall be a King.
Hiding himself, to all but the Secret, ill.
            to some, Blindness.
            to others, Loss of Children.
Image his seen in't, to a Father, a Son.
            to a Mother, a Daughter.
Many Suns seen, shew of Confusion and Discord, as, *&c.*
            to some, popular Joy.
Shining bright, to some, a Mind well pleas'd.
            to some, the Favour of Great ones.
            to some, an effectual Course of Reasoning.
About the Head, to Malefactors, Pardon.
            to others, Glory.
In on you in your bed, shews your Business is unexpectedly
    dispatch'd.
    Enter a House where he shines, get an Estate.
Scorching you, threats of your Prince's Tyranny.
Vanishing, to some Death or Blindness.
            Vid. *Disappear* supra.
Moon in general as the Sun, and only less Good or Ill, and by Women.
(2)   To some, she shews of the Wife and Female Relations.
            To some, of Instability and Mutability of Fortune.
    Seen in publick Places, of publick Import.
            with a bloody Cross, shew'd of a persecuting
                Church.
    In State, she shews the State Ecclesiastick ; 2*d* to the
                Sun, the Civil.
            to some, she shews of the Queen, and Depu-
                ty Governor.
            to some, she shews of being a Senator.
        ⊙ ☽ and Stars to *Joseph*, Father, Mother and Brethren.
Rising with the Sun and running with the Moon, foreshew'd one
    the Gibbet.
Delivered of a ☽ shining o'er *Britain*, shew'd *A.* having a Daugh-
                ter after Queen there.
        3 ☽'s like her self, 3 Daughters dying in a Month.
Many seen, threats with Confusion and Discord.
            Contending the worse.
            Vid. *My Book of Apparitions.*
    In private Vision, Divisions among Friends.

Moon. Many in publick Viſion, Diſcord about Queens, Churches or
(2)   puties.

     Image one's ſeen in't, to a Man a Son, to a Woman a Daught
         to ſome it threats a ſtrange, unſettled
         wandring State.
         to ſome it ſhews their Son fares ill or w
         as is the ☽ there.
         to Uſurers and Bankers ſeen in't, 'tis G
         and Profit.
         to the Secret, Diſcovery.
         to Saylors and the Sick, very bad.

Lighting a Candle at her, threats with Blindneſs.

Change becoming Blood, ſhew'd of the State Eccleſiaſtick alter
     Falling from Heaven, threats Sickneſs.
         to others, ſhews of the Death of ſ
         great Woman.

Appearing like a white Face, to a Virgin Marriage.
         to a Wife, a fair Daughter.
         to an Husband, a Son.
         to a Banker, &c. Good.

     Dark, threats Death of Female Friends, or Loſs
         Money.
         to others, Ill Voyages or Madneſs.
         to others, Sadneſs, or Treachery of great V
         men.
         turning clear is è con, and good.

Clear, is good to all.

At full to a fair Woman, gives her Lovers.
         to Villains, Diſcovery.
         to the Sick or Mariners, Death.

Shining about your Bed, Grace, Pardon and Deli
         rance by a Woman.
         to others, it gives a loving W
         to others, Profit by Merchand
         and Navigation.

     Colour Pale ſeen, ſhews Joy.
         Various, ſhews of Heavineſs or Loſs.
         Bloody, threats of Travel or Pilgrimage.
         to others, Peril.
         Purple, gives Profit or Increaſe.

New, gives Expedition of Buſineſs.
         Decreaſing ſeen, has ſhewn of a gr
         Lady's Death.

Greater ſeeming, promiſes Poſterity.
         Leſſer, threatens Decay.

Planets in general, ſhew to us as are their Natures.
(3)   to ſome they ſhew of Judges and Senators.
     Vid. *Aſtronomy* in *Science* in *Learning.*

Com

Comets feen, threat with publick Dangers, Fears and Changes.
(4)   To private Men they threat from Foreigners and new
            Officers.
         To fome, Danger of new Hereticks.
         To others, War, Peftilence and Famine.
Stars in general, fhew of Colleges and Congregations of People.
(5)   In the Scriptures, fome great Perfons.
         To Students, Secrets.
         And ☉ in publick Prophecy feen darkned, fhew'd of
            the King and Nobles ruin'd.
         ☉ and ☽ to *Joseph,* Father, Mother and Brethren.
         Vid. *Aftronomy* in *Arts,* &c.
Sorts, Signs, *Ram, England,*
         Virgo, France.
         Pyed Bull, Ireland.
Kind, fair and clear feen, is good to the Secret and Tra-
         vellers, and to all Profperity.
         Bright feen, promifes you of a fplendid Fortune.
         Dusky and pale feen, threats all Mifchief.
         Troubled feen, threats of Perils and Sorrows,
         Summer ones, caufe good from ill, *& è con.*
         Name, *Canis Ira Populi.*
Names, *Andromeda* threats with Chains.
         Corona, Honour from the People.
                  and fo all fhewing as are their Natures.
Beat by them, Death.
Becoming a Sun or Star, that is, a Judg or Senator.
Being as under the Houfe-heaves, breaks up Houfe-keeping
   where, *&c.*
Falling in general and clear, fhews Health.
         All feen, forefhew'd one bald.
         Seen to the Rich, Poverty and Sorrow, to the Poor
            Deftruction.
         On an Houfe, afflicts it with Judgments or Sicknefs.
                  To fome, that it be forfook or burnt.
         Ones Head, People talk great of him.
         A Sepulcher, fhew'd of a great Man dying.
Many feen to the Earth, fhew'd of great Battel and
         Slaughter following.
One feen and another rife, to a Servant his Mafter dy-
            ing and his Son fucceeding.
         To all, lofe Friends great or little, as are
            the Stars.
Into a Sepulcher, the Death of fome great Man.
From Heaven, and acting, fome great popular Man
         rifing.
         Into the Sea, ruining the People.
         At leaft, great Exchange of great Affairs,

Stars Flying in the Night ſeen, ſhew of vain Terrors and Expectation
(5)   the lighter and brighter, the worſe.

    Houſe, Vid. *Being* ſuprà, and *Shine* infrà.

    Moving ſwift ſeen, threats you Mad or Sad.

    Removing, ſhews the Poor in the People.

          Wandring diſorderly, threat of Sedition, Faction an
          Tumult.

    Robbing them, foreſhew'd Sacrilege.

          But to Students, the attaining of Secrets.

    Seeing them in general, threats Loſs to the Emperor or Lord.

          In an Houſe, threats Death to the Maſte

       Many in general, elſe gives Increaſe of Power and Joy.

    Shining in at an Houſe, threats Death to the Maſter, he is the Su
    there.

    Speaking to you, ſhews of great Events, but moſtly calamitous.

    Stealing, as Robbing, *ſuprà.*

    Vaniſhing, to the Rich Poverty.

        to ſome, Loſs of Hair.

        to villanous Deſigns only good.

    Weep before them, } gives ſome Grace at the Prince's Hand.
    Worſhipping them, }

C H A P. V.

Of Heaven and Air.

HEaven in general, Vid. *Spirits*, Chap. 1. ſuprà.
(1)   In the Scripture, ſhew'd the Government.

        Hoſts thereof, or the Stars ſeen, ſhew
          ſome Policy Eccleſiaſtick
          Temporal.

        Prince of them, the High Prieſt.

        $\odot$ $\mathcal{D}$ and Stars ſeen fine, orderl
        and clear, gives Health.

        Clear ſeen, gives the Knowledg of Secrets

    Aſcending, ſhews of great Difficulty and Grief, and th
        higher the worſe.

        To the Sick, Death.

        Jacob's Ladder with Angels, *Iſrael's* Di
        vine Approaches.

    Not too high, gives Tranquillity and Happineſs

    Fly thither as a Bird, gives great Preferment.

        to the Secret, Ill.

        to Servants, great Place.

Heaven

Heaven afcending, fee others ways to afcend there, reafon out their
(1)   ways to Riches and Glory.

Beating you, threats you Death.

Being there, fhews great Knowledg of Secrets.

    Having an Houfe, Death or great Noblefs.

    Heavenly Hall *A.* crown'd in, gave him a fine Fune-
ral.

    Tumbled down from thence, to *Cæfar* Death.

    Become a Sun or Star there, that is, a Judg or Senator.

Bird *A.* heard fpeaking to him flying thence, *A*'s Preferment;
Petition was heard.

Crown, Vid. *Falling* infrà.

Defcending thence an Angel feen cloth'd in Yellow, fhew'd of
a Plague-infection menacing.

Earth feen rais'd to it, gave an excellent Prince.

    Parch'd there, fhew'd of hot dry times.

Falling thence, a Dart wounded *A*'s Foot, he died, fnake-ftung
in that Foot.

    A Crown of white Flowers for your wearing,
fee Death near.

        Fire fpreading in Rays o'er the
Head, to *Adrian* Empire.

    Vid. *Fire* infrà *Chap.* 6.

Falling Fire thence, to great Men great Anger.

    to mean Perfons, danger from the great.

    to a King, War in his Dominions, or the
Government at rack.

Houfe having there, gives Death or great Glory.

Moving, fhews of fomewhat Myftical.

Man chain'd feen fit there or let down thence, threats with a
Tyrant.

    A Boy with a Whip feen there, fhew'd of a weak Prince
fet as a Scourge.

Paffing away feen, fhews of the prefent Government changing.

Sitting there, declares you of Happy News.

Speaking to you, fhews of great Events, but moftly calamitous.
Vid. *Bird* fuprà.

Sky touching Crown wearing, fhew'd *A.* of his Death near.
(2)   the Ground feen, fhew'd of Expedition of Bufinefs.

Falling feen, threats with Guilt or Crimes, and as if you wanted
Government defac'd.

Afcending feen, gives you Honour and Dignity.

Neck-piercing Swan feen, to *Socrates* fhew'd of *Plato* his Scholar.

Burning feen, threats of Difeafes or Wickednefs in the Dreamer.
Vid. *Fire, Chap.* 6.

Air. In general it ſhews of our Heart, Breaſt, Life and Religion.
(3)   So Air, projective States.

Fire, deſperate and paſſionate States. ⎫
Water, hazardous and venture-ſome States. ⎬ And all abſolutel ſuch as mere E lements.
Earth, ſure and fix'd States. ⎭

Weather-Glaſſes, Vid. *Goods.*

Minded, ſhew'd of a Monition to work, as th Weather offers.

Fair *A.* going in return'd back on't, he repair' his Prodigality.

State Calm, gives a Life and Manners peaceable and acceptable t all.

To others, it gives Buſineſs ſucceſsful according.

Clear is good to all, and takes away Deceit, and as if ſa no Fame, Superiority or Project againſt him.

to ſome, Wiſdom and Truth with Proſperity.

to ſome, Gain and Expedition.

to ſome, it ſhews them general Eſteem, and the very Enemies reconcil'd.

to all Deſigners good, but in Searches and Voyag chiefly.

Cold, threats with Want.

Hot, threats with Paſſion and Labour.

Red Sky ſeen, has threated with Wars.

Troubled and Cloudy, threats with Religious Errors and Fear

To others, Buſineſs with Diſpatch, but in Ange

Windy, threats with Contentions, as is the Plac where, &c.

Tempeſtuous, the ſame to great Loſs, in Circumſtance.

Tempeſts and Thunders, ſhew of all controlir changing Menaces.

Clearing after them tho, gives happy Iſſ in the end.

Dark, threats with Diſeaſes melancholy, and Tears.

To others, Obſtruction in Buſineſs.

Quiet, good to Aſtronomers and Prophets only.

To others, a quiet Life.

Actions, Circle of Drums ſeen in it before me, ſhew'd me of n Skill applauded, &c.

Eſcape to free Air from your Confinement, from Ol ſtruction to Freedom anſwerable.

Flying there, Vid. *infrd* in this Chapter.

Hanging in the Air a Man ſeen, ſhew'd of the Confiden tion of Apparitions there.

Be in an Houſe, die with good Fam

A

Air. Actions, hanging in the Air seeing Wheat, shew'd of a good Sea-
(3)   son for its sowing near.
                       Seeing the Earth, shew'd of dry Wea-
                       ther.
                       Vid. also *Hang* in *Posture.*
        Seeing it, declares of things incredible.
                to some, it shews of their ill Deeds conceal'd.
        Standing in it, projecting with an ill grounded Assur-
        ance.
        Taking the Air in Diversion, shews of making merry, as
        is the occasion.

Meteors in general, shew of Foreign and unexpected things of little
(4)   Moment.
        Chasms, Vid. *Voids* infra.
        Comets, Vid. *Stars* supra.
        Dews, shew of Learning, Grace and Blessing.
        Hail, Frost and Snow, Vid. *postea* in *Frost.*
        Mists thick and stinking, shew of palpable and pernicious
                Errors.
                Obstructing the Sight, blinding the Understanding.
Parelios declare of Women, and shew Foreign Affairs.
Rainbows in general are more specious than profitable, and
                more for Delight than Gain.
                To the poor good, it changes the Time
                and Air.
                To Princes, it gives Women and fading
                Dominions.
        Sort seen turn'd up and down, is very bad.
                Black, it threats Calamity and Destruc-
                tion.
        Posture, to the right side seen good, to the left ill.
                In the West, to the Rich good, to the
                Poor bad.
                In the East, good to the Poor and Sick.
                Over your Head or near you, gives you
                                Change of Fortune.
                                To some, Death and
                                Ruin of Family.

        Voids,   ⎫
        Whirlpools, ⎬ threat of Melancholy and Evils in Religion.
        Chasms,   ⎭
Clouds. Colour white, gives Prosperity and good News.
(5)   to the Secret, Discovery.
                to Travellers, a good Journey.
                        and if seen drawing upwards, a good
                        Return on it.
                Little ones seen lie on the Earth, shew'd of a
                little good to happen.
                        D 5   *Clouds.*

Clouds. Colour Red, Anger.

(5)   Obscure, ill Issue, Anxiety, and Trouble.

     Yellow, Trouble and ill Success.

     Black, Fears and Tempests.

Mounting seen, shew'd Travel, and to Travellers gave Return.

Flying above them, to *Julius Cæsar* shew'd Death.

Sitting or dwelling among them, threats of sudden Death.

     To some it shews vain Glory.

Clouded the Stars seen, is very bad.

Cloudy Jewels shew of Joy and Grief mix'd.

     Castles seen about one, shew'd to one of the Divine Protection.

Rain, shews to all Change, to the Ill Good, and to the Good Ill.

(5)   Clear, with Happiness.

     Troubled, Misery.

To Travellers Vexation and Tears.

To Tradesmen and Merchants Impediments and Spoils.

In at an House, threats Housekeeping Affairs in an ill Posture there.

     Every where, the Poverty and Calamity universal.

     Wetting your Bed even, to render you restless.

Falling, the Air clear, shew'd of Trouble unexpected.

Raining literally. *Vid. Grammar.*

Drink clear, to the Sick Recovery.

     Troubled, threats with Trouble and Sickness.

Washing his Hands in it, to the sick gave an healthy Sweat.

Moderate, seasonable, and clear, gives great Riches.

     To Messengers only Hindrance.

In little Drops, Gain to all Farmers especially.

     But then with Prospect as of time to come.

Sorts, Tempestuous threats with Hurt and Trouble.

     To the Miserable only Good, after a Storm a Calm.

     To Lovers Discord.

     To the Married Controversies.

     To Bargainers oppressing Contention.

Place. In a Way hard on you, troublesome and expenceful, but sure Hopes.

     Run for Shelter, stress'd for the present by it.

     To a fork'd great Oak, to a double Estate.

On your Brother's Garden, you seeing it from your Chamber-window, profit you against a contentious Enemy.

Wind. Common. *Vid. Sail* in *Water.*

(7)   Gentle shews of good News, and is good for all.

     A Fire left for it to blow up, a Debt left to be got by Reputation.   *Wind.*

Wind. Tempeftuous in general fhews of great Bufinefs with Fears,
  (7)   Labors, and popular Contentions.
                               To fome fudden Crifis's and Changes
                               above us, and out of our power.
                               In the Scriptures, Tumults among
                               the People.

Whirlwinds, parting Friends. Tumultuous, turns
of their Affairs.
Hurricans blowing: you away near, popular Chit-
Chat near confounding you.
Ordinary, to all Inconftancy with Brawls and Se-
dition.
                 To fome the Meffengers of the Mighty.
                 To fome great Fears, Labours and
                 Toils to Lofs and Difgrace.
Seen ill to all but the Poor and Miferable, to them
after a Storm a Calm.
Place. On your Enemies Garden feen, fhews fuch
                 Ill on your Enemies.
                 But you in't, your felf are fo
                 hurt thro Enemies.
Acting in general threats with Trouble from the People.
Againft you, popular Impediments.
With you, giving you Succefs.
Blowing down Chimney, the Fire about houfe, Quarrel
in Family to the damage of Houfekeeping.
Bringing Duft threats with Grief.
          Heat, Anxiety.
          Cold, Poverty.
Carrying you away, threats you wandring as is the Quar-
ter.
Hindring you, Paffions and Animofities doing fo.
Overturning Trees, Nobles.
          Herbs, People.
          Temples, Priefts.
          Houfes, Great Men.
          Towers, Kings.
Paffing thro Corn and not hurting it, gives Plenty.
          Doing Mifchief on it, a bad Year enfues.
Scattering Duft and darkning the fight, threated the Plague.
Terrifying you, popular Perfecution.
          Carrying you away, travel upon't according.
Thunder, Shews of Princes terrible Proclamations.
  (8)   Hearing fhews of good Tydings.
     To fome Contention, Strife, and Reprehenfion from far.
     Yet but as projective, threats to Earthquakes, to Princes
     taller Hurts.
And Lightning, to fome Gain, and a Change avoiding blafting
     Ruin.   *Thunder.*

Thunder and Lightning, to moſt States of great changes,
   (8)   to ſome approaching Sickneſs.
            to ſome the Anger of Princes with loſs.
Without Lightning threats Trouble and Falſhood to
    Servants.
In a dark and troubled Sky, Hurt from ſome great Diſplea-
    ſure.
Fighting ſhews Word-contentions.
      with Lightnings great Wars.
Waſting *Italy*, *Hannibal's* Emblem.
Thunder alone, oft the Words of Meſſengers.
Thunderbolt breaking ſomewhat down, to ſome has ſhewn De-
    ſtruction of Houſe and Family.
Striking a Pillar, Danger of Loſs.
           To Prieſts Loſs of Prieſthood.
           To Fathers Loſs of Children.
           To others Loſs of Houſe-Suppor-
           ters.
    Your Head, threats you Death.
        Houſe, threats you loſing Goods.
        Ground where you ſtand, conſtrain
         your Remove.

Lightning without Thunder threats with vain and cauſeleſs Fears.
   (9)   Seeing it gives Diſpatch, and is good to Men in Dignity.
      To the Ambitious Glory.
      To ſome Loſs of Children.
      It returns Strangers, and ſhews Natives to die at
        home.
      In Suits for Inheritance Loſs, elſe Gain.
      It forbids Enterers.
Paſſing thro a Town ſeen, blaſts your Deſigns there.
      Way, baulks your Hopes in ſuch a Way.
    By you in an unknown unfurniſh'd Houſe, removes
       you, as an Inhabitant, to your Glory.
      Without Tempeſt, removes to all their pre-
       ſent Abode.
Falling near without touching, ſhews you of Change of Place.
Before one, forbids Travail, or ſends Death.
At the Feet, ennobles the Poor.
      Deſtroys the Rich.
        To Parents Loſs of Children, it deſtroys
         Buds.
        Sitting in a Magiſtrate's Seat, it fixes
         you there.
        But being an Officer before, It dethrones
         you.
Touching one, it diſcovers Sins and Poverty.
    To Parents Loſs of Children.

                                     Lightning.

Lightning touching one, To Friends and married Folks Separation.
(9)   To the Unmarried it shews Marriage.
          To Kings and Nobles Glory.
          To others Loss of Goods.
     Striking your Ring, Bed, or Eye, Death to your Son or
          Wife.
          Outward Bed-post and consuming it, your
               Wife dies.
          A besieg'd City, rais'd the Siege.
          You lying down, is very bad.
     Burnt by it, but as if but touch'd, if not beaten down.
          Consum'd by it, Death.
          Lighting a Flame gives Glory.

Flying, In general shews of projective Exaltation above the common
(10)   Level.
          To many happy present Shifts, tho without solid
               Bottom.
          To some sudden Journeys or hasty News.
          To Captives Good.
          To the sick Death.
          To sedentary Traders and Scholars Ill.
          To some Blindness, as fearing to fall.
          To many Presumption in Reason or Faith, &c.
     Others seen fly, shews of their projecting, &c.
          Arm'd Men seen fly, promises you Victory, &c.
          Many seen fly, threats War or Plague, &c.
     Birds in general seen. Vid. *Birds* in *Creatures.*
          Ravens seen fly, threats of Complaints and
               Sadness.
          Crows and Birds of Prey seen fly in a troubled
               Air, shew'd of Anger with Loss and Misery.
          Over your Head Eagles seen fly, shews you of Honour.
          House an Angel seen fly, gives you Joy and
               Blessing.
          Common Birds seen fly o'er you, threats you
               Hurt by Enemies.
     Bell in the Air *A.* pulling down, shew'd of his commanding or
          reigning Sickness.
     Accidents desiring and unable, shew'd of Imprisonment and
          Constraint.
          Falling flat on't, your Project ends in Despair.
          Shot as in your Flight, treated by others as you
               have gloried.
          Trip'd up as flying, baulk'd in your Aims of Glory.
     High in the Air shews of sudden Journeys and hasty News.
          The higher the more stately, but more hazardous Project.
               The lower the surer, but nearer Experience.
          And down as one will, gives Facility in Business.
                                             Flying,

Flying High, and fall in your Flight, loſe a Certainty for a Project.
(10) Aided with Wings, to the Poor Riches.
    to the Rich Dignity.
    to Servants Liberty.
    Without Wings or Supports, threats with Fears or Dangers.
    To others Projects not ſure or durable.
On Eagles Wings, to Princes Death.
    To others, great Mens Favours and Travails.
On Horſeback, in a Project of great Strength and Uſe.
Leaning on an Iron Staff, ſupported by ſome ſure Great Man.
On a Man's Back, thro the Command of ſome reaſonable Courſe.
On a Chariot of Ropes, in ſome Project of reaſoning.
In a Chair, ſhew'd to one a chargeleſs Truſtee Law-ſuit.
In a Bed or Chair tho, to ſome Sickneſs.
    To Travellers has ſhewn of their Family going with them.
Poſture general, with your Feet ſpread before you, in a preſpoſterous Anxiety.
    Jumpingly, projectively thro many large Efforts.
    Deform'd ſeeming in't, threats you with Diſgrace and Contempt thereby.
    Ridiculouſly, projecting to expoſe your ſelf thereby.
    Backward, to Sailers Good.
    to others Idleneſs.
    to the Sick Death.
    Long, has ſhewn of Travail.
    Proſtrate, in Glory as to others, as to your ſelf in Deſpair.
    Upright and not too high, a ſafe and prudent Project.
Before your pitying Friend with Bravery in Adverſity.
    Enemy's Houſe projecting, to glory o'er his Enmity.
    A Miniſter over Pales, act a little in Conſcience Treſpaſs.
    Many as a Pigeon without Wings, be cenſur'd as idly innocent projective.
By, is as paſs in Travail.
Down from the Exchange-Top gloryingly, colour well your crack'd Credit.
    A Precipice to a leaded Houſe, to a worſe Oeconomy.
From Dogs, avoiding Calumnies and Reproach.

Flying

Flying Pofture. From Serpents, that is, fubtle and crafty Enemies.
(10)
    Others by Purfuit, and Conftraint, and with Terror, Ill.

    With Fear when not follow'd, projectively avoid things in vain.

In a Street, exceeding in publick Converfe anfwerably.

    Room, that is, exalted projectively in Converfe above others.

    An Hall, a Converfe according.

    Up and down, in feveral in Variety and Triumph.

Place near home threats with Wandring.

    To the Sick Death.

Over others, gives you Authority with them as Referee, &c.

    A Court to an inner Room, obtain a Court Office.

Oaks, exceeding old Age in projective Efforts.

Woods, projecting in fcorn to Trouble and Vexation.

Water, furpaffing Troubles by projective Efforts.

    By a Bridg with Caution.

    Cleverly with beautiful Iffue, and to good.

Houfes and forlorn Ways have fhewn of Sedition.

A fine Houfe alone, projectively compafs fuch an Oeconomy.

Unto Heaven or the Clouds, to the Secret Ill.

    to a Servant great Place.

    Heaven, &c. and not return on it, die with Praife.

    The Tops of Houfes, project within Hopes poffible.

    Thatch'd, command Tenants and Inferiors well.

    Another's Chamber, aim to command his private Defigns.

Athens's Academick Gate, fhew'd *Plato*'s Glory.

A pleafant green Mead high feated, full of Rivers, chofe Phyfician to a Noble.

A Beam in an Houfe from a Dog affaulting, tell a Dun you expect Rent.

With Birds, accompany Strangers, and be punifh'd with Malefactors.

C H A P.

CHAP. VI.

Of the Fire.

IN *general*. All the Elements ſhew us of Eſtates abſolute as are the
(1)   Natures.
         Air projective States.
         Water ventureſom and troubleſome States.
         Earth ſure and fix'd States.
         Fire deſperate and paſſionate States.
            Fiery Monſters oppoſe you angry, ſenſeleſs Courſe
               croſs you.
            Vid. *Rays* and *Glory* in *Spirits*.
Elementary, in general ſhew of Tumults, &c.
 (2)   Vid. *Comets* in *Stars*.
            Vid. *Meteors* and *Lightning* in *Heaven and Air*.
Sorts, moderate, fair and ſhining ſeen in the Heavens, ſhe
         of the Menaces of great Lords.
      Large, fair, and thick, the Approach of Enemie
               Sedition, and Tumult.
            To others Poverty and Famine from th
               Quarter ſeen.
      Clear, pure, and clean, not great or thick, threa
         Great Men.
Actions. Burning Trees and Graſs, Little and Great con
      ſum'd by it.
      Carrying it is moſt exceeding bad.
            And ſo ſhewing it openly is the ſame.
      Coming into a Ship, from that ſide a Tempeſt
         threatned.
      Falling and born unhurt in a Crown of Rays, t
         Adrian ſhew'd Empire.
            And hurling Puniſhment to the Dreame
               his Father or Son.
Torches and Flames falling from Heaven threat with Dan
      ger of Life.
      To others Hurts in the Head greatly.
      To others with burning Boughs, threated th
         burning of Woodſtacks, Colonies, and Trees
         Wars, Quarrels, and Sterility.
Coals ſeen fall from Heaven, ſhew of Great Men ruin
      and conſum'd.
      Bruſh'd off like Candles, Great Men ſee you angril
      but you eſcape.

Comm

Common. State orderly or calm, and seen well lighted in a Chimney, (3) good. (c)

　　So a Candle, &c.

　　Disorderly shews of things in Extremity and Passions.

　　　　For Mischief it threats speedy, swift, violent, and trifling.

　　Perfum'd, Great one worshipping to a Prince gave Victory.

　　Large in an House, shews of Extravagance or great Danger.

　　　　To some it shews of Anger or Sickness.

　　Moderate gives House-Plenty.

　　Little threats with Poverty, that is, have but little use of it, or to dress with it.

　　Troubled gives Heaviness.

　　Dead, to the Sick Death.

　　　　to the Well Poverty.

　　Crackling and sparkling with much Smoke, Anger, Dispute and bad News.

Actions. Blown up by the Wind, a Payment forc'd by Reputation.

　　　　In general, to many shews of old Quarrels stir'd up.

　　　　Down Chimney about House-Boarders, Quarrels to confusion of Housekeeping.

　　Burning well fortunates you to Honour and Profit, but regarding Housekeeping greatly.

　　Crackling and Sparkling threats of Anger and Infamy.

　　Going out strait, Hurt, if not Death or Banishment.

　　　　To some Family-Indigence and Necessity.

　　Kindled easily, to Women Generation.

　　　　And so it gives a Boy and an easy Delivery.

　　Make with green Wood, shuffle with bad Money.

　　　　On blowing vanishing, a Profit ceasing on Prosecution.

　　Quench'd soon, to the Sick quick Recovery. As further needless.

　　Run thro A's House, Fire in the middle of his House, bear his Anger without return, tho senseless.

　　　　Clothes burnt by't, Reputation hurt thereby.

　　Sitting by it shews of Desire, and if till out, in vain.

Place. At or by your Door without, make one be large in Charity and foreign Expence.

Parts. Brands carried about, shew'd of Endeavours for Quarrels.

　　Sea-coals seen, shews of hidden Malice withal, or else as other Fewel.

Common.

Common Parts. Seacoals. A Boat for it, a Convenience in the Trouble
thereof.

(2)

Seen in two Ovens to bake with, parted Boarders.

Coals treading upon, threats with greatest Miseries
from Enemies.

Going out shews Treachery to the Master.

Lighting a Fire from you in a Pot, to a Great
Man Servitude.

Eating them shews Good from the Master.

To some shews of Enemies speaking ill
of them.

Handling them unhurt, renders you fearless of
Enemies.

Seeing dead ones, shews of Expedition of Business.

Burnt by some, threats you with Reproach and
Shame.

Soot. Vid. *Chimney* in *Building.*

Flame splendid seen, gives Honour and Joy. This a
not in a Chimney.

Sudden Flashes, fierce Anger, hazarding Hurt

Quenching them, suppressing Quarrels.

Hurt by it, Danger thro medling.

Smoke. Vid. *Clear* and *Unhurt* in *Burning* suprà.

Smoke shews either as Fire, or Ignorance and Blindness

Obscuring the Sun, Errors darkning clearest
Truths.

Darkning the Castle from the City burnt
shew'd the commanding Citizens destroy'
made the Castle yield.

A smoky Window, a mean erroneous Prospe
of Oeconomy.

Burning. Unhurting and clear seen or having, gives great Glory or In

(4) famy on all consuming self-pre-
servative State.

To the Poor Riches or Inheritance.

To the Master Managery beyon
Treachery.

To the Rich Honour, Office and Dig
nity.

Vid. *Rays* in *Spirit.*

Provisions so and unconsum'd, famo
Plenty.

A Beard having so without Smoke, ga
one a wise Son without a Blot.

A Crown of such, to *Adrian* Empire.

An Army so, *Alexander*'s into *Persia.*

An House seen so, shew'd of vain Fe
where most secure.　　　　Burni

Burning. Perſons. Fathers ſeen ſo to the Son, threated the Son's Death:
(4)   *Alexander's* burning Army ſeen march, that is, his
         invincible one.

Lover, *A.* ſeeing his burning in a Pitcher, foreſhew'd
    of her Death by a Servant.

Unknown, *A.* ſeeing burn his Hand at a Candle,
    ſhew'd *A.* of his Servant departing.

Self feeling threats Danger.

    With Pain threats of Envy, Choler, and
      Debate.

    As a Coal, has ſhewn of a burning Ague or
      Fever.

    Unhurt, ſhews you greatly glorious or un-
      glorious, as above.

    Clothes burnt an ill Sign.

    On the Head, threats Deſtruction.

      Flaming and not hurting tho, gives
        great Glory.

    Your Fingers in making a Fire, dun one to
      your Diſprofit.

Goods, and not conſuming, gives famous Glory and Plenty
    too, as, *&c.*

Somewhat into the Fire flung, put it to the Iſſue of
    a deſperate Quarrel.

Trees or Woods ſeen burn, threats alſo generally the
    Dreamer.

Proviſions in an Houſe burnt, threat the Steward.

Cabinet Mrs. burnt, threats her Death.

    Her Cupboard the ſame.

Bed ſeen burnt, threats Death, Damage or Sickneſs
    to the Dreamer's { Husband or
                 Wife.

Stacks of Corn ſeen burnt, threat of Famine or Mor-
    tality.

    Not conſuming on't tho, ſhew great
      Plenty.

Furnace one ſeen burnt, ſhews you of travelling and
    wandring Removes.

    Hazardous, the ſame in hazard only.

Pillow on fire, ſhew'd to *Polycarp* his Martyrdom.

Chamber Chimney ſeen on fire, and then reaching to
    herſelf, ſhew'd one Death on't.

Gate ſeen on fire, threats Death to the Maſter or
    Miſtreſs.

Burnt Stones build with, reſcue good Notions from
    Oblivion.

Clothes burnt in paſſing a Fire, repute hurt in bearing
    Anger.

Burning. Dead Body burn, confound peremptorily a Roguery.

(4)   Houſe conſum'd, to ſome Death in Family, as is the Room burnt it your own.

To one it ſhew'd a Brother dying.

To ſome Adverſity, Trouble, and Law-ſuits.

To ſome Baniſhment.

Quench'd ſoon tho, with ſpeedy Recovery.

Your own Houſe by, your ſelf be an infamous Prodigal.

Crackling and ſparkling, the Infamy the worſe.

Engines playing, Reaſons of Prevention.

Burnt Houſe paſs by, exceed ſuch Miſery in your State.

Thorough in Anger, ſet aſide an Oeconomy.

Down and rubble, Cold, Poverty, or Baniſhment. If your own ſeen ſo.

Rebuilt fairer, coming into better Hands.

Burning ſee it, find Scandal thro your Eſtate waſting.

Sorts. Father's ſeen on fire, to a Servant be warn'd off by her Maſter.

Put out, no ſign left fully reconcil'd.

Own, to ſome has ſhewn of its falling.

Stop'd not mended, never rebuilt on it.

Enemy's ſeen burnt, glories you in what he is your Enemy.

Brother the ſame, you being out of it.

But you in it, threats you hurt by rivalling Intereſt.

A Counting Houſe ſeen burnt, ſhew'd of a Tithe by rate chang'd.

Two would extinguiſh it, vain Endeavours being made to prevent it.

Cities whole being burnt, threats you Deluge or Change of Place.

To others has ſhewn of Bankrupt Credit.

Your own Houſe only left ſtanding, perſonal Regard being only left.

One Houſe only burnt, one Trade only fails.

½ burnt by a Fire from _Charon's_ Houſe, a Conſpiracy there rooted out ½ its Inhabitants.

Parts in general. Vid. _Goods_ ſupra.

Houſe. Parts, Rooms, Kitchin burnt down, ſome Cook or Servant dies or removes, if your own Kitchin.

A Pillar on't only, ſome Rent only fails.   _Burning_

Burning House, parts, Rooms, Stable burnt; a Groom dies or warns off.
(4)   Hall Furniture burnt, Death or Hurt to
     Master or Man.
     Shop burnt, threats with losing Goods
      or Possessions.
    Stairs *A.* seen fired by his Son, shew'd such Son
     much hurt by them.
    Walls seen on Fire, shew'd of Sickness to fol-
     low.
    Windows fore ones burnt, shew'd of a Brother's
     Death.
     back ones, Death of Sisters.
    Door burnt seen, is good to the Wife, but bad
     to the Master.
    Top seen burnt down, threats Death to the Lord
     or Wife.

Light in general. Vid. *Sight in Sense.*
(5)   It shews of private Arts, as the Sun of common Rea-
     sonings.
    Christ thron'd in Light seen amidst great Darkness,
     shew'd of great Revelations.
  Sort. Clear in a House, to the Poor, Riches.
      to the Single, Marriage.
     to the Sick, Health.
    With a little Death's Head see, avoid Death
     menacing.
    Obscure and troubled, Heaviness and Death by Sickness.
    Put out seen, to the Sick Health, as a Watch
     Candle.
    Dying or going out, Death, except of a Watch Light;
     then Recovery, as needless further Use of it.
  In a Ship, gives Joy and Tranquillity to it.
    Afar off, gives a fair Wind and a good Haven, with
     no Tempest.
  Another's Hand, threats your Ill will be discover'd and punish'd.
    Put out, shews the contrary.
  Your own Hand try to bring down stairs, try to publish your
    private Notions.
    Hindred by others, Courses taken to obstruct you.
  Corps one seen on a River with Ships, shew'd me a *Londoner,*
    visiting me, that soon died on't.
  Lanthorn dark seen, foreshew'd of subtle Plots.
    The Light in it, shews the Dreamer's Spirit.
    Fair, gives Prosperity.
  Torches and Firebrands held by night, to young Folks Love and
    Marriage with Joy.
    To others, threatningly shew'd of Piracies, *&c.*
  Hold one only, is to the Secret Discovery.

Light. Torches burning clear, gives Happiness in sincere Friends:
(5)   Put out or darken'd seen, threats Sickness, Poverty or
                        Sadness.
                Of Straw carrying, gave Joy and good Management.
                Burning, *Asia* and *Europe* deliver'd of *Hecuba Paris's*
                        Mother.
Lamp of Brass, the Good or Ill durable, as, *&c.*
                Lighting it, gives Joy.
                        to some it reveals Secrets.
        Earth, good or ill, and reveals Secrets, as the other,
        but is less durable.
Candle in general shews of Princes, our Love, Soul, Studies
                        and Discipline.
                To others, Arts of reasoning in Obscu-
                        rities, as the Sun common.
                Making shews rejoicing.
        Sorts. A Wax Candle to a Lawyer shew'd of Chamber
                        Practice.
                        and seen to all, shews Gladness, as
                        of a good Message.
                Watchlight, to the Rich Poverty.
                        to the Sick seen put out, gives Reco-
                                very, as then needless.
                        Light another, renew
                                the Distemper.
                        Seen burn in your Chamber alone,
                                threats you with Indis-
                                position.
                        at a Door, threats you
                                in Attendance, as, *&c.*
        Lighting at the Moon, shew'd Blindness.
                In general, gives Joy.
                Two seen at *A*'s Head and Feet, threatned him
                        Destruction near.
                Not lighted seen, promises of Reward for some-
                        what past.
                Twice *A*. seeming, and still going out, shew'd *A*.
                        of his Search in Reasoning failing.
        Seeing in a Church, shew'd *A*. of reading a Sermon in his
                        Family.
                One alone lighted or in the Church-
                        yard, threats Death.
                Many *A*. seeing there with Laughter,
                        shew'd of his burying one Wife,
                        and marrying a second.
                In an House many lighted, to a Prince wise Ser-
                        vants.

Light. Candle feeing in an House, Dining-Room, to all promifes great
(s)   Joy and Mirth.

         Clear fhining feen on a Table or Ca-
            binet, to the Sick Recovery.
                to the Single Weddings.
       On an out Door Threfhold, fhew'd
           A. of tedious watching of Duns.

Put out feen, threats with Sicknefs, Sadnefs or Poverty.
         Eut of a Watch-light, to the Sich Re-
          covery.
      Darkned the fame, in lefs.
      Going out, to fome Death.
             to others, their Art at a Lofs.
             before an Attorny, to a Councel lofs
                of Bufinefs.
             thrice at anothers Houfe, your Art
                quite fails with him, as, *&c.*
             in a Church twice, fhew'd *A.* his
                Divine Reafonings failing, as im-
                perfectly purfued.

Handling, and not by way of Bufinefs, threats of Sick-
     nefs or Infirmity to follow.
Burning fair in a Room, fhew'd of good Reafonings
     offering.
           If by way of Search tho, fhews of Anger
            and Contention thro Artful Examina-
            tions.
      His Hand at it *A.* feeing a Man, fhew'd him of a
     Servant leaving his Service.
Finding, fhews of recovering fome good new Art of
     reafoning.
       A Friend brings you one in the dark, he fo
       aids your Diftrefs.
      You in the dark by a Candle, by powerful Rea-
      fonings difcovering you.
      Search, Vid. *Dark* in *Senfe.*
Carrying in the dark, reafoning artfully to difcover and
     reform others.
      Men ftriving to put it out, Courfes taken to
      fupprefs you.
      Brought in the Dark, fuch a Perfon appears a
      fullen Cavil, as, *&c.*

CHAP. VII.

Of Froſt and Snow, &c.

FROST in general, ſhews of Damage and Impediment, as thro
Poverty, &c.
To Travellers, Hindrance.
Worſe than Snow, as cauſing Loſs of Fruit.
Stops the Scent in your hunting, Want inter-
rupts your Dealings.
Be frozen your Sword, find Poverty, find
cool your Reſentment.
Impoveriſhed by it, diveſted of your Autho-
rity therefore.
Hail in general, threats Trouble and Heavineſs, and ſeen
fall the worſe.
to ſome, the Menaces of Robbers.
to ſome, it reveals Secrets.
To a Nation, War, Famine, Ruin, and certain
Loſs.
And Fire mingled with Blood, plunder-
ing Invaſions.
Ice in general, threats with great Poverty and Grief.
to ſome, Groans and Tears.
Walking on it, reſolving hazardouſly on ſuch
Troubles.
Sliding on it, projectively paſſing over ; Poverty,
Cares.
Paths of Ice, led by one, help'd by him to a
Winter Paſture.
With Snow ſeen, forbids Buſineſs, and backwards
travel.
To the Husbandman, and in ſeaſon
good, giving a good Year.
To Merchants and Soldiers, Fruſtra-
tion of Deſigns.
Snow in publick Dreams, publick Calamities.
In private Dreams, it ſhews of Hoſtile Endeavours
for Poverty.
Out of Seaſon ſtill, ſhews of Poverty and Im-
pediment.
But if it ſeem as in the Winter, the
Damage is the leſs.

Froſt

Froft. Snow in feafon and if little, Plenty; but much, Trouble, Want
and Enemies.

Seen in Patches, in a Garden gave pleafant
Froft, walk upon it.

A Country feen turn'd to it, and fo vanifhing, fhew'd A.
fo his own Family was to difappear thro Poverty.

A Mountain of it, a great Power of little Stay.

A Precipice of it mount, try at a Difficulty of Poverty
and Hardfhip.

Walk in a Snowy Place, defign wherein you are flighted
by Poverty.

CHAP. VIII.

Of Water-Actions.

Bathing in general, Vid. *Wafh* infra, and *Bathe* in *City.*
in Water naturally hot, to the Sick Health.
to others, Hindrance of Work.

Too hot, threats Trouble by fome in Family.
The hotter the Trouble, the worfe.

Cold, the fame as if too hot.

Temperate, gives Joy, Health and Profperity.

Clear, gives Joy and Diverfion.

Lakes troubled Water and abfurdly, threats great
Ills.

Clean to fome, has fhewn of purging Sins and
Corruptions.

Stinking, has fhewn of Shame and falfe Accufations.

Manner difturbed in't, threats with Obftruction of Remedies.

Decently, to the Sick Health.
to the Rich Profperity.
to the Poor Sicknefs.

With your Clothes on, threats you Sicknefs or
great Anger.

off without going in, Diftur-
bance, but of no continu-
ance.

Swimming in it, is ill in all Cafes.

Spring Bath find, difcover a noble Health-Courfe.

Bath in general, fhews of ill Conftitutions, Labour and Grief.

Seeing your felf there, threats you with An-
guifh.

E 4   *Bathing.*

Bathing. Bath in general, finging or dancing there, threats you with lof
of Voice or Society.

Seen empty of Water, hath threated of Labour in vain.

Drink there, be too infirm for fociable drinking.

Boiling, Vid. *Scalding* infra.

Breaking out of an Houfe Wall feen, threated with Trouble and Sadnefs.

Gather'd in Veffels on't, very bad.

But drying up, going off of it felf.

Bridg, Vid. *Building.*

Bubbling feen, threats with ftubborn Enemies.

Blood feen, fhewed of Contention to all forts of Murders.

Milling Claret as Chocolate, fhew'd one of ftirring up a
Cudgel Match.

Carrying in a Sieve, fhew'd of trufting a Rogue with Money, or being
robbed by Servants.

your Clothes the fame, but in Reputation more.

Falling out on't, it's utterly loft, otherwife not.

Dip, Vid. *Plunge* infra.

Drinking, Vid. *Drink.*

Drowned, Vid. *Dead.*

Falling into it, to fome Affliction, thro fome Flegmatick Difeafe.

A Pit or Well, threats of fome Accufation.

to fome, great Danger or Death.

Vid. *Fall* in *Action.*

Vid. *Carry* fupra, and *River* infra.

Ferryman, Vid. *Perfon* in *Grammar.*

Finding Water is good, and fhews Gain to all.

Something by Water, that is in Hazard and Trouble.

Flowing from a place unexpected, Care and Affliction according.

the Feet, to fome a Dropfy.

to fome alfo it has fhewn the Gallies.

Flung at one in his Way, fhew'd him of teafing Troubles offer'd to
prevent him in his Proceeds.

Houfe, Vid. *Houfe.*

Over Water have, that is, be in a troubled or fickly Oeconomy.

Overflowing feen in general, threats with exceeding great Trouble.

A fmall Spring becoming a Lake or River tho, gave great Increafe of Wealth.

A Mead fee by a rich Spring, have a prefent Wafte for a future
Good.

Falling from a fteep place over a neighbouring Plain, fhew'd
of fudden Riches ill got, to Oppreffion of others.

Vid. *Flood* in *Water.*

Pitcher, Vid. *Goods.*

Plunging

Plunging in it, to Fishermen is good.

to many, great Perplexity thro Distraction of Cares.

Shallow, in your Power.

Deep, beyond your Command.

Dipping a Lap-Dog in Water, shew'd of giving a Gentlewoman Physick.

Reflection, feeing your Image in Water, threats you with short Life.

Sailing in general, and Ships, shew of the Efforts of a wandring Fancy with great Doubt and Hazard, in oppofition to Travel by Land in Surety, and flying in Projects.

To Men, in Strife and Terror ill.

Defiring and unable tho, shews of great Hindrance,

Carried on board by another, be near as forc'd to run the risk of his Family Fate, and which is hazardous.

With a good Veffel and a good Cargo, and to a good Iffue beft.

But not refting at laft, the more danger.

Leave your Boat or Veffel, ceafe to venture fo hazardoufly.

As near finking, in Terror of mifcarriage at hand.

A long Voyage go afleep, anothers Labour proves your eafy Advance.

In 20 Veffels croffing the *Italian* Seas, shew'd a *Roman* Emperor live 20 Years.

By Land, shew'd *A.* of venturing at a Trade he was never likely to ufe.

Such Ventures are as dunging Land, &c. but hindred 'tis very bad.

In a Lake, shews of much Trouble with little Gain.

clear Water with Joy.

Torrents, threats with Mifcarriage thro ill Counfel.

Rivers with the Stream, gives great Prosperity.

The Sea quiet, gives good Succefs and great.

troubled, in great Neceffity and Tumult.

In a Tempeft in general, Vid. *Air fupra.*

On the Sea or a River, with Heavinefs and Anger.

Seeing a Ship endanger'd in't, only Peril.

In a Wherry, thro Voluptuoufnefs, as if in a Coach.

Shipwracks, threat Lofs with Tumult in great Affairs.

To Prifoners good, to others very bad.

Veffel not broke, tho 'tis recoverable, and your Hopes within retrieve.

Crying out on G O D as finking, gives Delivery on all fuch Extremities near.

Sailing

Sailing. Shipwracks. Hang'd on a Bough in the Sea by't, left out in ex
              ceeding Deſpair.

     Ships ſeen at Sea give eaſe, and is good to all, but from ſa
           moſt.

              Full of Goods, with greateſt Proſperity.

              In a Tempeſt is bad, tho your ſelf not in it.

              To ſome it ſhews Return from Travel or good
                News.

              Turning towards Land, Hazard becoming
                ſure.

        On dry ground, threats with greateſt Difficulties and
              Impediments.

              Vid. *Sail* general *ſupra.*

       Going from Haven, ſhew of good and ſlow Affairs,
             but as in hazard and commencing.

              To others Wandring, and Return from
                ſtrange Countries.

              Arriving at Haven, gives of quick Diſpatch.

      Shew of Family, Husband, Wife and Children, but then
            as in hazardous State, and ſo what befals the
            Ship, befals the Family alſo; the Ship being
            as the Houſe an Oeconomy, but as in Water,
            in Trouble.

              If Family be wanting, it ſhews of our Neigh-
            bourhood, College, or Relations, and to
            whom things are to befal according.

   Sorts. Great or fair ſee or climb into, ſhews of ſome no-
              ble Hazard to follow.

              With Charge and by Sea, the Hazard the bet-
                ter.

              Man of War, as others, but with Law and Con-
                troverſy.

              Drove to fight in one, forc'd to ſuch a po-
                pular Controverſy.

              Govern'd well, ſucceeding in ſuch hazardous
                Affairs.

              Tow'd in by a Boat, ſubtilly manag'd.

              Privateer, Enemies ſhew'd *A.* of Danger in
                great Affairs.

        Small Veſſels ſeen, threats of Sickneſs.

              Seen enter an Houſe and out again, the
                Bier and Death. (Water Tears.)

       Wherry going in, threats with ruinous Volup-
              tuouſneſs, as does the Coach.

               Seen on ground, ſuch an hazardous
                Pleaſure at a ſtand.

       Boat of another's be in, bear his like Misfor-
        tunes and Hazards.

                              Sailing

Sailing Ships. Sorts. Boat, pass a Water by it, escape a Trouble by
          such Expedient.

          Long one *A.* was in sunk in Mud, his Hog
          eat up his Chicken.

          Near sinking, an Expedient in Trouble near
          failing.

          Great one, shew'd of greater Affairs.

Plank swimming on designing, in want of all
     Necessaries.

Parts. Anchors shew of Surety, but withal threat of
          Impediments in such States.

          To the Guilty they give Security.

Arms shew of our Actions, Courage and Conduct,

Cables shew as Ropes below,

Castles on your side on a Rock, a Friend against
     such popular Troubles,

Deck Governor buried, threated of the Forepart
     of the Ship lost.

Fire seen in a Ship, shew'd of the Wind coming
          thence.

          To some Disgrace, as is the Person re-
          presented by the Part.

          Candles seen there, is good.

Forepart of it seen lost, threated the Governor
     thereof Death; & è contra, as *Oar* below.

Haven shews of our Friends.

Helm shews of our Council and Prudence in
     Action.

Keel shews of our Riches and Money.

Mast, the Master of the House or Vessel, if in a
     literal Dream.

Master shews of the Issue or End of all.

Oar losing, shew'd *A.* of burying a Fellow-rower.

Rocks shew us of cruel Men, and Men lov'd by
     constraint.

Ropes to Land and Cables, Debts and Imbargoes.

          Seeing of them, shews of News from Deb-
          tors and Factors.

Rowers shew Procurers.

Sands shew of Dangers.

Sails Fortune.

Servants shew of familiar aiding Courses.

Sea and Wind, publick Monuments in Strife, or
          the Circumstance of your hazard State.

          In other Cases, Princes and Magistrates.

Stem, the Beauty of the Business.

          Broke, to a Prince shew'd of Loss of
          Dominions in such hazard State.

                                        Sailing

Sailing Ship. Parts. Stern shews of our Friends and Aiders.
Scalding Pitch flung into, shew'd A. of vomiting up Choler.
Sieve. Vid. *Goods.*
Spilt in an House threats with Care and Affliction, as is the Quanti
Standing in it with a shrunk Belly, A. seeing his sick Horse, shew'
his dying of a Cold.
Swimming in general shews of much Labour in Business, of g
        Trouble, Danger, and Hazard.
      To some Sickness, as Colds, &c. and with
        bour, with Sweat and Snot.
      To many great Inconvenience, and the foc
          out on't the better, and so reco
          Overpowered by Waves, troubled
          yond Courage or Ability, as &
          With Facility, and Belly and Back
          pleasure, the Trouble the less.
  In a great Water strong and well, promises of long Life
       Lakes troubled Water, and absurdly with ill F
       tune too.
       Pond or River fall into, great Inconvenien
       but less popular and dangerous.
       Shallow Water, in your power, & è contra.
  In your Clothes, shews you of great Danger, as flying
         Enemies, &c.
       So hurt, of repute, as &c.
Up a River or in troubled Water, the worse.
      Against a bloody Stream, shew'd of one cur'd of
      Pleurisy.
Midwives Stoles seen in the Sea, foreshew'd to a Woman Childr
  that liv'd not.
Treading artificially, commanding Troubles.
Walking on it declares of Honour and Joy.
Washing in general. Vid. *Bathe* supra.
        Vid. also *Clean* in *Quality*, & *River* in *Water.*
The whole Body, is as banishing Care.
     To some it shews Health.
Your self in clean Water, Joy and Diversion, and to some wi
      Gain.
      foul Water, threats you with Accusation and I
        mage.
      in a deep Pit, the worse.
      Stream, shew'd to a *Mahometan* become
      Convert.
    The Sea shews of Loss and Damage, and is as cle
      ing your self popularly.
      But to a Seaman if pleasantly, Profit a
      Gladness.
  Parts. Beard threats Sadness.

                       Washi

washing Parts. Face shews repenting of Sin.
Feet is as Molestation cured.
To some it shews of Expedition.
Vid. *Feet* in *Body.*
Hand Right, shews of your declaring your Innocence.
To others vexatious Affairs.
Both in the Rain, to one sick gave a healthy Sweat.
Vid. *Body.*
Head shews of Deliverance from Danger.
Inwards to wash, *A.* receiv'd somewhat of a Minister, that is, she found she wanted Repentance secretly.
Plants, shews of ridding of heavy Cares.
Your Clothes, threats you Danger or Loss about Life or Body.
It opens to Reproof, and discovers Secrets.
Crevat for Holy-days, be at expence for Finery then.
A great one having, shew'd *A.* of losing his young Fowl.
Over and all clean, not troubled with Guests as others.
To the sick also a speedy Recovery.
New Sheets hanging to dry, shew'd *A.* of inviting new Boarders to live with him.
Dirt not coming off, is always the worse.

C H A P. IX.

Of *Water.*

[*N general.* As the Air shews of States projective, Fire States de-
(1) sperate and passionate, and the Earth States sure and fix'd, so the Water also shews us of States hazardous and troublesom.
Actions. Sailing is as venturing on prudent Hazard with an Oeconomy Assistance.
Swimming and wading, the same without an Oeconomy.
Seeing your Face in't, threats you with short Life.
Voice of many Waters, that is, many People.
Passing is as Trouble to all, and shallow in your power.
Deep, beyond your reach.
In Holes, hazardous.

In

In general. Actions. Serpents *A.* seeing in Water, shew'd of his E-
(1)   nemies distress'd.

      Sort, pleasant and good shews of Profit.

        Dry where accustom'd, Poverty.

        Dig and find none, act with Rogues and be punish'd.
           some, fortunates you.

        Running, Courses of hazardous Profit, but con-
           stant and dear as Thirst, and thus
           troublesom Revenues as still run-
           ning, *&c.*

           Great and universal, as is the Stream from
           a Spring to a River.

           To some also they shew Variances.

           To some also they shew of Tears.

      Colour'd seen, often threats the Eyes.

           A reddish River passing, threated *A.* of
           a Tempest.

      Standing, shews of some settled hazard Profit.

      Troubled much seen, shew'd of Humours.

      Dirty in an House seen, threats Danger of Fire.

           Clear gives Gain.

Sea, in publick Prophecy shews of the People, and as appearing,
(2)   so also they.

           In some cases also it shews the Religion, King,
           and People.

           Beasts rising thence, powerful Governments thence.

     In the Body it shews of the Thighs, Arms, and Humours.

     Fish. Vid. *Fish.*

     Fowls. Vid. *Birds.*

     Of Blood seen, shew'd of a great and ruinous War.

     Colour clear seen, is best.

           Sky-colour'd and waving moderately, shews of Joy
           and Facility in Action.

     Waves threatning, popular Commotions menacing.

           Bounded safe tho seen, promises Security.

     Seaman pass by, that is, venture at an Hazard greater than
        his.

   Acts. Being in, living in Care and Trouble.

           In Bed, lazy withal therein.

           Near Land and shallow, the Trouble the sooner
           help'd.

           In an Island, secure in such Trouble, but confin'd
           by it.

     Calm. Vid. *Tempest* inf a.

     Coming to *A's* House-Door seen, threated of his Death
           near.

           Next Neighbour Village, the same in Loss.

     Drown'd in't, join'd to a Whore.

                                    Sea.

Sea. **Acts.** Falling into it, entangled with Enemies.
(2)   Stars seen, threated of the Ruin of the People,
Hanging on a Bough in't, shew'd of unhappiest Despair.
Inundation of it fear, be in terror of some popular Con-
    spiracy.
            Drown'd Wheat so see, examine of your Wheat in
            such State, &c.
Near it be in an House, that is, in an Oeconomy full of po-
            pular Trouble.
                    Garden, that is, as to Plenty, State the same.
Passing it, shews Joy.
Riding on the Sea-side, transacting in a popular Course.
Seeing its Cliffs, threats of exceeding popular Dangers, as
            Robbers, &c.
            Catching Coneys there, shew'd of Robbers.
Speaking with it, threats Death.
Tempests threat of Dangers, Fears, and Hurts, and chiefly
            as to Merchandize.
            Calms give Idleness, but with Ease.
            Mean seen, gives great Business and a happy Life.
Swim in the Sea Midwives Stoles seen, shew'd a Woman of
    having Children dying young.
Walk on it, to a Woman dissolute Life, and to all accepta-
    ble Popularity.
            to some it declares of Honour and Joy.
            to the Traveller, Success.
            to the Batchelor, Marry or Whore.
            to the Servant a kind Master.
            From the People, Good, and the Judge Favour.
    Parts. Cliffs. Vid. *Seeing* supra.
            Waves shew of popular Commotions.
    Sea-side have a Garden by, be concern'd in some popular
    Managery according.
Standing Water, troubled seen, threats of some unexpected and hid
(3)   Trouble.
            Clear shews of Idleness and Pleasure.
            Overflowing your Banks, threats you losing your
                    Substance.
                    To others it shews a Wife or Child dies.
Lakes shew as the River, but without force, and States less
    considerable than Seas.
            A Swan seen there, shew'd of great Happiness
            and Wisdom.
    With Fish, with Plenty.
                    The Fish seen there, shew of lazy and un-
                    active Lubbers.
            Great, with Dominion, and so the greater the better.

Standing Lakes conſtant, and ſo ſhews not wilful Great Men, as do
(3) Rivers.

But as free from Great Men, ſo unactive.

More about his Houſe *A.* enlarging to e'ery Door, ſhew'd of his farming to have all of his own.

Your Pond about your Houſe, your more private Store ; as Mote more publick.

Pond great ſeen, hinders Travel, or elſe is as the Lake.

Your common one ſee dry, your Aid to others fails, &c.
Fiſh-pond ſtor'd, gives Plenty in abundance.

Empty ſeen, threats Want where otherwiſe expected.

3 paſſing by, ſhew'd *A.* of purchaſing an Eſtate for 3 Lives.

Of clear Water ſeen in a Field where was none before, to the Married Thriving.

To the Single Marriage and happy Children.

Seeing a little one, ſhew'd of enjoying the Love of pretty Women.

To a Woman ſhew'd her of her Deſires accompliſh'd.

Pit deep ſeen with clear Springs at bottom, hinder'd Journeys, but to no other Hurt.

Enough to draw Water at, waiting Alteration there in ſeeming vain.

With an Iſland in the midſt, and a Clock upon't, ſhew'd *A.* of Wet ſtopping him ſome daily Work, &c.

Dipping a Lap-dog in, ſhew'd *A.* of giving a nice Gentlewoman Phyſick.

Dig in a Field and find no Water, act with ill Men and be puniſh'd.

finding Water fortunates you.

Ditch *A*'s Bed ſeeming in, and Thorns his Pillow, gave him ſcandalous Riches with Care.

In general it ſhews Riches, but as thro Uſury and not Induſtry.

Dry, Ruin to all the Dreamer and his Houſe.
Troubled Water in't, Vexation.
Vid. *Fence* in *Earth.*

A. ſearching for a Chopping Knife in't, ſhew'd of his acting in a ſcandalous part-friend Errand.

Puddle *A*'s Houſe drinking out of, ſhew'd of his ſeeking Honour wherein Diſgrace would enſue.

Ciſtern of clear Water ſeen, gives great familiar Aid in Trouble.

It ſhews Change of Fortune by good Counſel, &c.

To the Sick, Health.   *Standing*

Standing Ciftern of clear Water, to the Defperate, Relief.
(3)   Foul or corrupt Water in't, è con!

High as your Head in Water, a Trouble elfe able
  to confound you.

Kept in by the Ciftern, your Friend fcreen-
  ing you.

Cleaning fhew'd of reforming Errors and Freedom
  of old Evils.

Of Blood plung'd in fo as fcarcely able to get out,
  fhew'd A. fick of a Pleurify, &c.

Running. Vid. *fupra* in general.
(4) Fountains feen dry, threat with Poverty.

See become a Brook, gives great Increafe of Riches.

Clear feen, fhew of a ferene Mind.

Drink of it is good, grow to Riches.

To fome fhews of matters done as to
  others, by which you gain.

Troubled falling into, threats of Accufation.

Clear falling into, gives Honour and Gain.

Sovereign one find, that is, difcover a gallant
  Courfe to anfwer fome end, as &c.

Running upwards feen, threated of unnatural
  Troubles.

Well dry. Vid. *infra* in *Brook.*

New feen in an Houfe or Ground, promis'd of a new
  Profit according.

Fountain feen fpring up there, the like.

Cleaning, threats with Injury.

Find in an unknown Garden and fh--- in't, find a new
  Credit and ufe it.

Bucket loft at bottom, fhew'd of one in Family dying.

Empty and the Wink down, fhew'd one his Suit for
  Juftice vain.

A Glafs full of Water thence given one, Marriage and
  Children.

The Giver the Matchmaker.

Fall into, be injur'd by a Profit fhould fupport you, as
  lofe by Merchandize.

Drawn at by Strangers yours, threats you with Death
  in Family.

To a fingle Perfon Marriage.

Clear, with Profperity and a Portion.

Troubled, fall fick and be troubled
  with her.

Stream dry. Vid. *Brook* infra.

Before your Door fee, confider of a Revenue at your
  Command.

Sailing with it, gives Profperity.

E   *Running*

Running Stream. Bathing in a clear one, ſhew'd a Convert of purging
(4)　　　　　　himſelf of his Corruptions and Sins.
　　　　　　　Stinking one, forbids as it ſelf bad.
　　　　　　　　　　　An Hen ſeen dead in't, the Drea
　　　　　　　　　　　mer's Soul hurt by't.
　　　　　　　　　　　A Woman taking it out it lives
　　　　　　　　　　　Truth eaſes her.
　　　Brook ſeen clear and clean, gave Joy and Gain.
　　　　　Riding in, ſhew'd *A.* treſpaſſing in his Art on another'
　　　　　Revenue.
　　　　　Jumping over one, expedienting a Trouble to you
　　　　　ſelf in flight of another's Revenue, &c.
　　　　　Dry ſeen, threats you of Poverty and Miſery.
　　　　　Walking in't, ſhew'd *A.* of loſing a Dinner.
　　　　　　　　　　To another ſhew'd him of
　　　　　　　　　　Profeſſion laid by offering a
　　　　　　　　　　gain.
　　　　　　　　　　Over one, ſhew'd *A.* retrieving a loſ
　　　　　　　　　　Stock of Drink.
　　　　　Troubled ſeen, threats with Damage by Fire, Law-ſuit
　　　　　and Enemies.
　　　　　　　　　　Vid. alſo *River* poſted.
　　Rivers and Fountains in Scripture ſhew'd of particular Na
　　　　　tions.
　　　　　　　　　　To ſome likens as to their Life, and ſ
　　　　　　　　　　drunk up is as Death.
　　　　　　　　　　To Students, 'tis their Courſe of Life and
　　　　　　　　　　Wiſdom.
　　　　　　　　　　Vid. *Blood* in *Body.*
　　　　　　　　　　Dirt of it dry eating, ſhew'd *A.* of miſſin
　　　　　　　　　　his Dinner and dining on Toaſt.
　　　　　　　　　　Dry.　Vid. *Brook* ſupra.
　　Sorts. Known found little and ſhallow, ſhew'd *A.* o
　　　　　　　　　finding the Liberal become niggardly
　　　　　　　　　A great Waſh of Clothes ſeen in it, pay
　　　　　　　　　ing Debts occaſioning it.
　　　　　The New River at *London,* ſhew'd of Exche
　　　　　quer Bills as fictitious.
　　　　　Of *Oxon* paſs by, exceed their Streams of Lear
　　　　　ning.
　　　　　Unknown ſail in, venture on an unexpected
　　　　　Courſe of Hazard.
　　　Side travel by, Deſign in ſome Courſe of Gain, as &c
　　　On the left ſide on a Precipice, ſhew'd *A.* of Loſ
　　　　　by gaming.
　　State clear and gentle, gives Security.
　　　　　To the Sick Recovery.
　　　　　To Students Wiſdom.

　　　　　　　　　　　　　　　　Running

Running Rivers. State clear, to Servants, Travellers, and Men at Law,
(4).   Ease.

Troubled, *è contra* to all.

Dirty and violent, threats with Trouble and Hardship from above.

Coming into an House threats it with Fire.

In general seen, shews of the Violence of an Enemy.

Hurried in it, forced accordingly.

To the Sea very bad, mob'd by it.

Pleasant and long, a continued Course of great Good.

Tending to *London*, of the best Converse and Commerce.

In a Boat, in a voluptuous hazardous Course.

Acts. Bathing. Vid. *supra.*

Being in and unable to get out, threats with great Evils and Oppressions, your whole Interest in such State.

Bringing us somewhat, shews of wilful Persons complying to us.

Carrying away Houses or Farms, Great Men oppressing.

To the Sea, to utmost Extremity.

Your self, to many threats them Sickness by Defluxions.

to others, Hurt by dilatory Law-suits.

Your Hat, threats you with ill Fame and Discredit.

Coming clear into an House, is as Profit by Great Men.

Vid. *House.*

By a Channel, the Good the more fix'd and great.

But troubled, is as the Violence of an Enemy.

By an House, gives Office, Honour, and Profit to the Rich.

Out of an House, to the Rich Liberality and Authority.

to the Poor an Whore, Wife, or Daughter.

to some, an ungovernable Family.

to some, Danger of Life or other Injury.

F 2   *Running*

Running Rivers, Acts. Groſs, Vid. *Travel.*

(4)   Fall into a River, miſcarry as to ſome yearly Revenue.

         Waſhing, Vid. *ſuprà.*

Floods ſeeing them, threats with Fear and Danger.

         flinging things down, threats Ruin.

Shew things neither good nor durable.

         But they leave Hopes for Amendment ſtill.

Paſſing them on Foot, or ſwimming, is ſtill good.

         Walking thro, as coming into a Room, ſhew'd *A.* Victor in an exploded Opinion.

Shew hard Judges, Maſters and Rabbles wilful as Rivers.

         Giving Trouble as is the Place overflowed.

Fiſh ſeen, ſhew of ſhort Life and fading Hopes.

Univerſal ones ſeen, threat Hereſy, Plague or Famine.

Falling from a ſteep Hill, and overflowing a Plain near, ill Riches ſoon got.

Torrents, threat of great Troubles, and are ſtill bad.

         But reparable, where Rivers not.

         Shoot *London* Bridg, paſs a critical Hardſhip.

         Soon over, elſe as a River.

Whirlpools ſeen, threat of dangerous Melancholy and Evils in Religion.

CHAP. X.

Of the Earth.

IN *General.* As the Air ſhews of States projective, the Fire of States (1) deſperate and paſſionate, and the Water of States of Hazard and Trouble, ſo alſo the Earth in general ſhews of States moſt fix'd and ſure.

It ſhews to us, of our Bowels and Feet.

         to ſome of their Father, Maſter and Country, & è con.

         In common publick Prophecy the State of the Church.

Place, Vid. *Country* infrà.

         Vid. alſo *Geography* in *Learning.*

World in general alſo, ſhew us Man and our ſelves.

In *general.* World in general alſo, and thus ſeen at an end, threats
(1)   us Death.
                          And ſo the Sea ſeen at *A*'s Door,
                              threated him near the ſame.

GOD the Soul.	Sea Fiſh Iſlanders.
Heaven the Head.	River Fiſh Inlanders.
Earth the Bowels and Feet.	Bears Germans.
Air the Breaſt.	Mice, *Alps* dwellers.
Sea the Blood and Humors.	Mountains, Flouts,
Trees, great Men.	Hills, Scoffs.
Towers, Kings. And ſo	Rocks, Mocks.
Herbs, People.	Gardens, Virtues in
Houſes, Nobles.	Rivers, a Diſpute.
Temples, Prieſts.	Fountains.

Actions. Crying, Vid. *Talk* infra.
(2)   Change, Vid. *World general* ſuprà.
         Earthquakes, ſhew of Popular Changes, as by the King's Edict,
                 &c.
                  Real alſo, as Thunder projective.
                  to ſome, Sickneſs.
                  to ſome Loſs, as is the Place where.
                  to ſome, Law-Suits and Loſs of Goods.
                  to the Indebted and Travellers, Good.
                  to others, Openings are Death and Loſs.
            Ruining his Country, ſhew'd one his Father
                  hanged.
            In his own Houſe, ſhew'd *A.* of the Prince's
                  Edict againſt him.
            Making *A.* a Tomb ſeen, ſhew'd *A.* of a Royal
                  Edict raiſing him.
            Falling Walls and Doors by it, Death and De-
                      ſtruction to the chief in the Houſe.
                  Mountain on a Valley, good Men op-
                      preſſed by ſome great Lord.
                  Palace overturned by it, to a King die,
                      or loſe his Dominions.
            Vid. *Move* infrà.
      Falling your ſelf to the Ground, degraded to the meaneſt.
      Gathering from the Ground Olives, threats with Labours and
              Pains.
            Money, attaining Plenty by ſtooping or ſneaking.
      Kiſſing the Earth, threats of Sadneſs or Humility.
      Levelling, Vid. *poſtea* in *Cave.*
      Lying on the Ground utterly dejected, as at others Command.
                  a Book paſs by, neglect an Inſtruction,
                  as with Contempt.

                  F 3   *Actions*

Actions.   Moving, Vid. *Earthquake* ſupra.
(2)   Under you, ſhews you that that Subject won't be judg'd by you.

Violently overturning your Perſon and Intereſt.

In general, threats you with Signs of Miſery, and Fear moſt abſolute.

Mounting to Heaven the Earth ſeen in publick Dreams, ſhew'd of a juſt Prince.

In private, get a Right unexpectedly.

to ſome, become impious.

Opened, Vid. *Holes* infra.

Divided Chaſms ſeen, have ſhewn the Death of great Men and Cattle Plagues.

To others, great Hurt to their Country.

Smelling well, promiſes you of good Fame.

Talking with it, gives great Riches and long Life.

to a Prince Victory,

to another, what ſaid is true and good.

In any Region, to a Stranger live and die happily there.

In your Houſe worſt, the Princes Edict againſt you.

From its Bowels, Death, Riches or Lamentation.

Crying out very ill, Death or Mourning.

Taſting ill or ſtrangely, threats of ill Men or Diſeaſes.

well, *à con.*

ill in its Fruits growing, threats with Scarcity.

Holes.   Place in your way, threats you with Interruption of Methods.
(3)   To others, ſtops their Journies.

With Water in you thro Wet, ſtopping Travel.

In your Chamber, threats with ſome Defect in your Family Oeconomy.

Ceiling, as to its Converſe Beauty.

In weak Ice, Danger thro ſome Courſe of Poverty.

firm Ice ſeen, aſſures you Want then, not hurtful.

Before an Houſe, hinders your Affairs, as is the Houſe.

A Tradeſman's Shop fruſtrated, *A.* dealing there.

Into a Goal Dungeon ſtand near, be in hazard of Debt.

Thro the Wall of an Houſe paſs, ſhift you as to ſome Oeconomy.

Vid. *Wall* in *building parts.*

State dark hide in, ſneak into obſcure Shifts.

A. got his Father's Ring out of, he retrieved his Brothers Honour in Diſpute.

Sneaking one, *A.* ſaw his Clothier in, he became ſcandalous in Apparel.

Holes.

Holes. State, Stinking into's Fathers Grave *A.* seeing, shew'd of his
(3)   Faults then dead, laid open.
          Deeper, the worse.
Actions, being in, to some has shewn of marrying a Widow.
          Levelling Ground, reconciling Difficulties.
               where it seems impossible to labour in vain.
          Opened seen in a Field, shew'd of the Secret of a Dis-
               pute discovered.
          Turf only, Vid. *Field.*
     Seeing wild Beasts in one, is good to the Secret.
          Sheep cry and run into Holes, shew'd of an in-
               nocent Sect persecuted.
Way under Ground walking in, in *Kent* beyond *London*, I saw
     there fine Line, Mortar, and the Passage there long, the
     Wind seem'd hard against me in't. This was on my essaying
     immediate Digestions in my Skills without a Diary.
House under Ground, Vid. *Room* in general, in *House.*
               Dwell in, to some die with ill Fame.
               Being in with a Minister my Divine se-
                    cret Skill, to hazard of my Health.
               Falling into by a Precipice, shew'd of
                    Death.
               Going down into by Stairs he could re-
                    turn by, studies getting Secrets, but
                    hazarding Health yet recoverable.
               Room West flying in, shew'd me of pro-
                    jecting to aid my Memory failing.
Cave, *A.* seeing his Neighbour Attorny have, shew'd him of a
     conceal'd Law-wrangle that in time appear'd out.
     Fall into, be subject to a crafty Design against you.
     A. seeming in such, seeing a Church above, shew'd
          A. of dealing underhand with a Minister.
     Under Ground *A.* finds Gold, that is, he is not yet
          in his true way to Riches.
     Vid. *Cellar* in *House, Rooms.*
Pits seen, threats with dangers at hand.
     Avoiding it, escaping them.
     Descending out of his Chariot into one, to *Domitian*
          his Death.
               Into one, threats to all great Loss and Da-
                    mage.
     Dig one, contrive some Roguery perillous to another.
               and fall into't your self, and have an Accu-
                    sation therefore.
     Falling into one *A.* seeing his Friend, shew'd that
          Friend dying.
     Fling one alive into one, imprison him.
               to others, Hindrance of Affairs.

Holes. Pits feen foundering your Houfe, an evil hazarding your Oecono-
(3)   nomy.
    Make one, fettle the Method to fome Roguery.
    A Door to one, fix a Refolution of Iffue in one.
        plank'd over Head, with Endeavours
        of Concealment.
    Vid. *Dig* in *Husbandry.*
    Shallow. Vid. *Swim* in *Water.*
Gulf feen, threat of Cattel Plagues, or great Mens Deaths.
    very great, threats as mifchievous to the whole
        Country.
        to others, has fhewn of devouring
        Taxes.
    Ditch, Vid. *Fence* in *Eftate.*
    Gutter, Vid. *Channel* in *City.*
        Cleaning, fhew'd of clearing Reproaches.
        Making, fhew'd of remedying Difcords.
Sorts in general, ftony feen, has fhewn of Famine, or quartering of
(4)   Soldiers.
        Black, has fhewn of Sorrow, Melancholy, and Weak-
        nefs of Brain.
Clay *A*'s Sifter became a Serpent of, that is, his hard Conten-
    tion at laft vanifh'd.
        Ground walking on, threats of grievous Sorrow and
        Peril.
Dirt, fhews of Trouble, Sicknefs or Difhonour, if it bedaub us.
    Caft on one, that is injurious Infamy.
    Dead in Dirt, confounded in Errors.
    Shoulders of it, is ill to all.
    Falling into it, Difturbance or Treachery by fome one.
    Mired, fool'd.
    Vid. *Stock* in *Travel.*
Dirty Water feen in an Houfe, threats it with Fire.
    if a Fountain, fo Tyranny and Hardfhip.
    River, Vid. *Water.*
    Place pafs, threats your Underftanding ill in contriving.
    Way and thorny, fhew'd of foolifh Labour to lofs.
    Way, Vid. *Travel.*
    Feet, threat of great Tribulation.
    Hands feen, fhews of our acting flovenly.
    Petticoat having to a Woman, fhew'd of her Pocket plen-
    ty mean.
    Vid. *Clean* in *Quality.*
Dunghil feen, is good to Husbandmen, or Men in publick Bufi-
        nefs.
        to fome, being invited to a Feaft.
        to fome, Heavinefs and Hurt.

Sorts. Dunghil feen, a white Hen on one, fhew'd of Difgrace by
(4) falfe Accufations.

Sleeping on it, to the Poor Riches.
    to the Rich, Office.

Walking by one, fhew'd of Sicknefs to enfue.

Sitting on one, threated one with a Fire.

Fighting on his *A.* feeing great Dogs, fhew'd of
 his moderating popular Quarrels.

A. feeing made in the *Weft,* fhew'd of his being
 ar prefent great Farm-Charges for future great
 good.

Dung foul'd with, threats with Injury from the Perfon by
   whom.

  By a Stranger, Reproach unexpected.

  In general, it threats Reflections on your
  Mind.

Heap'd on your Head, by the Rich great Gifts.
   by the Poor Contempt.

Pot carrying Stones, *A.* having, fhew'd him building
 an Oxftall of fuch.

Man's feeing is ill, but foul'd with it is worfe.

 Eat, Vid. *Eat* in *Victuals.*

 Vid. *fh*— in *Bodily Actions.*

 Child's foul'd with, fcandal'd as negligent in
 providing for Children.

 's Bed feen daub'd with it, fhew'd to *A.* his
 Wife dreft taudry.

Jakes chofe an Officer o'er, confin'd to a fla-
  vifh Regulation of Expence.

  Vid. *Jakes* in *Out-houfes.*

Vomiting it up, diverting neceffary Expences
 prodigally.

A. entering anothers Houfe, and finding him
 afleep, cut out his Fat and Excrement
 ftinking Guts, and carried them off; *A.* rob'd
 him.

Duft, Vid. *Wind* in *Air.*

 Vid. *Sweep* in *Domeftick Action.*

Gravel removing, fhew'd of Trouble and Returns of Money.
  out of ones Shoos, fhew'd of Confcience
  Offence as where, &c.

 mend Ways with it, that is, firmly rectify Mifunder-
 ftandings.

Quickfand ftand on, that is, be in an Affair of ruinous Hazard.

Rock fitting on, affures of good Hopes to the doubtful.

 Seeing, to the Rich, Care and Terror.

  to the Poor, Barrennefs, Mifery and Cruelty.

 Remov'd by Engines, fhew'd of difcovering Projects irrefiftible.   *Sorts.*

Lingua Tersancta.

Sand a Mountain of it seen, shew'd of a great Power of little stay.

Stones in general, Heaps of them, Vid. *Part* in *Quantity*.

seen to some, has shewn of Journies.

A Way stony, a Method of exceeding Difficulty and Hazard.

Earth stony seen, has shewn of Famine or quartering of Soldiers.

Pavement, Vid, *House, Parts*.

Seen and not cast, shew'd of disturbing Thoughts and Impediments.

Great ones, discover'd of ill hard-hearted Men.

With Marble and Mortar, shew'd of good Actions the best Monument.

Hard in general, shew'd of stable Security and firmness.

Sorts just siz'd ones, build with Reason in perfect Virtue, or with well form'd Notions.

Finely engrav'd, plain ones may be excellent.

Jewels, Vid. *Riches* in *Ornaments*.

Agats and worse Jewels, shew Workmen fine, but not the best.

Corals, shew of Sailing and troubled Affairs.

Divers colour'd and mean, shew of vain and popular empty Fellows.

Flints, shew of Men rude and harsh.

Loadstones, shew of Love, Folly, vain Thoughts, Wonder and Sailing.

Marble, neat and envious Persons.

Rocks, Vid. *supra.*

Touchstone shews of the Discovery of Secrets.

Whetstones shew of Encouragement without Aid.

Actions becoming a Mountain, shew'd of Christ's becoming a Church.

Casting, shews of injurious Speech.

In your Backside, of farming relating thereto.

To some, it has shewn of Journies, and as if pelted away.

Flung at, is as ill Fame.

Wound by it, chance Calumny.

To Fidlers, only good.

By many Profit and Mony, to others Flight.

Salt on Stones seen, shews of Pains and Materials fool'd away.

Sorts,

1

Sorts. Stones, Acts, falling from Heaven, foreshewed of publick Cala-
(4)   mities.

One only, it endured not long.
Breaking, as it fell, shew'd an ill
Man dying.

Fling, Vid. *Cast* supra.
Gathering together, threats of Sorrow or Sickness to
follow.
Laid in his Bed *A.* finding a sweaty one, shew'd of
his bedding his Wife weak and sick.
aside for your Defence see, have a Mishap as to
demand the Help of many.
Made of them having Clothes, threats Death.
Your Tongue of it, that is, quite useless.
Arms of it having, threats with Loss of
Victory.
Offer'd to Sale unknown seen, shew'd of Strangers
offering in publick Business.
In your own House in private,
&c.
Pavement, Vid. *House parts*, &c.

C H A P. XI.

Of Country and Place, &c.

COuntry Imaginary, Vid. *my New Jerusalem.*
(1)   Being in an Idle thought against *Africa*, shew'd *A.* of
using Exchequer Bills, a National shift.
Vid. *Unknown* in *Grammar.*
Vid. *Perfect* and *Imaginary* in *Quality.*
Native yours being in, that is, in Consideration of your pre-
sent Family State, as 'tis.
Enjoying it, to some has shewn an untimely end.
Foreign be in, that is, in Circumstance of fatal Family
Change.
Unknown or known is an Additament to either alike.
Vid. *Unknown* in *Grammar.*
State flourishing seen, and so fares it also with your
Father's Family.
first and then melt as Snow, it first
thriv'd and then vanish'd.
Street or City seen so, to a Citizen
the same.

Country Native. State ruin'd by an Earthquake feen, fhew'd one hi
(1) Father condem'd and executed.

Part. *London*, to an *Englifh*-man his beft publick Com
merce and Converfe.

A. Part known of it feen, in a way yo:
have experienc'd.

Unknown, fure and good alfo, bu
unaccountable.

Other Cities and Countries judg of, as *Eaft*
Weft, &c.

Or as they have been fortunate
as pendant, *&c.* Vid. *Grammar.*

So in general they fhew of meaner
univerfal States, as, *&c.*

Vid. *Cities* in *Habitations,*
infra.

Market Towns fhew of private Bargains.
Villages fhew of Neighbourhoods.
Northern Folks poor, Eaftern thriving, *&c.*
Home fhews of Tranfactions at our command.

Abroad fhews of things out of our power,
Foreign in general. Vid. *World* fupra in *Earth.*

Vid. *News* in *Language* in *Letters,*
It fhews of fatal, perfonal, or family
Changes, as is the Country.
Acts there, likens you in Circumftances, as
if there.

A. going there, took out his
Blood and gave it a Stran-
ger, he travel'd and made a
Stranger his Heir there.

From GOD. Vid. my *New Jerufalem* ;
that is, a State wholly model'd thro his
perfonal Prefence and Monitions.
Ifland being in, fhew'd A. Confinement home, as if in one.

To fome, be incompafs'd with Multitudes of Troubles and Dangers.

To fome, Separation and a religious
Life.

In publick Scripture Prophecy, it
fhew'd of Idols.

Be in with a fine Spring, retire to good Advantage.

Vid. *Being* in *Water.*

The leffer the worfe, and the narrower
your Affairs.

Sea-ward, the more dangerous.
Increafing feeming, the better.

Country Foreign. Iſland be in ſhipleſs for a Return, ſhew'd *A.* of his
(1)   Trade leaving him.
                                      for a ſeaſon only, for a time ac-
                                      cording.
                             One's Clock ſeen in a little one, ſhew'd of
                                   his daily Travel-work Wet ſtop'd.
Imaginary. Vid. my *New Jeruſalem.*
Europe. Scotch Lord *A.* marrying, ſhew'd of his being
                  in a Friendſhip with a poor diſtant ſtately
                  Perſon.
         Iriſh Man ſeem'd carrying *A.* away, a detri-
                  mental Courſe commanding *A*'s Hopes,
                  as Weſt.
         Woman, the ſame in Scheme or Reaſoning.
         Dublin walking in, to a Man in *England*
                  deſigning in Affairs in ill Command.
         Accompany *Iriſhmen,* be treated abſurdly.
         Coffee-Houſe being in, ſhew'd *A.* of be-
                  ing publickly talk'd of to Infamy.
Holland, ſhews of Induſtry and Trade-Advan-
                  tage, as, *&c.*
France, in Name only ſhews of ſome State free
                  and firm.
                             Fly there by Moon-ſhine,
                                   ſucceed in religious Projects
                                   thereto.
                      In Land and Circumſtance, ſhews as to
                                   its Government.
                             Sailing to her *A.* return'd a-
                                   gain in fear, he alter'd his
                                   good Thoughts of her State.
                             Walking there treated civilly as
                                   a known *Engliſh*-man, ſhew'd
                                   A. favour'd, or elſe the
                                   Laws in *England* as hard to
                                   him, as if there.
                      French-men two I ſaw ſate oppoſite to
                                   me, I ſeem'd oppos'd by an imper-
                                   fect Tyranny.
         Italy walking in with the Pope, ſhew'd me
                  paying another's Debt.
                             But this only if in Diſcourſe you
                                   own the Pope as Head there, or ſee
                                   Wood cut there, *&c.*
                      A Map of it ſeen, ſhew'd *A.* of a Mo-
                                   del of greateſt Plagues and Slavery.
                      Vid. *Papiſt* in *Religion.*

Country Foreign. Europe. Czar of *Muſcovy* ſeen threſhing my Corn, ſhew'
(1)   me of getting a Stock of Bees.

Denmark King I converſing, and he upon it re
proving my Clothes, I ſeem'd on't as goin
to pray as his Chaplain, after which ſtandin
as among his Women, I remov'd thence alſo
and on which an unknown I ſaw ther
ſcoundrel'd me as a mad Man ; this to ſhet
me Money failing to buy my firſt Coach
Horſes.

America. A. trading to a good Plantation there, ſhew'
his deferring his Corn-ſale till the Pric
rais'd, and as long as if ſo voyag'd.

Jamaica A. intending to live at, ſhew'd. of hi
reſolving to uſe Chocolate conſtantly.

New England Town A. paſſing, ſhew'd of hi
compaſſing a firſt-eſſay'd Trade, with Hope
of better Improvement alſo, as 'tis a Planta
tion.

Aſia. A. eſcaping from Egypt into the Holy Land, ſhew'
of his avoiding a Slavery near as great, to a
good a chance.

A. paſſing the Perſian Court to the Holy City o
Jeruſalem as Well, ſhew'd of his ſcorning the
Glory of the World for the Honour of G O D
even in all Circumſtances.

Jew. Vid. Religion.

Conſtantinople Streets I walk'd in, in doubt whe
ther a Slave or a Merchant, but at laſt ai
unknown Turk there, I thought my Maſ
ter, left me.   My Skill to confounc
Infidelity.

I walk'd there alſo in a dry Brook wall'd higl
on both ſides, my Courſe whe. e their Faitl
fails.

Africa ſail to, take a Courſe fundamentally deſertin
all your othe. Hopes.

Unknown Iſland againſt it A. being in, ſhew'
of his receiving Exchequer Bills.

Trade to be invited, that is, be tempted to
friendly but ruinous Dealing.

3 ſet on you there, having 2 more in
Boar, an Action deſign'd on botl
parts.

Struck by an Arrow of one, ſenſible o
Hurt by it.

Narrowly eſcape, at laſt take bette
Courſes.

Country Foreign. *Africa. Morocco* shews of a State partly desolate, partly
(1)   slavish, *&c.*

Things. Languages shew of contrary *Babel*-like Acti-
                ons and odd Impediments.
                        Vid. *Language* in *Learning.*
        Religions threat with Contention and Unsoci-
                ableness.
        Apparel the Saints seen in, gives you Good or
                Ill from thence.
                Wear your self, gives you good luck a-
                        mong such as wear the like.
                        to others Sickness or Treat-
                        ment as such a Stranger.
        Tomb making, gives Death, Travel or Marriage
                there.
        Silver Coin finding, shew'd *A.* paying a Debt.
                Under a Table, that is, spent already in
                Housekeeping.
        Nutmegs having, gives Profit from Strangers
                eat or not.
        French Hat offer'd *A.* to sell, shew'd him of a
                French Grass-Crop offered so.
                Marigold. Vid. *Crown* in *Ornaments.*
                Shoos wear, be prodigally nice in Actions.
                Grass seen, shew'd of good Husbandry
                        and Improvements.
                        sow in an House, remove a Tenant
                        for Gain.
        Persons seen in general, shew of new and strange
                Courses a whole Change.
        Turk married to *A.* seem'd, he prov'd resolv'd
                against publick Christenings.
        Spaniard trying to kill, trying to remove Jea-
                lousies in Converse.
        Princes. King of *France* offering *A.* Lozenges
                        tasting sweet, shew'd
                        A. tempted to Arbi-
                        trariness.
                        Attacks you, arbitrary
                        Tyranny threats you,
                        but as in *England* a
                        false presum'd, but
                        possible Tyranny
                        threatning.
                Alexander seen enter *Babylon* Temple,
                foreshew'd his conquering *Persia.*
                Elector of *Brandenburgh* offering *A.* a
                safe Welcome, shew'd his native
                Laws hard to him.   *Country*

Country Foreign. Perſons. Princes. Grand Senior and Emperor then in War
(1)

A. ſeeing meet, fore-
ſhew'd him of an odd
publick Quarrel.

Seiz'd by his Guards, his
Reaſonings in't reach-
ing A.

He threatens ſuch an abſolute wilful great Man
does ſo.

Grand Senior ſeeing on the *Holy Land*,
as I on the Shore, with a Fence between us, foreſhew'd me reſolv'd to
be good, tho under the Frowns of as
great a Tyranny.

Freeman made when not a Slave, Servant, or
Priſoner, Death.

Enemies ſeen fight you, ſhews you of popular
Enemies threatning you deſ-
perately.

In a Party abroad only, cruel
deſtroying Troubles near.

Near keeping A. from home,
Duns ſo on a Viſit.

Duels among them, ſhew'd A. of
popular Brawls to
his Loſs.

Fighting their Blows fall
on A. their Cavils to
A's Hurt.

Their Army beat, ſome popular
Ill o'erborn.

Free with their Geenral, familiar
with a great Enemy indeed.

Friends to A. but mutually Enemies, as *French*
and *Germans*, ſeen fight in A's Court,
ſhew'd A. of others Feuds on his account,
but horrid and mortal.

Place being in, not gone unto, engag'd in Circumſtances of unex-
(2)   pected Occurrence.

And gone unto, ſhews of what iſſues on ſome Deſign.

Poſture. Vid. *P.*

Proſpect fine, has ſhewn of a fine Diſcourſe.
Vid. *Appear* in *Sight* in *Senſe.*

Property. Vid. *Grammar.*
Vid. *Self* and *Another.*

Every where, ſhews of every where;

Place, being in Goal as a Prisoner with others, be chargeable as to
(2)   Debt.
                    Get out, avoid such Charge; but wake in't,
                    you must pay it.
          Vid. *Italy* in *Country*, &c.
Acts. Give place to another, humour him in Designs.
                    To shite, lend to aid his Expences.
     Mislaid *A*'s Hat, being shew'd of his Honour in question.
               Her Wedding-ring seen to a Wife, shew'd her at a
               Loss about her Husband.
     Picking things from the ground, getting contemptible
     Profits.
     Fly.   Vid. *Air* & *Travel.*
     Changed a known Room seeming, and a Table being where
          the Chimney stood, Converse instead of Oeconomy
          plenty.
Mountains in publick Prophecy, Temples.
               to others, Great Men and hard Works with Mise-
               ries and Fears.
               to others a miserable Life, but secure and at com-
               mand.
          Of Snow or Sand, a great Power of little stay.
          In some cases it shews of Kings and great Nations.
          Seen rising, shew'd of a great Man so.
          Fighting, shews of some great Men doing so.
                    Loss on't great Cattle, great Men.
                         Small Cattle, common People.
                         Corn and Grass, Men and Houses
                         destroy'd by it.
     Hills as Mountains, but less, and if flourishing, with Pleasure.
               To some an uneven Life.
               To some Heaviness and Trouble, as in passing
               them.
     Falling on a Valley seen, shew'd of a great Lord oppres-
     sing good Men.
     Flying unto, that is, fixing on a good and steady Resolu-
     tion of Advantage.
     Mount so as to wrestle the Devil, and see Death before him,
          shew'd *A.* attempting an Advantage of great Dif-
          ficulty, maugre Death and Despair.
          With Difficulty, Benefit by hard Labour.
          By Fingers fix'd in a Cart, rout thro a Farmer's Aid.
          Up-hill see one come to the left to you, that is, a
          Course offers, proving order'd to your good.
          Steep, hard to overcome.
          In a Street. Vid. *Street* in *City Parts.*
          Wake e'er on top, and so will be your Work unfi-
          nish'd.
                              G   *Place.*

Place. Hills. Mount, Return or tumble down is as bad.
(2) Seen mathematically lin'd, gave *A.* good Hopes by Wheat
Being upon gives you Strength, Wiſdom, Command, and
Profit.
Going down thence, threats you Decay in Affair
or Health, as,
Travel upon, deſign in Circumſtance of good Ad
vantage.
By a ruin'd Houſe in a Vale to the left
in a State leſs fortunate where ru
inous.
Downs high be upon, that is, command in a Freedom of Diſ
pute according, but poor, *&c.* tho large.
Adorn'd with Buſhes, mix'd with pleaſant leſſer Cares.
So they ſhew an univerſal Freedom of Diſpute, as
Field a particular one.
Heath high *A.* hunting upon, ſhew'd of his ſeeking Profit in
Reverſions.
Valleys ſeen, ſhew of the common People with Deceit and Op
preſſion.
Seen to an Houſe, ſhew of the Husbandmen.
Seeming pleaſant and fruitful, give you of the Love of
the common People.
Fly croſs to a Hill, project thro a preſent Abaſement to
a greater Grandeur.
Plain ſtand on againſt the Devil wreſtling you, and Death be
fore you, purſue your Deſigns maugre Death and De
ſpair.
Coming near up to Chriſt there rotting an Horſe by the
Touch, and a mad Woman beyond him to the left ra
ving, purſue the ſame near to greateſt Chriſt-denial,
and near to Madneſs.
Precipices walking on, threat with Poverty and Decay.
To ſome, threat of their nice Diſpoſitions
as dangerous.
Forc'd to climb a fearful one, ſhew'd to *A.*
Puniſhment by Juſtice.
Ground plain, tho ſeen behind, ſhew'd of a
good Retreat offering.
Doing Works thereon, eſſaying things of dif
ficulty.
Reach within, that is, a Difficulty within humane
Performance.
Falling into, threated with Danger by Fire.
Unhurt, a croſs Buſineſs evaded without
Damage.
Seeing her Husband fall from, ſhew'd to a
Wife Widowhood.

Place. Precipices. Getting down thence, escaping a Difficulty.
(2)

By a Cart, that is, a Farmer's Aid.

By a Ladder, that is, a regular means propos'd.

Looking from thence, Curiosity in ambitious Designs. Vid. *High* in *Posture*.

Place. An Hill, an hazardous Advantage to compass. Deep fall. Vid. *Fall* in *Action*.

Steep Stairs see to your Court, cause it to be hazardous approaching you.

to others dangerous dealing with you.

White Friers, being on one in, that is, in great hazard of Credit.

Garret one descend from, that is, get off some Difficulty as to Stock.

Church be on one in, that is, in a Difficulty as to some Minister.

To others, in fear of a Friend's Death.

Over Hog-wash getting down, shew'd *A.* of avoiding a Difficulty about keeping Hogs.

Estates in general. Vid. *Riches* infra.
(3)
Vid. *Farm* infra.

Purchase. Vid. in *Money*.

Of 50 l. per an. *A.* seem'd to have, in farming he got as much yearly by Barley.

Common all about *A*'s House seeming, shew'd him as wrong'd in his Property.

Well *French*-grass'd tho, that is, sacrific'd on a good prospect.

A's own Acre in his common Field, shew'd him of his proper Right in a common Dispute.

Lane *A*'s own. Vid. *A.* in *Travel*.

Pond *A*'s about his House found dry, shew'd him failing in others neighbourly Expectances.

Copse. Vid. *Wood* infra.

Desert. Vid. *Solitude* in *Company*.

'Tis as the Opposite to Neighbourhood, and if foreign the worse.

Trees usual in Deserts seen, predict of Solitariness.

Country lodg in, that is, be destitute as to all neighbourly Hopes.

King going thither in Robes, shew'd of Ruin to his Dominions.

Invited to trade there be, that is, a ruinous Market as in Trust is offer'd you.

Estates

Eſtates. Deſert. Invited in *Africa* unknown, ſhew'd as to a Woodſale.
(3)   Meet a Friend delivers you thence, ſuch a friendly Courſe reſcues you from ſuch Miſery.

Wilderneſſes but ſeen, threat a Deſertion of all Bleſſings temporal and ſpiritual, as, &c.

In oppoſition to Gardens, Cities, Neighbourhoods.

Fight Robbers there, that is, diſpute the Errors cauſing ſuch a curſed State, &c.

Farm good and well incloſ'd given one, ſhew'd him of a Wife according.

not incloſ'd, Pleaſure and Riches in a leſs proportion ſo.

Garden, Orchard, and Fountains pleaſant, a Wife chaſt with fair Children.

Sown to Wheat, Mony with Care and Labour.

Pulſe, threats of Affliction and Trouble, and leſs Gain.

Millet, gives vaſt Riches with eaſe.

To a Man in Holy Orders it ſhews Content.

Leaſe. Vid. *Riches* in general.

Rents. Vid. *Ibidem.*

Field in general. Vid. *Medow, Paſture,* and *Plow'd Ground* infra.

Leaving enter an Houſe, reduce the matter in diſpute to an Oeconomy Form anſwerable, and ſo

It ſhews of our private Manageries in diſpute in oppoſition to an Houſe, the ſame under rule.

So of all our Pleaſures and Delights with our Riches as ſo in diſpute.

An Horſe in a Field, an Eſtate or Art in diſpute ; but in Houſe under Oeconomy Rule.

Full of Trees or Cattle, a Profit according alſo.

A large Down or Heath, a Command or Diſpute as univerſal and large, but poor and mean.

A leſs Field, a privater State of Affairs.

A long and narrow Cloſe, an inconſiderable but durable Buſineſs.

State ſeen flouriſhing beſt, as ſhewing of Joy.

Firſt ſeen, and then dry, ſhew'd of perverſe Diſputes.

Barren, ugly, and dry, ſhew'd of Hopes ſubverted, and a Command of matter in diſpute to no Profit or Good.

To others ſhew'd of idle and fruitleſs Diſputes.

Eſtates.

Estates. Field, State seen fertile with shady Trees and fair Women,
(3)   gave Success in Love.

> Green and shady with pleasant Flowers and
> Birds, Pleasure and Content.
>
> A Well found in it, a new additional Profit.
>
> Full of Serpents and Weeds seen, threated of
> Want and Enmity for Aid.

Herbage turn'd to Gold, gives excellent Corn or Grass,
as, &c.

> Vid. *Keep Beast* and *Husbandry* in Do-
> mestick Action.

Grass high and thick, Profit without Labour at
command in the Dispute, as Corn thro
Labour.

> *French* Grass *A.* sowing in an House, shew'd
> his changing a Tithe-rate to Profit.
>
> A fat Medow, a Dispute of Want and
> Plenty.
>
> Poor heathy Ground, a trifling Husbandry
> Dispute.

Fallow, to a Batchelor his Mistriss.

Yally, a Dispute of somewhat troublesom and
ill-manag'd, but improvable.

Corn, a greater Increase, as Rent and Labour
too, and as Grass a lazy Rent.

> Seen, therefore is better than Grass.
>
> In a pleasant Day, promises of great Pros-
> perity.
>
> But seen ear'd 'tis best, or else it delays
> with Hopes.
>
> Sown in a dear time, Plenty, &c è con.
>
> High and thick, Profit, but with little
> Pleasure.
>
> Flourishing seen tho, Prosperity with Con-
> tent.
>
> A Wheatfield smelling pleasant walking in,
> to a Servant a pleasant Visit with her
> Mistriss.

Paths, a common one in yours, that is, a publick Course
for others in your Managery.

Fences, &c. Vid. *Infra.*

Actions. Assaulted by Death in a green one, shew'd *A.*
near Death in's Prime.

> Break into another's, take away his Husbandry.
>
> A Beggar seen break from *A*'s Field into
> his Garden, shew'd that his Want in his
> common Affairs would at last arraign
> his whole Estate Managery as strait also.

     Estate.

Field, Actions, called into it, prepared as against a Dispute.

Changes into an House, you turn your Dispute into a real Oeconomy.

Coming into his, A. saw a black Horse, he got the Command of such by a Contrivance.

Enter a new One, change the State of your Affairs in Dispute.

Husbandry in one, to a Farmer has shewn him of the like in another.

Leave your sick Friend in one, going into a 2d, despair of his hop'd for Health.

Open'd its Earth seen, discovered the secret of a Dispute hid.

A Turf A. cutting up there, he saw a Woman under it, he died in forcing to get her.

Seeing a Feast in his own, shew'd A. of a Feast he designed to make.

Sheep in one, shew'd A. of a Dispute about good Husbandry.

Stand stoutly in one, maintain stiffly your Dispute.

First Field, the absolute Dispute.

Second Field, the State as of Conscience, or on Endeavours failing.

Fences inclose your Court, retrench your expensive Resorts.

Inclosure good one pass to the right, have the full Benefit of a good Estate.

Inclos'd a property separate, and high by all lofty Distance.

In general, shew of wariness in danger.

Mending, shew'd A. of repairing his House Top.

Over an Hedg beat one, that is, command him by a Friends Help.

But he comes round at you, you are worsted, that Friend going off.

One run away with A's Child cross, one essay'd to fool him in a covenanted Expectation.

A Wainscot Fence only, a Guard thro a refin'd Conversation only.

Bounds enlarge your Mote to every Door Farm, to all Advantages.

Ditch cleaning, shew'd A. of killing an Hog.

Seeing another, by the like again in Expectation.

Estate.

Eftate. Fences, Ditch cleaning, feeing without Mud, yet not quite
(3)   fat enough.

Its Mud flung on a middle
Bank, fuch Hog kill'd divided in Sale.

Going over by a fmall Plank, fhew'd of Deceit
by a Lawyer.

Jumping crofs forcing thro Scandals and Difficulties.

Salt flung into one, fhew'd of a vile Ufe of
good things.

Horfe feen drink out of a fteep one, fhew'd A.
of gaining by hazard, as Gaming.

Hedges and Pales, Aids to the fearful.

To the Ambitious and Travellers, Stops.

To fome, the critical Point of Right and Property.

To the Right, Security from ill, & è con.

Keeping off a Stone, good reafon fencing
flander,

Thorny growing feen, fhew'd of a ftated
Intereft Obftruction offering.

Sheep jumping crofs one, run out of A's Backfide; A. loft Goods in Poffeffion by a
Wrangle.

Stiles climbing o'er, to fome has fhewn Marriages.

to others, putting their Affairs
in a new State.

to fome, attain juftly a new Property.

Stile a fecret way, as Gate a publick Courfe,
as, &c.

Gate fhews us the Stile, but more great and general.
Vid. *Door* in *Houfe.*

Alter your own by your Workman in Hufbandry, manage your Eftate in a new way.

Of his Field A. feeing flung down by an
Horfe, fhew'd of his Journy to a place fpoil'd.

A. feeing his Cart ftop'd at,
fhew'd of his hind Money
flufh'd deferting him.

Foreft travel to, refolve on a Courfe tending to Defolation and
Mifery.

Walking in, threats of the prefent Trouble.

And fo as in a Defert before, but lefs.

Trees feen cut down, fhew'd of an Affembly deftroyed.

G 4   *Eftate*

Estate. Forest being at a fine House there, Ruin thro dependant Hopes
(3)　　　　　on great Men.

Garden, Vid. *House-range* infrà.

Medows and Marshes seen, to Husbandmen and Shepherds if
　　　fruitful is good.

Pleasant and fruitful being, gives both Riches and
　　　Pleasure.

If on an Hill, Delight, Pleasure, and an happy Life
　　　to all,

Shew Plenty without Labour, as Corn Fields plenty
　　　with.

If low and wet tho, to Travellers Dangers.
　　　　　　　to others, Impediment and Delay
　　　　　　　thro mean State.
　　　　　　　to the Banish'd, long Exile.

Vid. *Valley* suprà.

Vid. *Herbage* in *Field* suprà.

Orchard, Vid. *House-range*.

Park fine see, please your self with the Laws of Confinement,
　　　as on your Wife, *&c.*

Lodg seen, has foreshewn of Melancholy or Drunkening.

Pastures profits with Cares and Pains, but less than arable.
　　　but Medows are as sheer plenty, and mere Rents, *&c.*

Plow'd Ground pass, travel a dirty Journy.
　　　　　to others, Design amidst great Impediments.
　　　　　Vid. *Domestick Work*.
　　　　　Vid. *Field* suprà, and *Corn* in *Vegetables*.

Wilderness, Vid. *Desert* suprà.

Woods in general, shew of Difficulties and Fears in Disputes.
　　　　　To the Young, Love-Fits.
　　　　　To others, Trouble and Crosses, as scratch'd
　　　　　　in passing.
　　　　　To some, Labour, Fear and Flight.
　　　　　To some, as the Desert above, but less.
　　　　　To some, hard Gain, as by Law, Hunting,
　　　　　　&c.

Seen in a Place of Houses, threats with Misery there.

Great Trees there, great Men but rustick.

Passing thro them is best, it shewing of teasing Diffi-
　　　culties in Designs overborn.
　　　　　Flying over them, projecting in Scorn to such
　　　　　Troubles.

C H A P.

CHAP. XII.
Of Building, and Bridges.

BRidg broken going over, ſhews Fear in a mean Expedient in Troubles.

Paſs over a River by, a means to get an Eſtate.

To ſome, he ſhews an end of Troubles.

waking e'er quite paſt it tho, continues it.

Falling on it, threats alſo with Obſtructions.

Paſſing a Ditch by a ſmall Plank, ſhew'd of Deceit by a Lawyer.

Narrow, threats your Methods as in greateſt ſtraits.

Wall like againſt the Sea, of ſecurity alſo againſt popular Troubles.

Building ſhews of an honourable Advance in ſome great Work or laſting Oeconomy, form Advance according.

A Church or Altar, ſhews of one of your Family made a Prieſt.

An Houſe in general gives Comfort, and ſhews of commanding a good Oeconomy Subſiſtance.

To a Maid and Batchelor, Marriage.

At *Oxon*, deſign an Houſe Managery well in Wiſdom.

An Hearth abroad and dwelling there, ſhew'd *A.* of dying there.

A Pillar of Bread ſupporting a ſlight Pile, ſhew'd *A.* of getting a Years Store on it.

A Labyrinth before his Court-Door, ſhew'd *A.* of confounding all Approaches to him.

Vid. *Church* in *Religion.*

Vid. *Houſe.*

Vid. *Maſon* in *Trade.*

Scaffold, &c. Vid. *Houſe-parts.*

Mortar, Vid. *Houſe-parts.*

Stone, Vid. *Earth.*

Throw down what you begun, undo what you at firſt deſigned.

Manner half finiſh'd, ſhews of Deſigns and Preparations only.

Stones loſe in your Mortar, Notions incoherent.

With equal ſized Stones, in juſt Truth and Virtue.

Maſon like your ſelf, threats you Trouble, Loſs, Sickneſs or Death.

Enemy his *A.* ſaw up all Night to build a dead Womans Houſe for him, that is, *A.* ſpied a Courſe offering that might be his Death.

Repair, Vid. *Mend* in *Action.*

A Cathedral Chappel Wall ſeen down, the Stones ſeen by, ſhew'd *A.* of reinſtating univerſal Chriſtianity.

CHAP.

CHAP. XIII.

Of House-parts.

ARCH A. faw a Madman fling on his Brother, himfelf prove diffociated by rafh Intereft Cavils.

-like Heavenly Engine A. feeing, fhew'd of his confidering of a focial Government Project.

Walk thro one into a Street, by a Friendfhip attain a new publick Converfe.

Beam of an Houfe feen fall, fhew'd of a great ones Death, of a Family or Oeconomy according.

Fly to one on a Purfuit, excufe your Payment fault by Tenants Failures, &c.

Ceiling fair and white, gives a Converfe according innocent and agreable.

with Holes in't, fhew'd of a Family Oeconomy's Defectivenefs to Shew or Repute, &c.

White-wafhing, fhew'd of Deceit and Fraud, as, &c.

Shews of the projective Beauty of our Converfe, as Floor of its Solidity, and Sides of its Defence.

Chimney alone, fhews of the State of our Converfation.

Vid. *Hearth* infrà.

Soot falling feen, or the Chimney firing, threats with Extravagance.

To others, quarrelling a good Gueft, chiefly if at *London.*

Vid. *Fire.*

A Table ftands in its place, a Converfe eats up your Oeconomy Plenty.

Departing a Room by one, fhew'd one of marrying off a Daughter.

Enter a Room above by one by Repute of an Eftate, command an Oeconomy as, &c.

A Weefel feen kill'd there, fhew'd of a Family Waft prevented, as in Wood, &c.

At his Street Door feen, fhew'd A. of confuming his Eftate in Charity.

Winnowing Corn by a Fire, fhew'd of threfhing for charitable Ufes.

Anothers make a Fire at, get fome Benefit there, or as is the Perfon.

The greater and larger the better.

Door, Vid. *Gate* infrà.

Floor,

Floor, Vid. *Ceiling* supr.

    Broke thro, treading upon, subsisting in a ruinous Oeconomy.

    Unboarded being in, shew'd of an unstock'd Farm, &c.

        Shite thence on anothers Neck below, ease such Stock
        want on them.

Foundation of a Gate seen sound, shew'd of a Business assured to be
    well begun.

    In general of our House, shews of our Friend and Kindred.

        Firm seen, gives the best Assurance to Men in
        doubt.

    Of *A*'s House seen worn down by a Cartway, shew'd of his
        Gentlemanship hurt by farming.

        Foundering, threated him in an Oecono-
        my would be ruinous.

Front none, an Oeconomy of no Credit.

    Beautify your own, live more splendidly.

    A sweating Tub seen there, an Oeconomy to be had by Labour.

Furnace ruin'd seen, threats Death to Master, Wife or Son.

    Falling down, Change of Family.

        Ruin inwards, they that remain.

        outwards, they that go off.

    Burning seen, shew'd one of Travel.

    Brewing, Vid. *Action Domestick.*

Gate in general, shews of our first Entrance in Business publick or
    private, as 'tis.

    Its Foundation found Iron Bar proof, your Entrance
    assur'd good.

    Academick *Athens* Gate a Swan seen pitch on, *Plato*'s
    Philosophy.

    Burning seen, threats Death to the Dreamer or Ma-
    ster of the House.

    New seen set up, that is, a new Resolution of per-
    mitting and forbidding.

    Of Iron stop'd at, that is, the firmest and hardest
    Resolutions obstruct you.

Sort looking, East advantageous, West detrimental.

    South, luxurious; North, laborious.

New one, to some a new Wife.

    to some, Strangers offering to controul in their
    Family.

    to some, the Death of the Master.

        Shut within, threatning Ruin to the Fa-
        mily also thereby.

    City being at, that is, in Overture of some publick Transac-
    tion State.

    Gate-House opening, a Profit of farming offering.

        Pass thro, compass a farming Profit.

    's Chamber-Door seen fly open to *Julius Cæsar*'s Wife, shew'd
    his Death.

                               Gate

Gate. Sort, An Hole enter by for a Door, have a Converſe by Shi¦
     not free Admiſſion.

       Parts, Door and Threſhold, ſhews the Wife, and ruin'd is ¦
         Death.

           Poſt right, the Husband.

              left, the Wife.

         Hinges, Health.

         Bolts and Locks ſeen, promiſe Security.

               filed to open a Door, ſhew'd of ſubtle A
                 tacks to alter a Reſolution.

           Locks are peculiar to Women.

     Keys ſeen, ſhew all is ſecure as they are held.

            Vid. *Keys in Goods.*

       Bar enfeebled, your Reſolution weakned.

           opened by anothers Son, his Expectation and your Hop¦
            on it alters it.

       Boards, not the Rails broke, a Reſolution chang'd in A¦
         pearance only.

           lying down, ſeeming neglected.

    Glaſs pan'd broke, ſhew'd of Reſolutions of Proſpect alter¦
      to Action.

   Actions between 2 Doors ſitting, ſhew'd a Woman of wanto¦
      Love, upon pretence of Marriage.

      Cut to Pieces ſeen, ſhew'd of debarring Reſolutions de
       ſtroy'd.

     Diſtant 2 Doors off, that is, 2 Days off.

     Entering *Cerberus* let in, ſhew'd of Death.

          Miſtake as you go, ſeek a Converſe by a wrong
            Courſe.

          One knocking to enter, that is, tempting your
            Reſolution.

          One undoing a Door, you open it and enter into
            a Room, that is, you have an unexpected Con-
            verſe by anothers aid.

         Turn one off or out of it, that is, diſmiſs him
            your Converſe.

            A Beggar ſo, that is, reſolve againſt
              relying on others.

         Another ſeen ſtand at your Door, ſhews you ſo
            precarious at anothers.

       Flung down, your Propoſals on Trial diſappointed.

       Off, Vid. *Diſtant* ſuprà.

       Open in general, Vid. *Open in Action.*

            Knock, Vid. *K in Action.*

         Seen open at a Judges Back, gives you your Will,
           as is the Controverſy.

           Before her, to a Woman would marry,
            a Seaſon offers.

                                 Gate

Gate. Actions. seen open fly his Chamber-Door, *Cæsar's Death.*
And not to be shut again, a Resolution
broke, not to be repaired.

Shews a Course offering at your Command.

Turning without a Passage, shew'd of a seeming
Condescension, but without Leave.

Shut on you seen, shews you some way rationally confined.

Up in anothers Chamber, with them confined in
Oeconomy, as, &c.

Call to have it open in Distress, seek to reverse
hard Resolutions.

Open seen on call, fair Liberty allowed to your
Want.

Not going out on't, not tho what you
can readily embrace.

Sitting, Vid. *Between* supra.

Turn'd to a Fire-Hearth, shew'd of an Estate wasted
by Charity, an Oeconomy for Door Guests. I

Hearth shews of our Friends Profession and Conversation, of our daily
Support, &c.

Stag A. seeing in a Chimney Corner, shew'd of his considering
to keep an Whore.

Vid. *Chimney* supra.

Build, Vid. B.

Mortar, see a Madman fling a Dab at you, your self by Rashness confound
Society.

Good seen, shew'd of excellent Works in composing.

Oven A's seeming Wood at top, advis'd him not to use Plenty, at at
present ruinous.

seen burning hot, shew'd A. of Change of place.

2 in an House, shew'd of a double Family join'd in House keeping.

Pit Coal seen in them to bake with, shew'd of hidden
Malice Quarrels parting them.

Paving a Patch before his Barn Door, shew'd A. of buying an Hog
to winter there.

Pav'd Court, a neat firm Reception or Approach.

Room or Stairs, that is, a mean and harder Oeconomy State, &c.

Pillars Northern, young Men of the House.

Southern, old Men.

Eastern, Males.

Western, Females.

Higher the Master, and lower the Family.

Of an House seen falling or ruin'd, threat of Death according.

Sort of Bread a slight Pile seen, shew'd of a Years Provision of
it made.

Pillars.

Pillars. Sort. Kitchin ſeen burnt off at Ground, ſhew'd A. of an Eſtate failing him.

Kept in Place by the Frame, ſettled however only on a Child.

Holding to ſome, has been as truſting in GOD, &c.

A. ſwarfing down as by one in his Fall, ſhew'd him by Rent ſupplying an ill Payment.

Roof, Vid. *Top* infra.

of his Houſe loſt, ſhew'd A. of loſing his Clothes.

ſeen fall, to Cæſir's Wife ſhew'd his Death.

Rain drains without it, ſhew'd A. of publick Taxes.

Scaffold falling with you, the Support of your Deſigns vaniſhing.

Built in anothers Court, in Deſigns relating to him.

Top in general, Vid. *Roof* ſupra, and *Fly* in *Air*.

Stone and Timber flung down, to ſome ſhew'd of Fences deſtroyed.

Burnt, threats Death of Wife, Lord, or his Friend.

to others, Loſs of Goods and Law-Suits.

Falling thence, that is, utterly broke and confounded in Houſekeeping.

down Top Ornaments of an Houſe ſeen, ſhew'd A. of miſſing of ſtately Goods.

Of Houſes A. walking or ſtanding on, ſhew'd of his uſing extreme Power over Families.

Untile the Church o'er the Miniſters Pew, uſe him with publick Scorn.

Anothers Houſe, redargue the Ineffectualneſs of his Oeconomy.

Wainſcot ſeen ſlight, ſhew'd of an Oeconomy or Converſe not ſecure or laſting in its ſuppos'd genteel State.

Of Cedar ſmelling well, that is, of Nobleſs and great Fame

Of Oak, not Deal, an Oeconomy durable and ſubſtantial. &c.

Altering to the better Change of Oeconomy or Converſe, as, &c.

Set out at your Back-Door, in a State of Scandal and Decay, &c.

Adorn'd with Pictures, the ſame glaz'd o'er with fair Imaginations.

The Images ſeen moving, falſe Hopes, and as if inchanted.

Wall ſhews the Dreamers Strength, Health, Eſteem and Riches.

Seen to Men in Doubt, it gives Surety.

Part build to its Height, a Work near finiſh'd.

The Scaffold breaking down, your Help about it failing

Wall'd out of a Place, denied abſolutely Communication accordingly.

Wall ſhews, Wall'd, An Hole offer'd to be broke, a ſneaking Admiſſi-
　　　　on only left.

　　State. Higher than your Head, a Security beyond Man's ordinary
　　　　　Power.

　　　　　Broken ſeen, threated the Sides of a Ship failing.
　　　　　Uneven, a Security of unequal power.
　　　　　Firm, a Security of greateſt Force.
　　　　　Mud one, Charles II. trampling on the Rump Parliament.
　　　　　Of Bones Human A. ſeeing about his Court, ſhew'd of his
　　　　　　living to bury moſt of his Reſorters.

　　Sorts Fencing, Vid. Fence in Earth.
　　　　　Houſe ſeen, ſhew'd of the Root and Foundation of a Fa-
　　　　　　mily Oeconomy, as, &c.
　　　　　Church-yard yours ſee down, threats you as unconſecrating
　　　　　　it.
　　　　　Church-walls A. ſeeing an Agreement wrote on, ſhew'd
　　　　　　him of a Miniſter's letting his Eſtate to board with him.
　　　　　City ſtanding on, expecting on the ſureſt Hopes of pub-
　　　　　　lick Tranſactions.

　　Acts. Sitting on a Wall, gives firmeſt Aſſurance.
　　　　　Standing on a Wall, commanding what was formerly a firm
　　　　　　Right in another.
　　　　　Burning in ones Houſe ſeen, ſhew'd Sickneſs, as &c. but
　　　　　　with Recovery.
　　　　　Break thro, by Law or Controverſy attain to ſome Right
　　　　　　of another.
　　　　　　　And as go in by the Door is directly, and by the
　　　　　　　Window by the by.
　　　　　Wrote out Tufes ſeen, ſhew'd of Dreams, Studies harmo-
　　　　　　nizing to good Monitions.

Windows in general ſhew of our Sons and Daughters, and Brothers
　　　　　　and Siſters.
　　　　　　　To others a publick Proſpect of Command riſing
　　　　　　　from their Oeconomy Managery.
　　　　State ruin'd ſeeing out of, threats you with Deſigns ru-
　　　　　　inous, as, &c.
　　　　　　Burnt Front-Windows ſeen, ſhew'd of the Death
　　　　　　　of Brethren, &c.
　　　　　　　Back-Windows, Death of Siſters, &c.
　　　　　Smoky, an erroneous and troubleſom Proſpect from
　　　　　　your Oeconomy.
　　　　　New finding in your Houſe, gives you of ſome new
　　　　　　Proſpect in your Affairs.
　　　　　Great, expreſs of Shewiſhneſs.
　　　　　Many, diſcover Secrets and render an Oeconomy un-
　　　　　　ſafe.
　　　　Parts, the Qualifications to ſuch Proſpects, as, &c.

　　　　　　　　　　　　　　　　　　　　Windows.

Windows. Kind. School-window *A.* would force out of his but can't, he's always a Learner.

Shop-window *A.* would go out of, that is, ſhuffle out of a bad Bargain.

House, the ſame as to ſome Oeconomy or Converſe.

Actions. Break in at one, have a good Proſpect of getting an Eſtate, as by Gift, &c.

Iron Bar looſened by one within for't, your Benefactor reſolv'd thereto.

Glaſs broke, preſent Proſpect ſcandalous, as, &c.

Enter an House by the Window, gain by indirect ways.

Thro the Door, by proper Methods.

Finding Money laid there, ſhew'd *A.* receiving of ſome lent.

Hearing thro the Glaſs, an Oeconomy Freedom, but in Obſcurity.

to others, perceive of an Oeconomy you are not privy to.

Lay things in. Vid. *Poſture.*

Open. Vid. *Action.*

Making to a Church, adding new Proſpects to Religion.

Seeing a Bird fly by 2 Windows, hearing of an Occurrence by 2 Intelligences.

one out of your own House Window. Vid. *Grammar.*

Shutting ſhews of Concealment in Converſe or Deſign.

Againſt a Storm, continuing your Oeconomy for all popular Commotions.

Stop'd to the left ſeen for warmth, a Proſpect for preſent Poverty laid by.

CHAP. XIV.

Of *House-Rooms.*

IN general, each Room and thing in't ſhews as to ſome Oeconomy or Converſe Branch as is the Room.

Various Rooms, various States of the ſame like Oeconomy, as in fix'd State.

Every Room. Vid. *E.* in *Part.*

In general, Endless Rooms he's in *A.* can't escape from, he is in an ill Oeconomy incurable, state it as he will.

　2 of a sort, the same Converse or Oeconomy State severally suppos'd.

　　3 of a sort, the utmost Perfection of Variety of Oeconomy States.

Quality neat, gives Gain or good Notion, as, *&c.*

　With a well-furnish'd Bed in't, Joy and Ease at pleasure.

　Unboarded, shew'd of a Converse or Oeconomy unpassable or not fitted for Action.

　　A Corner of it only, its Singularity only at present ill.

　Divided. Vid. *Part* in *Quantity.*

　Unknown. Vid. *Grammar.*

　Furniture. Vid. *Goods.*

Sort. Underground. Vid. *Cellar* infra, and *Holes* in *Earth.*

　　2 or 3 Steps down, a Secrecy or Roguery to a little degree.

　　2 down, an Art not quite conceal'd, but infamous.

　　Imprison'd in with a Physician, shew'd *A.* in a Malady dark to Remedies, but not dangerous.

　　　3 Strings leading the way thence, perfect Reasonings applied for Delivery.

　　Free Air back North, hard Labour and Industry the only Cure.

Over Water, in Sickness or Trouble.

Rush'd Rooms, a Life of Delicacy and Plenty.

Another's, his Way of Oeconomy, *&c.*

　　Leave his, that is, act otherwise than he.

Upper Rooms, your privater Oeconomy Managery, as by Contrivance and Expedient.

　Lower, your publicker Oeconomy Managery, or your personal Managery therein.

　2 or 3 Steps up, a Secrecy, Nobless, or Reservedness answerable.

Inner Room, a secreter Method.

　　So 'tis as a second Room, or the Equity of the Converse, *&c.*

　Having a Chamber within two Closets in *Oxon,* having a Managery dependant on a double ingenious secret Managery.

Dark, a wicked or foolish and ignorant Oeconomy of Converse, *&c.*

Open to the Street with Lace seeing, shew'd me of meeting with a travelling Lace-seller.

H

In general. Acts. Do ſomewhat in your Kitchin, that is, before your Cook.

Buy in another's Houſe, marry thence.

Enter by a Chimney. Vid. C. in *Houſe-Parts*.

Having Remnants in it be in one, that is in ſome Managery with a Taylor.

In it A. ſeeing an Owl and 2 Ravens, ſhew'd of his deſigning in a deadly and ſelf-deſolating Courſe.

Vaniſhing ſeen tho, it went off.

An half Angel threats you, a pretended Monition menaces you.

A. ſeeing 4 little Blackbirds, ſhew'd him of a little is determin'd, but to good Iſſue.

Looking on a Coffin before one there, ſhew'd A. of examining others fatal Predictions.

Purſued thro all the Rooms of an Houſe by a Snake, in terror of Temptations in all ſorts of Converſe, &c.

Shut. Vid. *Door* in *Houſe-Parts*.

Stand between the Rooms above and below, concern you doubly in Affairs.

Turn Perſons out of yours, diſcard Methods in your Oeconomy.

Apple-loft among Garrets, ſhew'd of a Collection of chief Rents.

Balcony ſtanding in, to a Woman running her ſelf into publickeſt Tranſactions.

See a Woman jumping from one to another, find her endeavouring for Marriage.

To ſome run from Chamber thither, proceed from private Family Tranſactions to publick and notorious ſhewiſh Declarations Oeconomick.

On a Stair-head ſeen, ſhew'd of a fair Rule for a private Conduct.

Fire make in it, that is, be ſhewiſhly expenſive.

Buttery in general ſhews of the Steward.

Vid. *Pantry* in *Kitchin*.

Better is promis'd you, that is, a fairer Houſekeeping is like to befal you thro Circumſtances appearing.

Diſcourſing in't, ſhew'd of Overtures relating to private Actions there.

Cellar. Vid. *Holes* in *Earth*, and *Rooms underground* ſuprà.

Shews us either of Secrecy or Roguery.

Fall into, be caught by another's roguiſh Plots.

Drawing Drink there, to a Maid ſhew'd of loſing her Sweat heart, a Tap-love offering only.

2 or 3 Steps down, better than underground.

Shops there, ſhew of ſecret or wicked Tranſactions according.

Cella

Cellar Shops. Huckster before an Apothecary within, shew'd of Extortion.

A Ghost seen coming thence into Passage, shew'd of a Cheat offering in drawing off Liquors.

Chamber-own. Vid. *Grammar.*

Becomes a Garden of the whole World, so your Managery the universal Culture of all Men.

Leaving, to the Sick Recovery.

to the Contemplative, Action.

Shiting in, threats with Sickness, Death, or Remove.

Door flying open, to *Cæsar's* Wife shew'd his Death.

Others. *Philizar's* being in, shew'd *A.* menaced with Arrests.

Other Lawyers being in, engag'd in some Law-concern according.

Physicians confin'd in, shew'd *A.* Sickness to a continual Regularity of Life.

Deaths seeing, considering of an Oeconomy to Sin and Perdition.

Temple one buying, shew'd *A.* of doing business *gratis*, and as if to buy Practice.

Sort. Antichamber to a Prison be in, that is, in great fear of Insolvency.

Consum'd by Lightning, your private Managery Designs quite subverted.

Great being in, that is, in a plentiful Family Oeconomy State.

Ill-floor'd, an Estate unstock'd or Rent ill paid.

Dropping between the Boards on't, Loss of Credit and Hurt by it.

Inner another's leave, that is, be of another mind in your secret Oeconomy Methods.

Master's be in, that is, in consideration of the whole Family Oeconomy, *&c.* as to its secreter Command.

Nursery. Vid. *Grammar.*

Opposite. Vid. *Against in Postures.*

To a Woman's being in, that is, in a Managery near as sedentary.

Sons elder, shews of our Inheritance Managery State.

Stately seeing the King or a Noble in, gives you Honour and Advance.

Atts. See a Book there, find some good Instruction thro some Family Managery.

Go down thence, leave private Application for publick Managery.

Tax-gatherers and Lawyers seen in one, shew'd of such Charges confounding such Managery.

Hear a Woman racket Chairs above in't, be in a narrow restless State.

H 2

Chamber. Acts. Turn one *Jew* from yours leaving 3, reject the Perſec
rion, but not the Eſtabliſhment of *Judaiſm*.

Another's Window fly at, project at his intimate Con
verſe.

Another has a Room in your Houſe, he fixes a Method
of Converſe with you.

Cloſet ſhews of our private and reſerveder Family Deſigns.
Vid. *Shedd* infra.

Have one in another's Room, carry on a private Deſign in the
Managery.

An unknown one at *Oxon*, that is, an unaccountable ingenious private Managery.

Another's having, ſhew'd *A.* of his Son their Godſon.

Being in a fair one of one unknown, ſhew'd *A.* of an unexpected Command of another's fine Cloſet-things.

Feeding his Oxen with Hay thence, leaving their home-labour
to uſe them abroad to advantage.

Dairy being in, threats you as a Milk-ſop.

To others has ſhewn of Divine Grace.
Vid. *Milk* in *Drink* and *Victuals*.

Entry. Vid *Paſſage* infra.

Galleries ſhew to us of Servants Chambers.

Long, tedious Services in Family Managery.

Puppit-play ſeen there, ſhew'd of many Servants throng'd in
a Bed.   Vid. *Paſſage* infra.

Garrets ſhew to us of Stables, Out-houſes, and Buildings for Goods.

Phyſicians being in, ſhew'd *A.* of examining his own Store
Medicines by him.

Window Precipice ſeeing out of, ſhew'd *A.* of fearing Ruin
thro building of Out-houſes.

Hall in general ſhews us of our Tenant's Wife and Equals.

Mean and large ſhut in, confin'd in a ſtately, but poor
Oeconomy.

Furniture, as Tapeſtry, &c. ſeen burnt, Death or Damage to the Maſter or Miſtriſs.

Stately being in, gives you an excellent Repute with
Tenants and Equals.

Throng'd by unknown ſeen, ſhews unaccountable Methods lead you much.

Heavenly crown'd in, gave a glorious Funeral.

Going out of it into the Court, diſmiſſing Treaty with
ſome Equals, as &c.

Jakes. Vid. *Houſe-range.*

Kitchin being in, to ſome Delight in Glattony, &c.
to others it ſhews of their Eſtate for Houſekeeping.

Act there, that is, do ſomewhat before your Cook, if
ſeeming your own you live in.

Burnt down, Death or Remove to the Cook or ſuch Servant.
                                                                Kitchin

Kitchin burnt. A Pillar on't burnt off only, some Rent Estate only fails.
In Religion it shews of Dogmas and Hypotheses.

Arrest one there, that is, accuse him for his Opinion.

Pantry for cold Meats, shews us of enforc'd Doctrines.

Run to it from Pursuers, answer a Dun that you expect Rent.

Scullery see a Man sit in your Brother's, triflingly cavil about side-wind Profits.

Milk-house. Vid. *Dairy* supra.

Nursery. Vid. *Own House* in *Grammar.*

Pantry. Vid. *Kitchin* supra.

Parlour many Candles seen there, gave great Joy and Mirth.

A little Dog seen in one, shew'd of a pleasant Entertainment by fine Ladies.

Gentlemen look askew on you there, you act as to appear ungenteel.

A's Tutor seen merry there, shew'd of his Study even to the Scorn of Company.

Passages to Chambers, shew Servants or Assistants.

Long shews of Length of time.

Meet one there, resolve to have no free Intercourse with him.

Come from Passage above to Passage below, go from Courses of Resolution to Action.

Below full of Men you can't stir, encumber'd by Workmen.

To the Kitchin A's Cradle seen in, shew'd of A's Sickness obstructing Housekeeping.

Door Persons knocking at, shew'd of new Transactions offering.

Lying idly in Bed with his Wife there, shew'd A. negligent as to Workmen.

With your Wife, taking a new Calling you, as, &c.

Scullery. Vid. *Kitchin* supra.   Shops. Vid. *City-parts.*

Stair-pace Fights shew of Estate Managery Disputes.

Find Money in, that is, turn Trade-stock to Pocket Money.

case vile, shews of Poverty.

Royal or Officers, gives Power with Authority.

New find, that is a new Method of Oeconomy.

Stone, a Managery of hard Fate. Vid. *Pavement* in *House-parts.*

2 or 3 Steps up or down. Vid. *House-rooms* in general supra.

Acts. Lost shews of the means of managing a Business vanishing.

Fling a Box at one coming up Stairs, shew him he is but a Guest.

Standing there wake, secure your private Oeconomy, where forc'd to publick visit Correspondents.

Drop Iron carelesly down there, lose hard Gains at Cards.

Stair-caſe. Acts. Purſued down thence, fear'd by great Dangers fro
        your publick Oeconomy.

        Meet one there, oppoſe for Secrecy his intermedlir
        in your Affairs.

        A Soldier would lie with *A*'s Wife and puſh him dov
        Stairs, ſhe'd oppreſs another, and ſcorn him
        withſtanding.

Store-houſes ſhew of our Poſſeſſions and Fields.

Study, Money ſeen lie there, ſhew'd of profitable Memorandums woul
        become ſuch,
        Vid. *Cloſet* ſupra.

Wardrobe, Vid. *Apparel*,

C H A P. XV.

Of Out-houſes and Houſe-ranges.

ARbours ſhew of our private Deſigns in publick Managements c
        plenty States.

        and Gardens ſhew of exceeding Plenty, as Houſes of bar
        Subſiſtence.

Backſides ſhew of foreign domeſtick Tranſactions and Servants, &c.
        Vid. *Street* in *City* in *Habitations.*

Fore-backſide, Tranſactions ſuch as are to your Credit and Good.
        Hinder-backſide *è con.*

        For Carts, ſhew of our publick Tranſactions for Husbandry
Vid. *Own Backſide* in *Grammar.*

Barn. Sort, old one ſeen, threats with Melancholy and Sickneſs.

        New unknown Oat-barn *A.* ſeeming to have with Logs at
        bottom, ſhew'd him of ſelling Oats e'er threſh'd.

Stored having, to ſome a rich Wife.
            to ſome Succeſs in Law,
            to ſome Merry-meetings.
            to ſome a Profit as great.

Paving a Patch before a Barn's Door, ſhew'd *A.* of buying an Hog
        to winter.

Seen in your way, ſhews of ſome farming Good in proſpect.

Deſcend the Wall naked within't, be near in deſpair about farm-
        ing.

Standing by, that is, conſidering of your Stock of Money.
        In't a Friend ſeen, promis'd of good Farming.

Threſhing in't the Czar of *Muſcovy* ſeen, bid civilly go off,
        ſhew'd of a good Stock of Bees got.

Court croſs'd. Vid. *Poſture* and *Paſs* in *Travel.*

Court in general. An House with no Court, a Trade-State defiring all
    Refort.

        With one, *è con*, State, *&c.*

    Sort. A Cottage pal'd in, *A.* having in his Court Front, fhew'd
        of his borrowing of a poor Man.

        To a Goal being in, that is, negligent in Circumftances, as
        tending to Debt.

        Papifts walk about, be as in the Approach to fome unreafo-
        nable Oeconomy.

        Little Sun, fhew'd one ill dreft for Receptions.

    Acts. Pafs thro anothers, by another Addrefs accomplifh your
        Affairs.

        Inclofing, excluding expenfive Reforts.

        Srop'd in entering anothers, threats your Bufinefs propos'd
        by him fails.

        Paving your own, fixing a fteddy courfe of Approach to
        you.

        Something threatning you in't, fome ill menacing in Oeco-
        nomy Approach.

            Come within a Gate-Houfe to it, thro fome
            farming Profpect.

            Efcaping from it into, building fuch ill Ap-
            proach well cured.

    Stairs to it render it the more ftately, and if fteep with danger.

    Own, Vid. *Grammar.*

Haytallanght, fhew'd of my keeping Horfes or Cattel.

    Affaulted there, accufed according.

Jakes, chofe an Officer over, that is, under great Trouble to regulate
    your Expence.

    full found, fhews your Expence already exceeds your Ability.

    Befhit feen, threats you fcandaloufly abus'd in your Expence.

    Vomit up Sirreverence, fpend your Rents e'er due.

    An Office drain a Revenue, clearing your Expence after laid out.

    Fair feen Eaft, a good Convenience to eafe Expence to Advan-
        tage.

        With Sheets of brown Paper for long Ufe.

    A. faw his Tutor go to from his Parlour drinking, *A.* prov'd
        eager to digeft his imperfect Studies.

    Vid. *Dung* in *Earth.*

    Vid. *Shite* in *Bodily Action.*

    Vid. *Clofeftool* in *Goods.*

Garden in general, fhews as to the Plenty and Splendor of our Eftate as
    it is.

        To fome, of their whole Eftate in little with its
        Ability above Neceffaries.

        To fome, the State of their publick Religious Mat-
        ters fo ftated.

    Puffing thro to a barren ftony Place, fhew'd *A.* of Sicknefs.

                                    Garden

Garden paſſing, walking there pleaſantly, gives you Joy and Diverſion in an Enjoyment beyond Neceſſaries.

Leaving to go into your Houſe, a Change from Plenty to Neceſſaries.

In a fine unknown one, delighting thee in Arrogancy.

Gathering Flowers there, conceiting high of thy ſelf.

Aſſaulted by a Tyger there, an Enemy according offering you violence in ſuch State.

Anothers walk with him in, be benefited thro his Eſtate.

Turn'd out of anothers, diveſted of Hopes in his Eſtate.

Get into a Lords Command at a great Man's Houſe in Plenty, and wake there, continue in it.

Walk thro a good Husbands, manage your Eſtate as he.

Gardener ſeen act, ſhews of your ſelf in the ſame Station.

Sort have at *Oxon*, learnedly or ſtudiouſly diſpoſe your Affairs to good, as, *&c.*

Own or Brothers, *&c.* Vid. *Grammar.*

Sea-ſide be in, be concerned in ſome popular Managery.

Kitchin, relating to plowing and ſowing.

Unknown finding a Well in ſh—in't, tick on a new Credit, *&c.*

Pleaſant one be in, that is unexpectedly in a good Eſtate Circumſtance.

State rude, ſhews of Deſigns according ruffled and diſappointed.

Hogs ſeen there, threat of careleſs waſtful Manageries.

Storms ſee on your Enemies, make his popular Claſhes hurt himſelf.

Parts there walks, ſhew Methods in ſuch State.

Vid. *Arbour* ſuprà.

Vid. *Apples*, &c. in *Fruit*.

Canal in't, to the King of *France* ſhew'd the Sea.

2 Iſlands there, *Britain* and *Ireland*.

Hunters and Spaniels, ſhew'd him of Armies and Men of War.

Ducks there, ſhew'd Iſlanders.

Eating their Eggs, deſtroying their Breeds and Plantations.

Walking with her Father in his, A, ſeem'd ſtung by a Snake and dying on't, to a Maid marry.

Orchard in general, ſhews of our live Stock in farming.

Break into anothers, get his Stock.

So of our main Product, as to Induſtry, as Garden, as to Pleaſures.

Orchard

Orchard in general. Apples and Quinces on Trees in't worth 50 *l.* such farming gain so.

To a Scholar, it shews of his Stock of Learning.

And as his Garden of the more Ornamental, so his Orchard of his more solid Stock therein.

Walking there, gives of Joy and Mirth.

Trees adorn'd by Roses on Rose Trees, stock gain as pleasant as reputable.

Keep Conies there that hide, pursue a Study or Husbandry you dare not own.

Pass by an Hog there to the left with Stags Horns with your Sword drawn, that is, challenge in Scorn in learning a stout bodied Rival, *&c.*

Labyrinth make before your Court Door, confound Men in their Approaches to you.

A Maze pass by to the Right, compass some puzling Affair to advantage.

Pigeon-House go to, design towards a projective fidling Familiarity.

spoilt, such Familiarities hurt.

Stable enter anothers, pay him Mony.

Going to your own, shews you of taking a Journy.

to some, has shewn of Warlikeness.

A. in anothers, his Horses kick'd at him, he refused his Mony as bad.

Beat by his Groom with Leather there, suppled by him to stoop for't.

A. pities a Prodigal in one unknown in his next Market Town, *A's* self proves as reduc'd.

Storehouses, shew of Fields and Possessions.

Summer-house looking out of, presents with Hopes of Pleasure, Plenty and Ease.

Yard, Vid. *Back side* supra.

C H A P. XVI.

Of House-State and Occurrences.

A CTS. Bearing with Labour, threats with a bad Wife or hard Business.
(1)

Break up anothers, get an Estate of another by Gift, *&c.*

Iron Window Bar remov'd for it by one within, they resolved thereto.

Vid. *Break* in *Action.*

Vid. *Water* infra.

A C T S. Bringing forth *Charms* feen, declared of a Confpirac
(1)   there hatch'd.

     Brought into it unfortunate Birds feen, fhew'd c
        crofs Affairs at Command.

        Handled thereon, to the greater Affur
        ance.

Burning feen, fhews of great Offence or Peril of Life.
     Vid. *Fire.*

Cleaning anothers, gaining by him.

     Your own, fhews you of Marriage or great Ex
        pence.

     White-wafhing it, attempts of Gain by Deceit.

Entering it with G O D, threats Death or great Sicknefs.

     anothers, and finding the Owner afleep, *A.* cu
        out his Fat and Excrement ftinking Guts, an
        carried them away ; that is, rob'd him.

Falling, Damage or Death to thy felf or Parents, *&c.*

Fire, Vid. *F.*

Having fomewhat in Houfe, that is, at full Command an
     Difpofe.

     A dead Ox there to cut up, that is, a Yoke to fe
        his ill Hushandry to keep.

Plaifter, Vid, *Clean* fuprà.

Sowing *French* Grafs in one, fhew'd of rooting out an i
     Tenant by way of Improvement.

Sweeping anothers, gives you Gain.

     your own, threats you Lofs.

Turn one out of it, that is, difcard him your Converfe c
     Oeconomy, *&c.*

White-wafhing, Vid, *Cleaning* fuprà.

Sort. Antient continuing in, increafes the Riches or Poverty of you
(2)   firft State.

     Repairing, fhew'd of paying Debts.

     Enlarg'd, gives Increafe of Eftate, Power or Family.

And unknown being in, fhews of Change of Air, *&c.*

     It ruinous, it threats Death.

     Vid. *Unknow* in *Grammar.*

Ruin'd in general, threats you with Fears and Vexations, if yc
     are in't.

     Vid. *Ruin* in *Action.*

     Parts ruin'd. Vid. *the feveral parts.*

Infirm, an Oeconomy not to be repos'd on.

Unfurnifh'd, with great Want of prefent Neceflari
     as, *&c.*

By a private Earthquake, Damage thro the Princes Edi

Flung down part by the Devil, threated one in Fam
     dying.

Raining in at yours, Circumftances fcanty to Scandal.

Sort. New building shewing one yours, acting boastingly as to your first
(2)   Managerys.

      Seen in general, changes the Poor to Rich.
                the Rich to Poor.
           to others it shews of some new Oeconomy or Converse.

Fair, gives an Increase of Power thro Industry.
      to others, a good Management therefore.

Lost among such in his native City, to *A.* hear of his
      Acquaintance dying there.

Double, shew'd of a Livelihood by Estate and Calling to.

    Poor Folks at one end, Gentry at t'other ; a Reversion
      after a mean Estate for Life.

    You Master of the best part of it, you act to the best
      in such Oeconomy.

Great, an Oeconomy of Nobless and Plenty.
    High, a lofty Converse or magnificent Oeconomy.

    Lodgings a Lawyer's there, a Lawyer belonging to such an
      Oeconomy.

Fair, Vid. *New supra.*

    Blesses with a delicate Family Subsistence and Converse.
    Old fashioned, shews of an Oeconomy absurd.

Firm of Stone, of good Durance and Ability.
    Freestone, the better.

A slight Pile, a Family Subsistence for a Year or so.

A Paper Building more firm, a Converse or Oeconomy also
    according.

Quality. Palace, rid your Shoos of Gravel before it, shews your Offence at
(3)   doings there.

    Stand in, do Actions worthy the Presence of a King.

    Royal Guard Room be in, consider of his Majesties War.

    In general it shews of a Converse or Oeconomy, of as
      great or equal Regard, *&c.*

    Opposite Chambers there, contrary Managery.

         A way between a common mean in the Case.

Over the Water, a sickly or troublesome Oeconomy.

Seat old with young Trees, an ancient Converse with new
    growing Hopes.

Country House, Vid. *Retirement.*

    Shew one to a Citizen, that is, a Profit can keep one
      for them.

    With a Cottage paled in in Frost, subsisting by
      borrowing of one Poor.

    A. seemed living at her Parents, her Husband's being
      but as a Country House; her Marriage to her Will.

Poor Man's being in, that is, in Circumstances indigent as he.

      To some, has shewn of mean Visitants.

    Thatch'd Houses flying to the Top of, projecting to
      command such Poor at Pleasure.   *Quality.*

Quality. Brick buildings, ſhew of the Cuſtoms thereof again repeated.

(3)   *Cupilo* reſiding in, that is, being in a Novel, but ſtately Form of Subſiſtence.

Property. Vid. *Grammar.*

(4)   Own, Vid. *Grammar.*

Home, Vid. *Grammar.*

Dwell among the Clouds, threats Death.

     abroad and build a Fire Hearth there, ſhew'd *A.* dying there.

     In Hell, ſhews of Wickedneſs.

       Paradiſe, declares of Celibacy.

       A Tomb threats with Death.

       Your old School, that is, be under Rebuke as heretofore.

         You Maſter, you rebuking others ſo.

     With your Phyſician, pitch on a courſe of great Security to your Health.

     With a King or Prince, gives you Joy and Advancement.

     At her Parents Houſe, *&c.* Vid. *Grammar.*

     At *Jamaica,* ſhew'd *A.* reſolv'd on a conſtant Chocolate Subſiſtence.

Houſekeeping Robbers ſet up for *A.* ſaw vaniſh, that, is, he found *B*'s Oeconomy to be deem'd no longer as a Cheat.

     In Church, Vid. *C.* in *Religion.*

Poor Folks at one end, Gentry at t'other ſeen, ſhew'd of a mean Cottage bought by a Gentleman.

Anothers, Vid. *Grammar.*

     being in or ſeeming as yours, likens your Oeconomy to be as is ſuch State.

     Stands in your Room, he vies with you in Houſekeeping.

       Whitewaſh'd, that is, cheatingly flouriſhed up thereto.

Known as where once perſecuted being in, threats you the like again.

     Seems nearer you than before, you imitate them.

     Adjoining to his others ſeen, ſhew'd of Buſineſs manag'd by *A.*

Strange be in, that is, another Courſe of Life preſents to you.

     Hanging in the Air, gives Death with great Fame.

     Under Ground being in, Death with Infamy.

     Wooden and darkened by Pitch being in, Death alſo.

     Vid. *Grammar.*

Without.
(5)
All about his feen common, fhew'd *A.* wrong'd in his Property.
   Set with *French* Grafs tho, to great Intereft, Improvement, *&c.*
River running before a Door bathing in, commanding a Revenue at Will.
Stars feen under *A*'s Houfe-Eves, fhew'd him of his Houfe-keeping breaking up.
   Falling on it, afflicts it with Judgment.
Sun falling on your Houfe, is Danger of Fire, or the Judges Sentence.
Owl feen fit on't, has threatned Death.

Within.
(6)
Furniture, Vid. *Goods.*
   Vid. *Wainfcot,* &c. in *Houfe-parts.*
   Unfurnifhed being in, that is, in a State ruinous according.
   Without Picture, without Projects.
Ravenous Birds feen enter, fwift Wafters devouring.
   Vid. *Grammar.*
Sun entering a Chamber, is very good or ill.
   To fome, it gives Children.
One comes to you in a new Houfe, you confult him in a new Converfe, you caufe the Approach of his Aid fo.
Trees feen in it, fhew of Strangers receiv'd in your Family if growing there.
   Green and rank, the worfe.
   Long liv'd feen grow in't, to fome has fhewn of long Life with quiet.
Water dirty flowing in an Houfe, Danger by Fire.
   Spilt in't, the Trouble proportionable to the Quantity.
   New Well found in't, a new Profit.
Breaking out of the Walls, Trouble and Sadnefs.
   Drying away, felf remedying.
   Caught in a Veffel, the worfe.
Full of it, an Oeconomy in Trouble or Sicknefs, &c.
River, Vid. *River* in *Water.*
   running out of it, to the Rich Liberality.
   to the Poor, a diffolute Family.
   into it, Profit by great Men.
   by a Channel, the Profit the more great and fure.

CHAP.

CHAP. XVII.

Of Houſe-ſorts.

Alehouſe, Vid. *Tavern* infra.
     Vid. *Village* in *Habitation.*

Bawdy-Houſe being in, threats with Trouble and Jilting as is there uſual.
     Force into one, attain to a Profit will near cheat you in the end.
     Entering unable to get out again, to ſome Death.
     Vid, *Whore* in *Woman, Grammar.*

Coffee-Houſe, ſhews of your publick Converſe, and your common Oeconomy State, free of all manner of regard.
     Seeming at on a Viſit, ſhew'd of Friends meeting, but without mutual Reſpects.
     Boarding there, ſhew'd A. thro Infirmity eating alone, but the Wall commanding all Reſort to him.
     Sneaking there A. ſeen, ſhew'd him eaſily banter'd by publick Company.
     Scrambling at its Entrance for Nuts and Almonds, ſhew'd of uncouth publick mix'd Greetings.
     Travelling to enquire about Apparitions, I came to a Coffee Houſe, where *D.* an eminent Friend Councel, and one *Fatma* there ſeemed to laugh and ſcorn at me, but I retorted ſharp on them; and ſo alſo I ſaw 2 ſlight Papers there, and then took *Fatman's* Place, &c. they ſeem'd to ſcorn my eldeſt Sons Hat, as old faſhioned, &c. This to ſhew me that my Skill at firſt ſcorn'd, will triumph with the moſt indifferent Converſant at laſt.

Caſtle ſeen burnt down, ſhew'd Death to its Maſter.   Vid. *War.*
     Of Clouds ſeen about one, ſhew'd him of the Divine Protection.

Corporation Hall Feaſt being at, ſhew'd A. of flouriſhing in great and general Dealings.

Cottages, ſhews of Poverty, Vid. *Houſe-ſtate* ſuprà.

Counting-Houſe ſeen on Fire, ſhew'd of Tithe by Compoſition Turn to kind again.

Eccleſiaſtical, Vid. *Religion* infra.

Exchange fall from the Top of, that is, be at greateſt Loſs in Credit.
     Going to, being in Deſigns of greateſt Profit and Advance.
     Dancing at the Back-ſide on't, hurried in publick Payment you can't anſwer.
     Go to buy fine things there, be in Plenty even to Prodigality

Gate

Gates. Vid. Door in *House-parts*.

Goal. Vid. *Prison* infrà.

Guild-hall, *London* seen, to a Villager shew'd him of his Parish-pound.

Hospital at *London*, a charitable Aid in the best Managery.

>　Kept by your Brother go to, seek Aid of an Interest thwarting you in your Distress.

>　At next Market-Town in your first Bargains.

Inn being in, threats you with Idleness and dear and hard Usage, and Business left a while unfinished.

>　The statelier the worse.

>　Vid. *Tavern*, &c. *postea*.

>　In circumstance, *&c.* shews of Journeys. Vid. *Grammar*.

>　To most it shews of Business will end by halves.

>　　So to some Death preventing of Attempts.

Own House becoming one, to *A.* shew'd him of Guests visiting him unbid.

Sorts. Unknown reside in, be trusted, but withal chous'd and extorted on.

>　　With a Prodigal, thro Prodigality be so us'd.

>　At *London* be at, that is, fail only in the Perfection of your Trade or Converse.

>　*Oxon*, fail as to the exceeding Subtlety of Managery.

>　Friendly to no ill Issue.

Innkeeper seen, threats of Misery and Dearness to all.

>　To the Sick Death.

>　Believe one unknown, delude your self with fair Pretences.

>　Hostess seen maundring, shew'd *A.* cheated with all Impudence.

Acts. A Bill brought you there, dun'd sharply, and if unknown with a Cheat too.

>　Jumping cross a Chamber with 4 Beds therein, shew'd *A.* of easily assenting to part with his Wife.

>　Fetch a Friend from thence, court a wrong Friendship to cheat you.

>　Coming to, shew'd of Business left ½ finished.

>　Hogs *A*'s seen there, shew'd of his taking order on his seeing them ill-us'd.

>　Oxen seen lie down there, shew'd of their Plow-work too hard.

Lodg in a Park seen, foreshew'd of Melancholy and Taverning.

Monastery *A*'s House becoming, shew'd him of bearing others Charges in Religion.

>　Vid. *Religion*.

Palace. Vid. *House-State*.

Parliament-Houſe going to ſee, to a Wife ſhew'd of offering to command her Husband.

     Her Head ſeeming bad dreſt there, his Command diſproportion'd for it.

     Adjourning to a Temple-Chamber on't, being content in her own juſt State at laſt.

Priſon ſhews of Impediments to rational Deſigns in Proſpects.

     To others of Debts and Benefits, they charge themſelves with as ſolemnly.

Parts. Window-Bars or Shackles ſeen broke, to a Priſone Delivery.

     Chains. Vid. *Goods.*

     Gives and Fetters on, to ſome have ſhewn of Friendſhips Shut ſeen, declare of Security.

Sorts. Court to a Goal be in, that is, uſe negligent Method leading to Debt.

     Dungeon waking in among Snakes, ſhew'd *A.* the noiſomeſt Sickneſs to Death.

     Inner Room to the left in a Goal *A.* entering, ſhew'd him by Law conſulting the Equity of a Debt.

     In a Church a Confinement thro Conſcience.

     In an Enemies Houſe teas'd, as fetter'd by a croſs Oeconomy unavoidable.

Goaler *A.* hearing threaten, ſhew'd of his uſing Caution againſt Debt.

     Letting out his Priſoner on parole, to a Student a preſent Relaxation.

     He gets Mony by it, he improves his Notions thereby.

Being in, to the Sick Continuance.

     to the Deſperate Recovery.

     to the Benefactor new occaſion of Benefits.

     to ſome mental Conſtraint thro Modeſty.

     His Wife only ſeen there, ſuch State in Idea more than Fact.

     Never eſcaping but waking in't, the more fatal.

     to ſome be charg'd in a Debt, if in Circumſtance. Vid. *Grammar.*

     Go into and not come out, pay ſuch Debt, but get out avoid it.

Impriſon'd by Robbers you fought, confin'd to Errors you oppos'd.

     Savages, Courſes anſwerably befetting us.

     Entering Bonds, to the Sick greater Sickneſs.

     Torment in't, to ſome Vexation thro tedious Studies.

rifon. Imprifon'd in an underground Room with a Phyfician, fhew'd
　　　　A. the Cure fought as yet to be fecret.
　　　　Among little Houfes A. feeming, he could not ef-
　　　　cape from, fhew'd him of others Roguery, De-
　　　　figns, *&c.*
　　Going out of it, to the Prifoner Continuance as a pendant li-
　　　　teral.
　　　　　to the Sick Death.
　　　　Haling your Enemy to it, having him at abfolute
　　　　command.
ofthoufe lodging at, offering at an hard Bargain as foon left as pro-
　　pos'd.
　-Boy bringing A. written and printed News, fhew'd me of my own
　　Meffengers bringing me Anfwers, *&c.*
ublick Buildings fhew of Authorities according. Vid. *London.*
eligious Houfe. Vid. *Religion.*
averns, Vid. *London.*
　　　　Shew of fair Fields and plentiful Poffeffions.
　　　　　To fome a State of Pleafure and Plenty without
　　　　　Care.
　　　　Be in as your own, be Mafter of fome fine Farm that com-
　　　　　mands fuch Plenty.
　　　　　　To all it gives them an Eftate fair to Lux-
　　　　　　ury.
　　Parts. Bar fhews of your publick Cenfure of Tranfactions.
　　　　Chamber-floor unboarded, your Farm let out.
　　　　Galleries above, private Refolutions of Tranfactions
　　　　there.
　　　　Paffages below, publick Courfes of Tranfactions in
　　　　farming.
　　　　Garrets full of fine Cabinets there, good Outhoufing
　　　　to fuch Farms.
　　Taverner fhews of your Tenant or Steward.
　　Feafting with Company there, fhews of Joy, Comfort, and
　　　　Friends meeting.
　　　　　The Dead there, threated of miffing fuch En-
　　　　　tertainment.
　　　　Drinking Sack there, gave a pleafant tranfient Pro-
　　　　fit.
　　　　Eating Bread and Cheefe there, the fame as to a
　　　　meager Profit.
　　Ale-houfe fhews of a leffer State of Gain, as a Tavern of
　　　　a greater.
　　　　In fcore there, at great charge for fuch a State.
　　　　Child unknown having unburied there, fhew'd A.
　　　　of a Rent unreceived.
　　　　Chambers being in, that is, in confideration of a
　　　　Managery at a Friend's.
　　　　　　　　I

　　　　　　　　　　　　　　Tavern.

Tavern. Ale-houſe. Chambers. Buffeted puſh'd about by a Giant there impos'd on thro his preſum'd Grandeur

Unknown. Vid. *Grammar.*

Weſtminſter-Hall. Vid. *London* and *Law.*

CHAP. XVIII.

Of Habitations.

IN general. Houſes ſhew of our Converſes and Oeconomies in form
(1) in oppoſition to Field ſhewing the ſame at large and in diſpute.

Single of *A.* private Converſe and Subſiſtence Method, *&c.* in particular, as, *&c.* and many various Methods, *&c.*

A great Hall, to Mr. *Poree* ſhew'd of th Converſe and Commerce of *Europe.*

Villages declare to us of great and mere Neighbourhood great or little as they are, or many Oeconomies coaſſiſting.

Market-Towns ſpeak to us of leſſer or private Bargains.

Fairs ſhew Advantages of Sales at time, as of Corn dea before Harveſt.

Cities ſhew of univerſaller publick Converſes orCommerces and in that are as large as Perſons, carrying in them al manner of Oeconomy Form, *&c.* and thus the Brid of Chriſt is equivalent to the *New Jeruſalem.*

Village, a fair one, that is, an excellent Neighbourhood.
(2) With a Church, comfortable in common bleſſing Enjoyments.

With an Ale-houſe, fraught with ſatisfactory common Plenty and Entertainment.

With Shops there. Vid. *City* infra.

On a Hill, a Neighbourhood poor and ſecure.

Quality. Vid *Market-Town* infra.

Sort. Eaſt to Advantage, Weſt to Loſs.

North to Poverty, South to Plenty.

South-weſt. Vid. *Quarter* in *Poſture.*

Known, a Neighbourhood in Circumſtance according.
Next *London.* Vid. *Unknown* in *Grammar.*
Next Brother's. Vid. *Brother* in *Grammar.*
Brother's, *&c.* Vid. *Grammar.*

Remote, a Neighbourhood diſtant from your Command Unknown. Vid. *Grammar.*

Where married, relating to Contracts.

Villa

Village. Acts. Stop at a Village in going to a Forest, chooſe Neigh-
(2) bourhood before Ruin and Deſolation.

Paſſing thro one to a Market-Town, ſhew'd *A.* ſomewhat lent him was after ſold him.

to the next Market, a Sale without
Talk or Delay.

Running thro one unknown, ſhew'd *A.* acting with ſlight
to ill Neighbours.

Fair being in, has threated of Pickpockets.
(3) to Servants it has ſhewn of merry Liberty Junkets.

Looking for it, that is choice advantageous marketting.

In a Mead, expecting an opportune Profit in
Cattel.

Market in general. Vid. *Literals.*
(4) At a Loſs in one *A.* ſeeming, ſhew'd of his Corn
falling in Price.

Towns in general ſhew of ſingle Bargains, as Cities of our publick Dealings.

Seen full of Inhabitants and Goods, gives
Plenty and Eaſe in Dealings.

Of ones own Country and Acquaintance, and
thoſe ſeen thrive is beſt.

Unknown ſhews of Bargains of unaccountable Iſſue.
Vid. *Grammar.*

Eaſt, to advantage, &c. as Village above.

Up-hill to great Advantage. Level, on the
Square.

Well-built, to good Oeconomy Support.

Long, a Bargain long in making.

Narrow Streets, Bargains going off for Po--
verty or Hardſhip.

Sort. Sea-port ſeeing gives of great and happy
Bargains, but with popular Hazards.

Road-town calling at a Smith's in,
ſhew'd *A.* of Iron Waggon-
work failing.

To others of Bargains immix'd
with Travel anſwerable.

Shops there. Vid. *City.*

Known. Brother's next Market-town, a Bargain thwarting you immediately in Intereſt.

And ſo for all others as the Circle demands. Vid. *Grammar.*

Beyond *London,* in a Bargain of good foreign
things if Sea-port.

To others a Bargain odd, foreign, and
overdoing Perfection.

Beyond. Vid. *B.* in *Poſture.*

I 2

...rket Towns known. Others as Eaſt, &c. or elſe a nomine, as the D
4)   vizes with Contrivances.

      Own in general, a Bargain at your eaſieſt Command.

        Neareſt, a Bargain of quickeſt D
         patch.

        Diſtant, a Bargain not ſo ſpeedily
         your power.

        Furtheſt South and beſt, a Bargain
          be had on ſure go
          value.

          A's departed Serva
           ſeen there, ſhew
           he'd be hired ag;
           for good Wages.

        Weſterneſt Market being at with
         Neighbour to ſee a Marriage, b
         gain where that Neighbour is co
         cerned, tho to ſome Loſs.

Next South,   A. ſeeing a Pit before a Wheel
         there, ſhew'd him ſome Whe
         Timber chance ſpoil'd.

        A Friend meets you there, ſuch P
         ſon literally aſſiſts your Bargain

        Market Beggar ſeen, ſhew'd of a Be
         gar with a Preſent of Apples.

        A's Sadler ſeen there beg in his Cha
         her, ſhew'd A. going thither
         foot.

        Being at, to a Servant ſhew'd her
          ſiring change of Pla

          Things appearing conn
           ry to her there, ſhe
           ſhe'l ſtay and
           change.

        A. walking there long, return'd
         laſt, bargain'd long Work at laſt
         niſh'd.

        A. as coming thence ſaw a Soldier pe
         on his Clothes as mean. He carri
         more Corn there than uſual.

        A. being at a Tavern there, ſhew
         him of an happy Copſe Sale.

        A. going thither cloth'd comica
         warm, &c. ſhew'd his forbeari
         going there, fearing Cold and W
         &c.

        Leaving it, but firſt going to examin
         a Neighbour's Garden, &c. ſhew
         the ſame.   Mark

Market Town own next South.
(4)

A. and unknown travelling towards the next South Market Town, they parted, the Unknown going strait, but *A.* trying an unknown By-way South, hoping to be there as soon as Unknown if he lost not the Way. First he passed by Oxen in a Wood, and then coming to a Village enquired the Way, he was told 'twas right if found, but he wak'd in going.

A. concluded to buy an Horse of his Friend immediately. A. suspended present Payment for him: He borrowed him the while to help his Oxen. By which the Bargain went oddly off foretold.

Unknown. *A.* entered an unknown Market Town South, and seeming as if going for *London*; but his Horse was near stock'd, till by force pull'd back at entrance. After seeing a Tavern there, he stay'd a little, and call'd for Sack, and then in going on turning round as North, he saw first a plain Church to the right, but on passing it prov'd a strutting Cathedral to the left: It appear'd as 6 a clock upon it, and as *A.* was thinking to return on't he wak'd.

A. bargaining to Advantage for Goods, was at a first Loss in wanting Money. A Delay was admitted. But it prov'd to undo all. For the Prebend was to sell the Goods, chang'd his Mind with Heat.

In the first Dream the Dealer is unknown, to shew *A.* his Bargain would be still at his command if he pleas'd, but an odd Course would cross it. In the second the Market it self is unknown, and as if said the Dealer will change his Mind and fly off at last.

Persons. Attorney's House seen thrive to the left there, worsts you in a Sale wrangle in controversy. Brother's Minister his, *A.* refus'd to let lie there, he would not sell against Conscience. Apothecary visiting there, shew'd *A.* of leaving a good Bargain as unjust to keep.

Wheeler }
Beggar } Vid. *Next South Market* supra.

Acts. Being in, that is, engag'd in some Bargain.

Market Town Aĉts. Going thither, being in Deſign or Purſuit of
(4)   ſome Bargain.
                    Loſe your way to't, miſtake your Method
                        in't.
                    Come to an Inn at firſt, conclude a time of
                        Delay in't, firſt at leaſt.
                    Paſſing tho it, fully accompliſhing your
                        Bargain, otherwiſe not.
                    Enter it only, begin a Bargain.
                    Ride thro one, by Repute of your Eſtate
                        command a Bargain.
                    Square go beyond to the left therein, al-
                        low above Right in't.
                    Thro a Viĉtual-Market, compaſſing the full
                        Command thereof.
            Lie in Bed with one there, be in negleĉt as to
                ſome Bargain.
            Fill'd with good Folks, a good Lot but with Tra-
                vel and Trouble.
                    ill Folks, threats of ill Eſteem and pub-
                        lick Infamy thro publick Dealings.
            Shiting there, threats of impious Shame and Diſ-
                covery.
            Sleeping there, ſhew'd Sickneſs.
            Wanting a Market, ſhew'd *A.* of his Commodity
                falling in his Hands.

C H A P. XIX.

Of Cities.

C *Ity* in general being in, ſhews of our general Tranſaĉtions of Life.
  (1)   Come unto. Vid. *Travel.*
                    Citizen being, promiſes of ſome good
                        Relicks of Fortune, as &c.
            Aĉts. Solitary being in a City, threats with Hereſy
                or ſingular Aĉion.
                    Walk up and down there, be re-
                        ſerv'd amidſt greateſt Cares.
            A Woman ſhutting out thence, ſhew'd *A.* gi-
                ving h's Pears out of his Orchard.
                    Having 2 Nieces, ſhew'd *B.* getting
                        2 Baskets of them.
            State ruin'd ſeen by an Earthquake, ſhew'd one his Father
                condemn'd and hang'd.

                                                    City.

City. State ruin'd. Known. seen so, threats War, Deſtruction, or Fa-
(1)   mine to the Country, as &c.

    Unknown seen so, to some has ſhewn Ruin to the
        Enemies of their Country.

    Beſieg'd being in, that is, under great and preſ-
        ſing Neceſſities in your publick Dealings.

Burnt all but his own Houſe in one unknown to A. ſhew'd
    his Credit loſt, perſonal regard all left.

    One Houſe only ſeen burnt, one Correſpondence only
        ſeen loſt.

    Old. Vid. Old in Time.

Waſt all near your Houſe, your preſent Deſigns not to
    profit.

    Flouriſhing at a diſtance, better Hopes in futuro.

Sort unknown, In general. Vid. my New Jeruſalem.

                Vid. Babylon in Revelation.

    See your ſelf in, engage you in a general unac-
        countable State of Tranſaction.

    Going out of it, Delivery therefrom.

    Fear loſing you there, find ſuch Tranſactions
        large to confuſion.

    Dwelling there, Death, Change of Country,
                    or Art.

            With Hills, amidſt Diſcords
                with Great Men.

            Populous, oppreſſing with ma-
                ny new cares.

Known, a Courſe of general Tranſaction according, and as
    unknown no way ſubject to our Diſcretion.

    Metropolis in general ſhews of the chief in ſort.

        Seen burnt down, threats of Ruin to the
            Country where, &c.

            To others, Famine, War, or
                Peſtilence there, &c.

            Vid. London infrà.

    Foreign in general. Vid. Country and Foreign in
                Earth.

            Shew of odd Tranſactions
                and out of command, as
                &c.

        Paris, thro Tyranny.

        Conſtantinople, thro Infidelity and Slavery.

        Rome, thro perverſe Impoſition.

        Dublin, thro ill Managery hurt, as the pro-
            perly ſecure.

Own is proper to us, as Known is qualified, and Unknown
    unenvied and unhelp'd.

City. Sort. Own, it ſhews of general Tranſactions States in our Powe
(1)   and not abſurd.

To ſome, it ſhews of the States of their Parents.

Native ſeen, flouriſh to a Citizen, and ſo will his Family thrive.

Loſt in unknown new Buildings there, hear of
Friends dying there.

Engliſh, City States to one living in *Dorſet* are as follows.

London as Metropolis gives a univerſal Perfection of the
Engliſh Genius in all publick Tranſaction.

Weſtminſter is good, but inferior to *London.*

It ſhews of a thoughtleſs Exiſtence in the
beſt Courſes or States.

Sarum, ſhews of an imperfect general Tranſaction
State, but hopeful withal, as Eaſtward and
toward *London.*

So as an Inroad toward *London,* it ſhews of a
preſent Stay in an imperfect general Tranſaction State.

Wells, ſhews of Detriment, as to the Northweſt.

It ſhew'd me of Garden Finery hurtful to my
Eſtate.

It ſhew'd me of Conteſt in chooſing a Pariſh
Clerk to the Loſs of Neighbourhood.

Briſtol, ſhews of general Tranſactions States in Poverty
and Want, as to the North.

So it ſhews of beſt Undertakings where Neceſſaries are wanting, as our 2d beſt City.

Wincheſter is perfect and notable, as to its School Tranſactions.

Sights there, Benefits thro learning of a Language.

Oxford in general, States for Learning moſt excellent.
Vid. *Univerſity* infra.

Cambridg is as a 2d to *Oxon,* or as *Briſtol* to *London.*

Bath is as a City of Phyſick,

Be there, that is, command ſuch a Good, &c.

Vid. *Bath* in *Water,* &c.   Note. All in their way
are to be conſtrued
as *London,* Chap. 20.

Parts. Alley of a Street come into, ſpoil the former Grandeur of your
(2)   publick Tranſactions Courſes.

Channel there *A.* could not croſs, ſhew'd *A.* of drinking Bouts
wherein he ſail'd.   Vid. *Gutter* in *Holes.*

Houſes there in general, Vid. *Houſe-ſorts.*

Having there, engag'd in a Portion of publick Tranſactions according.

Next Door to an Attorny, of Wrangle inſtead of Aid.   *Parts.*

rts. Houfes enter and poffefs one, command fuch a good or ill ac-
  cording.
2)
   Abus'd from thence, ill treated in fuch Cafe.
   Backyard this done in, that is, with relation to your
    fecret Managery.
   Shoomakers Shop towards the Street, Friendfhip to pub-
    lick Appearance for.
   As City fhews of the publick Tranfactions of our whole
    Lives, fo every Houfe, every Oeconomical Comport
    therein.
  Gate being at, that is, in Overture of fome general publick Bu-
   finefs.
  Shops, Place in her Marriage Town to buy at feeing, to a
    Wife fhew'd her Methods of Gain feparate
    from her Husband.
    In her Sifters Town, Methods of Advantage to be
    reap'd thro her Marriage there.
    In a Cellar having, to fome Trade in a conceal'd
    or unlawful matter.
     Huckfter without, Apothecary within, thro ex-
     tortioning.
   Sorts. Clothiers, as to general Repute.
    Belt-makers, as to Strength thro Union and Friend-
    fhip.
    Shoomakers, as to Friendfhip.
    Apothecaries, as to Remedies in Diforders.
    Semftreffes being in, to a Woman fhew'd of Needle-
     Work. Vid. *Trades.*
  Burnt feen, threats with Lofs of Goods and Poffeffions.
  Come into one, examine fome Bargain according in its
    Oeconomy Rule, *&c.*
    out of one, or of an Exchange, leave fome Bar-
    gain.
    Vid. *Going* in *Travel.*
  Creep between Bench and Form there, be overreached in
   dealings.
  Left long fidling alone in a Painter's, fhew'd *A.* fo cre-
    dited by an Apothecary.
    A dead Child brought in on't by a comical
    Woman, a Debt odly afk'd on it.
  Many feeing, gives Variety of Tranfactions, as, *&c.*
    To buy what you will at, that is, an Opportunity
    to procure by Merit, *&c.* as are the things.
  Stand in a Bankers as your own, lend Money as he.
     Your Friends, be as freely offer'd a
     Mony Loan as by him.
    Youth, leaping crofs the Counter juft as you
    are going out.
            Parts.

Lingua Terſancta.

Shops. Beans ſeen grow there, gives you a little Trade, and ⊙
fers that till they are ripe.

Chamber over it be in, that is, in care to obtain ſom
what as it is.

Sign near ſuch an one, that is, like ſuch a publick Tranſacti
State, as is the Houſe.

Of the Stags Head, a projective method to Gain only, a
without bottom.

Streets ſide croſs, chooſe the oppoſite Managery, as &c.

Weſt to the worſt, &c.

In general, Streets ſhew the free Intercouſe betwe
the various like Oeconomy State, as where, &c

Alley, Vid. ſupra.

Sorts own, Vid. *Grammar*.

Fair ſeen, gives a good publick Converſe or Co
merce.

Eaſt, to Advantage, &c.

Southweſt, &c. Vid. *Quarter* in *Poſture*.

Uphill, in a courſe thriving, and to command.

With fine Houſes, a Nobler publick Tranſacti
State.

Short or long, ſo in time according.

Flouriſhing the native Street ſeen, proſpers the C
tizens Family.

Known becomes unknown, experienced Tranſactic
become unaccountable.

In his Native City, ſhew
A. of his Friend's dyi
there.

Acts. Being in, ſhews of publickeſt Diſcourſes or Tra
actions.

Buying things, acting to Merit according.

Coaches, Vid. *Things* infra.

Croſs, Vid. *Walk* infra.

Diſcourſe a prudent Friend there, act pruden
in ſuch caſe.

Eſcape, Vid. *Walk* infra.

Flying there as you liſt, projecting in ſuch State
pleaſure.

But over Houſe Tops, is violently, ⁚
ditiouſly and immoderately pɪ
jecting in publick Tranſactions.

Lying down there, expos'd to publick Deriſion, ⁚
&c. in ſuch Intercourſe of publick Tranſactio

Phyſician known meet you in a Street there, ſu
courſe will be oppos'd by publick Remedy.

Paſs, Vid. *Walk* infra.

Refuſe, Vid. *Walk* infra.

Parts. Streets. Acts. Standing in being amidst publick Transactions, and
(2)   as worthy of them.

                     But your Feet naked and dirty there,
                     renders you notorious in poor pub-
                     lick foolish doings.

Talk, Vid. *Discourse* suprà.
Things, Vid. *Shops* suprà.
                     Coaches and Whores seen there, promise
                     of Plenty to Luxury by such publick
                     Transactions.
Walk in them with another, use his like methods
                     in such publick Transactions.
                     From your House, proceed from pri-
                     vate Managery to publick.
                 Thro it to a Lawyers Chamber, appeal from
                 ill publick dealings to Aid of Law.
                 Pass thro an Arch into it, by Friendship at-
                 tain such publick Transactions.
                     Down a Street in a Coach, treat others
                     finely.
                 Cross a Street, take the contrary part in
                 publick Transactions.
                 Escape to a Friend in't, such a course de-
                 livers you, as, *&c.*
                 Going out of Doors refuse, that is, choose
                     private before publick Trans-
                     actions.
                     To fight a Beggar, to go to Law
                     with one poor.
Whores, Vid. *Things* suprà.

CHAP. XX.

Of London *and the Universities.*

Londo**n** in general. Literal, Vid. *Grammar.*
                 As Home is what is proper to us, and at our full
                 Command, so
                 London is as our most perfect State in our publick
                 Transactions (to *English*-men.)
                 Walk there at Will, Skill to design at pleasure in
                 the most perfect manner.
                 House there, to some an Oeconomy, in opposition
                 to a Country one.
                   To others, an Oeconomy in best sort
                 answerable.   *London*

Lingua Tersancta.

a general. House, *London* like Stairs, an Oeconomy Addreſs
excellent.

Take an Houſe there, be in good Oecon
my Circumſtances anſwerable.

Have a Lodging there, the ſame as
Houſe, but leſs.

In a Tradeſman's Houſe, be di
abled wherein you'd trade.

Road *London* Gold found on, that is, Gain by
ordinary well skil'd method.

London Waggon *A.* driving over *B. C.* was angry
C. hinder'd *B*'s being a Vagabond.

Beyond *London*, a State exceeding the true Unive
ſal Tranſaction State.

Vid. *B.* in *Poſture.*

South-Eaſt, ſuch Ill to Good.

From *London* Weſt, is doubly bad.

Next Village, Vid. *Village ſupra.*

Aᵭs be in, aᵭ to the Perfection of Univerſ
Tranſaction.

Miſs buying there, fail in the Perfection
Gain, as, &c.

Diſcourſe there, tranſaᵭ ſolemnly worth
of ſuch State.

3 own Workmen be with there, implo
your Workmen true to univerſal Tran
aᵭion Rules.

Rats, Mice and Weeſels a Man ſeen ki
there, ſhew'd of Waſtes in beſt mann
prevented.

Perſons. Attornies there, *A.* heard had a Foreig
Plantation; *A*'s Friend was threated Suit thenc

Tavern *London A.* ſeem'd in with
fine Cabinets in the Garret, deſcending to the Chambers, the
Floors appear'd unboarded;
there he ſaw his Printer, and
paid away his leaden 6 *d.* and
ſhew'd his Enemy there a Picture Book explain'd, quoting
Ovid from the Creation.

My Fan
moſt profitab
I bought, an
after ſtock'
to furniſh n
Printing, an
Pocket Mon
to illuſtrate n
Skill.

Travel go thence Weſtward, worſt you in your general Tran
aᵭion State.

North, take a poor mean and ſelf-worſtin
Courſe.

A. paſſing on Foot by others on Horſebac
thro a Shop like an Exchange Weſt, an
where he was forc'd to creep between Tab
an

and Bench forwards; on Enquiry of the way was bid to go thro the Window; but strait, as seeing *Tyburn* before him on his going onwards, and a City Maid's offering her Service with Pockholes in Face, and Mans Clothes, he waked. This shew'd *A.* forbearing unjust Gain thro Breach of Agreements, and to the Ruin of his Transactions.

For *London* in a Coach and 6, advance you to greatest Plenty in best Methods.

Rob'd by the way, your Notions or Methods fail you

To many, the Spirit shews by this their best Course to good.

With 2 Friends, that is, by such like Interest seek your Preferment.

Left behind by them, that Interest will fail you.

Journey chang'd West, and from it, and so will such course.

With a Cheat, shew'd *A.* of Gaming.

Not quite to *London*, but staying at *Chelsey*, shew'd *A.* farming well, but imperfectly as not without the Use of Neighbourly Aids.

In an Hackney Coach on a Journey design'd, shew'd literally thereof. Vid. *Grammar.*

Walk there by Shops, command a Benefit according at Pleasure.

East, to all Advantages.

Northern, to a poorer State.

By Houses there, command publick Transaction Oeconomy States according.

Vid. *infra* in *Places Sorts.*

Place in general, Chang'd, Vid. *Streets* infra.

Temple seen chang'd to a Field, to a Lawyer shew'd of his leaving the Law to Farm.

Known act in as usual, find your self some way in the same State again.

A Place unknown there, a State unaccountable issuing well in publick Transactions best stated.

Known, a State will issue accordingly well in publick Transactions, so best stated.

London.

London. Place in general, known in an Hill with Advantage, a Vale to loſs.

         To the North in Poverty, to the South in Plenty.

         On the Rivers ſide, with Revenue, *& è con.*

         Out-parts, in Extremities of ſuch like publick Tranſactions.

         Between *Temple-bar* and *Weſtminſter*, ſhews of luxurious Idle States.

         Vid. *Strand* in *Particulars* infra.

         City it ſelf, ſhews of the very Standard of publick Tranſactions, as, *&c.*

         By-Streets, Vid. *Streets* infra.

Beaufort Street, *A.* hated her tame Sparrow in, ſhe would in Genteelneſs have been rid of him if convenient.

Cheapſide and *Cornhil*, the Standard Truth of beſt Trade and publick Tranſaction.

         Told any thing there, find ſuch a Truth thro ſuch a Knowledg State.

Churches fine *A.* ſeeing there, ſhew'd him diſcovering publick happy Bleſſing worthy God's Praiſe, *&c.*

Companies Hall a Field turning to, ſhew'd *A.* changing Tithe in kind to a ſociable moving rate.

Covent Garden Bullies I ſeeing ſtab'd by fat Men from a new Gate by, my ſelf eſcaping narrowly by flight from the Slaughter, ſhew'd me of my *Barth.* Fair Intereſt in the City in danger.

Exchange backſide on't dancing at, ſhew'd *A.* univerſally ex-poſ'd in Credit.

         Going to buy fine things there, being in a State of general Plenty anſwerable.

         A Crane ſeeing in a Shop over againſt the Royal Exchange, ſhew'd of my buying in my Farm Stock.

Eſſex Street walking up, I met Dr. *R.* coming kind up to me. I rode for walking to ſee my Grounds.

Fleetſtreet Bookſellers Shop I ſtanding in, envied by unknown, ſhew'd me reſolving to print theſe Books.

         Bridg meeting one upon, ſhew'd me next day a Dealer happy to all Buſineſs.

         Under it Pigeons ſeen fly, ſhew'd of good Society Aid, where once the worſt Enmity.

Ditch croſſing, ſhew'd *A.* of paying a King's Tax.

         In a mean Houſe by *S.* there, *&c.* that is, prove of Fate as he.

Fetter-Lane, *a Nomine* threats of Slavery.

London. Farthing Pye-House board at, subsist very beggarly.

Guild-Hall Transactions, publick Regulations of best publick
    Dealings. Vid. *Law-places.*

Hall, Vid. *Company* supra.

    London Feast seen, shew'd of my Farming first begun.

    Mayor's Feast *A.* seeing, and her Father's Provision for't
      noble, shew'd her Husband dunging his Ground much.

Holbourn is as our own Labour in the best Transaction, in op-
    position to the Defect imploying others in't.

Inn be at there, that is, fail only in the perfectest measures of
    publick Transaction.

Lincolns-Inn-Fields great flying into, shew'd *A.* projecting to a
      Repute, as of worthy living there.

      Flying from in a Chair thro *Jackanapes* Alley
      into *Chancery-Lane,* shew'd *A.* escaping
      free in a Knavish Trust Suit. Vid. *Place*
      in *Law.*

Leicester-Fields, A. seem'd on a Building of 1000 *l.* Charge in,
    waking there with his Brother-in-law. That is, *A's* Tenants
    time being out, he turn'd Farmer to all Advantage, except
    what the Laziness of Gentility, *&c.*

Market Victuals, *A.* sick passing talk'd of buying there; that
    is, he thriv'd beyond mere Necessaries.

Parliament, Vid. *Company.*

Palace Royal there, Vid. *King in Government.* Vid. *White-
Hall* infra.

Paul's Cathedral seen fine, shew'd me of a notable Progress
    in this Skill.

    Church-yard at a Painters there, *A.* seem'd trusted long
      fidling in, till at last a comical Woman brought in
      formally a dead Child. Mr. *B.* an Apothecary trans-
      acting as well with *A.* and as formally brings in his Bill.

Shop enter there, make a Bargain.

      Buy there, Vid. *Painter in Trade.*

    Vid. *City Parts general.* Vid. *Trades.*

    Goldsmiths passing there, and finding 2 Gold Rings,
    shew'd *A.* of his gaming, but to no good.

    Stockingmans as to Necessaries, *&c.* Vid. *Stockius*
    in *Apparel.*

    Friends be at, that is, be as kindly supplied as is
      the Person and Trade.

      Stand envied there, the same to your
      Glory.

    Pass by to the West, command such Symbol, but
    to your Detriment.

    Tradesman, *A.* hearing say he laid by a Sables Tipper
    for his Wife, shew'd *A.* prodigal on borrowing.

    Shews always so, publick Transactions of best Re-
    pute or Profit, as, *&c.* London.

London. Signs particularize the Shop, how and in what you advance.

Salisbury-Court A. purſuing his Wife in *London* Street loſt he in, and tho his Son appearing there, ſaid ſhe was in *Grain Corner,* yet on ſearch he could not find her there. Her Mo deſty ſuſpected, but ſpotleſs.

Strand the beſt Tranſaction in an ill State, or with a Tincture o Grandeur to Lazineſs, as leading to the Court, an as *Cheapſide* is the beſt in the beſt.

A. killing and fighting a great Throng there, ſhew'd o his commanding ſuch State happily.

The Streets from the *Strand* to the *Thames,* States de pendant on Revenues, as, &c. without Trade

A. ſeeming in a Whores Lodging there, and ſee ing an Image move there, ſhew'd his hearing : Play.

Street without Shops, a Life of beſt ſocial Plenty.

With Shops, of publick Tranſactions anſwerable.

Stand there, render you worthy of ſuch States.

Walk there, deſign actively worthy according.

By Streets, odd Courſes ſuch way circumſtanced, a: North with Poverty, &c.

Unknown new one ſeen, *London* Wall broke down from *Cheapſide* thro *Paternoſter-Rowe* as Weſt ſhew'd A. that dreamt it, tranſacting as for Conſcience, even to perfect Intereſt Loſs.

Somerſet-Houſe Palace A. walking about to ſhew one, ſhew'd of his giving one to underſtand that he could controul with State and Impoſition if occaſion, as bad as *Popiſh.*

Temple buy a Chamber at, to a Lawyer act as to merit Practice there.   Vid. *Law.*

-Bar ſtanding on, ſhew'd A. in a fatal Criſis, as the Weſt Point of *London.*

Weſtward Streets as out of the City; ſhew of worſer publick State Tranſactions. Vid. *Strand* ſupra.

Thames paſs in a Boat, engage you in ſome hazardous publick Tranſaction States in Succeſs as you ſwim.

Retired to a ſmall Channel, little Tranſactions appear ing where us'd to be the greateſt.

In a Canvaſe Boat landing thence at the *Temple,* ſhew'd me of my Dream Skill.

A. ſcaping from a long Boat ſinking there, a little car nal Managery A. ſlights.

Seen up in the *Strand,* ſhew'd A. that a meaner Tranſ action State would be cripled by yearly Accounts.

Trades, Vid. *Shops* ſupra.

Wall down, Vid. *Streets* ſupra.

Way, Vid. *Ibid.*

London. *Weftminfter-Hall* A. fling away a Law Book in, fhew'd of his
    rejecting a Member of Allegorick Skill.

    Palace-yard 2 Women feen fight in, fhew'd of a Re-
    ligious State Controverfy.

    A. leaving as feeing Cathedral Men hectoring enter,
    fhew'd him potent in Religion beyond national Efta-
    blifhment.

    A. paffing carried a Board thro it that the King lean'd on,
    A's fuffering for Religion is his Glory.

Whitefryers an Houfe be in there, that is, in a general Faule
    in your Oeconomy Credit univerfally.

    Fall off a Precipice there, Defpair in fuch State.

    Streets being in, fhew'd A. of receiving a ftrange
    Gift of Goods.

White-Hall walking before, defigning relating to the King.

    Meufe have a Stable and Horfe in, depend on a Sub-
    fiftence on the King.

    S. *James-Park* A. walking in with fine Company,
    fhew'd him his beft Diverfion fort as where he
    lived.

    A. emptying his Shoos of Gravel there is reprov'd by
    Soldiers, Force withftands his Religious Offences.

    A. affaulted by a little Soldier mounted on the Guard
    at *White-Hall,* purfued him running away by the
    Duck Pond Canal, where catching him, tho
    ftrong, he mumbled him to a Skin. My Skill as to
    Mr. *Force.*

Houfe. *Chrift's-Hofpital* Governor inviting A: to fit down by him,
    fhew'd A. in Charity aiding the Minifter.

    I feeing an Houfe on Fire at a diftance there, and at firft
    the Water playing ftrong, and the Fire near out; at
    laft I faw the Houfe nearer and the Fire worft, its Top
    being burnt, and fome ftole, fome Rafter burnt, tho
    I fcorn'd to take any; it feem'd in *Whitefryers.* It
    fhew'd my fcorning a fure, but poor and broken Huf-
    bandry, as plowing for others, &c. which might not
    be expected to my great Gain.

    A. would take an Houfe in *London,* but an Huckfter by
    fcorn'd him, as offering to buy Fruit of her, but after
    on his Return in fine Clothes, he gloried againft the
    Huckfter. Eftate help'd his Husbandry failing.

Neighbourhood. *Chelfey* A. fend 3 Workmen, two he diverts to
    idle Garden Finery, his Soldier Husbandry.

    A. faw a *London* Country Houfe with a Cottage
    paled in in its Front, the Paffage to it being
    round, Eaft to the Right, with an Iron Coach
    Houfe. He borrowed Money meanly, and
    kept a Coach with all Difficulty.

                   K   *Univerfity*

Univerſity come unto, Vid. _Travel._

(2)　　　Student being there again, to a Doctor ſhew'd of blundering to require it.

Being of the Sciences, to ſome ſhews of Chearfulneſs.

Contemplation delighting in, ſhew'd _A._ of the Miſchief of neglecting Buſineſs.

Studying Gowns Men ſeen in, ſhew'd of Converſe of Study in hand.

College ſee there, diſcover a Science worthy its Enquiry.

With thouſands of Students of vaſt variety.

Seen eating there, profiting themſelves according.

A Tutor ſeen there, that is, a chief method of Inſtruction therein.

An Atheiſt ſeen among ſuch Students, ſuch Tenants amidſt ſuch Science.

_A._ left fighting entering the Elaboratory flying, he ſlights their Inſtructions for new Projects.

Hall _A._ ſeeing full of Members fat and flouriſhing, he ſitting in State at the bottom, ſhew'd _A._ learn'd enough to be Founder of ſuch a Society.

Jealous of their Plate againſt Robbers, fond of their Opinions againſt Reformers, _&c._

House having there, gives you an Oeconomy thro ſheer Ingenuity.

Build one there, by a wiſe Enquiry fix an unuſual Oeconomy, _&c._

With a fine Garden to it, a Plenty to Luxury attending it.

Closet having there, ſhew'd of a ſecreter Managery of Ingenuity.

Inn be at there, that is, at a fault thro your Ingenuity of Managery.

Oxen _A._ ſeeing lie down at an Inn there, by putting Stags Horns between them and Horſes there, ſaw riſe again to Hay ; that is, by Horſes Aids _A._ prevented ſubtlely ſuch danger in his Oxen.

Waggons _A._ ſeeing there, ſhew'd of his reaſoning wiſely about keeping them.

Streets, paſſing from _Wadham_ to _Highſtreet_ there unknown, ſeem'd angry that in walking I dirted his fine Floor ; but I ſaying I was never there before ſince King _James_, paſſing by Muſick turn'd into the Street to the Right, an Apothecaries Shop there preſenting inſtead of a Bookſellers ; my Skill leaving the Rudiments of learning Eſſays its own Publication, and that by a Religious Remedy rather than Art.

Univerſity.

Univerſity. Phyſick Garden Anticourt in *Oxon* I walking to and fro in
(2)　　　reading a Book, at laſt after ſaw there a great Box-Dial
　　　　with the Giants there. This was to ſhew me by this
　　　　Skill commanding great Aids in Phyſick.

Note. this Allegory Chapter is near of infinite Change and Variety, for to a *Londoner* I conceive *London* Allegories, not as to
a Countryman ; and to every Foreigner his own Metropolis and
Univerſity is to be to him as *London* and *Oxford* to an *Engliſh*-man :
and ſo alſo to a Northern Man I conceive all varies in Allegory
alſo ; but as to that the Diſcretion and Obſervation of the Reader muſt ſupply where a greater Nicety of Dictionary would be
endleſs.

C H A P. XXI.

Of Qualities.

Ability in general, ſhews of Ability.　　　Vid. *Strong* infra.
　　　　　　Having things in your Power, aſſures you good
　　　　　　　Succeſs.　　　Vid. *Maſter* in *Grammar.*
　　　Can't, Vid. *Deſire* in *Paſſion.*
　　　　　　Act corporeally, that is, God won't let you re-
　　　　　　　ſolve mentally.
　　　　　　In part embrace, but without Power to ſpeak,
　　　　　　　Love but never to poſſeſs.
　　　　　　　　A. got to *M.* and could go to *L.* if
　　　　　　　　deſired, the thing tho unfiniſh'd yet
　　　　　　　　ſtill remained in *A's* Power.
　　　　　Climb a Precipice, fail in ſurmounting ſome
　　　　　　Difficulty.
　　　　　Fly when you deſire, is as Reſtraint in your
　　　　　　Glory and Projects.
　　　　　Eſcape from a purſuing Bull, be at an implaca-
　　　　　　ble Enemys Mercy.
　　　　　Lie with your Wife, threats you fruſtrate in
　　　　　　your Art.
　　　　　Find your way to an Houſe, that is, be out in
　　　　　　　your Methods to ſuch an Oecono-
　　　　　　　my State.
　　　　　　　Prayers in a Book, that is, finiſh
　　　　　　　your Deſires anſwerably.
　　　　Read, threats of Dotage.
　　　　Run an Hare ſeen, and ſo killed by the Dogs
　　　　　ſtrait, ſhew'd of a Diſpute ſoon ſtifled.

Ability. Can't speak Lovers met, shew'd of Parents breaking off the Match.

       Say your Prayers, frustrates your Desires.

       Or say them ill, is be frustrate in hottest Desires.

       Shut the Door against Robbers, resolve mentally against prodigal Errors.

Against, vid. *Contrary* infra.

Agility shews of Activeness and Readiness for Action.

Agreeable, vid. *Good* infra.

Artificial, vid. *Counterfeit* infra.

Aukward, is as aukward mentally.

Bending Trees as the Vine seen, shews of Men tractable and sometimes deceiving.

       Stiff an Hare seen on her hunting, foreshew'd of her being kill'd.

Better, vid. *Good* infra.

Big. vid. *Great* in *Quantity*.

Briskness shews of Quickness of Resolution.

Brittle things, as Glass seen, threat with Danger.

Clean seen things, shew of Delivery from Trouble and Disgrace.

       Make a Gutter, that is, clear Calumnies, and Reproach.

       Cistern, reform Errors, &c.

       Sword springing Blood, vid. *Prodigies* in my *Book* of *Apparitions*.

       Well threats with Injuries.   Vid. *Wash* in *Water*.

Clean making your Ears, shews you of good News approaching.

       Vid. *Ears* in *Body*.

       Teeth, promises you of fine Company, &c.

       Wainscot, rectify your hazarded Oeconomy Repute.   Vid. *House*.

Slovenly, that is, little and contemptible.

Nastiness in general is ill to all, and threats with Trouble and Disgrace.

       A Woman seen nasty, threats of a sordid Fortune.

       Saints seen nasty, shew'd A. of his Impiety hurting him.

       Beard. Vid. *Body*.

Dirty naked Feet have, that is, be poor and foolish in your main Actions.

       Foul Hands is as Loss and Danger in less Actions the same way.

       Wipe you on shiting, decently answer your Expence.

       Spotty Ring, shews of some Man nasty or infirm.

       Pitiful Face having, threats with Heaviness of Mind.

Foul'd with Dung, Injury from him by whom.

       By a Stranger, unexpected Reproach.

       with Man's Dung is worst of all.

                            Clea

Clean, Foul'd with Man's Dung, seeing it only, threats of things sordid with Desolation.   Vid. *Dung* in *Earth.*

Clear, Vid. *Clean* suprà.

Close, Vid. *Bind* in *Action.*

Cold, Vid. *Sense.*

Colour, Vid. *Sense.*

Contrary to Law acting, threats with Infamy.
        Vid. *Extreme* infrà.

Cylinder, Vid. *Figure* infrà.

Counterfeit Money paid *A.* shew'd him Hurt in Profit by Mismanagement.

    Handling, is a present, but rather seeming than real Relief in Money-want.

    Wine drinking shews in its way also as Money.

    Artificial things tho in general so, shew of heavy Cares and Dangers.

    The New River shew'd of Exchequer Bills.

    Vid. *Imaginary* in *Earth.*

Crooked, Vid. *Figure* infra.

Curious is as Inquisitive.

Custom, sing as you travel, live merrily.

    It shews also of Custom.

    Drinking Sack and Eggs, shew'd *A.* being ask'd to sing next day.

Decayed wooden heavenly Engine seen, shew'd of an erroneous Scheme of Government.

    Tooth loosing, &c. Vid. *Body.*   Vid. *Sound* infrà.

    Rotten Tree seen, shews of some decay'd Estate ; Oak, Inheritance ; Elm, Lease.

        Jaw-bone one having, shew'd him as sinful in Speech.

        Duck eating, patching and shuffling with refuse Project Services.

        Mouth, a Course of Speech vicious.

            Hid by the Nose, mollified thro personal regard.

Deform'd, Vid *Form* infra.

Degenerate *A's* Vine to a wild Vine seen, shew'd of his Life to come enuring miserably.

Different ways going from another, being angry thro various Resolutions.   Vid. *Divers* and *Variety* infra.

Difficult things doing, shews of acting in Straits and Contrivances.

    In passing a River, in dealing with wilful Folks, or in surpassing the Difficulty of some Revenue.

    Find things to be done, that is find your Courage near fail about them.   Vid. *Hard* infra.

Dirty, Vid. *Clean* suprà.

Divers, Vid. *Different* suprà, and *Variety* infra.

    Colour'd Flowers, Vid. *F.*

            Vid. *Garland* and *Crown* in *Ornaments.*

        As a Leopard, threats of Deceit.

Divers colour'd Horſes ſeen, ſhew of Deceit as to Eſtate.

Fiſh taking, threats with Poiſon or Deceit.

Vid. *Robe* in *Apparel.*

Dry, Vid. *Senſe* and *Brook* in *Water.*

Evil, Vid. *Ill* in *Good.*

Exceeding great, fair or ſtately things ſeen, has often ſhewn of Treaſon.

Excellent, Vid. *Good* infra.

Extreme bitter Taſt, threats with Death.

Ill, Vid. *Good* infra.

Mean Habit *Eſculapius* ſeen in, to a Phyſician ſhew'd him at a Loſs in Buſineſs.

Things diſcourſe of, imploy you as buſily about Trifles.

Shop'd and apparel'd *A*'s Clothier ſeen, ſhew'd *A.* himſelf cloth'd as ſcandalouſly.

Pavement before his Door *A.* making, ſhew'd of his buying an Hog to winter there.

Virgin *Mary* and Chriſt ſeen, Vid. *Saints* in *Dead.*

Ordinary, Vid. *Good* infra.

Moderate Fire on Hearth gives Houſe-plenty.

Little, is as Want.

Great, Extravagance.

Rain and ſeaſonable and clear, gives great Riches.

Fair, Vid. *Form* infra.

Faſhion, Vid. *Form* infra.

Fat, Vid. *Victuals.*

Fattineſs taſting, threats of Greedineſs or Sickneſs.

Beaſts wild ſeen, are not ſo deſperate or hungry as the Lean.

Rats ſeen, ſhew'd of Waſts in Servants rectifiable by Care.

Oxen ſeen, to ſome have ſhewn of a plentiful Year and Husbandry.

Lean ſeen, have ſhewn of Sickneſs or an Eſtate waſting.

Dead *A.* having in Houſe by him, ſhew'd of his having live ones to ſell.

7 fat Oxen and Ears of Corn eat by 7 lean, *Joſeph* and *Pharaoh.*

Birds ſhew of rich projective Courſes.

Having in your Lap, that is, at your command.

Catching, gives Gain according.

Flying away, your Hopes in it leave you.

Lean Cheeks and wrinkled, threats with Heavineſs and Care.

Aſſes, Labour with Heavineſs of Mind.

Fat è con. Joy thro Labour Gains.

Enemy, one malicious but haraſs'd.

A. entering another's Houſe and finding the Owner aſleep, cut out his Fat and excrement ſtinking Guts, and carried them off, that is, he rob'd him.

Figure,

Figure, Vid. *Mathematicks* in *Arts*, &c.

Square shews of Stability.

Round shews of Inconstancy.

To some it shews of Capacity and Security.

Fish and flat, vain Hopes.

About Travel, Design with superfluous Labour.

Turn a Stone, examine a Man or Notion thoroughly.

A great Ship *A.* sailing in a little Boat, shew'd his compassing the full Notion of Merchants thro a little Essay-hazard.

An House go, compass all the Parts of its Oeconomy.

By Long Galleries in a Tavern, thro tedious Services in a Farm.

A Sphere of Gold or Lead seen, threats of a most hard and unstable Fate.

Cylinder of Gold or Lead, as Sphere above, but less ill.

Curl'd Roots seen as of little Substance, threat of vain Hopes. Vid. *Hair* in *Body.*

Triangles shew of Defects.

Streight-way go, that is, use a direct or downright Course in a Business.

Crooked or about, Delay as to what side turning, &c. Vid. *Side.*

Rod having, threats you of vicious or lazy Delays in Managery.

Eel seen given *A.* shew'd him of a perverse Person offering him in Converse.

Fine, Vid. *Form* infra, and *Ornaments.*

Firm, Vid. *Decayed* supra, and *Sound* infra.

Flourishing Corn seen in a fair Day, gives you great Prosperity but with Labour.

Ugly and dry tho, threats with Misery and Hopes subverted.

Formal Intercourse, a Freedom in Affairs, but with all Caution.

Form in general of things, shews of their Powers and Operations.

Kings or Priests in their Robes seen going into obscure Places, is as Ruin to their Dominions.

A Ship wherein the Emperor *Nero* was led so by his Wife, the same.

Deform'd Horse shews of a mean or humble Friend or Wife, or Art, or Estate, as &c.

Things, to some shew of Wickedness.

Man, an active reasonable Course full of Errors and Imperfections.

Tail to your Horse or Ass seen, threats you Misery and Poverty *in futuro.*

Form

Form fair being, that is, in good Credit, Reſpect, or Power.
Vid. *Condition* in *Apparel.*
Countenance ſeen, gives you Honour.
Hands having, honours you for your Actions.
To ſome it has given faithful Servants.
Ears and many having, to Superiors has given good
Fame with Obedience.
Ugly is è con.
Woman ſeeing, ſhews of Truth.
Ugly ſeen, threats of Error with Infamy.
Things, Places, or Perſons ſhew of pleaſant States and Ope-
rations.
Baſon having, that is, a good Maid.
Creatures, &c. as Peacocks ſhew of Comlineſs.
Ways promiſe of Health and Proſperity.
Faſhion'd old ſeeing your Houſe, threats your Oeconomy as im-
proper.
Servant having, threats you of ſome hireling Ma-
nagery as abſurd.
Fine Rooms and fine Company ſeeing, ſhews of Proviſions for
ſuch.
Proviſions ſee at a Neighbour's, occaſion him Gueſts to re-
quire it.
Cloth'd ſeeming to a Wife, promis'd her Happineſs in her
Husband.
Foul things threat of matters ſordid with Deſolation.
Vid. *Clean* ſuprà.
Handſom, Vid. *Clean* ſuprà.   Vid. *Birds* in *Creatures.*
Woman ſeen, ſhews of Truth and good Fortune.
Ill-favour'dly devouring ſeeing one, threats you ſo oddly waſted
with Greedineſs.
Neat, that is compleat.
Rude, Vid. *Garden* in *Houſe-range.*
Spotted *A*'s beſt Clothes being, ſhew'd him ſullied in his faireſt
Repute.
Image *A.* ſeeing his in a Glaſs, foreſhew'd him ugly
Children.   Vid. *Jewels* in *Riches.*
Ugly Breaſt, a bad Conſcience.
Vid. *Breaſt* in *Body.*   Vid. *Hands* in *Body.*
Attendants ſeen going before one in Authority in ill-cut
Hair, ſhew'd him of Loſs of ſuch Authority.
Forward, Vid. *Raſh* in *Paſſion.*
Foul, Vid. *Clean* ſuprà.
Freely given, that is, receiving without Flattery, Service, or Pur-
chaſe.
Good in general, ſhews of Good.
Doing, to ſome ſhews Jollity.

Good in general doing. Hindred by a wicked Spirit, shew'd a
    Hypocrite hurting him.
   Vid. *Misfortune* in *Action.* Vid. *Malice* in *Passion.*
 Agreeable things having or buying, is good to all.
   Corn, Flowers, and all things else seem proper and in
   season, is good.
 Best Clothes spotted, A's best Repute spoil'd.
   Physicians see, discover of a best Remedy, as is the Ma-
   lady.
 Better shews better.
   To others it declares of things to be mended.
   Worse pass from to better, mend your Affairs, as *&c.*
 Ill State being in, threats you as it is.
    Seeing your Enemy or Brother in such, gives you Pros-
    perity.
    Seeing things in, shews you of Evils you flight for
    G O D's sake.
    Done you by a Friend, shews you of Evils will end
    well.
 Ordinary Leather Clothes shew of Poverty, but rich give Dig-
   nity. Vid. *Condition* in *Apparel.*
 Useful things having or buying, is good to all.
   Vessels of no use shew of Musicians, Fools, and Para-
   sites.
 Well all seeing, shews all will be so.
   Ready things seen, promises of a good Information in Bu-
   siness.
 Worst shews of the worst.
   Enemy see, have the worst Course crossing you possible.
   Place, Vid. *Country* in *Earth*, as *Deserts*, &c.
Green Wood make a Fire with, shuffle with bad Money.
   Trees cut down having, gives you Inheritance without Strife.
    Dry, with Strife.
Handsom, Vid. *Form* supra.
Hard and thick bark'd Trees shew of mighty Men.
   Things to some shew of Stability.
    to others have shewn of Poverty and Slavery.
   Vid. *Difficult* supra.
Heavy, vid. *Sense.*
High, vid. *Fly* in *Air.*   Hot, vid. *Sense.*
   Vid. *Posture.*   Hurt, vid. *Action.*
   Vid. *Precipice* in *Place.*   Ill. vid. *Good* supra.
Impotent, vid. *Ability* supra, and *Strong* infra.
Lasting *French* Marigolds seen, are good as the Colour lasts.
Lean, vid. *Fat* supra.
Liberty given you to act as you will, gives you your Desires fully an-
 swer'd.
Light, vid. *Sense.*

                 Loose

Looſe, vid. *Bind* in *Action*.

Mean, vid. *Extreme* ſupra.

Mix'd Friends and Enemies ſeen, threats of Miſtakes and Alterations

Moderate, vid. *Extreme* ſupra.   Ordinary, vid. *Extreme* ſupra.

Moiſture, vid. *Senſe*.   Vid. *Good* ſupra.

     Vid. *Rain* and *Water*.   Pale, vid. *Colour* in *Senſe*.

Naſty, vid. *Clean* ſupra.   Power, vid. *Ability* ſupra.

Neat, vid. *Form* ſupra.

Prepared, vid. *Deſign* in *Soul*.

     Horſes for the Race ſeen, has threated Death.

     Lion for the Fight, ſome great Man for a Diſpute.

     Self ſeeming for a long Fight, that is, for a long Diſpute.

     For eating Meat, for receiving Profit, &c.

     A Taylor taking meaſure of *A.* for a new Sute of Cloth ſhew him of a good plenty State near.

Pack up to leave your Home, reſolve as if ſo to do.

Ready, vid. *Victuals* and *Apparel*.

     See all things at your command, aſſures your deſired Su ceſs.

     A. having 4 Oxen to ſell, and a Chapman offering, waking in doubt, ſhew'd him receiving a Rent.

Proſperous your Friend ſeeing, gives you greateſt Happineſs.

Quiet, vid. *Action*.   Rotten, vid. *Decayed* ſupra.

Ready, vid. *Prepared* ſupra.   Rough, vid. *Senſe*.

Round, vid. *Figure* ſupra.

Rude, vid. *Form* ſupra.

Ruſty Iron, threats of Diffidence and Jealouſy in matters of Di culty.

Safe Horſe, that is, a truſty or ſucceſsful Art, Friend, or Wife.

     Eſcape, ſhews of a ſafe Eſcape.

Satisfied unſatisfied Thirſt, threats of eager Diſappointment.

Scandalous things ſhew of things ſcandalous.

Scorch, vid. *Senſe*.

Sharp in general, vid. *Senſe*.

     Sight ſhews of a good Underſtanding.

     Fruit gives a Life full of Trouble.

     Bodies feeling, threats with Grief, Poverty, Pain, and Diſea

Shining, vid. *Senſe*.

Skilful Singing ſhews of Joy, but ill threats of Scorn and Sadneſs.

     Farmer ſeen as doing a Work, ſhew'd of a good Seaſon fo then offering.

     Organs diſorder'd and ill plaid on, ſhew'd of Trees ſhe rob'd.

     Wind-muſick by Breath ill play'd on, ſhew'd of ſullen Quar

Slight, vid. *Weak* infra.

Slovenly, vid. *Clean* ſupra.

Slowly walk, that is, proceed with Difficulty, Hazard, and Fear.

Smartly be reproved, give Offence anſwerably.

                                      Sm

Smooth, vid. *Sense.*

Soft, vid. *Sense.*

Sound Life lead, that is, keep to your first Institution or Calling.
        Infirm shews of Travel, Change, or secret Study.
    Vid. *Decayed* supra.
    Firm things, as Iron, stone Walls, &c. seen, are all Assurance
      to Men in doubt.

Sour, vid. *Sense.*   Spotted, vid. *Form* supra.

Square. vid. *Figure* supra.   Vid. *Clean* supra.

State, vid. *Future* in *Time.*

Stateliness shews of Presumption or Stateliness answerable.

Stiff, vid. *Bending* supra.

Stout-look'd, that is, of a Carriage confident and bold in his Pretensi-
    ons of Speech, &c.
    Old Women, shew'd of a good old Fortune renew'd.

Streight, vid. *Figure* supra.

Strong, vid. *Arms* in *Body.*   Vid. *Ability* supra.
    Horse, a good Wife, Friend, or Art.
    Trees shew of Men stout or stubborn.
    Things in general promise of Assurance and Perseverance.

Stronger grown, that is, of firmer Resolution.

Weakness in general shews of Diffidence and Dereliction.
    Enemy weak, an ill Course easily cured.
    Window weak, a slight Prospect.
    Wife so, to a Priest a contested Living.
    Can't act, vid. *Ability* supra.
    A slight Pile of Building, an Oeconomy but for a Year,
      &c.

Stumbling Horse, an hazardous Art, Wife or Friend.

Supporting, vid. *Knees* in *Body.*
    In general it shews of Aid and Support.
    A Crown *A.* seeming, that is, being a chief Subject under
      it.
    A. seeing a Pillar of Bread supporting a slight Pile, shew'd
      of his buying in a Year's Provision of Bread.

Swiftly walk, confound Actions by hurry, or act without due regards
    and considerations had.
    Seeing another, shews of Overtures by surprize offering.
    Stars seen moving, threats *A.* as sad or mad.

Tall Horse, a stately Tenant, Wife, Friend, or Art.

Terrible, vid. *Passion.*

Troubled, vid. *Passion.*

Tired Horse riding, to one shew'd of desperate Love.
    Vid. *Weary* infra.

Vain Endeavours shew of vain Endeavours.

Variety of Clothes have, that is, be of various Reputes, &c.
      Meats eating has shewn of Sickness.
      Vid. *Different* and *Divers* supra.

Variety. All forts of Faces fee leave a Room, fcorn all Perfonatio
    forts in a Converfe, &c.

Ugly, vid. *Form* fupra.

Violent, vid. *Action* and *Rain* in *Air*.

Unable, vid. *Ability* and *Strong* fupra.

Uneven Wall in height, an unequal Security in power.

Unnatural, vid. *Abfurd* in *Soul*.

Unfetled Thoughts fhew Joy.

Untoward, vid. *Aukward* fupra.

Unufual ways flying in, fhews Sedition.

    Drinking Muftard ftamp'd, fhew'd A dying a violent Death.

    Meat eat that you would vomir, take unlawful Gain that you
    would reftore.

    A 3 horn'd Beaft, a Power ready for Deftruction.

    Vid. *Unnatural* in *Soul.*

Ufeful, vid. *Good* fupra.

Weaknefs, vid. *Ability* and *Strong* fupra.   Vid. *Action.*

Wearing down the Foundations of an Houfe a Cartway feen, fhew'd A
    of his Farming fpoiling his Gentlemanfhip.

    Vid. *Apparel* and *Crown* in *Ornaments*.

    Worn down Ways feen, threat with Inability of Methods, a
    &c.

    Your Garden walk near, your plenty State near loft.

Weary in walking, defpair in proceeding.

    Knees having, has fhewn Sicknefs.

Well, vid. *Good* fupra.

Wild Afs feen, has fhewn of good Fortune with Swiftnefs.

    Vid. *Beafts* in general.

    Lion feen, threats with Fire, Sicknefs, or fome great Oppreffor.

    Mules feen, threats you with Deceit in your own Houfe.

    Pears are good only to Husbandmen.

Wincing Horfe feen, threats with a troublefom Wife, Servant, or
    Friend, or Art, &c.

Wither'd Corn feen, threats you with Ruin and Mifcarriage.

    Rofes feen as foon withering, kill the Sick.

    Vine feen, threats of fome long Difeafe.

    Trees in general feen, to many threat with Deceit.

    Shooting forth at Root again, have fhewn Children
    in Age.

Worft, vid. *Good* fupra.

Wrinkled Woman feen, threats with a careful and fatigued Fortune.

    Seeming in a Glafs to a young Woman, gave her Succefs in
    Subtilty.

C H A P.

CHAP. XXII.

Of Vegetables.

IN general Creatures. Men shew of reasonable Courses.
(1)   Women, Opinions and Sciences.
                     Beasts shew of Passion and Appetites.
                     Birds as Beasts, but more swift and projective.
                     Fish shew of sullen and untractabler Persons,
                        Passions, and Appetites, both as mute, and as
                        living in Water the Symbol of Trouble.
          Plants shew less nobly of Works themselves, but as in States
                        progressive answering their Growth.
                     Long-liv'd as Oaks, durable according.
                     Herbs, *&c.* Methods of transient Profits an-
                        swerable.
                     Thorns, a Profit but of more Trouble and Pain
                        than Gain.
                     Growing in a Place improper, as in an House, is
                        bad.
                           in a Place proper, as a Garden or Or-
                           chard, *&c.* is best if good.
                     Thunderstruck has shew'd of some Person, Family,
                        or House ruin'd.
                           And burning out tho, thro famous
                           Acts.
                     Sorts, poisonous or ill smelling are still bad.
                           Ill as the Ewe Box *Rhododaphne* seen dry, is
                           still good, it shews an Ill failing.
                           Flourishing, *è contra.*
                     Fruitful and pleasant Valleys seen, shew of the
                        Love of the People.
                     Fish seen, shew Plenty.
                           Vid. *Mustard infrà.*
Stem, Plants without one, shew of vile Actions.
   (2)   Herbs without one, threat of short and triflingest Trans-
                        actions.
Blossoms, Trees seen beyond them, shew of Expedition of Busi-
   (3) ness.
Sap seen fall from a Tree, threats with Wounds and Lamentations.
   (4)   an Oak has shewn of a Great Man accus'd and Guilty.
               To some it shews the Blood and Riches.
               Vid. *Sap* in *Tree* postea.

                                                        Seed

Seed, Vid. *Viƈuals.*

(5) Muſtard Seed ſeen, ſhews of a Plentiful Increaſe.
Stamp'd and drank, ſhew'd *A.* of falſe Accuſations, er
to loſs of Life.
A. ſowing Flower of *London* Seed to kill Weeds againſt Whe;
ſowing, ſhew'd of his uſing things to clear Wine, come fro
thence as againſt that time.

Leaves moving, ſhew of Report and common Fame.

(6) Trees ſeen with them, ſhew of a thriving Chearfulneſs.
Of Herbs ſeen fall on the Sick, ſhew'd of Deceit and Wiles ;
gainſt them.

Flowers in general, ſhew of pleaſant Delights, as Fruit of Gain an

(7) Rewards.
Out of Seaſon tho, threats with Diſappointments.
But ending ill, ſtill as withering. Vid. *Garden.*

Aƈtions, Vid. *Roſe* infra.

Place ſhady adorn'd with Flowers being in, gives preſent Eaſe,
Pleaſure and Content.

Gathering in Seaſon, is Mirth and Jollity, but ſhort.
The more lively the better.
Out of Seaſon, White ſhews of Buſineſs obſtruƈted.
Yellow, not quite ſo bad.
Red, extreme bad, and to ſome
Death.

Roſes, to ſome has ſhewn of wanton Love.

Hold and ſmell unto is beſt, and if ſmelling well gives good
Repute.

Adorn'd with, enjoying ſome ſhort-liv'd Joy.
Poſies of them, to ſome ſudden Nuptials.
A Tomb ſeen with them, ſhew'd of an unjuſt and
untimely Death, as, &c. Vid. *Crown* in *Orna-*
ments.

Sorts. Quality lively, gives laſting Delight.
Languiſhing, fading.
Smelling well, of Glory.

Colours Green and Purple, ſhew of good Hopes.
Red, with Power and Chearfulneſs.
White, with Wiſdom and Innocence.
Golden, ſhews of Honour and the Princes Fa-
vour.

Roſes are good to all but the Sick, to them hazard of Death.
to others they ſhew Secrets revealed, as ſmelling ſtrong.

Red, ſhew of Joy and Recreation.
Seeing in Seaſon, is as Health.
out of Seaſon, is always ill.
Giving or receiving them alike, ſhews Joy.
Vid. *Crown* in *Ornaments.*

Roots in general, shew of hidden things.
(8)   Eating threats with Discord, and slender hidden Profits getting. Vid. *Root* in *Action*. Vid. *Roots* in *Victuals.*

      Scrap'd e'er eat, threats with Hurt thro Superfluity.

Salt seen flung on them, shew'd of destroying Men for their Inheritance.

Herbs without Roots, shew of vain Thoughts and useless Persons.
      to. new-born Children seen, it threats them of Death.

Driving away Ghosts by them, shew'd of clearing Errors by Truth.

Sorts. Parsneps given one, promis'd them of ordinary Fare, but with Health.

      Turneps given one, a slender Profit, from some deep Principles well reach'd.

      Carrots, &c. Vid. *Victuals.*

Rooted up Mulberry Trees seen, threated with Loss of Children.
      Other Trees seen, shews of Hopes frustrate, as, &c.

      A's Beard seen, threated him in great danger.

Fruit in general, shews of some Good long and lasting, as is the Fruit.
(9)   To some, Money the Fruit of their Labours.

      To a good Man Reward, but of Delight more than Profit, as not nourishing as Victuals.

      Ill Man Punishment.

To Beginners of Works, it promises an Issue.
      But their Profit in general is not lasting.

Acts. Degrees are see on the Tree, gather and eat.
      Eating of it to set your Teeth on Edg is very bad.
      Vid. *Victuals*. Vid. *Bodily Action.*

      Feasting on it A. saw his Wife, he discours'd entertainingly of his Art.

Have is Command only, eating is to full and sure Profit.

Seen fall from a Tree unripe, shew'd of an untimely Death.

Gathering is good, and gives Command.
      and eating many in a pleasant Place, is as great Riches and Prosperity.

      But going up a Ladder for them, is an ill Omen.

      A. looking for Kidney Beans on Hazles, shew'd of his expecting Boys good without Correction.

In Season gathered is Profit, as are its Qualities.
      Out of Season is ill, and Labour in vain for such Men.
      To some, Stripes, Trouble and Lamentation.
      To some, Vexation, Plague and Disappointment.

Fruit.

Fruit. Out of Seaſon, to ſome defers their Buſineſs as till then, a
(9)　　when in Seaſon.

Colour black, Lamentation, as Gain by Funerals, *&c.*

Yellow, threats with Grief and Diſeaſes, if eaten (
gathering.

Purple, Deceit.

Pale, Calumny.

Red, Loſs of Blood.

Quality unapt for eating, ſhews Poverty.

Noiſy on eating as Nuts, threat with Grief and Troub
in attaining.

Durable as Apples, a Profit firm according.

Periſhing, as Cherries, Strawberries, *&c.* ſhor
liv'd Pleaſures.

Rotten gathering, has ſhewn Adverſity and loſing (
Children.

Taſte ſharp, threats a Life full of Trouble.

Sour and unripe, ſhews of matters precipitant and il
to ſome, hard Rebukes.

Stinking, fulſome and filthy, have ſhewn of ill Hu
mours.

Harſh and bitter, to many Death.

Sweet eating, gives Profit with Delight.

to others, 'tis as good Diſpoſitions (
the Humours.

Unſweet as Acorns, is as Profit to your ſelf onl

Trees ſeen without Bloſſoms, ſhew of Expedition of Buſineſs.

Being among and pulling off Fruit, gives Riches and Prof
perity.

Apples, Vid. *Trees* infra, and *Orchard* in *Houſe-range.*

Gathering, threats Vexation from ſome one.

from the Top of a Tree, gave Advance a
midſt many Perſons.

Taking, threats of Anguiſh of Mind.

Giving threats Damage.

Eating ſhews of Choler or Labour.

Summer ones ſeen, ſhew of Joy and a good time.

Sour ones, threats with Noiſe and Sedition.

To ſome they ſhew Rents, and their Loſs the Rintal.

In Pies, they ſhew of Receipts defer'd.

2 ſet before me, I ask'd to fetch Apricocks, receiving *Lady*
Days Rent ; I wanted *Michaelmas* Rent alſo.

Almonds eating, threat with Difficulty and Trouble from their
cracking.

Apricocks ſhew of Rents, as Apples, but more voluptuouſly.

Blackberries gathering, ſhew'd of fidling loitering.

Cherries as Peach *infra.*

Buy at a Place, act to merit ſuch Pleaſures there, *&c.*
Frui

Fruit. Cucumbers give unexpected Riches, and the less the better.
(9)   To some they shew weariness with vain Hopes, as of no Nourishment.

Dates are excellent.

Figs eating out of Season, shews scurrilous Calumny.
    In Season is good, and gives Joy and Pleasure.
    7 black ones, Vid. *Time.*

Grapes in Season, shew of some excellent Benefit.
    In general, they shew of Subsistence beyond Necessities, as to Pleasure.
        And so also a genteeler Pleasure than Cherries.
    Ripe eating, gives Joy and Profit.
    Unripe eating, threats with Variances.
    White, a Benefit good and easy.
    Black, a Profit small and troublesome.
        to some, Poverty or Sickness.
    Bunch eating, shew'd of wet Weather.

Treading them, the Overthrow of Enemies, as the Vine press of bloody Vengeance to Gain, &c.

Gathering white is Gain.
    Black is Damage.
    Making Wine on't is Joy.
    Squeez'd overflowing in the King's Cup as held to him, *Joseph.*

Gourds, Vid. *Herbs.*

Mad Apples, shew of Madness.

Melons ripe, give Sickness.
    sharp, give Health.

Mulberries, threat with Stripes from their Colour.
    To others, they shew Fertility and many Goods and Children.
    Rooted up, Loss of Children.

Nuts, threat with Trouble from Impertinencies, as cracking.
    To others, Riches with Labour and Sadness, as in Circumstance.
    Cracking, threats the Dreamer Ruin by Feastings.
    Gathering, shew'd compassing a good Instruction thro Dreams, as their Allegory Difficult, first to be surpass'd.
    Hidden finding, shew'd of finding hid Treasure.
    Filbert is as the Nut, but more noble.

Walnuts looking, inquiring about Dreams.
    Tree *A*'s found dead on a Rock, shew'd of *A*'s Scorn of Dreams thro his Infidelity.

Olives seen, to some is bad.
    Gathering, to some gives Gain.

Oranges seen or eat, threats Wounds, Grief and Vexation ripe or not.

Oil gives Grace and Relief to the Sick and Miserable.

Fruit. Peaches and Cherries, &c. in Seaſon, ſhew of deceitful Plea-
(9)   ſures of Delicacy to no Benefit.
          Out of Seaſon, they are Calumny and Detraction.
              To others, Travel and Labour in
              vain.
        Are not ſo noble as Grapes above, &c. becauſe of them
         is made Wine.
Pears are good to all, and ſhew Plenty.
      Wild are only good to Husbandmen.
Phyſick Apples are of exceeding ill Omen.
Plumbs are greatly as Peaches above, but ſhew of Profit of a-
    nother Seaſon.
Pomegranats, ſhew of Stripes from their Colour.
          To others gathering them, is being enrich'd by ſome
          wealthy Perſon.
Pompions ripe, ſhew Diſeaſes.
      Sour, promiſe of Health.
Quinces are good, but with heavineſs from their Taſte as harſh.
      Vid. *Orchard* in *Houſe-range.*
Rayſins are always good, and moſtly by Women.
Strawberries give Profit from mean Perſons.
      To others, they ſhew of Heat of Mind.
Corn in general, as green or withered.   Vid. *Quality.*
(10)   Sowing.   Vid. *Domeſtick Action.*
      Field on't.   Vid. *Eſtate.*
      Ear'd well in a fair Day ſeen, gives Proſperity.
      Too thick ſeen, ſhews of Profit without Pleaſure.
      Gathering, gives Riches.
      Mean as Beans, &c. ſhew as Wheat, but with more
      Labour.
      Whole Barley caſt into *A*'s Mouth to eat, ſhew'd him
      Death.
Sort. Wheat is beſt, others are leſs good and with more Labour.
      Vid. *Bread* in *Victuals* and *Trade.*
      For our Children as a Bed of it, &c. ſhews of Males.
      Noble ſeen in a Ground, to a Farmer ſhew'd of a
      good Seaſon for it offering.
      Anothers ſeen overpowered by Oats, perceiving of
      his good Notions ſpoilt by Maggots.
      Green ſweet ſmelling walking in, to a Servant hope
      fuller Service promiſed.
      Meal ſeeing or handling, threats of Weakneſs or
      Sickneſs coming.
Barley Mowes making, ſhew'd of drinking Bouts.
          Horſes up to tread them by large Companies.
      Whole caſting into his Mouth to eat, foreſhew'd of
      Death.
Beans eating is ill to all, as groſs and ruſtick.

                                     Cor:

Corn. Sort. Beans eating is to many Diffension and Trouble in mean
  (10)   Profit as windy.
                          to fome Sicknefs.
            Found in ones Clothes, ill Repute from trefpaffing
              Neighbours.
            Seen grow in a Shop, defer'd a mean Trade Profit as
              till that Seafon.
            Cockle or Darnel fowing, threats of brawling Contention
              or Slander.
            Lentiles feen, fhew of Corruption.
            Peafe well boiled eating, gives Succefs in Affairs, as a Difh
              delicate.
            But feen grow, fhew of an impotent felf Subfiftence,
              as of weak Stalk.
            Rice eating, threats with abundance of Obftructions.
            Millet, threats with Poverty and Indigence.
State.   Ears of it feen grow from the Stomach, gave Children.
              In *A*'s Ears having and dropping into his Hand,
                fhew'd *A.* Inheritance as an Heir.
            Growing, the Wind paffing it and not hurt it, gives Plenty.
                          and hurting it, Famine.
            Standing to an Orator, fhew'd of his *extempore* Speech.
                  Lying hid in it, trufting to an *extempore*
                Speech *memoriter* to Benefit.
            Flourifhing in a pleafant Day, gives Profperity.
            Wither'd and poor, threats of Ruin and Mifcar-
              riage.
            Chaff *A.* beat an unknown Boy for putting into his Shoos,
              A. proves angry at himfelf for empty Pretences.
            Stacks feen burnt, has threated with Famine and Mortality.
                          and not confuming on't tho, has given
                          glorious Plenty.
                  Great, to a Farmer has fhewn Plenty.
                  Little, to all threat of Famine and Neceffity.
            Ufe gather'd feen, gives Profit.
              A Bed of Wheat, gave a barren Wife a Son.
              Pick'd in by Chickens feen, fhew'd of Children
                wafting Victuals.
              Wimming fhew'd of Charity, occafion to fpend it.
              In Sheaves, fhew'd Profit with Delay; you threfh it
                e'er you eat it.
            Literal, Vid. *Grammar.*
Herbs fhew Things or Actions of mere Growth or Progrefs.
  (11)   Of little Duration alfo, as Trees *è contra* of great.
                  Vid. *Crown* in *Ornaments.*   Vid. *Victuals.*
            Without Stem, Vid. *Stem* fupra.
      Seeing to Phyficians only is good.   Vid. *Root* fupra.
            Growing out of the Body, to many Death.
                          L 2   *Herbs*

Herbs ſeeing growing out of a part only its Loſs, or Death to them
(11)   thereby ſhewn.

     Leaves, Vid. *L.* ſupra.

Haymaker, Vid. *Perſon* in *Grammar.*

     Tallanght aſſaulted in, deſign'd againſt for Butchers Meat, or
     keeping of Horſes that eat Hay.

Weeds Thiſtle great *A.* ſeeing in his Paſture Ground, promiſed
     of a good Improvement offering there to him.

     And Serpents ſeen in a Cloſe, ſhew'd of Want and En-
     mity for Aid.

     Great pulling down, ſhew'd *A.* of expoſing and degrading
     a great Pretender.

     In Water, ill ſubſiſtent States in Trouble.

Cane, Vid. *Reed* infra.

Clown-all-heal *A.* ſeeing grow in his Parlour, ſhew'd him of lend-
     ing a Ruſtick Mony in Pity.

Daffadowndil having, ſhews Wearineſs.
         to the Sick Death.

Gourds, ſhew of vain and empty Fellows.

Hyſſop ſmelling, threats of Trouble, Labour and Sickneſs.

Lettice eating, threats of heavy Diſeaſes.

Lilies held or ſmelt to out of Seaſon, ſhews of Hopes fruſtrate.

Maidenhair ſeen, promiſes a dry Journy.

Mallows ſeen, threat with great Danger to the Sick.

Marjoram ſmelling, threats with Trouble, Labour and Weakneſs.

Muſtard ſeen, foreſhews of a plentiful Increaſe.

     Elſe eat or ſeen, is bad to all but Phyſicians.

     Stamp'd fine drinking, ſhew'd *A.* of Death by vi
     Accuſations.   olent

Nettles ſtinging, to young Folks little Love-croſſes.

Poppies Heads, ſhew Plenty.

Reed or Cane ſeen grow out of *A*'s Knee, foreſhew'd him a Fiſtula
     there.

Roſemary ſmelling, threats with Labour, Trouble and Weakneſs.

Saffron, ſhews of a Change of State for good.

     To ſome ſeen 'thas ſhewn of the Jaundice.

Sage ſmelling, threats with Labour, Trouble and Sickneſs.

Thiſtle down, ſhews of empty Thoughts, good to the Ill, and
     ill to the good.

Tobacco *Engliſh* grown *A.* taſting ſharp, ſhew'd *A.* of a Phyſician
     affronting him.

Wormwood, in Scripture Tyranny.

     Kill'd by it, that is, poiſon'd to it.

                                             C H A P.

CHAP. XXIII.

Of Wood and Trees.

WOOD (1) shews of our Gains and Rents, &c. and wanting it threats all Miseries.

Carrying it, shew'd A. of respect to one above him.

Carried away yours seen, threats you with Loss of Goods and Mony.

Stolen, Errors wasting your Estate.

Burnt with an excessive Fire, Necessaries spent foolishly.

Timber selling, having Debts indangering your Estate or Inheritance ; as Wood your present Mony.

Buying design in your Journy, aim in your Designs at Riches.

Measuring and buying, shew'd A. working some up to Uses.

Fine cut down seen and A. having it, gave him Inheritance.

Big or all shews the Proportion.

Green *fine lite,* dry after time.

3 Pieces not quite sawn asunder, an Estate for 3 Lives.

Turn'd, to Persons in hazard of Alterations.

Wrought fine, shews of Servants, Cooks, &c.

Fewel selling, threats with heavy Debts on your Person.

'Tis as present Mony, in opposition to Timber Estates ; Elm, Lease ; Oak, Inheritance.

Fire-wood, to some has shewn of the meaner Servants of an House.

Faggots trod in Dirt, little Revenues lost in contempt.

Fetching, gives Gain as is the Action and Circumstance after.

Mowe A's dancing on, commanding his Purse at pleasure.

Roots, shews of old useless Folks.

Vid. *Roots* in *Vegetables.*

Leaves, vid. *Vegetables.*

To some they shew Children, or if none, Words, and if dry, spoke of old.

L 3

WOOD.

WOOD. Rods hazle cut, prepare to buy Timber.
(1)   Flail-ſtick cutting, to a Labourer ſhew'd of threſhing next day.

Apparel having in general, hinders Motion and Travel.
     Shoos have, threats you with Poverty and Slavery.
Limbs, Arms having Wood, gives Victory from you.
     Legs of it, threats your Affairs all to the worſe.
         To ſome it has ſhewn a ſtiff and untractable Servant.
     Members, vid. *Body.*
Perſon, a Devil ſeen turn'd to Wood, ſhew'd *A.* his Deſpair threatning him vaniſhing.
     A Woman wing'd *A.* ſaw become Wood, an Angelick Scheme he was Maſter of became his Gain.

Trees in general in Houſe, vid. *Building.*
(2)   In Members, vid. *Humane Body.*
     Vid. *Crown* in *Ornaments.*
     Nurſeries of young Trees, little Methods of future Advantages.
         About an Houſe, attending an Oeconomy, as, &c.
Acts. Aſcending one, gives future Honour and Command.
         and eating its ſweet Fruit, foreſhew'd one Inceſt.
Becoming one, threats Sickneſs.
Climb, as aſcend.
Bird on one, vid. *Examples* infrà.
Burning near an Houſe, gives Proſperity if not conſum'd.
     Conſum'd threats Loſs of ſome one in Family.
Cutting down is Diſappointment in Hopes, and Loſs in Authority.
Fall from one, deſpair in ſome great Hope.
     to ſome Death near.
     to ſome Loſs of Favour or Offices.
     to a Prince it ſhew'd of his Nobles dying.
Felling, vid. *Cut* supra.
Fix'd to a Tree, chiefly if dead, the Torture of the Wheel.
     On one an Horſe ſeen, ſhew'd of Strength vow'd uſeleſs.
Growing out of the Body, threats Death or a Wound there.
         Whole Body, ſure Death.
     A Part, its Death, or the Party thereby ſhewn.
     Olive out of ones Head tho, gave him Succeſs in Philoſophy.

Trees.

Trees. **Acts.** Growing in your House, shews a Stranger receiv'd or
(2)   quarter'd in your Family.
                The bigger, ranker, and greener,
                the worse.
                So it a little defolates you.
        In a Garden or Field, &c. as proper, may be
        good.
        Slips from the Root, to a Prince Increase of People.
        To others Children in Age.
Planting shews of some new Work, or taking one into
        your House.
                With thriving Boughs, Gain accordingly ensuing.
Pull off ones Boughs, gives Victory o'er some Enemy.
                To a Prince, destroy his Nobles.
Rooted up, Hopes fruftrate, as &c.
Sitting on it Birds seen, vid. *The Example* infra.
Thunderftruck, Lofs of Children, or Ruin to some in Fa-
        mily.
Examples, *A.* faw a large cleft Tree, he liv'd long to fee the If-
        fue of his two Sons.
                White Poplar, that is, one Son a Porter
                hired of all.
                        All forts of Birds refting on't, im-
                        ploy'd in all Projects.
                Pine-apple, the fecond Son a Sea-Captain.
                Sea-fowls of all forts refting on him,
                trufted in all Merchandize.
        Vid. *Nebuchadnezzar's.*
Parts. Bark thick and hard, shews of a mighty Man.
        Top of an Apple-Tree gathering Apples from, gave Ex-
        altation before many.
        Boughs large and flourishing, Children and Family fo.
                Top, your eldeft Son.
                To *Nebuchadnezzar* his Empire.
        Scatter'd about, Rumors.
        Pull'd off, Victory o'er Enemies.
                        Clothes from Thorns, Reputation from
                        Enemies.
        Fruit, the Man's Riches from his Labour.
        From high Trees, famous Gain.
                Low, abject.   Vid. *Fruit* in *Vegetables.*
        Leaves in general shew of Beauty, Ornament, and Plea-
        fures.
                To others of Children, and if none, Words;
                and if dry, spoke of old.
        Vid. *L.* in *Vegetables.*
        Roots of a Tree feen firm, gives Affurance in doubt.
                To fome it shews of old ufelefs Folks.

Lingua Terſancta.

Trees. **Parts.** Roots of, To ſome the Offal of Eſtates, as *&c.* Nebuchad-
(2) nezzar, &c. Vid. *Roots* in *Vegetables.*

Sap in general ſhews of our Inheritance, Blood or Death.

Smelling ſweet, ſhews of Mony and great Riches
generally.

Wine to many ſhews Madneſs and ſhedding of
Blood. Vid. *Wine* in *Drink.*

Yellow threats with heavy Labour and Care.

White, Deceit.

Sorts. Ever-greens give a ſtable Condition.

Palm, Victory.

Laurel, Joy.

Myrtle, Love.

Cypreſs ſhews of Lamentations or Funerals.
To ſome of fine Women from their
Shape.

Fair, bloſſoming, or green, ſhew of Joy, Comfort, and
Delight.

Without Bloſſoms tho, ſhews of Expedition of Buſineſs; blight, Dangers over.

Quick growing ſeen, ſhew of quick Events, *& è contra.*

So alſo as the Fruits, *&c.* Vid. *ſupra.*

Deſert Trees ſeen, ſhew of Solitarineſs.

Garden Trees ſhew of Joy and Society.

Barren threat of Poverty and uſeleſs Perſons.

Fruit-bearing ſhew of Plenty.

Sweet, generally good.

Acrons, *&c.* to the Owners only Good.

Smelling ſweet gives good Fame, *& è con.*

Foreſt cuting down, ſhew'd a King of rooting out his
Nobles.

Qualities. Bending, vid. *Flexible* infra.

Binding as the Withy, is good in Friendſhip.

In fear of Priſons is bad.

Crown making is honorary, as are their Natures.

Broken ſeen, threats one in Houſe with Diſeaſes.

Old Stump, *Nebuchadnezzar.*

Burnt, vid. *Thunderſtruck* infra.

Cleft ſeen ½ Poplar, ½ Pine, vid. *Example* ſupra.

Crooked, corrupt reaſoning Men.

Crown making, vid. *Crown* in *Ornaments.*

Dry, vid. *Rooted up* infra.

Flexible as the Vine, ſhew to ſome Tractableneſs.
to ſome Deceivableneſs.

Great ſeen, ſhew of Honour.

Cut very great have ſhewn of Death.

Elm, a noble Leaſe Eſtate.

ees. Qualities. Great Elm bad at Root, one of the Lives in danger
   (2)   of dropping.

    Large and flourishing with thriving Boughs, gives
        Children so prosperous.

        To others as to *Nebuchadnezzar*, of Estate,
        &c.

    Long-liv'd as the Oak, shew of Inheritances and Be-
        nefits durable.

        Palm, Olive, and Vine also, give long Life.
        Growing in an House seen, give long Life
        with Quiet.

    Old shew of aged doting Persons.

        Scrubbed rooting out, conquering annoying Dif-
        ficulties.

        Wither'd seen, threats with Deceit.

        Springing at Root, Children in Age.

    Prickly shew of Thieves and Impediments.
        To some Enemies.

    Good also for Security as in Hedges.

    Vid. *Thorns* infra.

    Rooted up shew Annoy, Fear, Grief, and Hope lost.

    Spreading o'er the Earth, *Nebuchadnezzar.*

        Vine so, *Cyrus*'s Mother.

    Strong, solid, and erect, shew of Men stout and
        stubborn.

        And thorny, to some Thieves.

    Tall shew Men famous.

        Short, Men mean and base.

    Thunderstruck, threats with Annoy, Fear, Grief, and
        Hopes lost.

Abeles seen large and prosperous, give an Estate quick im-
    prov'd and soon gone.

Ash as the Elm below.

Apple-tree shews of some pleasant Woman.   Vid. *Fruit* supra.

Box seen flourish is ill, from its bad Scent and Unwholesomness,
    Dry shews of the Fall of some ill Man.

Bay-tree as in Scripture shews of a fair Wife and rich Affairs.
    A Crown of it to Poets, Physicians and Divines, Good.

Beech-tree seen, shews of wanton Women from its Shade.
    To others it threats of Pains and Labour from its
    Joynery Uses.

Briers pricking, to the Young has shewn of Love-crosses.
    Vid. *Thorns* infra.

Cedar, a powerful Noble of great Fame.
    An House smelling of it, an Oeconomy noble according.

Cotton-tree, shews one poor.

Cypress-tree shews of Patience and Lingring.
    To others of Funerals from Custom.

Trees. Cypreſs Tree, ſhews to others of ſome Princely Woman from
(2) their Shape.

Elm, &c. as without Fruit, Poverty to moſt but Joyners.

Fair and large tho, ſhew of Leaſe Eſtates, as Oaks
of Inheritance.

Ever green, Vid. *ſupra.*

Fir, Vid. *Pine* infra.

Foreſt Trees ſeen, threat of Deſolation.

Holly as ſuch, foreſhews Taverning or Melancholy.

Ivy ſeen, to many alſo has ſhewn the ſame.

Overgrowing *A*'s Church Porch on which *A.* ſeem'd lying on
a Bier, foreſhew'd *A.* a lingring Death.

Lawrel as the Olive.

To ſome he gives Health with Joy and Dignity.

Came from her, *Virgil*'s Mother.

Lote Tree, gives Tranquillity, and Evil forgot, *a Nomine.*

Medlar Tree ſeen, threats with Idleneſs and Remiſsneſs, *a Nomine.*

Myrtle Tree good in caſe of wanton Women, &c.

Mulberry Tree ſeen, gives Prudence and Gain, it bears Fruit
and Silkworms.

To ſome Conſanguinity, as its Fruit colour'd
as Blood.

Rooted out, is as Loſs of Children.

Vid. *Fruit,* &c.

Nut Tree climbing and gathering Nuts from, to ſome interpreting Dreams.

To ſome it ſhews of Covetouſneſs.

To ſome, it threats of Impediments.

To ſome, a Man of ill Fame and a Deceiver.

Oaks ſhew of Inheritances, as Elms of Leaſes.

So long-liv'd Ruſticks, known of many.

So Men chearful and eſteem'd.

To ſome, Divination and Divinity, as once ſacred to
Apollo.

Stately ſeen, gives Riches and long Life.

To ſome they ſhew Princes, rich Men, and old
Folks.

Cut down, antient Families rooted out.

Sap bleeding, ſhew'd of a great Man accus'd and condemn'd.

Olive Tree ſeen, pernicious to the Sick.

To ſome, a pleaſant Man or rich Woman.

To ſome, the Wife and Ambition, and ſo ſeen
flouriſhing is beſt, as in the *Pſalms.*

Coming out of the Head, gave Succeſs in Philoſophy.

Smelling to, to a Wife Children.

Maid, Marriage.

Man, Proſperity and good Enterprize.

Trees

Trees. Olive Tree, Olives bearing down, good to all but Servants.
(2)   Treading on them down, is Ill and Anger to
                                         all.
                                         Gathering them off the Ground, threats with
                                         Labour and Pains.

Orange Tree is as the Fruit.

Palm in the Hand shews Victory and a compleat Man, and so
    also as the Olive.

Peach Tree bearing to a Woman, foreshew'd her a Child of fine
    Manners, but short-liv'd.

Pear Tree is as the Fruit.

Pine and Fir Trees, to Mariners are good.
                                         to others they shew of Sloth and Fear.
                                         Vid. *Examples*, and *Trees Actions* supra.

Plane Tree, gives Pleasure and Ease.

Pomegranat shews of a rich Noble.

Poplar as fruitless, shews Poverty to all but Joiners.
    Vid. *Example* supra.

Thorns in general, Vid. *Prickly* in *Tree Quality*, supra.
                                         They shew of Grief and Injury, as also of
                                         Love.
                                         Seen growing, shew of perplexing Cares of
                                         little Profit.
                                         Good to Bailiffs and Robbers,
                                         others Ill.

A Pillar of them, Riches thro Care.

Walking on them, shew'd of the Destruction of Ene-
    mies.

2 in his Fingers shew'd A. of two Vexations about Mony
    Payments.

A Field seen full of them, a matter in Dispute full of
    Troubles.

Fall among them, that is, be perplexed with Cares of
    Weight and Loss.

Way thorny, Labour to loss.
                                         Stopping your Travel, such Perplexities obstruct-
                                         ing your Designs.

Vine shews of our Lives, its Boughs its Parts, and its Fruits our
    Bliss.
                                         Hence the Parable of Christ.
                                         To some, a fruitful Wife or Concubine.
                                         To some Plenty, but with Weakness, as born by
                                         others in its Growth.

Fruit, Mony.

Leaves, our Ornaments and Pleasures.

Turn'd to a wild Vine seen, shew'd one his Life to come
    all Misery.

Full of Boughs, Increase of Family.

Trees.　Vine thriving is as Increaſe of Family.
(2)　　　Withering ſeen, forethreats of ſome long Diſeaſe.
　　　Withy bending to lead *A.* over a Brook, foreſhew'd him a Widow
　　　aiding him in Expence.

CHAP. XXIV.

Of Creatures in general.

Actions hearing, Vid. *Senſe* and *Aƈtion.*
(1)　　Aƈting, Vid. *Aƈtion.*
　　　Dead or killed, Vid. *Dead.*
Sorts.　Vegetables, Vid. ſupra.
(2)　　Men ſhew of aƈtive Methods of Reaſoning.
　　　Women ſhew of Paſſive and Speculative Notions and Ideas.
　　　　　　So of Sciences, Schemes, Platforms and Proiects, *&c.*
　　　Beaſts declare of our Appetites and Paſſions with their plain Iſſue.
　　　　　So alſo of ſafe and ſure Tranſaƈtions.
　　　　　So of our ſettled Methods and Manners.
　　　　　So they declare of things preſent moſt.
　　　Birds ſhew Men of another Element, but pleaſant and delight-
　　　　　ful.
　　　　　　To ſome, of Merchants.
　　　　　　To all, of Projeƈts.
　　　　　　To ſome, of ſwift Occurrences without reaſonable
　　　　　　　Deſign.
　　　　　　They declare alſo of quick Futurities good or ill, as, *&c.*
　　　Fiſh ſhew of ſnaring and intraƈtable Enemies.
　　　　　to ſome of things paſt.
　　　　　to all, Matters in Trouble from their Element.
　　　　　　Sea publick, freſh Water private.
　　　　　　Dolphins excepted, ſhewing generally of ſome
　　　　　　　noble Strangers.
Kinds.　Males ſhew with Valour, Faith and Strength.
(3)　　　Females are milder, but with Treachery.
　　　Tame, Vid. *Birds* and *Beaſts* infra.
　　　　　Monkey having, ſhew'd *A.* of a Life of Voluptuouſneſs
　　　　　　to the fooling of his Perſonal Powers.
　　　Solitary ſeen is ill, *&c.* and the more the worſe.
　　　Poiſonous, threat with ſnaring and cruel Enemies.
　　　　　Conſiderable as Lig, *&c.*
　　　Inſeƈts exanguious or creeping things, are all of worſt Omen.
　　　　　Creeping, ſhew Deceit and Envy.
　　　　　Multitudinary as Locuſts, ſhew Conſpiracy.

Kinds.

Kinds. Infects changeable as the Maggot to a Fly, &c. feen, fhews
(3)   that fo the Dreamer have Change of Life alfo.
        Are of no Profit as uneatable.
        So in Allegory are moft imperfect as without Blood.
        A Fly under an Horfes Belly you ride, a grievous Menace
            from a Trifle; Senfe of peevifh Refentment in fome
            one.
    Inimical fhot crofs, Overtures rectified.
            Brought into your Houfe, fuch Ill at your Command.
            Headlefs feen, rendered without further Power of In-
            jury.
            Paffing you, Vid. *Ride in Pofture.* Vid. *Pafs in Tra-*
            vel.
    Monfters feen in general, threat with vain Hopes and Fears.
        Affaulting you, fuch Courfes menacing.
        Frights you from the left, the Abfurdity of fuch a
            Courfe is its own Remedy.
        Lies with firft, and then kill'd *A*'s youngeft Son; his
                new Husbandry prov'd deftroyed by its
                own Abfurdity.
                A. hardly efcaping himfelf, his whole Huf-
                bandry threatned by it.
    Sorts. Manlike enters your Hall, an abfurd Contract
                with Equals offers.
                With a Lump of Flefh for a Face, a
                    Courfe fcarce of feeming Reafon.
                Statues monftrous feen, have threated
                    great Trouble from Magiftrates.
            Child pafs of anothers, get advantage over
                them in a manner as abfurdly.
            Sheep feen without Eyes, fhew'd of an unjuft
                    Profit not to be own'd.
                    Mouths, fhew'd *A*'s Man
                    leaving him, that fed
                    them.
            Sea ones feen on Land good, it fhews of
                Popular Enemies in your power.
            Chymera, Lions Head, Goats Body, and Ser-
                pents Tail; that is, firft ftout, then luftful,
                and laftly treacherous and poifonous.
            Hippocentaur feen, fhew'd *A.* of bearing Twins
                foon dying.   Vid. *Fable in Literature.*
            Vid. *Bafilisk* in *Poifonous Creatures.*
            Hogs *A*'s own feen with Spurs, fhew'd *A.* of
                his Fowls eating away their Meat.

                                C H A P.

CHAP. XXVa
Of Inſects.

IN general they are as an Abomination to Men when ſeen, as of matter contemptible.

So they ſhew of Variances and Controverſies.

The Exanguious by much the more unnatural.

Magnitude bounds their Affection, and Action qualifies it.

A Fly under an Horſe, a miraculous little Evil.

Creeping things ſhew of Snares and Tricks, but mean an baſe.

In Multitude, ſhew Conſpiracies of little Enemies.

To ſome, Diſtraction from various Cares.

Vermin feeding, threats with Death.

Troubled much in killing them about you, give you Riches.

Stings ſignify as Thorns, Vid. T.

In the Body, to ſome Death.

Ears Ants going in, to Orators and Philoſophe good, the Peoples Attention.

Arſe Bees being in A's, ſhew'd of his Debts divertin his neceſſary Expences.

Ants ſhew to ſome the common People.

to ſome, Covetouſneſs and Contention.

to ſome, they threat ſhort Life.

to Saylors, great Dangers and other Hurts.

Winged, ſhew Nobles.

Their little Gains, Riches to all, eſpecially Nobles.

Brought from anothers Houſe by their means.

About the Body, threat Death or a troubleſome Life.

Near it only, ſhew to the Sick Health and Induſt again.

Entering the Body, threat it with Death or Blin neſs.

Bees ſeen in general are good, but menacing or ſtinging ; Enemi deſperate and popular, but mean.

Shew of People induſtrious, in oppoſition Waſps, &c. not.

The Czar of Muſcovy ſhew'd me of Be Vid. Earth.

To ſome they ſhew juſt Men and condemn'd of the that is, of the Juſt.

To ſome, Thieves.   B

Bees feen, to fome Men vile, but ufeful.
    To Dealers in them, Profit with Delight.
    To fome, Trouble from their Noife and Stings.
    To fome, fhew Sicknefs thro their Honey and Wax.
    Stock of them in *A*'s Room with an Hole in't, fhew'd
        him of others building on his ill
        Managery.
        A's Arfe the fame, *&c.*
    Beehive creeping into, fhew'd *A.* of Death and Diffolution.
Fighting, threats with Anger.
    Mutually with one another, is as Hurt of Perfons.
Find a Stock, to one defigning to be a Schoolmafter Succefs.
Fluttering over the Head, to Captains good, to others Ene-
    mies.
        Before Soldiers, *&c.* to fome Death.
        Beat them unftung, be courageous and
        fear nothing.
        About *A*'s Tenants Servants feen,
        fhew'd him of Floods on his Land.
Following them gives Gain.
Killing them and fhutting them up, Good and Profit to all
    but Countrymen.
King of the Bees feen, fhew'd of a Schoolmafter.
Making Honey feen, fhew'd of a Prince ruling well.
        In *A*'s Houfe, gave him Dignity and Eloquence
        fuccefsful.
Pafs thro many unhurt, compafs your Profit for all Popular
    little Confpiracies.
Poffefs your Hat, find the Fear of Popular little Enemies
    make you act difhonourably.
Stung by them, hurt by Deceits.
Settling on his Lips, to *Plato* fhew'd of admiring Auditors.
        On a Captain or Emperor's Head is good.
    Sitting upon one feen, fhew'd of the Hurt of Enemies.
Beetles, fhew to us wicked, nafty and lazy Fellows.
    to fome, Haters of Converfation.
Butterflies, fhew of empty Flatterers.
    if painted, Drolls.
Caterpillars feen, fhew to us of confounding Errors.
Crickets fhew to us Muficians, Flatterers, and ufelefs merry Fellows.
    To Men in Fear, vain Threats.
    To the Poor, Talk without Help.
    To the Sick, Thirft and Death.
Flees fhew to us great Troubles, but not perpetual.
Flies fhew us of Importunity.
    Seen, to Taverners threat of their Wine turn'd to Vinegar.
    Taking them, fhews of Wrong or Injury.
    Swarms of them, that is, unreafonable Enemies that will
    fcandal you.
                            Flies

Flies Swarms, to others naſty Troubles with Eaſe at Night.
>Sorts. Spaniſh ſeen, ſhew'd of an ungovernable barren Bu
>>gerer.
>>>To ſome they ſhew Poiſon.
>Gain, Fly in the main is ill as the Waſp and Hornet, but le
>>Engendring A's Horſe ſeen, ſhew'd him of a triflii
>>>Vilifier of his Abilities, but to dangerous Iſſ
>>>if he on his Back, and like to be ſtung by it.

Gnats ſhew of Trouble and Grief with Infamy, as Noiſy.
Graſhoppers ſhew as Crickets, but withal declare of Country-men,
>Vid. *Crickets* ſupra.

Hornets, Vid. *Waſps* infra.

Leeches ſucking, ſhew of Creditors devouring.

Lice many having, threats with Bonds, Sickneſs, Poverty or Gallie
>>At the Beginning of a Year or Magiſtracy, th
>>>more fatal.
>>Killing or caſting away, Delivery from Care an
>>>Heavineſs, and ſo Proſperity.
>>But waking among them is the more unhappy.
>Seen corroding the Fleſh, gave Plenty of Gold and Silver
>Between the Lips having, ſhew'd A. of trifling Abomi-
>>nation, as to Victuals.
>Pulls out a Cluſter of 4, and lays them on a Table ; A.
>>expoſing his ſecret Poverty in publick Dealings.

Locuſts ſhew of faithleſs, whiffling, miſchievous Fellows.
>Green with vain Hopes.
>Pale with Fear.
>Armies of them ſeen, threat with Sterility.
>>Flying, ſhew Peril more projective.

Silkworms, ſhew of Gains with great Labours.

Waſps and Hornets in general, as Bees *ſupra*, but worſe.
>Stinging, ſhew unjuſt Judgments condemning.
>>The more, the worſe.
>>To ſome they ſhew Thieves.
>Waſps in fatal Dreams ſhew of leſſer ill Judgments, as
>>a fine Galleys, *&c.*
>>Stinging is ill to all, as fall into ill and cruel Mens
>>>Hands.

Hornets, ſhew Men infamous from their Noiſe.
>>So ſuch as aſſault the Dreamer to diſcredit
>>>him.
>>Stinging, in fatal Dreams capital Puniſhment,
>>>as Death with Infamy, *&c.*
>>>Fatal generally, as 9 kill an Horſe.
>>Neſt running from, ſhew'd A. of paying a
>>>ſcandalous Parcel of little Debts.

Worms, Vid. *Silkworm* ſupra.
>Great ſtinking found in A's Coat, ſhew'd of his being a
>>Cuckold.   Worms,

Worms. Woodworm or Climex ſeen, is Trouble thro the Wife or
Concubine.

Glow-worms, Vid. *Tomb in Dead.*

Earth-worms ſhew us of Enemies would deſtroy us.

Bred in the Fleſh, threat with either Death or Corruption there.

To ſome Diſpleaſure at Familiars, as the Wife, &c.

Fleſh gnawing inwardly, ſhew of falſe Servants.

Void or vomit them, diſcover private Enemies and
avoid them.

Vomiting flat ones, Sh——g 4 long white ones,	Shew'd A. inventorying Goods to avoid	Deceits. Cheats.

CHAP. XXVI.

Of Poiſonous Creatures.

IN general. Seeing little ones threats with Misfortunes from ſecret
Enemies.

To ſome, Snares and cruel Enemies.

To ſome Men contemptible, but dangerous in Fact.

Stings ſhew as Thorns, but worſe.

Poiſon drinking, ſhews Puniſhment.

to ſome, dangerous Errors and Deceit.

to ſome, the ſame as dying or Death.

Sleepy Potion given A. by his dead Father, foreſhew'd him Death,

Handling it forbearing in Fear, ſhew'd A. leaving
ſomewhat dangerous as Poiſon.

Killing a Snake ſtinging her to Death, ſhew'd A.
marrying on Courtſhip.

Poiſon'd by a Papiſt, corrupted by Tyranny, &c.

Adder, Vid. *Snake* infra.

Aſp, Vid. *Snake* infra.

Baſiliſk or Cockatrice ſeen, threats preſent and ſudden Death, and
Loſs of Goods.

If at a diſtance and on a Tower, threats Ruin to the Country.

Standing by thee, ſhews thee to be the Ruin of many.

So he gives a wicked Prince ſpoiling his Country.

Cockatrice is the ſame as Baſiliſk *ſupra.*

Dragon ſhews of an ill King and Tyrant, as Lion of a good one.

To ſome, the Commander of a bloody Army.

To ſome, a Prince or Perſon cruel and proud.

M

Dragon

Dragon ſhews to ſome a Popiſh Prince, as poiſoning with Errors.
> Bringing forth one, who riſing againſt her drew forth her Bowels, *Nero's* Mother.
> Drove away by Thunder and Lightning, an ill Prince remov'd.
> Having his Eyes or Head, being Maſter of admirable Secrets or Jewels.
> Lain with, and bringing forth by a Dragon, *Auguſtus's* Mother.
> Kill one, remove ſuch a Tyranny in your ſelf or others.
>> Seen kill'd is the ſame but leſs.
> Seen, ſhews of ſome ſuch like Lord or Maſter.
>> But to ſome he gives Gain and Riches, as Gold and Silver, &c.
> Speaking often is great Good.
> Threatning, to all Danger.
>> to ſome the Deſolation of all.
>> to the Sick Death.
>> to ſome the biting of a mad Dog.

Frogs and Toads threat us with treacherous and fooliſh Perſons.
> to ſome Perſons liquoriſh and imprudent.
> to ſome the Gout and Hoarſeneſs.
> to ſome the Deſpiſers of Cuſtom, as (Land and Water.)
> Getting a Toad's Head is as Delivery from Poiſon.
>> So Freedom of back Pains and unknown Diſeaſes.
> Found in a Field the Earth open'd, ſhew'd Bawdy the Secret of a Diſpute.
>> Hiding again on it, that is, after ſtifled.
> Frogs ſhew of Abuſers and Praters.
>> Seen, is good to thoſe who live on Commons.
>> Beat with the Fiſt, gave Authority over Servants.

Serpents in general ſhew of implacable, ſubtle, falſe Enemies with ſure Loſs, as &c.
> to ſome Sickneſs.
> to the Sick ſtinging Death.
> to ſome Impriſonment.
> to ſome Deceit by a Woman, as the Wife.
> to ſome Enemies, fraudulent, malignant and impotent.
> to ſome Envy.
> to ſome long Life, Wiſdom, Treaſure and Magiſtracy.
> Seen in Water, ſhew'd of Enemies diſtreſs'd and powerleſs.
> Biting you, a ſubtle Enemy hurting you.
>> As lying in wait for you, a ſneaking deſperate Enemy.

Serpents biting you, To some troubled with a sharp venomous Humour.

> Leaving a Wound on't, Damage.
> A poisonous one; an Enemy tyrannical.
> A great one, some Superior.
> > A little one, an Inferior.
> > > Assaulted and not bit, a vain Effort.

Command his Head, have such an Enemy in your power.

Deliver'd of, covering *Albania* and devouring many *Turks*, *Scanderbeg's* Mother.

Fighting them, the Overthrow of Enemies.

Encompassing an Altar seen, gave the desired Success.

> Vid. *Crown* in *Ornaments.*

Flying from him, avoiding subtle and erring Evils.

Found with Weeds in a Close, shew'd of Want and Enmity for Aid.

Heard hiss, but not seen or felt, good as your Enemies, weak and fearful to appear.

Pulling him out of his Arm, shew'd *A.* ridding him of a false Servant.

Rul'd by him, exceeding bad.

> The Fall of *Adam* and *Eve.*

Wasting *Italy* behind him, shew'd to *Hannibal* his Captainship.

Persons: He shews Priests, Rhetoricians, and Physicians.

> *A's* Sister seen turn'd to a Serpent of Clay, shew'd him of his Divisions becoming contemptible.

Sorts. Adders fight, overthrow Enemies.

Asps and Adders to some shew of Mony, rich Wives, and Husbands.

> Assaulting and biting to Death so, is best and shews Marriage.

Snakes are as great Serpents, but less pernicious.

> To some they shew deceitful and erroneous Instructions.
> Seen in a Garden, threat of great Temptations to Expence there.
> > Come out of a Chamber in a City, is good to your main publick Transaction State.
> Assaulting you, subtle Temptations as is the Place where.
> > To some the Assaults of Enemies.
> Dead gives you Triumph over such Evils.
> Sting *A's* sore Leg and not to be cast off, shew'd *A.* Death of its Gangrene.

Scorpion poisoning, a false Teacher corrupting with Errors.

Serpents. Sorts. Viper ſeen, ſhews to us of Silver and rich Women,
                Biting, the greater Riches.
                Hid in a Woman's Breaſt, Rape or Miſ-
                  carriage as ſhe appears ſad or glad
                  therewith.

Scorpion, vid. *Serpent* ſupra.

Spider ſeen, threats you with ſome ſnaring Perſon.

Toad, vid. *Frog* ſupra.   Viper, vid. *Serpent* ſupra.

C H A P. XXVII.

Of Beaſts in General.

IN general. In Scripture and publick Prophecy they ſhew Kingdoms.
(1)   Their ſeveral ſorts ſhew of their ſeveral Qualities.
         Riſing from the Sea, form'd among the People.
In private Dreams, violent and brutiſh Inclinations and
         Paſſions.
         To ſome Tranſaction with ſuch as bears them
         in their Arms.
         Of quick Growth, of quick Events, *&c. e con.*
Poſture, on one ſide lying, a Power great but not active.
         Seen in Holes of the Earth, as Foxes and Co-
         nies, *&c.* is good to the Secret.
Place, as your Houſe ſeen in, vid. *Oxen* infra.

Sorts. Colour, vid. *Appearance* in Senſe.
(2)   White Horſe a weakly one, Friend, Wife, or Art, as *&c.*
         Ox is better than one black.
         Fox, a ſeeming innocent Beguiler.
         Calf *A.* ſaw his Cow have, that, is, one he
         would uſe, as one of that Colour was us'd
         before by him.
Form ſhews of their natural Operations.
         Magnitude ſhews to us as of the Power of a Man.
           With Gentleneſs, Terror without Miſchief.
           Great fighting as the Elephant, ſhews of a
           diſproportion'd Match.
Voices horrible ſhew Terror with our Cauſe of Senſe of it.
         Pleaſant ſhew of Delight.
         Mute are troubleſom, as unconverſable.
         Vid. *Voice* and *Speak* in *Action* infra.
Qualities unknown, unaccountable, as *&c.*
         Fat better than lean every way, and not ſo
         greedy.
         Thick-horn'd Beaſts ſhew of Fools.
Sex, Male ſtouter.   *Sorts.*

Sorts. Form. Sex, Female milder, except with Whelps.
(2)   Buck killing, shew'd A. putting off his Plowman.
              His Doe concern'd, his Sweet-heart sorry.
Wild naturally shew of our Enemies and Men ill by
      Nature.
Reclaim'd, shew of Enemies once, but now recon-
      cil'd.
Unknown, unaccountable.
Carried by a Woman in Bosom, Adultery.
              But against her Will, Sickness.
Following you in the dark, dangerous Discords
      thro Doubts.
Great and fair shew of Enemies noble and adorn'd.
Becoming tame seen, is best, except treacherous,
                    as the Fox, then hurt
                    thro your foolish Trust.
              Or poisonous as the Spider,
              Viper or Scorpion, shew-
              ing Insensibility of Danger.
      Tame Lioness and Whelps having in Pa-
              lace, to a King an hopeful Queen
              and Issue.
      Fox have, that is, a subtle dis-
              sembling Familiar.
              At home, that is, such
              one a Domestick.
      White Hare, an innocent Dispute
      at command.
      Taming Beasts, winning Favour of Ene-
              mies, or having them in Power.
      Oxen threats with grievous Sor-
              row.
Tame becoming wild is unnatural to all, and deserts all
      Hopes.
              To some it has shewn Men in Contract
              become separate.
Continuing tame, shews of mild Persons and
      Friends.
Sheep and Dogs seen wild is very ill, but Goats
      less ill.
Domestical purely, as Dog, Hen, &c. as to Fa-
      milies.
      Field tame, of Strangers.
Wild become tame, if generous as the Lion and Ele-
      phant, Good.
      If Carrion eating, threats Death.
      Monkey tame keeping, living to a self-
      fooling Luxury.
              M 3   *Sorts.*

Sorts.   Wild Robin-red-breaſt having tame, to a Wife her Husband
(2)   true.

Whelps ſhew of Men, as &c. and new-born ſeen are good to
all.   Vid. *Young* in *Time.*

Lioneſs ſeen with them, ſhew'd a King Felicity in Queen
and Children.

Wild Beaſts with their Young againſt you, are moſt
greedy and terrible.

Own Calf paſſing by, ſhew'd *A.* leaving Eſſays to farm
outright.

Of a Bear ſeen, promiſe of Change for the better.

A Sow with young ſeen, ſhews Fruitfulneſs, ſhe has many.

I'll gore him, ſays a Cow to a Calf, ſhew'd of a Land-
lord's rooting out his Tenant to farm himſelf.

Many, *A.* left a Gooſe, Fox, and Lion in his Backſide, he far-
med with ſubtle Checks.

Acts.   Aſſaults, vid. *Fight* infra.
(3)   Becoming men ſhew'd of Vices and Errors reform'd to Reaſon.

Men becoming Beaſts, Humanity turn'd to Rapine.

Beaſts eyed like men, Paſſions or Appetites colour'd with
Reaſon or acting with Reaſon.   Vid. *Change* in *Senſe.*

Climbing an Hill Oxen ſeen, ſhew'd of Plenty and further Proſperity.

Eating, vid. *Victuals.*   Engendring, vid. *Fly* in *Inſect.*

Fawning on you, vid. *Lion.*

Fighting ſhews of Railing and Slander.

Great to Diſadvantage in a match unequal.

Bit by a marble Lion, ſhew'd *A.* Death by a Viper in
ſuch a Statue.

Gor'd by a Boar, kill'd by one bearing that Arm.

Mutual fighting Oxen ſeen, a Diſpute of great Buſineſs.

Tearing us, threats us Puniſhment.

The Fleſh, to the Rich Loſs, to the Poor
Plenty.

Aſſaulted by Oxen, a grievous Strait, Hopes of Gain
threatning Ruin.

Kill'd by Beaſts, to Servants Liberty.

Vid. *Death* and *Dying.*

Beaſts ſeen, ſhew of ſome Power extinct.

Of Prey, greedy Deſigners vanquiſh'd.

Found under *A*'s Bed, threated him Death near.

Kill'd Ox, threats Danger.   Vid. *Fight* ſupra.

Lying down Oxen ſeen, ſhew'd of Plenty in Decay.

Piſſing *A*'s Horſe ſeen, his Art, &c. eas'd in his eager Expences.

Playing, vid. *Oxen, Rats,* and *Dogs* in *Beaſts.*

Riding Beaſts, having ſuch Deſigners in your power.

Running Oxen, precipitant plenty Joy.

Acts.

Ass. Running, vid. *Travel in Action.*
(3)　Sleeping, vid. *Oxen, Ass* and *Wolf.*
　　Standing, vid. *Legs in Beasts-parts.*
　　　　Oxen seen shew prosperous Plenty, as lying down
　　　　　fading and despairing.
　　Speaking, shews of things exceeding good, true and wonderful.
　　　　　　　　　To some tho, grievous Sorrow, as &c.
　　　　If one about your House, shews of Change in your
　　　　　Family.
　　　　To be interpreted with the Nature of the Beast.
　　　　It threatens the Domestick rather than the Master.
　　　　It shews of matter of mere Appetite or Passion issu-
　　　　　ing to reasonable Act.
　　　　Heard in general, it shews thee thy Enemies, &c.
　　　　　flying before thee.
　　　　I'll gore him, a Cow saying to a Calf, shew'd a Land-
　　　　　lord removing his Tenant.
　　　　Coach-Horses, shew'd A. of working them to farming.
　　Terrifying seen, is good only to Hunters.
　　　　Fear of them, as not hurting us, is Danger only.
　　　　Assaulting us, threats us greatest Evils.
　　Voice, mowing an Ox heard, shew of Strife.
　　　　Noisy in general shews of Acts of Defence against Ene-
　　　　mies.
　　　　Among themselves, mutual Resentments, as &c.
　　　　Vid. *Voices* in *Sorts* suprà.
Parts. Chang'd to Iron, Good as powerful.
(4)　　　　　　　But bears Miseries, or else why Iron.
　　　　　　Gold and Silver, Good as Rich.
　　　　　　Any thing else ill.
　　Belly Elephant's being in, threated A. with Death.
　　Blood, vid. *Drink.*　　　　　Claws, vid. *Horns* infrà.
　　Cunt-Calves give a Woman, charge her as an Whore before
　　　Marriage.
　　Dung and Urine seen is generally bad as an Abomination.
　　　　Of Horses seen, is good to Plowmen and Physicians.
　　　　In general it shews of Dissolution of Care and Expence,
　　　　　as is the Beast.　　　　Vid. *Dung* in *Earth.*
　　Hair'd like an Hog be, that is, die as he, or be contemn'd as
　　　　nasty and greedy as he.
　　　　Ass, shews of Servitude.
　　　　Lion, shews you terrible.
　　　　Hare, threats you Fear and Terror with a dread-
　　　　　ful Death. (Hounds)
　　　　Sheep, threats you kill'd by your Friends, and
　　　　　spoil'd for your Fortunes. (Christ thus us'd)
　　Hair seen by you and not growing on you, shews you act only
　　　　as they.

Parts. Hair ſeen. Fox's, craftily, &c.
(4)   Grown longer than ordinary, Riches in Repute 'tis their Clothing.

Heads 7 and 10 Horns, ſhew'd of 7 Governments or Polities, and 10 Powers or Kingdoms.
Vid. *Head* in *Humane Body*.
3 *Turks*, 3 Powers or Kingdoms to war by.
Vid. *Snake* in *Poiſonous Creatures*.

Hearts and Heads of Beaſt, often ſhew Lords of Societies.
Horns and Claws of a Beaſt in general ſhew of Arms.
To a Prince his Gariſons.
In Scripture, Kingdoms and the Lambs of Chriſt

Having Bullocks a Woman ſeen, ſhew'd of a Woman glorying in her Eſtate.
Like a Buck, threats you beheading.
An Horſe or Aſs, threats you with mighty Labours.
Ox, Goat, or Sheep, threats you beheading
An Hog threats you beheading with Wickedneſs and Luxury.
See another with ſuch, he is in ſuch Danger.
To ſome it ſhews of Dominion and Royalty.
To ſome attaining to act beyond their own Power in State, as &c.
Creatures wanting them, ſhew of ſome Friend or Enemy diſarm'd.
With ſtrong and thick Horns ſhew of fooliſh Men.
Cats Claws cutting off, preventing the Deſign of a Thief.
Goats or Stags Horns finding, ſhews of ſome little Gain.
Improper Horſes ſeen with Horns, ſhew'd of Strength ill applied.
A Boar with Stag's Horns aſſaults A. his Enemy in Diſpute as ſtrong would hector his Senſe.
Ivory ſhews of Grandeur from its Uſe.
Short Horns, ineffectual Force.
Cow goring a Calf, a Landlord removing his Tenant.
Bulls cut off, ſome great Man Diſabled.
Seen with too many, threats Diſcord.
Goring you is very bad and worſe than kicking.
3 horn'd ſeen, ſhew'd of a Dominion ready for Conqueſt.
Part

Parts. Horns. Actions. Sounding an Horn, forbids Law-suits.

(4) Seeing threats of Hindrance or Peril of Life if against you, or else Aid.

Vessels of Horns shew of our Infirmities and publick Acts.

Find them, is good or bad, as is see them above.

Growing much, is Preparation for Fight.

Making the Handle of a Sword or Knife, Rapine us'd with Humanity.

Becoming Iron shews of Surety of its Power.

Gold or Silver, that is, efficacious as Mony.

Legs Horses seen spancel, shew'd of an able Estate Managery Friend at leisure.

Marrow of a Lion finding, shew'd A. soon growing Rich.

Milk wild Beasts drink or suck, become ravenous in unjust Gain as is the Beast.

If not ravenous, it threats you Despoilment as they.

Dogs sucking, threats with exceeding Calamities and Fears.

Drinking it, generally threats with Grief and Diseases.

Of Birds or Serpents, shews of vain Hopes but wicked.

Of Fish, shews of a rare Fortune, or Deceit by Flattery. Vid. also *Drink.*

Skin of a Lion having, gives you Victory over some great Man.

Finding, shews you'l grow soon rich.

Leopard have, vanquish some cruel Deceiver.

The same also, as is the Nature of other Beasts.

Ox-skins stinking being amidst, shew'd A. slighting Farm Services. Vid. also *Humane Body.*

Acts. Skinning of tame Beasts, shew'd of A. mending Domesticks.

As to Enemies it gives Victory and Disarming.

Putting on a Dragon's, that is, becoming reputed proud, cruel, and covetous.

So being hated, shun'd, fear'd and persecuted of all.

Tail Horse's or Asses seen deform'd, threats of a poor old Age.

Quite off seen, threats of hardest Miseries.

Mov'd by a Cat seen, shew'd of Treachery.

Teeth of Iron, that is, of a Power confounding and devouring all. Urine, vid. *Dung* suprà.

Place. Closet, vid. *Ox.*

Tiger seen in a Garden, shew'd A. of a furious Enemy obstructing his pleasant Plenty.

C H A P.

CHAP. XXVIII.

Of Beaſts-ſorts.

APES ſhew us of Malefactors, Imitators and Deceivers.
　　　　To ſome, of Thieves and Flatterers.
　　　　To ſome, Sadneſs and Diſorder of Mind.
　　　　To ſome, Perſons angry and Slanderers.
Tame keeping, living to a ſelf-fooling Luxury.
Devoured by a Lion ſeen, gave Recovery to the Sick.
Vid. *Monkey* infra.　　　Vid. *Baboon* infra.
Aſſes ſeen, ſhew us of Slaves and good Servants.
　　　　　- To ſome, of Riches.
　　　　To ſome, of Malice, Stubbornneſs and Ignorance.
　　　　To Courtiers, Trouble, Labour and Contempt.
Fat, Gladneſs thro Labour Gains.
Lean, Labour with Heavineſs of Mind.
Sitting on his Crupper ſeen, threats of grievouſeſt Laboriouſneſs,
　　even to Deſpair.
Striving or Fighting ſeen, the Strife of Enemies.
Deſiring one is as Riches, and threats Poverty.
Tail deform'd, Poverty in Age.
　　Cut off, Miſery *in futuro.*
Gentle, is good for Friendſhip and Obedience.
Wild, promiſes of good Fortune with Swiftneſs.
Hearing one bray, threats Damage.
Seen ſleep, ſhews of the Tedicuſneſs of Sickneſs.
Falling from him, threats Poverty or Sickneſs.
Burſting ſeen, threats of perpetual Poverty.
Kicking, ſhews of ſtubborn Servants, and vexatious Rents
Baboon in general, Vid. *Ape* ſupra, and *Monkey* infra.
　　　　To ſome, he ſhews the Falling-Sickneſs.
Badgers ſhew of Deceivers, as they are lame footed.
Beavers ſeen, ſhew of ſuch as abuſe themſelves.
Bears, ſhew to ſome Men fooliſh, angry and ruſtick.
　　　to ſome an Enemy ſneaking, to the braver Lion.
　　　to ſome, the Wiſe Sickneſs, and Return from Travel.
Taken by him, ſhews Gain.
Seen with his young, threats of ſome furious Aſſaulter.
's Whelps ſeen alone, promiſe of Change for the better.
In Scripture, it ſhew'd a ſluggiſh Government rich and bold.
In publick Prophecy, it ſhews of *Germans* and Inlanders as there
　　bred moſt.
Great and lazy A. ſeeing fright him in his way, ſhew'd him
　　Vexation thro lazy Servants.
　　　　　　　　　　　　　　　　　　　　　　　Bears

ears Garden being in, that is, ſeeing, teaſing, &c. &c.
        Expecting Sport but none appearing, in vain, &c.
    2 A. ſaw paſs by her, ſhe gave way to an imperfect Surlineſs.

Boar, Vid. *Hog* infra.

Buck, Vid. *Deer* infra.

Bull, Vid. *Oxen* infra.

Camel ſhews of ill Men, Grief, Sadneſs and Death,
        to ſome, of Perſons crooked and perverſe.
        to ſome, mighty Aids in Labour, but withal ſolitary.
        to ſome, Princes from their Greatneſs, and ſo hard Jour-
            nies and Swiftneſs.
        to ſome, Diſeaſes from the Burdens they bear.
        to ſome, Patience, Abſtinence and long Life.
    Mounted thereon, threats you Straits and Confuſions, as in De-
    ſerts.
    She-one ſeen, has ſhewn of a Woman moſt wicked and deformed
        for his Wife.
            Have young by her, that is, ſuch another deformed by
                your Wife.

Cat ſhews to ſome, nimble Fellows, Thieves and Traitors.
        to ſome, Enemies, but not threatning your Life, and as to
            Houſe State only.
        to ſome, Adulterers and Harlots from caterwauling.
        to ſome, Melancholy and Sickneſs.
            ſo ſeen, with a Witch the worſe.
        to ſome, Houſe and Garden, Thieves ſtealing themſelves, and
            not letting others.
    Sorts. Tame having in Arms, ſhew'd *A.* commanding the Benefit of
        ſuch againſt Mice.
        Black one gnawing *A*'s Finger, foreſhew'd him Death by a
            Gangreen there.
    Acts. Caterwauling ſhews of Nightwalks, and ſtolen Love Plots.
        Eat his Fleſh, get a Thiefs Goods.
        Fight a Cat, proſecute a Thief.
            Kill him, hang a Thief.
        Have his Skin, have a Thief wholly in your Power.
        Moving her Tail ſeen, threats you with Treachery.
        Scratching you is ſore Sickneſs, Affliction or Diſgrace.
        Seen catch two Hares which ſhe skinned, to an Houſwife re-
            turn 2 ſwift Journies in a day.

Chameleon ſeen, ſhews of ſome Hypocrite.

Civet-Cat, ſhews of one of horrible ill manners.

Cows, Vid. *Oxen* infra.

Crocodile ſeen, threats from Pirats, Robbers and Murderers.
        to all, of Perſons Knaviſh and merciles.
        to ſome, Danger of Deſtruction.
        to ſome, an unhappy Iſſue or Offspring.

Coneys, Vid. *Rabbits* infra.

                                                    Deer

Deer in general, ſhew as the Hart and Stag, but leſs.
Vid. Stag infra.   Vid. Hunt in Diverſion.

Kill your ſelf, be Maſter of a good Trade, hazard Profit.
In a Park, ſhew'd of an Husband and Wifes Authority diſput
Chaſe, to Lovers threats of croſs Expectations.
     Kill'd by a Lion ſeen, ſhew'd of an hazard Gain bro
       to a Certainty.
Tame having, ſuch a Profit ſtrangely at eaſy Command.
     Leading A. near thro a Palace, to the Command o
      royal Approach.
Dogs in general ſhew of Faith, Society and Security, as alſo Serv
      for Cuſtody, &c.
     To ſome, the Fever Quartane.
     To Princes, Soldiers.
        Foreign ſent him, that is, ſuch Soldier
       To many, if great Enemies, powerful, furious
         ſlanderous, for they can kill.
         And ſo black and menacing, if great, h.
         ſhewn Death.
Property, your own ſhews of your Servants, Bayliffs and Frie
        Unknown, the ſame in Circumſtance un
        countable.
        Left on things, Affairs left to ſuch Perſ
        Cares.
        Standing by A. catch'd his Arm, on bla
        his Servant warn'd off.
     Anothers, ſhews of infamous Servants, of Enemies
        Overture.
        Barking at you, ſuch Enemies Inſults in Fa
     No Owner Servants in a Senſe, and yet not abſolute
     but elſe baſe, as, &c.
Colour white, ſincere and open Friends and Enemies.
     Red, angry and cruel, but not quite open, &c.
     Black, malicious, ſecret and unknown Enemies, &c.
     Various, deceitful and horrible, &c.
     Green or ſtrange, colour'd Men of ſtrange Manners.
Acts. Aſſaulted by a great black one, ſhew'd Death and Deſpai
      Purſuing you, the Danger of an Enemy.
      Others yours ſeen, ſhews you of En
      mies overthrown.
     Tearing your Clothes, Infamy with Injury.
     By one chain'd, a reſtrain'd Enemy threatning.
Barking others hearing, threats you with Slander.
     Own heard, ſhews you of the Approach of Enemi
Biting, threats with Injuries and Aches.
     To ſome, alſo Accuſations.
Dropping his into Water, ſhew'd A. in Trouble thro offer
   ing his Servant to another.
Dogs

Acts. Fawning on you, threats you with Craft from his Master.

Yours seen, shews of your keeping a good House.

Flying from them, avoiding Calumny and Reproach.

Giving them large Cheese Parings, Prodigality to ill Men.

Going to Chace, gives Imploy.

Returning thence abates Fear, but stops Work.

To Men in Law, it shews of hard Prosecutions.

Hearing, Vid. *Bark* supra.

Howling, threats with Grief.

Leap, Vid. *Assault* supra.

Playing with one, a good sign, the Favour of Adversaries.

Pursuing, Vid. *Assault* supra.

Tear, Vid. *Assault* and *bite* supra.

Chain'd, Vid. *Assault* supra.

Parts. Milk of Bitches drinking, threats Ills, Fears, and Enmities.

Flesh Dogs eating, foreshews Riches.

Kinds. Greyhounds coursing, swift Assaulters as to Interest.

Hounds, to Prodigals shew their Haunters.

You hunt, you so design, *& è con.*

Hunting, shews of a laid Pursuit or Law Suit.

With Noise, with Calumny, great Heat and Eagerness.

An Hare, a disputable lesser Gain in hazard.

A Stag a greater, *&c.*

Houshold one's seen, have foreshewn of Servants and Farms to come.

Hunters to some, Examiners swift and cruel.

Lap-Dogs, shew of Friendly Praters with Delight and Pastime.

Piss House ones, a self-confounding Finery.

Dipping one in Water, shew'd giving a nice Gentlewoman Physick.

A. saw his kill his Goose, he let his Pleasure destroy of his hard Services.

Pulling off his right Wing only, diverting a Dependance thereon.

Vid. *Lying carnally* in *Bodily Action.*

Mad Dogs shew of violent pernicious Men, but not lasting.

Bit by one, foreshew'd of a drunken fit.

Mastiffs, open and able Assaulters.

Playing at a Bull, shew'd of an Husbandry accus'd.

No keeping one for wild Beasts, shew'd *A.* his Enemies daunting, his Friends serving him.

Monstrous great and with fiery Eyes seen enter *A*'s Chamber, Death. *Cerberus.*

Dogs.

Dogs. Kinds. Spaniel seen trample on an Altar, shew'd of a sneaking Conscience.

        Setters, shew of Enemies waiting Advantages.

Elephant shews of a good Prince, but a wicked Woman.

        To some, Sorrow.

        To some, Men wise and powerful, grateful and kind.

        To some, Fear and Danger with Shipwrack.

        To some, Frights, Sickness and slow Affairs, but very great.

        To some, Men endued with good Manners.

    Mounted on one, Death.

    Kill'd by one, shew'd Death.

        one seen, shew'd of Grief without hurt.

    Being in its Belly, shew'd Death.

    Frighted by one, shew'd A. Sickness.

    Giving one to drink, shew'd A. waiting on a great Lord to advantage him.

Ferret seen, shews of some treacherous and irreformable Person.

Fox shews you of some common Female Enemy hurting you by Deceit.

        To some, of a little subtle Enemy lying in wait.

        To some, Deformity from his Skin.

        To some, Pains in the Belly.

    Seen in Holes, is good to Students of Secrets.

    Chain'd, threats of Prisons.

    Fight one, overcome some wary crafty Enemy.

    Breed one, support in your self a Method to crafty Gain.

    Tame see, discover some wary and crafty Dissembler.

        Having at your Home, that is, such a cheating Domestick.

        So a common Thief, as a Mouse and Weesel a Domestick one.

Goats in general shew as Sheep and Rams, but worse, and less beneficially.

        To some they shew of Plenty to follow.

        To some they shew strong Men, but foolish and stubborn.

        To some, Patience.

        To Navigators they threat with Rocks.

        To some, a cukolding Wife.

        To some, the Captain of a Ship.

    Bucks seen, to many shew of Happiness to follow.

    Young Kids seen, shew of Comfort.

    She-one seen, has threated of being rob'd.

Hart, Vid. Stag infra.

Hare shews of Fear, Softness, and all Evils to Death.

    So as the Stag also, but less.

    To some he shews of the Stone in the Bladder, or the Falling-Sickness.

    's hinder Legs as largest A. seeing, shew'd of his considering of Flight.

                                           Har

Hare, become one see your Son, that is, he becomes swift, fearful, or a
  Sodomite.
Hunting, to some shews of Melancholy or Taverning.
    With Hounds, a Dispute on Pleasure or Profit offering little,
      but eager.
        In your Field, peculiar as to your own Ma-
          nagery Right.
          1 follows 2 in Couples, 1 embraces, t'other not.
Leveret killing, stifling Inquiries in the *Embrio.*
Catching 2 and skinning them, shew'd *A.* of travelling 2 Journies
  swiftly.
Hedg-Hogs, shew us of passionate and fleering Time-servers.
Hogs seen, shew of Deformity, Gluttony and Idleness.
    To some, an unhappy Death thro Luxury.
    To most, at least Sickness thro Luxury and Laziness.
    To Royal Favourites they threat Disgrace.
  Headed and bristled as one seem, that is, live and die like
    one (their Clothes.)
  Hogs Trough, shew'd of the necessary House.
  Hogshead taken from one, shew'd him of his Gifts being
    rejected.
      Presented her by her Sweet-heart, to a Woman
        shew'd her she'd hate him as abominable.
Sorts. Barrow-Pigs as for fatting only, shew of *Epicureans.*
    For Persons they shew Collectors and Treasurers.
      So also Boys kept for Pleasure.
  Sow seen, shews of Fruitfulness, and of having many young.
    Breeding Pigs is Profit.
    Farrowing is to Perfection.
    Having in his Backside, shew'd *A.* of a Profit great
      enough to keep one, new found.
Sucking Pig biting *A.* shew'd him of Death immature thro
    Luxury.
    Seen killed after, for all Endeavours for Cure.
    Invited to eat, shew'd *A.* of a Rent paid next
      day.
Boar wild, to the Traveller Tempest and Shipwrack.
    to the Pleader, a strong and noisy Adversary.
    to the Plowman Sterility and Waste.
    to the Batchelor, a scolding Wife.
    With great Tusks, the Enemy the terribler.
    Goaring *A.* threated him Death by one bearing
      that Arms.
    With Stags Horns seen against *A.* shew'd him his
      Opponent would hector his Sense by Strength.
Acts. Gor'd by a Boar, kill'd by one bearing that Arms.
  Bit by an Hog, shew'd *A.* of cleaning a dirty way.
  Eating Ducks and Geese seen, shew'd of Servants spoil'd by
    hard Laws.   Hogs.

Hogs. Acts. Waſting a Garden, ſhew'd of Error and Hereſy.

          to others, ſhew'd of a careleſs waſtful Managery.

Dealing in them by way of Trade, threats Sickneſs.

12 Hogs A. ſeem'd to keep, that is, a numerous Train of Oxen to make Dung.

Seen on his Dunghil, ſhew'd A. of his ordinary Husbandry lucky.

Putting up a fatting, ſhew'd A. of making Preparation for a Dunghil.

Waſhing Diſhes for them, ſhew'd of ſucceſsful-mean Preparations.

Sheering them threats Damage.

Killing one, diſpoſing of a good Dunghil.

        's Fleſh eating; to the Rich, Proſperity ; to the Poor, Riches.

Kicking, that is, affronting ſullen, baſe Perſons.

Horſe in general, as rode, ſhews of our Wife, Friend, Tenant or Art.

And as well mounted; ſo under Command.

To ſome, ſo their Eſteem, Strength, Art or Fortune, &c.

Deſiring or borrowing, ſhews of wanting Riches.

As poſſeſt and in a Stable, Riches.

To ſome, he ſhews of their Conſcience and Religion.

To ſome, he ſhews Flight.

Literal, Vid. *Grammar.*

Many ſeen, declare of Gains according; or Hopes to follow.

But walking confuſedly has ſhewn of Trouble of Mind thro Confuſion in Arts, &c.

Kind. Horſes, ſhew Riches to a generous Nobleſs, as Oxen with Labour.

Geldings ſeen, have ſhewn of Accuſations.

        to others, Damage and Secrets to be reveal'd, as to Riches.

Colt jeer'd as not knowing, that is, cenſured as ignorant in the Myſtery of Riches, or Art in its firſt Riſes.

Mare well harneſſed coming into A's Houſe, ſhew'd him marrying a rich Wife.

Ill ſhapen with nothing, a Concubine with nothing.

Quality. Adorn'd, in ſplendid State.

Deform'd, mean and humble.

Fair, noble.

Fat, rich.

Gentle, with quietneſs.

Halting, threats of Affairs obſtructed.

Pacing, riding, gives a happy Life and ſucceſsful Affairs.

Pack-horſe paſs by, exceed your Formal Eſtate Methods, &c.

                                  Horſe.

Horse. Quality. Sadled seen, shews of Labour and like, as, &c.

Secure, with Safety.

Sick, evil.

Strong, good.

Stumbling, shews of an hazardous Fortune.

Tall, a stately Tenant, &c.

Tired, to a Lover has threatned Despair.

Unruly, shews unruly.

Well hors'd, that is, with a firm Assurance, as, &c.

Wild riding, succeeding in Government, but cast on't to Disgrace.

To some, Affairs of great Temerity.

To some, Success in desper a Affairs.

Held by the Main, at desperatest Difficulties therein.

Wincing, with Trouble.

Parts. Footed like one, shew'd A. Knighthood.

Hair'd or Headed as one seeming, is Servitude to all; their Clothes their Repute.

Hoof without, disarm'd, as, &c.

Tail fair having, gives an happy Issue of Affairs in Age.

ill, threats of Friend or Art failing at a dead lift.

Colour. White, to some Joy and a fair Wife.

to some, Good and Prosperity.

to some, Danger and Death if palish.

Racing on with the Dead, Death.

to some, Uncertainty.

to some, an innocent Friend.

seen or rode on alike, but rode is surest Command.

Bay as the Red below.

Black, threats of Sadness, and a Wife debauch'd.

to some, a Friend contrary.

to some, a rich Fortune, but with Strife.

Red, Prosperity; but with Contention and Trouble.

Grey as white, but less.

Roan, Prosperity.

Divers colour'd, to most, Deceit.

to some, Expedition of Business.

Furniture. Housing old and ugly, the graceful Managery of your Art ill.

Saddle fine A. wanting to visit with, shew'd him in Care for a Friend to blazon him.

A saddled Horse seen, shews of Labour.

Pillion carrying, fool'd in your Interest by others.

to others, your Friend serves others on your Account.

The dead behind you, threats you Death.

N Horse.

Horſe-Furniture. Pillion carry his Mother in Law who alighted firſt and
      he after, to *A.* a Daughter born at his Wife's Re-
      queſt, chriſtned her Mothers Name.
      Side-Saddle given a Woman, ſhew'd her of a good
      Horſe ſo at her Command.
Property your own, Vid. *Grammar.*
      Hors'd Servant ſeem'd to have, that is, a
      Friend to aid in Perſon and Eſtate.
      Anothers, Vid. *Ride* infra.
      Horſemen in the Revelations ſhew'd of Empe-
      rors.
      Among another's *A.* ſeem'd ſafe, that is, his
      Eſtate Managery hurt *A.* not.
      Others ride by while you on Foot, your Failure
      their Glory.
Bound and kill'd ſeen, Service by them put off for their Impo-
      tence.
Dead or kill'd, is every way unfortunate.
Dead, Vid. *Kill* infra.   Deſcend, Vid. *Ride* infra.
Falling, Vid. *Ride* infra.   Force, Vid. *Spur* infra.
Going freely, promiſes of Succeſs in Affairs.
Harneſs *A*'s own ſeen out of, ſhew'd of his being lock'd up
      without due Care.
Kicking you, Injury and Damage from ſome Man at Arms.
      till the Blood come, to great Loſs.
Kill'd Ox bound ſeen, ſhew'd of Service put off for their Impo-
      tence.
      Dead ſeen is generally unfortunate.
Led yok'd ſeen down Stairs, ſhew'd to a Maid hard Service.
      about, a mean Command of a Friend, but not as if rode.
Lent out, ſhew'd of a Tenant turn'd off.
      Saddle nor, the Eſtate kept in hand, and not let out again.
      Unruly till whip'd, ſuch Tenant ſo till ſued at Law.
Looſing him, ſhews of ſome good Advantage irrecoverable.
      In a Field, an Eſtate, &c. put to Diſpute.
      Frighting away as on a Frolick, unexpected-
      ly irrecoverable.
Mired. your Art or Eſtate at a fooliſh *nonplus.*
Mounted well *A.* his Horſe would not ſtir, an Inferior humblee
      but not obedient.
      And rode, commanded to Action.
Place, Vid. *Looſe* ſupra.
Piſſing. an Eſtate eas'd in Expence.
Prepar'd for the Race ſeen, has ſhew'd of Death.
Running, gives Proſperity and Deſires accompliſh'd.
      away with you, ſhews of unruly Inferiors.
      to others, unexpected Buſineſs diverting.
      On a white Horſe, Death.

               Hor

Horse riding in general shews of Command and change of Counsel.

So of our Art, Friend, Wife or Ship, as &c.
Vid. *Ride* and *Race* in *Travel*.

Manner. Behind as a Woman, be fool'd to others Command.

A fat fair one in a pleasant Place, Gain without Dispute.

Another's without Consent, threated A. catch'd in Adultery.

A Physician's, designing in a lame Business, or that will want Remedy.

A Soldier's, gives Recovery from Banishment.

To some be aided by a Stranger.

And sick on't, being stately and vex'd for it.

Place, thro a Town, heals the Sick.

To a Champion a Prize.

Out of Town, *è con.*

On the Seaside, in profitable and popular Designs.

Over a Man, designing with flight to some rational Course.

What mischief he does, such as in revenge ensues thro such neglect.

Her Master's Faggot-mow, to a Servant Imbezlement.

His Horse turn'd to a Tree, shew'd A. his Creditor died.

Descending voluntarily, quitting a good Hit.

Flung off, with Hopes of Recovery.

Lead him, still keep at Service Command.

Falling Man and Horse, Life and Fortune in danger.

Into Water, the Man and his Art in Trouble, &c.

But get out, avoid it.

In full speed, the mischief thro your own fault and hurry.

Off and breaking his Neck A. seeing his Ancestor, and his Horse coming to him, the Heir who mounted, shew'd A. of inheriting him dying.

Standing spancel, vid. *Legs* in *Beast-parts*.

Sliding fear, that is, be in terror of Dishonour, as &c.

Spurring your Horse, gives you Honour for Endeavours.

Wheels seen with no one riding, shew'd of a Carriage business.

Wanting is as Desire of Honour and Riches, and shews Contempt.

Yok'd led down stairs, shew'd of Maids put to hard improper Service.

Kid, vid. *Goat* supra.　　　　Lamb, vid. *Sheep* infra.

Leopards shew of swift and cruel Devourers by Deceit.

To some noble and adorn'd great Enemies.

To some Persons kind, but wicked and faithless Lyers in wait.

To some Strangers, Sickness, Fear, and sore Eyes.

Linx as the Leopard.

Lion

Lion in general ſhews of Princes and Great men noble and magnanimous.
>To ſome deſtructive Appetites menacing, but with Nobleſs and Gallantry.
>To ſome he ſhews of Strength and Valour.
>In oppoſition to Dragons, perverſe and Popiſh Tyrants.

Gentle ſeen, gives Good from ſome Superior of great Command.
>Be with in your Room, be uncontrolable in your Converſe, as &c.
>Carried by him, protected of ſuch an one.
>Fawning on you, ſome Great man's Favour.

Wild threats with Fire, Sickneſs, or ſome great Oppreſſor.
>Biting you, your Prince devouring you.
>>The Damage irretrievable.
>Defended from by your Miniſter, your Conſcience ſcreening you from ſuch Danger.
>Tearing you with his Claws, oppreſſing you to Ruin.
>Flinging you down, he takes away your Honour.
>>Beating out your Teeth, killing your Kindred.

Prepar'd to fight one ſeen, ſhew'd of a man ready for a Diſpute, or a deſperate Reſentment.

Killing and taſting his Fleſh, hazardouſly enrich'd by your Prince.
>>To a Prince devour his Enemies.
>Eat his Bowels, command his Secrets and Riches.
>Carrying his Skin, cheriſh'd by his Authority.
>Having his Claws, defended by his Guards.

His Young, ſhews of ſuch a Great man or Prince's Son.

Lioneſs as the Lion, but leſs and by Women.
>To ſome ſhe threatens Crimes and Accuſations.
>Seen with Whelps gave Felicity to a King in his Queen and Children, and as if ſo potent in ſelf-proviſion.

Manteager is greatly as the Monkey, but a more terrible and beſtial Counterfeit of a reaſonable Courſe.
>Eſcaping his Rape to a Woman, that is, a Thraldom according.

Monkey, vid. Ape ſuprà.

Moles ſhew us of men blind by Folly, as alſo Prieſts and Plotters.
>To ſome of Funerals.
>To ſome Blindneſs indeed.
>To the Secret Self-diſcovery.

Hills digging, enquiring into ſecret Prophecies.
>Seen above ground, ſhews the Secret of your Buſineſs diſcover'd, &c.

Mouſe in general, an unfaithful Domeſtick.
>>So a Thief and Tenant's Servant in Houſe with you.
>Too big-bellied to run into an hole, too proud to ſtoop to you.
>Playing, a truanting but not wronging Servant.
>In publick Prophecy he ſhews Mountaineers.

Mouſe

Moufe biting and tickling A. Fellow-members of a Society teafing A.

   Great one dying it ceas'd, the Prefident dying it ended.

Mules to fome fhew of Wives and Maids from their Tendernefs.

    White, fair.

    Black, ufeful.

    Mix'd, cunning.

  To fome Malice, and foolifh Imaginations.

  To fome Baftards and Divorces.

  To fome Difappointment in doubts.

  To fome Sicknefs, and Genitals failing.

  To Husbandry Good, great Labour, and long Life.

  To fome Barrennefs or Celibacy as to Procreation Crofs.

Run from him A. feeing another's he rode, freed him from a baftard Change.

   To a Stranger by chance.

  To his right Owner, the true Father.

Bringing forth feen, to the Happy Mifery.

    to the Miferable Happinefs unexpected.

Riding one, fhews you in a Bufinefs flow but fafe.

   Ambling or pacing, threats of Miferies and Croffes.

Wild or mad feen, threats you with Deceit in your Houfe.

Lofe one, if fuch as you have Lofs.

   If not, Delivery from great Trouble.

Oxen in general fhew of our main Subfiftence State, as Sheep of our lefs, and that in Labour as an Horfe in Plenty.

  Horns, vid. *Beafts-parts* in general.

  Oxskins ftinking paffing by, difmiffing ufelefs Farm-fervices as otherwife commanded.

Calf affaulted by, new farming Effays menacing.

  Own paffing by, leaving Effays to farm full out.

  Kill, vid. *Butcher* in *Trade*.

Cows feveral feen with a Bull, fhew'd A. of a good Farm Profit near.

  Saying to a Calf, I'll gore him, fhew'd of a Land-lord removing his Tenant.

Bull feen without Hoof or Horn fhews of fome one dif-arm'd.

  In general he fhews of plain rich Men, as Farmers, *&c.*

  Purfuing you, fome great Enemy threatning.

   Can't efcape him, be at fuch ones mercy.

   Efcaping from, fhew'd A. thriving well by Farming.

    To a Maid marrying above a Farmer.

  Baited to be Rabble following, fhew'd of a Great man expos'd.

  To Mariners he has fhewn of Hurt from Tempeft or the Top-maft.

         Oxen

Oxen in publick Dreams fat give a plentiful Year.

Lean ones threat a Famine.

Black menace of Danger.

3 or many horn'd, a Dominion weak by Diſcord.

Dead ſeen, threats of ſome very great Plague.

Sleeping or lying down ſeen, have ſhewn of ſome publick Calamity.

In private Dreams fat and chearful ſeen, they give plentiful
Rent.

Lean ſhew of Want.

Black carried by, ſhew'd A. Danger of Sick-
wreck.

Having to ſell and a Chapman offering, ſhew'd
A. of a Rent paid.

Lean paſſing by to the right, ſhew'd A. plowing better with Horſes.

Kill'd ſeen, threats Danger.

Lying down ſeen, ſhew'd of an Horſe's Death.
To others Deſpair in their greateſt
Support.

Place. A. feeding out of his Cloſet, ſhew'd him of
maintaining his Plow by project Husbandry.

A. ſeeing ſtand by his Bed-ſide, ſhew'd of his
farming well even in Lazineſs.

Acting ſeen in general is very good.

Aſſaulting you, an ill buſineſs, Hopes of Gain hurting.

Carried by one dangerouſly againſt his Will, ſhew'd A.
menace of Shipwreck.

Climbing an Hill ſeen, very good, ſuch Profit in advance.

Feeding them, ſhews of the Purchaſe of ſome good
Farm.
To others ſhews of ſome happy Plenty.

Fighting mutually, ſome great buſineſs Inconſiſtency in
Gain.

Hooking with the Horns, worſe than kicking.

Kicking you, Oppreſſion and Hurt by Great men.

Going to Water ſeen, a bad Sign.

Labouring ſeen is ſtill good, but in Herd Peril from Great
men.

Mowing heard, threats of Strife.

Playing gives Plenty.

Plowing gives Gain.

Running ſeen, is Joy thro Plenty.

Sitting on a white one, gives a quiet good Advance.
Vid. *Carried* ſuprà.

Standing ſeen is very good, and as lying down is bad.

Taming ſhews of great Sorrow.

Threatning is as Peril from Great men.

Oxen

Oxen acting. Sleeping feen is very bad, and is as Plenty diverted a while.

    Trampling on you, threats you as a Slave to Slaves.

    Yok'd, vid. *Domestick Action.*   Vid. *Grammar.*

Panther, vid. *Leopard* fupra.

Rabbits feen play about on Sea-cliffs, shew'd of Robbers.

    To Students in Secrets is good.

    Dead, shew'd *A.* of rancorous Swellings gone.

      Coath'd, shew of fuch Swellings broke.

    Keeping in Orchard that hide, following Courfes in Stock or Learning that you dare not own.

    Without Burroughs hunting with a Dog, shew'd *A.* of aflaulting Shufflers as without excufe.

Ram, vid. *Sheep* infra.

Rats shew to us of our Servants, and 'tis good to fee them play.

    Dead shew of Servants fick, or their Service laid by.

    Bold shew of fuch Servants prefumptuous.

    Gnawing a Box, Servants imploy'd to no Profit.

    Catch'd by a Cat, anger at them for loitering.

    Fat feen, shew'd of great Wafts rectifyable by Care.

Satyr *Alexander* purfuing, shew'd his making a Wildernefs of *Tyre* (Sa *Tyre*)   Vid. *Born in Bodily Action.*

Sheep shew of the lefler Plenty of the Earth, as Oxen of the greater.

    Many feen whether our own or others is good.

      Give Advance, *&c.* but feen sheer'd is beft.

    To all Plenty, and if feen orderly is excellent to Schoolmafters.

      But Profit with Tedioufnefs as Oxen great.

        White, Good.

        Red, Strife.

        Black, Death and Ignominy.

      In a Field, Plenty in fome Difpute of Husbandry offering.

    In a publick Dream they have shewn of Subjects.

Acts. Seen, shew of a lefler Plenty with Care, as *&c.*

      Feeding in a Vineyard, shew'd of Wafte and Lofs of Goods.

      Jumps o'er your Fence, you lofe fome Property you poffefs'd.

    Sheering, to fome shews Difeafes, and if black, Death.

      to fome Gain by Arts, and teaching Children.

      to fome Profit by Government, if well perfected.

      done, ruins all thefe Hopes.

    But shorn feen, threats Damage.

Ram shews of the King or Mafter.

    To fome the General of an Army.

    To fome the having Wives that are Whores.

        Sheep.

Sheep. Ram brought skin'd into an Houſe, ſhew'd of one dying in the Family.

Running at you, check'd by your Prince.

Seen, to ſome the Diſcord of Neighbours.

Ride him, and lie on his Horns, marry an Whore.

Lamb ſhew'd of the meek Kingdom of Chriſt.

Otherwiſe they are as Children.

Sleeping ſeen, is very bad.

Seeing them, gives of Comfort or Increaſe.

Feeding them or bringing them to Slaughter, threats great Torment.

's Fleſh ſeen to be ſold in Shambles, ſhew'd A. of a Divorce by Sentence.

to others it ſhew'd of a publick Proſtitute in Family.

Squirrels in general ſhew of mimick Juglers and Rope-dancers.

Hunting one and trying to find his Neſt, ſhew'd A. of trying to live by tricking, an unſettled inconſiderable Livelihood.

Stag ſhews moſtly of great Gain thro Subtlety and Hazard, as Gaming and Merchandize, &c. and as the Ox plain Profit.

To ſome long Life, and a known Whore a Husband.

To ſome a Great man, but cowardly and impotent, and as if ſaid fit for a great Prey,

To ſome he ſhews of the State of Shipping.

To ſome he threats Fears, &c. and with an Harp to Deſtruction.

But then to be one or ſit on one, is worſt of all.

Seeming one, to a Batchelor ſhew'd of living long in fear and doubt.

Breeding a young one, ſhew'd of Fornication with a Servant.

Horn finding, Gain tho but little, and that trading and hazardous.

Seen put between Oxen and Horſes, ſhew'd A. of merchantly poizing their Strength to their happy Plow-uſe.

Hunted by Unknown ſeen, ſhew'd A. of odd Courſes tranſacting in his Merchandize.

You falling before him, your Intereſt failing thereby.

Hurting you, Miſchief thro ſuch Courſes.

Down to ſtand for you, Aſſurance of Gain in ſuch Purpoſes.

Stood over A. down, ſhew'd A. oppreſſed by ſuch Venturers.

Kill and eat his Fleſh, or have his Skin or Head, inherit an old Man.

To a _Jew_ treſpaſs the Law.

To others vanquiſh ſome deceitful timorous Enemy.

Riding one, acting all in fear,

Stag

Stag. Running one seen, gives Subtlety of Spirit as by Merchandize.

Tygers shew of fierce eager able Enemies for Gain, forcing even to Death if press'd.

Setting on you, such an Enemy designing as is the Place.

So as the Lion also, but less generous and more active and furious, and an Enemy of the meaner sort.

Vear circling *A*'s Neck, not biting her, shew'd *A.* secure against Mice, that is, ill Servants as lazy, *&c.*

Unicorn is a Symbol between a Stag and an Horse.

Weesel seen, threats with some greater domestick Thief.

Driving from a Chimney Corner, shew'd of rectifying of Wood-wastes.

To some a bad Wife, Death, or Gain, *&c.*

Wolf shews some cruel and sordid Enemy openly hunting us.

To some he has threated of being rob'd in Travel.

To some he shews of the Year, and our State of Store-hay, *&c.* as against Winter.

To some he shews Menaces from Princes and High-way-men.

Fighting, contending with some furious sordid Enemy.

Killing the biggest of 4, shew'd of overthrowing 4 in a Lawsuit.

Riding, commanding or using, such an ill Course or Person.

Biting you, an open Enemy damaging you, as *&c.*

Sleeping, an open Enemy at present at least not to be fear'd.

CHAP. XXIX.

Of Birds.

IN *general* shew of Hopes with a swift Performance.
(1)   So of Hopes projective and not stable as Beasts.
Vid. *Creatures* in general.

Generally of Futurities.

As in size, so the Business.

Dead shew of vain Hopes.

To some also they shew of sudden Journeys.

Become one and fly into Heaven, gives Preferment on a projective Effort.

A Flight of them shew'd Law-suits.

Numbers of them, multitudes of things, as Suns, Days, Years, *&c.*

Colour. White, of good Omen.   Ashcolour, Sadness.
Black, ill.   Yellow, Anxiety and Jealousy.
Various, changeable. Brown Grief and Trouble.

In

In general. Colour. Red, Anger and Revenge.
(1)　　　　　Sooty, threats of Pain and Cruelty.
　　　　　Sky, great but diverſe.
　　Docible as Parrots, are good if well taught, if not, Fatigue.
　　　　　Prating Magpye keeping, ſhew'd *A.* keeping a ſcan-
　　　　　　dalous prating Servant.
　　Domeſtick ſeen, in fatal Dreams threats of Death untimely.
　　Fat catching, gives Gain projective.
　　Fearful, as Doves and Sparrows ſeen, is ill.
　　Gentle, as Peacocks and Swans ſeen, ſhew great Good,
　　　　Honour and a quiet Life.
　　Great ſeen, is good to the Rich, *&c con.*
　　　　　　　　In general ſhew Buſineſs and Perſons according.
　　　　　Small ſhew of trifling Hopes.
　　Handſom as the Peacock and Parrot ſeen, ſhew of Grace.
　　　　　Fair, powerful.
　　Home Birds live not out half their time, vid. *Domeſtick* ſupra.
　　Little, Vid. *Great* ſupra.
　　　　　And fat ſeen, to the Poor is good.
　　Multitudinary, as Storks and Locuſts ſeen, ſhew of Tem-
　　　　peſts and Enemies.
　　　　　Social as Pigeons, give of good Correſpondence.
　　　　　Vid. *Solitary* infra.
　　Noiſy ſhew of Dangers.
　　　　Quiet hinder Buſineſs.
　　　　Chattering that can't be catch'd, Contention,
　　　　　　　Soon flying away, ſoon quieted.
　　　　Vid. *Sing* infra.
　　Night-birds ſeen in an Houſe, threat it Deſolation.
　　　　　　To ſome croſs Enterprize, but fearleſs.
　　　　　　To Travellers, Thieves, Tempeſts or Loſs.
　　　　　　Seen, do no buſineſs next day, and left you be-
　　　　　　　come expos'd as an Owl, *&c.*
　　Ravenous Birds ſeen, ſhew us of Riches and Honour with
　　　　Care.
　　　　　　to the Poor Slavery, to the Rich Gain.
　　　　　　Eating Victuals o'er the Head. *Pharaoh*'s Butler's
　　　　　　Fleſh.
　　　　　　Carrion-eaters in general ſeen, threat of Death.
　　　　　　Dung-eaters, as the *Upupa*, ſhew of Naſtineſs.
　　　　　　And Crows ſeen fly in dark and cloudy Weather,
　　　　　　　Anger, Loſs, and Miſery.
　　　　　　In fatal Dreams they threat with Famine, thro
　　　　　　　their crooked Bills in old Age.
　　Sea-fowl ſeen or eat, to Sailors is Danger of Shipwreck,
　　　　but with Eſcape.
　　　　　　Sitting on a Pine-tree ſeen, ſhew'd one to have a
　　　　　　Son a Ship-maſter.

In general. Sea-Fowl eaten, to some Gain from publick popular Offices.

(1)   To some they shew of deceitful Persons living by the Waters side.

If on things lost they are seen, 'twill never be found.

Seagulls seen coming, shew'd of foul Weather approaching.

Singing-Birds, Vid. *Noisy supra.*

seen, are good for Delight.

Chirping, to some a good Sign and Ease in Business.

to others, trifling in Impertinencies, as, *&c.*

Solitary as the black Sparow seen, shew Hopes subverted, and the more the worse.

Social seen is good in publick Business.

Vid. *Multitudinary supra.*

Summer Birds, as Swallows, Martins and Nightingales, seen, shew us of Joy near, but short.

Small, Vid. *Little* and *great supra.*

Water-Fowl in publick Prophecy, shews of Islanders,

Vid. *Sea-Fowl supra.*

Wild coming gently into your Arms, is good.

Ravenous seen enter your House, threats you of Wasters devouring you.

Fowl shooting at, that is, aiming at Projects.

Get great ones, project to good Advantage.

Tame play with, divert you as triflingly.

Eating out of your Mouth, to your Loss.

Young shew of Trouble with the Beginning of Hopes.

(2)   Your young Turkeys see killed, find your new commencing nice Services fool'd.

Cock seen tread an Hen, shew'd of a little Profit in a day or two.

Vid. *Chicken* in *Cock.*

Eggs in general, Vid. *Victuals.*

Few, little Gains and handy Profit.

Plenty, have shewn Care, Pains, Noise and Law Suits.

to others, Differences and many idle Words, the first Seeds of Projects.

Broken sign an ill Sign, the Destruction of some Project in the Embrio.

Ducks Eggs, as to noisy Services.

Eat by the Birds as soon as laid, quick Repentance.

An Ostriches himself, shew'd A. recovering a dangerous Debt.

Find 6 Turkey Eggs and 4 Goose Eggs, to a Servant attain to be a good plain, not a nice Servant.

Young

Young Eggs feeing them, to Dealers in them is good.
  (2)   to others, moftly Quarels and foolifh Words.
      Setting Domeftick ones, fhew'd of planting a Garden.
              With Trouble, fhew'd of weary Haymaking.
       On them Fowl feen, fhew'd of good Hopes thereon.
          Young obtaining, is as greater Hopes.
              But grown, beft.
Neft of fmall Birds having in hand, to fome fhews truanting.
    It with Eggs and take them, gives fure Gains.
    Found feeling cold, fhew'd to Lovers Separation by Death.
       With young ones, gives Joy and Wantonnefs.
     To Maids they fhew of a ripe Virginity.
          And if the Young gone, loft.
     Vid. *Squirrel in Beaft.*

Parts. Beak fhews of our Riches and Suftenance for Life as form'd.
  (3)   Seen in hopeful Pofture, promifes of future good Iffue in
      Bufinefs.
     Long Devourers feen, threats of a poor old Age.
     To a Prince his Towers, and fometimes Riches.
Claws feen made into the Handle of a Sword or Tool, Rapine
     become Induftry.
     To a Prince, his Garifons.
Feathers fhew us of our projective Hopes and Ornaments.
       So they fhew, as are the Birds and their Colours.
     Naked Birds fhew of Trouble.
     Peacocks, as to empty Ambition. Vid. *Peacock* infra.
     Eagles, cruel and ravening.
     Pyes, flandering.
     Crows, fordid and hateful.
     Parrots, trifling.
     White feen on ones Clothes, fhew'd of Gladnefs.
     Peacock feen in *A*'s way, fhew'd its Vanity fhould ftop
     A's Defigns.
     Plumes of Feathers feen, fhew'd of Amendment of Fortune.
     Vid. *Wings* infra.
Headlefs fhot inimical feen, fhew'd of crofs Overtures defeated.
Quills rob a Bird of, that is, a Rival of Adherents in his Pro-
     jects.
Tail long, gives a Perfon of Beauty and Credit.
Wings of an Eagle, gives Swiftnefs and long Command.
       Other Fowl, gives Swiftnefs with lefs Command.
     Pluck your Goofes, correct your Servant.
       Quite bare, with exceeding blame.
     2 Covering *Europe* and *Afia*, *Darius*'s Government.
     A winged Woman feen, fhew'd of this Angelick Science.
Actions. Bounds fhew of hindred Hopes.
  (4)   Caged feen, fhew of Security.
       But fome in fome out *Omens* of proud Difcords.
                     Actions.

Actions. Caged Magpy seen so, shew'd of a scandalous prating Servant.
(4)   Abusive, as who keeps it, and where it hangs.

      Discage a Bird, to a Virgin threated her Maidenhead.

Catching Wild-Fowl, to some a Cold.

           to some, if fat, a good projective Gain.

      Vid. *Game* in *Diversion.*

      Chattering heard not to be catch'd, shew'd of Contention.

      A Peacock, interrupting some glorious high Flyer.

      A Sparrow-Hawk, is Gain and Command.

      Eatable Birds, shews of Pleasure and Profit.

      Find a Birds Nest is a good Sign.

      Lime Twigs and Glue, shew of the Return of Fugitives.

      Nets shew of Tricks as set for or against you betwixt Enemies.

Chattering, Vid. *Noisy* in *sorts.*

Dead, Vid. *Victuals* and *Salt,* ibid.

      In general, shew of Hopes vanishing.

      Vid. *Bittern* infra.

      Duck reviv'd seen, shew'd of a pleasant lost Service thought recovered.

Eating seen, promises you an happy Increase of Affairs.

      So a projective Support got, as is the Bird.

      Eat by you, Vid. *Victuals.*

      a rotten Duck, patching up with scandalous Services.

      Meat o'er the Head, *Pharaoh's* Baker.

      Vomiting seen, threats with Loss.

Entering an House seen, threats Loss.

      Ravenous, so swift Wasters devouring you.

Fighting mutually seen, threats you with Grief and Loss.

      With Men, Vid. *Eagle* infra.

Flying, shew of swift Dispatch.

      To the Right, shews Dispatch and Happiness.

          Left, is Misery and Disappointment.

      Over you, Vid. *Raven* infra, and *Eagle.*

      Vid. *Fly* in *Air.*

      Crossing you, Vid. *Bittern* infra, and *Travel.*

      Before you, relates to Matters you shall see.

      Behind you, shews of things you shall hear of.

      Many seen, to some has shewn of sudden Journies and Wandring.

          Birds of Prey in dark and cloudy Weather, Anger, Loss and Misery.

Having in Hand or Lap, gives assured Gain or Command, as *&c.*

Loosing or letting go, shews Damage.

Noisy, Vid. *Sorts.*

Sing heard, gives Joy, Delight and Love.

Actions. Sing heard. But a Crow ſo, is of worſt Omen.
   (4)   Sitting on you, Vid. *Ravens.*
             On a Tree, Vid. *Tree.*
             On ones Head, to *Pharaoh's* Baker Death.
                  and pulling off the Hair, ſhew'd to *A.* an ill
                  Death.
   (5)   Speak, Vid. *Raven* infra.
Eat ſeen, ſhews of needy Folks, and Trouble in vain.
          to ſome, Thieves and Way-layers.
          to ſome, fearful and miſerable Iſſues, (Night-Bird.)
          to Women with Child, good, ſhe ſuckles.
Blackbird ſeen, threats you Trouble, but ending friendly.
   Sparrow, Vid. *S.* infra.
Bittern ſeen, ſhews of ſome clamorous great Man.
         to others, as the Owl and Night-Birds.
     Croſſing *A's* Court 2 ſeen, ſhew'd the Approach to his Converſe
         ſo upbraided.
             To the Right, with no ill Deſign.
             Shot in paſſing, his End fruſtrate.
             Brought into Houſe after headleſs, ſuch croſs
             Fate commanded.
Cock in general ſhews the Maſter, but in a projective fidle fadle State
     as a Bird.
         to ſome, ſhew uſeful Familiar.
     Seen in an Houſe is good to thoſe who would marry.
             to the Sick, Inflammation, Heat and
             Tears.
             to the Poor, Happineſs in Family Care.
     Crowing heard, is as Proſperity to the Maſter.
         Another's heard, and ſo he vapours you.
         An Hen or Capon heard, threats of Sadneſs or
         Trouble.
     Spurs handſom with good Dignity.
     Fighting, threats of Noiſe and Trouble.
     Treading an Hen in the Dirt, ſhew'd of a little Mort-
         gage Eſtate in Purchaſe.
Chicken heard crow, ſhew'd Joy.
Own Fowl *A.* ſeeing his pick up others waſt Corns, ſhew'd of
         his advantaging him by others.
             Pick up his own waſtfully, ſhew'd of his
             own Children waſting Victuals.
Hen and Chicken ſhew of the inferior Domeſticks, as Cock of
     the Maſter.
           Seen and no more, threat with Damage as Chil-
           drens Waſtes, &c.
Caught or heard cackle, ſhews of light Joy.
Seen lay an Egg, gives Gain.
Hen careful, Dove gentle, Duck verboſe, and a Gooſe a uſe-
     ful Domeſtick, &c.   Cock

Cock. Hen white feen on a Dunghil, fhew'd of Difgrace by falfe Accufations.
　　　　Turn'd to an Hen, being in Difquiet.
Cormorant feen, to a Seaman fhew'd Peril without Death.
　　　　to fome, they fhew Deceivers and wicked greedy
　　　　　Perfons.
　　　　to fome, their Friends and Whores.
　　　　Seen on a Lofs had, threats it irretrievable.
Crane feen, fhews as the Stork below, as alfo Vigilance.
　　　　to fome, poor Folks.
Crows, fhew to fome Expedition of Bufinefs.
　　　　to fome, long Delay in doing Matters, as long-liv'd.
　　　　to fome, the Thief and Adulterer.
　　　　to fome, wicked and double-tongu'd Folks.
　　　Dying feen, promifes of a very great old Age.
　　　Sing heard, is of worft *Omen*, as fhewing of Sorrow and Sadnefs.
　　　Fear being fhot as fuch on Seed Ground, fear Cenfure as care-
　　　　lefs of Children to their Ruines.
Didaper greatly, as the Cormorant above.
Dove, Vid. *Pigeon* infra.
Duck fhews of fome verbofe Man or Maid Servant.
　　　　So of projective trifling Services.
　　　　　　In Street, in publick Tranfactions.
　　　　So as the Goofe, but lefs.　Vid. *Goofe* infra, and *Cock* fupra.
　　　　Wild feen, much as the Cormorant.
　　Rotten eating, patching up and accommodating with rotten, re-
　　　fufe Services.
Eagle in general, fhews of Princes and Kingdoms, but then as in States
　　　　projective.
　　　　to fome, of open Robbers.
　　　State threatning, fhews fome great Man angry.
　　　Gentle, fhews of fome great Good.
　　　Dead feen, to Servants and Men in fear, the
　　　　Danger over.
　　　　　　to others, hindrance of Action.
　　Seen, to the ambitious Good and Glory.
　　　　to the fearful, Hurt and Confufion.
　　　　he gives Succefs quick, but bloody.
Carrying, Vid. *Mounted* infra.
Drawing out ones Bowels, and fhewing them at a publick Affem-
　　bly, gave a Man a Son after famous.
Falling on the Dreamers Head, Death.
Flying, fhews of Change of Country.
　　　　To fome, Return of Strangers.
　　　　Far gives Bufinefs an end, tho not foon.
　　　　O'er your Head, Honour.
　　　　By a Woman big, fhew'd her Child of Honour.
　Mounted and flying on his Wings, to Princes Death.

　　　　　　　　　　　　　　　　　　　　　　Eagle

Eagle. Mounted, to the Poor great Mens favour, and Travel with Profit
　　　　to others, Change of Country.
　　　　Sitting on high ſeen, to the Enterprizer Succeſs.
　　　　　　　　to Strays it gives Return.
　　　　Over your Head, threats you Death.
Ficedula ſeen, ſhews of Paraſites.
Gooſe ſeen, ſhews of ſome thriſty Man or Maid.
　　　　　To ſome, of Honour.
　　　Eat a fat one, profit you by a good Servant.
　　　　Vid. Duck and Cock ſupra.
　　　Hen a careful, Gooſe an able, Pigeon a familiar, and Duck a
　　　　verboſe Houſe-Mate.
　　　Pluck his Wing, correct him.
　　　　　Quite bare, with exceeding great Blame.
　　　Seeing a Lap-Dog pluck off his right Wing, ſhew'd A. of lay
　　　　ing by Service for Pleaſure.
Gripe ſeen, to Potters, Tanners and Leather-Sellers is good.
　　　　　to Phyſicians and Patients 'tis bad.
　　　　　to ſome, it threats of Thieves.
　　　　　to ſome, ill Perſons dwelling abroad, and dangerous to all
Hawks ſeen, gives Succeſs as the Eagle, but leſs.
　　　　　to ſome, a violent Taker.
　　　　　to ſome, the Prieſthood or Nobility, as the Eagl
　　　　　Kingdom.
　　　　　to ſome, an open-Enemy, as a Kite a ſly one.
　　　Sort. Sparrow-Hawk catching, gives Gain.
　　　　　Falcon ſeen wild, ſhew'd of Thieves and Robbers.
　　　2 Hawks on a Seal, promis'd of Marriage with great Happineſs
　　　Hawking, profitable Projection of Deſigns at diſtance.
　　　　Hawk held in hand, gives ſure Succeſs.
　　　　　　Carried on your Fiſt walking, ſhews Honour.
　　　　　　Flying away ſeen, threats a Prince greatly.
　　　　　Catch an Heathpoult with one, get a Reverſion, &c.
Heathpoult catching by an Hawk, ſhew'd of getting a Reverſion, &c.
Hen, Vid. Cock ſupra.
Heron ſeen, threats Sadneſs, as a fighting and retiring Bird.
Jays, ſhew of needy Folks with Trouble in vain.
　　　　Hovering at A's Window, good chear Viſitants.
Icterus ſeen, gives Return of loſt Hopes.
　　　　　to others, Gold from its Colour.
Kite ſeen, threats with Thieves and Robbers.
　　　So a ſly Enemy, as an Hawk an open one.
　　　So ſubtle Enemies lying in wait.
　　　Leave ſomewhat to him, that is, willingly rid you of it.
　　　White aſſaulting A's Fowl, ſhew'd him of a 12 d. begging Drum-
　　　　mer approaching.
Lapwing yours ſhot, that is, your Surveyor cenſured in his Projects.
　　　Lam'd by it, that is, repreſented as imperfect.
Lark ſeen, ſhews of Cares and Fears, and a pleaſant Companion.　　Lark

Lark feen, to fome an unhappy Mufical Vagabondry.
Linnet, gives Delight from various little things.
Magpy in a Cage, fhew'd of a fcandalous prating Servant.
Nightingale, fhews of fome Mufician, Poet or Deceiver.
　　　　　So alfo as the Swallow, but lefs good.
Oftrich feen, fhews of Victory, even in Infuperables.
　　　　　to fome, Hopes in Defpair.
　　　　　to fome, he fhews of fome valiant or adorn'd Knight.
　　　Eating his Egg, fhew'd recovering a dangerous Debt.
Owl feen, to fome is Melancholy and Sicknefs, as is the Place where.
　　　　　to fome, Diligence and Watchfulnefs.
　　Crying threats Damage and Blame with benighted and delayed,
　　　but afterwards hopeful Defigns.
　　Eating feen, threats you as Tax-bit.
　　Fighting feen, threats with Grief Solitary.
　　Flying over you, Sicknefs, Imprifonment or Confinement worfe
　　　than his.
　　Kill'd feen is good, 'tis as the Fears of ill *Omens* over.
　　Sitting on your Houfe, Death.
　　　　　Anothers Houfe, fhews fome one there dies.
　　　　　Tiero's Spear, gave him Renown.
Partridges fhew of Men and Women confederate, but moftly wicked.
　　　　　To Gamefters flender and difputative Gain in quiet, and
　　　　　that projective.
　　　　　To the fingle, Marriage and Children.
　　　　　To Servants, Loyalty and Power.
　　2 feen, has fhewn of a prepofterous Venery.
　　Eggs eating, fhew'd of getting Riches from noble Women.
Peacock, fhews of fome noble pleafant Friend of Honour.
　　　　　to fome he gives Difpatch.
　　　　　to fome, Men famous in Magiftracy or Priefthood.
　　　　　to fome, marry a fine Wife and be in great Efteem.
　　　　　　　But tho rich and handfom, beware left a Shrew.
　　　　　to a Maid, a pretty Husband, but a Corquean.
　　　　　to fome, a true Affiftant, but angry and wandring.
　　　　　to fome, an Enemy, proud, crafty and clamorous.
　　Flying feen, to a rich Man fhews he travels in State.
　　Catching at one, fhew'd of affailing one proud of his natural
　　　Parts.
　　Hearing one cry twice, fhew'd A. of taking an imperfect ftately
　　　Journy.
　　's Feather feen hang at a Room Door, forbad A. to travel as
　　　idly, ftately.
Pheafants fhew of plain and fearful rich Men.
　　If filent, threat Death to fome fuch plain or fimple one.
　　Heard crow in a habitable Place as if chang'd to a Wood,
　　　fhew'd of Defolation by Death there.
Phenix fhews of things exceeding rare and excellent prefenting.

O

Phenix

Phen'x ſhews to others of things fabulous, a rare Youth, or decrepi
    Age.
Pigeons will ſeen, threat of Loſs and Melancholy.
        to others Wandring.
        to others Luſt, if cooing.
        to others ſhew of diſſolute Women.
      Tame in part, as Cock and Duck, &c. vid. ſupra in Gooſe,
        Duck, and Hen.
        So ſhewing of honeſt Women and good Society
        (in Flock)
        To ſome Delight at home, with Succeſs abroad.
        To ſome uſeful Familiars and Luſt.
     Vid. Pigeon-Houſe in Out-houſes.
    One alone, Chriſt.   Vid. Turtle infra.
Quails ſeen, threat with ill News from Sea, and Sedition.
    to the Sick Death.
    to ſome Ambuſh and Treaſon, the Fowler's Prize.
    to ſome Dangers from Company, and ſo croſs to Friend
    ſhip.
    One alone ſeen tho, not ſo bad.
Ravens ſeen, to ſome croſs Affairs, old Wife, Winter, and Death.
    to ſome a falſe Thief and Avowterer.
    to ſome of Graveſmen, Bearers, and Tanners.
    to ſome of Adultery.
    Aſſaulting you tread down, confound a death-menacing Pro
    ject.
    Flying in general threats with Complaint and Sadneſs.
    3 ſitting on one, and then flying round him thrice,
    ſaid he'd kill him, his Death.
    Over your head, threats you Danger or Damage.
    Poultry ſeen ſilently, ſhew'd of killing ſome
    of their beſt by miſtake.
    Shot flying fell, the Evil fear'd was eſcap'd.
    Seen pitch by 2 Windows firſt, 2 Letters of no
    tice for it.
Robin-red-breaſt reſting tame in a Woman's Breaſt, ſhew'd her of a
    Husband true to her alone.
Seagul, vid. Sea-fowl in general.
Sparrows ſeen, threat with Hurt from Friends impertinencies.
    to ſome ſhewing Lechery and Fruitfulneſs.
    Heard chirping, ſhew'd of trifling Impertinencies.
    Flying out of your hand, a certain Loſs.
    Deſert or a black one ſeen in a Granary, to a Farmer deſo
    lated his Corn-ſtore.
Storks ſeen at Weddings good, the young feed the old, this if
    alone.
    to ſome as Amulets, becauſe preſerving us from Snakes.
And Cranes ſeen in Flocks, ſhew'd of Thieves and Robbers.
                         Stork

Storks and Cranes, in Winter, Tempest; in Summer, Draught.
  To some change of Seasons.
    Seen alone, gives Return to Travellers.
Store seen, threats with a little Discontent.
Swallows seen, shew of change of Life.
    to some friendly Praters, and are good chiefly to Women.
    to some an unconstant Housemate.
    to some Friends prating and unconstant.
    to some they give a Wedding or Musick.
    to some an housewifely Wife.
    to some they shew matters out of Season.
    to some Change of Weather.
  Heard chatter about an House is as hurt by Flatterers.
  Seen coming, shew'd of good News approaching.
    So good in Eye-Diseases.
    Departing, threats with Evils near.
Swan shews of Men divine and sincere, and gives Joy.
  Seen to the Well, shews of a man Musick, or Musick it self.
    to the Sick Recovery.
    to Secrets Discovery.
  In a Lake shews Happiness.
    Rivers, is as good Advantage by watry Commerce.
  On dry Land seen, threated with Misery.
  Acts. Singing, to the Sick Death.
    Resting in the Lap to *Socrates*, *Plato* becoming his Scholar.
    Flying and pitching on the *Athens* Academick Gate, his proving a great Master after.
    Piercing Heaven with his Neck, sounding greatest Secrets.
Turkeys shew of nice and dainty Services, as the Goose of more useful.
  Your young ones kill'd, such Services fool'd.
  Driving to an House, shew'd of storing Apples.
  To some dainty domestick prating Fools and Gossips.
  Keeping is living with Plenty and Delicacy.
Turtle, vid. *Pigeon* supra.
    Seen alone, threats with Celibacy or Inconstancy.
      To others shew of Grief and Complaint from their murmuring.
Vultur seen, shews of Death, as also Royalty.
      to others he shews of Physicians.
Wood-pigeon, vid. *Pigeon* supra.
Wren seen, shews us of Honour without Profit.

CHAP.

CHAP. XXX.

Of Fiſh.

IN general ſhew of Perſons cruel, but malignant and dull.
(1)   To ſome of things paſt.
      To moſt of Trouble as living in Water.
         Sea, publick ; Freſh, private.
      To many, vain Hopes.
         And in groſs, Subjects, as dull, and ſpeech-
         leſs ; very contrary.
      Good as Food only.
      Fleſh of great ones brought into Houſe, Death in Family.
         To ſome brought home by themſelves, Victory
         unexpected.
         Moſtly thro Trouble or Ignorance
         conquer'd.
         Poiſon'd with what deſign'd for you,
         your Error reform'd.
      Place, vid. *Seen* in *Acts* infra.

Acts. Bought ⎫ both good, vid. *Fiſhing* infrà.
(2)   Caught ⎭
      Deliver'd of, that is, a Child mute or ſhort-liv'd.
      Eating is as Support got amidſt Troubles, as is the Fiſh.
         to ſome Sickneſs.
         to ſome Profit from Enemies.
         Vid. *Fleſh* ſupra, and *Victuals* Chap.
         Pickled ones, ſhew of Novelty and Delicacy.
      Fighting Conger Eel coming into A's Chamber, a popular Ene-
         my invading his Oeconomy, as ſpoiling his
         Servants.
         Twiſting about A's Legs, obſtructing his Works
         thereby.
         Cut to pieces flung down Stairs, Delivery on
         his Death.
         But returning noiſily flapping, ſhew'd an infa-
         mous Repetition therein.
      Fiſhing ſhews of ſeeking Profit in Trouble, and the Line De-
         ceit in reaſoning.
         To all eager Deſire, and with Gain if ſucceſsful.
      In deep Water, the Trouble the worſe.
      Catching Sea-fiſh is ill, and ſhews of popular Troubles,
      or Gain wherein you will raiſe the Mob about you.
      Taking many and great, Trouble to all but with Gain.
                                 Acts.

Acting. Fishing. Taking many, to Teachers 'tis ill, Fish are mute Scho-
(2) lars and perverse Hearers.
To Traders, idle Diversions.
With a Net in a River the best.
Little ones tho, shew of Heavi ess and
small Profit.
Nets seen, have shew'd of Rain and Change of Wea-
ther.
A Casting-net a comprehensive surprizing reas n-
ing to such purpose, *&c.*
Vid. *Diversion* supra.
Playing in the Sea seen, shews Security.
Given you, shews a Change of Fortune to Wisdom or Riches.
A crooked Eel threatning to bite *A.* an intract ble
Person offering in Converse.
Seem a Fish, that is, be a melancholy Dotard.
Pregnant of one, to a Woman shew'd having a Child
mute or short-liv'd.
Seen, to some shews of vain Hopes or Designs abortive.
In Multitudes has shewn Business troublesom
and inextricable.
By Orators threats them with flights, and so is ill.
On land, threats with things unnatural and unexpecta-
ble.
Stones, shews of things hard and heavy.
To some has shewn Bawdy and the
like Discourse.
Seafish seen on land, shew'd of troublesom
Enemies powerless, but most popular.
A's own Field, shew'd *A.* in ill Courses, as
to Talk, but never in Action.
In a Chamber is ill to the Sick or Master.
His Bed, to the Sailor shew'd Shipwreck.
to the Sick Peril by Humours.
Particular. Crab, vid. *Sea-crabs* infra.
(3) Crabs shew of mean, base, and wicked Folks.
Cuttlefish shews of Wariness in Danger.
Conger, vid. *Eel* infra.
Dolphin, vid. infra in *Seafish.*
Eel shews of Bastards and unaccustom'd Things and Per-
sons.
So of teasing and untractable Troubles.
So Persons also untractable, as slippery.
Conger, vid. *Fight* supra in *Action.*
Num-fish seen, obstructs all Business.
To some the Loss of Sense and Death.
Orcas shews of a cruel and tyrannous Prince.
Polipus seen, shews of some greedy Devourer.
O 3 *Particular.*

Particular. Polipus ſeen, ſparing neither others nor his own.

(3)   Sea-crab holding *A.* ſome naval Perſon or Power ſtopping *A.*

Sprats ſhew of Dainties and Delicacy of Life.

Whale ſeen, ſhews of a mild Prince.

         Swim, threats of Loſs, as *&c.*

Sorts. Alive ſeeing, is an ill ſign.

(4)   Eating them ſo, ſhew'd of unjuſt Profit.

Breathing ſeen, as the Dolphin and Whale, threats with Deceivers.

Colour changing, ſhews of Deceivers and Run-aways.

     Red, to Servants and Malefactors, Torments.

         to the Sick, Fever and Inflammation.

         to others it reveals Secrets.

Various or ſpeckled, to the Sick Poiſon.

     To others Deceit.

White ſhews of plain Men without hurt.

Black ſhews of Death, Lamentation, and Loſs.

Purple, of uſe in Negotiations and Gain, if not eat only.

Dead ſeen ſhew of vain Hopes and Deſigns abortive.

     Vid. *Eating* ſupra.

Devourers ſhew of unſatiable and untamable Gripers.

     Cruel ſeen threat of mercileſs Dangers.

Flat, vid. *Skinny* infra.

Flood-fiſh ſeen, threat with ſhort Life and periſhing Hopes.

Fruitful, foreſhew of Plenty.

Great, vid. *Small* infra.

Land or Water as the Sea-calf, ſhew of change of Condition.

Pool and Lake-fiſh ſhew of unactive lazy Lubbers.

River-fiſh ſeen, ſhew leſs good or ill than Sea-fiſh.

Round Fiſh, vid. *Skinny* infra.

Scale-fiſh to the Sick and afflicted ſhew Relief.

     to ſome Sickneſs or Impriſonment.

     to ſome Men bold or treacherous.

Sea-fiſh ſhew of Iſlanders and Coaſters.

     So of things popular.

     Seen play in the Sea, ſhew of Security.

     Great ſeen in the Sea, is ill to all, the Dolphin excepted.

     Catching them an ill ſign, 'tis Gain with popular Trouble.

     Dolphin ſeen, foreſhews of the Wind in the Quarter ſeen.

         On Land, is as Loſs of popular Friends.

     Monſters ſeen on Land ſhews of popular Enemies in diſtreſs.

Shell-fiſh ſeen, ſhew of change of Fortune.

                               Sorts.

Sorts. Shell-fish seen to some, Men rude, lazy, and a Prise.
(4) Skinny and round shew of vain Business.
    Flat-fish, as Flounders, shew of empty Gair.
Small Fish salted shew Waste.
    Pickled shew as of Novelty and Delicacy.
    Are Grief for Gain, as the Fisherman's Disappoint-
    ment. Vid. *Salt* ibid.
Speaking heard, shew'd *A.* of using unprofitable Servants.
    To some it has shewn of empty Pretenders,
    Fishes are mute.
Wanting Bones, threats with Weakness.

CHAP. XXXI.
Of Human Body.

IN *general* it shews of our most real and near State and Interest intire.
(1) In opposition to our Apparel shewing of our Re-
pute only.
Each Member shews of such State in its Branches.
    If it shew a Relation, it shews a mere
    Relation, and only just in his Post of
    Relation to you.
'Tis a Symbol more fatal and appropriate than that of
the World and things.
Chang'd is such fatal Change answerable.
    Vid. *Change* in *Sense.*
Members of Iron gives Success according, as strong and
    laborious.
    Yard *A.* having, foreshew'd him a Son
    that would kill him.
Ivory, of Vertue.
Stone, stiff and useless.
Gold, ennobled in Friend or Art, &c.
Glass, Peril in such case thro Folly.
Diamond, royal.
Dirt, contemptible.
Wood, that is, stiff, passive, and ineffectual.
Quality. Stiff golden Tongue shews Folly.
    Cut off, vid. *Leg.* Broke, vid. *Thigh.*
    Fat, prosperous.
    Lean è con.
    Swoln, false Greatness with Care.
    Fair, creditable.
    Ugly to Disgrace.
Great, of Power.

O 4

In general **Members.** Quality. Hairs loſt, Favourers gone.
(1)
　　　　　　　　　　Wound, vid. *Phyſick.*
　　　　　　　　　　Black, vid. *Fleſh* infra.
　　　　　　　　　　Like a Lion having a Forehead, gives
　　　　　　　　　　　　Male Children.
　　　　　　　　　　　　Serpent caſting his Skin, ſhew'd
　　　　　　　　　　　　A. Death.
　　　　　　　　　　　　Aſſes Ears *A.* ſaw pull'd out of
　　　　　　　　　　　　his Head, he remov'd his Im-
　　　　　　　　　　　　putation of Folly.
　　　　　Wanting, vid. *Noſe.*
　　　　　　　　　　Greatly ill, except as the Tongue, to a
　　　　　　　　　　　　Schoolmaſter on
　　　　　　　　　　　　a better Imploy.
　　　　　　　　　　　　Hand, to a Hang-
　　　　　　　　　　　　man on Prefer-
　　　　　　　　　　　　ment.
　　　　　　　　　No Feet having, foreſhew'd one's being
　　　　　　　　　　burnt.
　　　　　　　　　Loſt, vid. *Noſe* in *Body.*
　　　　　　　　　　To ſome loſe a Friend as is the
　　　　　　　　　　　　Member.
　　　　　　　　　　To ſome loſe an Imploy appen-
　　　　　　　　　　　　dant.
　　　　　　　　　　Ill always, but in change for the
　　　　　　　　　　　　better.
　　　　Multiplied ſhews either of great Aid or Confuſion.
　　　　Many, vid. *Numbers.*　　　Vid. *Feet.*
　　　　　　　　　Vid. *Hands.* Vid. *Privities.* Vid. *Head.*
　　Strange-plac'd. Eye in her right Breaſt, to a Mother
　　　　　　　　　　loſe her Son.
　　　　　　　　　　Shoulder, ſhew'd *A.* loſing
　　　　　　　　　　　his Shoulder.
　　　　　　　　　　Ears, ſhew'd *A.* being blind.
　　　　　　　　　　Falling into his Feet,
　　　　　　　　　　　ſhew'd *A.* Servants mar-
　　　　　　　　　　　rying his Daughters.
　　　　　　　　　Vid. *Eyes* infra.
　　　　　　　　Hands having in the Eyes ſhew'd of
　　　　　　　　　doing great things by Counſel.
　　　　　　　　Mouth *A.* having in's Fundament
　　　　　　　　　with great and fair Teeth in't to
　　　　　　　　　ſpeak and eat by, foreſhew'd *A.*
　　　　　　　　　Baniſhment for raſh Talk.
　　Strange Uſe. Privities *A.* feeding his with Bread and
　　　　　　　　　　Cheeſe, ſhew'd him his Ru-
　　　　　　　　　　in thro Whoring.
　　　　　　　　Feeding them with Porridg, vid. *Privities.*
　　　　　　　　　　　　　　　　　　　　In

In general. Members. Strange ufe. Privities fever'd of her Husband &
(1)　　making much of, fhew'd of her breeding his Son well
　　　　on his Death.

Whole. Wife have as a Man, that is, barren or Mafterlefs.
(2)　　　　Stone, that is, fenfelefs.
　　　　　　Sow or Cow, that is, an Whore.
　　　　　　Vid. *Like*, and as in Senfe.

　　　　　　's Inwards feen open and fair, fhew'd one his Trade-ftock good.
Afts. Carry Beafts. Vid. *Breaft*, Vid. *Carry.*
(3)　　　A Stock of Bees in Arfe, having Debts diverting neceffary
　　　　　Charges.
　　Hurt of it fearing, threats of violent Terrors of Mind.
　　Kifs, Vid. *K.* in *Bodily Aftion.*
　　Growing Trees thence, to fome either Death or Wounds there.
　　　　Boughs growing thence, to fome foolifh Children.
　　　　Olive growing out of the Head, boded one Succefs in
　　　　　Philofophy.
　　　　Vine Garland growing on the Head, fhew'd a Maid Death.
　　Out of the Knees, fhews Slownefs or Hindrance.
　　　　　　　　to the Sick, Death.
　　To fome, Death of a Friend, as is the Member.
　　Herbs, Vid. *Herbs* and *Corn.*
　　　　　Reed or Cane out of the Knee, forefhew'd a
　　　　　Fiftula there.
　　　　　Ears of Corn growing from the Stomach, Chil-
　　　　　　dren.
　　　　　　　　From her Breaft fell into
　　　　　　　　her Nature, fhew'd a
　　　　　　　　Woman lain with by her
　　　　　　　　Son, and killing her felf
　　　　　　　　upon it.

　　　　2 Wings covering *Afia* and *Europe*, to *Darius* Kingdom.
　　Maim'd your Head or Neck being, threats you Sicknefs.
　　Pofture in general, Vid. *Pofture* intra.
　　　　　Near the Body Ants feen, to the Sick, Health and
　　　　　　Induftry.
　　　　　　　　In it or upon it, threats Death.
　　　　　Flying many feen, threats of the Plague or publick
　　　　　　Calamity.
　　　　　Rifing from Hell feeing one with a Sword, threated a
　　　　　　Tyrant.
　　　　　Candles feen lighted at *A*'s Head and Feet, threated
　　　　　　him Death near.
　　　　　Sun feen rife out of her Womb, *Auguftus*'s Mother.
　　　　　Vomit Worms, difcover private Enemies and avoid
　　　　　　them.

Arms in general, fhew of our Brethren and Domefticks, *&c.*
　　　　　Right Arm blifter'd, to an Husband his Wife fick
　　　　　fwoln.
　　　　　　　　　　　　　　　　　　Arms.

Arms. State Parts. Muſeles ſhew Servants.

Elbow ſhews of our lighter Actions and Performances.

Arm-holes hairleſs, ſhew'd of poor Daughters.

If not, ſhews of Sickneſs, or Remove of Maids.

Pulling a Serpent out of its Fleſh, ſhew'd A. of ridding him of a falſe Servant.

Of Iron, gives great Victory or hard Labour.

Wood or Stone, gives Victory from you.

Diamond, Royal.

Dirt, contemptible.

Broke, to a King his Army hurt.

to others, Hurt to Brother, Son or State.

to a Woman, Widowhood or Divorce.

Cut off both, ſhew'd A. loſing his 2 Sons.

His Right one, to a Prince ſhew'd loſing his beſt Subjects.

Dried up is very ill.

Fair, ſhews of Ornamental leſſer Actions.

Foul, ſhews of Diſgrace, Strife and Loſs.

Great, ſhews of Power or Friendſhip.

Little is as Deſolation.

Hairy, ſhews of growing rich.

Little, Vid. Great ſupra.

Strong, ſhews Riches by Son, Brother or Servant.

to a Woman, gives her Husband rich in Power or Increaſe.

to ſome, Freedom of Priſon and Sickneſs.

Ulcery, threats Sadneſs with ill Succeſs.

Weak, threats with Torments.

Arſe ſhews of our Cares and Expences, as alſo our Indecencies.

Slapping a Farmer's Daughter's Arſe ſeeming fine and white, ſhew'd A. of getting by farming.

Pinch'd there, overreach'd in Expence you are engaged in.

Run with a Needle in there, jeer'd of Inſolvency.

Kiſs anothers put to you, bear the Teaſe of his Scorn.

Stock of Bees there, farm Stock Charges diverting neceſſary Expences.

Arteries ſhew to us of our Soul and Efficacy.

Back in general, Vid. Poſture and Behind ibid.

It ſhews of old Age and time to come.

Seen, threats with ill Luck in Futurity.

For Perſons, it ſhews of our Nephews and Uncles.

Bone yours ſee ſtrong, delight you in your Wife and Heirs.

to the ſingle it is Health and Joy.

Naked of Fleſh but heal'd, ſhew'd of a Brother's Love loſt.

Broke or ſcabby, threats you worſted by Enemies and ſcoff'd at by all.

Back

Back carry somewhat on it, that is, bear some Guilt.
   Anothers fee naked and Sunburnt, perceive of his liablenefs to
     Charge.
   Pinn'd about with Papers, jeer'd by others future Tricks.
   Plac'd with it fingle in a Corner, fet alone in Defiance.
   Turn to fomewhat, that is, fhew Contempt or Neglect of it.
Beard in general, fhews of our Authority, Joy and Gain.
       Having, to young Men Wifdom.
          to Children, Death.
          to others, old Age.
          to a Wife, a Son or Widowhood.
          to a Maid or Widow, an happy Match, and
           in which fhe to have her Will.
          to a Wife, be a Vixon, and wear the Breeches.
    Bearded Women feen, fhew'd of Bufinefs well done
     by improper Perfons.
     bearded feeming to a Wife, fhew'd her Divorce.
Chang'd ftrangely, Contention, Sorrow, Decreafe or Sicknefs.
Of Fire having without Smoke, gave A. Fame for a wife Son.
    and confuming, threats Trouble.
Great and neat, to Philofophers Wifdom.
     to a Child Death, but if near bearding 'tis good.
     to fome, be ingenious and pleafant in Difcourfe.
     Black and grey having, fhew'd A. fhrewd in
      Managements.
    Ugly being, and pull'd off by Boys, fhew'd A. of
     Anger, Care and Danger.
    Bigger than ordinary, that is, you richer than before.
    Large and thick, to Ambaffadors, Orators and Lawy-
      ers good.
         To others, Strength or Gain.
    Little, threats with Suits and Controverfies in Law.
Nafty or unfeemly, threats with Beftiality.
    to fome, Sicknefs.
    Wafhing it is as Sadnefs.
Cut or fallen off, Difhonour or Lofs of Parent or Friends.
   Dry, Joy.
   Pull'd up by the Roots, great Danger.
   Shav'd, Tribulation and Damage.
      to fome, as now ufual cuftomary Gain.
      to fome, alter Condition, Place, Office
      or Bufinefs.
      to a Woman, Marriage or Riches.
Belly in general, Vid. *Bowels* and *Inwards* infra.
   Fat, gives Increafe both of Riches and Children.
     Swell'd, rich in Efteem, not Reality.
   Lean, fhews of Children and Ufurers always craving.
    To fome, Delivery from ill Accidents.

                            Belly

Belly full of Crude and undigeſted Meats, ſhew'd of a Mind full of Error.

Felt aking, ſhew'd A. of Family Care oppreſſing.

Blood loſing, Loſs of Money, and the Veins full of it beſt.

Vomiting, corrupt Sickneſs to all.

Vid. *Vomit* in *Phyſick*.

Iſſuing out of ones Side, Death or Danger thro Gluttony to follow.

Noſe, threats Loſs of Riches and Decay.

Let at the Thumb, ſhew'd of Labour, &c.

Spitting it, foreſhew'd Sedition.

Letting, ſhews of Loſs of Riches.

Near to the Loſs of all, ſhew'd of a Father's Death.

With Joy, ſhews of pleaſant Expence, as build, treat Friends, &c.

By a Stranger, by Law or Violence he gets your Eſtate.

Taking out his own and giving it a Stranger, A. died, that is, he gave his Eſtate ſo.

Drunk with it, ſhew'd A. wanton in Murders.

Bloody Sword ſeen in an Executioners Hand, threated a Nation War.

Seeming A. ſite under a Death-watch in a Chamber, A. proceeded in a Courſe mortal.

Sea of it ſeen, threated great and ruinous War.

Killing without ſhedding Blood, Acts with conceal'd Malice.

Carrying, diſcovers the Secret.

River of it ſeen, ſhew'd of an incurable bloody Flux.

7 of Blood, 7 Years of War.

Ciſtern of Blood plung'd in, ſhew'd A. ſick of too much.

Sprinkling and bubling in ones Houſe, foreſhew'd of Cruelty and Tyranny.

Bones in general, Vid. *Dead.*   Vid. *Back* ſupra.

They ſhew of our Strength and Kin.

A Crown of dead Ankle-Bones wearing, ſhew'd A. Death.

Of dead Men and Tombs being among, ſhew'd A. of Gain by the Dead.

A Skull ſeen hang o'er A's Head, ſhew'd he went on in deadly Projects.

Approaching his Court wall'd with Humane Bones, ſhew'd A. hearing of his Reſorters Deaths.

Bowels own ſeen carried to Heaven and ſhewn, gave A. a Son after Emperor.

By an Eagle to a publick Place and ſhewn, gave A. a Son famous.

Bowels

Bowels own seen open and shewn, to some is as wicked Children and
　　　　　　　　Secrets disclos'd.
　　　　　　to some, Fear and Grief.
　　　Seen inwardly to one deserving well, Joy, &c con.
　　　Vid. *Vomit* in *Physick.*　　Vid. *Belly* supra.
　　　Vid. *Inwards* infra.
Breast in general, shews of our Valour with our Counsel and Secrets.
　　　Right seeming black, to a Woman shew'd her wicked
　　　　　to her Son.　　Vid. *Grammar.*
Hurt black, shew'd *A.* unnatural to her Son.
　　　Bloody or raw, be barren or lose Children.
　　　Breathing, hindred Action obstructed.
　　　Falling, to a Woman Death to her Children.
　　　　　to the Childless, Indigence.
　　　Plaisters having there, to a Woman big, defers expected
　　　　　Delivery.
　　　Sick and rough shews of ill Excuses.
　　　　　to others, imprudent Behaviour.
　　　Struck cross with a Sword, to the young Friendship.
　　　　　to the old, bad News.
　　　Stung there, Vid. *Snake* in *Poisonous Creatures.*
　　　Ulcery, threats of Sickness to come.
　　　　　to Women, sometimes Death.
　　　Wanting, threats Poverty to a Womans self.
　　　Wounded as struck *supra.*
State. Bigger than usual like a Woman's, to a Man Effeminacy.
　　　　　to a Child, Sickness.
　　　　　Plump only, promises long Life.
　　　　　Teats hanging down, gave fair Fields
　　　——— and Plenty.
　　　Fair, shew of Prudence and Children, and Possessions to
　　　　　come.
　　　　　To others, Health and Joy.
　　　Full of Milk shews of Profit.
　　　Hairy, to Men Success.
　　　　　to Women, Widowhood.
　　　Many having, to a Woman follow whoring.
　　　Opened, reveal'd Secrets.
　　　Ugly, shews of a bad Conscience.
　　　Whole and sound is very good.
Made of Iron, that is, cruel with Valour.
　　　Stone, helpless and senseless.
　　　Glass, threats of Folly and Danger.
　　　Gold, very just but fearful.
Paps great, give Children and Possessions.
　　　Sore, shew of Sickness to come.
　　　Falling, is as Death to Children, or Poverty.
Milk in them, to a young Woman childing to all Success.
　　　　　　　　　　　　　Breasts.

Breaſts. Milk in them, to a poor old Man or Woman, Riches.
     to a rich Woman, Liberality.
     to the Batchelor, a Wife and Children.
     to a Maid, Marriage.
         but if too old or young for it, Death.
     to Men active and Travellers, Sickneſs.
     to the Childleſs, married Children.
     to the Married, Widowhood, be Father and Mother too.
     Seeing Breaſts full of it, ſhews Profit.
Brain in general, ſhews of all Prudence and Learning.
Brows, Vid. *Eyes.*
Buttocks ſhew of Clowniſhneſs, as alſo ruſtick Servants.
     Seeing your own, is Infamy.
     Grown black, threats you with Shame and Damage.
     A Woman's naked, ſhew'd of Luxury and carnal Pleaſure.
Cheeks, ſhew of our Beauty, Grace, Honeſty and Love.
     Board thro finding, ſhew'd *A.* hearing of Blaſphemy Laws like to touch him.
     Bliſter'd or ſcabby, threat of wailing or mourning.
     Flat and wrinkled, Heavineſs and Care.
     Fair, Proſperity.
     Swell'd ſeen, threats of great and manifeſt Injuries.
     Bucca their Hollows ſeen, ſhews of Impudence and Scorn.
Complexion, Vid. *Face* poſtea.
Chin, the Foundation of our Joy, Gain and Eſteem.
     Double, that is, our Wife, Children and Secrets.
Ears in general, declare of Fame and Learning.
     Ants in them, Vid. *A.*
     Cleanſing them, ſhews of good News approaching.
     Cut off, Loſs of a Friendſhip.
     Left one accus'd, Innocence deſtroy'd, unheard.
     Right, Accuſer.
     To others, Diſgrace private, as the Noſe publick.
     Bite off a deſperate Man's right Ear, be more deſperate in good than he in evil in Repute.
     Change Eyes in the Ears having, foreſhew'd one Blindneſs.
     Ears having for Eyes, ſhew'd one Blindneſs alſo, *& è con.*
     Deform'd, ſhew of ill Fame, and the more the worſe.
     Full of Corn, ſhew'd *A.* of an Eſtate falling by Parents.
     Fair grown, ſhews they'l proſper to whom your Secrets are communicated.
     Having Aſſes, to Philoſophers Attention.

                Ear

Ears in general having Affes, to fome Servitude.

Lions, threats with Snares thro Deceit or Envy.
Hurting them, fhews of Secrets abus'd or ill News heard.
In them Ants having, to Orators and Philofophers Refpect,
others Death.

Lofing *con* to having many.

One-ear'd Child having, fhew'd *A.* of a Repute of Eftate
without Mony.

Many have, to the Rich is good Repute and Obedience, if well-
fhap'd.

to Artificers, the employing many Hands.
to Servants or Perfons at Law, Plantif or Defendant,
ill tedious Attendance.

One, Vid. *Lofe* fupra.

Stop'd, to a Prince be abfolute, hear no Petition.

to a Woman, whoring.

Elbow, Vid. *Arm* fupra.

Eyes, fhew of Knowledg, Jewels, Children and Injuries.

To fome, Fathers, Brothers and Religion.
To fome, Childrens Children.

Another's have, fhews Blindnefs or keeping his Children, or
Treafure.

Great, gives Grace and Profperity to your Sons.

Fiery, an Underftanding piercing all things.

In the Hands or Feet having, threats you Hurt as carelefs.

Fingers, fhew'd one Blindnefs.
Ears having, forefhew'd one Blindnefs.
Feet, fhew'd *A.* of Servants marrying his Daughters.
Vid. *Eyes* in *Members general* fupra.

Kill'd at them, deftroy'd in ones Profpects and Defigns.

Lofe one, lofe a Son or near Relation.

Shut at a Sight, become wittingly unfenfible of things, take no
care therein.

Number 3 or 4 having, is good to the Ufurer, but bids beware.

To one by Surplufage, it fhew'd Blindnefs.
To the Unmarried, Marriage and Children.
To a Cheat or Whore, Difcovery.

One-eyed, to fome fhews Herefy in Religion or other great Slander.

To others ½ the Lofs, as blind in both.
Right loft, lofe Father, Brother or Husband.
If but 2 Friends, the Right Eye the elder.
Left loft, lofe Mother, Daughter or Sifter.

Parts. Circle, fhews of our Children, Ornaments, and Temper of
Mind.

Pupil, fhews of our Children, Jewels, and Mind more
nearly.
White, fhews of the Strengh of our Children, and Rings.

Eyes.

Eyes. Parts. Crying Corners, ſhew'd of the Beginning of Joys in Children.

    Eye-Brows, ſhew of our Dignity and Ornaments.

        Naked, ill Succeſs, ſingle Combat and Grief.

    Eye-Lids, ſhew of our Schoolmaſters and Ornaments.

        Naked, threat with Shame.

  Blind, Vid. *Phyſick.*

    To ſome, loſe Children, Brother, Father and Mother too, or be ſick, as *&c.*

    To ſome, Needineſs of Mony.

    To the Poor and impriſoned good, not ſee their Miſery.

    To ſome, Sickneſs or falling into Sin.   Chriſt ſays, *The Blind leads the Blind.*

    To Travellers, a bad Return.

    To Traders, break their Word with Sedition therefore.

    To cunning Men and Loſers, ſeeking things ill.

    To Poets, a good time.

    To wiſe Men, Traders and Voyagers, Ill and Heavineſs.

    To Soldiers, ill Succeſs, tho with the Victory too.

    To the Sick, daily Expectation of Death.

        's Brother that travel'd return'd to ſee *A.* blind, ſhew'd his Death.

  Imperfect bleer-ey'd be, do a Crime and repent.

        Loſs of Eſtate threatned alſo.

    Weak Sight, bad Succeſs in Buſineſs thro imperfect Orders therein.

    Sore Eyes, ſhew'd of Children ſick.

    Troubled Eyes ſhews of Children ſick, or Want of Mony.

    Glaſs Eye remove, arrive to command your Affairs truly, without letting Interpoſals.

    Squint-Eye, ſhew of Perfidy.

    Motes in them hindring Sight, Imprudence arraigning your Affairs.

Face ſhews of Favour, as alſo Injuries and Hatred.

    So of our notorious, viſible and real Subſiſtence in the World.

    All ſorts of Faces, all kind of Perſonations in a Managery. Vid. *Looking-Glaſs* in *Goods.*   Vid. *Looks* in *Appearance* in *Senſe.*

  Own ſeen comely, gives you Honour.

    Black, Death.

    Red, Oppreſſion with many Crimes.

    Waſhing, repenting of Sin.

    Foul and pitiful guilt, with Heavineſs of Mind.

  Anothers freſh and ſmiling ſeen, gave a Friendſhip.

    Comely ſeen, gives Honour.

    Black ſeen, gives you long Life.

                              Face

Face another's green seen, threats you Heaviness.

    Meager seen oppose you, threats you Annoy and Poverty.

    Black, horrid, swarthy, and lean, a shrewd, malicious, and harass'd Enemy.

    Horrid Face *Esculapius* seen with, to a Physician shew'd him Business failing.

    Friend fair, he's faithful.

    Black, pale or sickly, false.

    Chang'd *A*'s seen, shew'd him alter'd in what might be expected of him.

    Cover'd, vid. *Cover* in *Action.*

Fat shews of useless Persons in Family.

Feet shews of our Arts, Riches, and Friends, and then those still of our greatest Aid and Support.

    To some of their House Foundations.

    To most of their greater Manageries.

    As their Hands the less.

Vid. *Legs* and *Knees* infra.

Children seeing, gives Joy, Profit, and good Health.

Sole of them shews of our greatest Poverty and Labour.

    Answer to our Hands for lesser Labours.

    Smelling rank shews of venereal Distempers.

    Scratch'd being by one there, threats of Flattery with Loss.

Bare, vid. *Naked* infra.

Broad seeming, threats of great Evils and hard Labour.

    Narrow having go not about your Journey, your Ability will fail in your Designs.

Brass have, walk in ways of Eternal Force.

Bit by a Serpent, Sadness thro others Envy.

Bound, vid. *B.* in *Action.*

Cut off, threats Pains and Damage.

    But if infirm before, recovers it.

Dirty, vid. *Naked* infra.

Hairy threats Hindrance.

Held by one, threats you with great Lets in your greater Operations.

    Tied by the Dead, Knavery hindring.

In the Fire shews Loss of Goods, Children, and Servants.

    To a Footman Success.

    Water threats with Colds and Sickness.

    But bath'd well, gives Honour and Joy from Servants.

Kissing another's shews of Repentance.

Many to them that want many's Help, Good.

    to the Rich Sickness, to the Poor Plenty.

    to Malefactors Imprisonment.

Feet many, to ſome Blindneſs, to ſome Danger of cripling,
to Merchants and Sailors good and great Help.
Vid. *Want* infrà.   None, vid. *Want* infrà.
Naked and white, Poverty with Innocence.
Dirty, Poverty with Trouble and Folly.
Rank ſtinking as dirty or worſe, and to ſome the Pox.
Bare, to ſome Sickneſs. Vid. *Shoos* in *Apparel.*
Narrow, vid. *Broad* ſupra.
Nimble ſhew of Joy and Amity.
Rank, vid. *Naked* ſupra.
Sore Feet walking with, ſhew'd Faſting,
Stinking, vid. *Naked* ſupra.   Tied, vid. *Held* ſupra.
White, vid. *Naked* ſupra.
Wanting threats of Moleſtation and Diſturbance.
To ſome it gives Humility and Succeſs.
To ſome Catarrhs and Defluxions. Vid. *Many* ſupra.
None having foreſhew'd one being burnt.
Water flowing thence, ſhews the Dropſy or the Galleys.
Vid. *In* ſupra.
Fingers in general ſhew of our fidling Actions and Faith.
Hairs growing thence ſhew'd Impriſonment.
Another's loſe and crying having, ſhew'd *A.* of a
preſent Payment urging he could not withſtand.
More than uſual, owe more than one would pay.
To ſome Wounds and fidling Arts.
To Men uſing fidling Arts, Good.
Too few threat of Impediments and imperfect Works.
Cut off, Loſs of Friends and Domeſticks.
None at all, attach'd for Mony without Bond.
Loſt, to ſome Loſs of Servants,
to Fidlers and Scriveners Loſs of Imploy.
to Uſurers Loſs by Intereſt.
to Debtors pay more than they owe.
Hurt, Thorn in them, Trouble about paying of Mony.
Bit, jeer'd about paying of Mony.
Cut by your ſelf or another, Damage.
Off, Loſs of Friends.
Burning them, Haſtineſs to Prejudice in Receipts.
One like a Lump of Fleſh having, ſhew'd Loſs thro
Change of bad Mony.
Parts. Nails ſhew of our conſtant Guard and Security.
Cutting or paring, ſhews grievous Perplexities of
Mind.
Pull'd off Miſery, if not Danger of Death.
Very long, Profit.
Biting threats with Wrangling and Vexation.
Thumb ſhews of our Letters, Strength and chief Ser-
vants.

                                   Fingers

Fingers. Parts. Thumb blooded there, shew'd *A.* of Labour.

Fore-finger shews of our Learning, Faith, and Religion. So of our present Offers and Promises.

Middle-finger shews of impudent and sordid Actions.

Ring-finger shews of our Wife, Children, and Dignity. Vid. *Ring* in *Ornaments*.

Little-finger shews of our Infants, Children, and lesser Cares.

Fist, vid. *Hand* infra.

Flesh eating, vid. *Victuals*.

Encreas'd, shews of Gain of Gold or Wealth.

Fatter, richer and fairer in Apparel.

Lean, to the Poor worse Poverty. to the Rich Decay.

Full of Scabs, Tetters, and Corns, rich.

Killing his Wife and selling her Flesh at Shambles, shew'd *A.* prostituting her for Gain.

Cut their Father to pieces and eat him, they inherited him dying.

Your own Flesh with Iron, threats you being grievous sick.

Colour. Yellow or pale, fall into Distempers by a long Fever.

White and fair is good, and shews of Innocence and Health.

Black, to a Woman Adultery and Divorce.

To others Cheating.

Breast, that is, as to her Son, &c. a Cheat.

Right Thigh so, that is, a Cheat as to her elder Brother, &c.

Forehead shews of our Authority, Dignity, and Affections.

High gives solid Judgment, Power   Wealth,

Fleshy gives Liberty of Speech, Strength and Constancy.

Hurt, threats your Wealth in danger of loss.

A Cut there well sowed up again, your Honour by a good Excuse retriev'd.

Of Brass, Stone or Iron, Good to Jesters, Vintners, and Ruffians.

To others it threats Hate and Irreconcilableness to Enemies.

Parts. Top of the Head, shews the Master and Chief in all things.

Crown shews of our Honour or Dishonour.

Hinder part shews of our secret Futurity and beheading. Vid. *Head* infra.

Gall shews of Choler, Melancholy, and Money.

To some of their Son or Brother.

Broken threats with Discord between Man and Wife.

Gall broken, to others Loſs by Thieves and Gaming.
Guts ſhew us of Children and Uſurers always craving.
    Ilia or ſmall Guts and Flank in general ſhew Daughters.
    Entering another's Houſe and finding the Owner aſleep, *A.* cut
      out his fat and excrement ſtinking Guts and carried them off,
      that is, *A.* rob'd him, *&c.*
    Pain or Sickneſs there, is Sickneſs indeed or Poverty.
    Vid. *Inwards* infra.
Hair in general ſhews of our Riches, Houſe-tiles, and great bodily
      Misfortunes.
      To a Prince Subjects.
      On Members, ſhews of Favourers as are the Parts.
      Wig, vid. *Apparel.*
    Seen only, ſhews of ſome unuſually ſeen Perſon occur-
      ring.
Hairy being, threats of Sickneſs after.
      On the Hand-joints, to ſome Chains.
           to others Hindrance.
      Legs long, threats Poverty and Ruin.
      Feet threats of Hindrance as to main Actions.
      Palm threats Labourers with Idleneſs.
      Arms promiſes growing rich.
          Arm-holes hairleſs, ſhew'd poor Daugh-
           ters.
      Tongue threats great Impediments, Diſeaſes,
      or Death.
      Eyebrows long pulling off, ſhew'd *A.* curing
      his Repute of Abſurdity.
Bald, vid. *None* infra.   Behind, vid. *None* infra.
Colour. White ſeeing, ſhews Friends.
      Red, envious Perſons.   Black, Enemies.
      Grey having, gives Gain, Profit, and Joy.
      To ſome Honour and Wiſdom.
Curling, to Women and Courtiers good Addreſs.
    to others puzling Debts and Sedition.
    Harſh and diſorder'd, Anger, Heavineſs, and Diſreſpect.
      ſhew'd to another being depriv'd of his Living.
    Not to be comb'd, ſhew'd Law-ſuits, *&c.*
    2 Feathers in his Hair *A.* finding gone, ſhew'd him of
    the Ornaments of his Actions failing.
Cutting another's, threats you Misfortune.
    By a Barber, is as Deliverance from Evil.
      Coming unexpected ſhew'd of a Tax unthought de-
      manded.
    By a Barber, ſhav'd by him ſhew'd *A.* Torments.
      Vid. *Shave* infra, and *Barber* in *Trade.*
    By your ſelf or another, is ſudden Heavineſs, Slavery,
    or Bondage.

                                      Hair

Hair cutting by a Stranger, to some Nakedness or Barrenness.

Right side, lose Male Kin, &c.

To Jesters and Men us'd to it, as Friers and Monks, &c. good.

To a Prince his Armies and Forces decreas'd.

Disorder'd, vid. *Curl* supra.   Falling, vid. *None* infra.

Growing shews of Liberty, as cut off Slavery and Bondage.

Harsh, vid. *Curl* supra.

Like an Hog, be in danger as he.

Horse, be in Servitude as he.

Sheep or Wool have, to some Imprisonment.

to some long Sickness, Fantasies, or the Itch.

to some the Ptysick and Consumption.

Long in general shews Fortitude.

To Women, Wisemen, Princes and Bishops, best.

To Princes, Victoriousness and their Subjects thriving.

Shaving threats Dethronement.

To some Honour and Power, but with Delay till so grown.

And black gives Increase of Wealth and Honour.

Like a Woman's having, to a Man shews of Cowardice and Effeminacy.

to others Deceit by a Woman.

Short and black shew'd of Grief and Sadness.

None, to those us'd to wear none, good.

to others a Mock or a Guile.

to a Prince Treasure exhaust.

to a Seaman Shipwreck.

to some, Shame, Barrenness, and hindrance in Affairs.

Behind, Poverty or ill Luck *in futuro*, or old Age.

To Men in Law, Flight, or Imprisonment, 'tis good.

Falling off threats with great Frights or the Plague.

To others Trouble and Loss of Estate.

Miserable to all but Women.

From Members best, &c.

Bald Woman seen, threats of Poverty, Famine, or Sickness.

Man seen, the contrary.

Right side, lose male Kin Favourers.

Left, female.

Condemn'd to Labour is shewn by having none.

Pull'd off the Head, Loss of Friends.

Poled, vid. *Cut* supra.   Pulled, vid. *None* supra.

Short, vid. *Long* supra.   P 3   Hair

Hair ſtaring a Woman ſeen with, ſhew'd of Diſcord.
    In Mourning to Death.
    Shav'd all, to Seamen Shipwreck.
        to the Sick recover tho deſpair'd on.
Hand ſhews of our Arts and Strength.
    Engrav'd ſeen, ſhew'd of happy Performances.
    Parts. Right, male Relations, Friends, Servants, and Goods to get.
    Left, Female Friends, Maids, and Goods got.
    Palm of the Hand ſhews of Day-labour.
    Back of it ſhews of Intermiſſion of Work.
    Touch'd by the Dead, ſhew'd A. ceaſing Work as
      fearing Death.
    Fiſt beating Frogs with, gave Authority over Servants.
Beating, vid. Fiſt ſupra.
Carrying a Crown of Gold in't, gives Honour and Dignity.
    a Stick in it, is as Sickneſs.
Cut off, Death or Separation of Friends, as &c.
    Both cut off, Impriſonment, or Sickneſs.
Colour white, to the Poor Friendſhip and Idleneſs.
    to the Rich Friendſhip.
Flinging away is as Prodigality.
Dropping things is negligent Loſs or heedleſs Expence.
Fair and ſtrong, to Tradeſmen Proſperity.
    to Fearers of Arreſts, &c. Ill
    to others honourable Imploys.
Filthy and foul threat of Loſs and Danger.
    To ſome Damage and Offence.
Feeling hectick, ſhew'd of preſent Indiſpoſition for Buſineſs.
Fingers, vid. Fingers ſupra, and Rings.
Handling things in general, vid. Poſſeſs.
    Fire hurting you not, renders you fearleſs of Enemies.
Hold ſomewhat in't, that is, command or act as is the thing held.
    A Rod, that is, be on Correction of Inferiors.
    A Sword, that is, be on Reſentments or Quarrels.
    Fling it away, reject ſuch Methods.
Hand-gout having threats with Languiſhment and Neceſſity.
Hard is as ſtrong, but not ſo good to the Rich.
Have in the Eyes, do great things by good Counſel.
Hairy threats with Trouble and Impriſonment.
    In the Palm is Idleneſs.
Held in a Fox's Mouth, ſhew'd A. of a ſubtle Enemy ſtopping
    his Actions.
    Without Hurt, Impediment only without other Damage.
Hinder'd, ſhews of Contempt with Deſigns fruſtrate.
    Burnt ſhew'd A. of a Servant for reaſons leaving his
    Service.
    Dead ſeen, ſhew'd A. of a Maid leaving him thro In-
    firmity.

Hands.

Hands. Hinder'd. Dead seen, to some has shewn of Inability and Poverty.

    Little, Vid. *Slender* infra.

    Looking on them, threats with Sickness.

    Many having, to Traders Plenty.

                to ill Men Captivity.

                to others, Children, Servants and Mony Store.

    Open, Vid. *Shut* infra.

    Saving you, your Actions defending you.

    Shut, left Covetousness.

        Right open, shews Liberality.

              Flinging from, is as Prodigality.

        Drop, Vid. *supra.*

    Strong, Vid. *Fair supra.*

    Shaking Hands with an Angel, being in perfect Command of Divine Messages.

              A Spirit the same, but to self-Delusion.

                    Feeling warm, and so of seeming Comfort and Aid.

    Stab'd in it, prevented of Aid Service.

    Slender seeming, shew'd A. of his Servants cheating.

    Stretch'd out in Aid by God to you, gives you all Joy and Success.

    Touch'd back of it by the dead, shew'd A. ceasing Work a while, as fearing Death.

    Wanting, to Mariners Trouble.

             to Juglers, very bad.

    Washing, shews clearing of Innocence.

             Dirt coming off easy, the better.

             To some it shews Disquietude and Vexation.

             In the Rain, to one sick gave an Healthy Sweat,

    White, Vid. *Colour* supra.

    Working with the right, good.

             the left, Ill.

Head in general, shews of the Father, Mother, King, Priesthood, Mind and Honour.

             To some, their Dignity, Power and Wisdom.

    Bare and uncover'd, threats with Dishonour.

            Vid. *Hat* in *Apparel.*

    Birds eating Meat thence, *Pharaoh's* Butler.

    Break anothers, have him in Contempt, as mean and beneath you.

    Childrens Heads Crows seen sit on, shew'd them hanging.

    Comely seen, shews of your Proceeding as with Wisdom.

    Cut behind by one unknown, shew'd A. of Memory failing.

            Vid. *Behind* in *Posture.*

    Dizzy, threats with perplexing Affairs.

    Fastned in a wooden Window, confin'd in a slavish Prospect.

    Ill drest, shew'd one of Authority defective.   Vid, *Apparel.*

                                          Head

Head looking back, ſhews of ill Enterprize, and returns Travellers.
    Set upon the Head the Heels upwards, ſhamefully expos'd.
    Waſhing it is as Delivery from Danger.
    White having, ſhews Gain.
  Little, threats of Contention about Quality.
  Large, to the Poor Riches.
        to the Rich, Dignity.
        to the Uſurer, Mony.
        to the Champion, Victory.
        to the retir'd Man, Pain and Anger.
        to the Servant and Soldier, Pain and long Servitude.
        to Judges and Orators, Charge and Reproach, with Loſs of
          Authority.
        to Men in Office the ſame.
        to the Sick, Headach, or a ſtubborn violent Fever with
          Heavineſs.
  2 or 3 have, to the Poor Riches, as able to maintain them.
        to the Rich, Contention with Kindred.
        to a Prince, Dominion ; to a Warrior, good Luck.
        to others, Company aſſiſting.
  Like a Beaſt, Vid. *Head* in *Beaſt.*   Vid. *Horns* in *Beaſt.*
    Dog, gives Servitude, Want and Miſery.
    Moor, gives Voyages and Diſpatch in Buſineſs.
    Lion, gave Male Children and good Succeſs in Enterprize.
    Elephant, Wolf or Leopard, good in Enterprize.
    Bird, ſhews of your not ſtaying in your Country.
    Horſe or Arſe, threats you with Servitude.
  Horn'd as an Ox ſeem, be beheaded as he.
Beheaded, loſe Father, Mother, Wife, Child or Farm, &c.
      To the Sick, Recovery.
      To ſome, Gain and overcoming of Enemies.
      To Criminals and Debtors, clears them.
      To Sailors on the Sea, Loſs of the Topmaſt.
      To Travellers, it gives Return.
      To Merchants and Uſurers, Loſs of Stock.
      To Princes, Joy and good Servants diverting Cares,
        but ſometimes Death.
      To Suitors for Inheritance, good.
              To others, Exile and Overthrow.
    Half done, that is, ſuch Occurrences befal you by halves.
      Cut off and recover'd again, gave Return from
        Baniſhment.
    By Sentence of Law, Delivery from Trouble and Miſchief.
      An Acquaintance, ſhews that he will ſhare with
        you in your Honour.
      Robbers or Murderers, is Loſs of Children, Rela-
        tions or Eſtate.
      A Youth, to the Sick, Death near.

                                                  Head

Head. Beheaded by a Youth, to the Healthy, attain Honour.

to a Woman with Child, have a Son, her Husband soon dying after.

For some heinous Offence, threats with Loss of Friends.

Beheading another, perfects Revenge, and gives Success in Business.

An armed Man being, signalized in the Service of some great Man.

A Pullet or Green-Goose, gives Joy and Recreation.

Beheaded seeing another, shews Sickness.

to others, Despair in Business.

Between the Hands, to a Batchelor Marriage and Children.

to the married, Loss of Wife and Children.

to some, it shews the Return of Friends.

to the Remover out of his own Country, good hap.

Trim'd well, it promises good Disposes of Affairs.

But if no other Head on, as if beheaded.

Heart, shews of the Husband or Wife.

To some, of Love and Life.

To some, also of their Parents or Children.

Precordia or Midriff about it, shews of our dearest Secrets.

Pain there, threats with some dangerous Disease.

To some, an intolerable Wife, &c.

None have, die, or be in the Power of thy worst Enemy.

Vigorous, gives long Life, Prosperity and Victory.

Hips grown stronger and larger, Joy and Health.

To one marrying, fine Children.

Black and blew, threat of Death, or hating ones Wife.

Broke, Affliction, Sickness, and Loss of Children.

Cut half thro, shews of Hopes accordingly lost.

Jaws shew of the State of Shops, Cellars and Ware-houses.

To others, of the Family.

Vid. *Cheek* supra. Vid. *Teeth* infra.

Bones, shew of our Cook and Baker, &c. that bear the Household.

Tore open, such Housing laid waste.

To others, their Family destroy'd.

Loosned only, Distress.

Rotten, shew of an House destroy'd by Sin or Poverty.

Swell'd by Diseases, shew'd of a Family increas'd to Loss.

Joints, shew them on whom the weight of some Business hangs.

Leg out, Vid. *L.*

Inwards in general, Vid. *Belly* and *Guts* supra.

To some they shew hid Treasure.

To some, Strength of Body and Riches.

Inwards

Inwards eat your own, be enrich'd by ſome Domeſtick.

     Anothers, get his Eſtate.

Voiding at Fundament, ſhew'd *A.* of ſome of his Family quar-
     reling abroad to his Loſs.

Diſeas'd, threats Body and Purſe conſuming.

See your own as dead, to the Poor Riches.

     to the Rich, Children.

     Seen of others, is Shame and Diſhonour, and
     to the Rich moſt.

's Wives *A.* ſeeing open and fair, ſhew'd of his finding
     his Trade Stock well.

Open'd and not ſeen, to the Miſerable Comfort.

     to others, Loſs of Houſe, Children, and
     Death if took away too.

To waſh them *A.* receiving Water of a Miniſter, ſhew'd her ſen-
     ſible of need of Repentance.

Kidneys ſhew of Brethren and Kindred.

Knees ſhew of our Strength and greater Operations.

Strong, to a Man Succeſs in Actions and Journies.

     to a Woman, Conjugal Obedience and Diligence.

     to others, ſhews of their Brethren or Children well.

Run by their Help, be happy in Undertakings.

     Weak *è con.*

Hurt there, Hindrance in calling.

     Cut or dried up, ſettledly.

     Grown well, gives Recovery.

     Weary only, ſhews Sickneſs.

     Trees growing thence, to the Sick Death.

     To others, Hindrance.   Vid. *Members general.*

Swell'd, ſhew Sickneſs or Buſineſs hinder'd.

Blooded in them, to Women immodeſt Deſires.   (Draw
     Flowers.)

     Streaming thro the Clothes, paſt all Shame.

Apples ſupplying their loſt Cap, ſhew'd *A.* of his Caſh
     help'd by Rent.

Reſting on the Knees, Submiſſion with Interceſſion.

     Walking on them for Feet, is Poverty and Loſs of Goods
     and Servants.

     Kneeling, ſhews of Devotion and Humility.

     To others, Trouble in Buſineſs.

     To a Crucifix, ſhew'd *A.* of turning Papiſt.

Vid. *Leg* infra.

Lap-Dog, Vid, *D.* in *Beaſt.*

     Have a Peacock there, to a Phyſician a glorious Patient.

     Pheaſant there, ſhews of a leſſer Profit.

     Flying away thence tho, is as miſſing the Offer.

Swan coming into his Lap, ſhew'd *Plato* to be *Socrates*'s Scholar.

Leg in general, Vid. *Knees* and *Feet* supra.
  Shew of our greater Actions and Aids, and the main
   Support of all.
  Right fuck'd by Leeches, shew'd *A.* of his Male Rela-
   tions drain'd by his Charges.
  Hinstep, shews of our greatest Strength we trust in.
Active, give Prosperity and good Journies.
Clean is innocent and prudent, but as naked, distressed.
Bound, shew'd Servants impeded.
Eroke, shews a Friend or Servant miscarries.
   By a *London*-Waggon, thro his likelihood of removing
   thither, or being a Vagabond.
Cut off, threats of removing a Family far.
   One cut off, a Kinsman removed to a far Country.
   Wooden having upon it, having ones Affairs to the
    worst by it.
   To many, some great Detriment in Managery.
Fleshy, in Circumstances able or happy.
Fat grown, gives Riches and powerful Kin.
Hair pull'd thence, Loss of Kindred or Favourers.
   Grown too long there, threats Poverty and Ruin.
Hurt, Vid. *Swell* infra.
Many and fighting having, gave *A.* a Family according, and in
 Discord.
Lesser grown, Ruin to your Kin or Livelihood, or your Art de-
 cays.
Rotten pocky seen, shew'd *A.* false, and therefore deserted of
 Friends.
Scabby, threats with fruitless Perplexity.
Swell'd, threats Loss by best Friends or Servants.
Leg wooden send one, assail him with Discord with his chiefest
 Friends.
Parts. Shin shews of our Familiars and meaner Friends.
  Calf of the Leg, our Glory and Safety.
  Ankle, shews of our meaner Domesticks and Servants.
  Hinstep, shews of our greatest Strength we trust in.
Lights shew of the Husband and Wife.
Lips shew of our Words and Grace, as also our Health.
   Vex'd at Lice between them, teas'd with trifling Abomi-
   nations.
  Fair and large, gives you a lovely Wife and Children, and Allies
   of Kiss-Mates.
   In ill States, hurts their Affairs.
  Hair-lip'd Person meets you, a double dealing Course opposes you.
  Vid. *Mouth* infra.
Liver shews of the Dreamers Son, Food, Profit, Pleasure or Riches.
  Your Enemy's find, overrule him and his Treasure.
  Burnt or dried, threats Death or Wealth wasted. (The Bloods
   form'd there.)   Lungs

Lungs ſhew of the Husband or Wife.

Marrow is as the Liver.　　　　Vid. *Bones* ſuprà, and in *Dead.*

Member, Vid. *Privities* infra.

Milk, Vid. *Breaſt* ſupra.

Milt ſhews of Pleaſure, Laughter, and Houſhold Stuff.

Mouth ſhews of our Shame, Dignity or Health, our Weal or Woe.

Rotten within, a Proccedure of Wickedneſs or Sin.

Hairy, ſhew'd of ſlandering.

Have in Fundament, Vid. in *Members general* ſupra.

Privities, Vid. *P.* infra.

Actions dumb, Vid. *Phyſick.*

Rings put to it, intruſted with great Secrets.

Saw his Servant put his Girls Arſe to hers, ſhe talk'd obſcene of the Girl.

King ſee, give you ſomewhat thence, be benefited by his Edict.

Speaking proud things, acting preſumptuouſly.

2 edged Sword coming thence, ſhew'd of a Truth and Prediction irreſiſtible.

Shut as not able to eat, ſhew'd *A.* of ſudden Death.

Wide yawning at him *A.* ſeeing, ſhew'd him of a Proclamation after him.

Wider then ordinary your own ſeeing, ſhews you'l be richer, and your Family greater.

Parts. Uvula ſhews of our Speech, as alſo our Nephews.

Chaps under, ſhew of our Life and Puniſhment, (hanging is there.)

Pits under the Chaps, ſhew of our Death, as alſo of our Wives and Daughters Ornaments.

Muſcles ſhew of the higheſt Honour and Principles of Action.

Navel ſhews us of our Parents and Country.

Loſt, threats with Death of Parents.

Having none at all, ſhew'd Baniſhment.

Pain there, danger to Father and Mother.

To others, danger as to Inheritance or Baniſhment.

Nails, Vid. *Fingers* ſupra.

Neck ſhews of our Pleaſure, Wife and Strength.

Awry, forbids Travel, and returns Travellers.

Bound yours ſeeing, beware of giving another Credit after.

Golden Bunch ſeen behind there, ſhew'd one of an excellent Futurity after him on his Death.

Impoſthum'd, threats with Sickneſs.

Thick, to a Man proſpers him in all Strength.

Slender *è con.*

Tied by another, threats you as ſubject to him.

A. ſhiting on anothers from his unboarded Floor, ſhew'd of his laying his Managery Expence on them.

Nerves ſhew of our Auxiliary Powers.

Noſe

Nose in general, shews of our Ornament and Decorum, and Personal
    Regard.
      To some, it shews of Authority.
        2 having, threats Discord with domestick Kindred.
Big to Deformity, is living in Plenty, but with popular hate.
Blowing Snot out of it, shew'd A. venting flashy rude Thoughts.
Diseas'd or stinking, threats with greatest Infamy.
      Polypus there, threats with great Infamy to self
      or Friends. ———
Fair and great, shews Subtlety in Sense, and Providence in Af-
    fairs.
      - To others, great Acquaintance.
      To others, shews of discerning of Plots
      well.
      Lost *è con.*
In the Mouth, threats with Loss of Smell.
Laying hold of anothers, shew'd Fornication.
Lost, Vid. *Fair* supra.
None at all, threats with Accusations of Falshood, and to some
      fly for it.
      To a Perfumer, Loss of Trade.
      To some, want of Sense, and Hatred of Betters.
      To the Sick, Death, Sculls have none.
      Cut off, shews of Disgrace publick; as the Ear private.
Scent lost, to a King danger by one of his nearest Subjects.
      to a Woman, her Husband deceives her.
      to a private Man, he's notoriously cuckolded.
Nostrils fair, give Prosperity and quick Sense.
    Right stop'd, branded as wanting Sense.
    Hairs in them, shew of Troubles from great Men.
      To some, Infamy as to quick Sense.
      Pull'd out, Delivery from such Ill, but with Labour and
      Pains.
Palat shews of our Cook, Comfort, Life and Judgment.
Paps, Vid. *Breast* supra.
Privities shew of our Riches, and Vigor of Mind and Body.
      To some, of Esteem.
      To some, of their Parents, Whores, Wives and Children.
    Of Iron, gave a Son that kill'd his Parent.
    Stone, threats with a Rupture.
    Husband's sever'd taking care of, to a Wife shew'd her care-
    ful of his Son on his Death.
Vigorous shews of our Estate, Circumstance and Courage as clear.
      To a Man, Male Children.
        Woman, Female Children with good Repute.
        King, long Life, and a good Son and Heir.
      Little, threats with Infamy and Shame.
      Handled, shews of our Vigor of Mind and Courage de-
      monstrated.
                      Privities

Privities vigorous handled ſeen ſo by another, is as handled, only leſs.
      Seen in publick, ſhew'd A. his Villany diſcover'd, and near
        puniſh'd.
Female Parts, judg of by the ſame Rule as a Man's.
      Womb in general, ſhews of Sons and Daughters.
        Sun riſing out of her Womb, *Auguſtus*'s Mother.
        Its Entrance declares of Female Pleaſures.
        Eating Porridg there, ſhew'd A. conſuming her
         Revenue on her Luſt.
        Wheat growing in her Breaſt A. ſaw fall in there,
         ſhe was lain with by her Son, and kill'd her ſelf
         on it.
Stones out, your Courage near overwhelmed.
      Swell'd is as heavy Care of Wife, Child or Whore.
Member ſtanding, to your ſelf Strength, Idleneſs and Leachery,
        to your Sons, Luxury with Stubbornneſs.
        With an Hole in't, great Diſgrace and Trouble
         on it, as thro Preſumption, &c.
        3 together having, ſhew'd A. becoming a Free-
        man being a Prentice.
      Strong and fair, ſhews our Wife and Children pleaſe
      us.
      Long, ſhews of a good Wife and Son.
        Short *è con.*
      Cut off, Poverty, or your ſelf or Son dies.
      Maim'd, beat by your Enemy, or your Child ſick.
      Held in your Hand, Chaſtity.
      Swell'd is Son or Wife troubleſome.
    Big overgrown, threat of a troubleſome and ſcandalous Son.
    Languiſhing, ſhews an Eſtate decaying, idle Sons, and Strength
      failing.
     Anothers ſeen ſtand and ſpend at him, to a Father ſhew'd a
        Daughter born.
        Handle, to a Schoolmaſter good, teach his Children.
        A. ſaw his Daughter naked and piſſing, he guarded her
        Modeſty narrowly.
Reins in general, ſhew of our Sons and Strength.
           To others, of their Brothers and Couſins.
Ribs ſhew to us of our Companions and beloved Females.
    Large and ſtrong, give you Delight in your Wife.
    Broken upper, Diſſenſion with Wife to Diſgrace.
      Lower, with other Female Relations.
Shoulders ſhew of our Brethren and Familiars of great Power.
     Of Gold, ſhews of famous Power.
        Ivory, Power obtained by Virtue.
        Diamond, Royal Power.
        Dirt, is ill to all.
        Glaſs, threats with Loſs of Authority.

                              Shoulder

Shoulders firm, give good Luck, Strength and Prosperity.

To Prisoners bad, shewing of enduring much.

Broken, Death to Brethren, or Familiars of great Power.

Lean, their Poverty.

In Pain or swell'd, is Trouble by Relations.

Fleshy good to all but the imprisoned, to them Continuance.

Forc'd on as held by them, necessitated in Affairs by such Persons.

Skin in general, shews of our Guard and Ornament.

Fleaing his Son for a Bag, foreshew'd his Father being drown'd next Day.

Cast at a Serpent, die.

Black having as a Moor, to a Woman Adultery.

Skinny Fish seen, shew'd of a vain Business.

Skinned your Tongue being, threats you with Poison.

Of a Christian seeing, shew'd A. commanding the full Power of a Christian.

Mumbling a Man to a Skin, attaining to the full Perfection of a reasoning, as &c.   Vid. *Skin* in *Beast* and *Commodity.*

Soles, Vid. *Feet* supra.

Spleen in general, shews of our Pleasure and Laughter.

Hurt, Oppression thro Care.

Enlarged, shew'd A. invited to a merry Meeting.

Stomach in general, shews of the Storekeeper or Steward.

Corn growing as from it, Children.

Wounded in't, to young Folks Love Tidings.

to old Folks, ill News.

Teeth in general, shew of our Family and Strength of Body.

So of our common Meat-Mates, as &c.

With Blood coming out a Relation dies, without not.

To others, has shewn of such an one expected to dine abroad.

Of Iron, that is, all devouring and cruel.

to some, it shews hard living.

Gold, with good Attendance and good Speech.

to some, Sickness of Choler.

to some, an House burnt.

Silver, to the Learned get Mony by Talk.

to the Rich, expensive Hospitality.

Tin, Shame.

Ivory, neat.

Wax, sudden Death.

Glass or Wood, threats a violent Death.

Lead, threats with Dishonour or Sorrow thro Speech.

Growing ill or wagging, shews Sedition in House.

Strong, big and white, shews you terrible to Inferiors.

Longer than ordinary one seen, Trouble by Relations.

Teeth

Teeth growing longer, hindring Speech, threated with Inheritance
Suits.
Bloody, threats the Dreamer's Death.
Gnaſhing, threats great Fear or Anger.
Grating againſt his Tongue, ſhew'd A. his Miſery ended
by his Speech.
Sorts. Upper, the better kin of an Houſe.
Under, the inferior.
Foreteeth, the Chief of an Houſe and young Folks.
Side-teeth, Servants.
Fore-teeth out without Blood, ſhew'd A. of
a Friend's Son dying.
Right ſide, male Kin, & e con, or old Folks if all Wo-
men in an Houſe.
Eye-teeth ſhew of Children mid-ag'd, Friends and Trea-
ſure.
Great Teeth ſhew of old Folks and little Goods.
Goods, Cheek Teeth, hid Treaſure.
Eye-teeth, of common value.
Foreteeth, of ordinary Goods.
Come out in general, leave your Houſe or Church, &c.
With Blood, loſe a neareſt Relation.
to ſome expeſt ſuch dining abroad.
No Blood, loſe a familiar Friend only.
With Grief, one very near to you.
With no Grief, of remote Concern.
As ſtanding on Temple-Bar, to great Hazard Loſs.
14 out 2 Pieces at the right ſide all left, ſhew'd A.
all his own Corn too bad to eat, and therefore
buying.
Drawing out, to ſome Death.
to ſome have the Tooth-ach.
to ſome loſe Friends thro Quarrels.
Drawn out by others, ſhew'd A. that they
got away one of his Family.
Drawer, vid. Trade.
Taking out his left ſide ones, ſhew'd A. feeding daintily
for Health.
Becoming Dice, inheriting Life would be loſt by
it elſe.
Saying he'd keep them as long he liv'd, that is,
uſe ſuch Care.
In your Hand or Boſom, Loſs of Children.
Getting others upon't, Change of Condition, as &c.
Black or rotten and out, Death of old Folks.
Long hollow is drawn, one long expeſted leaves
you.
See ſuch of another's drawn, have a Gift or Le-
gacy there.   Teeth.

Teeth coming, black. To others Delivery from Anger or Evil.

    None at all have, to Servants Liberty.

      to Merchants Gain.

    All loft, to the Sick quick Recovery; if but one, flow.

    to fome Death, others Exile:

    to fome long Life as then toothlefs.

    At a blow, fhew'd of the Houfe's lofing all its Inhabitants.

      Recover'd again, Change of States

Some lofe with Grief, that is, our deareft Intimates.

    To fome Lofs of Goods.

    Great Teeth, hidden Treafures.

      To others fome Thing or Veffel of lefs import.

    To Debtors a Debt acquitted.

Temples fhew of our Wifdom, Authority, and Time of Life.

Thighs grown big and ftrong, promife of a real Plenty and Advance:

Well-fhap'd, to fome happy Journies.

    to a Woman Comfort by her Children.

Eroke, to a Maid marry a Stranger and live at diftance:

    to a Wife Widowhood or lofe her Children.

Wound there, difturb'd by Relations.

Elack and blue, to a Man die a Foreigner and out of Friends Aid.

    Right being fo, fhew'd one wicked to his Brother.

Seeing a Woman's naked, gives Health and Joy.

Hipps fhew of our Servant-Maids and Stewards.

Throat fhews of our Strength, Brothers, and Safety of life:

    As to fome, their Victuals and Pleafures.

Cut by a Knife, Injury from fome one, if not to Life:

    And not dying on't, gives Hopes and good Succefs in Bufinefs.

    Another's cut, do him Injury, as &c.

Toes, the utmoft part of them fhews of the utmoft Extremity.

Tongue declares of our Speech and Efteem for it.

    Hairy threats great Impediments, Difeafes, or Death.

    Black, fooner; white, later.

    To others Slander.

    Tied or bound, Impediments and Poverty there, no free Speech.

    Set forth, fhews flander.

Skin'd threats with Poifon.

Lofing, Mifery, Imprifonment, or Poverty, (as Tied *fupra*)

Swell'd, Lofs from Speech, or Sicknefs to Self or Wife.

    In mouth in houfe, near Death thro ftifling Notions.

Q

Tongue ſwell'd in mouth. Coming into Air large but flippant on D
               courſe, noble and free.
    Of Iron, ſharp and piercing.
      Gold, with grave Eloquence.
           But if ſtiff, proud in Folly.
     Stone, quite uſeleſs.
Veins ſhew of our Rents and yearly Profits.
Womb, vid. *Privities* ſupra.

C H A P. XXXII.

Of Senſe.

IN general Seeing is to act and order Courſes to appear, as are t
        Perſons.   Vid. *Looks* infra.
     Hearing is to ſuffer.
     Taſte
     Touch } are common.
     Smell
Sight in general ſhews of active Conſiderations, as are the things ſe
 (1)   To others it ſhews mental Diſcovery and Re
           lutions thereon.
Quality. Sharp ſhews of a good Underſtanding.
     Clear ſhew'd of a fine Proſpect ſeen.
     Firſt clear then dim, your Underſtanding betters
       Study, or you order more clearly.
     Steddy, examining things throughly.
     Obſcure and doubtful of things, threats of great I
       ſolution.
     Abrupt ſhews of Interruption, as &c.
     Hinder'd, Vid. *Hinder* in *Action.*
Manner. Into a Court, examine into ſome Approach to an Oe
     nomy.
     Prying narrowly ſhews of Guard and ſtrict Search.
     Go to ſee a place, that is, examine the Power of it.
       Another, quarrel and prove his Strength.
         And return on it, alter Meaſu
         thereon.
       The end of a Walk, proceed in a meth
       to a Concluſion.
     Your ſelf ſee another do ſomewhat, that is, take
       der for it ſo.
     Viewing from far the Chancellor ſeen, ſhew'd *A.* of
       quiry Relief near.
     Standing ſtill ſee hunting, ſee a violent Proſecution
       or againſt you.   *Si*

Sight. Manner. Standing. You going in't, you active thereto as follow-
(1)   ing.
    Things. Taking order of, or occasioning things according.
        To others a prudential Direction or Consideration
        according.
    Beasts. A Lion, discourse a King or Great man.
        Vid. *Beasts.*
    Beggar, vid. *Person* in *Grammar.*   Dead, vid. D.
    Figures, vid. *Mathematicks.*
    Gun *Wiltshire,* consider of a good Course in Resentment
    us'd there, to use it your self.
    Hell, to the Miserable Joy, as its Plagues going off.
        to the Happy Misery according ensuing.
    House-court see, consider of the Addreis to some Oeco-
    nomy.
        Brother's ruin'd seen, shews of your Interest Ri-
        val distress'd.
        You in't, your self hurt by rival
        Interest.
        Shop Booksellers see, be in consideration of some
        good Advice.
        Of Law, as to Law.
    Knife or a Sword see, and no more, quarrel but all may
    be well.   Lightning, Vid. in *Air critically.*
    Man, Vid. *Person* in *Grammar.*
    Person, a Man, that is, a reasonable Course offers that
        you so order, *&c.*
        Seen acting so, measures issuing thereon
        so, *&c.* from you, *&c.*
        A Woman see fling by a Book, in your Opinion
        scorn some Instruction.
        A Beggar see, that is, your self be in Want and
        troublesom Expectation.   Dead, vid. D.
        's House, vid. *supra.*
    Lion, vid. *Beast supra.*
    Play acted, vid. *Diversions.*
        A History reacted, take measures as to see it re-
        peated.
        A Tragedy, quarrel to hazard such a fatal Change.
    Swords, vid. *Knives supra.*
    Appearance bright, that is, self-evident and clear.
        Iron gives chearful Assurance in Difficulty.
    Vid. *Looking-glass.*   Vid *Colour* and *Obscure infra.*
    Shining Sun seen, gives of present Ease in Necessities.
        Stars, give a splendid Fortune.
        Moon the brighter, the better Profit in Merchan-
        dize.
        Obscure *e con:*

Sight. Appear, diſappearing abruptly things ſeen, ſhews Deſigns weakly
(1)   alter'd.

       Thro Miſts, thro Errors.

       Enemy's Sword ſeen, his Reſentment chang'd.

       Vid. *Vaniſh* infra.

       Gradual a Man ſee appear perfect from Lines mathema-
         tical, a growing Examination, as &c.

As, Vid. *Like* infra.

Askew a Friend looking, ſhews he acts diſmiſſing due regards
       to you.

       Gentlemen ſee look on you, that is, your ſelf act ungen-
        teely.

Bright, Vid. *Appearance* ſupra.

Change, Vid. *Alter in Action.*

       Greater, Vid. *Great in Quantity.*

       Manner. Thro reading a Book find a Change, cauſe
         ſuch thro purſuing ſuch Inſtruction, &c.

     Perſons. Servant to a Torch ſeen, threated one Blind-
         neſs.

       Enemy, to a Child a bad Courſe to gain.

         to a Woman an ill Courſe poſſible of
          a noble Uſe, becoming as a Scheme
          at your command.

       Friend ſo, the ſame.

         Seems mean, the Aid offering, as &c.
         proves contemptible.

       Beggar to another's Boy, others Hopes prove
        to help your Wants.

       Siſter to a Serpent of Clay, your Diviſion be-
        comes trifling.

       Woman *incognito* proves a Queen, your clouded
        Fortune ſhines, &c.

       Scholar become again at *Oxon*, diſpute again as
        when there.

         Prefer'd ſeem there, be learned as to
         merit great Eſteem.

    Man to a Woman, to the Poor Succour.

         to a Scholar ſcheme things, but act
         to others pleaſure.

         to ſome Change of Place.

         to the Rich Loſs of Power.

         to Magiſtrates very bad, model things,
         but act at others Wills.

         to Labourers Sickneſs.

         to Servants leſs Labour.

         Vid. ſupra *In general Enemy*, &c.

     Seen in female Apparel, monſtrous. (*Hermaph.*)

    Woman to a man, to a Maid marriage.

                               Sight.

Sight. Change. Woman to a man, to a Wife a Son.
(1)   to a Mother Widowhood.
                                      to a Servant Pains as a Man.
      Become Gold, to the Poor Riches.
              to Slaves be ſold.
              to the Rich Plots.
              to the Sick Death.
        A Tree, to ſome Sickneſs.
                to ſome Joy and Profit.
        Braſs, to Soldier Victory.
              to a Servant Liberty.
              Forehead only ſuch, Shame to all but
                Jeſters.
      Iron, threats you prodigious Miſeries.
      Cloth, beat one to force him to act reputably.
      Stone, threats with receiving Blows and
        Wounds.
      A Beaſt, ſhews of Humanity turn'd to Rapine.
      A Bird flying into Heaven, be preſer'd thro
        Projects.
      A Sun or Star, that is, a Judg or Senator.
      Earth is Death, except to Potters.
      Fire, be inglorious or ſick of an Ague or Fe-
        ver.
      Fair or ugly exceedingly, is both alike evil.
      Age, young to old in ſucceſsive Ages, ſhew'd
              A. of being in ſuch State childleſs.
            Becoming young, threats Sickneſs and
                Weakneſs.
                V. *Cradled* in *Child,&c.*
              Old, better'd in circumſtance,
                but with Infirmity.
      Bigger grown moderately, gives Increaſe of
                Goods.
            Immoderately, threats Death.
          Fight an Enemy till he become a
            Child, quarrel to Gain, *&c.*
      Dead become when alive, play the Knave.
          Your Friend ſeems, that is, he ceaſes to
            be ſuch.
          A fair Woman turn'd to a Carcaſe, an
            Opinion proving ill.
              Man ſo, a rational Courſe proving
                as abominable.
          Appearing for Perſons alive, ſhew of
            Cheats.
          Self ſeeming, vid. *Dead.*

                    Q 3   *Sight,*

Sight. Change, become dead self seem, and buried on't, be imprison
(1)   as a Rogue.
                                          But if alive, unjust[l]
    Parts. Teeth lose and get others, change yo[ur]
        Condition.
            Eyes falling into A's Feet, shew'd Se[r]
            vants marrying his Daughters.
            Leg A's stepping into a Pit became Ma[r]
            ble, he died of a Dropsy.
    Beasts become tame or wild, vid. *Beast.*
            A's Calf seem'd like another he had, [&]
            gave him the same Usage.
            Men shew the Savage or Appetite turn[ed]
                to Reason.
                    Only eyed as Men, in appea[r]
                    ance only or in acting not
                    designing.
    Man becomes a Fish, that is, a melancholy Dotar[d]
                    a Beast, to a Servant Reprehensi[ve]
                    of his Master.
                    an Hart, threats his Life full
                    Snares and Fears.
                    an Eagle, to a Combatant ga[ve]
                    Victory.
                    a Bull as being his Arms, it shew[d]
                    him treated with Family Civili[ty]
                    a Crow on Seed-ground, a Destroy[er]
                    of Children.
                    a Countess to Bread, an Estate
                    Glory to Necessity.
                    an Harvest-woman to a Greyhoun[d]
                    a Tenant to an Enemy.
            Monster to a Farmer's Daughter, an Error
            Husbandry Profit.
            Deer you hunt proves another's Boy, your Ga[me]
            proves their Expectation fool'd.
            Horse under him becoming a Tree, shew'd
                his Creditor dying fail'd him.
                    Chang'd for another, your Friend alte[r]
                    his Service.
                    to an Ape, your Strength or Rich[es]
                    es proves a Foolery.
    Place as chang'd so, alters your Circumstance in Actio[n]
                Vid. *Place.*
    Things. Cloke to a Coat, your shifting Affairs to
            more creditable.
            Clothes fine becoming Rags, threats you Povert[y]
            Corn to Gold, gave excellent Farming.
                                                    Sigh[t]

Sight. Change. Things. Country A's seen chang'd to Snow and then melt
(1)   away, shew'd so of his Family also vanish-
             ing.

Door turn'd to a Chimney, shew'd *A.* of his
       Estate consum'd in Charity.

Field seen first green then dry, shew'd *A.* of
       the Perverseness of his Temper.

Garments changing for Office, to some Death.
             Vid. *Cloke,* &c. supra.

GOD, vid. *Spirits.*

Grass to Gold, gives excellent Farming.

Hair, Vid. *Beast.*

Hermaphrodite, vid. *Grammar.*

House yours seen, and so is your Oeconomy or
       Converse State like to be.

Jewels all to Pearl, to a Wife Widowhood.

Journy change, and so your Designs in Busines.

Mony in pocket to Brass, and so your Plenty to
       Debts.

Moon to Blood, Ecclesiastick State alter'd, *&c.*

Prayers his finding alter'd, shew'd *A.* of his
       Expectation crost.

River seen turn'd to a Ditch, shew'd of a Reve-
       nue fool'd away.

Side left, *&c.* vid. *Posture.*

Smoke, vid. *S.* in *Fire.*

Spring small becoming a Lake or River, unex-
       pected Riches.   Street, vid. *City.*

Timber to Persons shew'd of an Estate in dan-
       ger.

Times and Laws, that is, Customs and Manners.

Victuals seen chang'd to Marble, threated *A.* Death.

Water sail'd over boldly turns to a Pavement, a Course
       troublesom proves firm by Agreement.

Writing Funeral Tickets to blank Paper, shew'd the Sick
       Recovery.

Colour in general, vid. *Creatures.*   Vid. *Apparel.*

Coloured Water threats with bad Eyes.

White is open.   Black, secret.

Red, *&c.* indifferent.   Various, deceitful.

Black threats Grief, Fear, Anger and Misfortunes.

But if decent, shews of Gravity, Modesty, and
       Dignity.

Cat gnawing the Finger, shew'd one a Gangrene
       there.

Clothes wear, to some Joy.

           to some be of wicked and deceitful
           Repute.

Sight. Colour, Black Clothes, Vid. *Robes* in *Apparel,*
(?)   Clouds, Vid. *Air* ſupra.

Figs eating, Gain with Sorrow, as by a Friends Death.

Fleſh, Vid. *F,* in *Body Human.*

Horſeman, ſhew'd of an Emperor rich, but ſevere in Diſcipline.

Ox Danger, Vid. *Ox* in *Beaſt.*

Rainbow ſeen, threats with Calamity and Deſtruction.

Sun ſeen, is as Deſtruction to the whole Family.

Duskineſs, threats Grief of Mind, Doubt and Trouble.

Green bright, ſhews of Joy, Hope, Chaſtity and Honour.

    Dull, threats Poiſon, Deceit or Sadneſs.

    Seen your ſelf, threats you Heavineſs,

    Wood, Vid. *Quality* ſupra,

Pale, Vid. *infra* in *White.*

Purple, ſhews of Anger, Dignity, Ambition and Bloodſhed.

    Obſcure, ſhews of great Pride and Cruelty.

Red, threats as bloody,

    Garments wearing, ſhew'd bleeding.

    Fruit eating, ſhew'd of Loſs of Blood.

Ruſtineſs, ſhews of Diffidence, Grief and Cruelty,

Sad colour'd Clothes, of melancholy Repute, *&c.*

Sky bright, ſhews of Dignity, Gravity and Majeſty.

    Dull, threats with Grief, Deceit and Poiſon.

Various, ſhews of Changeableneſs, Immodeſty and Deceit.

    Colour'd Horſe, a deceitful Eſtate.

    A ſtrange colour'd Dog, a Man of ſtrange Manners.

White and pale, to ſome threats Death.

    to ſome, threats of Enemies cruel and malicious.

    Your Familiar ſeen, ſhews he envies you.

    Thy Friend ſeen, gives thee anxious, but happy Cares.

Splendid, ſhews of all good, Human and Divine.

    Crown of Flowers falling from Heaven for *A.* to put on, his Death.

    Hair'd being, that is, full of pure Wiſdom.

    Hen ſeen on a Dunghil, ſhew'd of Diſgrace thro falſe Accuſations.

    Horſe, that is, one tender and weak.

                      Sight.

ight. Colour White and Splendid Horseman crown'd, shew'd of an innocent Emperor.
(1)

  Kite, an hypocritical sly Robber by
   Project.

  Wolf the same, more open and great.

Yellow, shews of Folly, Impudence, Deceit and Riches.
  To others, Anxiety, Torment and Jea-
   lousy.

  Cloth'd Angel, shew'd *A.* of the Plague Infection.   Vid. *Apparel.*

  Fruit eating, threats Diseases gathering not so
   bad.

  Golden, shews of Dignity.

Darkness is ill to all but the Secret.
  to the Sick, Death.
  to Malefactors, Chains and all Impediments.
  to some, Fear, Despair and ill Deeds.
   Hence said Christ, *They loved Darkness,*
    &c.
  to some, Sorrow or Sickness to follow.
  to many, Ignorance with its Hurts and Expectances.   Vid. *Clouds* in *Air.*
  Vid. *Night* in *Time.*   Vid. *Candle* in *Fire.*
Full of it, that is, invisible Confusion thro Error.
  To others it shews Quarrels thro sullen Reserve.
In the Dark hearing Spirits, shew'd of caterwauling
  Cheats.

Dark Day, that is, an unhappy State.
  Light put, Vid. *L.* in *Fire.*
  Room an Oeconomy or Converse wicked, or
   foolish, or ignorant.
  Sun seen, shews the Government chang'd, or the
   King dead.
  To others, horrid private ill State.
  By Smoke, Errors clouding clearest Truths.
  Moon seen, shews the Queen dies, or the Church
   alters.
   To some, has shewn Danger
   by great and treacherous
   Women.

Acts. Fight in it, wrangle about blind Cavils.
  Lose your way in't, become blinded in your
   Course by Passion, &c.
  Pursued in't by wild Beasts, in Terror of
   Enemies thro Ignorance, &c.
  Thron'd in Light in the midst of Darkness
   Christ seen, shew'd of greatest Revela-
   tions.

           Sight,

Sight. Darkneſs. Acts. Travel in't, deſign in Ignorance, &c.
(1)   Diſappear, Vid. *Appear* ſupra.
Light great, to the retired Trouble.
     to the Sick, Death.
     overgreat, threats with Blindneſs.
To ſome, Piety, Wiſdom and Honour.
To Bondmen, Liberty.
To Artificers, Perfection.
Lighter growing, that is, freer of Sin and Error.
Vid. *Appear* ſupra, and *Fire.*
I ike Beaſts four-footed walking, threats Sickneſs.
     Head and Ears, Vid. *Body.*
     Hair, Vid. *Body.*   Vid. *Hog* and *Horſe* in *Beaſt.*
     As a Dragon voic'd, that is, falſe and Tyrannical.
     An Horſe footed, gave Knighthood.
Chamber as yours *A.* has, that is, a private Oeconomy
     in like Circumſtance.
Perſons dead being like, threats you a wicked Life.
         See others, they are ill.
     Father like, that is, a courſe as tender and good.
London Stairs, an Oeconomy Addreſs beſt in ſort.
Perſons. Devil like unto ſee one but friendly, that is, a
     courſe thought of Deſpair proves good to you.
     Friend like unto one ſeems, that is, ſuch a
     Courſe will not prove ill.
     Vid. *Enemy* in *Grammar.*
     Vid. *Another* in *Poſſeſs.*
Chamber like your Brothers, a Managery near thwarting
     you in Intereſt.
Acts. Like to be kill'd but prevented, gave Delivery from
     danger.
     A. will not return or do the like, ſhews of wrong
     done.
     A. has 2 white Coach Horſes and 1 too little, that is,
     1 weak and ill match'd.
     As *Hercules* fulfil his Labours, to a Woman be burnt
         as he.
         To a Man it gives renown'd Ex-
         ploits.
     Another ſuffer, that is, partake of his Crimes,
     G. did fall from a Precipice, that is, miſs of his
     like Hopes.
As before fell a Lamb, ſhew'd *A.* of having another again
     ſo to ſell.
Your laſt have a Calf, that is, one you'l uſe as you did
     that.
Looks in general, Vid. *Seeing* above.   Vid. *Face* in *Body.*
     Vid. *Looking-Glaſs* in *Goods.*

                   Sight.

*Sight.*Looks in general. After another, shews of mental Expectation
(1) as &c.

On your Hands, threats Sickness.

For your Children in Distress, take care of
them as if so.

Back, Vid. *Posture.*

Quality Pale, Vid. *Colour* supra.

Sneaking, shews of Efforts sneaking according.

Slight, shews of slight Treatment according.

Smiling God departing on whipping *A.* shew'd
him sick and recovering.

Your Friend seen on ill threatned,
shew'd of its issuing happily.

Creditors seen, shews you'l thrive to
deserve Trust.

Vid. *Laugh* in *Passion.*

Terrible, shews of being powerful and mighty.

Stern and shrewd Men, threat of Guilt and
hard Examiners.

Troubled, shew of want of Mony, or a Stink.
To some, their Children sick.

Pleasant Friend sees you, your Behaviour anfwer to all Expectation.

Stranger seen, shews of some new
Course of Ease and Plenty offering.

Stout Persons seen, shew of a Carriage confident and bold.

Sneering at you seeing one, threats you acting
ridiculously.

Askew Gentry looking on you, shews of your
acting ungenteely.

Obscure, Vid. *Colour, Darkness* and *Appearance* supra.

Presentations, threat with Doubt and Irresolution.

And troubled Light seen, threats Heaviness and Death
by Sickness.

Sun seen, is bad to all but the Secret.

By Smoke, Error darkning clearest Truths.

Overlooked ones Works seen by the dead, shew'd *A.* of his never ending them.

Unless in Place unknown, then Delay for
a while only.

By another, is as peep'd at beneath.

From a Chamber Window, in others private Manageries.

Peeping at you another seen, shews of his trying to trick you.

To others, it threats them in a constant Regard, as is
the Person.

Prospect into a Garden have, be in Consideration of some plenty
State; *Sight.*

Sight. Proſpect from high have, be ambitious in curious Deſigns.
(1)   Of a City, ſee ſome Hope of a univerſal Good or Con-
        verſe appear near your Command.
        Houſe at a Diſtance, an Oeconomy poſſible
        hereafter.
        To ſee a National Battel, a Security againſt preſent
        Hurt near.
        From his Cloſet Window *A.* ſeeing his Rival at his
        Door, ſhew'd of his making him as beg thro his
        Managery.
        Fine of 3 Coaches ſeen, ſhew'd *A.* of a ſtately Viſit
        for 3 Days.
Seeming Childleſs, threats with danger of loſing them.
Shadows ſeen, ſhew of dark Imaginations.
        Of a Mountain, the Preſence of a Power protecting.
Shew fine, a noble and hopeful Proſpect.
Shining, Vid. *Appear* ſupra.
Tranſparent things as Glaſs ſeen, reveal Secrets.
Vaniſhing Appearances imaginary on view, great Expectations
        coming to nothing.
        Vid. *Diſappear* in *Appear* ſupra.
        Sheep follow'd vaniſh'd in *Weſtminſter-Hall,* *A.* loſt a
        Profit in a Wrangle.
        Death ſeen, ſhew'd *A.* of its fears going off.
        Fire your wooden one vaniſhes, your Profit hop'd for
        fails you.   Vid. *Fire.*
        Garden paſt vaniſhing, ſhew'd *A.* of his Servant leav-
        ing him, ſupporting his plenty State.
        Horſe under you, your Repute for Learning ceaſing.
        Ghoſt vaniſhing *A*'s Wife appear'd, the Cheat as ima-
        gined prov'd his proper Art.
        Men, reaſonable Courſes.
        Places, Circumſtances or States anſwerable.
        Perſons. *Xerxes*'s Olive Crown overſpreading the Earth,
        his vaſt Army proving defeated.
        Purſuers, that is, Terrors dreading you ceaſing.
        Alexander entering *Babylon* Temple in a *Perſian*
        Robe vaniſh'd, he got the Empire but ſoon
        died.
        Robbers ſet up for Houſe keeping vaniſh, that
        is, the Thought that *A.* ſubſiſts as a Cheat
        only goes off.
        Wife *A*'s vaniſhes, that is, her Aid becomes
        uſeleſs, as &c.
Robbers, Vid. *Perſons* ſupra.
Stars ſeen, to ſome loſe their Hair.
        to the Rich, Poverty.
        to the Poor, Death,

                                Sight.

Sight. Vanifhing Sun feen, threats Death, Blindnefs, or Lofs of a Child.
(1)   Wife, Vid. *Perfon* fupra.

     View, Vid. *Profpect* fupra.

     Vifible Hound fee hunt, perceive of anothers Servant purfuing you.

         Hear another not feen, a 2d joins him as you'l find by Report.

         Unfeen dead calling you, threats you Death near. Vid. *Dead.*

Hearing. To all is fuffering, and fome obeying.
(2)   To all paffive, as fee active, and fo often fhews of Expectation and Wifdom.

     Sounds in general, to many of News and Meffages.

     Out of hearing, Vid. *Diftance* in *Quantity.*

     Overhear another in Difcourfe, prevent his Transactions as in Defign.

         You unknow fear, be cautious againft odd Methods fooling your Actions in Prevention.

    Creatures, Vid. *Beafts.*

     Speaking, that is, matter of Appetite iffuing to reafonable Action.

     Affes braying, threat with Damage.

     Birds noify, fhew of Danger near.

     Cock crowing, gives Profperity.

     Dogs barking, fhew of Enemies Overthrow, if your own, &c.

     Hens cackle and Geefe cry, gives of Profit and Difpatch in little Family Projects, &c.

     Ravens croaking, threats Sadnefs.

     Serpents hifs, but neither fee nor feel them, fhews of powerlefs Enemies.

     Swallows chattering about an Houfe, threats of Hurt by Flatterers.

    Things. Bells, Vid. *Religion.*

     Report, act as giving Credit thereto.

     Clocks ftrike, fhews of Infamy and miffing of time.

     Shaking things about you, threat Deceit as where dreamt.

     Thunder and horrid Noifes, threats with Terror and Diftrefs.

    Perfons, Vid. *Difcourfe* and *Grammar.*

     A Woman racket Chairs in a Chamber above, be in a reftlefs Oeconomy.

     Your Wife fcold, threats you with great Diforders and Torments as might occafion it.

     Loud Speaking, fhews of paffionate Action.

     A Goaler threaten, that is, avoid Circumftances menacing Death.

     Another ceafe to hear, that is, regarding him ceafe.

                             Hearing.

Hearing. Persons. Another speak in answer unto, conform your Measure
(2)   of Action according.   Vid. *Discourse,* &c.
    A rich Man chide a Spunger hear your self, avoid of
        occasion of the like.
    A Voice and no Body seen, Delusion with false Pretences.
                From Heaven, such with relation
                    to Religion or Government.
                Vid. *Invisible* in *Spirits.*
    Fatal said to be heard, threatned of a desperate Issue.
    Intelligible hearing, shews you'l stay in your native
        Land, as unintelligible shews Travel.
    Like a Dragon, that is, an Effort of Action of Tyran-
        ny offering, &c.
        God's hearing, teaches Secrets; and shews living
            well.
        As of many Waters, that is, of many People.
    Pleasant and no Body seen, shews Joy.
            to some, Reconciliation or Oppression of Ene-
                mies.
            to some, the same as if sung, or occasion'd by
                ones self.
    Shrill, shews of a Temper desperate and exhaust
        with Deceit.
            Your own seeming so, threats you such Impe-
                diment in your Affairs.
    Slender, threats with Deceit.
            Made by your self, shews you of Impedi-
                ments.
        Unpleasant, shews of ill News or compel'd Fears.
    Passion, crying foreshews Grief.   Vid. *Cry* in *Passion.*
        Howling Devils heard, *Fra. Spira*'s Despair.
        Sighing heard, bodes ill Events to your self or Friends.
        Laughing, forethreats of Sadness and Complaints.
        Groans, shew of Trouble and Anguish.
    Singing sweet, shews of ill News and Friends Complaints.
            Your self, you also shall sigh and cry.
        To others, it shews of Deceit, and Passions long issuing.
Smelling shews of good or ill Fame, as is the Scent.
(3)   To some, it shews of their first Attempts.
    To some, it discovers Secrets.
    To some, it shews of their Favour or Hate.
    Vid. *Nose* in *Body.*
    Extensive, and so the Fame.
    Lost, Vid. *Nose* in *Body Human.*
        Of Cheese to *A.* that is, his Repute of chusing it faild.
    Sorts, good praise, and the greater the better.
        Bad, Slander and Infamy, and the greater the worse.
        Cedar an House smelling of, that is, an Oeconomy great and
            stately.
                                    Smel.

Smell. Sorts. Odors golden Vials of them, ſhew'd of the Prayers of the
(3)   Saints.
          Perfumes fine ſmelling, to a Prince Death.
                              to a private Perſon, Health.
          Stinking Breath having, threats univerſal Hatred.
               Miſts, that is, wicked Errors.
               Oxskins, ſhew'd of uſeleſs Farm Services.
               Water bathing in, ſhew'd of Shame and Accuſa-
                    tions.
               Drinking, threats of violent Diſtempers.
               Worms found in *A*'s Coat, ſhew'd him infamous
                    Adultery in his Wife.
          A. entering anothers Houſe and finding him aſleep, cut out
               his Fat and Excrement ſtinking Guts, and carried them
               off; that is, *A.* rob'd another.
Taſting in general, threats with Pain and Torture of Mind and Body.
(4)   Things, *Alkermes* ſhew'd *A.* of paying an Apothe-
               caries Bill.
               Ill to Exceſs, Death.
               Elſe not.
               Moderate, Loſs of Friends.
          Aſtringents, threats with Grief, Cold and Fear.
          Bitter Fruit, or other things if exceedingly ſo, threats Death;
               Moderate, Death of Friends or Loſs of Goods.
               Little, threats us only Grief of Mind.
          Fattineſs, ſhews either of Sickneſs or Greedineſs.
          Inſipidneſs, threats with Falſhood or Vanity.
          Saltneſs, ſhews of Prudence and Pleaſure.
               To others, of Slander and Lazineſs.
               Salt taſted inſipid, threats either Madneſs or Deceit.
               (Chriſt's Words.)   Vid. *Victuals.*
          Sharp, threats with Torture of Mind and Body.   Chriſt's
               Cup in his Paſſion.
               Forcing Tears, the worſe.
               Wine, ſhew'd *A.* of a Son's Funeral.
               And four as Vinegar, labour for Suſtenance.
                    Bitter, threats Death by hard Diſeaſes, if exceſſive.
                         Of this ſort are Muſtard Seed and red
                         Pepper.
               Tobacco of *Engliſh* Growth taſting, ſhew'd *A.* dange-
                    rouſly quarrelling a Phyſician.
          Sour Apples, threat with Sedition and Noiſe.
          Acids, ſhew of Venery and ſhort Pleaſure.
          Harſh, to ſome pleaſant Labour.
                    Fruit taſting of, to ſome Death, if exceeding.
          Sweets in general, ſhew of Subtlety.
                    They give as well Grief as Pleaſure.
          Meats eating, ſhew'd of reading Romances.

                                             Taſting

Taſting. Sweet Meats ſeeing, foreſhew'd *A.* of a Preſent of Oranges.
  (4)   Wine drinking, gave good Succeſs in Law.
         Things eat, taſte a reaſoning as delicious.
             to ſome, be oppreſt with many Cares.

Feeling in general, and handling, ſhew of our Love and buying this
  (5).   Vid. *Hands* in *Body.*
      Things, Leeches ſucking you, ſenſible of Extortioners devour
         you.
        A full grown Child in her, to one big, ſenſible of
         time near.
        Figures, Vid. *Mathemat.* in *Quantity.*
        Pain, ſhews of Danger or Wickedneſs, as is the Part.
  Touch another, ſlander him.
        Touch'd by him, ſo ſlander'd.
  Touching a fair Woman, ſhews of Pleaſure with Profit.
        Anothers Houſe Foundation, cenſuring of his Subſiſter
          Frize Coat, examining of his ſheepiſh Spirit
          Repute.
        The dead, gives Infirmity, but with long Life.
        The Sky a Crown wearing, ſhew'd *A.* of Death near
        Vid. *Stroke* in *Action.*
  Touch'd by Lightning, diſcovers Sins in Poverty.
        Vid. *Lightning* in *Air critically.*
        By a great Man to receive Warmth, becoming great
         help'd by him.
        By *Jupiter* deſcending in Lightning, *Alexander's* Fathe
        Belly.
        By a Woman in Mourning, ſhew'd *A.* in Terror at
        Tooth's breaking in his Head.
  Qualities Cold, threats with Impediments in all things.
        To others, Loſs, Diffidence and Numneſs.
          Vid. *Air* in *Froſt.*
        Brought by the Wind, Poverty.
        Meat eating, Matter in ſuſpence finiſhing.
        Bread, Vid. *Heat* infra.
        Warmth *è con,* ſhews of Riches and Comfort.
  Dry, Vid. *Liquid* infra.
  Figures, Vid. *Mathemat.*
  Hardneſs generally threats of Poverty and Slavery.
         To ſome, Stability.
        Soft things, ſhew of all good, and are bett
        than ſmooth.
  Heat moderate, gives Proſperity with Diſpatch and Pr
        dence.
        Exceſſive, threats Grief and Heat of Mind.
        Sun ſcorching, Tyranny confounding.
        Burning, threats Dangers from Paſſions, Fevers, *&c*
        Hot Bread, gives Riches with Trouble.

                             Feelin

Feeling. Qualities. Heat. Hot Bread, carrying it threats with Accufa-
(s)   tions.   Vid. *Cold* fupra.

Heavinefs threats with Labour, Care, and Injury.
    In Prudence and Stability 'tis only good.
    Vid. *Quality.*   Vid. *Tools in Trade.*
    To fome Grief, Poverty, and Difeafes.
    To fome old Age and Impediments.
    Heavy Friend preffing *A.* fhew'd him fick
      with Recovery.
      Enemy the fame with Danger and
      worfe Iffue.
Lightnefs fhews of Inftability, a quick come and go.
    To fome Facility of Action.
    A light Blow by a Magiftrate, a trifling for-
      mal Difgrace.
      Coffin, a trifling Fear of Death.
Liquidity fhews of Inconftancy if moift.
    Drinefs fhews of Aptnefs for ufe.
      To Rottennefs, Age, Poverty,
      and vain Labour.
    Dry fee your River, Pond, or Fountain,
      be your felf poor or die.
    Leaves, Words fpoke of old.
    Ditch feen ruin with Water, Riches.
    Tree cut down having, fhew'd *A.*
    Inheritance after Controverfy.
Sharpnefs threats with Grief, Poverty, Pain, and
    Difeafe.
Smoothnefs gives Relief to all forts of Mifery.
    'Tis Patience under ill.
    To fome chance Help.
    Rough Breaft fhews of ill Excufes and
      a bad Confcience.
      Hair approaching, a furly Dun
      for Mony.
Steddinefs fhews of Prudence, if not unpleafant.

C H A P. XXXIII.

Of Bodily Action.

Awake, vid. *Sleep* infra.
  Belching fhews of uttering carelefly abominable and abufive
    Words.
A's Finger being, fhew'd him jeer'd about Mony Payment.

R

Bit

Bit *A*'s Finger. Rats gnawing a Box, ſhew'd *A*. his Servants about a gain-
leſs Work.

    Biting your Nails threats you with Wrangling and Vexation.
        A Madman's Ear off, being more mad in Repute than he.
        Chewing of Gold gives Gain, Profit, and Joy.
By Words, affected by them.
    A Cat, cheated by a ſly Thief.
        A black one gnawing *A*'s Finger, ſhew'd him dying of a
          Gangrene there.
    A Dog, threats with Wounds and Accuſations.
        A Spaniel, caught in a ſneaking fawning Trick.
        Vid. *Dog* in *Beaſt*.
    A Fox holding *A*'s Hand in his Mouth unhurt, ſhew'd of a cun-
    ning Enemy's preventing his Actions.
    A Lion, devoured by your Prince.
        Of Marble, ſhew'd *A*. poiſon'd by a Viper in ſuch Sta-
        tues Mouth.
    Mice, teas'd by Fellow Collegiates or Houſematcs.
    Serpent, hurt by a ſubtle Enemy.
        Vid. *Serpent* in *Poiſonous Creatures*.
    A Viper, to ſome great Riches.
    Wolf, hurt by an open Enemy.
Born again, to a poor man Maintenance from Friends.
    to the Miſerable Good.
    to the Servant the Love of his Maſter.
    to the Tradeſman want of Work and Change of manners.
    to ſome great Trouble and Servitude.
    to the Rich man loſe the Rule of his Houſe.
    to the Sick man Death.
    to the Traveller Return.
        Of his own Mother, ſhew'd him inheriting her
        dying after.
    to the Combatant Vanquiſhment as impotent.
    to the Husband with a Wife big, a Son like him.
        Not with Child, ſhe dies.
    to ſome Eſcape of great Dangers.
    to the Sinner Converſion.   (Our Saviour to *Nicodemus*.)
    Reentring their Mother's Womb, to Travellers ſhews Return.
    Miſcarriage, to a married Woman ſhews her Husband's Affairs
        failing.   Vid. *Grammar*.
        Have Flowers only, if with Child, be indiſ-
        pos'd but recover.
    Bringing forth a Stork, that is, one will ſupport Father or Mo-
    ther.
        Serpent devouring *Turks* and covering *Albania*,
        Scanderbeg's Mother.
        Viper threats the Mother Death in Labour.
        Satyr, that is, a man powerful, but wicked and
        tyrannical.   Born.

Born. Bringing forth a Spider shew'd of one who would kill his Parents.
        Vid. *Deliver'd* in *Woman* and *Child.*
                Seeing Children born, threats with damage.
                        An House bring forth shew'd of a Conspiracy
                        there.
                        A Mule, vid. *M.* in *Beast.*
Breathing shews of Delivery from Trouble and Anxiety.
                Stinkingly threats with the Hatred of all, and as if allego-
                ried all your Discourses hateful, *&c.*
        Hindred, to some drowning.
                        to Rogues a Prison.
                        to others Freedom of Action obstructed.
        Very greatly shews either of Death or deceiving some body.
Breed, vid. *Action.*   Bring forth, vid. *Born* supra.
Coughing threats Diseases and Disgrace thro ill Gains.
Deliver'd, vid. *Born* supra, and *Child* in *Grammar.*
Devouring, vid. *Eat* infra, and in *Victuals.*
Dream, vid. *Sleep* infra.   Vid. *Divination* in *Spirits.*
Drinking, Vid. *Drink.*
Eating, vid. *Victuals*, and *Dead* and *Bite* supra.
                to some Gain.
                        And hard of Digestion; lasting.
        Fruit or Victuals is fullest Enjoyment, as having is Command
        only.
        At Privities, vid. *Members* in general, and *Privities* in *Body.*
        Devouring is better than eating, and greater Gain if by your
                self.
                        Another seen, threats he preys on you.
                An Ape a Lion seen, gave the Sick Recovery.
                Many *Turks* a Serpent deliver'd of, covering *Albania,*
                Scanderbeg's Mother.
                        Fish seen, shew of untractable and untamable Enemies.
Farting shews of doing things shameful, and wilfully publishing them.
                to some it threats of great Fears and Pains in the Belly.
        With no ill Smell, shew'd only of disorderly Words.
Feeding, vid. *Action* and *Eat* supra.
Gnashing the Teeth, vid. *Teeth* in *Body.*
Gnawing, vid. *Bite* supra.
Groans hearing, threats Trouble and Anguish.
        In publick Dreams they shew of an active Care of others Mise-
        ries.
Growing bigger shews of Might and Power.
                Stronger, that is, of firmer Resolution.
        Full grown, of Perfection in its Nature.
        Vid. *Son* and *Heir* in *Family.*   Vid. *Herbs* in *Vegetables.*
        Worms kill e'er grown to Dragons, prevent the Commencement
        of Tyranny in your self.
Hiccough, to the Well Sickness, to the Sick Death.
                                R 2

Hiccough, to others exceeding Grief.

Hunger in general ſhews us indigent, laborious, and ingenious.

　　　　To moſt Deſire of Gain.　　　Vid. *Eat* ſuprà.

　　Fill'd being with Bread, ſhew'd *A*. purchaſing a good Farm.

Kicking is as beating with Contempt.

　　　　Hogs lying down, quarrelling, baſe and ſullen dejected Perſons.

　　Aſſes having, gives ſtubborn Servants and vexatious Rents.

　　2 ſeen kick ſo in Bed as forc'd to have Bedſtaves, ſhew'd of their lazy Quarrels offenſive to others.

Kick'd by an Ox, hurt by Great men to Slavery.

　　　　Another: ſtabled Horſe, treated ill by him in your Mony Payment.

Kick'd *A*'s Horſe being at an Inn by Rogues, ſhew'd him of his Purſe fool'd.

Kiſſing in general, vid. *Farewel* in *Words*, and *Lying* infra.

　　　　It ſhews of an hopeful Greeting and Meeting to an Iſſue according.

　　　　Leſs than lying with, *&c.*

　　　　Kiſs taking, gives Joy and Gain to you in ſuch manner.

　　　　　　giving threats you Damage by helping others ſo.

　　To ſome ſhews ſudden Nuptials.

　　To ſome Hoſtile and Fighting as the uſual Signal.

　　To ſome benefit others to their own Loſs.

　　　　And wipe the Mouth on it, with Contempt after.

　　To an old Man Scorn and Deriſion if from improper Perſons.

In Lechery, to ſome give or take a Benefit, as *&c.*

　　　　to Men and Women mutually alike.

　　　　Heartily, cordial therein.

　　　　By an unknown Whore, in an odd unexpected Courſe.

　　　　A Boy, threats with naſty Deſires.

Things. The Earth threats with Sadneſs and Humility.

　　　　A Tomb, bury a Child or publiſh a fair Book.

　　　　Eternal Verity, come to a true underſtanding of things.

A Member of ones own, return'd one his Son from Travel.

　　　　If your Son at home, threats his Sickneſs.

　　　　　　Having none, it promiſes one.

　　　　Another's Feet, ſhews of Repentance.

　　　　Arſe, provoke him to ſcorn you.

　　　　Your Forehead being by another, ſhews he admires your Capacity.

Refuſed kiſſing by one, fail'd in ſome expected Benefit.

Perſons. Kiſs'd by another ſee your Wife, threats ſhe'l give you occaſion of Jealouſy.

　　　　But he kiſſing another after more nearly, ſhew'd him naught to another after, tho not with her.

　　　　　　　　　　　　　　　　　　　　Kiſſing

Kissing Persons. Dead, to the Sick Death.
        to some Secrecy, to some Fasting.
        to some Infirmity with long Life, and as if laid
           take leave of the Death you were near.
  Father own, presents you with as entire a Friendship.
  Daughter own in Lust, help a weak Friend.
  Enemies, threats with greater Enmities.
        But with speaking it may be a Reconciliation.
  Kings, gives Gain with Joy.
  Great Persons, shews of Consolations.
  Schoolmaster, be vex'd with one too nice for Instruc-
    tion.
  Servants, shew'd *A.* borrowing their Wages.
  Woman kissing a Woman, threated her cross'd in her
        Love.
        a fair one, to a man shew'd hitting off
        a noble Opinion.
        a great Lord's Lady of vast Stature,
        Respect for some end.

Laughing, vid. *Passion.*
Leaping shews of Affairs prosperous.
  With Pain, abrupt profitless Procedure.
  On a Mountain best.
Lying down, vid. *Posture.*   Vid. *Rise* in *Action.*
  Carnally with, vid. *Kiss* supra.
    To Emission, acting to the fullest Expectation of your
      Reason, as is the matter.
      With Beasts, sacrificing the Hopes of your
      Reason to appetitive Courses according,
      and therefore wicked.
  Modesty is Modesty if in Circumstance.
  Lain with is passive, as lying with is active.
    By a Monster, fool'd in a Profit expected thro
    a Course absurd.
    By a Dragon, shew'd *Augustus's* Mother's Con-
    ception.
    By a Man till the Blood come, to a Maid
    shew'd contracting a Marriage after child-
    less.
    By Stars, gives you Power.
    By Spirits gives you Wisdom.
  Lying with others in general shews of Delight and Pro-
    fit.
    Would but can't, frustrates Desires.
    All, makes you contemptible thro Facility.
    Rich and old, Gain.
    Poor and young, Loss.
    Enemies, overcome them or be reconcil'd.

           Lying

Lying carnally with Friends, make ſome Bargain with him.

        Familiars, has ſhewn taking them into Houſe.

Adultery ſhews of doing abſurd and hateful things.

        To ſome of hunting and fowling.

        To ſome Poiſoning, Cheating, Forging, or For-
          ſwearing.

        To ſome future Debates for Wrong in great Con-
          troverſy.

        To *Iſrael* by the Prophets Idolatry and Corrup-
          tion.

Unwilling to commit it, hating to cheat on borrowing.

One would debauch your Wife, that is, cheat and
    miſlead your Art.

Pleas'd to be kept by a Citizen's Wife, borrowing
    Mony thence.

A's Member ſeen publickly in an Adultereſs's Mouth,
    ſhew'd him publickly cheated and expos'd in't.

Buggery with Inſenſibles, as Plants, Stones or Earth, Death.

    Plants lie with, gain by them; but lain with by
      them is Death, that is, become Earth.

    Poiſonous Creatures, threats Poiſon.

        To be lain with by them the ſame.

        Lain with, and bringing forth by a Dra-
          gon, *Auguſtus*'s Mother.

        Serpents, Death with Horror.

    Beaſts uſual, threats with Diſgrace and Danger.

    In general threats of Infirmity.

    Cows, ſhew'd of receiving Profit by them.

    Sows, 'tis not ſafe.

    Wild Beaſts, favour wicked Men.

    Male Creatures, be offended by them.

    Lap-bitch, indulge a Gentlewoman in Sin.

        Seen ſmell to *A*'s Codpiece, ſhew'd
          of his being indecently immo-
          deſt.

    Perſons. Males ſhews of doing things abſurd, and
        with great danger.

        With Emiſſion of Seed, capital
        Puniſhment thereon.

        To others Strife and Deceit of
        the Devil.

    A pretty Boy ſhews of idle Pleaſures, as
      Poetry, Chymiſtry, &c.

    Deform'd Man or old Woman, threats of
      grievous Deformities.

    Self, bear great Torments, or be confus'd
      in Buſineſs.

        To ſome lie with Kindred.

                       Lying.

Lying. Buggery with Perfons. 's Wive's Luft A. faw fo ftrong as to
    have Puppies by a Dog, fhew'd him
    ftooping to beggarly Profits in his
    Art.

Frigging forefhews ones lying with fome Familiar.
    With ones Hand, lie with ones Maid.
      Without Emiffion, only talk Bawdy to her.
    Another if you are a Schoolmafter, fhews you teach-
    ing his Children.
    To others do fome degenerate Office for them.
Inceft fhews of doing things wicked, irreverent and unnatural.
    With a Daughter, good, if rich fhe'l maintain her Father.
    a Mother, fhews Nature propitious, and difpatches
    Bufinefs.
    To *Julius Cæfar* Empire.
    To the Sick Health.
    Relations, threats with Injuries and Mifchiefs from
    them.
Infant known lie with without Emiffion, he fickens.
    With Emiffion, threats his Death.
    Unknown gives an abfurd Aid to Impotence.
Pimp'd to by the Rich and Elder, gives greateft Hopes.
    Young and needy threats with Defigns againft
    you.
Prodigious, with Saints, die fhortly or live a religious Life.
    Spirits or Stars forefhews Death.
    Dead Perfons if known help their Heirs.
    Unknown, overcome an Enemy
    or die.
    C—n A's lain with by the
    Dead, vid. *Play* in *Diverfion.*
    Known would lie with her, to a
    lying in Woman narrowly ef-
    cape Death.

    Furies } threats Death with Horror.
    Devils }
    Stars lying with you, gives Power.
    Spirits, to fome Wifdom.
Ordinary with your own Wife or Concubine, Pleafure, Profit,
    and Benefit.
    Wife, ufe regularly your Art to fome good.
    To others threats of fome grievous
    Strife. Vid. *Wife.*
    Her Husband, to a Wife ill News, if not fo in-
    deed.
    A Whore, act irregularly, tho to tend it in your
    Art.

Lying. Raviſh your Mother, tyrannize o'er your Country and die for it, (*Julius Cæſar*)

'd *A*. ſeeing her Mother in Law and near kill'd, ſhew'd of the Tyranny over her near ended.

Threatned by an old Man offering Gold, ſhew'd *A*. bleſs'd by her Husband in like Plenty.

Being, to ſome Women is as forc'd againſt their will to ſomewhat.

Eſcape ſuch Rape, that is, avoid ſuch Force, and if Marriage promis'd on it, thro Agreement.

Sucking your ſelf, Poverty or Loſs of Wife or Children.

Women in general as unlawful threats Danger, and near as to fly the Country.

With a Man to a Woman as bad.

In Bed only, vid. *Bed* in *Goods*.

Lain with till the Blood came, ſhew'd to a Maid contracting Marriage, but childleſs on't.

Deſiring it but with Inability, is Diſappointment.

With Averſeneſs ſhews ſhe hates you.

Lying with all ſhews Facility and doing every ones Buſineſs.

Sort. Whore beſt next the Wife, as free of Danger of Revenge.

Fair and rich clad offering her ſelf, ſhews of excellent Adventures.

She offering, beſt, the Courſe is in your power ; you offering, è con.

Old, ragged, and deform'd, threats with Heavineſs and Sorrow.

A Servant, threats of Damage by that Servant.

Known rich Woman, get by her if not with Luſt.

You offering, and not they, is the contrary in all.

Strangers threats as great Dangers as if ſo, as Friends Revenges, &c.

To ſome if in Bed only, receive ſuch into Family.

Handſom threats of Deceit, and expect Jilting thereon.

Moors or deform'd Perſons, threats of Diſcontent or Sickneſs.

Whores, gives Pleaſure with a little Charge.

To ſome Gain, vid. *Whore* in *Grammar*.

In a Bawdy-Houſe and not be able to get out, Death.

Lying

Lying with Women. Sorts. Sifter threats of Sorrow, Division, or Damage.
     Except a Domestick, &c. and then li-
      teral of Friendship, if in Bed only.
    Virgin, Sorrow.
    Widow known, shews of attaining to her
      Inheritance.
     Unknown, advantage another by
      your Labours.
Miscarriage, vid. *Born* supra.
Pinch'd by the Dead that he murder'd, shew'd A. teas'd in Conscience
 to Distraction for it.
Pissing, to some Ease of Care and Burden in earnest Expences.
   to some Coition from Similitude.
   to most as shite, but less and lighter.
   Against a Wall, gives Assistance in Business.
     His Screen in his Hall, shew'd A. rashly guilty in Beha-
      viour to scorn his best Equals.
     His Wainscot, shew'd A. by having many Children ful-
      lying his Plenty.
      And not fouling it, managing the Charge
      well to Ease.
   Drinking Piss threats Sickness.
   Piss'd on by another, he eases his Expences with Contempt on
   him.
   Piss house Lap-dogs seen, shew'd of a self-confounding Finery.
   Horse seen, vid. *Action* in *Beast.*
   's Tutor's Wife seen, shew'd A. eager even to Expence to pro-
   secure his Study.
Pulse feeling your own, threats you Sickness.
   Another's, is as inquiring into his Secrets.
     To some it has given so the King's Secrets.
Rape } Vid. *Lying* supra.
Ravish }
Reentring your Mother's Womb, vid. *Born* supra.
Rise, vid. *Lie down* supra. Vid. *Action.* Vid. *Bed* in *Goods.*
Shite in general, vid. *Jakes* in *House.*
   Vid. *Dung* in *Earth.* Vid. *Closestool* in *Goods.*
   Vid. *Piss* and *Dung* in *Beasts.*
   Manner orderly gives Ease in answering ordinary Charges.
    Wiping you on it, to Decency.
    Fouling you with your Dung, Contempt thro foolish
      Expence.
      to others heavy Sickness.
Shiting Convenience in a Closestool by the Fire-side, shew'd one un-
   active thro Visits.
    Remov'd decently, carried off well.
    Pot and hiding it, shew'd A. disappointing Com-
    pany, but making it up.   Shiting

Shiting convenience in your Clothes, compell'd Expence to repute
          Hurt.
          Falling on them, a preſent Scandal thro
          ill Payments only.
          Pocket full of it, that is, Pocket Mony
          thro beggarly Payments.
Vid. *Looſeneſs* in *Phyſick.*
Perſon one riſes to let you, one lends you to help your Expence.
Wife ſeen, Vid. *Grammar.*
Place convenient, as in the Fields, is good, and ſhews of Eaſe,
          of Care, and Expence.
          To others, Joy, Profit and Health.
In his Coach, ſhew'd *A.* working his Coach Horſes at
          Plow for Gain.
          Your Chamber, threats Sickneſs, Di-
          vorce or Remove.
In an unknown Garden *A.* finding a Well ſh——in't,
          he tick'd on an unaccountable Credit.
From Chamber thro your Parlor others ſeen, ſhews of
          eaſing their Expence to your Converſe Loſs.
In Church or Market, threats of impious Shame and
          Diſcovery.
          Publick Places, forbids your being there.
          Jakes and wipe ones ſelf, ſhew'd *A.* of cleaning
          Dung well.
Sighs in general, foretel of Loſs of Goods or Sickneſs.
          and Groans hearing, threat with Trouble and Sihkneſs.
Sleep in general, Vid. *Dream* in *Art.*
          Dream free as if awake, have cleareſt Mo-
          nitions.
          Not in a matter, be unworthy the
          Monition.   Vid. *Watch* in *Aſtion.*
Shews to Doubters Security, and reſt from Care.
          to others, Hindrance.
Creatures, a Wolf ſleeping kill'd, ſhew'd of a Winter Store Hay
          got well in.
          Oxen ſeen ſleep, threat of great Calamity.
          Aſſes ſeen ſleeping, the tediouſneſs of Sickneſs.
Perſons dead ſeen ſleep, gave one an eaſy Death.
          Among the dead ſleep, live among Debauchees.
A. entering anothers Houſe, and finding the Owner
          aſleep, cut out his fat and Excrement ſtinking Guts,
          and carried them off; that is, rob'd him.
Place in the way, threats ſudden Death, or great hindrance.
          As climbing e'er on Top of an Hill, ſhews of
          your Ambition's failing.
          Church, gives Divine Help and Aid beyond Hope.
          to the Sick, Health.
          Sleep.

Sleep, Place in the Church, to the Sound Sickness, or great Business.
 On his Barns mowe his Fan by, shew'd A. neglecting his threshing there.
 Church-yard, to the Sick Death.
 to others, Hindrance.
 Market, threats Sickness.
 On a Dunghil, to the Poor Riches.
 to the Rich, Office.
Posture, standing before his Church Door, in Expectance of Parish Transactions next Day.
 Leaning on Pales, trusting on a Protection or Fence, &c. as.
 A failing a long Voyage so, anothers Labour prov'd his Dispatch.
 Time at Noon Day, neglect Business or die in prime.
Hag or Nightmare, shews to some an Apoplexy.
 to Women, Marriage.
 to some, be ruled by Fools.
 to some, silly, drunken, ungovernable Fits.
 Hagrid, to the Sick deadly.
Sleepy seeming, that is, being dull and insensible, as &c.
 To others, shew'd of sitting up late.
 Waking again, gives Operation and Action.
Knowing you sleep, assures you of great Vigor of Mind.
 Heeding Lapses.
 To all, Assurance of not being deceiv'd.
Potion given one by his dead Father, gave him Death.
Waking in general, the Spirit is surpriz'd by none; and wake how or when we will, the Spirit either wakes you, or ends his Discourse e'er others do.
 Lie unexpected when in Health, *Ahasuerus's* Fate, and bids beware.
 Early secure, projectively great Hazard.
 Long e'er sleeping, act in a Source of Caution.
 At Midnight, an unexpected Monition of Divine Caution.
 In the Morning, shews of Cautions of Remedy.
 Thro Dreams of howling Devils surrounding him, *Francis Spira's* Despair.
Can't sleep, be in State of dangerous Doubts next Day.
 As fearing to hear a Death-Watch, thro a restless Care for Health.
Seem when not so, nor can't wake your self, be deluded against all Expectation.
 Can't sleep fearing Robbers, restless fearing Errors.
 Sleep.

Sleep. Waking feem, Wake and fleep by turns, have fine Thoughts mix'd with obscure.

In an unknown Surprize, be confounded in an uncertain Expectation.

Frighted as your Chamber chang'd, surpriz'd as your Managery confounded.

Matters imperfect, that is, you cease to see them more finished.   Vid. *Grammar*.

Seeing your self, shews you warn'd against Fraud.

Would wake but can't, fail wittingly in Designs according.

Seem as unwilling to sleep, be in fear of Danger or Deceit.

Inability to sleep, threats you of horrid Crosses next Day.

Smiling, Vid. *Looks* in *Sight* in *Sense*.

Sneezing, threats of unexpected Events and Diseases in the Head.

To others, Delivery from Evil, thro Calumny from its Noise.

Snorting, shews of Idleness and heavy Sickness.

To others, Delivery from Calumny.

Spew, Vid. *Drunk*.

Spitting, shews of Affronts and Disparagements.

Spit upon being, that is, in Contempt answerable.

Your Daughters Face, scorn some Debt as contemptible.

Blood, shews of Sedition.

Starting in general, shews of great Doubt and Irresolution.

Step, Vid. *Action*.

Sweating, Freedom from some great Care or Disease.

To others, Fear or Labour.

Tub seen before an House, shew'd of an Oeconomy amidst great Labours.

Thirst, Vid. *Drink*.

Tickling one another, that is, mentally grieving each other.

It shews of teasing and fretting mentally.

Tickled by Men, as not wearing Stays, to a Woman teas'd, as of loose Behaviour.

Trembling, threats of great Uncertainty and Irresolution.

Vomit, Vid. *Physick*.

Wake, Vid. *Sleep* supra.

Watch, Vid. *Action* and *Passion*.

Wink'd at by another, that is, baulk'd or refused, as &c.

Yawning, threats with tedious Idleness, short Confinement, and ill News.

To some, the Desires of *Venus*.

C H A P.

CHAP. XXXIV.
Of Posture.

IN general. One prostrate rises, one in Despair becomes further active. Ill things seen with you, are of good *Omen* if against your Enemies.

A Serpent surrounding an Altar, gave a Sacrificer Success. Vid. *Crown* in *Ornaments.*

Above, Vid. *High* infra.

About, Vid. *Fly* in *Air.*　　　Vid. *Incompass* infra.

Your House all seeming common, threats you abused in Property.

An Estate walk, that is, examine into its Nature.

An House and Garden lead by another, following their Example in Managery.

The Sick, Emmets seen crawl, gives them Health and Industry again.

But upon them, threats Death.

You fling your Snot, that is, vent publickly your private offensive Opinions.

Against you another travels, that is, he opposes or stops your Designs.

On a white Horse, with Power and Innocence.

Speaking, shews you'l provoke him so to do, *& e contrà.*

With you another faces or moves, that is, such a Course aids.

Things, Vid. *Wind* in *Air.*

A Hare runs against you, a Dispute is usher'd to thwart you.

A bloody Stream swimming against, gave one Cure of a Bloody-Flux.

Torrent walk against in a Room, maintain a Singularity in Converse.

The Wind go against, design'd contrary to popular Impediments.

Opposite House, the contrary Oeconomy.

To some, it shews of Vying and Contention.

High and North, poor, but in good Circumstance.

Low and South by a River, with good Revenue, but in ill State.

Against.

Againſt. Oppoſite to you another ſtands, that is, oppoſes you, and the higher the worſe.

    Sits ſnearing, that is, acts ſettledly to oppoſe you.

    An Attorney ſtands, that is, a brawling Brangle ſtops you.

    2 French-men ſee ſit, that is, find an imperfect Effort of Tyranny menacing.

    A Fox in a String, that is, a contrary Roguery, but under Check.

    Northward come at an Enemy, that is, to their Loſs.

    Shore a Piper ſeen play on, encourag'd Julius Cæſar to Conqueſt.

    Ground croſs a way againſt a Butchers Wood ſeen in, ſhew'd of fat Cattel.

    Chamber croſs a Street, that is, a contrary univerſal Oeconomy.

    To a Woman's be in, that is, be indiſpoſed or unactive as they.

Thruſting you Perſons ſeen, that is, Methods preſumptuous hindring you.

Throng'd by the dead, ſhew'd A. narrow'd in Action, near to pine away by it, as they did.

Among, Vid. Company and Meet.

    Stinking Ox Skins being, that is, diſmiſſing Faith Services as uſeleſs.

    Pigeons finding A. ſhew'd him acting at the Deſire of diſſolute Women.

    Logs and Coal walking, Deſigns to Profit, but amidſt Malice and Envy.

Aſide puſh ſomewhat, that is, lay it by in Scorn in your reaſoning.

    Puſh'd his Coach ſeen, ſhew'd A. of deferring his Journies with it.

Back, Vid. Human Body.

    Return, Vid. Travel.

Acts brings ſomewhat, that is, returns to ſome former State according.

    Pelted with Dirt, ſcandaled to deſert your Methods.

    Going, undoing what you are then about.

    Turn'd in paſſing a Palace Chamber by a waiting Woman, baulk'd A. in his ſplendid Aims according.

    Back a Grave-Stone on him ſeen, ſhew'd A. narrowly eſcaping Death.

Looking is as repenting.

-wards flying, to Sailors good.

    to others, Idleneſs.

Begin, Vid. B. in Action.

Back-wards go and then go another way, that is, proceed a new, but on first leaving some former Method.

Bishops turn'd streight, A. puts on his Hat again, he has Respect for Ends only.

Place Way travel, use some by or indirect Method.

Side of the Exchange dancing, shew'd A. greatly expos'd in Credit.

Behind hairless, threats you Poverty and ill Luck in old Age.

To Men in Law and Flight, 'tis Good and Escape.

You in general, shews of Matters you'l hear of, now past.

A great wasting Serpent seen, shew'd to *Hannibal* his Captainship. Vid. *Leave* in *Action.*

An Angel sitting, you steddily presuming your self a Divine Messenger.

Another being, that is, excell'd by him.

But if you pursue him, you are Victor.

Hide you, Vid. *Action.*

The Curtain a Play acting another, Resentment ready if provok'd.

A Coach ride, that is, have a mean Hand in great Performances.

Hinder part of A's House only left standing, all but his Settlement threatned.

Before in general, Vid. *Hanging* infra. Vid. *Forward* and *Cross* infra.

Another being, that is, excelling him.

But if pursued, threats you being vanquish'd.

Fall down so, despair in such Course menacing.

Walk direct, and order Methods according.

Meet another, oppose his Designs.

Persons your Enemies House seen mean, fly Project to Grandeur in scorn of him.

Hide, that is, be shamefully at a Fault wherein they your Enemies.

Robbers hiding to escape, is avoiding Error and good.

A Minister fly o'er Pales, trespass the Bounds of Conscience Property.

Known Persons act, act in regard to them.

The Lord Keeper A. fidling before, shew'd his acting to be accountable to him.

All your Relations affronted, that is, to the Knowledg of all.

Strangers dancing, shew'd of Shame and flirting Quarrels.

Your pitying Friend fly, be brave in Adversity.

2 boast, act with Glory, but not where perfectly known.

Things. A Tavern walking before, shew'd of a profitable Treaty in Hand.

His Parish Church Door standing, shew'd A. of publick Parish Business Attendance.

Before

Before you ſee Matters, Vid. *See.*

Dead Bones lie and wake ſtopping, ceaſe a Death-me-
nacing Courſe.

A Man ſtand, that is, a reaſonable Courſe offering.

An Houſe fired, forbids your direct Proceeds, as of
ruinous Oeconomy.

An Horſe ſtand, Vid. *H.*

A Coffin reſt to look on, that is, examine of others
Fatalities.

A Raven, Owl and Angel threatning you from an Eaſt-
ern Window, that is, find Death, Oblivion, and pretended Divine Monition would offer to divert your
Oeconomy, &c. as deadly.

Behind, Vid. *Back* ſupra.

Below, Vid. *High* infra.

Between in general, Vid. *Head* in *Body.*

You and others ſee Woman ſit, that is, find Opinions obſtructing your Intercommunication.

2 Doors ſitting, ſhew'd of wanton Love to a Woman free
with a Man, ſo as not known whether married or not.

2 Enemies Houſes travelling, ſhew'd *A.* in want of Entertainment in Deſigns, &c.

A. trod on a Serpent, Wheat between, thro Plenty he commanded an Enemy.

Stags Horns ſet between Oxen and Horſes, ſhew'd *A.* of merchantly poyſing their immix'd Uſes.

Him and an Hog he would fight *A.* ſeeing Wood laid, ſhew'd
A. wagering Contention with his Antagoniſt.

Beyond you ſee another, that is, in Advantages he ſo far exceeds you.
Vid. alſo *Before* ſupra.

London things, that is, more than the true Standard of publick
Dealings will allow.

At a Sea-port Market buying things, ſhew'd of getting
good Foreign things.

Next Market *A.* being ſeem'd on it coming home, *A.* prov'd at
a Loſs in a Bargain he could not fix to a value.

By, vid. *Near* and *Sit* infra.   Vid. *Paſs* in *Travel.*

Corner being in, that is, in a deſperate Iſſue of Defiance.

Of a Room ill boarded ſeen, ſhew'd *A.* Singularity in Converſe
at that time would be ill.

Croſſing a Ditch by a ſmall Plank, ſhew'd of Deceit by a Lawyer.

Way, Vid. *Way* and *Paſs* in *Travel.*

Yours ſee one, that is, intercepting your Deſigns, as meet
is oppoſe.

A Friend from the Left to the Right, find of a
kind Aid preventing your Care.

An Enemy from the Right to the left, find an ill
Courſe avert your Hopes.

/ Croſſing

Cross Way. Yours see a mad Woman, her like Rashness prevents your Proceeds.

You cross anothers way, you obstruct them so, &c.

A Chamber pass, compass the Command of a private Managery answerable.

The Exchange pass, that is, command all the Plenty of it.

A Corn Field an Hare seen run, shew'd of a good Husbandry Dispute.

A Tomb denying a Beggar, shew'd A. refusing sneaking thro Plenty at hand.

Down from Heaven tumbled, shew'd to *Cæsar* Death, that is, his Government proves ended.

Stairs running hurrying, an Oeconomy change.

Your Gate seen flung, your Entrance according in somewhat propos'd sails.

A Town going briskly in a Coach, shew'd A. giving an expenceful Treat.   Vid. *Lying* infra.   Vid. *Break* in *Action.*

East, vid. *Quarter* infra.

Facing, vid. *Against* supra.

Foreright looks, shew us of Hopes direct.

Vid. *Side* infra, and *Opposite* in *Against* supra.

Forward shew of proceeding, as backward reversing.

Sit in a Coach, command honourably.   Vid. *Before* supra.

From in general, vid. *Travel* and *Fall* in *Action.*

Vid. *Prospect* in *Sight* in *Sense.*

Lower Ground fling a Ball, start a Dispute about Humility.

Your Physician travelling, threats you with Sickness.

His Orchard to his Church-yard paving his way, shew'd A. reaching his Wisdom to Divinity.

Court to City travel, design ungenteely from better to worse.

One House to another go, change Circumstance of Oeconomy answerable.

Scullery to Parlor inviting one, shew'd A. of another inviting him from trifling Interest Cavils to a free Converse.

Hanging in general, vid. *Over* infra.   Vid. *Condemn'd* in *Law.*

Washing hang'd up, vid. *Wash* in *Water.*

Himself seeing one, that is, acting to utmost Despair.

Cut down dead on it, to full Issue.

He falling so you fall on him, the Despair affects you in the end.

No reviving, no Alteration likely.

Before the Room Door he was in A. seeing a Peacocks Feather, shew'd A. his Travel would be but in vain shew.

On a Bough in the Sea, shew'd of exceeding Popular Despair.

Beam in an unknown House, depending on Rents in a Mony Want.

In the Air Wheat seen, shew'd A. of a good Season for its sowing offering.

S

Hanging

Hanging in the Air a Man ſeen, ſhew'd of conſidering of the Reaſon of Apparitions there.

Over a clear ſhallow Water, that is, being in ſuſpence on ſome leſſer Trouble you can evade.

Jeruſalem a fiery Sword ſeen, ſhew'd of its Deſtruction near.

Up ſee a dead Carcaſe, that is, be ſenſible of ſome Abomination ſet up.

Goods, ſhews of ſome matter of Profit in ſuſpence.

High in general, vid. *Precipice* in *Place.*

Within a Man's reach, a Difficulty within Human Endeavours to compaſs.

Higher end of a Table ſit at, Command in chief in ſome ſocial Oeconomy.

Than others fly but the ſame way, project as they but freelier.

Top of a Wheel ſitting on, threats with Decay.

Bottom ſitting at, promiſes Advance.

As your ſelf have a Daughter, that is, a Debt to your whole Worth.

Water ſeen in a Ciſtern, ſhews you of Trouble skreen'd by a Friend.

Dance or fly, ſhews of great Efforts with Hazard, Fear or Danger.

Fence, a lofty Separation.

Of Wainſcot, as to Converſation and Oeconomy.

Fling a Ball from lower Ground, that is, raiſe a Diſpute about Humility.

Fly, vid. *Air.*

Houſe, ſhews of a lofty or ſtately Oeconomy.

The Sun ſeen, ſhew'd A. of riſing early to make the Day long.

Trees, their Fruit ſhew of famous Gain.

Low, mean, &c.

In in general, vid. *Fall* in *Hurt.*

Fire or Water, vid. *Feet* in *Body.*

Water A. ſeeing his ſtick Horſe ſtand with his Belly ſhrunk, ſhew'd of his dying of a Cold and Surfeit.

A Place or Shop, in Command of Circumſtances anſwerable.

Without, travel in ſuch State without Deſign.

Thro, travel by Deſign as is the Place.

A Room, that is, in Command of a Converſe or Oeconomy State, as &c.

Seeing others there, ſhews of their like Methods.

At a Window there hear another, that is, have a Glimpſe of anothers Oeconomy.

A Cupboard A. ſeeing a Book of Prodigies, ſhew'd him of a Bargain of Cupboard Goods he bought, and which he left as abominable.

An Entry met by one, that is, oppos'd by his like Reaſoning in ſome Family Tranſaction.

In

In an Entry a fine House in a Forest being, shew'd *A.* endanger'd Ruin thro Hopes on great Men.

Incompass'd by Beggars, surrounded by Courses of Necessity.

Enemies, threats you with grievous perplexing teasing Cares, and those issuing contrary too.

A Serpent an Altar seen, gave the Sacrificer Success.

Ravens, vid. *R.* in *Birds.*

Inward falling, vid. *Furnace* in *House-parts.*

Clothes, that is, his surer and secreter Repute.

Room of an House enter, vid. *Room* in *House.*

A Prison enter, consult the Equiry of a Debt charged on you.

Kneeling, vid. *Knee* in *Body.*

Laid in general, vid. *Action.*

In a Window your Hat see, a Regard on some Prospect offering.

Mony seen taking up, shew'd *A.* of receiving some lent.

Chaff seen put in *A*'s Shoos, shew'd him accus'd of idle Pretences.

Leaning on a Pale, trusting on some Protection of Right, as &c.

Standing, expecting with a Reliance according.

On Hands and Elbows as sitting, shew'd one destitute, idle and forlorn.

And if sick, they die.

Over another sitting, that is, oppressing him in some of his settled Methods.

Standing against a triple Stone Mausoleum in *Huts-Street,* shew'd me in Expectance to tend a Country Funeral of *Russel's,* living in *London.*

Low, vid. *High* supra.

Lying down, vid. *Prostrate* infra. Vid. *Bed* in *Goods.*

Vid. *Rise* in *Action.*

It threats Idleness, Grief, Death and Despair.

Place on the Ground, that is, being in Despair and at others Mercy.

With another upon you, at his Mercy.

With an Ox upon you, your Labour and Care in Despair with you.

With your Wife on you, your Trade or Art in Despair too.

On a Floor naked, the same restless Want and Despair as is the Place or Oeconomy.

Dunghil, despairing as to Farm Expences.

Bed in a desolate Place, lazily submitting to Ruin.

With your Wife, in a Passage negligent as to Work. Vid. *Bed* in *Goods.*

Lying. Place. On your Hall-Table Robbers ſeen, threats you of careleſs Waſtes, &c. ſuffer'd divert-
ing your Revenue.

Ornaments ſeen, ſhews of their being ſacrific'd to Family Neceſſity.

Pins many new bought ſeen, promiſes you of Plenty.

In a Ditch and prone, is grievous Sadneſs.

With a Pillar of Thorns tho, gave Riches by
ſneaking ſaving, there the Dung is waſh'd.

His Desk ſhut up, that is, retir'd from publick
Tranſaction in deſpair to Writing, &c.

Manner. Side, Vid. *S.* infra.

With the Dead, Vid. *Dead.*

In your beſt Clothes, tho your Eſtate good, your preſent Purſe State bad and in deſpair.

In his ſtudying Gown on bed, ſhew'd *A.* Deſpair in that
Studies Succeſs.

Self in a croſs way, deſpair near even to Self-murder.

Down. Things. A Sword againſt you ſeen, perceive of a Reſentment now ſlighted that may revive.

A Door ſeen, ſhew'd of Reſolutions of Obſtructions contemned.

His Plow-Cattel ſeen at an Inn, ſhew'd *A.* in
more work with them than finiſhable.

Cattel. Oxen ſeen threat with great Want and Calamity.

Shew'd alſo of an Horſe's Death, 'tis fatal
to Cattel to lie down.

Mounted, vid. *Upon* infra, *Ride* in *Horſe,* and *Hill* in *Earth.*

On an Eagle, to Princes and Great men Death.

to the Poor welcomes him to Great men.

Elephant, threats Death.

A Camel, threats with Straits and Confuſions, as in
Deſerts.

High Place others below, that is, having advantage of
Wiſdom, &c.   Vid. *Proſpect* in *Senſe.*

Mounting ſeeming to Heaven, to the Sick Death.

The Earth ſeen to Heaven, ſhew'd of a juſt Prince.

High before others, ſhewing others boaſtingly of
your Power.

Naked Birds ſeen, ſhew Trouble or project States monſtrouſly defective.

Devil ſeen naked, threats Miſery, but otherwiſe Riches.

Sword or other Weapon receiving ſo, may ſhew your Wife dies.

But with the Sheath, ſhews ſhe ſickens only.

Self being, threats you Loſs of Goods, Houſe, and Pleaſures.

In the Church very bad, mad.

Bathe with good Company, Joy.

Seen by others the worſe, your Poverty or Diſrepute pub-
liſhed.

                                                     Naked

Naked Self. Parts. Arms seeming so, that is, destitute in your Methods of Action.

Feet so, to some threats with Pains or Sickness.

to some Scorn and fears of Poverty.

Walking barefoot, shew'd *A.* imprudently catching a Cold. Vid. also *Feet in Body.*

Man seen is worse than a Beggar, except to a Woman, &c.

Moor seen threats you Sadness, Melancholy, and Damage.

Unknown seen so, threats you with unaccountable Fears and Terrors.

's Tenant seen so, shew'd *A.* of his own Husbandry failing.

Husband seen so to a Wife, gives her Success in Business.

Embracing as so, when not with her, ill News.

Woman 's Wife seen so, shew'd *A.* Deceit and his Contract expos'd.

Seeing her self naked, shew'd her Widowhood.

Embracing as so tho not with him, shews him of Joy and Profit.

Others fair seen naked shew of good Luck and Success.

Common ugly seen so, shews of ill Luck and Repentance.

Your Whore seen so, threats you Peril by her Craft.

Painted seen naked is as the real, but less.

Servant seen naked, gave *A.* Joy in home Concerns.

And impudently whorish too, shew'd her flinging off her Service.

Near in general, vid. *Coming* supra.

Vid. *About* supra. Vid. *Quantity.*

Nearest way to a Place stop'd, your direct Method, as &c. hinder'd.

Market-town go to, that is, bargain immediately.

Next Neighbour doing a thing, shew'd *A.* himself next day supplying Defects, &c.

Another you can't fit, that is, you can't establish your Resolves as to him or thro his Assistance.

Kneel to pray, that is, such can't aid your Expectations.

At call *A.* seeing his Maltman, foreshew'd *A.* of much Sider unexpected.

A Physician being, that is, in good Assurance of a Remedy, as &c.

A River, that is, a profitable Succession or Revenue, if with good Circumstance.

Have an Estate, that is, an Estate teas'd with obstinate great Mens Quarrels.

Neat.

Near. Place, your Houſe flying ſhews of Wandring.
to the Sick Death.
2 Doors off, 2 Days off.
Near his Fan in his Barn ſleeping, ſhew'd A. neglecting
threſhing there.
Near the Sea bē in a Garden, that is, be concern'd in a
popular, &c. plenty State.
His Barn A. keeping a Magpy caged, ſhew'd him of
having a Servant prating ill thereof, &c.
The Head a Crown over it, and not touching it.   (Protector
Cromwell)
North, vid. Travel and Quarter infra.
Oppoſite, vid. Againſt ſupra.
Over in general, vid. Hanging ſupra.   Vid. Upon ſupra.
And overbeat one, expoſe a Courſe or Perſon anſwe-
rable throughly.
Another flying, gives you Authority over him according, but
projectively.
Get or go, that is, exceed or ſubject him to your Me-
thods.
Stand as he lies, oppreſs him in Deſpair.
Your Miniſter's Pew untile the Church, treat him ill.
Lean as he ſits, oppreſs him in his fix'd Courſe.
You a Rainbow ſeen, ſhews you a Change of Fortune.
To ſome Death and Ruin of Family.
To ſome Change for the better.
Vid. Rainbow in Air.
Plate ſeen hang in a Room, ſhews you Suſpenſe of turning
Goods to Mony, as ready Mony.
Birds ſeen fly, threats you prejudice from Enemies Projects.
An Owl ſeen fly, threats you Sickneſs or Impriſonment.
Angels ſeen fly, gives you all Joy, Comfort, and Bleſſings.
Things. A Ditch jumping, ſhew'd A. of forcing thro a ſcanda
lous Difficulty.
Water, have a Cloſet or Nurſery, that is, be your ſelf or
Children ſick or in Trouble.
Houſes and forlorn Ways flying over, ſhew'd of Sedi-
tion.
Hill and Vale travelling over, gives Advance thro La-
bour.
An Houſe deſcend, proceed in neglect and flight of an
Oeconomy, as &c.
Dominions a Vine ſeen overſpreading, Cyrus's Mother.
A Garden Hedg where you are, ſee one run away with
your Child, he tries to fool your Plenty, &c.
Outward, vid Inward ſupra.
Proſtrate, vid. Lying down ſupra.
Before 2 Men, humbled for 2 Faults.

Prostrate. Witch asking A's regard, foreshew'd him regard to a despis'd Fortune-teller's Counsel proving considerable.

Fly in a Room, be in glory in your Concerns as to others, tho as to your self despairing in your Projects.

Face downwards lie, that is, be in a most disconsolate State for Hopes.

Quarter East, West, &c. vid. Travel.　　Vid. Pillar in Buildings.

A Door opening East advantageous, West detrimental. South voluptuous, and North laborious.

South is to Luxury and Plenty.

North is as to Poverty and Hardship.

East travelling is good, it increases Virtue and Riches.

Standing with ones Back in the East is good also.

Your Friend seen so, the same.

Back in East in the West Streets of a Village I saw three Corps pass by me, this shew'd me of my recovering of my broken Leg, as if said you'l live where many die.

West Corner set your Back in, stand in defiance of the worst. to others Rest, as Content in Despair.

Pass by one westward, act more self-detrimentally than he. West from home, act to loss of good Command and Property.

London to the worst, as to the Perfection of publick Transaction.

West of you see Cattel, that is, be in ill Condition as to matter of Estate, as &c.

A Dunghil, be at a present expence for future Good.

Another standing, that is, in worse Circumstances, as &c.　　Vid. also Side infra.

☞ Note, This is of singular use and regard in all Dreams whatever.

Round, vid. About supra.　　Vid. Figure in Quality.

Side in general turn, that is, alter your Course, as &c.

So the right Side of the Body, Male Relations.

Left, Females.

Upper Side shews of Masters and Elders.

Middle shews of Equals, &c.

As the Quarter of the World shews the good State of things in themselves, so their Sides represent of their appropriate States as to us.

Before shews of Futurities with our direct Hopes.

Behind shews of what's past, vid. Back supra.

But to him that turns about it shews of Futurities on Change of State.

Right in general shews of Courses to our present Good.

Side

Side, right in general. Ill things feen there is ill Iffue at laft, or an Evil out of Good.

A Scithe or Pickax feen there, an all-confounding Force aiding, &c.

On it pafs by another, that is, exceed or negleft juftly fuch Courfe according.

Lying down on right Side looking foreright and deadly, to the Sick Death with Eafe.

Left Side ftep to, that is, err in your Proceeds, at leaft for the prefent.

Fine Grounds feen there, fhew'd of a good Husbandry neglefted.

A Monfter frighting Boys thence to the right, Abfurdity curing an ill Courfe.

A Scithe or Pickax feen there, fhews of fome great Force to your Hurt.

Good feen there gives Good out of prefent evil Courfes.

Hat laid in a left fide Window, an Honour on fome profpeft given, but in a State of Detriment to you.

Perfons feen there, Courfes to be deem'd efforting to your worft, as &c.

to your right è con. as is the Perfon and Charafter.

Travel in general, vid. *Pafs* in *Travel.*

One meeting you ftops to the left, your Oppofer errs.

Walk in a Village to the left and thro it, evade the ill of a neighbourly Converfe, as &c.

Pafs by things to the right, exceed or barely negleft Courfes, as &c.

Left, do the fame in Scorn.

On a Hill-road by a ruin'd Houfe in the Vale below to the left, by good Advantages efcape a State otherwife as ruinous.

Forward go, proceed in a direft Courfe.

Turn to the right, alter for the better and eafier.

Left è *con*, for the worfe and harder.

Turn up hill to the left, the prefent worft Courfe will be beft at laft.

Down hill to the right, the prefent beft Courfe ends ill.

Short to the right, take a better Courfe without delay.

Stand againft one coming from the right, oppofe a defign'd Wrong.

Meet one coming from the left, oppofe one overdoing Amendment of matters.

Sitting shews of being in some steddy fix'd Course, as standing is expecting, and walking about shews of seeking Alteration.   Vid. *Chair* in *Goods.*

Birds on a Tree, Vid. *Tree.*

Distance, Vid. *D.* in *Quantity.*

To many when with no other Circumstance it shews Infirmity.

Or leaning seeing the Sick, denies the Recovery.

In a Chimney-corner, after tedious Infirmity.

Rising thence, and not returning tho, gives Recovery indeed.

Seat fall from, lose your Office.

Can't get in again, irrecoverably.

Have in a Room within a Court of Justice, that is, an Office in such a Court.

With an Angel, that is, deeming your self as much establish'd to be a Divine Messenger.

Women, contenting you in Theories without Intent of Practice.   Vid. *Company.*

Between 2 Doors, shew'd a Woman of wanton Love, &c.

Under a Death-watch in a Chamber bloody, wilfully continuing in a Course will be deadly to you.

Upon a Rock, assures of good Hopes.

Well, promises an assured good Issue.

Dung, threats with a Fine.

Cloud, threats Death.

Dirt, threats with Poverty and Disgrace.

A Chair of State shew'd of a lazy Acquiescence in neglect, as &c.

On his Crupper an Ass seen, shews of over Laboriousness, and as to a *Nonplus.*

A. 3 Ravens seen, and one saying he'd kill her, shew'd A. her Death.

An Eagle or Dove, gives Honour, as &c.

Between, vid. *B.* supra.   Forward, vid. *F.* supra.

By a Fire shews of Desire, and if till out, in vain.

Man seen, shews of some rational Establishment.

To some it shews of little Labour and long Expectation.

The Back against an Hedg, a flight Shelter to some Trouble.

At a Table to Meat, compos'd to some Method of Profit.

At the lower end of a College-Hall the Members all formal before A. shew'd A. as fit to be an Instructor or Founder there.

At the Table of a Man of Power, gives you Joy and Gain.

Sitting.

Sitting your ſelf by a ſcandalous Perſon, threats you as ſettledly deemed ſuch.

Louſy Companion, be fixedly treated as ſuch.

Talking with ſuch, tranſacting as if in ſuch State.

You or lying in the Church, ſhews to you of change of Apparel.

Suffer one to ſit by you, that is, admit of ſuch a Courſe to your Freedom and Imitation.

South, vid. *Quarter* ſupra.

Standing ſhews of Expectation and inſtant Neceſſity.

In a Place, that is, being worthy of Abode and Expectance, as is the Place.

Still on the Watch, being in obſtruction for a ſpace.

Your ground dead Bones before you, ſtout in your point maugre Death.

In his Coach, ſhew'd *A.* keeping one without uſing it.

On a Rule ſhew'd *A.* of living well and Chriſtianly.

Among Women, being in a Converſe of a trifling Deſign, or of mere Theory.

In a Bookſeller's Shop, ſhew'd *A.* of having a Book to publiſh.

Upright hinder'd by Wood or Wall, threats with ſlaviſh Subjection.

Struck ſo with a Sword or Knife, to a Prince Danger of Death or Slavery.

To ſee Hunting expected, an Intereſt proſecuted, as *&c.*

Following it your ſelf, your ſelf endeavouring in ſuch a Deſign.

Againſt Purſuers, reſolving againſt threatning Dangers.

A Cart driving againſt you, reſolving againſt a Farmer menacing.

Speaking on it, ſhew'd of Iſſue thereon.

Manner ſitting you, others ſtanding, they on Expectation only where you fix'd.

Corn good ſeen to an Orator, ſhew'd him of an effectual *extempore* Speech ro great Profit.

Another ſeen by your Bed-ſide, ſhews of your Phyſician and Sickneſs.

Before you, a Courſe in obſtruction anſwerable.

At your door, threats you as in want of his Aid.

A Prophet before you, ſhews you as intent on his Imitation.

Ready with right Hand in Pocket ſee your Debtor, he pays you then.

An Hermaphrodite ſeen before her, ſhew'd to Queen *Mary* Popery.

Steddily viewing one, that is, examining him thoroughly.

In general Steddineſs ſhews of Prudence if not unpleaſant.

Strutting

Strutting ſhews of boaſting.

At another, that is, comparatively boaſting with him.

By a Fire's ſide, as to Eſtate ability, &c.

Cathedral ſeen, ſhew'd of a vaunting Prebend.

Surrounding, Vid. *Incompaſs* ſupra.

Throng'd } Vid. *Againſt* ſupra.
Thruſt } Vid. *Puſh* in *Action.*

Towards the Church your Houſe Foundation, the Solidity of your Converſe as to Religion.

You an Hare ſeen hunted, others purſuing their Intereſt to your hurt.

Turn, vid. *Side* ſupra.

Under, vid. *Over* ſupra.

Your Mother or in her Belly being, Death.

Departing from, being under a Cart, gave an End of Slavery.

Bed Beaſts found, threated of Death ſhortly enſuing.

A Death-watch *A.* ſitting bloody, ſhew'd him ſubmitting to a Cauſe would gradually be his Death.

A Table *A.* found ſomewhat, that is, belonging to Houſe-keeping already ſpent.

Foreign Mony, that is, he paid off ſuch Debts.

Ground travel, gives Obſcurity and Enquiry of Secrets.

Hiding a Veſſel of Water, ſhew'd *A.* of falling into ſhameful Decay and dying in't.

Houſe-eaves the Stars ſeen, ſhew'd *A.* of breaking up Houſe-keeping.

Upon in general, vid. *Fall* in *Action.*   Vid. *Mounted* in *Action.*

Things. A Camel being on, that is, in Straits and Confuſions as if in a Wilderneſs.

An Houſe-top ſtand or walk, that is, uſe the Extremity of Power on ſome Family.

to others command an Oeconomy anſwerable with Eaſe.

An Elephant, vid. *E.* in *Beaſt.*

A Stag, perſecuted with Fears and Snares.

The Clouds being, ſhew'd *A.* Travel, and to ſome Death.

Bed *A.* finding Chocolate, ſhew'd *A.* of having it by her Husband.

You an Houſe falling, that is, you being oppreſt with ſome Oeconomy.

Get from under it, eſcape at laſt.

Childrens Heads Crows ſeen ſit, ſhew'd of their being hang'd.

Table things ſeen, ſhew'd them after ſpent in Houſekeeping.

Jewels ſeen there, ſhew'd of their being after ſpent for Neceſſaries.

Many Pins lately bought ſeen there, ſhew'd *A.* of Plenty at hand.

Upon

Upon *Athens* Academick Gate from *Socrates*'s Lap a Swan pitching
  Plato's Glory.
Salt flung on Stones, Work and Pains fool'd away.
   Roots, ſhew'd of deſtroying Men for their Inheri
    tance; it kills them.
   A Ditch, ſhew'd *A.* of a vile uſe of good things.
Up upright fly and not too high, that is, excel others as much.
   Standing hinder'd by Wood and Wall, ſhew'd of ſlaviſ
    Subjection.
   In general ſhews of attaining to a full Freedom
    as &c.
With, vid. *Againſt* ſupra.
  ―in your Seat another having one, that is, he having advantag
   over your ſettled Courſe.
   Yard another having one, that is, your Eſtate being en
   cumbred by others Manageries.
   Cloſet *B.* having another, that is, a ſecret Managery de
    pendant on yours.
   You have the Key, you command all.

C H A P. XXXV.

Of the Soul.

SOUL in general ſhews of our GOD, Will, Wife, Child, or Friend
  beloved.
   A. cried out on *B*'s Spirit would carry her a-
   way, *A.* remov'd fearing *B*'s Slights in Love.
  Imagination ſhews of Contrivance for Futurity.
   To others it ſhews of Painting or Po-
    etry.   Vid. *Thought* infra.
  Memory learning things by, ſhews of gathering
   up things by degrees.
   Remembring what was learnt, ſhew'd of
   diſpoſing things in order.
   Remember'd or put in mind, as in cir-
   cumſtance, may be literal.
   Something given you to remember *A.* by,
   that is, a Benefit offers to you thro *A*'s
   good Example.
   To ſome it ſhews of Hiſtories, things paſt,
   Monuments, and Wiſdom.
   To ſome Grief, as only to be re-
   member'd, is unhappy.
  Forget your Dreams, alter your Purpoſes,
  as &c.
          Soul

SOUL. Memory forget accompanying a rich Man, cease esteem-
ing Riches as in themselves lovely.

Your Name, conclude to alter it.

Find another, the new
Name you take.

To some, it shews of things of little
Concern, (as *Nebuchad. &c.*)

An Inscription of a Gravestone he came
out of, to *A.* narrowly escape Death.

Understanding in general, shews of the Worship and
Honour of God.

Intelligible Voices hearing, shew'd *A.* continuing
in his own Country.

Contrary, shew'd Travel.

Vid. *Reason* and *Thought* infra.

Will, vid. *Offer* in *Possess.* Vid. *Desire* in *Passion.*

Will not shews will not, or an Incapacity rational thereto, as under greater Engagements. Vid. *Refuse* in *Discourse.*

Willingly buying Jewels, shew'd of great
Profit and Pleasure.

Unwillingly shew'd of compell'd
Expence and uneasy Gains.

Leave given, shews of Permission.

Unwilling to commit Adultery, not designing a Cheat.

Your Friend see that won't speak, find of
a good Course offering, but not to Action.

Your Dog won't run at Conies tho' set on,
your Servant proves baulk'd in dunning
Shufflers.

Carried by a black Ox as designing him ill,
and against his Will, shew'd *A.* Shipwreck.

Abruptly, vid. *Improper* infra.

Be in a Place going thither, shews of a Design accomplish'd.

Without going thither, shews of Occurrences
unforeseen.

Absurdity, vid. *Improper* infra.

Accepting shews of accepting.

Accepted being in fine Company, shew'd *A.* of acting genteely.

Agree, vid. *Willing* supra, and *Reconcil'd* in *Quarrel.*

Believe not a matter, that is, act as if not so believing.

Care being in, threats with Necessities, and the greater the greater.

Leave a Child, cease to regard him.

With a Watcher, but not absolutely.

Cautious Persons meet you, Reasons of Caution oppose your Designs.

Using Caution generally is Literal.

Censured, that is, censured or esteemed.

Choosing,

Chooſing, vid. *Honour*.

Circumſtance ; crown'd without Robes, ſhew'd *A*. Deriſion.

    Dancing wanting Muſick, threats you Monyleſs.

    Vid. *Dying* in *Dead*.

    A Fly under an Horſe, a miraculous little Ill.

    Gold have in Female Plate, that is, be rich, but not in what is
      apt for Uſe.

    Lightning without Thunder, ſhews of vain Fears.

    Night-Cap having on in Church, ſhew'd *A*. of venting his Re-
      ligious Crudities in publick.

        -Gown have on at the Bar, be exploded as a *Virtuoſo* Law-
        yer.

Conclude, vid. *Reſolve* infra.

        That is, Matters are in a reaſonable Chain of Cauſes, as if
        ſo.

Confuſ'd unſettl'd Thoughts having, ſhews Joy.

    Walk alone in a Place, that is, be diſcontent to ſee a Change
      in Circumſtance anſwerable.

    Walking about many Horſes ſeen, ſhew'd of Confuſion about
      Arts and Riches.

    Singing in the Church hearing, ſhew'd *A*. of Religious Diſ-
      putes.

Conſent. Riding anothers Mare unconſenting, ſhew'd *A*. catch'd in A-
    dultery.

Deſign, vid. *Thought* infra.

    To buy things but loſe the way, ſhew'd *A*. Mony failing.

    Privately to ſee another, that is, to examine his Tranſactions.

    To go to a Feaſt, that is, be near to a Capacity of Plenty.

    To be married where 'twas never done, ſhew'd *A*. beginning a
      Contract never after finiſh'd.

    Intend a thing in general, that is, take Meaſures as if ſo but
      finiſh them not.

    Expedients failing, ſhew of Deſigns defective.

    Carried by a black Ox, as deſigning him Ill, ſhew'd *A*. Ship-
      wreck.

    Unclothing you laying by, care for Pleaſure.

             With no Deſign of putting on again, threats
             Death by Obſtructions.

Diſcretion ſhews of Diſcretion.

Diſtinguiſhing Books into Sorts, to a Student ſhew'd doing the ſame as
    to Notions.

Doting Perſons ſeen, threat your Affairs with their like failure.

Doubtful things, ſhew Matters doubtful.

Doubting ſhews doubting.

    Perſons meeting you, Reaſons of doubt oppoſing your Deſigns.

        But ſuch Perſons ſeen baffled, ſhews of ſuch Doubts
        as fooliſh.

    A Matter you wake, you refrain Procedure according on
      Scruple, as *&c.*   Doubting

Doubting whether you such a Person see one, that is, act as to merit
    such Doubt.
    2 seeing of Diet, and his Physician one of them who eat on
    it, shew'd A. such Diet wholesom.

Examining shews of examining.
    By a 2d View, shew'd of a more deliberate Consideration.
    See how things will issue, suspend your Proceeds as if so.
    Anothers House and Gardens, that is, his Estate and Stock.
        Closet or Trunk, that is, search the Secrets of
        his Breast.
        Find what wanted there, to a Lover Re-
        turn of Love.
        Others Gloves there, he seeks after
        others Loves.
    In suspicion, be jealous of your self, as if you so
    to be examined.
    Whether substantial or no, that is, a Course
    whether a Cheat or no.
Thoroughly, and things changing on't, shew'd of Matters
    issuing otherwise than expected.
Expected. Unexpected things coming, threat with Surprize.
    Stay in Travel, unthought of Delays in Designs.
    Till others, asham'd with just Cause.
    Things not coming, shew of vain Terrors invading.
    Gold unexpected found in hand, shew'd A. possest of a Gain
    unthought.
    Can't sleep in fear of Robbers, the Terrors of erring invade
    you to disturb your quiet Care next day.
    Expect another, be in want of a Course according.
    It raining the Air clear, shew'd of Trouble unexpected.
Extravagant Journy go, undertake a Business as extravagant.
Feigning things, threats with Strife and Variance.
    Vid. *Quality.*   Vid. *Lie in Discourse.*
Folly, vid. *Person Sort in Grammar.*
Forbear going to a Place, resolve to cease a Design.
    A Challenge offer'd in Street, shew'd A. refusing going to Law.
    Dreaming of A. refrain essaying him in a matter.
    Loving fair Women, but forbearing them, shews of virtuous
    Actions.
Forget, vid. *Memory.*
Forsaken Sweetheart seen, threats of vain Designs and Disappointments.
    Vid. *Lover in Grammar.*
Giddy being in general, threats with Perplexity.
    On a Precipice, shew'd A. delay of Accounts to danger of
    forgetting.
Impossibilities shew of vain Hopes, and frustrate Expectations.
    Seen done by God, promise of things unexpected.
Improper, vid. *Ridiculous* and *Unnatural* infra.

                                    Improper

Improper Ornaments wearing, threats with Deriſion.

    Earth talk with, vid. *Earth.*

    Ship ſeen on dry Ground, threats of greateſt Impediments.

    One Man robs many, that is, by Complaiſance anothers trifling Errors paſs to many.

    An Horſe ſeen on a Tree, ſhew'd of Strength reſolv'd or vow'd uſeleſs.

    Way impaſſable go, that is, deſign in a method impracticable.

    Reconcil'd ſeeming to ones Friend, threats with falſe Hopes and Flattery.

    Seek Kidney-Beans on Nut Trees, expect Boys good without Correction.

Intelligible, vid. *Underſtanding.*   Vid. *Knowing* infra.

Intention, vid. *Deſign* ſupra, and *Thought* infra.

Knowing in general, vid. *Strange* infra.   Vid. *Grammar*, the Head unknown.

    Be with Child and know not the Father, ſhew'd to a Woman marry a Stranger.

    By Hearſay, ſhews of things known by Hearſay.

    That you ſleep, gives you greateſt Vigour of Mind.

    Anothers Name, that is, his declared Reſolution.

            Papiſt's Name, ſhews the ſame as to Popery.

    Know you your Rival won't, that is, you become contemptible, as &c.

Miſtaking a Woman lain with for his Wife, but found hating her, ſhew'd A. reconcil'd to his Wife.

    A Letter is wrote to a Prodigal, and thought to S. that is, S. prov'd unexpectedly a good Husband.

    Rectified, ſhews of Courſes freed of Error.

    A Door, that is, your Approach in ſome matter.

    A. for his Brother, ſhew'd Matters iſſuing better than expected with A.

    See a Miſtake, mend the matter.

Offer, vid. *Give* in *Poſſeſs.*

Opinion ask'd, ſhew'd of Opinion ask'd.

Order, vid. *Shite* in *Bodily Action.*   Vid. *Command* in *Words.*

Soul, Order in general ſhews of Order.

    Liſting of Soldiers, to the Sick Death.

            to others, Anger.

    Vid. *Place* in *Earth.*

    Order your Garden, manage your Eſtate Affairs to Plenty.

    Putting a Ring on a Maid's Finger, ſhews of reſolving to marry.

    Garter ſeen tied up by a Man, ſhew'd a Maid Marriage.

    Head firſt, and ſo downwards, anſwers in time according. (*Nebuchad.*)

    Bow fine A's Houſe ſtanding in, ſhew'd of his viſiting great Men.

Soul order. Foreparts of an Horse first; Hinder and Tail last in time, &c.
Pretending shews of pretending.
Prudence shews of Prudence.
Reasoning in general, forethreats of great and various Cares.
Refrain, vid. *Forbear* supra.
Regard, vid. *Neglect* in *Passion.*   Refuse, vid. *Will* supra.
Resolving shews of resolving.   Vid. *Will* and *Conclude* supra.
Ridiculous: A Doctor giving a Glyster, shew'd of his Repute eclips'd.
    King being or seeming, and play with Boys, that is, become
        others Mockery.
    Seeing a Client asking to change 6 *d.* to a Counsel Slights.
    Singing in publick, to the Rich Shame.
            to the Poor, Folly.
    Fly sillily, project as sillily.
    Things in general, threat with Mockery.
    Designing to travel 5 Miles in the Dark, pursuing a Purpose ig-
        norant of the Means.
    Woman see, that is, an aukward Opinion presents.
    Riding a Dog, being in want of Necessaries in Business.
    A King's Officer setting a Gold Button on *A*'s best Clothes,
        shew'd his Credit crack'd.
    4 Oxen *A.* having to sell, and a Dealer to his Mind, but want-
        ing one to sell for him, shew'd him in needless Doubts as to
        a Gain expected.   Vid. *Improper* supra, and *Unnatural*
        intra.
Search, vid. *Examine* supra.
Shrewd Men surveying you, threats you doing what's liable to such
    Censure.
Thoughts unsettled shew Joy.   Vid. *Intention* and *Design* supra.
        Thoughtful, that is, puzlingly engag'd in distracting Affairs.
            To some, it shews of things in present Action.
        Thinking and pale see your Friend, have anxious, but suc-
            cessful Cares.
            To kill you see a Woman, find of a Scheme hazard-
                ing your Ruin.
Truth, vid. *Lie* in *Literature,* and *Appear* in *Sense.*
Uncertain Terrors, threat with great Evil.
        Somewhat removing to take up hid Mony, shew'd *A.* of setting
            aside all Excuses to borrow.   Vid. *Fair* in *Quality.*
Undecent, vid. *Ridiculous* supra.
Unexpected, vid. *Expect* supra.
Unintelligible, vid. *Known* supra, and in *Grammar.*
Unknown, vid. *ibid.*
Unnatural in general, vid. *Breath* in *Fish.*
        Vid. *Wild* and *Tame* in *Beast.*   Vid. *Ship* in *Water.*
        Vid. *Unusual* in *Quality.*   Vid. *Improper* and
            Ridiculous supra.
    Fish seen on dry Land, shews of things against Expectation.
                T   Unnatural.

Unnatural. A Mole ſeen above Ground, diſcovers deepeſt Secrets.

Horſes ſeen with Horns, ſhew'd of Strength fool'd with Imprudence.

Drinking Muſtard ſtamp'd, ſhew'd A. a violent Death.

Marry your Siſter, live and die a Batchelor.

The Image of Chriſt crucified, ſhew'd A. becoming a Nun.

Woman being kiſs'd by a Woman, ſhew'd her loſing her Love.

Tree ſplit ½ Poplar ½ Pine, vid. *Tree*.

Wooden Clothes having, forbids Travel.

Members plac'd, vid. *Members* in *Body general*.

Serpents ſeen in Water, ſhew of powerleſs ſubtle Enemies.

Water ſeen run up Hill, of grievous ill *Omen* ; (horrid Troubles.)

Willing, vid. *W.* ſupra.

Wiſdom ſhews of Wiſdom.

Wiſeman talk with, act as thro the Reſult of good Counſels.

Would, vid. *Will in general* ſupra.

CHAP. XXXVI.

Of Company.

SOcial Actions if proper, ſhew of Company indeed.

Abſurd are generally Allegorick, vid. *Grammar*.

Dancing Company ſlighting, that is, Company in great Mirth.   Vid. *Grammar*.

A. ſeem'd in Houſe with a mean King, he was concern'd to pay a King's Officer a Tax.

He durſt not ſpeak to him, he could not uſe any Liberty about it.

Accompanying a King, threats you Servitude, *&c.*

with A. uſe his like Methods in your Actions.

Acquainted with Soldiers being, ſhew'd A. of deſperate Fortune, and as near to become one.

Act by you ſee an Angel, that is, let a Divine Meſſage Preſumption do ſo in you.

Admitted into an inner Room, entertain'd or attaining to a more ſecret Oeconomy State.

Bed, vid. *B.* in *Goods*.

Before you, vid. *Poſture*.

Coming, vid. *Walk* infra, and *Travel*.

Conſpiracies having againſt you, threats you with ſuch indeed.

To ſome, Trouble from near Relations.

Conſpiracies

Conspiracies scatter them, break the Troubles causing them.
Conjoint Actions shew of Conjoint Actions.
Seeing many going together opposite to him, shew'd *A.* of Conspiracies.

Disappointed Hope, gives Grief.
Eating a Pie at a Bankers, shew'd *A.* treated where he would borrow.

Discourse in general, vid. *Speak* infra.
A Thatcher shew'd *A.* a Corps light in a River with Ships, the *London* Hatter that call'd that Day on *A.* the next News that *A.* heard of him was, that he died.
A. heard a Minister say, that he lov'd his Wife for reading the Whole Duty of Man ; *A.* became self-pleas'd as answering every way a good Conscience.

Diversion, vid. *D.*
Drinking to one at Enmity, foreshew'd a Reconciliation.
Eating, vid. *Bodily Action.*
Embracing, vid. *Passion.*
Encourage, vid. *Presence* infra.
Entertaining as a Bed-guest his Brother's Parish Minister, shew'd *A.* leaving Gain for Conscience.
Not suffering him to lie at the next Market Town, refusing wicked Bargains, *&c.*

Faction, vid. *Conspiracy* supra.
It shews of Faction, and such Persons of such like Courses.
Put on their Clothes, become liable to their like Repute.

Familiar, vid. *Free* in *Passion.*
Failing on Summons, shew'd *A.* of failing on Summons.
Follow, vid. *Travel.*
Guests having or receiving, threats with Envy or Deceit.
Vid. *Grammar* and *Visit* infra.

Hal'd by others, vid. *Action* and *Dead.*
Haunt or frequent you see some, shew'd *A.* kind to them, as to occasion it.
Vid. *Inchantment* in *Spirit.*
Vid. *Dead* and *Visit* infra.

Introduc'd by another Man, a Course directing you, as *&c.*
a Maid, your State gives you the Treatment of such Opinion.

Invitation shews the Offer of things presented.
Of one passing by in a Place unknown, shew'd *A.* of treating him well in Discourse.
You go to invite one, another offers to invite you.
Of one to discourse, shew'd of the Offer of a good Bargain.
To a Tavern, in a Design of plenteous Living.

Invitation

Lingua Terſancta.

Invitation to a Table before you, ſhews you of ſome Profit offer'd you.

    By a Friend to come to his Houſe, *A.* being then in Mourning, ſhew'd *A.* ſick and recovering on it.

    To a roaſted Pig, ſhew'd *A.* receiving a Rent next Day.

    To a Piece of Beef by the dead, ſhew'd *A.* of one in Family taking Phyſick.

    To Supper by *Ceſar* then dead, ſhew'd one dying as he did after him.

    a Tenant, ſhew'd *A.* of one would borrow Mony of him at Intereſt.

    Hercules invited *Alexander* from the Walls, and he took *Tyre.*

    Of your Enemy, vid. *E.*

Lying with, vid. *Bodily Action.*   Vid. *Bed* in *Goods.*

Meeting, vid. *Travel.*

Mutually tickle, that is, aggrieve each other.

    Support, that is, aid each other.

    Diſcourſe each other, that is, be equally bold and free in a full Tranſaction together.

Preſence of an Angel encourages you, the Preſumption of your ſelf's being a Divine Meſſenger ſupports you.

Salutations from Perſons known, ſhew of diſtant Hopes, and bid beware.

Shewing, vid. *S.* in *Action.*

Single Combat, to ſome has ſhewn Marriage.

    to ſome, Law-Suits, and the Aggreſſor Plantiff.

Soliciting ſhews of ſoliciting.

Speaking not heard as God, accompanying Death.

    A Man with you, a Courſe to no actual Iſſue, only chit chat.   Vid. *Diſcourſe.*

Surrounded by Devils, horrideſt Deſpairs.

    Ravens, vid. *R.* in *Birds.*

Throng'd by a Prodigal, narrow'd in Circumſtance thro his like Fault.

    Multitude, your Abilities obſtructed thro a Variety of Cares and active Courſes.

    Neighbours your Hall ſee, act to attract their Reſort.

    Servants there, act ſo as to have good Choice.

    Vid. *Dead.*

Treat, vid. *Feaſt* in *Diverſion.*   Vid. *Gueſt* ſupra.

Viſits in general, ſhew of vain, proud and idle Diſcourſe of Affairs, as *&c.*

    In a Coach, ſhew'd of vain, proud and idle Diſcourſe of Honorary Purchaſes.

    In anothers Chamber, try his like Managery.

Viſits

Vifits in general, it fhews of Efforts you defign not to reft upon.
(1) With a Phyfician's Wife, fhew'd *A.* of torbearing Vifits in Refentments.

One dead, defign in an Expectation threatned *as* groundlefs.

From an idle Perfon, threats you to be like him, at leaft for a while.

Your Debtor, be under ftraits thro Mony Payments.

Perfons infirm in State, threats you fo alfo diverted.

Vid. *Own* and *Unknown* in *Grammar.*

Known and unknown great Men at Tables, fhew'd *A.* of a ftately impofing Treatment.

One rid out an Oculift, fhew'd *A.* of going a Journey for a Friend.

The Dead, fhew'd *A.* Prevention of Work thro wet Weather.

A *Papift,* fhew'd *A.* a Difcourfe of fuperftitious Obedience.

With another, fhew'd of blind Impofitions as to him, *&c.*

A Familiar to thy Bed, fhews of thy Phyfician.

His Brother's Minifter and Butcher, fhew'd *A.* admitting all rival Intereft Confcience Doubts.

Unto fhews of active States from your felf, as from is paffive from the Impulfe of others.

Known or unknown, vid. *Grammar.*

An Attorny, be engag'd in a Wrangle for a while.

A fick Man, fhews him idle, and not your felf fo.

His Phyfician who feem'd tree, fhew'd *A.* taking Phyfick to good Iffue.

Unknown dead calling *A.* C—n, fhew'd *A.* foolifhly fuffering himfelf infirm for a while.

A pleafant entertaining Friend, gives you Plenty and Pleafure.

A Town-Clerk, bufy you about others Good, not your own.

An idle Prodigal's Houfe, be your felf in Oeconomy like him.

An unknown Brother an Apothecary in a Market Town, fhew'd *A.* leaving a good Bargain as unjuft.

One dying, fee of his altering his State.

Or be in Oeconomy like him for a while.

Place. *A's* dead Father looking in upon him in Bed, fhew'd him of a wicked Benefactor's charging him, as with neglect.

Waiting on another, that is, acting at his Pleafure.

In Bed, that is, having Patience with their neglect.

But their own Bed is fatal.

Vid. *Shewing* in *Action.*

From Action till another comes, deferring your Refolutions to his Difcretion.

T 3   *Vifits.*

Viſits. Waiting on a Boy to School, ſtriving to diſcipline one with Ten-
(1)   derneſs to Obedience.

    Benefactor uphill to ſhite, benefiting your ſelf thro
    eaſing his Expence.

Walking to his Wife in a great Hall *A.* ſeeing Beggars, ſhew'd
him teas'd in a Debt for 2 Coach-Horſes.

Welcome, vid. *Words.*

With a vigorous Man act, ſucceed with Vigour.

    An Enemy dance, effort as to the utmoſt with them, as in
    Contention, &c.

Poſture in general, vid. *Poſture.*
(2)   Before you an Attorny with a Phyſician ſtands, that is, a
    Wrangle ſoon cured croſſes you.

    2 boaſt, act with Glory, but not where well known.

By you an Attorny ſtanding, that is, you being teas'd with
uneaſy Wrangles.

    Others ſeen act you ſtanding by, ſhews of things done
    to your ſlight.

Sitting with Tenants, that is, becoming reputed as of their
-     Rank.

    With a louſy Companion, becoming treated as ſuch.

    Known dead Robber, that is, being fix'd in a
    ſure erring Courſe to Loſs.

Quality. Women riding or converſing with, threats with Fooling,
(3)   Deceit, Trifling, or Misfortune, as verſing you
in what will vaniſh into Schemes and Opinions
only.

    Men converſing *è contra* is profitable, for it iſſues ſtill
to Action.

Women ſee ſate between you and others, that is,
find of Opinions rendring you of various
Eſtabliſhment.

    Full-fleſh'd, well-featur'd, and fair cloth'd,
and pleaſant-look'd tho ſeen, are beſt as
happieſt Schemes.

Great men ſhew of Servitude and Awe when ſeen in ill Circumſtance.

    Viſit with them be as greatly attended as they, pre-
figuring withal of a greater Reality *in futuro.*

Seeming our Equals, ſhew of good Courſes aſſiſting us.

Admitted into a Room among them, being induſtrious as to merit ſuch a Preſence.

    a Chamber with the King, gives Ho-
nour and Advance.

Dine with them, be honour'd *in futuro* as to be of
their Rank.

Flattering them, gives Servitude with Hope.

                              Quality

Quality. Great men. Threatning you, shews you plagued by such Power.
(3)   Popes and Bishops seen tho, threats us with
         Fear and Reverence most.
    A Major seen shew'd of hectoring and ruling with
    boasting.
Attendance great having, gives Honour and Respect according.
    In ill-cut Hair seen go before him, shew'd *A.* Loss
    of Place.
Fine Company seen in *A's* House, foreshew'd him of Enter-
    tainment for such.
    To others shew'd them drest as for such Recep-
    tions.
    Accepted be by them, that is, act genteely and
    avoiding Meanness.
    Being among such shew'd of How-do-ye Visits
    from such.
    Follow them, imitate their Courses as is the
    Place where.
    One only seen eat, shew'd of putting off a de-
    sign'd Feast.
         But another Coach coming waking,
         shew'd *A.* resolving to go on with it.

C H A P. XXXVII.

Of Company Number.

Single seen in a City threats you with Heresy or greatly exploded
  (1) Singularity.
    Act so, that is, use Methods peculiar and of no Imitation.
    By your self, proceed singularly and in your peculiar
    Courses.
      With one more, he's your Genius and you
      imitate him.
      With many, shews your using Prudence and
      following a common Course.
    Privacy to some is as Retirement thro Weather.
      Retiring Persons seen, threat you the same Fate with
      Want.
      Retire with another, be secret in his like Method.
        An Adulterer to a Woman in who-
        ring.
      A Woman incognito *A.* saw took for a Queen,
      his desperate Fortune at last he found flou-
      rishing beyond Expectance.
         T 4   *Single.*

Single. Privacy. Houfes feen burn inwardly threat of fecret Family Ruin.

(1)   Private Earthquake of it feen, fhew'd of the Prince's Edict againft *A*.

Private way, an unufual Courfe.

Intentions fhew of fecret Actions.

Statue having, fhew'd *A*. excelling in's private Managery.

Dancing being at, gives Joy and Careffment of Friends.

Publick threats you as expos'd to all.

Solitude in general, vid. *Defert* in *Earth*.

Being there in great Sadnefs, threats of Mifery and Poverty as left of all.

By choice fhews of leaving Bufinefs for Pleafure.

To all but Men retiring and Students ill, to them leifure.

To the Poor Mifery and Danger, if not Death.

To the Rich Lofs of Friends and Family, as Death of Wife, &c.

To the Sick and Criminals Death as in Circumftance.

Solitary Creatures as the Eat and black Sparrow feen, defolate all, &c.

Circumftance. A little Houfe in it, an Oeconomy to the fame purpofe.

A little Boy feen with you there, your happy Genius if a Student.

With Grafs, Herbs, and Springs tho, to Women has fhewn Study to come.

Deer and wild Beafts gentle, gives a Life of Eafe with Security.

Ghofts and domeftick Beafts, fhew'd *A*. of being a Monk.

Lions and Serpents fhew'd *A*. of becoming a Thief.

Bare and empty is more horrid than all.

Ee with one he commanding, that is, thro God's Providence be forced to bear his like Humours.

You mafter, that is, your felf act fo as to be born in his like Humours.

Two.

n. Posture. Before } vid. *Posture.*
2)   By you }

Sit with a Robber, be in a fix'd and stared Course of
    Error.
            Who flings you into Water, to your
                personal Trouble.
    Standing by you, that is, being in an establish'd Course
        as is the Person.
    Walking with one, that is, designing in a Course as is
        that Person.
                Pragmatical and presumptuous in an
                    House unknown, that is, your self
                    being so in all Oeconomy States.

Angel shake hands with, Vid. *A.* in *Spirit.*
    Travel with, vid. *Ibid.*
Another act see, vid. *See* in *Sense.*
    Travel with, that is, design in his like Methods, *&c.*
Brother travel with, design in a Course will cross you with others
    Interest.   Vid. *Brother* in *Grammar.*
Cheat travel with, design to your self Deceit, or to cheat others,
    as *&c.*
Chrift walk with in Streets, appear in publick Converse and
    Transaction like him.
Discourse, vid. *D.* in *Grammar* and *Words* infra.
Doting, vid. *Old man* infra.
Dead man, vid. *Dead.*
            Go about Business with, design in vain in a Concern.
            Call to go with you, expect no finishing Issue to be
                in such matter.
                He follows not on Call, matters are better
                    than expected.
            Brother dead yok'd with and forc'd to draw as an Ox,
                shew'd *A.* Death.
            Do business with, be condemn'd by others as doing
                what you did not.
            Known see act, that is, your self act as they did
                when alive.
Father-in-law walk with, design in an hard and slaving Method.
    Vid. *Grammar.*
G O D be with, be pure.   Vid. *G O D.*
Humoursom Person accompany, either humour or be humour'd,
    as who of you appears Master in his like Circumstance.
King, Vid. *King* in *Government.*   Mother, Vid. *Grammar.*
Known acting or seen act, shews you imitating him.
    Vid. *Grammar.*
Neighbour act with, that is, transact in a neighbourly Course,
    as *&c.*
Old doting Man or Woman standing by you, that is, you your
    self also expecting as a Dotard.   *Two.*

Two. Pope converſe with, that is, awe or be aw'd with Reverence, a:
(2)　*&c.*

In *Italy*, and withal calling him Lord, ſhew'd *A.* of paying another's Debt.

Romantick Princeſs travel with, deſign in a glorious and obſolete
Courſe.

With Don *Quixot* going, ſhew'd of deſigning ſeemingly as fooliſh as he.

Shoomaker arreſted by, ſhew'd *A.* under Cenſure of Friendſhip
broke.

Sick, vid. *Grammar.*　Spirit, vid. *Spirit.*

Siſter, *&c.* act with, that is as Brother above but leſs.
Vid. *Grammar.*

Spunger be in Chamber with, that is, live by ſpunging.

Son one weeping with, ſhew'd a Father the others Death.

Sun riſing with, and with the Moon going her Courſe, ſhew'd *A.*
the Gibbet.

Tenant's Wife travelling with, ſhew'd *A.* deſigning in an Intereſt
Method too ſharp for him.

Tutor travel with, deſign in a Courſe wherein you'l be repri-
manded.

Unknown, vid. *Grammar.*

Act with, purſue an unaccountable Courſe.

A little Man, the Method the more contemptible.

A fair, fat, pleaſant-look'd Man, that is, be
in an odd Courſe of Plenty.

Giving *A.* Gold, and his Breeches
full of Chocolate Cakes, Plenty
alſo accruing thereby.

Young man ill-cloth'd *A.* diſcours'd, who firſt going back and
then forwards, at laſt went off well-cloth'd ; this ſhew'd *A.*
firſt ſettling his Accounts, and then his Arrears paid buying
him Clothes.

Wife being with, that is, in conſideration of your Art, *&c.*

Three. You and 2 more act is beſt, that is, you act with full Endea-
(3)　vour.　Vid. *Doubt* in *Soul.*
Vid. *Numbers.*　Vid. *Unknown* in *Grammar.*

A. was defended from the Devil by an Angel he talk'd with, the
Thoughts that he was a Divine Meſſenger emboldned *A.* to
act tho againſt the Law.

His Mother yok'd and forc'd *A.* to draw as an Ox with his dead
Brother, dying ſhe buried him with him.

A's Father-in-law back in Weſt drank a Glaſs of Blood to *A.*
but *A*'s own Father ſtood oppoſite to him ſmiling back in Eaſt.
A. narrowly eſcap'd that day Death.　(Both Fathers dead)

1 Friend ſeen come, a 2d alſo ſeen to follow, ſhews you of
great Good or Miſery to follow.

Three.

Three. A. in bed with a Madman and Hermaphrodite, enrol'd moſt to
(3) the Hermaphrodite, that is, A. being lazy and deceitful ; mad
and ; monſtrous in Temper, yet in the main appeared moſt
of the laſt ſize.

A. walking with his Tenant and Lawyer on plow'd Grounds,
ſhew'd of his purſuing, ſuch an Eſtates Controverſy in iſſue.

Leacher with Chirurgeons A. leaning of, ſhew'd of his having to
do with a Rival was lame,

2 Women travel with, deſign only as to Opinion, &c. and that
imperfectly,
2 Girls is ſtill worſe.

Walk with a prudent Friend to a projective one, oneto in a
Courſe, ſigr.

2 Boaſt before, aſt as with Glory, but ſee where well known.

Bear a rich Man chide a Sponger, avoid the Approach of ſuch
Impraction your ſelf.

One comes to you as talking with another, ſecond Courſe offers
in aid to your firſt.

With a Phyſician fee one, that is, ſuch a Courſe will be remedied.

Man and Wife travel, deſign with Prejudice.

2 Domeſticks lazy and unactive in Bed, that is, idled
thro their means.

Your Lawyer and Friend go towards Leave, thro their
Intereſt ſeek to prefer you.

Frugal Friend and Siſter aſt, that is, partly led by
Frugality, partly by Devotion.

Fut, 3d. Number.

(3) 4 unknown ſtand before you, that is, a Diſtreſs of Counſel
offers.

Fight with, conteſt in a matter of Conſpiracy.

This ſhew'd A. by plotting for 4 confounding all.

4 acting together, ſhew thus always as of your Action or Counſel, but ſeverally they ſhew the Interference of ſo many reaſonable Courſes or Perſons, &c.

4 Beggars before you, a State of perfect Want threats you.

2 Women and 2 Girls, a Council of Science, &c. imperfect.

4 Jews ſeen in a Chamber, A. beſtirr'd down one that floated,
that is, A. confined the Perfection of Judaiſm.

3 breaking the few ſtay, he allowed however the Juſtice
of its Eſtabliſhment.

A's Bailiff and 2 unknown would buy a Bed for him at a rich
Man's, that is, ſuch Bailiff for his own Benefit would tempt
A. to Laziness, as on occaſion of his being rich enough.

A. Friend, and one known with 2 unknown A. ſaw at Cards, A.
avoiding a Cheat offering, colour'd partly with Friendſhip and
Acquaintance.

Four. St. *Peter* noiſy, a Captain huff'd him to ſneak, whilſt I with M:
(4) ſes left the Room; I choſe rather by *Moſes*'s Meekneſs t
preſerve my Conſcience, than St. *Peter*'s Raſhneſs to deny i

Introduc'd by one I paſſed by an unknown Lord, and ſaluted h
tall Lady in a Room, in craft like the Introducer, I neglecte
my own Honour to magnify my Wife for a turn.

One run away with *A*'s Child, his Wife going with him; one abu
ſing his Expectation would have fool'd him in his Contrac
alſo too.

A. ſtop'd by one to be rob'd ſaw 2 come to his Aid, this ſhew'
A. an imperfect cheating Conſpiracy.

A. ſate at Cards with 3 Divines ſtanding, that is, *A.* in a fix'
Courſe dealt with them unbelieving, *&c.* —

Many in general, Vid. *Fairs.*   Vid. *Numbers.*
(5)   Vid. *Multitude* in *Numbers, &c.*

Friends and Enemies ſeen mix'd, ſhews of Miſtakes an
Alterations.

Acting with, deſigning in a common way.

     Helping you, various odd Methods call'd to you
     Aſſiſtance.

Unknown and his Enemy dancing in *A*'s Barn he ſeeing g
off, ſhew'd *A.* of his Harveſt brought in.

Coming among on riſing Ground, that is, being in a com
mon way to advance.

Wife's Friends ſeen with *A.* ſhew'd of his own neglectfu
of him.

A. ſeeing her 4 Sons dead going before the Virgin *Mar*
ſaw the other 2 alſo follow after; this ſhew'd of the
dying of the Plague, as had done the 4.

Others acting ſeen, you ſtanding by, ſhews of things don
to your flight.

Apoſtles ſeen in conference about *Julian*, 2 comforted th
reſt.   (His Death on it)

With your Friends pray, that is, obtain your commor
Deſires.

     Neighbours hunt, that is, uſe their like commor
     Methods to Gain.

A. ſaw a Play, and his Wife and Siſter ſate oppoſite to ſe
it alſo, that is, an Intereſt Diviſion offer'd in oppoſition
to the fatal Iſſue *A.* was proſecuting.

Among the dead ſleep, live with Debauchees.

     Robbers being, that is, in a various Courſe of Waſte and
     Prodigality.

     Servants feaſting, ſhew'd *A.* of borrowing their Mony.

     Tombs and dead Bones being, ſhew'd *A.* of gaining by
     dying Friends.   Vid. *Fly* in *Air.*

Publick Prayer hearing, gives a publick Relief.

     Correction to a Servant, ſhew'd of Idleneſs cnred by
     hard Service.   *Many.*

Many. **Publick** Death gives Servants and private Men publick Power.
(5) Applause having, shew'd *A.* publick Cenfure and Condemnation of Juftice.

  Funeral in a City feen with Counfel attending, shew'd *A.* of a great Debt paid off.

  Shiting as in a Church or Market, threats with impious Shame and Difcovery.

  Singing, to the Rich Shame, to the Poor Folly.

  Dancing shew'd *A.* of being expos'd in publick.

    Vid. alfo *Private* fupra.

Rabble confounded amongft, perplex'd amidft Variety of Methods.

Societies. 7 Men with Coronets feen, shew'd of the 7 United Provinces.
(6) Senate-houfe has shewn of the Parliament.

  Convocation-houfe feen, has shewn of the State Ecclefiaftical.

  College you belong'd to feen exalted, celebrates your Learning.

  Of Apoftles feen confult, to *Julian* shew'd his Deftruction.

  Court fine feen with a Taylor Judg there, shew'd *A.* of going to a Receiver General a Mercer.

  Parliament faid to do fomewhat, if in circumftance 'tis literal.

  Acts of Parliament shew of the publickeft determin'd Refolutions.

  Bufy feen, shew'd *A.* confulting divers short Notes and Opinions.

    To others a Confult of many call'd to their Aid.

  A.'s Brother walking crofs him before it, shew'd him in Intereft Difputes law'd by others.

  Go to fee, that is, queftion another's Power, as *&c.* and as if you would alter his Laws.

    Remove thence to a Temple Chamber, being balk'd therein, remain content in plain Juftice.

  Seen at a Church or Feaft, shew'd of Beaux ruling in Clothes.

  Man chofe for London, shew'd *A.* by Confcience forc'd to publickeft Difcoveries for *Englifb* greateft Good.

Affemblies in general threat with Trouble and Confufion.
(7) Vid. *Feafts* in *Diverfion.*

  Vid. *Fairs* and *Markets* in *Habitations.*

  With many being, shews of having a common Fate.

  Drinking-Bouts feeing, has shewn of being at Merry-meetings.

  Great Companies feen in clofe Debate, threat of Confpiracies as for or againft you, *&c.*

          Affemblies.

Aſſemblies. A Ring of mean Women *A.* ſtanding amidſt, ſaid, Hapr
(7) they who are in GOD's Kingdom, ſhew'd *A.* of being
Godfather to a mean man's Child.
Many well apparel'd and chearful ſeen in a Church, ſhew
of an happy Wedding.
Ill-favour'd and ſad ſeen, and your Friends apar
threats Death.
Bowels *A*'s ſhewn to an Aſſembly, gave him a famous Son

CHAP. XXXVIII.
Of Self.

SELF in publick Dreams ſhews of our publick Wiſhes, Intereſt
(1) and Deſires tho large as Kingdoms.
Vid. at large in St. *John*'s Revelation, and Mr. F
re*'s Dreams, *&c.*
In private Dreams it conforms narrower, as is our Vie
Deſigns, and Hopes.
To ſome their peculiar Temper and its Iſſue
oppoſition to others.
To ſome it ſhews of Self, Wife, Children, ar
Parents.
To ſome of our GOD, Will, or Friend belove
Do buſineſs then in expectation, that is, ſee it done in i
Zeal.
To others do it in their peculiar Courſe of H
mour.
Kill your ſelf, your ſelf be the Cauſe of ſome great Chan,
of Good or Ill unto your ſelf.
Vid. *Kill* in *Dead.*
Judg being, gives you your Suit obtain'd.
Dreſſing ones ſelf is as Eaſe from Trouble, and Leiſure fro
Diverſion.
Own proper things in circumſtance are ſtill literal.
(2) Unproper give at leaſt ſureſt Comman
Vid. *Grammar.*
Chamber, vid. *C.* in *Houſe.*
Dog ſeen ſhews of your Friend or Bailiff, as another's another's.
Dwell, vid. *Home* in *Grammar.* Vid. *Grammar.*
Field *A.* ſaw a black Horſe come into, that is, by contrivance
got the Command of one to himſelf.
Having an unknown Houſe in my own Mead, ſhew'd me by co
trivance enabled to get ſome Houſe-goods that were then
my Cuſtody.

O

Own Flesh eating, threats with greatest Grief.
(2) Funeral seen gives you great Honour, but short-liv'd.
Hogs see at an Inn, be concern'd to see them ill car'd for.
Home, vid. *Home* in *Grammar.*
Horse see another ride, find he commands your Estate.
 He and your Horse get off safe, his Right and yours too
  farewel.
 Seen expire, shew'd *A.* of ceasing its Use, as keeping a Coach.
House seen entred at a new Door, vid. *New* in *Time.*
 Vid. *Grammar.*
Lane, vid. *Grammar.*
Name proper, shews to you your self and all belonging to you.
 Elotted cut seen, is of horrible Portent.
Picture seen well drawn, promises you long Life.
Right Hand *A.* saw cut off, that is, he fell by the Hand of his Bro-
  ther.
Sake a thing done for, shews of ones occasioning it.
Shop seeming stand in, that is, help another, as is the Trade.
Staff in *A's* Hand struck at thrice by an Hornet, shew'd *A.* of a
 cunning Knave's striving to fool his Managery.
Trees seen without Fruit that had some before, shew'd *A.* of
 gathering them in next Day.

C H A P. XXXIX.

Of Another.

Nother seen in a strange Place, shews of such Courses of yours
 as is the Place and Person, but in odd Circumstances.
 's Property, vid. *Brother* in *Grammar.*
 London Waggon the best sort of such hard
  Work.
 Father-in-Laws Hat, a slavish Honour.
 Brothers Crevat, a Repute thwarting you in
  Interest.
 Unknown, vid. *Grammar.*
 Prudent Friend's studying Gown wear, use the
  wisest Courses in Study.
 Virgin *Mary* seen with a great Bush of Hair,
  shew'd *A.* of Gain.
Acting, vid. *Action.*
 Act with another, act in their Method.
 For another, that is, do what will turn to
  others Benefits at last.

                              Another.

Another. Acting. Act. See another you ſtanding by, that is, nicel
              let ſuch a method turn in you
              Actions.
        You aſſiſting, adding your own hu
             mour'd Managery thereto.
      Againſt you ſee one, that is, ſuch a Courſ
        God has ordain'd ſhall croſs you.
      See another, vid. *See in Senſe.*
Able a meek Man *A.* ſaw able, tho himſelf not; that is, b
  Meekneſs *A.* might attain what his own Humour can't.
Brother, vid. *Grammar.*
's Daughter in Bed with, that is, idly gaming for another
  Mony.
's Bed lie on, that is, be lazy where expected active by him
's Book ſee, that is, be in want of ſome Inſtruction he car
  furniſh you.
        Biſhop *F*'s delivered me to peruſe, ſhew'd me
          choſe a Godfather.
's Dog ſeen, ſhews of your Enemies Servant or Procuter.
's Chamber, vid. *Known* and *Unknown* in *Grammar.*
's Child, vid. *Man* in *Grammar.*
's Clothes wear, that is, rival them, or uſe their Repute o
  Intereſt.
      So, to ſome get their ſure Friendſhip.
Court, vid. *Grammar.*
Diſcourſing, that is, acting with relation to him.
      To others, act as he uſually does.
      Vid. *Diſcourſe* and *Grammar.*
Diſtracted and raving ſeen as a Domeſtick, foreſhew'd him
  grievous Miſhap.
Dreſſing, that is, paying him Service.
      To ſome tho, command their Repute withal.
's Enemy differ with, that is, differ with them as they did
  with that Enemy.
Exalted to Office ſeen, threats you with Trouble.
Fall from, that is, leave him in his Party.
   -ing off his Horſe ſeen and breaking his Neck, ſhew'd a
    dying.
        His Horſe coming to *A.* who mounted, that is
         inherited him.
's Goods uſing, to the Rich Poverty.
        to Rogues, Succeſs in Roguery, as none will
         lend them.
        's Plate ſeeing, ſhew'd of Envy, as deſiring their
         excellent Methods.
        's Hay your Horſe eats, that is, the Horſe you
         treat of you'l buy.

Another's Hand fee with a burning Light in't, your Facts will be dif-
    covered, &c.
        But put out there, the contrary.
   's Hair cut, that is, benefit him, but to your own Hurt.
   's Having, vid. *Poffefs* infra.
   's Help, vid. *Action* and *Nurfe* in *Grammar.*
   's Horfe riding without leave, fhew'd *A.* of being caught in
        Adultery.
        He riding yours, he commands your Eftate, or
        cuckolds you.
   's Houfe, vid. *Grammar.*
        Make a Fire in, that is, act to get an Occonomy
        good by him.
        Being in, that is, fubject to the Control of his Me-
        thods in your Oeconomy.
        Shiting in, fhew'd *A.* of paying him off his Debt
        in Scorn.
        His Barn, fhew'd *A.* of fettling the
        Charge of his farming there.
        Sifter's be in, that is, in a Converfe of Difcord and
        Divifion.
        Phyfician's be in, that is, in a Converfe of Remedy.
        Minifter's, that is, in a Converfe of Divine Cafuifm.
        that married you, as to Marriage, or
        fome Contract.
Kill, vid. *K.* in *Dead.*
Kills your Lice in your Head, that is, rids you of your beggar-
   ly Cares.
   You, that is, a change of good or ill to you, is accord-
   ingly from him or fuch like Courfe.
Kifs, vid. *Bodily Action.*
Like, vid. *See* in *Senfe.*
Looking-Glafs Enemies fee your felf in, contend with a Kinfman.
Name know, that is, his exact Power refolves and Intereft.
   Like yours heard of, gives you fome ftrange unexpect-
   ed Ufage.
Offend, vid. *O.* in *Action.*
Place come into, that is, fucceed him in Time and Manner.
Room, vid. *Houfe* and *Grammar.*
   's Seal poffefs, that is, become his Heir.
   's Servant, that is, his like Method of Service.
        Vid. *Brother* in *Grammar.*
   's Shop ftand in as Mafter, command the Benefit of his Trade.
   He ftands in yours, you give him the like Freedom
   with you.
Sick your Fellow Neighbour Tradefman feen, threats you
   wanting Bufinefs.

Another fick, you're dead on't and carried to his Grave, threats yo
leaving your Houfe on't.
's Son give a Sugar Plumb to, fool him in his Expectation.
Suffer as another, become as an Acceffory to his Fault.
's things feen, vid. *Book* fupra.
Vifits you, vid. *Company.*
Unknown, vid. *Grammar.*
Wheat near overrun by Oats, his good Notions near fpoi
by Fancies.
Wife marry, that is, contract a Friendfhip with her.
Works of *Hercules* finifhing, forefhew'd a Woman's bein
burnt.

CHAP. XL.
Of Poffeffion.

IN general, vid. *Poffefs* infra.
Borrowing is Literal, and fhews as is the thing borrowed.
Vid. *Lend* infra.
Mony of others, to a Student fhew'd of fhort Notes Colle
tions.
Talk of borrowing, &c. lend your felf as to deferve it.
Buying in general, vid. *Sold* infra.   Vid. *Painter* in *Trade.*
To fome it fhews as borrowing.
To fome, full Command and free Ability to procure things
To fome, get a Friend by Services.
To fome, merit as by Power or Service without bargai
ing.
Manner willingly, fhews Pleafure.
At a Place, that is, get a Profit according, or anfwer
ble.
Preparing or going for it, fhews of Endeavours for Gai
Refus'd in what you would buy, baulk'd in what yo
would merit.
Unwillingly, fhews of compell'd Expence.
Offer'd cheap, a Benefit eafily atchiev'd.
Dear, that is, be at fome great Lofs in its A
tainment.
Handling things only, is as Treaty without Gain.
Of you fee others, fhews of your doing fo of them
Seek to buy and find not what defired, if in Circu
ftance Literal.
Refufe on the Tradefman's Offer, the Inftructic
wanted you have got.

Buyi

Buying. Manner. Seek the Exchange vaniſhes, your Managery ſhould
enable you fails you.

Deſigning but loſing the way, ſhews of Mony Diſappointment or ill Managery.

Go to buy Timber, that is, deſign for Riches.

Hinder'd, ſtops communication according.

Perſons. Of a dead Butcher Meat, to the Sick Loſs of Stomach.

A lazy Prodigal buys of *A.* to pay him in Counters,
this ſhew'd *A.* trifling away his Gains.

You buy of ſuch 7 Acres of Wheat, you ſpoil ſuch
lazily.

Things in general, to ſome attain things thro Benefits, or by
good Methods.

See another buy things, your ſelf command
ſuch Plenty alſo.

Agreeable and uſeful is good to all.

A new Head at the Exchange, ſhew'd *A.* her
Husband thriving to her Glory.

Apartment in anothers Houſe, ſhew'd *A.* of marrying
there.

Chamber in the Temple, act to merit full Practice there.

Common for all to ſhite, doing Buſineſs *gratis*,
and ſo eaſing all in Expence.

Cherries at a Place, acting to procure Pleaſures, as *&c.*

Cheſt, vid. *Iron* infra.

China, attaining Riches to Delicacy.

Chang'd to Bawbles, deceiv'd in ſuch Hopes.

Bed rich, acting to deſerve a ſtately Wife.

Poor Man's buying, ſhew'd *A.* of awing a Lodging from him.

Of a rich Man, ſhew'd *A.* being lazy in proſpect
of Riches.

Gloves ſhew of amorous Diſpoſitions.

Jewels unknown, gave Benefit by Hands unexpected.

Vid. *Jewels* in *Riches.*

Iron Cheſt, have Mony to keep by you as in one.

News offer'd to be bought, acting to occaſion ill Reports.

Proviſions, to the Poor Plenty.

to the Rich, Expence.

Victuals of the Dead, to the Sick is as Loſs of
Stomach.

Salt, get a Friend by Benefits.

Fiſh, good.

A Pheaſant, viſit where a Treat requir'd in
Return.

A Whiting in Market, to the Sick recover
to eat one.

Buying things. Rich things, vid. *Bed* ſupra, and *Silk* infra.

Silk talk of buying, be in Circumſtance of Plenty anſwerable.

Sword rich, act to procure a Reſentment ſure and good.

Timber, raiſing Mony.

Victuals, vid. *Proviſions* ſupra.

Unneceſſary things, threats with Prodigality.

Neceſſary, vid. *Proviſions* ſupra.

Wheat 7 Acres buying of a Prodigal, ſhew'd *A.* of ſpoiling his Plenty, &c.

Sold ſee things offer'd ſneaking, threats you ſo bargaining.

A. ſeeing his Mare for a while, ſhew'd *A's* Wife waiting for a Reward as a Nurſe.

Handling things only, ſhews of Treaty without Profit.

Sweat Meats offer'd by a Woman, that is, a Scheme to Delicacy, but with hard Labour. Vid. *Handle* infra.

Sold be ones ſelf to one who would change Condition, good.

to ſome, Marriage.

to ſome, Miſery or Travel.

to the Rich, Loſs of Honour.

to ſome, Sale indeed.

Selling things, to ſome, loſing Friends thro Unkindneſs.

Timber, threats you with Debts endangering your Eſtate.

To others, act as to neglect Eſtate Gain.

Salt, ſhew'd *A.* of loſing a Friend thro Intereſtedneſs.

Evil things, acting to attain better.

Windows cheap, offering of good Proſpects readily.

Neceſſaries and unwillingly, threats with great Poverty.

Unneceſſaries, ſhews Riches.

And if unwillingly, with Hate of Buſineſs.

Drop, vid. *Handle* infra.

Finding things, ſhews of a mental Diſcovery of the Means to attain them.

Upon Bed find Chocolate, &c. that is, have it of your Husband or Wife, &c.

Can't find what you want, be baulk'd in hotteſt Expectations.

A bold Man ſeen and that was not after to be found, ſhew'd of a confident Strain in a Letter blotted out.

Finding

Finding things. In your Coat, that is, your Reputation is ſo mark'd as what is there found.

Books in a fine unknown Houſe, thro ſuch a future plenty State get ſuch, *&c.*
Vid. *Old* and *New* in *Time.*

Altars, ſhews Joy and the Bleſſings of God.

Beaſts Horns, Hoofs or Claws good, it ſhews of ſome Enemy disarmed.

Birds Neſts, a good Sign.
Claws or Beaks, ſhews of ſome Enemy disarmed alſo.

Candles, diſcovering ſome new Arts or Reaſonings.

Claws, vid. *Beaſts* and *Birds* ſupra.

Combs gives you Eaſe under preſent Preſſures, and is as by way of Diverſion.

Corn Oats 30 Buſhels near waſte, providing Hay enough in Place.

Deeds, diſcovering of Methods to Profit worthy of them.

Gloves his own again, ſhew'd *A.* of a Quarrel reconcil'd.
Woman's in his Box or Cheſt, to a Man his Miſtreſſes Favours.

Gold under Ground, ſhews the Dreamer is not yet in his true way to Riches.

Hat yours at your Beds-feet, that is, retrieve your Diſhonour thro Neglect.

Horns, } vid. *Beaſt* ſupra, and *Stags* infra.
Hoof, }

Jewels yours dropt, that is, your Liberty, *&c.* before loſt to you.

Liquorice in a Foot Path, that is, ſomewhat as chewable in one.

Major out, ſhew'd *A.* of trying induſtriouſly to outvote another.

Mony on the Ground, ſhew'd of Want and hard Labour, or Gain, thro means contemn'd of others.
In general, ſhews of Envy or Hatred to come.
Laid in a Window, receiving ſome well lent.
Put in your Hand unexpected Receipt, or Relief by a Friend.
Treaſure loſt and hiding it for fear, ſhew'd *A.* Loſs by a Woman.
With Joy when not ſo, is as Grief thro Expectation.
In a Tomb, ſhew'd of learned Books and Secrets.
Under ſomewhat, ſhew'd *A.* of ſetting aſide all Excuſes to borrow.

Removed ſomewhat, threats you deceiv'd in Aid expected, as *&c.*

Rings which were claim'd again, ſhew'd *A.* Loſs by Gaming.

Stags Horns, gives hazard Gains tho little.

Under Table ſomewhat, that is already ſpent in Houſe-keeping.

Finding Words unknown on a Bed, difcover horrid Iffues attendin
     Lazinefs.

Lofs in general, to the Rich Ill.
       to the Poor Good, as having to lofe.
     Of things evil is ftill gcod.   Vid. *Clothes* infr
         'Tis as tortur'd in Defire for Perfons, as a
           the things loft.
     Self feeming among new Buildings in her Native Cit
         fhew'd *A.* hearing of Friends dying ther
       Vid. *Old* and *New* in *Time.*

Of Birds let go, threat Damage.
       Seen not to be caught, are Damage alfo to all.
Clothes, to fome is as Lofs of Fame.
       to fome, it avoids Anger.
       to Servants and Debtors, 'tis Acquitment and Fre
       dom.
       Woollen loft are good to all, it fhews Gain in La
       and Controverfy, (fheepifh.)
Eye, threats of a Son or dear Friend dying.
Friend, that is, fome pleafant profitable Courfe according
Hat, that is, your Honour, or the Cover of fome Houfe (
     Wall.   Vid. *H.* in *Apparel.*
Horfe, fome Art, *&c.* irrecoverable.
Jewels, fhew of fome trifling Lofs if unknown.
     If your own, threats you Slavery, and as being an
     thers.
Keys, threats Anger.
Means, threats of your Bufinefs failing.
Members, vid. *Body.*
Mule having one, fhews of a real Lofs, or elfe is as Deliver
     from Ill.
Name, that is, Life, Circumftance and Riches.
Nofe, to a Perfumer his Trade.
     to others, Lofs of good Fame or Death.
Papers of Juftification, to one accus'd in Law, acquitte
     him the next day.
Rings, threats Lofs of Wife, Tenant, and Goods too often
          to others, fome grievous Deceit.
          to others, Lofs of a Lover or Relation.
       Find it, retrieve all.
       Father's finding, fhew'd *A.* retrieving his Br
       ther's Honour.
       Sealing, that is, your Profpeĉt to fome Inher
       tance.
       Wedding, one turn to hate Husband or Wife.
Roof threats with lofing your Clothes.
Scent to a King, fhcw'd danger by one of his greateft Cou
     tiers.

                                       Fin

Find Loſs of Scent, to a private Man his Servant cuckolds him.

to Cheeſe, ſhew'd *A.* his Loſs of Repute in judging of it.

Shoos, to ſome be bed-rid, or have Pains in the Feet.

to others, exceſſive Poverty. — Vid. *Apparel.*

Way with the dead, and not find it again, Death.

Fear out ih't, ſhews of Cautions againſt Miſtakes in your Methods.

Friend anſwers you, you calling, ſuch Methods retrieve your Error.

Wife, to ſome the Loſs of ſome Ring.

to others, her Care or Aſſiſtance as failing plagues you.

Gone and married to *A*'s pitying Friend, ſhew'd *A*'s Pleaſure in his Wife near loſt.

Loſt in a bad Place is good, it ſhews her acting to be of better Circumſtance.

Woollen, vid. *Clothes* ſupra.

Getting Store of Goods gives Profit.

to Exceſs, threats Hurt.

to ſome, Burden and Trouble with Deſire fulfilled.

Things with Difficulty, that is, thro great mental Application.

By help of a long Pole, thro a tall Man's Aid.

Another's Clothes, attaining to a ſure Friend.

's fine Clothes and Image from her, ſhew'd *A.* of ſeparating a Wife from her Husband.

Papiſt's Pſalm-Book from him, baulking the Glory of Popery.

Giving in general, ſhews attributing, as is the Thing and the Giver.

Better than taking, except from Perſons above us.

To ſome it ſhews attaining by a Courſe, as is the Perſon.

Thus receiving Gold is good, giving it is bad.

Vid. *Meſſenger.* Vid. *Send* in *Travel.*

Place to another, that is, letting things be done to his Will.

From God, vid. *Spirit.*

He puts a Benefit in your Power, as *&c.*

A Romantick habited Woman receiving Dates. Eating ſuch thereon recover'd the Sick.

A Servant Mony, by ſuch Service gain it.

A kind-look'd unknown Man broad pieces, ſhew'd *A.* a good Courſe according, giving him Plenty, his Breeches too with Chocolate Cakes, to all Freedom and Daintineſs.

Your Brother, have Benefit tho againſt anothers Intereſt.

A good Husband, ſhews your good Husbandry profiting you

Giving from one literally, ſhews he attributes ſuch matter to be in your Power.

The King or Queen gives great Joy.

The Dead is good, and Benefit from their Imitation.

Chriſt-Bread given to *A.* gave him a miraculous Increaſe of Plenty.

Unto the Dead ſomewhat, threats you Death or great Loſs.

Way, ſubmitting to act wickedly.

Chriſt's Nurſe, vid. *Chriſt* in *Religion.*

Another ſomewhat, ſhews you of Gain, as able there-to.

To ſome, put it in their Power to gain, as &c.

A Beggar ſomewhat own you, enjoy anſwerably ſome-what as beggarly.

Dogs large Cheeſe-parings, be prodigal to ungratefu Perſons.

3 is as being abſolutely liberal, as &c.

An Elephant to eat or drink, waiting on ſome great Lord to benefit him.

Unknown honeſt Man ſomewhat, that is, in Conſci-ence forbear it.

Manner. Another gives for you, that is, in Complaiſance you admit, as &c.

Freely, vid. *Quality.*

Preſenting one, that is, making him an Offer of a Bar-gain, as &c.

Your ſelf, threats you Damage.

Receiving *e con,* is Joy and Gain.

With Pictures, acquainting him with good News.

Preſented by her Lover with an Hogſhead, ſhew'd *A.* ſhe'd hate him.

With a Garland of Flowers, to ſome has given Succeſs in Love.

Offer'd is as commanding.

Offering is as ſtooping generally.

You offering others ſomewhat, ſhews they will you.

Being fineſt China, that is, being in Circum-ſtances of greateſt Plenty.

Things *A.* ſeeing to be ſold at his Door, ſhew'd himſelf of ſuch Neceſſity, &c.

News to buy, News occurs to Advantage, as &c.

Your Daughter, to another give him a Profit, with a Daughter a Dowry.

Giving. Manner. Offering you an Horſe to go Weſt ſee your Banker Friend, that is, find your Eſtate bad near to Remove.

Her ſelf to lie with you a fine Woman, is good. You her, bad.

His Service to you ſee one, threats of your being in want of ſuch a Servant.

Receiving from Perſons above us is good, or elſe is ill.

Vid. *Preſent* ſupra.

Vid. *Beggar* in *Grammar.*

An Angel by you, that is, attaining thro a Divine preſum'd Meſſage.

The Dead, Vid. *Dead.*

A Woman, threats Damage.

The Dead, is good to all; to ſome benefit thro Wood-ſales.

To others good thro their Imitation.

Mony ſhews you in want of ſuch a Sum to lay it out.

A Crown to the Royal Blood, has ſhewn inheriting it.

A Debt by a Creditor, from the Sick Death.

A Letter, meet a Friend or find a new one.

To ſome it has ſhewn of a Buſineſs not to be done without it.

From your Father, befriend one in Family regard.

To ſome it ſhews a Friend receives a Letter for you in your buſineſs.

An hard Blow in the Neck, to a Combatant Vanquiſhment.   (running away.)

Things. All to a religious Houſe, ſacrifice all your Intereſts to Piety.

Bracelets as Rings below.

Book given you, that is, ſome noble Inſtruction attain'd, as *&c.*

As flying, in ſome Project, *&c.*

Calves Privities to a Woman, that is, repute her a Whore.

Cheeſe by one, that is, a ſlender Benefit of troubleſom Iſſue.

Eel crooked given you, that is, an intractable Perſon offering you in Converſe.

Keys a Bunch of them to ſome that ask'd them, Liberty to Captives.

Knife give to another, that is, charge him with Injuſtice and Contention.

Leg wooden ſend one, ſhew'd him in Diſcord with Friends.   Giving.

Giving. Things. Memorandum Paper mine deliver'd me torn, ſhew'd of
my Neglect therein, &c.

Mony, 10 ſ. give one, refuſing him your 100 l. Big
that is, make his Notions ſome Allowance, but refuſe him your full Aſſent. Vid. *Mony.*

Paper expected clean is given you ſcribled, a Tempe
expected pure proves involv'd.

Privities, vid. *Calf* ſupra.

Ring ſhews Damage.

To others a Gift and Honour.

Spectacles given you by one rob'd, that is, you appea
in his Error.

Water give a cold Glaſs of it to one, that is, Marriage
with Children.

Clear from a Well, a Wife with a Portion.
To his People, to a Miniſter teach
them well.
Troubled, Hereſy.

Woollen Apparel give another, hector him from hi
Right.

Handling ſhews of our Power and Command, &c.

To others of their Love and buying things.

To ſome an Eſſay, as what Eſtimate to make of matter
Vid. *Buying* ſupra.

Have in Houſe is oeconomick poſſeſſive Command
handling, perſonal.

Bread one ſeen, ſhew'd a Baker.

Birds who fly away upon't, certain Loſs on Projects.

Female Garments, gives a Wife or Whore.

Fire unhurt, ſhews your Enemies can't hurt you.

Glaſſes threats with Perplexity and Danger.

Gold gives Joy, Profit, and Gain. Vid. *Mony* in *Riches.*

Jewels for ſale and not buying them, gives a good Treaty only

Lights and not be in buſineſs, threats you Sickneſs or Weak
neſs to follow.

Mony, vid. *M.* in *Riches.*

Pepper threats fighting with Enemies.

Pocket-mony, being in circumſtance of Plenty, but in deſig
or Expence.

Poiſon, being in Tranſaction of ſomewhat as pernicious t
Health.

Privy Members ſhews of Chaſtity.

Another's, to ſome teach their Children.
By another ſeeming ſtout, ſhews they'l ap
prove your Vigour of Mind.

Drop a meaſuring Rod, ceaſe Building.

Recover Mony drop'd, retrieve Expence ſquandred.

Vid. *Fall* in *Action* and *Find* ſupra.

Havi

having ſhews of our Deſire of having, and our Suppoſal of things as had.
>In houſe is as poſſeſs.

Lord Keeper ſee have your Letters, be queſtionable by him for ſomewhat.

Poſture. In Lap a tame Swan, to *Socrates Plato* his Scholar.

>Peacock to *Cardan* the Pope offering to be his Patient.

>to others thro perſonal Merit command ſome great Projector.

In Breaſt a Robin-red-breaſt tame to her alone, to a Wife a chaſte Husband.

In Hand Mony, to ſome Aid from a Friend.

>to others unexpected Gain.

>Gather'd from the Ground ſhew'd of Want and hard Labour.

In Arms a crying Child, to a Woman Grief thro Loſs of Parents.

Place. In a Field ſomewhat, that is, in diſpute.

In an Houſe ſomewhat, that is, in full Command and Poſſeſſion.

>Vid. *Handle* ſupra. Vid. *Grammar.*

In Backſide a Sow and Pigs, that is, a Profit as good at command.

>A Baronet Couſin's fine Horſe, find a way to maintain ſuch by a Cheat avoided.

>A Fowl and Chickens after her, aſſures ſuch on ſetting her.

>In Coop as in proper Place, aſſures her hatching.

>V. *Numbers* and *Grammar.*

In his Stall a Yoke of Oxen, ſhew'd *A.* 2 expected to be bought came home that day.

In his Chamber, &c. Vid. *Grammar.*

Manner. Thoſe to a Woman drink White-wine, &c. for them, but in vain.

Neighbours viſiting you, take meaſures as therefore.

Fine things come from *London*, ſhew'd of Materials thence to make ſuch.

Things. A young Bullock, ſuch an one pawn'd to me that after prov'd mine.

A Tomb to Servants Liberty, to others Land.

No Son gives Plenty with Eaſe.

Tame Cats in a Window, things as good in proſpect as where, &c.

A Book of Bp. *F*'s deliver'd me and which I perus'd, ſhew'd me choſe a Godfather.

>Having

Having. Things. Sope, Snow, and Salt much in his Garret, ſhew'd
his Farm-ſtock between Poverty and ſubtle Manag
puzling him greatly.
Hireling Waggoner he, that is, uſe as great an improving Drudgery
in Study Tranſcription, &c.
Hackney-coach have, that is, be in an honourable Courſe
a time.
Hired Houſe have, atchieve a new Profit.
Common as others.
As a Lodger, in part only.
Lend, Vid. Borrow ſuprà.
Your Horſe, turn off your Tenant.
-ing his Chariot to one, ſhew'd A. of lending his Horſe to an
ther.
Give freely is as an abſolute Uſe according.
Loſe, Vid. Find ſuprà.
Mark Trees, lay claim of Property, as &c.
Miſs ſomewhat expected, be deceiv'd in ſome Truſt.
Hunt an Hare that eſcapes, miſs of earneſteſt Deſires.
Offering, Vid. Diſcourſe.   Vid. Gift ſuprà.
Own, Vid. Self and Another ſuprà.
Poſſeſs in general, Vid. Have ſuprà.
Bees poſſeſs your Hat, Vid. Bees.
Son ſee poſſeſs a Place, your ſelf arrive after to co
mand it.
Dead ſeen poſſeſs a Place, ſhew'd it transfer'd to He
An Horſe, that is, Riches, &c.   Vid. Horſe in Beaſt.
Place. Brother's Garden, have an Eſtate that Debt won't
you enjoy.
Houſe the ſame as to an Oeconomy.
Vid. Grammar.
Dead's Houſe, Vid. Grammar. ?
A Living to a Miniſter on his Expectation of it gave
him.   Vid. Place in general.
Preſenting, Vid. Give ſuprà.
Property, Vid. Grammar.   Vid. Self and Another.
Receive, Vid. Give ſuprà.   Recover, Vid. Handle ſuprà.
Selling, Vid. Buy ſuprà.
Send, Vid. Travel.   Vid. Gift ſuprà.
Stealing, Vid. Take infra.   Vid. Robber and Thief in Perſon.
Reſtore, Vid. Take infra.
Take away Leeches from your right Leg, ceaſe Charges on your m
Relations.
Taken away your Clothes being, that is, you being rob'd in yo
Fame.
Key ſhews of your Means propos'd ſailing.
Clock ſhews of the Intermiſſion of your dai
Work.
Tak

e. Taken away your Watch the same in less.

        Victuals from before you, threats you Circumvention and Loss.

    By the Dead Clothes or Victuals, threats Death or Sickness.

        Mony or Jewels, Death of Son or Wife.

A Wolf any thing, that is, opprest by an Enemy.

GOD, Vid. G.

A Bear shews Gain.

$\frac{1}{2}$ of him, shew'd A. Loss of $\frac{1}{2}$ of his Estate, and dying too.

Out of the Dirt, deliver'd from Trouble.

Restoration of Sight desiring, shew'd of Loss of Children.

    Soul the same as to Wife or Child.

Stealing, to Cheats good, to others Punishment as such.

    The richer the things and firmer guarded the worse.

It shews of lying, deceiving, and taking unlawful Pleasure in Danger.

Salt shew'd getting Wisdom.

Riches shew'd A. of Dung wash'd away in waste, turned in on his Grounds.

Persons. To Priests, Prophets, and secret Students, Sacrilege is good as to Riches and Prophecy.

    To others Dangers and ill Pleasures by deceit.

Stolen your Goods being, threats you losing somewhat dear.

    Wood threats you Waste on your Estate.

Corn A's by his Servant, shew'd of his Waste in sowing it.

A's Horse at an Inn unknown, shew'd him cheated openly of his Mony.

    To another shew'd him fool'd in his Estate.

    Seen demanded of him as stole, shew'd him asham'd to use his Profession laid by.

    Vid. *Robber* in *Grammar.*

Surrender of your Person requir'd, shews of Endeavours to slave your Will and Designs.

hriving shews of thriving.

urn out, Vid. *Action.*

CHAP.

CHAP. XLI.

Of Riches.

E. (1) *State* in general, vid. *Eſtate* in *Country.*

Prodigal dreaming of his former Plenty, promis'd its Return.

Rich man ſeeming in his former Miſery, the like.

Leaſng it out, ſhews of its being troubleſom to your Managery.

Another Parſon *J. F.* hear of, that is, ſuch another Plurality Man.

Lay out 6000 *l.* in a Purchaſe, that is, improve your Eſtate 300 *l. per an.*

Tranſactions in one Eſtate befal you in another.

Rent examin'd found poor, ſhew'd *A.* Mony wanting and hard to be got.

Rich ſee your ſelf, threats you with ſuffering Injuries.

Riches deſiring, to ſome Sickneſs in the Belly.

Falling from a Shop, ſhew'd of a Dunghil waſh'd away.

Purſe having in hand with Mony in it, gives all Affairs at command,

Profit. Unprofitable Office having, ſhews of Trouble without Gain.

Sailing in a great Ship with Charge and by Sea is beſt.

Treaſure dug in the Earth, Evil great or little as is the Treaſure to Death.

Finding under ground, ſhews the Dreamer yet is not in his true way to Riches.

Poor man's Houſe be in, that is, in an Oeconomy indigent as his.

Carried by the Rich good to him.

by the Poor the Rich being, *e con.*

Corn ſeen threats you of Ruin and Miſcarriage.

Poverty in general, to the Poor and Rich Good.

to Flatterers moſtly ill.

Vid. *Beggar* in *Grammar.*

Prodigal ſeeing in Neceſſity, threats the ſame befalling your ſelf alſo.

Eating on you, threats you with unneceſſary Expence.

Buying idle things, ſhews you of being fool'd of your Mony.   *Eſtate*

Eftate. Prodigal dreaming of his former Plenty, promiſes ſome way
(1)   of its Return.

Metals, Gold to ſome ſhews Snares, Diſeaſes, Difficulties, and Ho-
(2)   nour.

To ſome Cares of Weight and Value with Fear, Anger,
and Sorrow.

To ſome good Fortune, but holding it in hand ſhews
you falling from your Wiſh.

To ſome talk of great Affairs, as Silver of leſs.

To the Scholar noble Truths.

       In Coin to his Gain.

       In Medals, in Preſents to pleaſure his
       Friends by.   Vid. *Medal* in *Ornaments.*

Members. Shoulders of Gold, famous Power.

       Teeth of it, Succeſs to Orators and Taſters.

         To ſome Hurt in their Houſe by Fire.

         To ſome Sickneſs thro Choler.

       Bunch of it ſeen in *A*'s Neck, ſhew'd of bet-
ter Times to follow on his Death.

Seeing it ſhews of happy Times to follow, and that
therein is to be your Gain, as *&c.*

Have it in hand, command ſomewhat as valuable.

       Lewidores ſhew'd of a Copyhold E-
ſtate.

       Guineas, Inheritance.

In an High-way, command Riches thro a common method of Affairs.

Handling it gives Joy and Gain, but tending toward Expence.

Holding it threats with falling from your Wiſh.

Chewing it gives Joy and Gain.

Expect 16 *l.* Gold from the Spirit, that is, the
Perfection of Grace.

State. In female Plate, your Eſtate in ill Circumſtance.

Spoon gold buy, attain to live deliciouſly.

Tools of it, that is, efficacious as Mony.

Coin into Medals, to a Scholar ſhew'd printing
and preſenting his Books.

Smith's Shop be in, gain or deal directly in Mony.

       To ſome great matters, and others Poiſon.

Silver ſhews of Heavineſs and Sorrow.

       So as Gold above, but leſs good or evil as in cir-
cumſtance.

       Seen eat ſhews of great Advantage.

       To ſome diſcourſe of great Affairs, as Gold of
greater.

       To ſome Tumult from its Sound.

       To ſome Honour, Trouble, Care and Jealouſy as
in getting it.   *Metals.*

Metals. Silver Tools, *&c.* efficacious as Mony.
  (2)   Teeth of it gave Profit by Eloquence.
            To the Rich great Expence thro Hoſpitality.
      Seeing and not handling ſhews of greateſt Strife
           follow.
        Handling it, to ſome Sadneſs.   Vid *Mony* infr

Jewels ſhew of our Children, Books, and Delights from our Love
  (3)   them.
      To ſome of rare and unhop'd of Goods.
      To ſome their Freedom and Liberty.
      To ſome Poetry and ſparkling Witticiſms.
        — Poliſhing them is as arguing Oratorically.
      To ſome Words Divine.
      To ſome Perſons wiſe, honeſt, and innocent.
          And ſo Prieſts cheerful, *&c.*
      To Widows and Maids Marriage.
      To the Married Children.
      To Fathers and Mothers Purchaſes and Riches.
      To Traders Confuſion of Accounts, as the Value moſt
        unknown.
Acts. Chang'd all to Pearl, ſhew'd to a Wife Widowhood.
      Buying unknown ones, profit thro Hands unknown.
          Offer'd to Sale only, ſhew'd of unknown pub
           lick Offices made.
        In your own Houſe, profit by ſuch.
          If only handled, Treaty without Gain.
    Loſe Jewels you have not, be greatly concern'd at ſom
        little Loſs.
        The beſt you have, threats you Slavery an
          becoming another's.
        Drop'd find again, retrieve your en
          danger'd Freedom.
      Put to your Mouth, entruſts you with great Secrets.
Sorts, Vid. *Ornaments* and *Stones* in *Earth.*
      Of great Value, Books of great Secrets.
      Carv'd and engrav'd, vid. *Trade Carve.*
      Ear-rings ſhew of Perfection in Curioſities and Secrets.
      Scepters and Staves having, give Authority according.
      Breaſt-jewels threat with Calamities and Troubles.
Kind. Amethiſt, Tranquillity.
      Carbuncle, Honour.
          Broken, deſtroy'd.
      Diamond, Victory.   Emerald, Riches.
      Jacinth, Joy and Valour.
      Jaſper, Hope and true Friendſhip.
      Pearls, Wiſdom and Religion.
         to ſome Tears from their Shape.
      Margarets, Wiſdom and Religion.
         Treading on them, bad.   *Jewels*

Jewels. Kind. Saphir, Divinity.
(3)   Philofophers Stone, vid. *Arts* and *Sciences.*
        Chriftal fhews of fine and rare Books as of mean price.
                On a Table A's Wife breaking by handling, *A.* on it
                tied with the Yarn of a torn Woman's Stocking, this
                fhew'd *A.* redeeming a pure Notion by Chaftity.
        Shoulders of Diamond fhew of Royal Power.
        Colour. White give Wifdom, Divine Pleafure, and Innocence.
                Various give Sweetnefs and Joy.
                Black fhew Study, or Joy with Grief as Inheritance.
                        Diamond have, atchieve a noble Courfe of Stu-
                        dy with Grief.
                Cloudy give Joy and Strength with Grief.
                Golden, Honour with Envy, and Emulation with Power.
                Green give Hope with an honeft Wife and Friend.
                Purple, Study, Dignity and Wifdom.
                Red, Gain with Danger or Blood.
Mony fhews to us things valuable, and as good as Mony.
(4)   Vid. *Medals* in *Gold* fupra, and *Ornaments.*
        to Scholars of good Notions.
        Sorts. Guineas fhew of noble Plenty and Inheritance.
                Broad Pieces Plenty to Surplufage.
                Lewidores have fhewn Copyhold Eftates, and moderate
                        Plentys.
                5 *l.* Pieces fhew of a grander Plenty.
                1 *l.* is a noble Plenty, but not fo genteel as a Guinea.
                1 *s.* is a leffer State of Pocket-mony.
                        With an Hole in it fhew'd of 6 *d.*
                        A 12 *d.* Book read, purfue an Inftruction of trifling
                        Gain.
                5 *s.* as a Crown is fomewhat more grand than the Shilling.
                Pence fhew of trifling Gains fcarce worthy Care.
                Half-pence fomewhat more inconfiderable than Pence.
                Farthings fhew of mere trifling Gains with great Trou-
                        ble as is in change.
                        Finding, fhew'd me difcovering a Convenience
                        of Fruit us'd to be bought with fuch.
        Sum. 60000 *l.* the King giving; fhew'd *A.* vainly promis'd a
                Payment of 60 *l. per an.*
                Vid. *Purchafe* infra, and *Great Sums* infra in *Alphabet.*
                Vid. *Eftate* in *Earth.*
                2 *s.* or 2 Guineas is repugnant *a numero,* Vid. *Numbers.*
        Borrowing fhew'd *A.* of borrowing ftudying Notes.
        Brafs feen, threats with brawling and Difcord as in change.
                Turn'd to Brafs feeing your Pocket-mony, fcances your Plen-
                        ty to nothing.
                        Rub'd coming good again, reftores it with Pains and
                        Cares.
                                X   *Mony*

Mony. Clip'd offer'd for Faggots, ſhew'd *A.* leſs than worth offer'd for Wood.

Counterfeit Guinea paid you, rob'd by Miſmanagement in Profit. Make the Man change it, alter your Methods to avoid it.

Foreign findine, ſhew'd *A.* of paying of Debts.

Found in general, ſhews of Envy or Hatred enſuing, as Riches gain'd where the Title doubtful.

On the Ground threats with Want and hard Labour.

In *A*'s Chamber, *A.* gives it you, but with Submiſſion and ſtooping.

To a Student, Notions and ſhort Notes.

Found put in your Hand, Aid by a Friend or unexpected Receipt.

In your Hand as a Friend ſhews you, he ſhews you of a good in your Command.

To others, any precious thing diſcover'd.

Given you broad Gold by a kind-look'd Man, that is, Plenty attain by a good Method.

By a Servant, by ſuch Service procure it.

Great Sums receiving, that is, being under a Care as wanting ſuch.

To others, be at the ſame Trouble as to receive ſuch,

Clip'd Mony among, that is, ſome withheld your Receipt. Vid. *Sums* ſupra.

Handle, conſider of Expence, and with Anger if took out of Pocket.

If there otherwiſe, it ſhews Gain.

Joy for Mony found when none, Grief thro Watching.

Leaden, that is, bad Mony, or not paid in time.

Lend, vid. *Poſſeſs.*

Little Gold and Silver having in Pocket, gives happy Affairs and Pocket Mony plenty.

Long Mony have, that is, ſome defer'd longer in your keeping. and old *A.* having lying on a Table, ſhew'd of expected and unthought of Receipts.

New Mony find, that is, ſome new Profit.

Old Mony, ſhew'd of expected Payments.

Receiving, ſhew'd *A.* deſiſting an intended Expence.

And obſolete finding, ſhew'd *A.* diſcovering an abſurd but valuable Profit.

Paid for a Snakes Skin, that is, ſav'd by avoiding a pleaſant Temptation.

Paying ſhew'd borrowing, and as on which one muſt pay.

To ſome, lending ſomewhat Monys Worth, and Goods to be return'd.

Deſiring, ſhews you'l want Mony wherewith to pay.

Inſolvency, Literal, as *&c.*

Mony. Paying in Counters, choufing with foolifh and empty Expecta-
(4)   tions of Gain.

        Debtor feeing have Bills not yet paid, threats you defer'd
         in Receipts.

        Payable and he not having, fhew'd *A.* of his Husbandry
         failing.

        A's once vanquifh'd Enemy got one Friend to pay ano-
         ther Money. this fhew'd *A.* getting fuch an ones Goods,
         and forcing him to buy more.

        Paid you in a Court of Juftice, a Receipt to be expect-
         ed after waiting and wrangling.

           Out of a Book, attaining fuch Mony by fome good
            Notion, *&c.*

Pick up, vid. *Find* fupra.

Pocket full having, fhews you ordering Affairs to want it fo.

        To *A.* fhew'd him killing an Hog, and having much
         Monys Worth by him.

        Moderately gives Freedom from Debts, and Eafe.

Mony drop, fpend it heedlefly.

        Handle, be in Circumftance doubtful of fpending
         your Plenty.

         You walking up Hill in a Street, your Purchaf-
          ing narrowing you.

Purchafe ; 6000 *l.* lay out in one, fhew'd *A.* improving his Eftate
    300 *l. per Ann.*

Put, vid. *Find* fupra.

Receiving, fhew'd bargaining to want fuch Receipts.

Sums, vid. *in general* fupra, and *Great* fupra.

Turn'd, vid. *Brafs* fupra.

Wanting Weight having, fhew'd *A.* of his Notions failing.

Wrong Sums paying, fhew'd *A.* of his Bufinefs failing of Suc-
 . cefs, but moftly in Appointment.

C H A P.   XLII.

Of Ornaments.

IN general fhew of either Power or Derifion.

     Fair, vid. *Quality.*

     Fine, vid. *Quality.*

        Beggars meet you, that is, a credita-
         ble Method of borrowing affails you.

      To a Woman, her Husband's Love.

      To Widows and Maids, Marriage.

      To the married, Children.

In general, shew fine. To all, Plenty and Eafe when good and
proper.

To Servants, Eafe in Service.

Fine Servants having, living in a ftately
Oeconomy.

Noble Tomb feeing, shew'd A. attaining to a Book
of excellent Wifdom.

Stately Bill, vid. Inn in Building.

Actions shew of Defigns clear, plain and po-
fitive.

Oak feen, gives Riches, Profit and long Life.

School enter, be difciplin'd by one, but with
Grandeur.

Perfum'd Fire worfhipping, to a Prince Victory.

Your Head being, shews you haughty to your
Affociates.

To a Woman, wear the
Breeches.

By the Indians, live in good
Repute.

Perfumes receive, receive honouring News.

Pofture ; Lying on his Kitchin Table his feen to A. shew'd
his facrific'd to Family Neceffity.

Sorts. Ribbons and Plumes of Feathers, give a bare Amendment of Fortune.

Curl'd Hair vid. H. in Body.

Vid. alfo Apparel.

Church ones feen fall from an Houfe Top, shew'd
A. of miffing a Bargain of a Minifter's Goods that
he expected.

Adorn'd with Flowers a Tomb feen, shew'd A. of
untimely Death.

In general, shews of fome
short-liv'd Joy.

With Spoils Venus Temple caufing, shew'd
to Pompey his Overthrow.

Bracelets lofing, threats with fome grievous Deceit.

Give or receive is much as Ring below, but more confiderable.

Banner feeing, threats you opprest with fome great Crimes.

Breaft-Piece, vid. Jewel fupra.

Colours, vid. Enfign in War.

Crown in general, shews of Glory or Derifion, as &c.

So it shews in a publick State of Envy or Hate, &c.

Brought one by the Prophets and Apoftles to A. shew'd
him Martyrdom.

Crown'd by an Emperor, shews Joy.

a dead Perfon, gives Security.

To fome, 'tis Death to follow.

Crown

Crown in general. Crown'd, Crowning his Wife, to a King shew'd recovering some Dominions her right.

In an inconvenient Place, Disgrace.

In *Aulâ cælesti*, Death with a fine Funeral.

Without Attendance, Dangers, Fears or Snares.

With Attendance, Derision.

Heads so many see, that is, foresee of so many Successions of Kings.

Making by Bees is honorary according.

One from the Crown be, that is, in great Freedom with a Master Philosopher.

Gold on the Head gives Favour from the Prince.

To some fine Presents.

Carrying in your Hand, gives you Honour and Dignity.

Falling off has shewn dethroning, and Loss of Hopes and Dignity.

New one having, to a Prince gave him a Son and Heir.

Over the Head not touching it, great Power without the Honour.   (*Cromwel.*)

Receiving, to an Heir of the Crown inheriting it.

Without Robes evil, to the Sick Death.

to the Secret, Discovery.

to the Poor, want of Support, and Derision.

to a Magistrate good, others Danger.

Worn, to some threats Wrangling and Contention.

to some, being adorn'd with singular Powers of Truth.

to some, Danger of Life.

Herbs. Cresses shew Patience.

Featherfew and Marjoram, Sickness to all.

Sweet Bazil, Sickness to all.

Time,   ⎫ To Physicians good.
Savoury and   ⎬ To Gardiners good.
Melilot,   ⎭ To others Labour and Wandring.

Parsley or ⎫
Smallage, ⎬ To the Sick Death, as by a Dropsy.

Smelling as Mint, shew of Diseases difficult and unknown.

Ill, *&c.* is very bad.

Daffodil and ⎫ Ill.
Cypress,   ⎭

Flowers in season generally good, as shewing of Joy and Ease.

Presented to them, to some Success in Love.

Vid. *Garland* infra.

Crown. Flowers in Seaſon, White ſeen falling from Heaven, ſhew'd to *A.*
of his Death near.

Amaranthus, renders inſuperable.

Flower de Luce, ſhews of Delay in Hope.

French Marigolds good, eſpecially in Law-Suits, the
Colour laſts.

Lilies wither'd, bad.

Mallows, to Gardiners and Husbandmen good, to
others Labour and Wandring.

Roſes as ſoon fading, kill the Sick.

Smelling reveal Secrets, but to good Repute.

Elſe in Seaſon, generally good.

Violets white out of Seaſon, worſe than blue.

Yellow, ſo leſſer Incommodity or Evil.

Purple ſeen out of Seaſon, threats Death.

In Seaſon ſeen, are ſtill good.

Trees. Ivy threats with Bonds, Madneſs, Love, Priſons and
Hanging.

Lawrel, Wiſdom.

Myrrh, as of Olive.

Myrtle gives Honour and Victory, &c. but not great.

To ſome, Love.

Oak or Hay, as the Palm.

Olive, to ſome gives a Daughter, and Concord with long
Life.

So alſo of the marrying a Maid, it
given.

Palm or Olive, ſhews of marrying a Maid.

To ſome it gives a Son, with Victory and long
Life.

Vine, to ſome proſperous Succeſs.

to ſome, as the Ivy above. (Vid. *Trees.*)

Wicker over the Head ſeen, bleſs'd with an happy complying Temper.

Things. Corn, gives proſperous Succeſs.

Dead Ankle Bones, Death.

Fruit, Apples give Joy.

Jewels in Gold, vid. *Gold* ſupra.

Metals threat with great and difficult Buſineſs.

Lead, very bad.

Onions good to the Wearers only.

Particolour'd wearing, ſhew'd of the Temper of the
Air.

Salt and Brimſtone, threated with Touble from great
Men.

Stones threats with difficult Buſineſs.

Sulphur ſhews of Infamy.

Serpent of Gold with Gems having on, ſhew'd *A.* pre-
ſiding o'er wiſe Men. Crown.

Crown. Things. Wax is ill to all.
Candles, to the Sick Death.
Wool threats with Poisons and Prisons.
Diadem seen generally shews of Royalty.
To some it shews of Gain or Honour.
Earrings. vid. *Riches* supra.
Favours Wedding seen, to the Sick shew sure Death Symptoms.
In Friendship they promise it most sure.
Garland of Flowers, or Fruit in general, shews Joy and good Repute
with Continuance, as are the Flowers, *&c.*
Divers Flowers wearing, shew'd A. an Equality of Temporal Goods neatly enjoy'd. Vid. *Crown* supra.
Of Gold, to a Maid shew'd happy Marriage.
to the poor Man and Servant, Ill.
Of a Vine growing on the Head, foreshew'd A. Death.
And Ivy threat still Sickness or Prison.
Mace, vid. *Officer.*
Medal in general, vid. *Gold* in *Riches* supra.
Of a Tyrant's Remove given you by a Friend, Hopes of imposing
Slavery remov'd, *&c.*
Inscrib'd *Non nobis Domine,* &c. sent me in Gold from the Spirit
by a Minister, shew'd me of my Skill.
Patches giving a Man to a Woman, shew'd of her encouraging him to
be naught with her.
Plumes of Feathers, vid. *Birds.*
Ribbons seen, promise of Amendment of Fortune.
Rings in general, shew of our Faith, Dignity, Wife or Secrets.
To such as are without Wife, Dignity or Son,
Parents.
To some, the Year as round.
To some, Dignity or Magistracy.
To some, their own Gain.
Of Iron, shew of Goods with Labour.
Holding such, gives Security.
Amber, } *&c.* good only to Women.
Ivory, }
Gold with Stones, Good, Honour and Riches,
&c. thro Personal Atchievement.
Without Stones, Pains without Profit.
But this, as is the Person.
Hollow or little, greater Hopes than
Profit thro Error.
With Jewels buying, gives a Wife, Son
or Dignity.
Broke, Hurt to your Son
or Wife.
Falling out, your Son departs far.

Rings in general.   Gold   with   Jewels falling ſoon taken up, ſtays not long.

                     Red, faithful and ſtout.

                     Green, wiſe and amiable.

                     Sky, pious and chaſte.

                     Golden, malignant and fraudulent.

                     Spotty, naſty or infirm.

                     White, pure or ingenious.

                     Dark, humble but rich.

                     Precious,   noble   and   of Fame.

Breaking, threats loſing Power, Wife or Child.

           To ſome, Loſs of Lovers or Relations.

Buying, gives you a Wife, Son or Dignity.

Loſt, Loſs of Tenants, Goods, Wife, Father or Eyes.

           To ſome, Change of Stewards.

           To ſome, ſome grievous Deceits.

Jewel out loſt, full as bad.

           To ſome, Priſon or Slavery.

           Falling out and not found, a Son travelling and not returning.

           And found, returns ſoon, or goes not as propos'd.

Father's find, retrieve the Honour of your Brother in Diſpute.

Dropping in Hay, to a Maid threats her Virginity.

           off the Finger, to ſome Diſappointment in Love.

Putting to the Mouth, entruſting with Secrets.

           On a Maid's Finger, ſhews you reſolving to marry her.

Sealing loſe, that is, miſs of your Proſpect to ſome Inheritance. Vid. *Seal* infra.

Slipping off to a mean Maid, ſhew'd of her virtuous Actions cenſured.

Wearing one, ſhews Dignity and Felicity.

           As many, ſo many Sons to a Prince.

Wedding-Ring have on the Finger, to a Maid ſhews Marriage.

           Miſs, to a Wife be at a Loſs what become of her Husband,

           Loſe, quite hate her Husband.

           Chang'd to Lead, melancholy Iſſue, and very bad.

           New *A.* ſeeing putting on upon his Wife, ſhew'd him of danger of Death near.

Scepter ſee held by a Dog, find Royal Command in a baſe Perſon.

           Beat with it by the King, that is, benefited by him.

           Under an unknown one, that is, under as unaccountable a Controul, as is the Place.

           Mercurial or with Snakes intwin'd having, gives Authority of cunning Managery.   Seals

Seals in general shew of Inheritance.

    Have another's, be his Heir.

    Give another yours to keep, make him your Heir.

    Seal'd with a Lion, *Alexander's* Mother's Womb.

Sealed Letter from a Prince Dignity.

    Another's shews Business or Secrecy.

Book, that is, a set Instruction enigmatically hid.

Man, that is, one mark'd out for a purpose.

Womb Woman's being shew'd her with Child, things seal'd not empty.

Ring lose, that is, fail in your Prospect to some Inheritance.

    Vid. *Heraldry.*   Vid. *Ring* supra.

    Throw away yours, be destitute and despairing in all your Power.

    Find it again broke and useless, retrieve it to shew again.

Stately, vid. *Quality.*

Turbant seen shews of Royalty.

C H A P. XLIII.

Of Apparel.

IN general they shew of our Repute only, as our Body of our real State.

(1)

    Making, Vid. *Taylor* in *Trade.*

Sort. Outward shew of our ordinarier Repute.

    Inward our secreter and truer Esteem.

    Vid. *Wastcoat* infra.

Nakedness threats of extreme Poverty. Vid. *Naked* in *Posture.*

Having on, so are you reputed.

Drest being by another, that is, at their Pleasure in your Repute.

Put on, take such a Repute on your self.

    To your Quality is best.

    Rich, overvalue your self.

    Your Head as to your Wit, but not without Controversy.

Matter shews us of the Quality of such Repute, as rich or not.

Manner, Member as to its Actions, &c.

    Long, tedious, troublesom, and stately.

        Not past the middle Legs, a doubtful Business not quite blameless.

    Loose, a Repute easily own'd and slightly cast off.

In

In general. Manner. Looſe Linen Sheet as lying down cover'd with,
  (1)   ſhew'd *A.* as deſpairing in Poverty.

Seam or Pleat, the Coherence of the Reputation.
       Unſown, incoherent.

Lining, the ſecreter Stability of ſuch Repute.

Circumſtance, full of Beans ſeeming, ſhew'd *A.* as ſcan-
       dal'd, as his Hogs eating his Neighbours Beans.

In his Bar-Gown, being order'd by another in his,
       to a Counſel Slights.

Come out of Bridal Chamber in Mourning, to a
       Wife ceaſe Embraces for Health.

Compoſition. Bier Clothes dreſt in, threats Death.
  (2)

Leather fair may ſhew Dignity, but mean Poverty.

Linen threats Death, Sickneſs, Poverty or Trouble, as our
       Skin Garment.

Narrow, ſcantieſt Poverty.

Looſe Sheet, like abſolute Poverty.

Robe like Poverty at command.

Fair with other Clothes, proper Riches.

Fine Sleeves on, ſhew'd *A.* of being on
       conſideration of fine Vails.

Point, to the Poor Work of more Nicety than Profit.
       to the Rich Plenty to all Luxury.

Sack-cloth, a Repute of Poverty and Humiliation.

Silk promiſes Riches and Honour.

Stone threats Death.

Velvet Coat wear, be in Repute of Riches and Grandeur.

Winding Sheet dreſt in, Death or near.

Wood threats Death, and hinders Journies and Voyages.

Shoos of it have ſhewn of Slavery and Poverty.

Woollen and little, Anger and Loſs in Law Contentions.
       Sheeps Clothes.

In Strife therefore better loſt than kept.

Gives long Journies, a Priſon, or Servitude.

To others Navigation, Poverty, or Miſery.

Your Sheep's Coat felt, your ſheepiſh Spirit in
       Repute examin'd.

Condition. Ornaments edg'd with Silver, give Honour and Greatneſs.
  (3)

Beſet with Jewels give Principality with Royalty.

Painted ſhew of Victors, Fools, or Players.

Figure woven, threats with Diſgrace.

But if precious, ſhews of a fading
       Dignity.

Faſhion looſe, a Repute or Benefit precarious.

Scanty, poor and mean.

Cloſe as faſt on, or with Sleeves, at ſure command.

Large with Plenty in its ſort.

Rags fine Clothes on your back turning to, threats you with
       Poverty.   *Condition.*

Condition. Rags feeing her Head drefs'd with in a Looking-glafs, to the
(3)   Sick Death.

Rich gives a Repute of Ability or Wealth.

Fair chang'd yours for better, and fo is to be your Repute
          according.

          to Rags, threats you of Poverty.

Having on, gives you Credit and Refpect, and Company anfwerable.

To a Woman gives her Husband's Delight in her.

To a Maid and Batchelor, where in purfuit by them,
Marriage.

To fome as in circumftance literal.

To fome if new fhews of Preferment.

          Of going to Church.

Torn fhew of Poverty, Damage, and ill Succefs.

          Woman's Stocking feen, fhew'd *A.* of flighting female
Pleafures.

Ill-favour'd having, threats with Mockery.

          to Jefters only giving Succefs.

Ill-cloth'd feeing the Dead, threats you with Evil.

          Little and dirty Clothes, good to thofe of floven'y
Trades ; to others very bad.

Common, deferve not regard.

          But feen in publick in them, threats with
Chains or Madnefs.

          Strip'd campagn Stockings wearing, fhuffling
with mean Coach-horfes.

          Strong and feafonable, as Summer for Summer,
&c. good.

          Beft fpoil'd, your choiceft ordinary Repute fa-
tally hurt.

          Gold Button fow'd on them by the King's
Officer, fhew'd *A.* of Credit loft.

New, bad to thofe in Law, and Servants defiring Liberty.

And nafty, fhew of fome new Trouble approaching.

And good, to fome Honour.

In general change of Repute, and good or bad, as *&c.*
but with Gain.

Put on, to a Virgin Marriage.

Lofe or find, vid. *Time.*

Old and clean gives Delivery from antient Troubles.

          Torn Shoos falling off, fhew'd of Poverty and Dif-
trefs.

          Worn, vid. *Girdle* infra.

          Unfown, vid. *Seam* fupra *in general.*

Quantity. Warm to a Woman expectant, fhew'd Delivery
as in Bed fo.

          Thin-cloth'd, to a Prince fhew'd Happinefs and
Eafe of Care.   *Condition.*

Condition. Quantity. Loaded with Clothes *A.* ſeeing his Farmer's Wife,
(3)   ſhew'd of ſuch Farmer's overſtocking where
                       in common.
                       Scanty and white, ſcandalous in Poverty.
Colour in general. The Body in black while the Head in white, ſhew'd
(4)   *A.* of acting ill with a good Deſign.
          Scarlet, to the Rich and Servants Honour, Dignity, and Autho-
                       rity.
                       to the Poor worſe Miſery, if not Captivity.
                       to the Sick Death.
                       to ſome Prieſthood or Royalty.
                       to ſome Heavineſs or Sickneſs, as an Ague, *&c.*
          Sad-colour'd, of melancholy State.
          White in general Good, Joy, and Happineſs.
                       to Prieſts and Cooks good.
                       to Malefactors Diſcovery and Trouble.
                       to ſome if Linen, Poverty ; and the ſcantier the worſe.
                       to the Sick Death, as generally Burials in it.
                       to the Juſt an innocent Life.
                       to Mechanicks want of Work.   Vid. *Linen* ſupra.
                       Covering the Feet, ſhew'd of a Soul entire in Truth
                       and Purity.
          Black in general ſhews of Care, Poverty, and Shame.
                       To the Sick Health, but if poor Death.
                       To the Secret and Plotters generally Succeſs and Joy.
                       To others generally ill.   Vid. *Mourning.*
                       Seeing his Debtor cloth'd in Black, ſhew'd *A.* of getting
                       nothing by him.
                       Your ſelf in it, if long and ugly threats of Grief.
                       Women meeting *A.* in it with cover'd Heads,
                       ſhew'd him of Deceit oppoſing him.
          Sky-colour'd threats with Diſeaſes.
          Yellow ſhews of Impudence.
                       Cloth'd Angel calling *A.* ſhew'd him of a Plague In-
                       fection offering.
                       Golden threats with Grief and Torments.
                       Put on, ſhews of Envy or Heavineſs.
                       To ſome Folly, Impudence, and Government.
          Green is good and full of Hopes.
          Red ſhews of Anger, Blooding, and Slaughter.
                       Not deep tho, is Joy with Anger and Cruelty.
                       To ſome it ſhews Sickneſs and Indiſpoſition.
          Purple threats with Sickneſs and Trouble, if not Death.
                       To the Sick ſharp Humours and Choler.
                       Not deep, Joy with Anger and Cruelty.
                       To rich Men and Servants good Advance.
                       To poor Men Danger or a Priſon, *&c.*
          Divers-colour'd, to Players good, others Trouble, *&c.*

                                                            Colour.

olour. Divers-colour'd, to the Sick Humours, to the Secret Discovery.
(4)   In Merry-meetings good.
                     Wavy gives Riches in Age.
        Sun-bright, that is, transcendent in glorious Truth.
Actions. Broken shew'd *A*'s Body wounded in the same place.
(5)   Vid. *Rags* and *Torn* supra.
        Eurnt, an ill sign, threatning Injury and Reproach thro Paf-
        fion.
        To others Loss in Friends by Law-suits and by Deceits.
Cut in pieces, shew'd *A*. of his House falling.
Dressing your self is good, it shews you at leisure for Diverfion.
                Combing your self is as Delivery from ill
                Times and bad Affairs, but in thought moft.
        Another, that is, paying him Service and Attendance.
                His dead Miftrefs's Head half way, shew'd
                A. near incapacitated for Amours by In-
                firmity.
        By another, at their command in your Reputation.
                Garter put on by a Man, to a Maid shew'd Mar-
                riage.
        Half undreft before a Man fee a Woman, that is, of
        doubtful Repute.
        Put on your Cloke, put your Affairs to a Pofture of
                Concealment.
                Clothes fee the Dead, and pull them off
                again, threats you dying in them.
                New, to the Sick pray to G O D for Recovery.
                to a Virgin Marriage, to fome Preferment.
                Taken only to put on shews Lofs.
                Vid. *Pull off* infra.
        Having on shews fo you are reputed, as putting on shews you
        taking fuch Repute on you.
        Loaded with Clothes *A*. feeing his Tenant's Wife, shew'd of
        fuch Tenant overftocking on ground in common between
        them.
        Loft Garments is Damage and Lofs of Fame.
                But to the poor Debtor, and Servants in Mifery,
                Freedom.
                Stolen by one handling Bread, shew'd *A*. of a Baker's
                Calumny.
        Pull off your felf, lay by your Dignity.
                Pull'd off by others, your Dignity is forc'd
                from you.
                A red one gave return from Banifhment.
                With Delight, laying by Cares for Pleafure.
                With no defign of putting on again, Death by Cold, &c.
        Up a Woman's literally examine her Power beyond repute.
                Her Legs found pocky on't, she deferted by
                Kindred as fo'fe.   *Actions.*

Aᐸions. Put on, vid. *Dreſs* ſupra.
 (5) Spoil'd, vid. *Broke*, *Burnt*, and *Cut* ſupra.
    Stolen, vid. *Loſt* ſupra.
    Swim in them, vid. *S.* in *Water Aᐸion.*
    Taken away by force, threats you Death or fatal Deſtruction.
     Privily is but as Slander.
    Torn away from you, takes away care.
     Ey Dogs ſhew'd of Infamy with Injury.
    Walk in a Morning-gown, proceed in a Courſe of Study as in
     the Place.
    Waſhing, vid. *Water.*

Perſonal. Another's wear, command his Intereſt.
 (6)   Getting, attaining to a ſure Friendſhip.
     Brother's take care of yours, ſupport in your ſelf
      a ſelf-rivalling Repute.
     They wear yours or your Wife's, they command
      your Intereſts.
     Cheat's wear, act on ſuch a preſum'd Repute.
     Getting away her fine Clothes and her Image, ſhew'd
      A. ſevering *B.* from her Husband. Vid. *Grammar.*
   Armour Clothes promiſe of Soldiery, and the richer the
     better.
     To ſome they threat Death.
   Factious knaviſh Parties Coat putting on, brings you to ſuch
    a Repute.
   Female. Torn Woman's Stocking ſeen, ſhew'd to a Man ſlight
     of Female Pleaſures.
     Handle, buy, or have in Houſe, ſhews of having a
      Wife or Whore.
     Wear, to ſome Sickneſs.
      to ſome Effeminacy and Laſciviouſneſs.
      to ſome Folly with delight, and the richer the
       better; to Players Applauſe.
      to a Batchelor a Wife.
      to all in Merry-meetings, Joy.
      to the Husband Loſs of Wife.
      Vid. *Change* in *Senſe.*
   Former, vid. *Own* infra.
   Foreign wearing, gives you good Hopes from thence.
     To ſome has ſhewn Sickneſs or Treatment as
      Stranger.
     Alexander ſeen enter *Babylon* Temple in *Perſian* Robe
      (he conquer'd it on it.)
   Gown, vid. *Robe* infra.
   Lawyer, Vid. *Law.*
     In Bar-gown, being rul'd by another is ſuch, to
      Counſel undervaluing Treatment.
   Maiden, Vid. *Former* infra in *Own.*

             Perſon

Perfonal. Man's wearing, to a Woman wear the Breeches, and the
(6)   richer the worfe.
        Mourning in general, Vid. *Funeral.* in *Dead.*
                        Vid. *Chamber* in *own Houfe* in *Grammar.*
        Others. Husband feen in Mourning in his own Church,
                and about to marry his Wife in White there,
                and who was then near her Delivery ; this
                fhew'd fuch a Wife fearful of Death, yet ef-
                caping Travail. Bringing into the Church her
                Child and not marrying, fhe efcap'd Death.
        Servant unknown meeting *A.* fhew'd him inter-
                rupted to tend a Funeral.
        Woman unknown touch'd by, fhew'd *A.* in ter-
                ror at a Tooth's breaking in his Head.
        Women unknown following *A.* in his native
                Street, fhew'd him in caufelefs Fears of Death.
        Wife feen in M — with torn Hair, fhew'd to *Va-*
                lentinian Death.
        Self being in, threats you in great concern at the *Fear*
                of your Death near.
                        To fome concerns for Friends as well as
                        themfelves.
                Lie down on bed fo, be negligent every
                        way thro fuch Fears of Death. ...
                So be invited by a Friend to come to his
                        Houfe, fhews you Recovery by his Aid.
                Come out of Bridal Chamber in Mourning,
                        to a Wife ceafe Embraces, as fearing
                        Death.
        Things, vid. *Mourn* in *Paffion.*
                Room with Scutcheons enter, follow wilfully
                an Oeconomy in the end will be deadly.
                Coaches a paffing before *A.* fhew'd him of vifit-
                        ing one fick in 2 days.
                Flag treading on, triumphing over the Terrors
                        of Death.
        Own, vid. *Anothers* fupra.   Vid. *Grammar.*
                Maiden drefs her felf in, to a Wife forbear her Huf-
                band's Society in State.
        Priefly promifes the Priefly Office.
        Quaker's of Repute as he.
        Robe or Gown loofe or apoftolical, judg of it by the Co-
                lour.   Vid. *Colour* fupra.
                Morning or Students Gown wear, be engag'd in fome
                        Courfe of Study, as *&c.*
                        Prudent Friend's wear, ufe his pru-
                                denter Courfes of Study.
        It fhews us of Reputes of States eafily laid by as
                loofe, *&c.*   *Perfonal.*

Perſonal. Royal promiſes of greateſt Hopes.
(6)   Strange wearing, to ſome Travel.   Vid. *Foreign* ſuprà.
    Students, vid. *Robe* ſupra.
    Sumptuous, to Rich and Poor good.
        to a Woman Pleaſure.
           And with many Colours Profit too.
        With tawdry Lace, more in Shew than Sub-
        ſtance.
Travelling wearing, foreſhews of Journies.

C H A P. XLIV.

Of *Apparel-ſorts.*

APron angry at a Servant's, that is, for refuſing to carry things in her Lap.

Fine for your Credit, &c. ſtately for your Honour.

Bodkin, Vid. *Head-dreſs* infra.

Boots or cloth Stockings having good, promiſes happily to future Journies.

Buttons for Sleeves given a Servant, that is, Vayls for Service.

    Clothes, the Security for our Reputation, as &c.

      Needleſs of Detraction to it.

Breeches new having gives Mony Store to them who want it.

    To ſome they ſhew of the Wife, Modeſty, and obſcene Pleaſure.

    Shiting in them, ill Fame thro Failure in neceſſary Expence.

Caps 2 wear, hide one ill Repute by a Crime in another. V. *Hats* infra.

Clokes ſhew of Concealments in our private Deſigns.   Vid. *Coat* infra.

    Sickneſs if Purple.

Royal ſhew'd the Queen.

Put on yours, take to a Repute of Concealment in your Affairs.

To ſome it ſhews of Soldiery or Sadneſs.

'd Perſons ſeen, threats your being teas'd with Excuſes.

    Shew me ſeeking to be of no certain reproof; an hiding Garment eaſy on, eaſy off.

Yours chang'd to a fine Coat, your Shifts become creditable.

You wear one, you deceive with a falſe Appearance, & e con.

Coat Frize, vid. *Woollen* ſupra.   Vid. *Riding-hood* infra.

Fine ſeen hang'd up to be given him, ſhew'd *A.* of a Gift and Benefit promis'd him.

And Waſtcoat *A*'s ſeen all in holes, ſhew'd *A.* of Straits every way reflecting on him.

Waſtcoat ſhews of our more ſecret publick Repute.

                       Coat.

Coat *A.* finding great stinking Worms in his Coat he could not shake off, shew'd him his Wife an Adulteress, and yet he unable to get rid of her.

Great one, shews of Journies.

> Of mean Leather wearing, to some Souldiery and Postilioning.

> With an Hood, shew'd of a monastick and solitary Life.

Codpiece smelt to by a Lap-Bitch, shew'd *A.* of being indecently immodest.

Crevat sent *A.* by the Spirit, shew'd him Profession open of his Favour.

> It shews of our Face, Countenance or Appearance, Repute, *&c.*

Fan shews of Diversion and Leisures, as to take the Air, *&c.* and therefore prosperous.

Garter tied by a Man, to a Woman has shewn her Marriage.

Girdle, to some shews the Daughter.

> Girt with it, gives Safeguard to the Person.

> Of Gold, shews Dignity in Youth.

> > To others, Sincerity, Gain or Envy.

> Silver, gave profitable Journies.

> Cut off, shew'd of Dispatch in a Journey.

> > In Pieces, shew'd of Envy and Discord.

> Old one girt with, shew'd of Labour and Pains.

> > Worn much having, threats Damage.

> New one having, gives Honour.

> Loosing it, shew'd of Sedition of Faith.

Gloves on your Hands, honour.	Gentlemen mostly wear them.

> Finding, shew'd of reconciling of Quarrels.

> > Rich, as with Silver Fringe, *&c.* gave Pocket Mony Store.

> And Stick fetch from a Place, disown of your Abode there.

> Buying, shew'd of amorous Disposition.

> New putting on, has shewn Marriage of self or Friend.

Gown, vid. *Robe* supra in *Ap.* general.

Handkerchief, to some gives Joy, as what wipes away Tears.

Hat. Parts. Brim none before, shew'd of Opportunity prevented by Dispatch.

> > Behind, shew'd Prevention of after Claps.

Sorts. Straw-hat Woman seen, shew'd of a common Country tittle tattle presenting.

> Beaver fine have, be in Prospect of a fair Repute.

> *French* offer'd *A.* in Sale, shew'd *A.* of a Crop of *French* Grass so offer'd him.

> Diadem and Turbant shew of Royalty.

> Fine one chang'd for a mean one, shew'd *A*'s Set of Servants grown worse.

> New lac'd having, changes Affairs to Plenty.

> > Officers for a little time only.

> Bread, shews of Profit but not great.

Y

Hat.

Hat. Sorts. Broad, to ſome, the Prieſthood, or the Cardinalate.

　　　　　Hindring the ſhining of the Sun, ſhew'd A. the
　　　　　next day as cloudy.

　　　Mounteer, ſhews of an active, unſettled, imperfect Repute.

　Hatter treat, be expenceful in Ornaments ingenious.

　　　　's Houſe ſeen on Fire, ſhew'd of Controverſy about Maſter-
　　　　ſhip.

Acts. Chang'd yours to an Officers, your Honour become precarious.

　Deſtroying anothers, ſhewing Scorn to his Honour.

　Flapping, your Honour or Maſterdom failing.

　Laid in a Window by ſeen, ſhews of your giving Honour
　　from ſome peculiar Regard.

　Leave in fear as poſſeſt by Bees and Waſps, fearing little Ene-
　　mies be forc'd to diſhonour.

　Loſt, to ſome the covering of their Houſe or Walls failing.

　　　　　To ſome, their Honour in queſtion.

　　　　　Seek in a Market Town, ſtrive to ſalve your Sale Ho-
　　　　nour.

　　　　　Found at a Beds Feet, your Diſhonour thro Lazineſs
　　　　retriev'd.

　Put on in anothers Preſence, ſlight him.

　　　　　Anothers Back turn'd, reſpect him for by ends only.

　Pulling off, ſhews of giving Reſpect anſwerable.

　　　　　Bareheaded being, threats you with ſome diſhonoura-
　　　　ble State.　　　　　Vid. Cap ſupra.

Head-Dreſs Female wearing, to a Man Folly and Laſciviouſneſs.

　　　Broke in its Ornaments, to a Woman great Loſs of Power
　　　and Diſgrace.

　　　Adorn'd in it too much, vexing others by your Pride.

　　　New one buying at Exchange, to a Wife Plenty thro her
　　　Husband's Managery.

　　　With Rags, ſhew'd A. comforting her ſelf where Death on-
　　　ly was in proſpect.

　　　Bodkin Silver buying for it, to a Maid ſhew'd her by Pride
　　　hazarding a Quarrel.

Hood wearing, foreſhews Prieſthood or Monkery.

　　　　　Sky or Purple, gives great Riches, or a more noble
　　　　Prieſthood.

　　　And Scarf wearing, to a Woman ſhew'd her as deem'd a Shuff-
　　　ler.

Jacket, vid. Coat ſupra.

Mounteer, vid. Hat ſupra.

Lining, vid. Apparel in general ſupra.

Night-Cap wearing, to ſome threats Wounds and Diſeaſes.

　　　　　To ſome it ſhews of tedious and puzling Vexations.

　　　　　In Church, ſhew'd A. of venting his Crudities in
　　　　publick.

　　　　　　　　　　　　　　　　　　Night-

Night-Cap *A.* dropping his in the Exchange, shew'd him sullying his
 Glory by his hard care supporting it.

 -Rail a Domestick's tearing, shew'd *A.* of doing the like to her
 Head Clothes.

Clothes seeing one drest in, shews of their being rude to you.

Petticoat long trim'd having, to a fine Woman gave her a Coach.

 To others, a noble Subsistence, even to Superfluity.

Pins abundance new bought seen on a Table, gave great Plenty.

Pocket find yours full of Mony, threats you'l want it.

 Empty when before full, shews you'l purchase.

 Vid. *Mony in Riches.*

 Book in it, that is, continuing duly a Prosecution of Notions, *&c.*

 Little Silver there is good, as shewing of agreeable Pocket Mony
 at Command.

 Shite in by others, enrich'd by scandalous Gains from others.

 Drink finding there, shew'd *A.* of correcting his Error in spend-
 ing too much upon Drink.

Ribbon, vid. *Ornaments.*

Ridinghood want, be in desire to go some Journy.

 Have on, be in consideration of some such Journy as certain.

Scarf, vid. *Hood* supra.

Shoos in general, shew us of Foot Journies and Diseases.

 To some of their main Pocket Mony State.

 As Stockings of our Oeconomy State.

 Vid. *Feet in Body.*   Vid. *Stockings* infra.

 Buckle sell somewhat for, that is, part with it for a Trifle.

French wearing, that is, being prodigally nice in Actions.

Sorts. New and good, to a Prisoner Liberty.

 to others, Change of Repute for good
 but with Pain.

 to some, Profit and Honour by Servants.

 to some, Comfort from some new and good
 Course offering.

 Old Shoos and Stockings having, threats Sadness.

 Seeing only, shews Loss.

 Torn or falling off, heaviest Poverty and Distress.

 Cut in pieces, Riddance of Troubles.

 Cleaning, ridding of Impediments in your Affairs.

 Gravel in them, touch'd with Scruples of Conscience, as is the
 Place where.

 Have Chaff put in them, be censured as frivolous in your ways.

 Loose and go barefoot, have Pains in the Feet, or be bed-rid.

 Mending, to some has shewn of Foot Journies.

 Put off, shews of Decrepidness or Lasciviousness.

Shift seen in, to a Woman acting immodestly.

 Before a Domestick, literal, *&c.*

 Her self, to a Maid is as Danger to a Virginity.

 Y 2   Shift.

Shift. Shifting, to ſome Travel, Change of Country, or hard Lodging.

Shirt ſhews of our Wife, Whore and Secrets.

     Run about in it, be in great hazard of Sickneſs and Death, thro
       Colds, &c.

Sleeves in general, ſhew us of Plenty with Eaſe, as being moſt worn by
       Gentry.

     Scattering pick up, retrieve former Finery and Plenty, (as in
       Viſits, &c.)

     Buttons of Silver given a Servant, ſhew'd her of Service Rewards.

Slippers ſhew of ſhuffling, and uſing Expedients for Pocket Mony Shoos.

Smock, vid. *Shift* ſupra.

Socks ſhew of Pleaſures and Pomp, but with Deceit, as noiſeleſs.

Stays not wearing tickled by Men for it, to a Woman Scandal, as of
     looſe Carriage.

     Wear, to a married Woman is good, promiſing of an eaſy Life,
       and Ability to go dreſs'd, &c. —

Stockings, vid. *Shoos* ſupra.

     Thred Stockings having on, gives great Plenty.

     And Shoos new having, ſhews of Affairs like to be proſperous.

     Holes within Shoos only, paying off all but Servants Wages.

     Old *A*'s ſeeming, but his Shoos good, ſhew'd *A*. of his Pocket
       Mony plenty, but Houſe State bad.

     Woman's torn ſeen, ſhew'd *A*. of ſlighting Female Pleaſures.

     Wanting them, that is, in want of Neceſſaries anſwerable.

       Angry at Servants therefore, remediable find it by em-
       ploying Workmen.

     Strip'd Campagn wearing, ſhew'd *A*. ſhuffling with ſcoundrel
     Horſes in his Coach.

Stomacher in general, ſhews of Dignity, Magiſtracy, and a Wife.

         White, fair.

         Sky, ſad.

         Red, troubleſom.

         Yellow, rich and grave.

         Green, chaſte.

         Black, angry and cruel.

Waſtcoat, vid. *Coat* ſupra.

Wig wearing, ſhews of your owing more than you are worth.

     A neat Bob one, a clever little ſhifted Debt.

     A mean old one, a trifling old Debt.

C H A P.

C H A P. XLV.

Of Goods.

IN general, seeing a Ship at Sea full of Goods, gives Prosperity.
    Prudent Friend's studying Gown wear, use the prudenteſt Courſes of Study.
    Houſhold in Diſhonour, threats your Eſtate as ſo.
    Houſe ſeen naked, threats you as wanting Mony to buy ſuch.
    Full of Lumber, an Oeconomy of trifling Benefit.
    Empty of Goods, deſtitute of Mony for Family Uſes.
    Hall Furniture, as Tapiſtry or other Movables, ſeen burnt, is Death or Damage to the Maſter.
    Common ſee fetch'd away by another, pay Debts, as &c.
    Stolen away, threat you by Error miſſing ſomewhat dear.
    Stuff, Parcels and Packets of it having, generally good.
    To Fliers, it threats with Surprize and Delay.
    To Dealers and marrying Perſons ſeen, it gives Plenty.
    Fail in packing it, that is, in the Managery.
    Catching others with Goods, &c. is good to Surprizers.
Andirons ſhew the Life.
    Bright give a ſplendent Fortune.
Baſon fair, ſhews a good Maid.
    Eating out of it, the Love of her.
    Broken, threats her Death.
    Seeing your Face in it, having Children by her.
    Gold or Silver having, ſhews you marry her.
Bed in general, ſhews of the Husband or Wife.
    To ſome of Lazineſs, as the Coach of ſtately Prodigality.
    3 Beds, perfect Lazineſs.
    Vid. *Lie down* in *Poſture.*   Vid. *Grammar.*
State. Well furniſhed, gives Eaſe, Joy and Diverſion.
    Fine purchaſe, act to procure or merit a noble Wife.
    Little Bolſter ſize lie on, be lazy to Poverty.
    Foul'd, ſhew'd *A*'s Wife in Diſgrace.
    Fired, threats Damage, Death or Sickneſs, to Husband or Wife.

Y 3   Bed

Bed. State. Of Corn if of Wheat seen, promises the barren Wife
        Son.

Cradle bedding his Wife in, shew'd A. lying with her when infirm
        Apothecaries Wife angry at it, against all Physick Rules.

Parts, vid. *Blanket* infra.

        Head scape to from fighting, skreen you from the Wife by
        the Husband.

        Feet anothers wait at, with Humility attend their Delay.

        Posts fired unconfuming, gave A. Sons fortunate.

        Curtains seen hurt, threated the like to A's Coach.

        Sticks for Cords having to the married, shew'd Separation
        for Sickness.

Another's lying in, lazy towards them where expected active.
                Another so in yours e con.

        2 kick in their Bed, so as to want Bed-ftaves, their lazy
        Janglings prove to others Offence.

Company full of Boys, others restless Expectations craving on you
        With your Wife in Bed at an Inn, rest careless ½ way
                in your Art use.

                Domestick, shews you making each other idle
        The dead, vid. D.

        Anothers Daughter, shew'd A. idly gaming for
                anothers Mony.

                Maid, to a Physician entertain'd long in
                his Family.

        A Woman in Glory, thro divine Studies become
                idle to other things.

        A mad Woman, to a Woman big shew'd her De
                livery.

        A mad Man and Hermaphrodite, madly or mon
                stroufly idle.

                Turn to the Hermaph. but mostly mon
                ftrous.

        A's Brother seen sick in Bed, shew'd him of his Rival
        Interest at present worsted.

Own former rising from her Husband out of her Bridal Bed, to a
        Wife shew'd her forbearing Embraces.

        Lying with another besides her Husband in her Maiden
                Chamber, to a Wife shew'd her debating of her
                2d Marriage.

Present a dead Body A. seeing in her Guest Chamber-Bed
        shew'd of her hearing of such a likely Guest's
        Death.

        Man seen by A's Bedside, shew'd him of his Physi
                cian, and threated him Sickness.

                Physician seen so, shews of your Illness going
                off easily.

        Push'd by her Bed-fellow out of Bed, exhorted by
                him to part for Sickness.   Bed

Bed. own. Present seen trimly made, shew'd to a Lover a fair Wife.

Lover found in Bed with her in't, shew'd she married him.

Dead making them, shews of Sickness to us or Friends.

Place at an Inn lie with a lazy Prodigal, be dun'd as if so.

Push'd out of Bed by him there, near rudely us'd on it.

In dirty Water A. saw her Bed and plaid there, she was concern'd how her Husband was to lie.

In his Stable assaulted as lazy in Bed, reproach'd by his Groom as remiss.

In your Passage lie in Bed, be negligent as to Workmen.

With your Wife, as to your Art.

Actions. Flying in't, shews of Sickness or Travel with Wife or Family.

Lying down in't, vid. *Posture* and *Bodily Action.*

In Mourning, negligent generally thro the Fears of Death.

A's Mother-in-Law seen, shew'd of his Scheme of Slavery failing.

With another, has shewn of boarding them.

Expecting, that is, expecting in laziness.

In your studying Gown, despairing lazily as to Study.

Laid in it A. finding a sweaty Stone, shew'd of his bedding his Wife sweaty and infirm.

Lengthen anothers, excuse their Delay and Laziness.

Rise from, vid. *Action.*

In a Market Town, cease idling as to some Bargain.

Bed with another, cease idling in such a Course.

Sitting on Bed watch'd by another, treated as most negligent.

Stifled near in the Clothes, opprest by Husband or Wife, as &c.

Travel thro one, designing in a matter caus'd an unexpected staying out all Night.

Turn'd up and down, Disorder between Man and Wife.

Under it Beasts found, threated of Death shortly ensuing.

Walking on Beds, shew'd A. a Business thought easy proving hard.

Besom seen, shew'd of a Washer-woman, &c.

Blanket cloth'd in, shew'd A. of Prophecy with hardship.

Rug cloth'd in, to some Madness.

Box, vid. *Trunk* infra.

Brass, vid. *Tools,* &c.

Bundles,

Bundles, vid. *Parcel* infra.   Vid. *Stuff* in *Goods general.*

Cabinet, vid. *Coffer* infra.

Candle ſhews the Man, as the Candleſtick the Woman.

    Candleſticks golden, holy Churches.   Vid. *Fire.*

Carpet ſpare, that is, give one leave to pick Stones as off your ground.

Cart in general ſhews the Dreamer's Life, and going well gives Succeſs.

    Sitting in it, declared of great Gain to follow.

    Carried in your own, to ſome gives Children of good behaviour.

        to ſome good command.

        to Travellers Surety with Slowneſs.

        As if blindfold, commanded by a Farmer.

    One and not drawn in it, to ſome Death.

        to ſome hardeſt Gout.

Faſtned or drawing in it, Servitude or Sickneſs to all.

    And yok'd with his dead Brother by his Mother, ſhew'd *A.* Death.

    Among Oxen and drawn by them, being at your Tenant's command.

    But coming from under it, ſhews an end of Slavery.

Drawn in one by Men, gives you Authority over many.

Going without a Driver, to a Farmer ſhew'd his Hind leaving him.

    Stop'd at a Gate, ſhew'd one his Carriage Weather ſtop'd.

        To another his Carter idling thro Mony Plenty.

    Seen with fine Horſes, gave a Life in excellent proſpect.

    Cattel looſe and running away, a farmerly Profit expected failing.

    Paſſing a narrow Road, ſhew'd of an ill State of Farming.

    His fetching Faggots, ſhew'd *A.* viſiting a Benefactor on horſeback.

        Friends doing the ſame, he meeting you.

Dung-pot yours ſee ſtock'd, find your Farm Improvements near in deſpair.

Waggon ſeen at *London,* vid. *L.*

    Oxon, ſhew'd *A.* of ſtating rationally how to keep them.

    Deſcend a Precipice by a Waggon, get off a Difficulty by a Farmer.

    Full of ſcarlet Cloth driving, laying laborious Foundations of laſting Fame.

    Waggoner being, that is, laborious in ſome exceeding formal tedious Method.

Chains ſeen ſhew the Wife, Love, Priſon, Impediment and Slavery.

    To a Servant being bound in them, ſhews Liberty as worthy of them.

Bonds ſeen ſhew of mutual Love.

Chain'd to a Poſt, incapacitated for Action.

    Dog aſſaults you, a reſtrain'd Enemy oppoſes you.

                  Chains.

Chains. Chain'd Man feen let down out of Paradife, fhew'd of a Tyrant.
      In general threats of dealing with one wicked.
Chair, vid. *Sit in Pofture.* — Vid. *Couch* infra.
  Of State feen fhews of lazy Acquiefcence in neglect.
  Stool fling at one, declare you won't fettle in fuch Methods.
  Flying in fhews of Sicknefs, Neglect, or Travel with Family.
      to fome projective Command, and controuling
       in State in Affairs.
  Hear a Woman racket them above you, being below, be reftlefs-
   ly fhifting in your Fortune.
  Chairs and Stools walking on, refufing Sedentarinefs for Health.
   Sitting there and fpeaking thence, fhews of things dog-
   matical.
Chariot fhews of ftately, lazy, and prodigal Proceeds, as the Bed of
   mere Lazinefs.
   To fome often rode in, threats of idly dying a Beggar.
   State with neglect.
   Travel in, defign glorioufly to the full Capacity of ones
    Circumftances.
  Own rais'd on Leathers feen, fhew'd *A.* of buying new Harnefs
   to it.
   Set afide, fhew'd *A.* of his Journy put off.
   Stock'd in Ice in his Backfide feen, fhew'd *A.* of his laid
   up in Winter as ufelefs.
  Afcending into fhews Honour.
  Being in, to the Sick Death.
  Come out of, to fome offend Elders.
     to fome Degradation of Honour as a Criminal.
     to *Domitian* it fhew'd him dying from's Empire.
  Defire a Chariot's ftanding near a Painter's in a City, want a
   Tradefman's Applaufe to blazon you, *&c.*
  Drawn by Men, be in command of Men to your State, as others
   do Horfes or Eftates.
  Drive with Leopards, *&c.* good only againft great Enemies.
   Thro Deferts, threats with Death at hand.
  Get into by a Dungpot, keep one thro farming Aids.
  Lending fhew'd of lending an Horfe to an Equal.
  Overrun by another's, oppreft in his Courfes of Grandeur.
  Ride in't with 4 Horfes, to an Olympick Racer be beat; the
     Horfes are foremoft.
     to one keeping one, good.
     to others Danger of Ruin thro Prodi-
     gality.
   Horfes running away with *A.* fhew'd him of his Ser-
    vants vaporing.
    Unruly, alfo fhew'd of Servants, Hirelings,
    and Coachmen fo.

             Chariot

Chariot. Ride in't with 2 Girls, deſign lazily prodigally in a trifling opinionative Courſe.

Behind it, have a mean hand in ſome great Performance.

Fearing the Wheel catching you, that is, Interruption.

Paſs in a Coach with 2 black Horſes by the Attorny General to the right, ſhew'd *A.* proſecuted by him for a fine Book.

Briskly down a Town, ſhew'd *A.* of treating others gloriouſly.

Sitting forwards, commanding in chief or the moſt honourably in it.

Staying at an Inn, your Buſineſs at a ſtand for a time.

Shite in your Cloſeſtool ſeeming in your Coach, farm with its Horſes to Profit.

Standing ſtill Coach be in, that is, keep one to appearance only.

Sedan being in, to the Rich Delicacy.

to the Poor Diſcredit.

to ſome die an idle Beggar.

Coach, Sort. Mourning, Vid. *M.* in *Apparel.*

Of Ropes in the Air flying in, deſigning in ſtately Projects.

Philoſopher's with a Divine in't being in, ſhew'd me of this Study.

Prodigal's borrow, uſe his ſtately ruinous Courſes.

Jupiter's ſent to the Houſe of *Veſpaſian Nero* ſaw, and ſo the Empire went.

Carrying more Company, that is with 4 Horſes, where it went but with 2 before.

With many Arms painted on it, ſhew'd of the Grand Jury.

Hackny or hired, a Procedure of a commoner ſort, but for a time only.

With various-colour'd Horſes, of deceitful Preſentation.

And 6 Horſes travel in toward *London,* that is, with powerful vigor aim at Plenty.

To others in Glory, preſume at the Standard of Truth and Notion.

Poſtilion ſhews of ventureſom, forward, and bold Courſes.

Seeming, being a mean daring Leader according it Trouble.

Acting ſhews of raſher Wi Attempts.

Chariot

Chariot. Coach, Sort. 4 white Horses in't, shew'd *A.* of rectifying 4 garden Beds-disorder'd.

Coach-man commend, find the Gardiner proving good.

½ Ox ½ Horse see pass by him, shew'd *A.* of a Farm for 3 Lives offering him in Sale.

Monster in one ½ Hog ½ Ox assaulting *A.* from his Harness, shew'd *A.* of one ½ a Tenant and ½ a Labourer designing against him.

Chest, vid. *Coffer* infra.

China Ware given *A.* by one, shew'd him of Chocolate sent him by them to drink.

Offer'd you in Sale, that is, Riches to Delicacy.

Chang'd to Baubles, baulk'd in such Expectation.

Chopping-knife, vid. *K.* infra. Cistern, vid. *Water.*

Clock, vid. *Watch* infra.

to some dilatory Operations.

to some it threats of Opportunities lost.

Eroke, Danger to all, chiefly the Sick.

In the less pieces, the worse.

Counting forenoon Hours in it best, it gives Opportunity.

The earlier the better.

On a Church, with relation to a Minister.

Heard strike, threats you with Infamy.

Standing still, shews of Obstruction for a space.

Taken away, shew'd of Intermission of such Work.

Close-stool, vid. *Shite* in *Bodily Action.*

Shiting in in a Room by a Fire-side and no more, shew'd *A.* of living delicately.

Seeing remov'd, to one sick recover'd his Looseness.

Full, threats with Sickness or Business obstructed.

Having in his Coach, shew'd *A.* keeping his Coach-horses to plow.

Shite and wipe there, to good effect.

Coach, vid. *Chariot* supra.

Coffer and Cabinet shew of the Mistress and Steward.

Keeping Writings shew of the Course of our Lives.

Broke behind, to a Mistress of an House shew'd her Steward leaving her.

Burnt, threats her own Death.

Shew yours open to one, discover some Secret to him.

Iron Chest buying, shew'd *A.* of keeping Mony by him.

Open'd theirs to *A.* being, shew'd of *A*'s having Presents thence.

Couch lying on, idling thro Visits. Vid. *Chairs* supra.

Cushions shew the Wife.

Dish

Diſh eat off, take a Profit formally, as &c.

Dungpot, vid. *Cart* ſupra, and *Dung* in *Earth*.

Faggots, vid. *Wood* in *Vegetables*.

Frying-pan ſhews of a Woman given to talk and hurt.

Furnace, vid. *Houſe-parts*.   Gold, vid. *Riches*.

Hangings, vid. *Tapeſtry* infra.

Harneſs *A*'s Horſe ſeen out of, ſhew'd of him as lock'd up without due
Care.

Hour-glaſs ſeen out, ſhew'd *A*. of his Time miſpent.

Horſe-litter ſhews greatly, as the Chariot before.

         To ſome of Infirmity.

Houſeholdſtuff, vid. *Goods in general* ſupra.

Jointſtools, vid. *Chair* ſupra, and *Bier* in *Dead*.

Jug, vid. *Pot* and *Pitcher* infra.

Key ſeen in an Houſe, gives an handſom Wife or a good Maid.

       to others it ſhews of all in Security as is the
House.

Given the Dead, threats you loſing your Command thro Infirmity.

Have to an Houſe, command an Oeconomy or Converſe according.

Of a Place given one, that is, a full command thereof.

Snatch'd from you, ſhews of ſome means propos'd failing you.

Held in your hands, ſhews you of firm Agreements.

       By another, to Travellers and Deſigners is croſs.

Of the bottomleſs Pit given *A*. ſhew'd him a great Teacher
of Errors.

Find, that is, a ready Remedy in Obſtructions according.

Take out of your door, forbid ſome one your Freedom.

Of her Trunk broke, to a Servant ſhew'd her means of ſecret
Managery failing.

Loſing threats with Anger.

       Loſt, to an Houſekeeper his Steward, Maid, or Daugh-
ter proves debauch'd.

A Beggar has the Key of your Barn, you bring in your Harveſt on Credit.

       Taking it from her, paying ſuch off in ſcorn, if
rudely.

A Bunch given to them that ask'd them, ſhew'd *A*. of Liberty
to Captives.

Knife, vid. *Cut* in *Action*.   Vid. *Fight*.

    Seen only, threats with Quarrels and Contentions.

    Taking ſhews of thine Enemies ſpeaking ill of thee.

    Give one to another, attribute wrong to him.

    Pen-knife fight with, that is, contend in a cloſe, but deſperate
Quarrel.

    Chopping-knife ſeen, ſhew'd of more full and blunt Diviſions
and Quarrels.

                             Lanthorn

Lanthorn or Light feen fhews of the Dreamer's Spirit.
    Vid. *Candle* fupra, and *Light* in *Fire.*
Looking-glafs in general fhews us of juft mental Reflexion from Cir-
                cumftances.
           to a Dreamer of Prediction.
           to fome great Self-value.
                  Tricking ones felf up in it, o-
                  vermuch Self-value.
           to the Single Love, and their Sweethearts
            fhewn by it.
           to the Married the Image feen in't, Chil-
            dren.
           to the Afflicted Comfort.
           to the Sick Health, if not in bad circum-
            ftance.
    Seem in't in general, vid. *Looks* in *Sight* in *Senfe.*
           Deform'd threats you of Heavinefs, Care, or Sick-
            nefs.
           Pale, to the Sick threats of unhappy Symptoms, but
            with Recovery.
                worfe than *A.* that is, tho really fo.
           Due proportion'd, to the Single Marriage.
                to the Married Children.
           Other than you are, threats you a Cuckold or Whore-
            mafter.
                  To others be a reputed Father of Baf-
                  tards.
           Dead threats you Death.
           Double gives you a Son like you.
           Crown'd, that is, honour'd.
           Ill-drefs'd, that is, in bad circumftance.
           Head drefs'd in Rags, to the Sick Death.
    Image there, to fome the Son, Brother, or Friend.
           Changes fides of things feen in it.
           Bewitch'd or difappearing, threats their Evil or Death.
    Enemies feen in, to one fhew'd of quarrels with Kinfmen.
           A dead Man feen in one, fhew'd of Death to a Son.
    Barber's look into, marry a Whore.
           Your Face feeming fpotty in it, you having ugly
            Children by her.
    Bafon, vid. *B.* fupra.
    Moon *A.* feeing his Face in, forefhew'd him of a ftrange va-
        gabond Life.
    Water feeing your Face in, threats fhort Life to your felf or
        Friend.
Parcels, 4 Bundles of Mr. *F.* troubled with 3 gone and 1 with her,
    forefhew'd *A.* deliver'd of a fourth Child by him.
Peftle the Man, Morter the Woman.

                                      Peftle

Peſtle pounding Pepper, ſhews of Melancholy.

Pillar on Fire, to *Polycarp* ſhew'd Martyrdom by Fire.

   Of Thorns under one, gave him Riches thro Care.

Pitcher ſeen full of Water, gives Comfort in Adverſity.

     Broke and Water ſhedding, Mother and Child die.

        Not ſhed, the Child only lives.

        Not broke, the Water only ſhed, the Child only dies.

    A's Lover ſeen burning in it, ſhew'd *A.* of her Death by a mean Servant.

Plate ſtealing fear'd at *Oxon*, that is, their Standard Notions corrupting.

    Noble ſeen in an Houſe, gave excellent Notions of Oeconomy Profit.

    Handling, ſhew'd of ſelling Commodities as valuable and ſure of Sale.

       Church Plate among, that is, religious Notions.

    Vid. *Gold* and *Silver* in *Riches*.

    For drinking have, that is, be rich in what may make Drink.

Platters ſhew of our Eſtates and Actions.

    As what is on them, ſo is our Health and Ability to eat.

Poles clambring over, to ſome Love Intrigues.   Vid. *Rod* infra.

    Getting ſomewhat by, that is, by the Aid of ſome tall Man.

Poſt chain'd to, that is, diveſted of Authority.

Pots, vid. *Pitcher* ſupra.

    Shew of our Life, and as chang'd for the better judg.

    Jug flinging at one, ſhew'd *A.* of bribing him by Mony to drink.

    Braſs, vid. **Tools.**

Purſe fine, an happy Command of Mony.

    2 ſpoils all by Repugnancy.

Riding-hood, vid. *Apparel.*

Rod in general, vid. *Stick* infra, and *Poles* ſupra.

    Vid. *Beat* in *Arms.*

    Having in hand, ſhews of Power according.

White one, ſhews of Authority of Controul, as given or receiv'd.

Diſtorted, ſhew'd of vicious Delays.

In a Schoolmaſter's Hand ſee, be in Terror as under as ſtrict a Controul.

    A Whip having, gives good Authority over Servants and Inferiors.

       Loſt or left behind, threats you defective in ſuch State, &c.

Acts. Struck at by an Hornet yours, ſome Rogue eſſaying to fool your Managery.

    Drop'd out of your Hand, Power accordingly loſt.

       Meaſuring one, about building, &c.

    Carried by another ſeen, ſhews you ſlaving your ſelf to ſome Authority according.

Stick and Gloves fetch from a Place, diſown your Abode as 'tis, &c.

    Broke, to the well Sickneſs, Palſy, &c. find a uſe of it before neglected.   Rod.

Rod. Stick broke, to the Sick Recovery, as to forbear uſing it.

In your Hand, ſhews of Sickneſs.

Fighting with, contending in Mony Expence. Leſs than an Horſe, labour, &c.

Catch away anothers, get ſome of his ready Mony.

Rug, vid. *Blanket* ſupra.

Saddle, vid. *Horſe* in *Beaſt.*

Skreen in your Hall, your intimateſt Neighbours and Protectors of your Repute.

Scruitore as the Cabinet ſupra.

Have in a fine Houſe, that is, a rich Oeconomy with Deeds and Tenants ſupporting it.

Scive carry Water in, truſt a Rogue with Mony.

Falling out on't, you loſe it.

Sheet winding, vid. *Dead.*

Her lying in ones ſeen worn and torn, ſhew'd to a Woman big her Midwife lying in at the time.

Shelf new to hold Mony, finding diſcovering of a new Courſe of Profit.

Spectacles find a good Pair, hit off a true Light to ſet your Converſe in.

Given you by one rob'd, convinc'd of erring to Loſs in his like Circumſtances.

[Fictitious Eyes have, be at others Controul in your Affairs.

Removing them ſee clear, alter ſuch ill State to full Command.

Spoon Gold buy, attain to live delicately.

Staff, } vid. *Rod* ſupra.
Stick, }

Stool, vid. *Chair* ſupra.

Stuff, vid. ſupra in *Goods general.*

Table ſhews of the Wife, and to ſome of Farmers.

With a Baſon on it, ſhew'd of Baptiſm.

Stands where the Chimney was, a Converſe, &c. is in the place of your Oeconomy Plenty.

Sit at it to eat, be in a compos'd Method for Profit.

With the King of *France,* be in a Courſe you approve his Conduct in.

At the higher end, command in chief in a Profit or Converſe, &c.

Along with others, that is, be in ſuch a State with many more.

With a great Man, gives you Merit and Joy.

In a Law Court, have an Office according.

With a Phyſician talking of Dreams, tranſact in them ſafe in Health.

A's a Phyſician ſeen dine at, ſhew'd of one in Family abſent, taking Phyſick.

Remove anothers Son from yours, withdraw his Hopes from depending on you.   Table

Table hinders your correcting your Child, a Table Companion does ſo. Higher one, a further and grander State, &c.

Upon a Table things ſeen, ſhew'd of what would be ſpent in Houſe-keeping.

't old and new Mony ſeen, ſhew'd of expected and unexpected Receipts.

Robbers ſeen lie in *A*'s Hall, ſhew'd him of diſcovering of Tenants wrongs.

Under it, ſhews of what is already ſo ſpent.

Miniſter has a fine one, that is, a noble fair State of things in a Religious Converſe.

Put Lice from your Head thereon, expoſe your ſecret Poverty in your publick dealings.

Leave yours ſee a Friend, find ſuch a courſe wanting to your Profit.

Victual carried from it, deceit in Profits.

Tapeſtry ſeen in general, threats with Treachery and Deceit, as too oft a falſe Partition for overhearing, &c.

Dividing a Room, vid. *Divide* in *Part*.

Fair and open, ſhew'd of good News.

Torn, threats of ſhort Life.

Old and coarſe ſeen in *A*'s Houſe, ſhew'd of Falſeneſs in his Dealings.

Tea-Boxes ſhew of luxuriant Plenty, ſuch as Tea-Drinkers poſſeſs.

Tobacco-ſtopper find a carved one, that is, a fiddle ſaddle prating Method of Diverſion.

Pipe break, offend the petty Niceties of mutual Converſe.

Treſſels bearing your Tables, Farmers.

Trunk, vid. *Coffer* ſupra.

Holding Writings, ſhews of our Courſe of Life.

Carried into *A*'s Barn ſeen, promis'd well for his good Husbandry.

Box fling at one coming up Stairs, ſhew them they are but Gueſts.

To a Servant as if a Cloſet, it ſhews of his private Concerns.

Have Wax in Box or Trunk, that is, have occaſion to write private Letters.

Search anothers, examin his Secrets, &c.

What found there is the Diſcovery.

Broke up, to the old Death.

to the young, Loſs of Modeſty.

Tub ſweating, vid. *Sweat* in *Phyſick*.

Veſſels in general, vid. *Drink*.

Repreſent, as they contain Wine, Oil, &c.

Vid. *Plate*, *Pot*, and *Pitcher* ſupra.

Catch Water in one, vid. *Water* in *Houſe*.

Made of Metal, ſhew of the Conſtancy of our Life.

Horn, ſhew of our Infirmities and publick Acts.

Earth, ſhew of our meaner and private Actions.

Veſſels made of Glaſs, ſhew of frail, open and uncertain Actions, and
　　　　ſo ill to all.　　Vid. *Glaſs in Commodity.*

　　　　　Gold with Odours, ſhew'd of the Prayers of the faith-
　　　　ful.

Narrow mouth'd Glaſs ſeen broke, ſhew'd *A.* an end of Evils.

Fair for drinking, ſhew'd of excellent Servants.

　　　　Keeping Jewels or Mony, ſhew the Wife.

　　　　　　Ointments ſhew of wiſe Men, Prieſts or Stew-
　　　　ards.

　　　　　　No Uſe ſhews of Perſons uſeleſs, as Muſick Fools, Para-
　　　　ſites.

New, ſhew of ſome young Perſons.

Broken and the Water pour'd forth ſeen, ſhew'd of an old Man
　　dying.

Waggon, vid. *Cart* ſupra.

Watch broke, to moſt their daily Work diſorder'd.

　　　　Vid. *Clock* ſupra.

　　　　Own let fall and hurt taking up, ſhew'd *A.* of riſing early.

　　　　Taken away, ſhew'd *A.* Intermiſſion of his daily Work.

In Cart Work, the Caſe the Horſes.

　　　　　the Ballance ſpoil'd, the Way wet and Carter
　　　　idling.

　　　　　the Spring having no Catch as wound up, ſuch
　　　　Work endleſs.

Weather-Glaſs conſult, act as a Time-Server.

Wood, vid. *Vegetables.*

CHAP. XLVI.

Of Drink.

IN general. Drink ſhews of ſwift and earneſt Gain, as Meat of ſolider
(1)　　and ſoberer.

　　　　To another, that is, be reconcil'd to him.

　　　　To by unknown, ſhew'd *A.* of an unaccountable Re-
　　　　conciliation offering.

　　Thirſt, a more vehement Deſire of Gain than Hunger, as
　　　　admitting no Delay.

　　　　Without finding Drink, Buſineſs failing us in hot-
　　　　teſt Deſires.

　　　　Exceſſive, threats often of ſome hot Diſtempers,
　　　　chiefly if lying on our left ſide.

　　Drawing Drink in a Cellar, to a Maid ſhew'd a falſe Sweet-
　　　　Heart (Tap-Love.)

　　　　Vid. *Piſs* and *ſh*— in *Bodily Action.*

In general. Brew, that is, do somewhat towards it, as fetch Malt, &c.
but not finish it.

East shews of Separation, talk of it to a Joyner, that is,
design in a Friendship will end in Separation.

In Gold, Silver, Earth or Horn, shews of Tranquillity.

In Pocket have, spend your Pocket Mony on Drink, but see
its Error.

In Glass as brittle, threats Danger and reveals Secrets.

Broken, threats Death of Friends or Shipwreck.

Narrow mouth'd one seen broke, shew'd A. of an
end of Evils, and his scanty Subsistence.

Sorts. Water threats Care, Poverty and Sickness.

Hot, shews Hindrance in Affairs, and Sickness.

Rain, vid. R. in Air.

Very much, threats with Want without Hope.

Clear is a good Sign, and gives Health and long Life.

Dirty, threats with Actions in greatest Straits.

Stinking, threats with violent Distempers.

Clear giving to his People, to a Minister teaching them
well.

Up a River, shew'd A. Death.

Blood drink or draw in general, is good and gives Riches.

¼ a Glass drank to by's Father-in-law, shew'd A.
his Life in danger.

Lions, by Force.

Wolves, by Rapine.

Apes, by Craft.

Dogs, by Flattery.

Foxes, by Craft.

Cats, by Snares.

Dragons, by Tyranny and Sin.

Storks and Wild Geese, by Merchandize.

Cranes threats Poison.

Bats, Gains by keeping Houses, Castles and Towers.

Bullocks, Poison or Gain by Fields.

Sheeps, Gain by Artifice.

Vipers, Endeavours for Craft Gain, but vain.

Various. Urine shews of Sickness.

Wormwood, threats Sickness or grievous Sorrow.

Oil, threats of Poison or Sickness.

Salt, shews Preposterousness.

Mustard stamp'd, shew'd A. falsly prosecuted, ever
to Death.

Poison, threats Punishment.

Spiced drinking, take care of some Enemy, 'tis no
help Digestion.

Strong Waters of several sorts, shew'd of various
kinds of Poetry.

Sort

Sorts. Various. Strong-Waters so content in high Speculations, and with Pepper to Madness. Vid. *Still* in *Domestick Action.*

Milk. Sorts, vid. *Beast* in *Creature.* Vid. *Beast* in *Human Body.*

Of Birds drinking, gives vain Hopes.

Of Serpents drinking, shew'd of vain Hopes, but wicked.

Of Fish, as without Milk, shew'd of Flattery to worst Poverty.

Of Dogs, shews of Calamity, or Gain by Flattery.

Common Drink is joyous, and an extraordinary good Sign.

Skimming Milk Bowls, gives Maids their Desires, have them about them they'd treat so.

Sack-Posset, vid. *Victuals.*

Cheese, vid. *ibid.*

Butter, vid. *ibid.*

Cream seen shed on one, shew'd him of Grace from the Holy Ghost.

Custard eat, Profit in exceeding Grace, but eat in a Feast, it mixes its Symbol.

Wine moderately is good, and gives Security and Chearfulness, if what you are us'd to.

To others, Sickness.

Much is ill, and shews of Contention and Quarrels.

To some, be in the Company of Drunkards.

A Glass given you, a competent quick Profit offer'd.

A full Treat denied, a thorough Gain withheld.

Sorts. Sophisticate, is a good Sign.

Sweet, gives Success in Love and Law.

Mix'd, to the Rich Plenty, to the Poor Sickness.

With Water, shew'd of the Study of Moderation.

Sharp, shews of Poverty.

Kind. From Trees unproper, shews of Idle Expectation and Deceit thereon.

Corrupting soon as Cherries, &c. shew'd of Luxury.

Cherry-Wine, gives Aid from luxurious Folks.

Cotton Tree, from Men laborious and Artificers.

Mulberry Wine, Aid from Men wise and prudent.

Peach Wine, good from sad Men.

Perry gives Help from Rusticks.

Pomegranats, good from Strangers and Men perfidious.

Quinces, Aid of Artificers and Workmen.

Sider gives Aid from great and wicked People.

Slows, from crafty subtle Fellows.

Strawberry Wine, Help from mean and poor Folks.

Drunk, to Men in Buſineſs Blunders to Diſhonour, but withal be born in them.

to ſome, Aſtoniſhment.

to ſome, Sickneſs.

to the Sick, Death.

to Malefactors, Diſcovery.

to the doubtful, it rids Fears and Torments.

to Men, as to Honour or Prudence very bad.

to ſome it increaſes Eſtate, and recovers Health.

to Men in Pain, it abates its Senſe.

Fear alſo good, to others Folly.

Spewing on it, forc'd Returns of ill Gains.

Pain at Heart by it, cheated by ill Servants.

Thro Sack or Muſcadel, Gain by ſome great Lord, (ſweet.)

Water, Boaſts of variety of Wealth without Ground.

Blood, murdering to all Inadvertency.

Ale, to a Gentleman Confuſion thro mean Cares.

Wanting t'other Barrel, producing little borrowings on it.

March Beer the like, but in midling Sums.

Without drinking, threats you of ill Actions of Gain endangering the Law.

And not ſpend 3 d. at an Alehouſe, a Gain queſtionable, as too cheap.

And pain'd at Heart or inwards, rob'd by Servants.

Drunkards great, ſwift Gainers of little ſtay.

Seen drink in A's Parlour, ſhew'd A's allowing ſwift Waſters to devour him.

Drinking Bouts ſeeing, being at merry meetings.

Be at, to a Drinker be ſenſible of the prodigal neglect of Buſineſs by it.

Of Wine, has ſhewn of Madneſs, and ſhedding of Blood.

Treated with it, ſhew'd of a mad, flaſhy and drolling Wit.

White ſhew'd of Muſick, and in Church in Conſort with a Miniſter.

Sweet, gave Succeſs in Law.

Sharp taſting, ſhew'd me of burying a Son.

Drunk with, ſhew'd A. maz'd amidſt profitable Cares and Charges.

Claret milling as Chocolate, ſhew'd A. of making a Cudgel Match.

White-Wine gives Health.

To Women, it ſhews them at a Loſs in their Menſtruums.

CHAP.

C H A P. XLVII.

Of Victuals.

IN general shew of the Master of the House.
(1)
        To some of Necessaries, as Gain to Subsistence, not
          Riches.
        Plentiful tho, gives an happy Subsistence.
Sorts. Variety eating, threats Loss.
        Except in Feasts, vid. *F.*
        Rarities and Dainties buying, blesses with
          Plenty.
Child's eating, shew'd *A.* Confinement home by bad
    Weather.
Nourishment Roots good for, shew of Support in
    Business.
Of strong Smell, add of good Fame or Infamy.
Bread and Cheese, hard Subsistence.
Venison, Daintiness with hazard.
Beef greater, Mutton lesser Plenty, but more pru-
    dent and sure.
Plentiful shews of great Subsistence Gains.
        Little threats with preposterous Actions.
    Turn'd to Marble shew'd *A.* of Death.
Hunger shews Want, and eating Gain upon it.
        Vid. *Thirst* in *Drink* supra.
        Avers'd at Victuals being, to the Sick threats Death.
        Or if accustomed, Hurt.
Procuring buying, to the Poor Plenty.
        to the Rich Expence, and Want remind-
          ing the Care of Necessaries.
        But the richer so, the better.
        Market of it passing thro, commanding a
        Plenty according.
        Vid. also *Buy* in *Possess.*
Eating shews of the Labour and Profit.
        But devouring is best, attaining to your
        full Desires, as &c.
Sought for shews of vain Desires of Gain as to
    Provision only, and not full Plenty.
Set on Table shew'd of a Profit ready for Re-
    ceipt, as eating is Gain.
        Divided on Table, to Prisoners Tor-
        ments.

In general. Procuring. Set on a Table divided, Frogs ſeen ſo, ſhew'd them
(1)　　　　　　　　　　　　　　　　　　ſelves torn in pieces
　　　　　　　　　　　　　　　　　　To ſome the Gout.

Refuſe to eat on it, that is, accept
the Gain.

Snatch'd away e'er eat, Circumvention and Loſs.

Prepar'd by ones ſelf beſt, it ſhews of Profit thro Induſtry

Not ready threats with delay in Gain.

Eating ſuch, prepoſterous and
haſty Gain.

Dreſſing without eating defers your Gain.

Scrap'd Victuals e'er eat, threats of Hurt.

Kept hot in Oven, profit under continual command

Cold Meat new heated, Profit continued on to fur
ther Expectation receiv'd at laſt.

Having an Ox in houſe dreſs'd and ready to be
cut up, ſhew'd *A.* of ſome by him to ſell.

Roaſted Swines Fleſh eating, to the Poor ſpeedy
Profit.

Seen in houſe not eat, ſhew'd of
ſuch Profit defer'd.

Meat eating, to ſome fall into Sin.

Greedily at a Feaſt, to ſome
has ſhewn Sickneſs.

Fleſh ſeen, ſhews damage.

Haſh'd Mutton eating, ſhew'd *A.* paying Debts that
waited his Leiſure.

Bread without Leven, threats of a Buſineſs hard
and heavy.

Hot, Riches with Care.

Cold, Riches with Eaſe.

Ready to bake ſeen, ſhew'd the Sick firſt a
Fever and then recovering.

Eating in general, vid. *Bodily Action.* Vid. *Dead.* Vid. *Vomit* in *Phyſick*
(2)　　　　　　　Feaſting, vid. *Diverſion.* Vid. *Invitation* in *Company.*
Grace, vid. *Religion.*

It ſhews Gain in Pocket or Wiſdom, but yet ſo as but to an
ſwer Occaſions of Support, &c.

To a Glutton it reproves them.

Devouring, better than eating, and more profitable.

Fiſh ſeen, ſhew of untractable and untamable Gri
pers.

An Ape a Lion ſeen, gave Recovery to the Sick.

Dreſſing without eating defers the Gain.

See others eat, ſhews they gain, and rudely rudely.

Out of a Baſon, ſhew'd *A.* of Love to a Maid Servant.

Seeing the Meat you have eat, threats you with Loſs.

Things. Beans threat Sickneſs as heavy, ruſtick, and windy.

Eating

Eating. Things. Books to Bookfellers and Scholars good, or elfe fudden
  (a)   Death.

Coals, good from the Mafter.

Corn Ears, *Jofeph.*

     Unground, fhew'd A. Death.

Dung with Bread with delight, gave A. a profitable
  publick Office.

Eggs Oftrich's, recover a dangerous Debt.

    Other threats with Trouble from the Care in't,
      and at beft but the Embrio of a Project got.

Embalment of the Dead, fhew'd me profiting thus thro
  G O D's fatal Predictions on others.

Fleas fhew'd of Difquiet.

Fruit to fet your Teeth on edg, an ill Omen.

    Apples fhew Choler.

    Roots threat with Difcord.

Metals. Gold chewing, fhew'd Joy and Gain.

     10 Guineas of a Workman, gaining fuch
      by him.

    Iron gives long Life, Strength and Victory.

    Silver threats with Wrath and Anger.

     Seeing others eat it, gives great advan-
      tage.

Milk as Drink *fupra.*

Pot-herbs threat Sorrow.

Unaccuftomed things you'd vomit up, unjuft Gains you
  would reftore.

Stars, to Aftrologers good.

Trafh, vid. *Dung* fupra.

    As Stones, Dirt, *&c.* threats with grievous
     Troubles for Gain.

    Skin, Leather, Dung, Bones, *&c.* threats
     hardeft Poverty, as bad near as in Sieges.

Variety of Meats theats with Lofs.

Manner, eat Porridg at her C—— to a Woman, wrong her Children by a fecond Match.

Meat, fupping in a Town he befieg'd, fhew'd A. doing it in
  Chains, being took in his Affault.

    With *Cæfar*, that is, being murder'd as he was.

    With *Saturn*, be imprifon'd.

    With the Dead, threats extreme Poverty or
     Death.

    In your Parlour, fhews you of eating delicately.

Dine with great Men, live in Character of Command
  and Plenty anfwerable.

    Turky having for Dinner, fhew'd A of a delicate
    projective plenty State.

Table, vid. *Goods.*

Eating.

Eating. Table, Victuals carried from it, vid. *Goods* ibid.

(2)   Others. Prodigals ſeen eat on you, threats you with unneceſſary
             Waſtes.

           The greater Eater the worſe.

         Birds eating o'er the Head, *Pharaoh*'s Butler.

         Owl ſeen eat, threats you as tax-bit.

      7 fat Ears of Corn and 7 fat Oxen eat by 7 lean, *Joſeph*.

Fleſh of a Man unknown, conquering a Courſe with advantage
           by the Victory.

             Known, threats you with extreme Neceſſity.

             Parents, ſhew'd to *A.* his Death and his inhe-
             riting him.

             Hang'd, enrich'd by foul Practice.

             Son's or Brother's worſt, except thoſe Parts
             us'd by them in their Arts, then be main-
             tained by them.

             Your own Fleſh, threats you with extremeſt
             Grief.   Vid. *Human Body.*

     Creatures. Beaſts, ſure Gain.

             Birds, projective Gain.

             Fiſh, Gain amidſt Troubles, *&c.*

         Lions, ſubduing a ſtrong Man to Profit.

         Serpents, conquering one falſe and crafty to
         good.

         Fiſh alive, ſhew'd *A.* of unjuſt Gain.

             Flat as Flounders, ſhew'd *A.* of Profit leſs
             than expected.

             Great, to ſome has ſhew'd Defluxions and
             Melancholy.

         Kine 7. *Joſeph.*

             Beef changing to Cale-ſtumps, ſhew'd
             A. of a Profit offer'd at, vaniſhing to a
             Trifling.

         Mutton Neck of *A.* ſoen, and ripping up his
         Belly on't, ſhew'd of his breeding a Duck
         and loſing him.

         Gooſe fat, gives Profit from ſome Servant or
         project Service.

         Carrion threats with Sadneſs and grievous
         Straits.

Fleſh in general ſeeing much, beware of thine Enemies.

(3)   Man's have and eat, be enrich'd at another's loſs.

         Vid. *Eat* ſupra.   Vid. *Human Body.*

     Birds ſhew of projective Gain, vid. *Birds.*

         Little and green Geeſe are good to all, allegorying of Dain-
         tineſs.

         Sea-fowl, threats of Shipwreck, or gives Gains by Cuſto-
         mers.

                                           Fleſh.

Flesh. Fish, gives Gain amidst Troubles, as &c. vid. *Fish.*
(3)　Having, to some gives Gain from crafty Persons.
　　　　　　to some Victory o'er Enemies in quality, as is the
　　　　　　Fish.
　　　Great ones eating is good to all.
　　　　　　To some tho it shews Defluxions and Melan-
　　　　　　choly.
　　　　　　Little has shewn of Enmity among Friends from
　　　　　　their little Bones.
　　　　　　Flounders and Soles fried, empty and trouble-
　　　　　　som Prospects of Profit.
　　Dolphin eating, enrich'd by a dead Friend.
Beasts dress'd by ones self is best, as shewing Profit thro In-
　　dustry.
　　　　　　Eat by others off the Spit e'er ready, diverted by
　　　　　　Charges e'er due.
　　　　　　Raw eaten, foreshews of somewhat lost or forgot.
　　　　　　　　In general it shews of either Abomination
　　　　　　　　or Difficulty.
　　　　　　Cold Meat eating, shew'd A. of matter in expec-
　　　　　　tation finished.
　　　　　　Porridg of it, vid. *Infra* in *Alphabet.*
　　　　　　Vid. *Butcher* in *Trade.*
　Parts. Fat or Lard eating, shew'd A. of burying a Pa-
　　　　rent.　　　Vid. *Fat* in *Quality.*
　　　　　　Neat's Tongue eat, be at a Treaty of Land in Sale,
　　　　　　and in your power in vain.
　　　　　　Loin of Veal eat, compass the full power of a
　　　　　　new Farming.
　　　　　　Shoulder of Mutton eat, get a slenderer Farm
　　　　　　Profit with Fear.
　　　　　　Neck refuse for to eat of a Leg of Mutton, thrive
　　　　　　well in full midling Cares.
　　Dead of himself, but fine Meat, find an Hog, that is,
　　　　discover a neat but profitless good Husbandry.
　Sorts. Beef and Mutton eating, to some Loss, Lamenta-
　　　　　　tion, and Anger.
　　　　　　　　To some living on the main Stock,
　　　　　　　　have just plain Subsistence and
　　　　　　　　that's all.
　　　　　　Devouring Beasts eating, shews of Power with Sin.
　　　　　　　　Great and not devouring, as Bull, Ele-
　　　　　　　　phant, &c. Power with Sin left.
　　　　　　Dogs eating, foreshew'd of Riches thro Flattery.
　　　　　　Hogs Flesh eat, to the Poor Riches.
　　　　　　　　to the Rich Poverty.
　　　　　　　　Chiefly if roasted it shews quick Profit.
　　　　　　Bacon seen cut, shew'd of ones Death.
　　　　　　　　　　　　　　　　　　Flesh.

Fleſh. Beaſts. Sorts. Hogs. Bacon, eating it as ſalted, ſhew'd of Gain
   (3)   with murmuring, as receive a
                              Rent delay'd with grumbling.
           Serpents eating, to ſome give way to Luxury and
             by Induſtry maintain it.   Vid. *Blood* in *Drink.*
           Sheep and Goats eating, ſhew'd of Juſtice with
             Fear.
                Lambs, vid. *Sheep* in *Beaſt.*
           Small Creatures, threats of Imbecillity.
           Stags, to a *Jew* ſhew'd of treſpaſſing the Law.
             to others gain by hazardous Voyages, *&c.*
           Veniſon eat, get good from Enemies ; or as Stags,
             but leſs.
           Vipers eating, threats with Plague or Poiſon.
Salt in general ſhews of Prudence and Defence.
   (4)   To ſome of Durance as to their familiar things.
           To ſome of Pleaſure.
           To ſome of Barrenneſs.
           To ſome of a Friend prudent, but angry.
Accidents. Melted in an Houſe, threated with Loſs of Rents.
           Inſipid, threats of Madneſs or Deceit, not Folly.
           None having in your Houſe, threats of all your Af-
             fairs as fooliſh.
             Full of it, gives Riches thro Wiſdom, and with
               Pleaſure.
            Stealing it, ſhews of getting Wiſdom. (Chiefly an-
              tient.)
Buying Salt, getting a Friend by Benefits.
           Selling it, by Intereſtedneſs loſing one.
Drinking it ſhews of prepoſterous witleſs Action.
Eating much threats with Scandals and hearing of Evils, *&c.*
           Shews of a vile uſe of good things.
           It Birds ſeen, ſhew'd of good Counſel ill us'd, or made a
             Project.
            Sharp, not wiſe.
            Self-deſtructive too, for it kills the Birds.
Flung in the Fire, a ſharp Trial of Wit.
             Noiſy on it, Tumult thereby.
             If conſum'd, ſuch Attempts made in vain.
             Leaping back, ſhew'd of nothing done.
        A Ditch, ſhew'd of a vile Uſe of good things.
On Roots, ſhew'd of deſtroying Men for their Inheritances.
On Stones, ſhew'd *A.* of Work and Pains fool'd away.
Scattered in a Houſe or City, threats it Deſolation.
Heaps of it ſeen, ſhew Grief, and a dangerous Commodity, as
           melting.
           Finding, that is, an Aſſembly of ill wiſe Men.
Fleſh eating, threats Grief for Gain and Pleaſure thro Neglect and
           Delay.   *Salt*

Salt Flesh eating, ready if before you
(4)   Eaten in future.
        To some Invitation from your wisest Neighbour. (Salt,
            Wisdom.)
    His own powdering, shew'd A. quarter'd at the City Gates.
    Too salt to eat, your Profit delay'd in Vexation, so as to be
        refus'd or rather profitless in the end.
Fish, confirms Hopes and Fears, and gives them Issue.
            Vid. Fish in Flesh supra, and Fish general.
    Little ones threat of Waste and Poverty.
            But pickled as Anchovies, shew Delicacy.
    To some old Faults and a new Punishment.
    To some, so many Pieces, so many Wounds.
    To him that carries them off or eats them, worst.
    To most of old Grudges, and if small with Poverty.
    Mushrooms shew of Aid to Mischief before.
            To some Danger without Gain.
Applepy, Vid. Tart infra.
Bread in general, vid. Corn in Vegetables.
            Vid. Supra in Victuals prepar'd.
    Eating gives Gain.
        Poor Mens threats Poverty.
        With Sugar, gives good Fortune and Riches.
        Cutting largely on't seeing a Woman, promises you of a
            plentiful Fortune.
        Dip'd in Hony, gave Wealth with Wisdom.
        Fill'd with it, shew'd A. of purchasing a good Farm.
    Sorts. Barly is good to all, giving Profit with Health and Con-
            tent.
        Cutting it, shews of rejoicing.
        White, to the Rich good.
            . to the Poor Sickness.
        Mean, to the Poor a careless Life.
            to the Rich Despair, as not further able to com-
                mand dainty Indulgence.
    Loaf last cut, shew'd A. his Faggot-pile last begun.
    Ready to bake having, shew'd to the Sick a Fever, and then re-
        covering.
    Without Leven seen, shew'd of an hard and heavy Business.
    Handling it one seen, shew'd of a Baker.
    Hot, Riches with Trouble, or a Subsistence in Shifts.
        Carrying it threats with Accusations.
        Cold, with Ease.
    Old shews of a mean and hard Livelihood.
Butter, Vid. Milk in Drink.
        Gives Prosperity and Gain with Sweetness.
            to some the Priesthood, chiefly if eat with Hony.
            to some so, it threats Prodigality.
                                                Butter

Butter eating, to one it gave a happy Meffage.

Cake gives Pleafure and great Festivals, if very great.

Making as eating, &c.

With Hony eating, fhew'd A. of Death to Pleafure and Flattery.

With Butter eating, gives a lazy voluptuous but gainful Life.

With Cheefe eating, threats with fome Plot or Cheat, a Contrariety offering you in Banter.

Capers, Olives, and Confections, to moft evil from their fidling Care.

To fome Difeafes alfo as other Pickles.

But in a Feaft they add Delicacy to Profit, and are good.

Cheefe frefh eating, fhews of Gain or Favour.

Salt ill as hard to digeft, and the Food of the Poor.

It threats with Deceit whether eat with Cake or alone, except to the Poor.

Vid. Milk in Drink and Cake fupra.

Parings large given to Dogs, fhew'd of a cheated Liberality to ill Men.

Given you, a mean Profit offering of troublefom Confequence, as poor Mens Diet.

Eat or have it, be fool'd both in a mean and ill Profit as hard to digeft.

Cinnamon fhews of Riches, Dignity, Beauty, and Felicity.

Comfits give Joy and Profit.

Confections, vid. Capers fupra.

Eggs in general, vid. Birds in Creatures.

Shew Mony, chiefly if hid.

To fome Hopes and Works projective begun.

Eating, Trouble from our Care about them.

To others Strife.

Roafted, the better.

Partridges, enrich'd by fome noble Woman.

Seen hang by a String o'er a place, fhew'd a Treafure under.

Setting them, Oppreffion thro Cares and Fears of little value, as in gardening, &c.

Young coming on it, near Perfection.

it in general, vid. Vegetables.

Cucumbers pilled, fhew good Succefs as genteel, and a Dainty.

Grain in Portage bad (Peafe excepted) they fhewing Expedition of Bufinefs.

Pulfe fhew of hard Bufinefs and Men intractable.

Beans are ill to all, as grofs and ruftick.

As hard to digeft, they threat Troubles and Diffenfions in Cares.

Onions and Garlicks good to have, but bad to eat.

Eating, to the Sick Recovery, but if but few, Death.

Pompions good in Friendfhip as fpreading.

To others they fhew of vain and empty Fellows.

Fruit,

Fruit. Radishes as ill smelling, shew of ill Counsel.

Gruel the same as Bread above.

Herbs in general, vid. *Vegetables.*   Vid. *Crown* in *Ornaments.*

Of strong Smell, reveal Secrets, and cause Anger and Reports.

Good Nourishment give Support in Business, but then withal not great.

Medicinal, as Beets, Mallows, Burrage eating, shew Dispatch.

And as keeping the Body soluble give Ease in Trouble, and are as if said remedial Gain.

Purging eating, good to those who are in Debt.

Sallads eating, shew of Sickness or Evils that will happen.

To others, Trouble and Difficulty in Managery, as hard to digest.

To others, Novelty of Opinion, and if diverse with Controversy.

Cabbage shews a Man of a great Family, but not noble.

To Taverners and Vine-Workers Ill, to all a very mean Subsistence, poor Mens Gardenage.

Coleworts eating, shews of Vexation poor and windy.

Moss gives a total Discovery, all's above Ground.

Mushrooms eating, threat with Poisons, Snares and Flattery.

Give a total Discovery, all is above ground, and as upstart.

Salted, shew'd of Aid to Mischief before.

To some as troubling the Belly, Sedition in House.

So vexing, Creditors abroad.

Puffs seen, declare of the Discovery of Secrets.

Smallage in general, threats with Sickness.

To the Sick, Death.

Potherbs eating, threat Sorrow, as us'd as medicinal Correctors, &c.

Honey taking, beware of Enemies.   Vid. *Butter* and *Cake* supra.

eating with Butter, shews of luxurious Prodigality.

Bread gives Wealth with Wisdom ; Bread Wealth, and Honey Wisdom.

Milk and Milk Meats, vid. *Drink* and *Butter* and *Cheese* supra.

Mushrooms, vid. *Herbs* and *Salt* supra.

Nutmegs give Profit from Strangers eat or not.

Pap shews the same as Bread or Gruel, but with more Infirmity.

Pepper threats with fighting and Grief, that is, using a Victual or Gain that wants such Aid to digest.

Handling, threats Fights with Enemies.

Eat Beef stew'd with it, command a good Instruction, but withal so tending.

Pastinaca threat with great Disgrace or Death.

Pickles, vid. *Capers* supra.

Mushrooms, vid. *Herbs.*

                                                    Porridg

Porridg of Meats, the Skim of Profits, not all the Subſtance.
  Of Grains are all bad; Peaſe excepted.

Potherbs, vid. *Herbs* ſupra.

Pies, ſhew of Joy and Profit.
  Apple-pies ſhew'd of Rents due, and as kept cold for a long time.

Roots in general, vid. *Vegetables.*
  Eat, threat of Diſcord.
Of ſtrong Smell, reveal Secrets, but with Labour.
    To others, threat with Domeſtick Jars.
   Good Nouriſhment, ſhew of Support in Buſineſs.
Scrap'd e'er eat, ſhew'd of Hurt thro Superfluity.
Curl'd ſeen as of little Subſtance, threat with vain Hopes.
Carrots eating, good to Suitors for Inheritance. (Pull'd up by
  the Roots.)

Sauce good eating take care of ſome Enemy, 'tis a Digeſtion Aſſiſtant.
   Cake with Honey or Butter eating, ſhews of lazy Voluptuouſneſs.

Spice eating or drinking, take care of an Enemy, &c.

Sack-Poſſet eating, to Women ſhews of goſſiping.
    to Men, of enjoying their Love.

Sugar eating with Bread or without, gives good Fortune.

Sweet-meats, vid. *Taſte* in *Senſe.*
   Eat, to ſome read Romances,
    to ſome, it ſhews of Liquoriſhneſs.
    to ſome, 'thas ſhewn being invited to a Feaſt.
   Refuſed them, being baulk'd in what ſo hop'd for.

Tarts, vid. *Pies* ſupra.

Vinegar drinking, threats Sickneſs or grievous Sorrow.

C H A P. XLVIII.

Of Paſſion.

IN general Paſſions ſeen with falſe Cauſes, often ſhew of the
 Contraries.

Admiration ſhews of things preſenting, worthy thereof in Circumſtance, &c.
   You be admir'd, that is, you are in ſuch Circumſtances.

Affection in general, vid. *Dying* in *Dead.*
   Childleſs ſeeming and not ſad, ſhew'd *A.* as happy as if ſo.

Anger in general, vid. *Fighting.*
   Kill ones ſelf, to ſome literal by Gluttony, &c.
   Beat another fulfil your Deſire on him, have all Free-
    dom deſirable with him.
   To Lovers, it gives Enjoyment.

              Ang

Anger in general, Hard Words, vid. *Words*.

If without cause, shews of pure Anger and Injuries coming.

To others, it threats Envy, unjust Actions, and Grief enough to cause it.

At a Tyrant, refuse to obey some accustomed Lust or Fault.

Servant, shew'd *A.* of commanding a Friend he imploy'd with Pride.

Your Cook, shews your Fare mends, and is correct of what it was.

Angry see your Tenant, threats your Estate is in ill Condition.

Husband at your Frugality, shews you how he thrives to live more great.

Master, threats your Service will be in fault.

Parents-in-Law, threats you with implacable Hatred.

Servant, shews your giving occasion to vex some Hireling, *&c.*

To some, of their Estate Managery as troublesom.

King, is ill to all.

An indulgent Person, shews you thwart his Courses, and are too rough.

One unknown, shews you as vex'd at your self for erring.

An Apothecaries Wife, to one sick shew'd trespassing Prescription Rules.

Vid. *Revenge* infra.

Arrogant Fellow be troubled with, that is, have just Cause of Offence at such like Proceeds.　　Vid. *Insolency* infra.

Asham'd, vid. *Shame* infra.

Boasting, vid. *Discourse*.

Bold being, shews of acting freely.　　Vid. *Free* infra.

Brisk Person waiting on *A.* shew'd of a bold forward Person writing to *A.*

Bustling your Enemy seen, shews you prosperous as to provoke him to it.

In a Room among Company, shew'd *A.* idly fooling away time in Company.

Care, vid, *Soul*.

Cheerful Oxen seen, gave a plentiful Husbandry and Profit.

Friend seen gives you good, as is that Friend's Capacity.

Enemy seen threats ill Luck, as that Course triumphing over you.　　Vid. *Merry* infra.

Civility, vid. *Contempt* infra.

Shews of Civility, as Rudeness of Rudeness.

Maundy and hectoring an unknown seen, shews you submitting to odd Compliances according.

In eating as to Profit, either in Gain or Instruction.

Civil see another, that is, receive real Kindness from him or her.　　Civility.

Civility. Civil be to others, that is, your self do benefits as if so.

Rude to you Company seen, threats you some way incapacitated for them as sick.

Others see find, Acts done by them you might justly think so.

A rude Beggar meets you, a beggarly rude Course obstructs you.

Comfort having, to the Poor good.

to the Rich, Mishap. Vid. *Applause* in *Honour.*

Comforting the Sick, gives Joy and Profit.

Vid. also *Pity* infra.

Concern having, shews of being in Straits according.

Contempt in general, vid. *Civility* supra. Vid. *Slight* infra.

To some, Sickness, as at such time Persons are too often neglected.

To some, Study of Ease with Calamities gone.

Plain, to many has shewn unjust Oppression.

Hiss'd at being publickly, threats with the heaviest Contempt.

To hiss e em.

Contemning Religion, threats greatest Misfortunes.

Fleer'd at by another, treated with Contempt as if so.

Sneering Fellows passing by you seen, threats of your acting to others Scorn.

Assaulted by 2 such, design'd against in 2 Rogueries.

Kiss one and wipe your Mouth on it, receive a Benefit, and after contemn it.

Scorn'd being, that is, in Circumstances deserving it.

To be answer'd, that is, treated as beneath any Regard.

To some, it has shewn Retirement and Sickness.

Scorn your Enemy, that is, be in Circumstances enabling you thereto.

Content. Discontent shews of things cross, as is the Place where, &c.

Vid. *Confus'd in Soul.*

Countenance, vid. *Favour* infra.

Courageous, that is, resolute and positive.

Courting beautiful Woman, threats with Crosses and Vexations.

An old Woman gave Riches in Marriage, but with Discontent.

To others, a profitable Bargain offers, but a little shameful.

Coy is as shy *infra.*

Cross A's Husband being, shew'd of his being prodigal, and so incapacitating his Kindness.

A Friend find, that is, find him not act with that kindness you might expect.

Cruel Fish seen, threat with Danger.

Crying in general, vid. *Hear* in *Sense.* Vid. *Words.*

Maid seen, foreshew'd A. Joy.

Crying ſelf ſeeming, has foreſhewn Joy and Laughter, and as if ſaid by the Spirit, I will ſhew you a Cure of Crying.

Seeing others, ſhews that they want your Regard.

Howling ſee your Enemy, proſpers you to the utmoſt.

Child having in Arms, to a Woman ſhew'd her Grief for Loſs of Parents.

Owls heard, threat with Damage and Blame, and as if in Deſigns benighted.

Sheep heard and running into Holes, ſhew'd of a good Sect perſecuted.

Out Murder, that is, ſeeking a deſperate Aid in a great Diſtreſs.

To all, ſhews of great Danger with Application of Aid ſought.

With Jeſts, ſhew'd A. of merry Bouts.

Delighted with things, ſhew'd A. uſing them as if he were ſo.

In eating, to the Glutton ill Conſequence thro ſuch Crime.

Eating Bread with Dung with Delight, gave A. a profitable Office.

In Contemplation, to the Student ſhew'd his being plagu'd thro Neglect of Buſineſs.

Deſire in general, vid. *Want* infra.

It ſhews of the Loſs of ſomewhat can't be had.

Another ſee deſire to buy of you, you ſo deſire of them, &c. be in that Circumſtance of want.

Would borrow 2 *l.* of A. this ſhew'd A. fail'd in finiſhing 2 *l*'s worth of Work.

Aſſes is as Riches, and ſhews Poverty.

Book yours to be printed, ſhews of your Notions as formally exploded.

Coach ſtanding near a Painters in *London*, ſhew'd A. in want of B. to be a blazoner of his Honour.

Kingdom of God, ſhew'd A. of falling out with his Miniſter.

Honour is to be in want of an Horſe.

Horſe is as to want Honour, and ſhews Contempt.

Payment of Mony, ſhew'd A. in want of Mony for a Debt.

Reſtoration of Sight, ſhew'd to A. Loſs of Children.

Soul, threats you Loſs of Wiſe or Child.

To the Uſe of his Art, ſhew'd to A. the Loſs of his Wife.

Riches, ſhew'd to A. Sickneſs in the Belly.

Seeing your Shoulder, but cannot be blind on that ſide.

Deſpair, vid. *Hope* infra.

Deſpiſe, Vid. *Contempt* ſupra, and *Slight* infra.

A Book, neglect the Uſe of ſuch Precepts, as &c.

God, ſhews of greateſt Miſery or Good, as to tempt us to it, &c.

Crumbled brown Bread in Pocket, be better'd to ſcorn a mean Eſtate.

Differing ſhews of differing.

A 2   Diſplea

Diſpleas'd, vid. *Satisfi'd* infra.

Diſtracted, vid. *Raving* infra.　　　Vid. *Mad* in *Phyſick.*

Diſtreſs ſhews Diſtreſs.　　Vid. *Misfortune* in *Action.*

Diſturb'd, vid. *Action.*

Diverted by another, that is, alter'd in your Courſe by a Method, as is the Perſon.

Embracing, vid. *Farewel* in *Diſcourſe.*

　　　　To ſome, ſhews of ſudden Nuptials.

　　　　By a Ghoſt, deluded in hotteſt Deſires by a Cheat.

　　　　A. laying Farewel, I muſt leave the Company of Men, ſhew'd *A.* dying on it.

Enemies ſhews of Reconciliation.

Father and Son ſeen, ſhew'd *A.* of a Tutor as kind to him.

Iron ſhews of Impriſonment, or teaching Fencing.

Without Power to ſpeak, falling in Love, but never to poſſeſs.

Your Guardian Angel, having a Divine Meſſage as to your Preſervation.

One known, entertaining a Courſe as cordially as is the Perſon.

　　　　Your Brother's Miniſter, admitting heartily of all Rival Intereſt Caſuiſm.

Encourag'd by an Angel, a Divine Meſſage Preſumption heartning you.

　　　　A Friend, a Courſe as is that Friend encourages you.

Envious being, threats of anxious Loſs to your ſelf, and Proſperity to others.

　　　　Enemies ſeen, gives you greateſt Joy and Proſperity.

　　　　J. N. ſeems envious, that is, you'l prove happy in what he rivals you.

Fail, vid. *Want* infra.

Faithfulneſs ſhews Faithfulneſs.

Familiar, vid. *Free* infra.

Favour'd by the Judg ſeeing your Adverſary, threats you as loſing your Aim.

　　　　Countenance another, ſhews of Countenancing, &c.

Fawning Lion ſee, find of ſome great Man favouring you.

Fear in general, vid. *Terrible* infra.

　　　　It generally gives good Succeſs, tho with danger.

　　　　It's always much better than Hope.

　　　　To ſome, Hurt and violent Terror of Mind.

　　　　To ſome, if violent, Deſtruction, but then upon ſome Act occaſioning it.

　　　　To ſome, be ſenſible of a juſt Cauſe for it.

　　　　To ſome, great Enemies, Strife and Sickneſs.

Of Perſons, Thieves caution againſt erring.

　　　　A Servants Spoil, ſhew'd *A.* ſuch Servants doing well.

　　　　Of their ſhooting you, of their Cenſure.

Of Beaſts not hurting us, ſhews only Dangers.

　　　　Aſſaulting us, ſhews great Evil.

　　　　A Lion, be ſenſible of the King, or ſome great Man's Anger.

Fear

Fear of Beaſts. A Lion, but without Hurt, becauſe only Fear.
  Of Fire burning *A*'s Hall Stone-Chimney, ſhew'd *A.* vain Fear of
      his Wife's Death.
          A's Furnace, hazard too, *&c.* vid. *F.*
Flattering, vid. *Flatter* infra, and *Wheedle* in *Words.*
Fleering, vid. *Contempt* ſupra.
Fondled by Parents and old Relations, threats of their indulg'd Errors
      plaguing us.
  Fond Perſons accompanying, ſhews of being fondled.
          Seen angry, threats of your offending in Rough-
              neſs, as *&c.*
  Vid. *Wheedle* infra, and *Flatter* in *Words.*
  Vid. *Fond Perſon* in *Grammar.*
Forward, vid. *Free* and *Raſh* infra.
Free in general your Friend ſeen, ſhews of your Affairs going eaſy.
          Horſe going, ſhews your Affairs ſucceeding well,
              according as *&c.*
          Too free his Son, ſhew'd to *A.* Anger at his Son's
              Rudeneſs.
  Familiar the King ſeen, ſhew'd of another great Perſon ſo.
          Being with an Angel, ordinarily preſuming your ſelf as a
              Divine Meſſenger.
          Strangers being to you, ſhews of ſome taking too great
              Liberty with you.
Frighted, vid. *Action.*
Gentle, vid. *Dead.*
          Lion ſeen, ſhew'd of a ſuperior Kind.
              And tho great, ſo 'tis Terror without Hurt.
          Eagle ſeen, the ſame in its way.
          Wind gives good News.
          Walking, proceeding with Pleaſure and Advantage, as *&c.*
Glad, vid. *Joy* ſupra.
Grieving, vid. *Sad* infra.
          Sorry, ſhews of Actions occurring worthy of Sorrow.
          Moaning threats the like.
          To ſome, Hurt or Loſs of Mony.
          Without Cauſe, ſhews of pure Grief and Wrongs coming.
          For abuſing another, threats you in Terror of Revenge, and
              ſo repenting.
          With one Son, ſhew'd a Father the t'others Death.
Grievouſly is grievouſly.
Groans hearing, threats with Trouble and Anguiſh.
Hatred in general, vid. *Love* infra.
          Shews of having Cauſe therefore.
  Ill to all, we have need of all the World.
          Without Cauſe, ſhews of pure Hatred.
  Of another, find your ſelf in Circumſtances therefore.

* Hatred

Hatred. Hating a Perſon known, threats you as receiving Injury of him, &c.

Unknown, be angry at your ſelf for erring.

Of Victuals, threats you either Death or great Hurt.

Heartily ſhews heartily.

Hector, vid. *Huff* infra.

Hope ſhews of a good Beginning, but withal ſtill it threats of vain Deſire.

To all of vain Expectation, and as Pity ſtill bad, and as if ſaid, that matter will end in Hope only.

Diſappointed, threats Grief.

Deſpair ſhews of Deſpair, and helpleſs Miſery worthy the occaſioning of it.

Huffing another ſhews of ſubduing him to your Will.

See unknown, ſtoop to odd Methods according.

All in Learning, that is, exceeding all in Learning, &c.

Vid. *Words* in *Literature.*

You your Creditor ſeen, ſhews you in want to borrow Mony of him.

A. Officers ſeen in the King's Name, ſhew'd A. of good Conſcience moving, &c.

Jealous in general be, that is, act with Caution.

Your Enemies ſeen, ſhews of your Affairs as proſperous.

Of Quarrels being, taking care to prevent them.

Of his dead Son A. ſeen, ſhew'd B. reacting what cauſed ſuch Jealouſy in A. once.

Of ones Wife's Whoredom, to ſome of their Friends Verity.

to ſome their Abuſe in their Art.

Indulgent, vid. *Fond* ſupra.

Inſolence another's defy, that is, prevent his like Efforts againſt you.

Joy ſhews of happy Circumſtances, and as ſuch as may merit it.

Bonefires make, be bold in a clear Conſcience.

Vid. *Sad* infra.

Without Cauſe, pure Joy.

Great, to the Sick Death.

to ſome well, a Child born.

to ſome Marriage of Self or Brother.

Sudden or ſurprizing at the ſight of ſomewhat, Marriage or Friends Approach.

For Mony found when none, Sorrow.

Rejoice to ſee your Enemy, be in circumſtances to ſcorn his Miſchiefs to the utmoſt.

Joyful Parents ſeen, to ſome Return from Baniſhment.

to ſome Happineſs in Life or Manners, not Riches or Honour.

Friend ſee, be proſperous in what he is your Friend.

Enemy ſeen, threats you miſerable wherein he your Enemy.

    D ſeen, gives you all

                                                                    Kind

Kind ſhews of doing friendly Acts, as is the Perſon kind.

Lamenting in general, vid. *Grief* ſupra, and *Weep* infra.

GOD ſeen, threats with publick Ills and a wicked Prince.

For Parents as dead again, gave *A.* Joy and Gain again, as before by their Deaths,

Sighing is as lament, but for leſſer Ills.

Laughing in general, vid. *Contempt* ſupra.

Vid. *Smile* in *Looks* in *Senſe.*

To ſome it foreſhews of Tears and Sadneſs.

To ſome in good Circumſtance Gain.

Your ſelf, threats you with Strife and Variance.

Hearing it, threats you with Sadneſs and Complaints.

Strangers and mocking at you, threats you Self-vexation and Diſappointment.

Love in general, vid. *Hate* ſupra.

It ſhews of Grief and Loſs, things loſt are moſt lov'd.

Verſes ſay, tranſact with Women anſwerably.

Loving another, giving him Uſage as if ſo.

Lov'd being, ſhews of being or doing things acceptable to the Humour of the Perſon.

Words to that effect, as make you his Heir, &c. that is, ſuch Courſe will reward you, &c.

Courting beautiful Women, threats with Croſſes and Vexations.

Bring one a Sweetheart, offer him a Friendſhip.

Paſs'd by by a former Sweetheart, ſcorn'd in fierceſt Deſires, as &c.

One greatly belov'd heard of as dead, ſhew'd of an Aid greatly deſired wanted.

Another for a good cauſe, be pleas'd his Actions are according.

Malice ſhews of Malice.

Malicious Perſons ſhew of their miſchievous Courſes.

Maundy, vid. *Saucy* in *Civil* ſupra.

Merry in general, vid. *Joy* ſupra, and *Cheerful* ſupra.

Being, threats with Heavineſs.

Bouts, vid. *Diverſion* in general.

The Dead ſeen, is good againſt the Terrors of Death.

A dead Prince ſeen, ſhew'd of vain Hopes to follow.

Moaning, vid. *Grief* and *Lamentation* ſupra.

Mourning in general, vid. *Apparel.*

Woman ſeen with her Hair diſorder'd, ſhew'd *A.* of his Wife dead.

Mourners ſeen, threat with the Death of ſome Familiar, as &c.

Sword *A's* ſeen chang'd to a plate one, ſhew'd *A.* of his Suffering turn'd to noble Action.

Neglect one envying you, that is, be happy in what they miſerable to ſcorn their Reſentment.

Of Religion, ſhew'd of greateſt Heavineſs to follow.

Neglect

Neglect. Regard not Comforters, feek to rectify your Mifhap.

    Regarded not by an Enemy fneaking away on a queftion ask'd, fhew'd of its iffuing well.

Nice Perfons feen, threat you afflicted with fuch like Courfes.

Pity in general, bodes ill without any manner of good.

    From GOD, threats with moft exceeding Mifery.

        One dead in whofe Houfe he was, to the Sick fhew'd the Infirmity he had would end in Death.

One in Mifery, threats it fo befalling your felf.

A Prodigal in a Stable, be in a reftlefs Want of Mony your felf.

Of an unknown Perfon, fhew'd A. of concern in another's cafe.

One in your next Market Town, be at a Lofs to anfwer your ready Bargains.

Pitiful Face having, threats with Heavinefs of Mind.

A Hare hunted pity, be in great fear of your Iffue in fome Difpute.

    Your felf being fafe, fear of another's Iffue in dangerous.

Hogs by Children feen, fhew'd of the neglect of feeding fuch Hogs cured, and fo pity good.

Pleafant, vid. *Joy* and *Delight* fupra.   Vid. *Satisfied* infra.

Pride, vid. *Vain-glory* infra.

    Vid. *Arrogancy* and *Infolency* fupra.

Racketing, vid. *Buftling* fupra.

Rafh in general, vid. *Free* fupra.

    Man and his Houfe, vid. *Grammar.*

Go abroad out of doors, to the weak Sick catch a Cold as if fo.

Order his Garden, to the recovering Sick fhew'd him near well for Affairs again.

Be free about Houfe, to the defperately Sick threats Death near.

    To the Recovering gives greater Strength than expected.

Walking weakly, to the Bed-rid gave an hopeful Advance toward Recovery.

    Barefoot, fhew'd the Sick of a Cold.

Putting your Feet in cold Water long, threats you with a Cold.

Walking naked about a Room, to the Sick gave a Cold.

Buy a Whiting in a Market, to the Sick recover as to be able to eat them.

Raving or diftracted feeming, threats with heavieft Misfortunes as requiring it.

Rejoice, vid. *Joy* fupra.   Regard, vid. *Neglect* fupra.

Repenting fhews of having caufe therefore in your Judgment.

    See another repent, treat them as if fo.

    Vid. *Complain* in *Words.*

Reputed being an *Oxford* Scholar, to a Counfellor fhew'd him writing himfelf a Gentleman.

Revenge in general, vid. *Anger* fupra.

                      Revenge.

Revenge. See one angry for an Injury, find him actually resent it.

    Another's preventing, shew'd *A.* first of offending them, and then disabling their Resentment.

    Riding o'er one unknown who struck his Horse, shew'd *A.* neglecting a Course to his Wife's hurt.

Rude, vid. *Civility* supra.

Sad, vid. *Grief* supra, and *Sigh* below.

    See your Physician, threats you fooling away your Health.

    Enemies seen good, it prospers you wherein they are your Enemies.

    Friends seen ill, it shews you are unhappy in what they are your Friends.

    Saints seen, threats that your Impiety hurts you.

    Parents seen, very bad ; it threats your Affairs distress'd.

        Father worst, as wisest, desperatest Sickness.

        Mother seen so, threats you with Sickness, but little.

Satisfied being, shews of being satisfied.

    Pleas'd gives Expectation answer'd, *& e con.*

    Vid. also *Pleasure in Diversion.*

    G O D seen or pleasant, gives all Joy.

Saucy, Vid. *Civil* supra.   Scorn, Vid. *Contempt* supra.

Severe-look'd Men see pry on you, do Actions liable to hard Enquiries.

Shame shews of Shame, and doing things worthy of Shame.

    Asham'd be to do as others, refuse literally such Action on such account.

    Catch'd doing what asham'd of, shew'd *A.* of Discourse reflecting as by the by on such things as he had done.

Shy in scorn, vid. *Contempt* supra, and *Slight* infra.

    Your Enemy seen, shews you some good Hit near, if but well minded.

Sigh, Vid. *Lament* supra, and *Bodily Action.*   Vid. *Groan* supra.

Slight, Vid. *Contempt* and *Despise* supra.

    Beggars, be not in the Want you might seem.

    To some, 'tis as tricking.

    A. passes by me to *B.*   *A.* transacts with me, but mostly for *B's* sake.

    Passing thro dancing Strangers, shew'd me as unhospitable to a Merry-meeting.

    Rude to Gentlemen in a fine Room, slighting of a noble Course of Entertainment.

        You see others, that is, be treated by them as if so.

        For Birth, literal.

    Slighted at a great Man's Table seeming, shew'd *A.* of Offence for Opinion.

        By Men in Office, that is, by Persons in all Pomp and Form.

        By his Mother asking her of his Health, shew'd to *A.* 'twas in no danger.

                Slight

Slight. Slighted by Looks, shew'd of Discourses and seeming Actions.

Sneaking seeing a Sharper, shews of your preventing or outwitting such Tricks.

In a Street, as to publick Converse.

Your Enemy, felicitates you wherein he is your Enemy.

Your self, threats you someway outdone or expos'd as &c.

Your dead Enemy away, shews you good as is the Place and Person, but unexpected.

Sneering, vid. *Contempt* and *Laugh* supra.

Sober Verses fix'd, solemn Notions forcing Sobriety.

Sorely, vid. *Grievously* supra.　　　Sorrow, v.d. *Grief* supra.

Stern, vid. *Severe* supra.

Submitting to another shews of suchlike Submissions indeed.

Suffer, vid. *Affliction.*

Surpriz'd seem'd as caught doing what asham'd of, shew'd A. hearing Discourse reflecting as if so sideway.

Teasing, vid. *Vexing* infra.

Terrible, vid. *Fear* supra.

That is, powerful and mighty.

Enemy seeming, that is, appearing malicious and mighty.

Wind, that is, Persecution of popular Vogue.

Image of another's see, that is, approve of his surly ways.

Terror without Hurt, shews of Danger without Damage.

Uncertain, threats with dangerous Circumstances.

From Beasts tho, is good to Hunters.

Troubled being, receiving occasion as therefore.

to some it shews Sickness.

With 4 Bundles of her Husband, 3 gone and 1 with her, shew'd A. deliver'd of a live Child by him that day.

Going about, designing in Affairs of Perplexity.

Looks, to some want of Mony.

to some has shewn of being in a stink.

Much in killing many Lice, gave great Riches.

Travel shew'd of Sickness.

Fire seen, threats with Poverty and Sickness, or at least Heaviness.

Water seen shews Vexation, but a Pond or Lake seen so is as unexpected.

Rivers seen so, threat with great Annoy and Discontent, as &c.

To some the Violence of an Enemy.

Vain-gloriously strutting before others shew'd A. of acting prodigally.

Vexing Persons escape from, ease you of Cares oppressing you.

Unknown escape from into a Room, shew'd A. of making him a Closet.

Vexing

Vexing Perſons unknown eſcape from in general, that is, from odd
        Methods preſenting.
Teas'd by a Spirit punching with his Finger, treated as a Chea
       to your great Uneaſineſs.
By the Devil, being under continual Efforts of Deſpair.
       To ſome in good Shape he has ſhewn of
       happy Gain.
Affairs, that is, croſs and ſufficient to perplex and teaſe one.
Unkind, vid. *Croſs* ſupra.
Wanting, vid. *None* in *Quantity.*
     Parts. Hair, vid. *H.* in *Body.*
       Noſe, vid. *Body.*
       Fingers, vid. *Body.*
       Bones Fiſh ſeen, threated of Weakneſs.
       Breaſts a Woman ſeen, ſhew'd her of Poverty to herſelf.
    Perſons ſeen, ſhews the Dreamer is ſo far defective of his Me-
       thods.
       One wants to buy of you, that is, you ſo want to buy
       of another.
       Failing on Summons ſhews of failing on Summons.
       His Wife, to an Husband ſhew'd him in diſtreſs in his
       Art or Contract, or her Intereſt.
    Vid. *Deſire* ſupra.
    Things. Your Whip or Sword, that is, indiſcreetly loſe your
       Power.
       A Staircaſe, that is, find the means of your Buſineſs
       failing.
       A Door and Bar againſt Lions purſuing, ſhew'd *A.*
       failing to pay a potent Creditor.
       Victuals in a Room, be in an Oeconomy of no Profit.
       Curſes the Bible ſeen, promiſes you all Happineſs.
       Troubled with 4 Bundles of her Husband, 3 gone
       and 1 with her, ſhew'd *A.* deliver'd that day of
       her fourth Child.
       A Ship to carry him from an Iſland, a good Market
       for his Corn.
       A Market, ſhew'd *A.* of his Corn falling in his hands.
       Apples ſeeing his Trees, ſhew'd *A.* of gathering
       them in next day.
       Scales to weigh with, ſhew'd *A.* at a loſs how to va-
       lue a Bargain.
Watching, vid. *Action.*
Weeping in general, vid. *Cry* and *Grief* ſupra.
    If for ſome cauſe, ſhews of Joy for a good Act.
    To ſome Favour once loſt reſtored.
    Sad without a Cauſe, has ſhewn Grief with a Cauſe.
    Your Son ſeen, threats you Misfortune.
       Vid. *Son* in *Grammar.*

                    Wheedling,

Wheedling, Vid. *Flattery* in *Words.*

One, threats you in want of Aid as is the Perſon.

To all it ſhews a Mind dejected, and a croſs Fortune.

Wonder, vid. *Admiration* ſupra.

CHAP. XLIX.

Of Action.

IN general, Vid. *Ability* in *Quality.*
(1)   Things ſeen done, ſhew of ſomewhat towards them done, but denies their Perfection.

By your ſelf, ſhews of ſomewhat wherein you imploy others.

You whip your Son, you make another do it.

Another, ſhews of what done by your ſelf. Vid. *Grammar.*

That a big-bellied Woman was deliver'd, ſhew'd only of a Nurſe come to her.

Field had ripe Wheat in't, ſhew'd of ſowing it to Succeſs there.   Vid. *Grammar.*

Seeing, vid. *Sight* in *Action*, and *Beggar* in *Grammar.*

Hearing Hens cackle and Geeſe cry, gives Profit and Diſpatch in Buſineſs.

Swallows chatter about an Houſe, ſhew'd of Hurt by Flatterers.

Serpents hiſs, not ſeen or felt, ſhew'd of Enemies powerleſs.

A Cock crow, ſhews Proſperity.

An Aſs bray, threats Damage.

Beaſts. A Lion carried by, protected by your Prince, *&c.*

Mare fine and well-ſaddled coming into A's Houſe, ſhew'd of his marrying a rich Wife.

Ugly and unaccoutred coming in, ſhew'd of taking a mean Concubine with nothing.

Spurring your Horſe, honoured for your Endeavours.

Mule carrying Books ſeen derided, ſhew'd A. of his pious Intentions hinder'd.

Aſs ſeen ſit on his Crupper, threats with Laboriouſneſs.

Elephant give to one to eat or drink, benefit ſome great Lord.

h

In general. **Beafts.** Oxen feen eat 10 Ears of good Corn, Slavery en‑
(1)   ing, 10 Years of Plenty.
           7 fat eat up 7 lean. *Pharaoh.*
Infects. Bees fettling on *Plato's* Lips, fhew'd him of ad‑
           miring Auditors.
Eirds in general, vid. *Birds.*
           Fighting fhews Adverfity to your Projects.
           Flying on the Head, fhew'd of prejudice by Enemies.
           Crows feen fit on Childrens Heads forefhew'd them
                hanging.
                And Birds of Prey feen flying in dark Wea‑
                      ther, Lofs and Mifery.
                      Eating o'er the Head, to *Pharaoh's*
                      Butler, *&c.*
           Swan feen reft on *Socrates's* Lap, forefhew'd him *Pla‑
                to* a famous Scholar.
                Flying and pitching after on *Athens* Academick
                Gate, a great Mafter.
                His Neck piercing the Sky, *Plato* fearching
                greateft Myfteries.
Infenfibles, Vid. *Salt* in *Victuals.*
           7 fat Ears of Corn eat by 7 lean, *Pharaoh.*
           A Barly‑cake beats down a Tent, *Gideon's* Con‑
                queft.
           Church‑Ornaments feen fall off an Houfe‑top,
                fhew'd of a Bargain of Goods of a Minifter
                going off, tho the Goods were in poffieffion
                to *A.*
Perfons. Another comes to you, that is, you go to him.
           Vid. *Self* and *Another.*
           Beggar, Vid. *Grammar.*
           Friend feeing injure you, fhews of Injuries wil
                end to your good.
           Enemy *e con.*
           Known feen act, and fo will be your Courfe as is
                that Perfon.
           A's Phyfician feen prefcribing, fhew'd *A.* of taking
                Phyfick and happily.
           Crown his Wife, to a King fhew'd recovering a
                Dominion her Right.
           Thriving Man feen, fhews you in a Courfe alfo
                fuccefsful as his.
           Efculapius feen draw ones Humours together,
                fhew'd *A.* an Impofthume there.
           Dead Bifhop feen ftrike the Ground paftorally
                thrice, gave *A.* Victory there.   Vid. *Dead.*
           A Soldier would lie with *A's* Wife and pufh him
                away, this fhew'd *A.* tempted by her to op‑
                preffion.   *In*

In general. Circumſtance. Unable for Action, that is, mentally reſol
  (1)   againſt it.
            Ill to be done ſhews Danger ; but done, Hu
             & e contra.
            One handling Bread ſtole *A*'s Clothes, t
             ſhew'd a Baker ſlandering *A.*
            Direct, vid. *Grammar.*
                    Sup in the Enemies Camp, that is,
                    a Priſoner.
                    Departing out of Priſon, to a P
                    ſoner ſhew'd Continuance.
            Near done in hopes, not yet finiſhed a
             therefore good.
       Variety. Seeing a Croſs carried along, threats you Sadneſs
          Practiſe what you have learn'd, proſper in yo
           Profeſſion.
          Carrying and giving is better than receiving a
           being carried.
          Teaching more advanc'd Scholars than he had,
           a Schoolmaſter ſhew'd great Self-improvement
          Buſineſs doing in general, ſhews of our Deſire
             do it, but fruſtrate.
                Wrong done, ſhew'd of Care without Su
                ceſs.
                Setting others Boys about it, ſhew'd
                Neglect iſſuing to others Hopes.
                His Plow running too deep, ſhew'd
                undertaking too much Plowing.
                Managing of great Concerns threats wit
                Obſtructions.

Abuſe, Salt ſeen flung in a Ditch, ſhew'd *A.* of a vile Uſe of goo
    things.
Aid, vid. *Help* infra.
Alter your Prayers, change your Deſires.   Vid. *Change* in *Senſe.*
Amendment ſhews of good Alterations according.
Begin the King's Health to prodigal Drunkards, encourage Waſters o
    you.
         A thing backwards, diſcover of its End before you find its B
         ginning.
Bind, Vid. *Rope* in *Commodities.*
         Binding Trees as Withy, *&c.* in Friendſhip good.
                 in fear of Priſons, bad.
                 in Sickneſs alſo Joy is very bad.
         Bound hand and foot, that is, diveſted of all Powe
           and Authority.
             Such Binding undone, your threatne
            Power retriev'd.
          Your Neck ſeeming, beware how you give
         thers Credit.   Bin

Bind. Bound Lion feen brought A. fhew'd him of a great Enemy taken
    Birds feen, threat with hinder'd Hopes.
    Legs feen by an Eel, fhew'd A. of Servants hinder'd
    by Enemies.
Loofe Apparel, loofe Reputation.
Tied your Hands being behind you, fhews you difabled in Actions.
    A's Feet by the Dead, fhew'd of Knaves obftructing his
    greater Actions.
    Chains, vid. *Prifon* in *Houfe-forts.*
Bounded Water by a Ciftern, fhew'd of a Friend skreening A. from
Trouble.
Brawling feeing themfelves, to fome has given them Gain.
Breaking up anothers Houfe, fhews of getting anothers Eftate.
    Vid. *Walls* in *Building.*
    Window the Iron Bar loofe, thro fome Profpect of their
    in your Power.
    Unknown inviting you in, by an unexpected Method en-
    couraging.
    Down of Altars, threated of Death to follow.
    Into anothers Field, getting away his Husbandry.
        Orchard, getting away his Stock.
    A Lord-Mayors Houfe, unwarrantably prefuming on his
    like Authority.
Out of a Wall Water feen, forefhew'd of Trouble and Sad-
    nefs.
In two a Pillar of Bread feen, fhew'd A. buying in a Years
    Provifion of Bread at twice he defign'd at once.
    A Chriftal feen by A's Wife's handling, fhew'd A. immodeft-
    ly confounding his Purity, &c.
Breach making, fhews of Reconciliations.
Broken Arms, vid. *Body.*
    Bafon yours feen, threats your Maid-Servants Death.
    Bridg going over, fhews of Fear, or Expedient o'er Revenues
    and Troubles failing.
    Clothes having, to fome has fhewn Wounds in the fame
    Place.
    Clock feen, is Danger to all, efpecially the Sick.
        Into the leffer Pieces, the worfe.
Coloffus feen, fhews of fome learned Man dying.
        Pieces, left his Scholars.
    Eggs feeing an ill Sign, project Embrio's foil'd.
    Gall being, threated Deceit between Man and Wife.
        Vid. *Human Body.*
    Houfe, vid. *H.*
Key having to his Trunk, to a Servant lofing fome Aid in
    his Secrets.
    Leg having, fhews your Friend or Servant dies.
        To others, Bufinefs by them mifcarrying.
                Breaking

Breaking. Broken Leg Left being by a Plow, to *A.* a Carters Meſſage breaking his Siſters Friendſhip.

     Thigh ſeeming, to a Maid ſhew'd her marrying in a ſtrange Country.

     Printed Papers ſeeing, finding good Inſtructions from ill Treatments.

       Of the Bible ſee, find good Inſtructions from imagin'd Inconſiſtencies there.

     Ring ſhews of loſing Power, Wife or Children.

       To ſome, of loſing a Lover or Relation.

     Staff, vid. *Goods.*

     Sword anothers ſeeing, ſhews of his Power or Reſentment deſtroy'd.

       Tip on't, the preſent Sharpneſs of its Reſentment only remov'd.

     Thigh, vid. *Leg* ſupra.

     Tree ſeen. threats one in Houſe with Diſeaſes.

     Trunk, vid. Goods.

     Veſſels, vid. *Goods.*   Vid. *Baſon* ſupra.

     Walls ſeen, to a Seaman threated his Ships Sides.

       Vid. *Wall* in *Building.*

Breeding a young Stag, Fornication with ſome Servant.

     A young Fox, allowing your ſelf in an indirect crafty way of Gain.

     A Sow ſeen breeding Pigs, ſhew'd of a good Profit, but farrowing gave it Perfection.

Bribing, procuring by Merit, Overawing, or Reſpect.

Brewing in his Hall, ſhew'd *A.* buying Grains for his Hogs.

Buffet, vid. *Puſh* infra.

Burden loaden with, ſhew'd *A.* Sickneſs.

Burſting Aſs ſeen, threats with perpetual Diſcord and Poverty.

Buſy being, that is, reaſonably convinc'd you ought to be ſo.

     Your Enemy ſee, diſcover and prevent a Courſe would hurt you.

     Officious your Friend ſeen, threat you with Flattery.

Carry, vid. *Travel.*

Caſting in general, vid. *Fling* infra.

     Stones, that is, ſpeaking injurious Words.

     Dirt, that is, aſperſing with a more ſticking Infamy.

Catching fine Birds, interrupting glorious Projectors.

     A Sparrow-Hawk, gave Gain.

     Rats a Cat ſeen, ſhew'd of Anger at Servants for loitering.

     Fiſh if many and great, ſhews of good Profit.

     Mony another dropping it, gaining by his unheeded Expence

     Your Arms ſee your Maſtiff for a Stone caſt at him, from your Baily, &c. threaten to leave you for Words, &c.

Cauſe Fire out of *Charon's* Houſe burnt ¼ the City, a Conſpiracy there deſtroy'd ⅓ its Inhabitants.

     Slighted, for Birth literal.

                                  Cauſ

Cause. Joy without cause, pure Joy.

For Mony found when none, Sorrow thro Miftakes.

With Child and know not the Father, to a Woman fhew'd marrying a Stranger.

Ceafing, vid. *Leave* infra.

Change, vid. *Sight* in *Senfe.*

In general, fhews of Change as is the thing.

Climb, vid. *Afcend* in *Travel.*

Clip'd Mony bid for Faggots, that is, lefs than worth.

Command, vid. *Words,* and *Mafter* in *Family.*

Compel, vid. *Force* infra.

Confum'd by Lightning, Death.

Cover'd in general, vid. *Hide* infra.

Your Father's Nakednefs, aid and credit out his Poverty.

Bodily from you fee fomewhat, that is, mentally conceal'd.

Up in a Cart, that is, manag'd by a Farmer in the dark.

The Earth feen by her Iffue, *Cyrus*'s Mother.

2 Wings covering *Europe* and *Afia, Darius*'s Kingdom.

Veil'd Perfons feen, fhew of conceal'd Refolutions and Refentments.

Women in black with cover'd Heads meet you, Courfes of Deceit oppofe you, or Schemes that are afham'd to be known.

Cut in general, vid. *Fight.*   Vid. *Knife* in *Goods.*

Vid. *Wound* in *Phyfick.*

Clothes. Old Shoos to pieces, mafter Inconveniences of Poverty.

Vid. *Clothes.*

To pieces, to fome has fhewn their Houfe falling.

A Thred one feen, fhew'd of his peremptorily interrupting fome Courfe, &c.

Parts. Your Fingers cut or fee them cut by another, threats you Damage.

Flefh with Iron, threats you with fome grievous Sicknefs.

Throat being by another, receive Injury, &c.

You cut anothers, you do him Injury, &c.

Forehead fow'd up well again, a Difgrace eafily excus'd.

Off your Ear being, threats you fome Friendfhip loft.

Left Ear, deftroy your accus'd Friend unheard.

A Bit of Flefh from the Belly by a Butcher, abates Pride as if fpaid, &c.

His Leg being, to one fick of the Gout, fhew'd Recovery.

To others, travel for ever away, or be at a Lofs in their Arts.

Vid. *Privities* in *Body.*

Perfon. Their Father to pieces and eat him, fhew'd *A.* and *B.* his Sons inheriting him on dying.

Cut.

Cut. Perſon. Self by Seamen ſeem, your ſelf be reputed as great a Beggar as to ſome hazard Trade.

     A. entring anothers Houſe, and finding him aſleep, cut out
his Fat and Excrement ſtinking Guts, and carried them
off, that is, rob'd him.

Beaſts. Horſes or Aſſes Tail ſeen cut off, threat of Miſery *in futuro*, as to ſuch Riches States.

     Bulls Horns ſeen cut off, ſhews of ſome great Man diſ-
abled.

     Cats Claws cut off, ſhew'd of a Thief diſabled.

     Bacon ſeen cut, ſhew'd of an Acquaintance's Death.

Things. Doors cut to pieces, Reſolutions deſtroy'd.

     A Flail cutting, to a Servant ſhew'd threſhing next day.

     Cutting up a Turf in a Field, *A.* ſaw a Woman under it,
he died in trying to get her.

     Early Bread, ſhew'd Rejoicing.

     Down Trees ſeen, ſhew'd of Loſs of Authority, and
Hopes diſappointed.

     Having a dead fat Ox in Houſe fit to be cut up, ſhew'd *A.*
having 2 to ſell, ill to keep longer.

Danger get out of, that is, ſecure ſome hazardous Point.

     A Fly under an Horſe, ſhew'd of a miraculous little Ill.

Deliver'd at Stake, ſhew'd *A.* of making Reſtitution of Wrong with
Diſgrace.

     From Enemies perſecuting you, gives you Glory and Tri-
umph.

     Dangers, literal, as *&c.*

     Deliver your Son, free your Expectation, *&c.*

Deſtroying a Place, ſhews of a Deceit, as *&c.* as a ſelf-vacating of a
Power of Circumſtance, *&c.*

     To ſome, a Deſtruction of a State of things, *&c.*

     A Book, confounding the Method to have it.

     Vid. *Ruin* infra.

Dip a Lap-Dog in Water, make a Gentlewoman take Phyſick.

Dip'd Bread in Hony eating, give Wealth with Wiſdom.

     Vid. *Water Action.*

Directing us one ſeen, ſhews us of a Friend aiding us, as *&c.* or a
Courſe aſſiſting, *&c.*

     Directions wanting, being at a Fault for Aid, *&c.*

     Vid. *Tools in Trade.*   Vid. *Words in Diſcourſe.*

Diſturb one ſick by working, affront one to Diſhumour by your Methods.

     In a Chamber by a Barns Door, *A's* Servant about an Hog.

Diſturb'd ſhiting by his Creditors Daughter peeping, ſhew'd *A.* fearing
common Expence for his paying Debts.

     Preaching, to a Miniſter ſhew'd his Pariſhioners ſlighting his
Doctrine thro Quarrels.

Diverſion, vid. *D.*

                                                      Done

Done things, vid. *Action general* supra. Vid. *End in Part.*

Drawing out his Bowels an Eagle seen and shewing them in publick, gave A. a famous Son.

Drop in general, vid. *Fall* infra.

Iron down Stairs, shew'd A. losing hard Gains at Cards.

Your measuring Rod out of your Hand, shew'd A. carelesly desisting building.

A Ring in Hay, to a Maid threats her Virginity.

Vid. *Ring* in *Ornaments.*

Mony another catching, that is, be larger in some Expence than design'd.

Handled and get it up again, retrieve the hazard of some Expence Mischief.

Ease great, to the Sick Death.

An House on Fire easily put out, a ruinous Course easily averted.

Embrace, vid. *Passion.*

Endeavours shew of Endeavours. Vid. *Try* infra.

Waking endeavouring in literal Dreams, assures you Success.

Endeavouring an Horse seen, shews the Estate will get free of it self.

A Dog seen, assures such Service will deliver it self.

Your self wake, assures you God will prosper you.

Fall in general, vid. *Drop* supra. Vid. *Rise* infra.

Vid. *Lightning* in *Air* critically. Vid. *Lying down* in *Posture.*

Let something, offer it to another where 'tis accepted, but then upon his sneaking.

Before another, that is, despair of opposing him or his Course, as &c.

Deep down, threats with greatest Miscarriage unto Despair.

Unhurt to your no Personal Damage.

From another, that is, leave his Party or Errors.

Heaven a Dart seen and wounding A. in the Foot, shew'd him dying Snake-stung.

An House Top tearing, being sensible of Danger of breaking up House, &c.

A Tower, despairing of surest Hopes.

A Precipice, missing in some Difficulty.

But catch e'er down, recover from Despair.

A Tree, miss of some great Hope of Inheritance, &c.

Your Horse and break your Neck, lose your Dignity and die.

An Ass, threats with Poverty or Sickness.

His Throne unable to get in again, to a Prince Dethronement irrecoverable.

Seat the same, to a private Man of his Office.

Into a Ditch or Pit being, cast in a Law-Suit.

Seeing his Father so, shew'd his Death to A.

Bb Fall

Fall. Let into a Dairy-Room, where confin'd in Deſpair under Ground, ſhew'd *A.* puzled with a Dairy-man's Roguery in a Bargain.

Dirt, threats with Diſturbance or Treachery from ſome one.

Water, vid. *W.* and *River* ibid.

To ſome, it threats a Flegmatick Diſeaſe.

To ſome, Death or Danger to their Perſon.

A troubled Fountain, ſhew'd of Accuſation.

A Well have, Injury by what ſhould aid you, as Loſs by Merchandize, &c.

A clear Fountain, gives Honour and Joy.

Your Hand ſee ſomewhat, find ſomewhat become yours, as by Title.

Off your Bed your Clothes finding, threats you with Change of Lodging.

Crown from your Head, threats you Loſs of Dignity.

Old torn Shoos feeling, threats you in preſent greateſt Poverty.

Hair, vid. *H.* in *Body.*

On you Cream finding, gives you Grace of the Holy Ghoſt.

An Houſe ſeen, oppreſſes you to Ruin.

Get from under it, recover your former State.

Upon the Ground in general, threats with Diſhonour and Scandal.

Another falling ſo, deſpair thro anothers Deſpair.

A Bridg, deſpairing in Obſtruction to your ſelf and others.

The Ground from on high, is as Diſtreſs in Ambition.

Going off pretty well on it, ſhuffling off the Misfortune.

Falling. Things. Dirt from Houſe Tiles, ſhew'd of Scandal about tiling Houſes.

Crown of white Flowers from Heaven for *A.* to wear, ſhew'd him Death near.

Fire from Heaven on him in Rays and not hurting him, to *Adrian* Empire.

Beam of an Houſe ſeen, ſhews of ſome great Man in the Oeconomy dying.

Church Ornaments from an Houſe Top ſeen, ſhew'd *A.* miſſing a Bargain of a Miniſter's Goods.

Fruit unripe from the Tree ſeen, ſhew'd of an untimely Death.

Houſe Pillars ſeen, threats ſome in Family Death.

Senate Pinnacle, ſhew'd *Cæſar's* Death.

Roof ſeen, to *Cæſar's* Wife ſhew'd his Death alſo.

Falling. Things. Riches from a Shop feen, fhew'd of Dung wafh'd a-
way in Waft to a Farmer.

Your Account Book fee, retrieve your Defpair as to
keeping your Accounts.

Unhurt, without Damage interfering.

Moon feen, fhew'd of a great Woman dying.

Mountain on a Valley feen, fhew'd of good Men oppreft
by a great Lord.

Sky feen, threated with Guilt and Crimes.

Afcending tho feen, has given Honour and
Dignity.

Sun on an Houfe, Danger of Fire or Hurt by the
Judges Sentence.

Stars feen from Heaven and acting, fhew'd of a great
popular Man rifing.

One feen fall and another rife, to a Servant
fhew'd his Mafter dying and his Son fucceeding.

Perfons. Husband feen fall off a Precipice, to a Wife Widowhood.

His Eyes falling into his Feet, fhew'd A. his Daughters
marrying his Servants.

An Eagle on A's Head feen, forethreated him Death.

Manner. Man and Horfe feen fall, threats Life and
Fortune in Danger.

Running in full fpeed, the Mifchief thro your
own Fault.

Faftned in general, vid. *Bind* fupra.

To a Cart and drawing in it, Servitude or Sicknefs.

Tree chiefly if dead, threats with the Torture of the
Wheel.

In Dirt, fettled in abfolute Trouble and Difgrace thro Folly,
&c.

Shovel'd away tho, promifes Remedy.

Stak'd down, abfolutely confiu'd.

Fidling before the Lord-Keeper with Writings, fhew'd A. doing fillily
what accountable before him for.

Finifh'd, vid. *End* in *Part.*   Vid. *Done* in *Acts general.*

Fling in general, vid. *Caft* fupra.

Off Lice from your Clothes, avoid Poverty, as *&c.* in Repute.

A Ball, raife a Difpute, and if high to Advantage.

A Serpent low, reject fome fubtle Enemy with Contempt.

A Box at fome coming up Stairs, fhew them they are but Guefts.

A Sword out of your Hand, reject the Ufe of fome Refentment.

Down, vid. *Building.*

Away her Arms *Minerva* feen, to *Domitian* threated Deftruction.

A Ball feen, fhew'd of a Contention Occafion avoided.

Fling away a Shilling matter, not of fuch an Expence for a Purpofe.
One into a Pit, caufe him to be imprifoned.
Your Snot about, vent your offenfive Crudities in publick.
Flung down headlong from Heaven, to *Cæfar* ftabbing.
By a Lion, threats you with Lofs of Honour.
Lofing your Teeth on it, that is, your Kindred.
His Field Gate feen, fhew'd *A.* of his propos'd Journy baulk'd.
Into a Veffel of fcalding Pitch, fhew'd *A.* of vomiting Choler.
The Fire feeing himfelf, fhew'd *A.* fick of a Fever.
Somewhat, fhew'd of putting it to the defperateft Iffue.
Your Ruler flung at one is return'd, that is, your Orders by him are obey'd.
A Bit of Bread at *A.* feen at the Houfe of the dead, fhew'd *A.* too fick to eat a Bit in Company.
A Dab of Mortar by a Mad-man at you, your Rafhnefs uncements Society.
Part of an Arch Mortar the worfe, and as of a Court Door in regard of fome Oeconomy Approach.
Off your Clothes feeming, to fome lay by Care for Pleafure.
With no Defign of putting them on again, Death.
Horfe, lofs in fome Command, but with Hopes of Recovery, &c.
From his Throne a King feen, fhew'd of a Cuftom fubverted.
Forcing bodily, anfwers to refolving or compelling mentally.
Vid. *Break* fupra.
Compell'd, acting as by Intreaty, &c. at the Pleafure of another.
By the Shoulders, fhew'd *A.* of his Brethren requiring, &c.
Into an Houfe, by Law or Menace attaining to fomewhat anfwerable.
Bawdy-Houfe, a Profit of a corrupt and dangerous Nature.
To climb a fearful Precipice, punifhing by Juftice.
Forc'd by a Pain at Heart to ceafe flying, mov'd thro a bad Wife to ceafe projecting, &c.
From an high Hill of good Profpect to a Valley, from Command to Poverty.
At a Noble's Chappel, a Piety of Grandeur impelling, &c.
Away by one, conftrain'd by reafonable Defires according.
On Shipboard to ferve their Family, Advantage in Hazard.
Your Clothes from you, threats you Death or Deftruction near.

Frighted,

Frighted, vid. *Threat* infra.   Vid. *Terrifying Beasts* in *Creatures.*
   Shews of some just Occasions accordingly for it offered.
   Fright your Horse, put your Estate in a State of Despair.
  By another, that is, having an Aversion to his Courses.
   An Elephant, threats with Sickness.
    Vid. *Ghost* and *Spirit* in *Spirits.*
 | Others Girls seen by Madmen, find your Positiveness confounding
   others imaginary Hopes.
    Boys seen from the right by a Monster, shew'd *A.* shun-
    ning an Absurdity to Profit.
Gathering, vid. *Prepare* in *Quality.*
   Things by degrees, shew'd of learning by Memory.
   Together Arrows intending, wicked Deceits as to some one.
   Flowers gives Mirth and Jollity, and the livelier the better.
   Stones and laying them aside for Defence, having a Mishap
   may require the Aid of Many.
   Up Gold and Silver from the Ground, threats with Deceit and
   Loss.
   Fruits in Season gives Profit, as are their Qualities.
    Out of Season ill, and shews of Labour for such Men.
    Apples seen, threats with Vexation from some one.
Grasp a thing, command it at pleasure.
Hal'd, vid. *Forc'd* supra.
   By a Waggon as travelling, being at the Command of an Hind.
    Officers, vid. *Proceedings* in *Law.*
    Devils, vid. *D.* in *Spirits.*
    Many unknown, odd Reasonings perswading and moving
    you.
   To a Place unknown by the Dead, threats with violent Illness.
    Overcome by them in it, Death.
    Drawing your self back, Recovery.
Handle, vid. *Possess.*
Hasting by *A.* Crowds seen, shew'd him of a neglectful Treatment.
   Away about Business, pressing swiftly on in Designs.
Haunted, vid. *Spirits* and *Company.*
Help in general, vid. *Fly* in *Air.*   Vid. *Lead* in *Travel.*
    Vid. *Deliver* supra.
   Remedies us'd, be indispos'd according.   Vid. *Physick.*
Help'd by a Friend unknown, an unaccountable Course aiding.
   Miller, Aid thro hardest Labour.
   False Gods, gives Aid as are their suppos'd Power.
   Person unknown with a Sword, deliver'd by an unexpected
   Force.
    In general, in Circumstance of odd aiding
    Courses according.
  To get things, vid. *Get* in *Possess.*
 With a Sword driving away a Quack would beat him, shew'd *A.*
 deferring Physick by a Journy.
     Bb 3   Help'd

Help'd to deſcend a Precipice by a Cart, to get off a Difficulty by a
    Farmer.

    Aſcend from the Sea by a piece of a Ship, help'd in
    Straits by a Domeſtick.

Perſons. A younger Son from falling, ſecure a doubtful new
    Husbandry to Profit.

    A Divine order his Books, diſpoſe in Method ſome di-
    vine Subject anſwerable.

Hiding in general, Vid. *Cover'd* ſupra.

    It ſhews of mentally concealing, &c.

    Behind *A.* let his Methods or Intereſts conceal and
    protect your Methods.

Your Apothecary ſee, your Remedy in ſome ill for a while
    will be dormant accordingly.

Your ſelf, threats you with Flight or Obſcurity.

    In a Den from a Genius deſcending from Heaven,
    to *A.* by Retirement avoiding a Plague-Infection.

    In ſtanding Corn, truſting to an Oration *extempore.*

        From Robbers, ſecuring your Purpoſe from
        Error thereby.

    From an Enemy, being in ſhame as to ſuch Circum-
    ſtance wherein he's your Enemy.

    In a Tomb, ſhews of your acting wickedly.

    Rotten Mouth by your Noſe, covering your corrupt
    Speech Deſigns by your perſonal regard.

Your Son ſeen, threats your Expectation near at a loſs.

Things. Words. Vid. *Words.*

    Sun ſeen, ſhews of Secreſy, Blindneſs, or Loſs of
    Children.

        By Smoke, ſhew'd of Errors darkning
        cleareſt Truths.

    Somewhat under 2 Saddles, by 2 Journies procuring it.

    Veſſels and Water underground, falling a publick Spec-
    tacle to decay.

    Mony got for his Wife's Fleſh ſold at Shambles,
    ſhew'd *A.* proſtituting her for Gain, and go-
    ing off on it.

    Seek it ſetting aſide ſomewhat for it, borrow it
    againſt all Excuſes.

    Viper found hid in a Woman's Breaſt, threats her Rape
    or Miſcarriage.

Your dirty naked Feet, your beggarly fooliſh Tranſactions
    conceal.

Hinder'd going out of ones Houſe, to the Sick Continuance.

Sight by Miſts, Conſiderations obſcured by Error.

    Houſes, Converſations and Family Oeconomies, doing
    the like.

Entering a Room the Door being wanting, your Addreſs fails
    or is miſtook.
                                Hinder'd

Hinder'd by another, shews your Proceeds obstructed by him, or such a like Course.

Ringing a Bell by a Spirit, Frustration and Loss in publick Undertakings.

Kept from home almost by foreign Enemies, asham'd to return near for Duns.

Being like to be kill'd only, shews of Deliverance from some great Danger.

Breathing, to some Drowning.

　　to Rogues it has shewn Imprisonment.

Unknown Woman in Mourning prevented A's Actions, the Opinion of Death near discouraging him.

Taking the Sacrament, shew'd A. of an Hypocrite hurting him.

By an Enemy seeming, gives you Expedition of Business.

Finding Paper by Writings, shew'd A. vainly looking for a Security where all his Estate settled.

Holding things in hand, that is, acting, discoursing, or designing according.

　　A Rod see a Master, subject your self to such a Discipline, &c.

　　A Sword see your self, shews you in pursuit of some Revenge &c. or Resentment.

Held by one unknown, obstructed by an odd Course, as &c.

An Iron Ring, promises you Security, but with Hardship.

A Pall in hand she could not make snack, shew'd A. Recovery of Infirmity, but not cleverly.

A Pillar, shew'd A. of trusting in GOD.

Gold, threats you as falling from your Wish.

　　That you have in hand you know not whence, command somewhat as good.

A Plow, shew'd A. of directing its Managery.

A Sword in hand, threats you with Law, War, or Dispute.

A Scepter in hand, gives Royal Power.

Your Privities in your hand, shews of your leaving Procreation.

A Light in hand, assures you good Information, and that you are Master of your Art.

　　To some accomplish their Ends, and enjoy their Wishes.

　　To some enjoy their Loves.

　　To some overcome their Enemies.

Held by another, threats you with Designs obstructed.

　　to the Sick Continuance in't.

　　　　Except very ill, then live

　　to some their Designs discover'd and punish'd.

Holding. A Light held by another, to some their Light put out *e con.*
      The Dead, prevented by Knavery.
       Devil, if well-shap'd, gives Gain.
    Another, is as commanding him at pleasure.
      's Hand, prevent somewhat he'd do.
      's Feet, the same in greater Actions.
     As to strengthen him, shews of aiding him.
     A stubborn Woman before you in a Field, having her
      Fate in a Dispute.
      Till she stink, till of scandalous Disrepute to
      you.

Hurried, Vid. *Forc'd* supra.
Hurt, Vid. *Misfortune* infra.   Vid. *Threat* infra.
   Vid. *Body in general.*   Vid. *Ability* in *Quality.*
  Ill to be done shews Danger; but done, Hurt.
  Leg by a Plow, Pride thro Farming affronting Relations.
  Parts. Ears being, shews of ill News approaching.
    Fingers, Vid. *Body.*
    With Iron, Damage as to Desolation.
  Altars breaking down, shew'd *A.* of Death to follow.
  By a Man, that is, literally ; or a Course as is that Man.
    Friend, have an Hurt that will prove to your good at the
    last.
   A Stag fearing, in terror of hurt by Merchandize.
  Your Son says Boys hurt your Trees, that is, it appears your E-
  state Profits are diverted by others.
  Embalment seeing not hurt by the Carcase, shew'd of G O D's fa-
   tal Predictions adorable to us, tho the Ends of wicked Men ap-
   pearing therein are abominable.
  Unhurt his Account Book seen fall, shew'd *A.* retrieving without
   damage his Despair in keeping Accounts.
Ill, Vid. *Hurt* supra, and *Misfortune* infra.
Imitating another, shews imitating him.
    To others mocking them.
    Vid. *Like* in *Sense.*
Inclose your Court, retrench expensive Resorts to you.
Interpose in a Difference is literal.   Vid. *Reconcile* in *Fight.*
Interrupted Travel shew'd of Business left imperfect.
    Prayers being by the Devil, shew'd *A.* of losing a Child.
   Snap up another in Discourse, by counteracting prevent his
   Actions.
Jumping shews of irregular Efforts, as walking of plain Proceeds.
   Fly jumpingly, project by gradual Efforts.
    O'er Men Servants lying down, project to avoid their
    too hard Labour.
   Thro a Gatehouse, resolving forthwith on a Farming Method.
   Cross a Ditch, forcing thro a scandalous but gainful Difficulty.
   Jump'd at by a Dog, abruptly assaulted by an Enemy.
               Jumping

Jumping out of his Pen *A.* feeing Sheep, fhew'd him at a lofs in Goods fetch'd from him.

Down on an Houfe-leads off a Precipice, falling abruptly to a worfe Oeconomy.

Knocking at *A*'s Door one heard, fhew'd him of admitting a new O-verture.

Heard at your Bed-fide, Vid. *Grammar.*

Another's Houfe-door, fhews you of wanting fome Con-verfe or Dealing there.

Your felf at a Gatehoufe, that is, making fome new farming Overture.

Laid to the Mouth, Vid. *M.* in *Body.*

In his Bed *A.* finding a fweaty Stone, fhew'd of his bedding his Wife infirm thro Sicknefs.

Afide Stones for his Defence *A.* feeing, forefhew'd him a Mifhap might require the Aid of many.

Leave in general, vid. *Part* in *Travel.*

The Sick, be in defpair as to their Condition.

Your Husbandman behind, aft your felf unhusbandly.

Another, ceafe to regard him if literal.

With a Watcher, not abfolutely tho.

Behind the Dead, efcape the Cheat or Difappointment fear'd.

A Robber, defift fome erroneous Courfe to certain lofs.

Others, fhews of Negleft or Contempt as is the Perfon.

In a Room, ceafe Tranfaction with them as is that Room.

A Judg, aft illegally even to Controverfy.

A green Bough Death feen, fhew'd *A.* of his Death ef-cap'd in drowning by fuch a Bough.

Your Whip, be fomeway at a fault in your Command.

A Chamber, vid. *C.* in *Houfe.*

A Tavern, as told, for *Glocefter* Folks, part with a Revenue de-fign'd for the Poor.

Poifon you handled for fear, forbear a Courfe offering as perni-cious to Health.

Left all Curfes out of the Bible, forefhew'd to *A.* all Happinefs near.

Fire to be blown up by the Wind, Mony to be got by Repu-tation.

By your Husband, that is, he in that proves of no Aid to you.

Behind by a good Husband, threats you failing in your Huf-bandry.

Your Phyfician, fhews you in fome matter without Remedy, as *&c.*

Ceafing ill Promifes, all good near.

From feeming as dead, fhew'd of avoiding Knavery.

Fighting, fhew'd *A.* of yielding in a Difpute.

Leave

Leave. Ceaſing from hearing another pray, leaving to regard his D
           ſires.
           Men to converſe Women, that is, go fro
             Action to mere Theories.

Loaded with Clothes *A.* ſeeing his Tenant's Wife, foreſhew'd of ſu
   Tenant's overſtocking.

Make, Vid. *Trade.*   Vid. *Domeſtick Action.*

Mangled Meat have in houſe, have Farm-profits order'd againſt all Di
   cretion.

Means, by your Hand ſave you, by your Actions preſerve you.
       Vid. *Cauſe* ſupra.

Melted in your Houſe Salt ſeen, threats you with Loſs of Rents.

Mending things faulty, gives you an happy Uſage of them.
       Fences ſhew'd of repairing Houſes.
       His Shoos, ſhew'd *A.* going Foot-Journies.
       His Houſe, ſhew'd *A.* paying of Debts.
       A Baſe Viol carrying to be mended, ſhew'd of ones Humou
         reprov'd as grum.

Misfortune, to the Rich Miſery.
       to the Poor and Miſerable good, as capable of it.
         Vid. *Good* in *Quality,* and *Hurt* ſupra.
       Time to be done is Danger.
         Done is Hurt.
         Told to outlive it, ſhew'd *A.* that day ſomeway avoi
          ing it.
       Meet a Friend in it, that is, ſuch a Courſe aids you as is th
         Perſon.
       Complaining thereof, ſhews of Amendment, and as uſual
         follows.
       Befalling your Brother or Enemy ſeen, promiſes you all good.
       Miſerable ſee your Enemy, that is, be your ſelf happy where
         he's your Enemy.
       Done you by a Friend or his Wife, ſhews you of an Evil end
         ing well.
       Aiding others afflicted by Robbers, helping to rectify their e
         forc'd Errors.

Miſs your Blow at a Snake, fail of overcoming an Enemy.

Miſtake, vid. *Soul.*   Model, vid. *Platform* infra.

Moving in general, vid. *Quiet* infra.
       Swift the Stars ſeen, threats you mad or ſad.
       The Tail a Cat ſeen, threats with thieviſh Treachery.
       The Heaven ſeen, declares of Myſteries.
       Leaves ſeen, foreſhew'd of Report and common Fame.
     Motion in general ſhews of Change and Inconſtancy in Event.

Neceſſary, unneceſſary things buying, threats with Prodigality.
       Your Tenant ſeen in neceſſity threats your own Husbandry i
       A three-horn'd Beaſt ſeen, ſhew'd of a Dominion ready f
       a Conqueſt.

                                    Negle

Neglect shews of Neglect.

Offending another, to a Boy shews beating as Revenge follows.

       to a Youth Vexation from some one.

       to an old Man teasing from foolish Behaviour.]

Offer, Vid. *Endeavour* supra.   Vid. *Possess* and *Discourse.*

Officious, vid. *Busy* supra.

Open, Vid. *Shut* infra.   Vid. *Door* and *Window* in *House-parts.*

Another's Door, reverse his Resolutions.

Your Door to another, admit him so far in your Oeconomy Resolves.

A Door seen open to *A.* at a Judg's back, shew'd him the Controversy to be at his will.

Shew some Chest or Coffer, that is, afterward discover some Secret.

Room to a Street entering, shew'd *A.* of conversing a travelling Pedlar.

Earth of a Field seen, shew'd of the Secret of a Dispute discover'd.

Cut, vid. *Cut* supra.

Your Ancestor's Tomb see, find his Life examin'd after his Death.

To others Death of the Master or some one in Family.

Breast seen, shew'd of Secrets reveal'd.

Fair Tapestry seen, shew'd of good News.

Your Grave and come out, retrieve you miraculously from Death.

Your Window keeping to view, that is, becoming shewish of your private Affairs.

Opposing mentally is actually resisting.

Bodily is mentally or by Discourse.

Oppress'd by one unknown, ruin'd by false Counsels.

Perfect } Vid. *Done* in *Acts general.*
Perform'd }

Permit, vid. *Suffer.*

Persecuting shews hating.

Persecuted, forc'd in Designs to another's will.

Picking in eating, fidlingly nice in choice of Profit.

Up Guineas in Street-dirt, enriching you to the Scandal of your publick Converse.   Vid. *Gather* supra.

Pickpocket, vid. *Person* in *Grammar.*   Place, vid. *Laid* supra.

Prepare, Vid. *Quality.*   Vid. *Victuals.*   Vid. *Gather* supra.

Platform of the Devil destroying, shew'd *A.* escaping Death.

Preserve you from Hurt often is literal.

Your Malt, secure your Maltman unoffended.

Vid. *Defence* in *Fight.*   Vid. *Sister* in *Grammar Person.*

Press'd being by a Friend, gave Sickness with easy Recovery.

Enemy, gave Sickness with great Danger.

Preventing shews of preventing.

Pull

Pull off a Thorns Boughs, gives you Victory over fome Enemy.

    Off your Clothes your felf, voluntarily lay by your Dignity.

        To fome lay by Cares for Pleafures.

        By others pull'd off, fhews of your Reputa
tion or Dignity forc'd from you.

Down fome mighty Weed, expofe fome great Pretender.

    A Bell flying in the Air, fhew'd to *A.* of commanding
reigning Fever.

Rooted out your Beard being, threats you with great Anger.

        Hair off your Head, threats you with Lofs o
Friends.

Punch'd with the Finger by a Spirit, teas'd with Imputation of bein
a Cheat.

Punifhment, beating and chiding Inferiors alike, promifes of their A
mendment.

    Bearing bodily, being under great Tribulation mentally.

Pufhing another, that is, exhorting him.

    Down one unknown, fhew'd *A.* of rejecting falfe Counfels.

    Back a Wheel approaching, removing a new Change of For
tune coming.

    Afide fomewhat, laying it by in ones Reafon in fcorn.

Buffet, Vid. *Fight.*

Pufh'd down by a Prodigal, ruin'd by his like Courfes.

    About by a Gueft, confounded in Freedom thro his Gran
deur and Refpect.

    Out of Bed by her Husband, to a Wife fhew'd of his Ex-
hortation to part for Sicknefs.

    Away by a tutelar GOD or Saint, threats your Fate ac-
cording helplefs.

    Throng'd by the Dead, near pin'd to Death by knavifh Methods.

    Thrufting againft you fee another, that is, find him pre-
fumptuoufly rude and daring.

Put, vid. *Laid* fupra.

Quiet, vid. *Lake* in *Water.*   Vid. *Move* fupra.

    Air, vid. *Air.*

    Seeing things is ill to all on Changes expected.

    Shews of our Confideration of things unapt for Action.

    Birds feen fo, fhew of Impediment in Bufinefs, as clamorous
ones fhew of Danger.

    An Horfe ftands on your mounting, and fo will your Tenant o
Friend be in your Obfervance.

Raging Sea feen, to Bufinefs threats Trouble.

    Vid. *Paffion* and *Mad* in *Phyfick.*

Raife, vid. *Rife* infra.   Reach, vid. *High* in *Pofture.*

Reflexion, feeing your Image in Water threats you with fhort Life.

    Vid. *Looking-glafs* in *Goods.*

Remedy, vid. *Help* fupra.   Remove, vid. *Travel.*

    vid. *Mend* fupra.

                Repetition,

Repetition, vid. *Former* in *Time.*

> Doing things again that were done before, shews of rectifying Omissions.
>
> Mock'd *A.* seem'd, as his Prayers repeated by a Ghost, this shew'd *A.* deluded in hottest Desires.
>
> Reenter his Mother's Womb, to a Traveller shew'd returning home again.

Rescue, vid. *Deliver* and *Help* supra.   Resist, vid. *Oppose* supra.

Rising from Bed with another's Daughter, ceasing from gaming, *&c.*

> Ceasing from Neglect, as *&c.*
>
> Vid. *Bed* in *Goods.*
>
> With him seeing a good Husband's Children, shew'd *A.* himself so every way industrious also.
>
> A Bier in a Church or Church-porch and run away, recover when given over.
>
> And not go off, deceives you with a seeming hop'd Recovery.
>
> The Dead seeming lying by you, desert your Colrogues.
>
> Rais'd on Leathers *A.* seeing his Coach, shew'd of his buying Harness to it.
>
> Stars, vid. *Fall* supra.
>
> Mountain seen, shews of some great Man appearing.
>
> Raise another upright, encourage him, as *&c.*
>
> Beasts out of the Sea, Governments from among the People.
>
> Rise and strut, that is, become active, and challenge and boast from Despair before.
>
> Stand on your Feet, perfects your Recovery from your dejected State.
>
> From lying on the Ground, from lowest Despair, as *&c.*

Rub your Pocket-mony looking like Brass till it become Silver, with Care and Pains retrieve your Pocket-plenty.

> 'd Rooms, shew of a Life of Delicacy and Plenty.
>
> Wheat till it have Scroff, shew'd *A.* treating his Friends to the Waste of his Plenty.

Ruffle others Boys, be rude to others Expectations.

Ruins, vid. *Destroying* supra.

> Vid. *Repair* in *Build* and *Mend.*
>
> Undoing a Man threats Sickness, and is as destroying a Constitution.
>
> Well-wink seen broke down, shew'd *A.* of Justice failing.
>
> An House seen on fire before you, forbids of your direct Proceeds, as *&c.*
>
> *A.* seeing one pull down his new Building, shew'd of his wittingly destroying his new Livelihood, *&c.*
>
> Of a Tomb seen, threats you with Banishment.

Ruins of a Furnace, vid. *Houſe*.

A Timber Fire of it ſeen made for *A.* ſhew'd of his getting a Treat, and ſpare Loan of Mony.

Window looking out of, threats you with a Proſpect of Deſigns unhappy according.

Foundring an Houſe ſeen, ſhew'd *A.* in a Method deſtructive of an Oeconomy Subſiſtence.

Save, vid. *Preſerve* ſupra.

Scrap'd Roots eating, threats Hurt thro Superfluity.

Scratch'd with Nails being, threats with Hurt fear'd from the Perſon by whom.

Another is deceive him, *& e con*, ſcratch'd being by him.

The Soles of your Feet being, threats you Loſs and Flattery.

Seek in general, is as mentally apply your ſelf in Care, as *&c.*

To buy ſomewhat and miſs it, be in Straits according.

Victuals, ſhews you fraught with vain Deſires of Gain, and as what will but get Victuals.

Your Husbandman, try to mend the Management of your Affairs.

Hat in a Market Town, that is, your Honour in doubt in ſome Sale.

Seiz'd by the Grand Senior's Guards, ſome great Man's Reaſonings fixing on you.

On in a Church-yard, ſhew'd *A.* of a Miniſter's Deſigns diverting him.

Shake off is as fling off *ſupra*.

Shelter'd from Rain by an Oak, aided in farming Charges by a Rent.

Shewing in general ſhews of acting, as in Poſſeſſion and with Glory.

Another ſomewhat, acquainting thereof till they deſire it.

A Cheſt or Coffer open, that is, diſcovering ſome Secret to him.

A way, directing him in a Method.

A Bill, acquainting him of its Uſe till he deſire it.

Your Buttery, make them long for your Entertainment.

Your Legs fleſhy and clean, diſcover to him how firm your Subſiſtence.

A Lord's Buttery, make them deſire ſuch a Fare of you.

Perſons. One Servant an ill Action of another, giving them exemplarily to ſee the ill Effects of it.

Somerſet-houſe as you walk about its Courts, act as if approaching to an impoſing Grandeur.

The dead ſomewhat, glorying in what you are fool'd by Knavery from claiming.

A dead Counteſs his upper Rooms, ſhew'd *A.* thinking to claim a neglected Royalty which he durſt not proceed in, when he offer'd at it for anothers Roguery.

Shewing

Shewing. Perfons. A Tradefman a Country-Houfe, fhew'd *A.* offering him a Profit could keep one.

A good Husband your new Purchafe, find it proving greatly to your good.

A Phyfician your Houfe rectify thoroughly, Matters in Diforder there.

Shewn by one his Stable, acquainted by him of his Riches.

His Property fhews of anothers fo glorying.

Her dead Father Meat not ready, her Apothecary by hiding on it fhew'd *A.* her Maid warning oft in Anger, becaufe chid for not faving Dinner for her Matter.

Things. A Funeral Ticket by an Angel, premonifh'd of a Friend's Death.

A Book and Receipt by his dead Father, literally *A.* found it there.

A new Pair of Shoos by an old Woman, to a Servant factioufly leave a prefent Service, as fhe had done others.

Shewn a Provifion Store by one unknown, find your own Straits remind you thereof.

Chambers by a fine Woman, difcovering a good Management of Plenty.

A Corps light in a River of Ships by a Thatcher, fhew'd *A.* his *London* Hatter calling on him, and who foon after died.

Gold in Hand by a Friend, convinc'd by him to have fuch Gain at Command.

A fine Houfe and Garden by the dead, imitate them, *&c.* to Profit.

You things by your Sifter, threats you baulk'd in Expectation according.

Shifting threats with Neceffities.

Shutting a Door, making fome negative Refolution.

Vid. *Door* and *Window* in *Houfe.* Vid. *Open* fupra.

Prifon Door feen, declares of Security.

A Window againft one, flightly hiding ones Defigns from them.

Up in a Room, confining in a private Converfe or Oeconomy State, as *&c.*

Himfelf in his Box, to *A.* fhew'd him retire himfelf from publick Avocations.

Taking out the Key, prohibiting difturbing Approaches on it.

Sliding your Horfe fearing, that is, your Art or Glory being in an Eclipfe.

Your Self on Ice, fhews of your hazardoufly flipping over Poverty Cares.

Snatch,

Snatch, vid. *Take* in *Apparel*.   Vid. *Take* in *Poſſeſs*.

Spoil, vid. *Waſt* infra.

     Suffering, threats with Loſs of Place and Ruin.

         By others, bearing their Charges.

     Anothers Hat, ſcorn to reſpect him.

        Sword, diſable the Virtue of his Diſpute or Reſentmen

Spur'd as an Horſe being, threats you Danger from ſome Man at Arm

     he forces your Intereſt.

       Till the Blood comes, threats with the greater Loſ

Steeping ſhews of a regular gradual Courſe, as flying ſhews of aimin

     at the End without the Means.

     Wide, ſhews of large Efforts in a reaſonable Courſe.

     Off a good Cawſy on a drown'd Marſh, ſhew'd of deferrin

     for Increaſe a good Husbandry Profit.

     His Leg into a Pit and it becoming Marble, foreſhew'd to *A*

     his Death by a Dropſy.

Stopping ones Ears, to ſome hear no Petition.

       to a Prince, Abſoluteneſs.

       to a private Man, alter Reſolutions.

       to a Woman, be debauch'd.

     At a Gate, ſhews your Entrance in ſome Buſineſs is reſolutely

     withſtood.

     A Chamber Window for Warmth ſeen, ſhew'd *A*. of a Ma-

     nagery laid by for Poverty.

     In Deſigns thro Company, new Courſes altering your Aims.

       An Angel, the Imagination of being a Divine

       Meſſenger ſo diverts you.

      Travel by one, ſuch a Courſe offers to obſtruct your

      Methods.   Vid. *Way* in *Travel*.

     In fatal Dreams, ſhews of your Death and the Manner.

Strengthning ſhews ſtrengthning.

     Vid. *Strong* in *Quality*, and *Help* ſupra.

Striking, vid. *Fight* and *Thunder* in *Air*.

Strive, vid. *Struggle* infra.

Stroke in general, vid. *Touch* in *Senſe*.

       to ſome, it threats Flattery or Sickneſs.

       to a Villain, Torments.

Strok'd by a Witch, threats with her Faſcination like Fortune.

Struggling with a Man, mentally ſtriving againſt a Courſe.

     So it ſhews of Good and Increaſe, *&c.* unleſs overcome

     therein.

Suffer as another, become as an Acceſſory to his Fault.

     Carrying is better than to be carried.

     Another to ſit by you, admit his Intereſt or his like Courſe to

     your Freedom.

       Apparel you, give them leave to model your Repute.

In Hell, threats with being wicked and diſcover'd.

Permitting or ſuffering alſo is literal.

                                     Suffer.

Suffer. Permiting another to kneel by you at your Prayers, that is, he
&c. proves of Aid to your Wants.

Take, vid. *Apparel.*　　　　　　　Vid. *Possess.*

Terrified by Devils, confounded by Despairs.

Threatned, vid. *Fright* supra.

　　　Eeing, the Ill appears or Circumstance of Fear, as &c. but no
　　　more.

Threatning to bite him A. feeing a crooked Eel, shew'd of his fearing
an intractable Person's exposing him.

Throng, vid. *Push* supra.

Thrown, vid. *Flung* supra.

Thruft, vid. *Push* supra.

Tied, vid. *Bound* supra.　　　　Vid. *Rope* in *Commodity.*

Tormented in Prison, vex'd with tedious Studies.

　　　Tortur'd to be, is to pray, &c e con.

Cut by a Knife, griev'd mentally in short Quarrels.

　　　　By a Woman unknown, rais'd thro a weak Conceit.

Torn Clothes, vid. *Apparel.*

　　　Womans Stocking seen, shew'd A. of slighting Female
　　　Pleasures.

　　　Have yours so, threats them so in Fact, or your self
　　　wounded there.

　　　　　To others, 'tis as Delivery from Care, or Loss
　　　　　of Reputation.

Paper of Memorandums seen, shew'd A. of retrieving such Methods once neglected.

Tapeftry feen, shew'd A. of short Life.

Shoos old falling off having, threats of greatest Poverty and Di-
ftress.

Garments a Woman seen with, shew'd A. of Misery and Poverty.

By wild Beasts, threats you with Punishment and Scandal.

　　　Ones Flesh only, to the Rich Loss.

　　　　　　to the Poor, Plenty.

　　　　　Till Blood come, being had to Justice by it.

　　A Dog, threats Injury with Infamy.

　　A Lions Claws, threats with Oppression to Ruin.

Tearing away a Lions Claw, shew'd of vanquishing a mighty and
domineering Enemy.

Tortur'd, vid. *Tormented* supra.

Treading on things, shews of their Subjection and Contempt.

　　Down Thorns, overcoming of Enemies.

　　On a Serpent, commanding a subtle Enemy to your Power.

　　　Coals, threats with very great Evils, and is as contemning
　　　others Malice.

　　　A Badger, commanding a greedy Deceiver as lame to
　　　your Pleasure.

　　　Mourning Flags, triumphing o'er the Terrors of Death.

Oxen on you feen, threats you as a Slave to Slaves.

　　　　　　　　Cc　　　　　　　　　Trying,

Trying, vid. *Endeavour* ſupra.
　　　In general, it ſhews of trying.
　　　To deſcend a Precipice, to avoid a Difficulty.
Tumbled down from Heaven, to *Cæſar* Death.
Tumbling in Bed, that is, reſtively lazy and out of Humour.
Turn one out of your Room, that is, diſcard him your Converſe c
　　Managery.
　　'd out of a Friends Garden, rejeɛted in your Intereſt in his Eſtate
　　Away a Pack of Gameſters, that is, reſiſt ſome ones ſmooth
　　　Tricks.
　　Back a Grave-Stone lying on you, narrowly eſcape Death.
　　To the Left, vid. *Side* in *Poſture.*
　　A Papiſt out of Church near, ſhew'd to *A.* Power given near t:
　　　unchriſtianize Popery.
　　From one to another, that is, regard ſuch a Courſe moſt.
　　Hard Words had *A.* turning off his Man, ſhew'd to *A.* ceaſing im-
　　　ploying as if ſo.
Venturing ſhews of venturing.
Violent being, that is, reſolv'd.　　　　　Vid. *Rain* in *Air.*
　　　River or Fountain ſeen, threats of Tyranny and Hardſhip.
Unhurt, vid. *Hurt* ſupra.
Uſe a Prodigal's Coach, be in his ſtately ruinous Courſes.
　　Uſe or your Religion omitting, threats you of great Heavineſ
　　　following.
　　One kindly, by Aɛtions perform'd ſeem as ſo to do.
Wait, vid. *Time* and *Company.*
Wake, vid. *Sleep* in *Bodily Aɛtion.*
Waſte in general ſhews Waſte.　　　　Vid. *Spoil* infra.
　　　　Vid. *Salt* in *Viɛtuals.*
　　Seen made by his Tenants Servants, ſhew'd to *A.* of his own
　　　Husbandry failing.
　　Wheat ſeen ſown too thick, ſhew'd *A.* of a good Husbandry
　　　overdone.
　　A Fountain ſeen overflow a Medow to the Right, ſhew'd *A.*
　　　of a preſent Loſs for future Good.
　　Fowls ſeen hurt *A*'s Corn in Barn, ſhew'd him of its raining in
　　　to hurt it.
　　　See yours pick up others waſt Corns, find your Family
　　　　help'd to their Loſs.
　　See another root up his young Trees, deal ſo falſly alſo by your
　　　own Profit Hopes.
Watching in general, vid. *Sleep* in *Bodily Aɛtion.*
　　　　It threats with Error, and being diſcovered on it.
　　　To the Rich, Trouble and Diſgrace.
　　　To the Poor, Riches.
By Night, threats with grievous Expeɛtations of Trouble.
　　　　To the Rich, great Affairs, but deceitful or ticklish.
　　　To the Poor, Diligence with Subtlety.

Watching by Night in the dark, and with Diſtraction, threats you as
　　fool'd in Expectation.
　　Watch-Light, vid. *Candle in Fire.*
　　Perſons watch another out of ſight, ſee to the end of a Matter.
　　　　You ſee another, prevent the Efforts of his Ex-
　　　　　pectations.
　　　　A Tyrant, ſecure you againſt Terrors.
　　　　His Sweet-Heart ſee a Lover, your ſelf alſo fol-
　　　　　low ſome Opinion as zealouſly.
　　Watch'd as a Thief, threats you as loſing your Aim.
　　　　By another, threats you as under great Care to pleaſe
　　　　　him.
　　　　In Shiting, about Expences.
　　　　One ſitting by you as you lie on Bed, he expects
　　　　　on your fix'd Lazineſs.
　　　　Force from one watching you, anſwer or excuſe you
　　　　　to ſuch Expectance.
Wearing, vid. *Ability* in *Quality.*

C H A P. L.

Of Diverſion.

IN general, all Things or Men pertaining to Recreations ſeen, are good
　　to all.
　　　　Challenge,　　⎱ Vid. *Cards* and *Lots* infra, &c.
　　　　Win, loſe, &c. ⎰ Vid. *Pleaſure* infra.
Eall ſhews of Diſputes and Quarrels.
　　Flinging, raiſing a Diſpute.
　　To ſome alſo it ſhews the Whore, that alſo is from one to many.
　　Golden chooſe before a wrought one, that is, a Profit in Diſpute
　　　before Pleaſure.
　　Seen with a Bull painted on it, ſhew'd of the *Iriſh* War Diſpute.
　　Tennis ſeen, ſhews of long Noiſe and Quarrel for Wealth.
Bear-baiting, vid. *Bear* in *Beaſt.*
Birding ſhews of future, projective and empty Hopes and Pleaſures.
　　Vid. *Birds.*　　　　Vid. *Nets* infra.
Bopeep with another, try to deceive him.
Bowls ſeeming at, ſhew'd to *A.* riding gently abroad.
Bull-baiting, vid. *Bull* in *Beaſt.*
Cards playing at have all the Trumps, gives you Joy and a good Lot.
　　　　Others ſeen, he that is towards you is for you, but op-
　　　　　poſite againſt you.
　　　　Challenge in it, is as Challenge.

Cards win at with a Phyſician, ſhew'd *A.* obtaining at laſt to recover his Health.

Loſing at, threats you with great Hazard by Roguery.

Paſs by ſome ſet at Play, ſcorn of ſome ſolemn Trickers on you.

Catch Birds, vid. *Birds* ſupra.　　　　Fiſh, vid. *F.* infra.

Cheſs playing at is as at Tables, and ſhews of Gain by Lying and Deceit.

　　Seeing others play, threats you ſo loſing.

　　　　Vid. *Tables* infra.

To a Prince, it ſhews the Field prepar'd for Battel.

　　Gameſters, Generals.

　　Cheſsmen, Souldiers.

　　　　Taking many, that is, Priſoners.

　　Cheſs-board loſt, threats the Army gone by Plague o Famine.

　　　　Broke, deſtroy'd by the Enemies Aſſault.

Chuck-farthing ſtopping to ſee, ſhew'd *A.* of his Buſineſs marr'd by idling.

Cock-fighting, vid. *Fight* in *Cock* in *Birds.*

Dancing, ſinging, leaping or running if neat, ſhew of Proſperouſneſs

　　In general, ſhews of ſome great Affairs or Friends dying.

　　　　To the Captives, Liberty.

　　　　To the Malefactor, hanging.

　　　　To the Child, it threats being deaf and dumb.

　　　　To a Servant, beating.

　　　　To the Sick, raving.

　　　　To a Sailor, Danger of drowning.

　　Alone, to ſome Madneſs or Folly.

　　　　to Sailers, Tempeſt ; to the Sick, raving.

Company with an Enemy, flurt it with her in Quarrels.

　　With a Skeleton, threats with Death.

　　At a Wedding, ſhew'd of Sickneſs.

　　Follow'd by a dead Man in't, Miſery and Death purſuing your Mirth.

　　Slightly paſs by dancing Strangers, diſregard merry Meeting.

　　Slighted by dancing Strangers, that is, in all Pomp and Mirth ſlighted.

　　For Family, 'twas literal.

Privately with your Friends, gives you Joy and Careſsment.

　　But before Strangers, threats of Shame and flirting Quarrels.

Manner ; the much Motion in't ſhews of deceiving or Dotage.

　　Without Muſick, threats you'l be in want of Money

　　To the Tune of *Pythagoras*, in imitation of his Methods.

　　Learning, eſſaying in hazardous great Difficulties.

　　　　　　　　　　Dancing

Dancing. Place on high, ſhews of Fear and Danger.

To ſome, great Endeavours to little Good.

To Offenders, grievous Puniſhment.

In the Air, ſhews of artificial but hazardous Actions.

On a Mountain, gives happy Succeſs to Grandeur and Eminence.

At the Backſide of the Change *London*, ſhew'd *A.* moſt publickly expos'd in Credit.

Seeing 2 Women, ſhew'd *A.* imperfectly buſy about Opinions to the neglect of Buſineſs.

A known Friend a Phyſician, and 1 unknown, ſhew'd a fooling with his Health, but yet in Safety.

To the Tune of *Pythagoras*, in imitation of him.

One dance a Jig, cauſing one by Hardſhip to ſhew all his Shifts.

Turning round he falls, your Trial fools him.

He tries again, he eſſays a 2*d* Effort.

Dice playing at, to Gameſters Joy, others Idleneſs.

You play you cheat, ſee others play they cheat.

To moſt they ſhew of Debate, and Noiſe about Mony.

To ſome, winning by them has given Inheritance.   (Dead Mens Bones.)

Exerciſe. Top whipping, promiſes of Health with Pains, *&c.*

Feaſt in general, vid. *Victuals*, and *Eat* in *Bodily Action.*

See and not eat, threats Poverty, a Plenty you can command, but not to uſe.

Eat too, gives you Plenty that you uſe.

Shews of Preferment, or ſome Friend dead, or a Rent paid.

Treat another, act to magnify their Judgment.

Manner. In a Tavern with Company, ſhews of Joy and Comfort.

A. being to ſay Grace inſtead thereof run off to ſhite, that is, Debts interrupt *A's* Plenty.

With Plate and Sweet-Meats, a Profit ſufficient therefore as an 100*l. &c.*

Some laid up cold, the like again in future Expectation.

Little Sweet-Meat Glaſſes in it broke, trifling Delights in't miſcarrying.

Perſons. Others ſeeing in your Houſe, threats you of Prodigals waſting you.

At a Feaſt, ſhew'd *A.* of paying them Mony.

Seen made by the dead, ſhew'd *A.* of a Profit by a Woodſale, *&c.*

Among his Servants, ſhew'd *A.* of borrowing their Mony.

Cc 3   Feaſt.

Feaſt. Perſons. 's Wife *A.* ſaw with a Diſh of Fruit, this ſhew'd *A.* d
      courſing pleaſantly of his Art after.
           Treated by a Chirurgeon's Wife with Cherry-wir
                ſhew'd *A.* eating ſome of his ov
                made Sweetmeats.
                London ſtately Friend, ſhew'd *A.* carri
                abroad in his Coach to be air'd.
           Company feaſting leave, ceaſe to encourage ſuch Inte
           courſe Society.

Fiſhing ſhews direct Gain with Strife.   Vid. *Fiſh* and *Nets* infra.

Fool, vid. *Pool* and *Expoſer* in *Perſon* in *Grammar.*   Vid. *Trick* inf

Fowling, vid. *Birds* ſupra, and *Game* infra.

Frolicks ſhew of Injury, vid. *Trick* infra.

Gaming, vid. *Birds* ſupra, and *Hunt* infra, &c.
           It ſhews of fulfilling ones Deſire with Trouble and Hazard.
           Gameſters ſeeing, foreſhews of venturing at hazard, or bei
                aſſail'd by ſmooth Tricks.
                They ſhew of Gain ſo to us, if ſucceſsf
                and not againſt us.

Gins ſhew of Deſigns and Deceits for or againſt us, as held by us
           others.

Hunting in general, vid. *Dog*, *Stag*, and *Hare* in *Beaſt.*
           It ſhews Strife for Victory, and Gain without da
                ger of Life, but moſtly for Honour.
           Others ſeen, threats you under Snares.
           You hunt, you ſnare others.
      Breathleſs ſee your Game ſtand, attain to your Intereſts (
           others.
           Miſſing your Game, fruſtrates your Hopes.
           Turns to another's Boy, proves to be as anothe
           expected Inheritance.
      Going to, to ſome Diverſion or Gaming.
           to ſome Law, War, or Quarrel.
           to ſome Accuſation of others.
      On a Horſe for Mony.
           Your Horſe drinking out of a deep Ditch on it, w
           hazardous Gain.
           Froſt ſtopping the Scent, Poverty interrupting tl
           Deſign.
           With a black Dog, in malicious Deſigns and Calumnie
                Your Neighbours, uſing their like Methods (
           Gain.
      Of an Hare that eſcapes, miſſing ſomewhat earneſtly expec
           ed of little Profit.
           To ſome hunting indeed.
           To ſome Melancholy and Taverning.
           Seen ſtand ſtiff to the left on hunting, ſhew'd h
           took but kept by others.

                                     Hunti

Hunting of a Bear, Lion, Boar, or Panther, endangers your very Life
in the Suit.

Tame Creatures, ſhews of your preying on Domeſticks.

Foxes, deſtroying little tricking Deſigners.

Squirrels, ſtriving to live by jugling and tricking.

Deer, to Lovers threats with Croſſes.

Jeering and playing threats with Fighting.   Vid. alſo *Jeer in Words.*

To ſome it ſhews of deceiving ſome body.

Another, being in Circumſtances to treat him with a Scorn anſwerable.

Jeer'd by an Enemy, that is, being in a Fault worthy, *&c.*

For telling 40 Stories in an hour, for uſing equivocating Deceit, *&c.*

A Slut, ſhew'd of making ſuch a Rebuke in diſcord to one.

A. flung one would kiſs her into a River, as waſhing ſhe daſh'd a Man approach'd her.

Kite raiſe in T-Fields, have a topping Diverſion thence, if then there.

Lots have drawn at by you and your Siſter, that is, in Family Regard have a Benefit.

Gratis, a ſeeming Chance in ſuch regard without Purchaſe of Flattery or Service.

Win, have your full Expectation therein.

China, be receiv'd on't into a great Family to live ſumptuouſly.

A Side-Saddle, the Privilege of an Horſe too to ride at pleaſure.

Maſquerades ſhew of Cheats or fooling, from jeſt proving to earneſt.

May-pole ſeen ſet up, foreſhew'd *A.* of a ridiculous Building, *&c.*

Merry-bouts being at, to them that gain by them gives Gain as if ſo,
Returning e'er any thing done, threats of vain Expectation in the matter.

Nets ſeeing are ill to all but Seekers of Runaways.

to hold them, ſhews of troubling others.

In general. ſeeing them held threats you with Trouble.

Hidden, horrid Danger from ill Men.

Fiſhing ſeen, ſhew of Rain or Change of Weather.

Catching Birds or Fiſh gives Gain.

So full to break, a little the more exceeding.

Vid. *Fiſh.*

Lime-twigs and Glue ſeen, foreſhew of the Return of Fugitives.

Nine-pins playing at, threats you with either Fraud or Strife.

Play in geernal, 'tis as fooling in earneſt, Vid. *Jeering* ſupra.

With Children ſhew'd of wanton Love.

With Dogs is a good ſign.

To a Child is good, but to a Man 'tis ill.

Seeing Oxen, gives Eſtate plenty to Luxury.

Rats is good, it ſhews Servants diligent and cheerful.

Dogs, ſhews of the Favour of Adverſaries.

Play ſeeing Fiſh in the Sea, gives you Security.

    Son *A*'s ſeen taken by Play-fellows into an Hall, and there clad rich and crown'd with Laurels, foreſhew'd himſelf on it after crown'd indeed.

Play-things, vid. *Trifles* infra.

Plays ſhew of fatal Changes coming unexpected, and from trifling Iſſues like Jeſts.

    Married to a King in one, to a Wife ſhew'd her Huſband renown'd.

Comedies ſeen acted, give a cheerful Iſſue of Affairs.

    But if in ill circumſtance, they threat with Deceit, Vanity, and Calumny.

Tragedies, threat Fights, Injuries, and a thouſand Ills to the Life.

    Of *Paris*, pernicious Efforts thro a raſh Copulation.

    Of *Abraham* and *Lot* leaving their Fathers Houſe ſeeing, ſhew'd *A*. himſelf near under ſuch Fate.

    Hell ſeen acted, threated *A*. hopeleſs Grief in hotteſt Deſires.

    A Man ſeen call'd off the Stage by a Ghoſt, to a Woman ſhew'd loſing her Lover by a Cheat.

Manner. *A*. with his prudent Friend by and pleas'd ſaw a dead Groom-porter there, who ſaid he had lain with *A*'s unknown Couſin.   *A*. by Diſcretion, *&c.* quite eſcap'd an unaccountable Deceit, *&c.*

    A Show at *A*'s Houſe, and whence he kept whom he pleas'd, ſhew'd of his diſcarding ill Boarders.

    Seeing 2 or 3 ſhort ones acting, having ſome Friends dying young.

    A Dictator wanting, ſhew'd of an Infant dying.

    A. would ſee a Tragedy, *A*. would act to provoke a fatal Change.

Scenes underſtand as the Plays, but leſs.

    They ſhew of Projects, heavy Cares, Pains, Dangers and Contentions, as *&c.*

    Behind the Curtain already acting, the Method already reſolv'd on as you ſhall act.

Place. Seen at an Inn and ſtrait left, ſhew'd *A*. of juſt eſſaying an ill and fatal Diverſion.

Ticket receive for it, have a ſolemn notice about it.

    to others be in a ſolemn Capacity for ſuch iſſue.

    Vid. *Token* in *Diſcourſe*.

Perſons. A Set of Players viſiting me, ſhew'd me of ſending for News Letters.

    A Friend ſeen acting, that is, doing ſomewhat fatally and odd.

    Your ſelf forc'd on a Stage of Ice, your ſelf forc'd thro a dangerous State.

                                     Plays.

Plays. Persons. Queen's Theater-Actors seeing become Puppets, shew'd A. of fooling Symptoms thought fatal. ⸺ ⸺ ⸺

  A Physician Puppet seen dance, as to Physick Skill.

Pleas'd seeing your Judg, shews your Dispute going easy.

  Taking the Air on a delicate colour'd Horse, shew'd A. glorying over others in Skill.

  Shady Trees and fair Women seen, gave Success in Love.

  Pleasant-look'd Man seen, promis'd to A. of wise Methods to Ease and Plenty.

  Fields seen with good Corn in a pleasant day, shew'd to A. Prosperity.

  Adorn'd with Flowers and Singing Birds, gave Pleasure with Ease and Content.

  And fruitful Valleys seen, gave the Love of the People.

Puppet-play seen in a Gallery, shew'd A. of Servants ridiculously throng'd in Lodging.

Questions and Commands playing at, foreshew'd of Joy and Merrymeetings.

Shittlecock playing at, to Parents shew'd them both beating their Son *Will,* a nomine.

Sing, vid. *Musick* in *Arts,* &c.

Tables in general, vid. *Chess* supra.

  Playing at, threats with Debate and Noise about Mony.

  Winning is best, and shews Victory over Enemies.

  Losing is as beat in Controversy.

  Seen only, threats with Sedition and Noise.

  Giving over Play, to the Sick is ill.

  Lost shews of the Loss of Evils, and Hazard becoming certain.

Top-whipping shews of Pains with Health ensuing.

  To others Labour with good Hopes in the end.

Trifles, a carv'd Tobacco-stopper finding, discovering a pretty prating Converse.

  Her Ginger-bread Clogs doing well, shew'd to a fine Woman her Daintiness becoming her well.

Tricks shew of cunning Designs in hand, as where, &c.

  Vid. *Fool* and *Exposer* in *Grammar.*

  Banter, vid. *Words.*

  Trick'd being, shew'd A. of acting ridiculously as to become thereby thereto liable.

  Get the Trickers House, that is, outwit the exposing Plotter.

Wager contend for, that is, act in Rivalry as earnestly as if so.

  Be willing to lay, have most reasonable Cause of Opinion according.

            C H A P.

CHAP. LI.

Of Travel.

IN *general* it shews of carrying on some mental Design, as &c.
(1)　　A travelling Beggar meet, be in want in a present Design only.

What pass'd by is as compass'd and commanded.

Land-travel shews of Designs firm-bottom'd.

On foot, in poor and mean Designs.

　　Vid. *Walk* infra.

On horseback, by Strength of Estate and Person.

In a Coach, in Designs of lazy Grandeur and Splendour.

Coach
Sedan } to many has shewn dying a Beggar
Wherry } 　thro idle Vanity.

Upon an Ass, with small Gains.

A Camel, with great Gains.

An Horse, in Honour or in Vigor.

　　Vid. *Horse* in *Beast*.

An Elephant, in Power.

A Lion, in Security.

A Deer, in Fear.

A Dragon, in Terror to others.

A Serpent, with mean Subtlety.

A Wolf, with Ravening.

　　To some 'tis as commanding a ravenous Enemy.

Flying shews of projecting acting without sure Ground of Experience.

Upon Birds, gives swift Dispatch.

　　A Griffin, promises Royalty soon.

　　Ducks, Geese, and Pigeons, in Fear.

　　Hawks, with Boldness.

　　Swan, poetically or philosophically.

Vid. *Fly* in *Air*, and *Birds*.

Sailing shews of a Course hazardous, and good or bad, rugged or smooth.

　　The meaner the Vessel, the worse.

Vid. *Water-Actions*.

In the Night threats with Trouble and Melancholy.

Side turn'd to, vid. *Posture*.

　　　　　　　　　　　　　　　　　　　　Compa

Company in general, vid. *Company.*
(2)   With a Friend, act in a Course will issue as friendly.
        Many, dispose your self to a common State of Life.
        A forsaking Sweetheart, in a Business will thwart your
          hotteſt Wiſhes.
        A foot Philoſopher, threats your Deſigns defective in
          Wiſdom, Art, or Riches.
        Don *Quixot*, act ſeemingly as romantically.
        Your Wife, deſign about your Contract, Profeſſion, or
          Art.
    Single, vid. *Company.*
    For your Brother, in a Buſineſs will croſs you in Intereſt.
        Siſter, in a Buſineſs of Diſcord and Diviſion,
          thwarting in Scheme.
    Wait on a Juſtice on horſeback, have occaſion ſo to do.
        Boy to School, ſtrive to diſcipline ſome one to O-
          bedience.
    Leave ſome one behind, proceed with Negligence to ſuch like
        Courſe or Perſon.
        A Mountebank ſo, ſhew'd *A.* ſick for want of his
          Noſtrum.
    See a Friend go Weſt, perceive of a Courſe going ill as is that
        Friend.
        Merchant lie ſhort of a Town, your ſelf buy not as hop'd
        for there.
        Judg about to travel hear of, your ſelf conſult Hiſtory in
        Aid, as *&c.*
Ways in general ſhew of our Methods in our Deſigns at large in oppoſi-
(3)   tion to Fields of Diſputes at large.
    Sorts. Another's climb into Heaven by, that is, uſe their like
        Methods to Riches.
        Bad ſhews of a Buſineſs troubleſom or dangerous.
        Broad, Methods with Plenty and Eaſe.
        Narrow *e con,* of Difficulty, and Hardſhip, and Want.
          Vid. *Narrow* in *Quality.*
        Crooked, with Croſſes or Diverſions to the beſt or worſe
        Courſe from the direct, as *&c.*
        Dirty and thorny, a Courſe fooliſh and troubleſom, as
          Law, *&c.*
        To Buſineſs very obſtructive.
        Fair and plain promiſes of Health and Proſperity.
        Firm, that is, a Method ſure.
        Green Ways, Courſes idle and unfrequented.
        Ice, vid. *I.* in *Froſt.*
        Known ſeen, the Good or Ill therein accuſtomed is again
          renewed to you.
        Long or Short, that is, ſo in time according.
        Narrow, vid. *Broad* ſupra.

                                      Ways.

Ways.
(3) Sorts. New one ſeen in a known City, ſhew'd *A.* of an unaccountable State failing his beſt publick Tranſactions.

No further way, no other viſible Method reaſonable in that matter.

Own, vid. *Grammar.*

     Vid. *Poſſeſs* and *Self* and *Another.*

Round about, long in time.

Stony, a Courſe of great Difficulty and Hazard.

Streight, direct Courſes.

Thorny, vid. *Thorns* in *Trees.*

Uphill to advantage, *& e con.*

Watry, a Courſe careful and with Trouble.

Wore down on one ſide, erring.

Alter, pave foot, a fair Correſpondence according moſt firm.

     Vid. alſo *Buildings.*

A ſmooth way, fix a pleaſant ſettled eaſy Method.

From *A*'s Orchard to his Church-yard, *A.* reaching his Learning to command holy Diſputes.

Pitching ſhews of making a firm, but meaner Agreement.

Gravelling and guttering, ſhew'd of rectifying Miſunderſtandings.

Widening, encouraging of greater Intercourſe.

Dug up, ſhew'd of ſuch Methods or Journies obſtructed.

Line out a way to the King, take meaſures of Approach to him or GOD.

Kind. Cartway private offer'd *A.* foreſhew'd him an Horſe offer'd for a Journy.

     Publick dirty ſeen, ſhew'd one diſtreſs'd for want of an Horſe.

Cawſey ſtepping from to a drown'd Mead, ſhew'd *A.* leaving a preſent Surety for a future Improvement.

Croſs ways ſhew of new Methods diverting former Courſes.

Highway be in, that is, in command of ſome common Method ; and tending to *London,* of the beſt ſort.

     A's Man ſeen at plow there, foreſhew'd him at work at hire.

     Between *A*'s fine unknown Houſe and Summerhouſe ſeen, ſhew'd him of his Plenty maintain'd by farming.

     Riding on a Ridg there his Company vaniſh'd, it ſhew'd *A*'s Pride unſociable, *&c.*

     Sleeping there, ſhew'd *A.* idling, *&c.*

     Finding Treaſure there, enriches you in a common way, as farming, *&c.*

     Uphill and Eaſt going there, is good, *&c.*

Lanes ſhew us of Buſineſs common and of Time, but of little Variety.

Ways. **Kind.** Lanes dirty, to some Law-suits.
(3)   Come to others there, arrive to be of their Fortune
                     in such State.
           Paths in your Field, common Courses for others in your
                     peculiar Manigeries.
           Parish own ways walk in, design as to your publick Parish
                     Business.
                 Met there by one, becoming oppos'd in such Pa-
                     rish Proceeds.
           Private Backways, shew of indirect Courses.
                         Over Walls and Pales, Courses of
                             Wrong and Presumption.
                 To some they shew of Methods peculiar to their
                     own Affairs.
           Thorowfare see one angry for your making his House, that
                     is, for spunging on him.
                     Permitted to have in a Place, shew'd *A.* of a
                         bare Possession of an Intercourse.
           Walk Royal walking in, shew'd *A.* concerning himself in
                     Royal Transactions.
                 A deep Politician's seeing with Reverence, shew'd
                     me with great hazard fathoming in Reason deep
                     as he.
Place in general, vid. *Place* in *Earth.*
(4)   In what Place or Posture we rest, so end our Affairs
                     according.
                 Part firm only before a Tradesman's Door, Security
                     in borrowing there only, &c.
           Fatal where you stop there, Death.
                     If waking immediately, Death unexpected.
           In Solitude, in Study.
                 Cities, amidst Business.
                 Mountains, among hard Labours.
                 Seas, on great Meditations.
                 Villages, shew'd of dying in Misery and
                     Poverty.
                 Rivers, in Pleasures or Obstructions.
                 Publick, shew'd *A.* of dying publickly.
                 A Place unknown with many, in War or
                         Plague.
                         Who seen travel with you,
                             die also.
                     Single, die in some singular Method
                         or Fate.
           Ascending shews of Difficulty, but with Gain and Honour.
               Descending is as with Ease and Loss.
           Before a Tavern, with relation to some State of Plenty.
               Vid. *Posture.*
                                                                Place.

Place. Between 2 Enemies Houſes ſeeming, ſhew'd *A.* at a loſs in his
(4)   Deſigns for Entertainment.

Beyond, vid. *Further* infra.

      Your next beſt Market Town being, that is, overdoing
         in your bargaining, and to the Left to your Detriment,
         &c. turning up Hill to the Right at laſt, proving to
         your Profit in the end.

By Hill and Vale, gives Advance thro Labour.

      A down Ground to one plow'd, deſigning change to a
         Matter of Improvement.
      3 fine Houſes at a diſtance, ſhew'd *A.* of diſcourſing
         how he had compaſſed 3 good Farms, *&c.*
      A fired Houſe, threats you as having exceeded its Miſery.
      A poor Man's Child, ſhew'd *A.* of compaſſing what might
         have ſeem'd his Gain, *&c.*

From, vid. *Poſture.*

      One Houſe to another going, ſhew'd of Change of Oc-
         conomies according.

Further, vid. in *Alphabet* infra.

In a Foreſt, in Circumſtances of Deſolation.

      Street be with another, uſe the ſame Methods of publick
         Converſe as he.
      Garden being with Pleaſure, gives Joy and Proſperity.
         Of Flowers, of meer Pleaſure.
      Holy Ground, a good Sign.
      Dry Brook walking, ſhew'd *A.* of loſing a Dinner.
         To another it ſhew'd the chance Uſe of a Profeſſion
         laid by.
      The Dirt or among Thorns walking, threats of Folly or
         Sickneſs.

On an Hill, with great Advantage.

        By a ruin'd Houſe in a Vale to the Left, which
         Courſe wanting were ruinous.

Over, vid. *Upon* ſupra, and *Fly* in *Air.*

      A Stile climbing, foreſhew'd *A.* Marriage.
      Things going, commanding with a Subjection according.
      Dead Children walking, deſigning on the Ruins of others
         Expectations.

Out of a Village go, that is, deſert all further Neighbourly
    Tranſaction.

Thro a Wood, amidſt Cares, *&c.* but paſſing them is beſt.

      Market, vid. *M.* in *Habitations.*
      Fire paſſing, bearing anothers Anger with Patience.
         Clothes burnt on it, to Damage of Reputation.
      Water in a Boat, paſſing thro Methods compaſſing a
         Trouble.
      Bryers and Buſhes, amidſt Hindrances.

Places. Thro a Parish running, acting in flight to a Neighbourhood.
(4)   Vid. *Pass* in *Travel-Acts,* and *Company.*
          An House go, compass an House-keeping Profit, *&c.*
          Westminster-Hall A. carrying a Board that the King lean'd
               on, shew'd of his glorying in the Pillory.
Towards a Place go, that is, only reduce your self a little near-
     er to it in Circumstances.
Under Ground, shews of Obscurity or Wickedness.
          Vid. *Cave* in *Earth.*
Unto known Places, renews to you the like Entertainment, as
     is there usual.
          London, gives of the best Commerce or Converse, as *&c.*
          Oxford, gives of the Perfection of Learning.
          Deserts, threats with Solitude and Desolation.
          Your rash Friend, act so as to be near as rash as he.
          Vid. *Come* infra.
          The East, with Increase.
               West, with Decrease.
               South, with Weakness.
               North, with Strength.
Upon a Precipice, threats with Poverty and Decay.
          Eeds, shew'd of a Business thought easy proving hard.
          The Sea, gives you Power with the People.
          Thorns, promises you of the Destruction of Enemies.
          Logs and Coals gives Riches, but with conceal'd Malice
               and Envy.
          Anothers Faggot-mowe, wasting on his Estate at plea-
               sure.

CHAP. LII.

Of Travel-Actions.

Approach, vid. *Coming* infra.
     Arrive, vid. *Unto* supra, and *Come* infra.
Ascend in general, vid. *Place* supra.
          It shews of Difficulty with Gain and Honour.
               Vid. *Clouds* in *Air,* and *Descend* infra.
     A Cathedral Steeple, to a Minister attain a Church Prefer-
          ment.
               So high, so great Preferment in that Diocess.
     Heaven or Sky seen, vid, *Air.*
               The Sky seen, promises of Honour and Dignity.
     Ladders, vid. *Tools* in *Trade.*
     Stairs, vid. *House.*

                                        Ascend

Aſcend Oxen ſeen, ſhew'd *A.* of great Plenty on a farther Advance, &c.

Climbing a Tree and eating its ſweet Fruit, ſhew'd *A.* doing Inceſt with a fair Kinſwoman. Vid. *Tree* in *Vegetable.*

Over a Wall into a Court, forcing irregularly into an Approach, &c.

Stile, foreſhew'd one Marriage.

To all, ſome great Change of Property and Condition.

Out of the Sea by a Piece of a Ship, ſhew'd of Help to the Maſter in Diſtreſs by one in Family.

Avoid a Danger, ſecure an hazardous Point.

Company, diſlike ſome reaſonable Methods offering.

A Carcaſe, abhor ſomewhat abominable.

Back, vid. *Poſture.*

Before, vid. *Poſture.*

Beyond, vid. *ſupra* in general.

Bringing in general, ſhews bringing.

A Winding-Sheet to you ſeeing the dead, threats you with their like Death.

To the Left, vid. *Side* in *Poſture.*   Vid. *Wind* in *Air.*

Back any thing, that is, returning it to its former State.

Somewhat to us Rivers ſeen, ſhews of wilful Perſons complying with us.

A Lion bound to you ſeeing ſome, ſhews of ſome great Enemy in your Power.

Brought into your Houſe ſee a Bittern, find a clamorous Enemy in your Power.

One a Crown ſeen by the Apoſtles and Prophets, ſhew'd him his Martyrdom near.

Carrying in general, ſhews of Command, and ſo to carry is better than to be carried.

Things, to ſome ſhews of glorying in them.

Home ſomewhat of yours ſee another, threats he abuſes you in Property.

Rivers, vid. *Water.*

Armour ſhews you of Safeguard or Honour.

Beaſts in Boſom, to a Woman Adultery with her Husband's Enemy.

Againſt her Will, threats her with Rape or Miſcarriage.

Bible ceaſing, that is, leaving to reſpect it.

Blood, diſcovers the Secret.

Bows, ſhew of Deſire or Torment.

Bread hot, threats with Accuſation.

Coffin on his Left Shoulder, ſhew'd *A.* of being melancholy.

Crown of Gold in your Hand, gives you Honour and Dignity.

Dead Body to a ſtrange Place, threats you Sickneſs.

Without returning again, Death.

Carrying Devil, to ill Men the Cross.

to good Men, Danger from wild Beasts.

Falcon on your Fist as walking, shews you Honour.

Garment Royal, shew'd *A.* of an Exaltation ending in his Ruin.

His Mother-in-law's Scarf, shew'd to *A.* Attendance with an unreasonable formal Reverence.

House your own with hard Labour, threats you with a bad Wife or hard Business.

Musick a Base-Viol to be mended, shew'd *A.* in fear of Reproof for grum Carriage.

Water in a Seive, trusting a Knave with Mony.

Your Clothes, the same.

To some, it has shewn of being rob'd by Servants.

Carried in a Cart, commanded by a Farmer.

Drawn by Men, gives the noblest Command.

Born by Men in one, shews Death, or the Gout irrecoverable.

Coach, to a Racer shew'd Loss for the Horses went before him.

Waggon red Clothes seen, shew'd *A.* as getting Materials for lasting Honour.

Vid. *Cart* and *Coach* in *Goods.*

By Parents, promises Delivery from Slavery.

A Lion, protected by your Prince.

The Poor, to the Rich Ill, *&c e can.*

A Mule Books seen derided, shew'd *A.* of his good Intentions hinder'd.

Away by the Wind, baffled from all Certainty by Reports.

A black Ox against his Will, shew'd *A.* Shipwreck.

Another *A.* seeing his Child, shew'd of his preventing anothers baffling his Expectation.

His Wife going with him, his Contract fool'd also.

Another your self seeming, shews you of all your Hopes in his Power.

A. entering anothers House and finding him asleep, cut out his Fat and Excrement stinking Guts, and carried them off; that is, *A.* rob'd him.

Along seeing a Cross, threats you with Sadness.

Coffin, threats you in an ill Conduct that near menaces your Death.   Vid. *Wood.*

Change your way, that is, alter your Methods.

To the Left, *&c.* vid. *Side* in *Posture.*

Climb, vid. *Ascend* supra.

Coming in general, vid. *Unto* in general.   Vid. *Go* and *Remove* infra.

Vid. *Place* in *Earth,* &c.

Into a Place, engaging your self to be in such Circumstances:

D d

Coming

Coming into a Place, being there without going, that is, being engag'd undeſigningly in ſuch State.

Another's Place, that is, ſucceeding him in time.

An Houſe dirty Water ſeen, threated A. of a Fire.

Your Brothers Pariſh, engaging you in a Neighbourhood
interfering in Intereſt.

Near unto dead Bones lying before you, purſuing a Courſe near
unto Death.

From the Weſt, &c. vid. *Place* general.

Out of a Coach, degrades you from Honour on a criminal Account.

Up to you to aſſault you, vid. *Fight*.

Down from Paradiſe a Man ſeen, ſhew'd of a good Prince appearing.

But chain'd ſo, ſhew'd of a Tyrant.

Things. Swallows ſeen, ſhew of Weddings and good Times near.

Peacock into the Lap, to *Cardan* a famous Patient offering.

A Wheel to you ſeen, ſhews you of ſome new Change of
Affairs approaching.

2 Horſes to you, that is, 2 to be kept for you.

One falling off his Horſe and breaking his Neck, his Horſe
came to A. on it, who mounted; that is, he dying A. inherited him.

A Bull came to A. who ſeem'd another. (Creſt) Family Invitation.)

A young Mare coming into A's Houſe well accoutred,
ſhew'd of his marrying with a good Portion.

Perſons. You bolt in among others, you are call'd to patronize,
&c. by Surprize.

Devils ſeen, ſhew of Courſes of Deſpair approaching.

To you ſeeing another, ſhews of your ſeeking to him in
Aid or Converſe.

As you ſit at Table, you ſend for
them as Tenants.

Servant for a Doctor ſeen, ſhew'd of his going to ſuch
Patient as if ſo.

New Maid ſeen, the old being to depart, ſhew'd of the
old's leaving her Service indeed.

Husband ſeen come for a Woman ſeparate, ſhew'd of her
removing her Dwelling.

Couſin living far off ſeen come for A. ſhew'd A. as wanting to go to her.

The more urgent ſhe, the more earneſt A. to
be gone.

She ſtays for A. A's Suſpence of ſuch Remove.

Going home without A. ſhew'd of A's
altering her Mind.

Creeping in narrow Holes as on all 4, deſigning in greateſt Straits and
Shifts.   Croſs

Cross, vid. *Posture* and *Pass* infra.

A River, to some thwart wilful Folks.

to some, act neglecting anothers Revenue.

Your Way see one find a Course, obstructs your Designs according.

Fleet-Ditch going, shew'd A. with Difficulty paying off a publick Tax.

A Lane, shew'd of going a Journy.

A Street or Channel, vid. *Street.*

A Vale fly, project beyond a present straitned State:

To an Hill, with Hopes of future Good.

One crossing your Way you pass on after, that is, your Designs proceed for all such Reasons of Obstruction offering.

Departure far, and taking leave of Friends, threated A. Death near.

A. heard his sick Wife taking her leave, but not thoroughly; she died not, but grew worse.

A. packing up as to depart from Home, shew'd of his resolving as so to do.

A's Brother being to go to *Constantinople*, shew'd of his Credit being good, Rival Interest being vanish'd.

Out of an House from one, shews of your refusing Intercourse Oeconomick with him.

Anothers Garden, cease of Expectance on his Estate:

Your own House, vid. *Grammar.*

The World, remove to some desolate Place.

Westminster-Hall to a Counsel, shew'd of his ceasing Law-Practice.

From being under a Cart, Freedom from Slavery to a Farmer:

Fleering Men, acting to avoid Tricks against you.

Company, shews you as at variance with their Courses.

Spirits. God see depart smiling on whipping A. gave him Recovery of Sickness.

Ill Genius A's seen depart, shew'd him of Sickness ceasing.

From her holy Place *Minerva* seen, shew'd to *Domitian* helpless Ruin.

Persons. A new Maid being come, A. seem'd to be to depart, this shew'd A. a Servant departing that Day unthought.

Your Physician seen depart, threats you Sickness:

To the Sick, Death.

Friends heard of as far off, shew'd to A. of seeking to Enemies for Aid.

Rival comes and you are to be gone, that is, find he's prefer'd before you.

Colonel Kinsman heard of as gone away, shew'd to A. of his being at a Fault in a Command, &c.

Enemy from a good Place seen, prospers you according in its Command.

Departure. Perſons familiar ſeen from you, ſhews you leave his like Courſe. Vid. *Leave* infra.

Deſcend in general, vid. *Aſcend* ſupra.

-ing from Heaven an Angel cloth'd in Yellow ſeen, ſhew'd of a Plague Infection.

An Horſe voluntarily, quit an Art or Eſtate, *&c.*

Deſcending a Precipice by a Cart, getting off a Difficulty by a Farmer.

Into Hell and return, to the Great Misfortune with Remedy.

to the Poor, weak and good.

In general, it threats with Eaſe and Loſs.

Over an Houſe, that is, in a Courſe with neglect of Oeconomy Rules.

Deſigning to buy Timber, in a Method to attain Riches.

Directed by one, gives you of Aid and Advice in your Courſe, as *&c.*

Drawing faſtned in a Cart, threats you with Sickneſs or Servitude.

Got in among Oxen and drawn by them, ſhew'd *A.* ruled by his Tenants.

With their Corn, delayed at their Will, and till their Harveſt in. Vid. *Oxen* in *Domeſtick Action.*

Driving Chariots with Leopards, commanding great Enemies.

Another back, baulking his Deſigns againſt you.

To the end of a Room, to all Extremity of Converſe, *&c.*

Away Hogs, ridding of waſting Errors and Miſtakes.

Ghoſts, clearing of Cheats.

By the Roots, by the Examination of Truth.

By Words and Croſſes, that is, ſuperſtitiouſly.

A Dragon ſeen by Thunder and Lightning, ſhew'd *A.* of an ill Prince remov'd.

Fowls from Corn, prevent the Occaſion of ſuch Miſchief.

Oxen from eating Barly in the Straw, ſhew'd *A.* of ſecuring his Corn as he eat the Straw, *&c.*

Others Boys waſting your Garden, fooling others Ends on your Eſtate.

A Devil aſſaulting you, avoiding a Conſpiracy or Perſecution threatning.

Driven by unknown to fight in a Man of War, ſhew'd *A.* of his being forc'd into popular Quarrels.

Enter, vid. *Go* infra.

Eſcape, vid. *Fly* infra.

In general, it ſhews a mental Avoidance of Ill.

From Thieves, that is, wronging Errors.

Fly without Fear, avoid in vain.

With Fear, avoid for good Cauſe. Vid. *Purſue* infra.

Out of an unknown great Houſe, avoid Engagement in an unaccountable great Oeconomy.

Things. Horſe leave eſcaping, find the Eſtate will be free in its own Courſe. Eſcape.

Escape. Things Dogs seen escape, the same as to some Centinel Guard Service. I

A Bird letting go, threats Damage.

An Hare hunted by you escapes, you prove baulk'd in hottest Desires.

Pursued by a furious Bull, you can't escape at an implacable Enemies Mercy.

Permitting Pigeons, not prosecuting ill Women.

To a Ministers House, that is, by a conscientious Oeconomy avoid an Ill, as *&c.*

From beating, free your Will of others Tyranny.

Neighbours Ghosts, that is, his like teasing Cheats threatning.

Place, vid. *P.* in *Earth.*

A Spaniel would bite you, avoid a Course of sneaking fawning.

Watching Pursuers to a Pantry, shew'd *A.* making Excuse to a Dun to stay till a Rent paid him.

A Wolf to a fine House, shew'd *A.* of getting Plenty of Winter Stores.

To be among Gentlemen, that is, thro being one become free of an Ill, as *&c.*

A Beds-head from fighting an impertinent Man, shew'd *A.* skreening himself from a Woman's Quarrel by the Power of her Husband.

Fetch Paper from another, get Instructions, as *&c.*

Meal and a Bed-stead from *France,* wish for their Subsistence, but hating their Government.

A Book from a Booksellers, shew'd me taking Order to print one.

His Stick and Gloves from a place, shew'd *A.* of disowning his Abode there, *&c.*

A Genealogy from a Painter, shew'd *A.* of choosing an Apothecary as to blazon his Credit.

A Writing from a Church Clerk, shew'd *A.* of choosing a Clerk because able to write.

Printed Papers from a Printer, shew'd *A.* printing a Book,

An Handkerchief gives Joy, it wipes away Tears.

'd back by your Wife, alter'd in Resolutions by your Profession.

Go to fetch somewhat, that is, endeavour to procure it.

Receive what you go for, succeed in your Enterprize. Vid. *Dead.*

Another comes to fetch you from your Home, Necessity urges you to live nearer to them. Vid. *Come* supra,

Fetching Goods from *A.* shew'd *A.* of preparing to pay him a Debt.

Them Death seen, to the Sick Recovery.

Somewhat for a Superior, shew'd *A.* of receiving a Reward answerable.

Fly, vid. *Escape* fupra. Vid. *Purfuit* infra.

Following in general, vid. *Purfuit* infra. Vid. *Imitation* in *Dead*.

    Gentle, is as Imitation.

    Violent is as Purfuit.

    Another, that is, giving him Place or Precedence.

        One Friend a 2*d* feen, fhews you of great Mifery or Happinefs.

        A Woman, purfuing a weak and foolifh Fortune, an Opinion only, &c.

           Unknown in Mourning in her Native Place, fhew'd *A.* of weakly fancying his Death near.

        A Domeftick, that is, making your mental Court or Application to him or her.

        Your ftout Friend, have Succefs as when ufually he your Leader.

        The Dead, imitate their Actions as when alive.

        Many being, guided by a publick and open Example.

        Your Brothers Parifh Minifter, purfue your Confcience tho againft Intereft.

        To fome, be of their Train or Affiftance.

        A Lord, purfuing a ftately Courfe.

        Parents, fhews you of their Slander or Imitation.

           Mother-in-law, obey a felf-ended Commander.

    Bees as to hive them, gave *A.* Profit by a School.

    A Coach and 4 Horfes following a Coach and 2, fhew'd *A.* of keeping 4 for his Coach where 2 were too weak.

    Follow'd by another, threats you as in dread of his Threats.

        You follow him, you would terrify him fo.

        A Rabble, expos'd in many publick Methods.

        The Devil, threats of Governments, or Confpiracies menacing, or Defpair thro Wickednefs.

        A Beggar, being in Terror of Want at hand.

        In a Dance by a dead Man to a Marriage, fhew'd of Death and Mifery purfuing it.

    Expecting another, fhews you in want in your Proceeds, as &c. is the Perfon.

Forfake, vid. *Part* infra, and *Leave* in *Action*.

From, vid. *Pofture*, and *Travel in general* fupra.

    Weft to Eaft, is beft.

    Better to worfe, is bad.

Further travel, defign what is beyond another, as &c.

    See another, fhews he fo exceeds you, &c.

    Vid. *Beyond* fupra.

Going in general, vid. *Defign* in *Soul*. Vid. *Prepared* in *Quality*.

    With Dogs a hunting gives Imploy.

    About in a great deal of Trouble, defigning in Uncertaitny enough to caufe it.

                                  Going

Going off, vid. *Depart* supra.

　　To find the Mayor, shew'd *A.* of striving by Voting and Faction.

　　　　Invite one, that is, find another proposes somewhat to you.
　　　　　　He comes to you, you propose to him.

　　Your Stable, shews of your going some Journy.

　　A Place in general, changes your Circumstances as is the
　　　　Place.

Out of your House without hindrance in a Morning, gives you
　　　　Success.

　　A Shop, shew'd *A.* of leaving a Bargain, &c.

Over, vid. *Cross* supra, and *Posture.*

Marching, *Alexander*'s burning Army seen, shew'd of his invin-
　　cible Conquests.

Enter another's House, command its Freedom.

　　　　　　By a new Door, thro presumptive Li-
　　　　　　　　berties.

　　　　　　Into his Granary, kill his Cat,
　　　　　　　　&c.

　　Into a Market, begin a Bargain Treaty.

　　　　His Hall seeing a Monster, shew'd *A.* of avoiding
　　　　　　an absurd Treaty with a Tenant offering.

　　　　Smith's Shop, that is, being in want of his Aid
　　　　　　or Work.

　　　　　　On horseback, as to the Cure of some Horse.
　　　　　　　　Wake there, threats you without
　　　　　　　　　　Remedy.

　　　　Place in general, command such Circumstances
　　　　　　according.

　　　　A Field, begin a Dispute or Husbandry Managery.

 . Another's House and finding the Owner asleep, he cut
　　　　　　out his Fat and excrement stinking Guts, and
　　　　　　carried them off, that is, rob'd him.

　　　　　　Hall surpriz'd by fine Company there, this
　　　　　　　shew'd *A.* quoted by the Owner of it to a
　　　　　　　Testimony.

Different ways from others, shews of Anger upon Mistakes.

Give way to another, humour him in his Methods.

　　　　　　With muttering, ineffectually and to appearance
　　　　　　　only.

Hal'd, vid. *Forc'd* in *Hurt.*　　　Haste, vid. *Action.*

Jump, vid. *Action* and *Hop*, &c. in *Diversion.*

Leave, vid. *Action*, and *Part* infra.

　　　　　　Vid. *Despair.*　　　　　Vid. *Behind* in *Posture.*

　　A Chamber the Dead entering, cease a Course as fearing Death.

　　A Place you fight in, give ground according in some Dispute.

　　A Chamber going into a Street, proceed from a private Oeco-
　　　　nomy to publick Action.

Leave your Table see Friends, that is, find such Aids to your Profit failing.

Left behind, that is, excell'd according.

By a Friend, shews he ceases further to aid you.

By one hors'd, exceeded by them thro their Art or Managery.

Coach'd, in a more stately Course.

Leave your Wife behind, cease to give her Aid, &c.

Fine Company feasting, cease to encourage such like Entertainments.

Led by another and not know where, threats you deceiv'd in Expectation.

Your Sister, in a Course tending to Division.

A Physician out of Town, find your first Onset in Business wanting Remedy.

And follow another, being instructed by him.

About an House and Garden, with relation to Estate an Oeconomy Managery.

By the hand by the Dead, if to a Place unknown, it threats you Death.

Losing your way, the means of your Business fails you.

Turn to the right or left, vid. *Side* in *Posture.*

Not finding the way back, to the Contender Oppression.

to the Servant Continuance in Slavery.

to the Seeker vain Expectation.

In the dark, Blindness in your Methods thro Passions, &c.

Meet in general, vid. *Drive* supra. Vid. *Side* in *Posture.*

Another, oppose or cross his or his like Designs.

Being met is so, you are oppos'd also.

Meet thee at *Philippi, Brutus's* fatal Obstruction.

A dead Man, a Course obstructs you as was he when alive.

In Streets, in publick Converse or Transactions.

A Staircase, oppose for Secrecy ones Managery in a Design.

An Entry, oppose all publick Oeconomy Transaction with them.

A Coach, in stately Proceeds.

In Visits, shews of pursuing Ends of Civility, as is the Person.

His own dead Body to be buried out of an Inn, shew'd *A.* not quite remedied in his imperfect Affairs.

Met by a Lawyer, oppos'd by a Wrangle.

Friend in a Desert, shew'd *A.* his Misery in a good State of Remedy.

Singing Men coming out of a Cathedral, shew'd *A.* benefiting a Minister to his own hindrance.

One and stopping on it, lays your Designs aside.

Return on't, shews you'l undo all that was done before.

Me

Meet. Met by one and stand your ground, resolve against such Opposition.

Overrun by another's Coach, oppress'd by him in his Courses of Grandeur.

Seen your Son so, threats your Expectation so hurt.   Vid. also *Run* infra,

Overtake another, vid. *Pursuit* infra.

That is, exceed him in Methods.

Overtook by him, threats him so exceeding you.

Part from another in Travel, use other Courses in Designs.

At a River, with wilful thwarting.

Coffee-house, that is, vary in publick
Censures and Converses.

Company in a Room, use other Methods of Oeconomy.

You see your Father, that is, cause a Friend or Care as kind
to defert you.

Turning to the South, as chusing Pleasure.

You standing back in East, you seeking for
Advancement only.

Parted by force by the Wind, separated by a violent popular Crisis.

An Angel, cease further acting as if you presum'd your self
a Divine Messenger.   Vid. *Leave* in *Action.*

Pass thro another's Court, thro another's leave accomplish your Designs.

Church by Scoffers to the Tower, scorn Shame to fly to GOD.

Dancing Strangers, rudely slight civil Merriment offering.

An Inclosure to the right, receive a full Lease Benefit of
farming.

London Streets, drive some great and generally approv'd
Transaction.

To the West, of ill end, *&c.*

A Victual Market, compass a full and thorow Command of
Victuals.

Multitudes to one, that is, lay by all Excuses to attain your
End.

Places, exceed the Benefits proposable by such States.

But as pursued, *e con.*

France and *Rome*, and told so also *Cromwel*, that is,
he hector'd them.

A Torrent, vanquish a common Vogue, *&c.*

A Town and see a Judg beyond, shew'd *A.* discovering
Cheaters of him to good Hopes of Cure.

Down hill in a Coach, shew'd *A.* of treating others
gloriously.

Villages to Cities, is good.

Deserts, threats of the utmost Miseries wilfully
pursued.

Pass

Paſs thro Woods, is better than to reſt in them, for it rids of offenſive Difficulties.

Toward the Weſt, act moſt ſelf-detrimentally.

By his own Barn to the right A. enter'd his Houſe, by farming he got his Livelihood.

An Ironmonger's, vid. *Trade.*

A Ghoſt to the Eaſt, ſhew'd A. of eſcaping Death thro Care.

Pack-horſes, ſhew'd A. of exceeding your formal Artiſts, &c.

A Book on ground, neglect an Inſtruction anſwerable with Contempt.

An Houſe on fire, that is, proceed in a Courſe will exceed its Miſery, and end well.

Oxford Rivers, exceed their Fountains of Learning.

Oxen in a Wood, ceaſe the Neceſſity and Trouble of their Uſe.

Ox-skins, ſhew'd A. aiming at the good of farming without the Labour.

Perſons. Others Boys, exceed Mens common Expectations.

One that has cheated you, mend your Eſtate not to feel its Hurt.

You have outwitted, ſecure to your ſelf the like Advantage again.

Another looking fine, ſnare him with Appearances.

Attorny General, vid. *Officers.*

Huckſters, that is, deal harder than they.

A Boneſetter's Houſe, ſhew'd A. great among his offended Kindred beyond a meer Reconciliation.

Soldiers many threatning, ſhew'd A. of ſecuring himſelf againſt Robbers.

Gentlemen in a fine Room, exceed ſuch like Methods in Converſation.

To others, ſlight ſuch gentlemanly Tranſactions.

Side, vid. *Poſture.*

Paſſing you things ſeen, ſhews you of active Overtures made you, or Benefits and Courſes beyond our preſent Command.

Away the Heavens ſeen, ſhew'd of Change of State.

A Bull ſeen by A. with a torn Coat to the right, ſhew'd A. of hearing of one of that Arms acting ill.

Oxen lean by him A. ſeeing, ſhew'd him of his uſing Horſes doing better.

Perſon. Dead King ſee paſs by you, your ſelf act as by an Authority extinct.

By A. a Schoolmaſter ſeen, ſhew'd A. of his reading his Book with Delight.

Place. Croſs A's Court a Bittern ſeen fly to the right, ſhew'd A. of a clamorous great Man blaming him, but not with ill Intent.

Shooting him, ſhews your preventing his Scandals approaching you. Paſs.

Pass. Place. Thro *Asia Alexander's* burning Army seen, shew'd of his conquering it.

Snakes seen pass out of a Chamber, shew'd to *A.* of Temptations to ill Managery going off.

Passing by an unknown Mourning Coach seen, to the Sick shew'd of causeless Fears of Death.

His *Quondam* Master seen to *A.* shew'd of Disappointment in hottest Desires.

You crump'd Men seeing, threats you with cross Affairs thro perverse obstructing Courses.

You Men hors'd seen you being on foot, threats you as in Derision, as Artless or Estateless, &c.

Proceeding further on a Journy, on further Issue, as &c.

With Trouble, to some Sickness.

Pursued long, that is, long under Expectation of Terrors or Threats. Vid. *Follow* supra.

Thro all the Rooms of an House, in all the Branches of Converse or Oeconomy.

Streets, thro all publick Transaction States.

By another, being in expectation of Clamours and Threats according.

So it hinders your Command of what you pass.

A Bull, some great Enemy threatning.

You can't escape from, you being at some implacable Enemies Mercy.

Wild Beasts in the dark, devouring Wranglers assail you amidst Doubts.

Monsters, shew'd *A.* dreading senseless and unreasonable Wrongs.

A Dog, expecting with Fear the Assailments of a Slanderer.

Opening at you, &c. that is, publickly approaching you.

Men would hang her, shew'd *A.* in danger of being charg'd with Theft.

And Women in general, that is, being afraid of such Persons, Courses, or Opinions.

Kissing the Fairest it ceas'd, satisfying the Best 'twas over.

Unknown, be in terror of some unexpected Course.

Follow'd by Blood, discover'd by self-apparent Circumstances.

Dead, threats you of their like Death menacing.

to some it shews of imitating their ill manners.

to some be in terror of their Reproaches as when alive.

A dead Bishop, shew'd *A.* of the awe of doing wickedly vexing him.

Pursuing others, shews of our overcoming or clamouring.

Pursued.

Purſued. Purſuing one that fool'd you in a Suit againſt him formerly
         tho, threats you ſo fool'd again as before by him.
         Overtake the Purſued, command your terrified
         Enemy as in your full Power.
     Purſuer A's vaniſh'd on his talking to a Great Man.   A's Dun
         went away on his Excuſe of Rents.
         Stand againſt, that is, reſolve againſt threatning Dan-
         gers.
Race is good to all but the Sick, to them the Goal is Death.
     With others, ſhews of vaunting Contention, and who is foremoſt
         is beſt.
     On foot is perſonal Contention.
      Horſeback is as Contention with Eſtate too.
         Outride your Enemy, overcome him in Art, but
         hardly.
     You fly while he walks, you act ſillily projective while he goes
         ſure.
     With the Dead on a white Horſe, ſhew'd A. of Death.
     Vid. *Ride* and *Run* infra.
Raining hard as he travel'd, to a Farmer ſhew'd great preſent Expence
         to future Gain.
     Flying for ſhelter on't, ſhifts us'd in it.
Removing in general ſhews of Change of Place. Vid. *Coming* ſupra.
     A thing, mentally reſolving ſome Change as to its State.
     From *London* Weſt, a Change from beſt publick Tranſaction
         State to worſe.
     His Library, ſhew'd to A. of his Backſide of live things
         chang'd.
     Somewhat hiding Mony, ſhew'd to A. ſetting aſide all Ex-
         cuſes to borrow ſome.
     Joiners Tools to do ſomewhat, ſetting aſide all Friendſhip
         to do it.
     A Cloſeſtool decently away after ſhiting, ſhew'd A. of pay-
         ing off Debts orderly.
     A dead Body, concealing a ſcandalous Knavery.
     A Coffin ſet by his Bedſide in a Houſe unknown, ſhew'd A.
         laying by the vain Fears of Death.
  'd your Glaſs Eye being ſee well on it, Aws being gone, com-
         mand your Affairs truly.
     Finding ſomewhat, threats your being deceiv'd on ſome Aid
         expected.
     A's Friend heard of as nearer to him, ſhew'd A. of an hap-
         pier Command of ſuch a Friendſhip
         Aid.
         Further, *e contra.*
     Ludgate heard of, ſhew'd Danger to one Son, to a Father
         having three.
     To a ruin'd Houſe ſeeming, beware of a Remove indeed
     out if tolerably ſettled before.   Retreat,

Retreat, be baulk'd in a Design, forbear a Course as someway most manifestly inconsistent.

Returning in general, countermanding former Resolves.

Where you stand on return, in such State is your resolv'd Retreat.

Things happening on return, shew of Occurrences intermediate on such change.

From hunting, abates Fear, but stops Work.

A Place you go to, repent you of your first Designs.

E'er your Desire there answer'd, threats you fool'd in Expectation.

White-Friers, retrieving your endanger'd Credit.

To a Place, new stating things in an old Light, or a Recontinuance of deserted Methods.

Street, to publick Intercourse, &c.

Things found gone thereon, matters failing on a second Essay.

Down from an House, from an Oeconomy to a free Dispute.

To his Parent seeing a Prodigal, shew'd to *A.* himself also such a Welcome in a sort.

Go and would return but fail, design to undo somewhat, but be withstood.

In a narrow dangerous way seem that you can't return, be catch'd in an unhappy Course that you can't reverse.

Your Ruler flung at *A.* see him return, find your Orders by him obey'd.

Riding, vid. *Upon* supra *in general.*   Vid. *Race* supra.

Upon a Horse, vid. *Horse* in *Beast.*

A Dog, threats you with want of Necessaries.

A Ram and lying on his Horns, shew'd *A.* of marrying a Whore.

A Wolf, gives you some mighty and wicked open Enemy in your Power.

A Mule, pursue a Business flow but safe.

To many it has shewn of Flight.

Rob'd in your Journy seeming, frustrates you in your Designs according thro Error.

Run in general, Vid. *Race* and *Overrun* supra.

Vid. *Escape* and *Pursuit* supra.

To some Folly, Hurry, Rashness and Decay.

To a Woman Disgrace and Damage.

To some if steddy, Dispatch and Gain.

Easy, Command and Joy.

Inability to run, shews Sickness, Hindrance, and Loss.

To some Affairs hard to accomplish.

Persons seen, threats of Strife and Contention.

Vid. *Race* supra.

Run

Run Beasts seen, shew of Troubles.

    Ram, Vid. *Ram* in *Beast*.

    Hare or Hart seen run, gives Address to Wealth by Subtlety.

    Horses seen run, give Prosperity and Accomplishment of Desires.

    Lion seen, gives Courage, Dispatch.

    Asses threat seen run, Misfortunes.

About Enemies seen is good, it shews you their Envy.

    Friends seen is bad and Loss, you are their Care.

After your Enemy, gives you Victory and Profit.

Against one another People seen, has shewn of Wrangling and Discord.

    Children which can speak seen, has shewn of Joy and fair Weather, their Play-time.

    Arm'd tho with Sticks, has shewn of War and Dissension.

Away on a charge, leave your Pretences.

    From Pursuers, slight Expectations, as &c.

    With your Child see another, threats he tries to fool your Expectation.

    Your Wife going with him, notwithstanding your Contract.

From you a Mule seen, Vid. *Mule* in *Beast*.

In a Palace, declares to you of Sorrow.

    Church, gives you Joy.

    Market or sleep there, gives you Sickness.

On a white Horse, has shewn Death.

Over by another, opprest by him, or such a Course, &c.

Round about, vid. *Round* in *Quality*, &c.

Thro a Parish to the left, shew'd A. of acting slightingly, and hurrying to Neighbours.

Seek, v'd. *Fetch* supra, and *Find* in *Possess*.

Sent *Jupiter*'s Chariot seen to the House of *Vespasian*, shew'd him after Emperor.

A young Man to *Hannibal* from *Jupiter*, foreshew'd him his Captainship.

Clouts and Physick having from *London*, to a Woman big, shew'd of sending for a Tender thence.

A's Sister sent for her such a day, that is, she sent for her then as A. required, and to her Felicity.

Send your Man for your Friend gone West, thro his Service retrieve the ill exprest thereby.

    Goods, be in a Capacity to command what thereby shewn.

Sing as you go, live honestly and merrily.

Sleeping in the way, to the Sick Death.

                              Step,

Step, vid. *Action.*

Stock'd, vid. *Dirt* in *Earth.*

> *A's* Tenants Cattle seen at his Close Gate, shew'd to *A.* his Title to some Lands to be in doubt.
>
> *A's* Horse as entering a Market Town seeming, shew'd of *A's* Mony failing him in a Bargain.

Stopping in general, vid. *Action.*

> Proceeds voluntarily, desisting from Designs.
>
> > In passing a Place, in commanding Circumstances, as &c.
>
> For a while, being at a stay for a while.
>
> Vid. *Chariot* in *Goods.*

Stop'd e'er at your Journies end, your Business resting unfinish'd at least that day.

> From flying, hinder'd in projecting, but not always.
>
> Interrupted or waking e'er a Matter ended, the same.
>
> By a Friend, a Delay ending well.
>
> > Ghost, hinder'd by a Cheat.
>
> Oxskins you can't remove, Obstruction thro a Farm Course you can't compass.

Summoning shews of Summoning.

Taverns on the way, Diversion Oeconomies occurring in your Proceeds.

Thorowfare angry at *A.* for making his House, that is, for spunging there.

> > To others, Vexation at some ones taking too great Liberties there.
>
> A Parish run slightingly, act with Scorn and Hurry to Neighbours.
>
> A Lane walk, design to Perfection in some common Method.
>
> Vid. also *Pass* supra.

Turn, vid. *Action* and *Side* in *Posture.*

Walk in general, vid. *Way* supra.

> Jump, vid. *Action.*
>
> It shews of Discontent and seeking change, as sitting shews of mental fixedness.
>
> By Water, gives Security.
>
> > But thro it, threats Trouble.
>
> On Clay Ground, threats with grievous Sorrow and Trouble.
>
> Persons. To a Gentleman Detriment thro mean Designs, especially if a long Journy.
>
> With a Spirit, designing in a self-delusive Action.
>
> With one sick, taking measures as for their Cure.
>
> Vid. *Company.*

Beasts confusedly many Horses, shew'd *A.* of Trouble of Mind about Riches.

Manner. Pleasant and without Hindrance, gives Success in Business.

Walk.

Walk. Manner. Horse unfurnish'd in hand, in want of Mony.

Slowly, threats with a hard Method.

On Water, declares of Honour and Joy.

Gently, shews of taking your Pleasure in moderate Actions.

But others seen on Horseback by, as comparative, is ill, &c.

Swiftly is as doing Business in great Confusion.

To some if steddily, it shews of Gain.

Weary of it, despairing in a Course answerable.

Posture. On the Knees for Feet, threats Poverty, and Loss of Goods and Servants.

With 4-footed Beasts, or on all-4, threats Sickness.

Sore Feet, shews you of Fasting.

Over Logs and Coles, gives you Riches, but with great Envy.

On Pew Tops off from a Precipice in a Church, shew'd A. just escaping from burying his Wife.

Wandring over Plains, } To Lovers, great Disappointment.
In Plains, } To others, unaccountable Confusion in Designs
In Woods, } with great Grief.

CHAP. LIII.

Of Words-sorts.

A, That is, *A.* literally.

Abjure your dead Father haunting you, act as never to acknowledg a wicked Benefactor more.

About or concerning, is literal as is the Subject.

Accusing in general, shews of sullen Resentment for things.

By Letter, that is, very solemnly and formally.

vid. *Chide* infra.

For divorcing his Sister, for breaking his Neighbours Contract.

Accounting, shews of taking Mathematick Measures to certainty.

Acquainting another threatning, giving *A.* conceal'd Awe according.

Tell another somewhat, act so as to let him understand it of you.

To others let your Experience, let him understand it.

Told be that you should know such things, that is, they will appear so in Fact to you.

Advising you a Minister heard, shews of your acting as Conscience is directing.

Advising

Advising you hearing a Woman to Virtue, shew'd *A.* of Poverty assailing him.

Unknown Persons, shews you as following unaccountable Methods.

A Friend, shews you as acting to good Issue in a Course, as is that Friend.

Your Brother, shews you cajol'd to a Course that wrongs you in Interest.

Another not to marry a *Roman* Dame, shew'd *A.* the Adviser so shrew bit.

A Schoolmaster, shews you pretending to direct one who thinks himself too wise for you.

In your Profession, relates more to them than your self.

A Boarder-taker not to leave off, shew'd *A.* teas'd near to forbear House-keeping.

And after disown it, that is, be slightly in such Circumstances as you advise of.

Affection, vid. *Love in Passion.*

Affirming, vid. *Answer infra.*

It shews of acting evidently, and so as to give others Assurance as strong.

Double, shews of acting first by Inclination, and after by Consideration, as are the Words.

Aim shews of the Aim.

Answer made you on your crying out, relief at Hand on your seeking.

Any Demand, shews you of things issuing to your Desires therein.

None made to your Question, threats your Matters therein will be crost.

Refus'd by your Enemy sneaking away, assures you Success, as &c.

One opposes you tho, threats such Course will obstruct your designed Actions.

You answer on Call, you perform as expected, & e con.

Vid. *Call* and *Question* infra.

On Demand, gives Actions corresponding according.

Apology, vid. *Excuse* infra.

Appeal shews of appealing, or acting thereto indeed.

Argument; outargue another, that is, act better as Experience shews.

Ask, vid. *Demand, Inquire* and *Question* infra.   Vid. *Answer* supra.

Bantred being, that is, treated as one of mean Parts, and so unworthy Transaction.

Bawdy writing to a Woman, shew'd *A.* using too great Freedom in his Letter to her.

Believe, that is, act as to be suppos'd believing according.   Vid. *Soul.*

Bid is as Command infra.

Blame, vid. *Chide* infra.

E e

Bleſſing heard, ſhews of your doing one good, and as if anſwerable to require it.

    A. unknown hearing in his Barn, ſhew'd A. acting kind to Workmen, by farming to his own Good.

You bleſs another, you occaſion him Bleſſings anſwerable.

Vid. *Curſe* infra.

Boaſting in general, ſhews of vainglorious Actions, as are the Words.

    So be in Circumſtances glorious as to occaſion it.

    Hear another, find him in Circumſtances according exceeding you.

    To ſome it has ſhewn a ſtern and haughty Carriage, importing as are the Words.

    With Prodigals, Thieves and Waſters, threats your ſelf alſo being vainly riotous.

    Before 2, ſhew'd A. of boaſting indeed, but not where perfectly known.

By ſhews by.

Caution ſhews of Caution.

Call in general, vid. *Anſwer* ſupra.

    It ſhews of Extremity, and ſeeking Aid on it.

    Call. A. ſeek the Aſſiſtance of his Perſon or like Courſe ; but acting with A. aſſures Command of ſuch Aſſiſtance.

A dead Man to come after you, be in a Deſign your ſelf thinks vain.

    A ſelf-Murderer act ſo, as if deſigning to do like him.

One to aid, you make Application according in Fact.

To have a Door opened, that is, a Freedom according allow'd.

One back, that is, paſſing by you make one alter his Courſe that would ſlight you.

-ing for Aid of St. *Chriſtopher*, and being unhelp'd on it, ſhew'd A. being drown'd.

Another to you, that is, by a Courſe of Force make him imitate you.

    Father, that is, own him to have acted as ſuch for you.

One known, that is, ſeek in Fact for Aid, as is the Perſon.

    Your Miniſter, follow your true publick Conſcience.

Crying Murder, ſhews of ſeeking Aid in worſt of Dangers.

    On ſeeing a Souldier, for fear of robbing.

    In a Pantry Door, ſeeking Remedy to ruinous Hurts thro Rents unpaid.

In Womb heard, vid. *Child* in *Grammar*.

Your Son hear, act to ſecure your future Expectations in Danger.

                  Call

Call ; crying out is as feeking new Aid on your Defpair occafioning it,
&c.

Called Coufin, being deceiv'd in fome Courfe.

    Eeggar by one, that is, created by him as if in Po-
       verty.

    Anfwer no, that is, act to falfify it.

Lion, gives you Victory and courageous Succefs.

Boy,   }
Fool, } be treated as fuch.

Shews of Affairs, alfo requiring your Prefence as if fo
call'd.

Out of an Houfe, threats you as mov'd to change your
    Oeconomy.

    By a Woman, as in a fudden Fit of Paf-
      fion, or thro fome Scheme.

Your Garden into your Houfe, tempted to lay
by your Plenty for a plain Oeconomy.

Into the Field being, that is, being in Circumftances
that require you to prepare for a Difpute.

By a Friend, warn'd accordingly of a good Opportunity
at hand.

Unknown Perfon, your felf follow unaccountable
    Courfes.

    3 fo, fhew'd A. oddly fick.

One known to follow him, exhorted him thro his
Succefs to imitate him.

An Angel coming from Heaven cloth'd yellow,
fhew'd A. of a Plague Infection offering.

An evil Angel or Demon, Death if not feen.

    Or if feen, Death with Defpair.

Your eldeft Son, threats your Inheritance in Diftrefs.

Perfon unfeen, vid. *Hear* in *Senfe.*

    Seen, warns you of fome Opportunity, as
is the Perfon.

Dead, Death if not feen, and in manner as they
died.

    Thrice, yet if fay won't come, not die.

    The Call is deadly Symptom appearing in
Fact, and the Denial Skill repelling.

    If feen, Death too, if follow'd to Place de-
folate and unknown.

Anceftor, act contrary to his will.

Son, Wife or Friend, and fay I come alike;
die and be at reft.

Virgin *Mary*, and fay you'l go   (Die)
Innocence.

Ee 3   Gall

Call. Called by, dead, Cardinal *Woolſey* thrice ſeen walking in his Chamber, to Archhiſhop *Laud* Death.

By your Sirname only, ſome one elſe may die and not you.

Cannot come ſhe ſaid, that is, ſhe prov'd actually diſabled from coming.

Calumnies, vid. *Slander* infra.

Cares not for you one ſays, that is, he acts every way to ſlight you.

Cenſured, that is, eſteemed.

Charge, vid. *Command* infra.

Charm againſt Snakes heard, gave Relief againſt ſubtle Enemies.

Chide, vid. *Accuſe* ſupra.

It ſhews of Impediments with Severity and Hate.

You chide another, you proceed ſo, &c e con.

Blaming Inferiors, gives you of their Amendment, as is the Blame.

Hear your Brother, ſhews you of jealous Intereſt ſtopping your profitable Proſpects.

An Eccleſiaſtick Judg, do what is worthy of his Reprimand.

A Tradeſman, be dun'd by a Meſſage in an hurry.

An Apothecaries Wife, ſhew'd acting preſumptuouſly and againſt Rule when ſick.

His Aunt Guardianeſs, ſhew'd *A.* of his Eſtate ill managed near to deſerve it.

The Founder, to a Viſiter gave him Recovery after Miſcariage.

The dead, the ſame.

A noble Youth chides *Xerxes* to war with the *Grecians,* that War prov'd his Puniſhment.

Civilly is civilly.

Commanding, ſhews cauſing things to be done as if ſo.

Of active Reſolutions occurring.

So of Actions iſſuing purſuant, and as if ſo commanded.

Refuſe or ſtand againſt, commands Defeat controlling proceeds.

Maundring is as impudent Control to ones Will.

Shews of Trouble and unruly Diſorders occaſioning thereof.

Seeing others, threats you with Trouble from Anger and Power.

Commanded in Bar-Gown by another in ſuch, to a Counſel ſhew'd him mean Treatment.

Hear of anothers ordering, refer you to ſuch an Equity.

Bid go to his own Country, foreſhew'd to *A.* Death.

Surrender your ſelf by an Enemy, ſhews he ſtrives to ſlave your Will.

Commanded.

Commanded. Bid run by a Robber, be urg'd by a prodigal Courſe for to
    borrow.
Commend, vid. *Praiſe infra*
Compariſon, vid. *Match in Quantity.*
        Vid. *Unknown Perſon in Grammar.*
     Shews of our acting variouſly from the common Road.
     If to your Credit and Advantage, it gives you Succeſs accord-
       ing.
     A's Country Plow beat his Coach and 6 at *London*, this ſhew'd
      A's Country State paying him beſt.
     All Fools at *Oxon* but *A.* this ſhew'd *A.* excelling in their like
      Learning.
     Comparing an Amethiſt Ring on his Finger to *A*'s Diamond one,
      ſhew'd *A*'s Poverty thro Religion great, as *B*'s thro Negligence
      and Softneſs.
Complain in general, vid. *Chide* ſupra.
     Hear your Friend, eaſe him according.
     It ſhews alſo of Ills meriting ſuch Complaints.
     Complaint of Ill, to ſome Amendment according, and as uſually
      thereon follows.
         Hear another, ſhews Matters mending to you in their
         like Circumſtances.
     Words of Pity are true alſo tho by an Enemy, for he may pity.
Concerning, vid. *About* ſupra.
Confeſs a Fault, act as if you eſteemed your ſelf ſo faulty.
Conjure, vid. *Spirits.*
Conſult, vid. *Inquire* infra.
Contradiction, ſhews of Matters iſſuing, as is the Contradiction to the
    contrary, *&c.*
Cry, vid. *Call.*
Curſe, vid. *Bleſs* ſupra.
     Another, ſhews you of the Ills of your Curſes befalling him.
     God, be in Circumſtances miſerable according.
Demand in general, vid. *Queſtion* ſupra.
     Why, *&c ?* that is, act ſo as if calling Matters ſo in queſ-
      tion, *&c.*
     Replies are as confident counter Actions.
     It ſhews of acting on a preſumptuous Suppoſal, that ſome-
      what is our Right.   Vid. *Anſwer* ſupra.
     Dead Parents demanding thy Child, thou not denying, he dies.
             (Family Diſeaſe, *&c.*)
             Denied and departing angry on it, threats
               him hard Recovery.
             But they replying, they will have
               him, he'l die for all.
     Thine Horſe as ſtole ſee one, that is, find them acting as if
     preſuming thy Profeſſion laid by.

Commanded Mony by a Prodigal for riding in his Coach, that is, thy
  felf being in hazard of thy Eftate thro ftately Lazinefs.
Denying fhews of acting as in Denial.
Departing anfwers to admitting others to Commands anfwerable.
Directed by your very dead Brother, your contrary Intereft proving con-
  fiftent to you.
Difowning fhews of acting thereto.   Vid. *Name* infra.
Difputing with Party and Judg too, threats you as beat in Controverfy.
    With a Philofopher, gives you Profit and Wifdom too.
      Of eating, *A.* hearing between his own Aunt and own Doctor,
        and his own Doctor feen eat on it, fhew'd that the Diet
        doubted on Experience would not hurt.
Drolling at your Defigns hear one, find them to be acted againft, as fo
  expofing them.
Dream told a thing is none, that is, find your Dream Monition will
  prove more than a meer Fancy or Imagination.
Enemy, that is, a Courfe as hurtful as fo.
Enquire, vid. *Enquire* infra.
Entreating, threats you acting as yielding and overcome.
Examine, vid. *Enquire* infra.
Exclamation, O the Devil fay, that is, find your felf in horrid Defpair.
    Vid. *Call* fupra.
Excufe making, fhews of offending according to occafion it.
      For a thing, fhews of your acting fo as to fhew you
        diflike it.
      That you would not fteal, that is, do a Wrong as bad.
      To your Creditor, prodigally incapacitating your felf
        from paying him.
Exhort, vid. *Advife* fupra.
Expos'd being in your Parlour, that is, your Converfe with Superiors
    being fullied.
      Another being, fhews of his Cavils render'd contemptible.
Extempore fear to fpeak, confult others in your Actions.
    Declaring, fhew'd *A.* of paying Mony without Aid.
Farewel heard or faid, is good to all on new Undertakings.
    To a Lover, Good.
      But from a Friend fick in Bed, if not abrupt, it threats
        of his Death near.
    A Phyfician bidding *Efculapius*, fhew'd to him of his Practice
      failing.
    Bid and embraced by *A.* faying he muft now forbear the Com-
      pany of Men, he then died.
    Not bid by your Friends on your defign'd Travel, threats of
      your Defigns failing.
    Bidding your Phyfician as departing, threats you of Sicknefs
      approaching.
Flattery in general, fhews of a bad Fortune.
    To Flattery, is to be bafe.

                                        Flattery

Flattery in general, to be flatter'd is to be cheated by the Person by whom.

    Is good to none but those who use it, to them Gifts as therefore.

    By a fair Woman, gives you good Fortune.

    Dead Enemy, threats you with Deceit.

    Mother in-law, shews of some awing Wheedler fooling you.

    To others, Banishment.

Follow shews Follow.

Forbidding, shews of actual Hindrances answerable.

    Proceeding thro an House, Baulks in Oeconomy Designs according.

    A. his young Son seen to cast his Snot about, shew'd A. of Scandal hindring him venting his Projects.

Fully shews fully.

Future things shew of things future.

Happiness shews of Happiness.

Hear good News at A. be told Matters will issue well for you there.

Heir one will make you, that is, such a Course will be a full Reward in it self to you, or your full Wish 'twill answer.

Hope such a thing is so, be your self incapacitated to see it so.

Good shews of Good.

I. is literal of I.

Jeer'd be, as where's your Sword ; that is, be at a fault in your Virtue as worthy of such Jeer.

    By a Neighbour, that is, be in a common reputed Error.

    Vid. *Jest* in *Diversion.*

    Shews of Treatment, with Circumstances of Contempt answerable.

    Jeer a Justice, act as above him, and with Contempt to his Power.

Jeering. Reflect on anothers Work, act so as to confound his Projects in it, and to neglect and slight them.

Jeer'd being by others, threats you so acting as to be deem'd worthy thereof.

    A rich Man for somewhat, that is, acting somewhat fooling your Hopes to Riches.

Ill shews literally of Ill.

Enquire a way, learn a means for somewhat according.

    And have no Answer, gives you very ill Issue, you will not skill the Method.

    The Truth of Facts, that is, act so as to secure warily the Mistakes of such Facts.

    For a Magistrate, take some Measures solemnly to rectify Disorders, as *&c.*

Enquiring in things evident, threats with Deceit and Mistakes as if you had need so to do.

Intent shews of Intent.

Interpreting

Interpreting Scripture, shew'd *A.* of receiving Tithes.

Irony, Vid. *Banter* supra.

It shews of it.

Knowing not of a matter said, that is, your Actions shew you as not concern'd in it.

       Told to know of such things, that is, they will actually so appear to you by relative Facts.

Latin, Greek, &c. Vid. *Numbers* and *Languages.*

Letters D. J. C. Dead Jewish War *Cyrene.*

       Happy as B. blesses, C. curses.

Little shews of little.

Love, vid. *Passion.*

Lying in general threats with Fear, Death, Grief, Idleness, and Despair.

       To some 'tis as defrauding and jeering.

       To all but Players Hurt.

       Unto Strangers is least hurt.

       About what it is, in that is threatned your great Danger.

       To be belied is greatly to be deceived or applauded.

Mocking Boys beating, shew'd *A.* of repelling others impos'd Charges.

       By Repetition, Vid. 2 infra.

          By an Apparition in your Prayers, beguil'd thro a Cheat in your Wishes.

       Vid. *Contempt* in *Passion.*

Muttering shews of acting maliciously, and pursuing confus'd and unaccountable Ills against whom, &c.

       Your self, shews you stifling your Resentment as in fear, &c.

       Hearing another, frustrates you in your Expectations according upon them.

Name is still Allegorick, where there is no Circumstance to oppose it.

       Gold Dr. opposes you, that is, an Offer of Riches would thwart you.

       Domitian assaulting *A.* shew'd him of House-robbers menacing him.

       Southby is prosperous as *South.*

    Allegorick. *Gravesend* near, that is, a Correspondence near hazarding Death.

       Ridout an Oculist coming to see, shew'd *A.* of his going in a Journy of Survey.

       Julius a Friend stopping *A.* shew'd of the Month of *July* for Heat doing it as friendly.

       A Taylor nam'd *Bland*, a Carpenter making Gritboards.

    Literal in part, *Mimas* Mount, that is, not that which you know, but another of the Name.

       Cambises seeing *Smerdes* his Brother thron'd, kill'd him upon't, but another bearing that Name for all got away his Crown after him.

Name

Name Proper shews the Man his Property, and all that belongs to him.
   F. Bishop's Books having, shew'd F. of the same Name
   being a Godfather.
      Sirname call'd by only by the Dead, shews of another's
      like Death, not yours.
   Ludgate heard of as remov'd, threated 1 Son of 3 with Sickness
   to a Father.
      Travelling from it, shew'd the same.
Another's know, that is, fathom his utmost Resolutions.
      Papist's the same as to whole Popery.
      Take on you, sneak thro fear as to be of his Character.
Change yours, alter your State according.
      Disown it, fatally sneak from your true Character, &c.
      Vid. *Letters* in *Language* infra.
Forget yours, change it for another.
         Find another, it proves the Name you'd take.
            Fix'd on such, lay the Bent of your For-
            tune on its Issue.
   Losing, threats of Life, Circumstance, and Riches.
            Blotted out, threats of a most grievous Portent.
   Named in sleep was *Jovinian*, and made Emperor after upon it.
New shews of things new.   News, vid. *Hear* in *Sense.*
None is literal of none.   Of shews of.
Offer'd be a thing, that is, be satisfied in your Thoughts that 'tis at your
   command.
Order, Vid. *Command* supra, and *Soul* in *Man.*
Perfuaded by your Brother, the Submission of a thwarting Interest
      moving you.
      Relations being, threats you as in Circumstances dange-
      rous to need it.
Positively is positively.
Prayers, vid. *Religion.*
Praife a Courfe, that is, actually fet others in ufe of it.
      Commend fomewhat your felf, or hear it commended by proper
      Perfons, find it after deferve well at your hands.
      Commended be by one, act fo as in his Way or Courfe to de-
      ferve it.
      Another, act to shew he deferves fo of you.
Preach, Vid. *Sermon* in *Religion.*
Proclamation heard made, shew'd A. of hinting at a fecret but folemn
      Refolution to others.
      Reading one fet out by the King, to a Wife shew'd hear-
      ing of a folemn Refolution made by her Husband as
      to publick Affairs.
Promifes shew of Changes of Affairs, and Performances anfwerable.
      To follow the Dead calling, to die on Sicknefs prefenting.
      'd a better Buttery, shew'd to A. of a better Houfekeeping on
      Boarders coming.
Queftion, Vid. *Demand* fupra.   Queftion

Queſtion ask'd you by one you meet, ſhews he acts to expect you alter your Courſe.

Ask an Angel who anſwers you, you preſuming your ſelf a Divine Meſſenger ; this Intercourſe between your own reaſoning and divine Preſumption offers.

Anſwer'd being, gives aſſured Hopes, or that Courſe will ſo perform to your Expectation.

Vid. *Anſwer* ſupra.

Opinion as'd, ſhew'd *A.* of Opinion ask'd,

Ask another, be inform'd by him as if ſo ask'd.

Wak'd before you are ask'd, perplex'd with a doubtful Unwillingneſs.

Dead Judg hear ask you if you need him, be tempted your ſelf to judg wickedly.

Railing Papiſt hear, find unreaſonable mute Impoſitions obſtruct your Deſigns.

Fool call another, that is, act ſo, and as if you thought him ſuch.

At another ſeem, be treated by him as to require it.

Vid. *Slander* infra.

Rebuke, vid. *Forbid* ſupra.

Smartly is as ſmartly.

'd by G O D, being in a fault to him as ſo deſerving.

Another, that is, under an awe anſwerable, and as if ſo rebuk'd.

A King you'd converſe as cloth'd ill, the Grandeur you would awe others by proves abſurd.

A's ſecond Marriage by his firſt Wife threatning to fetch the ſecond away, ſhew'd her Death alſo.

Your Son, act to ſecure your Expectation in hazard.

Another acting, that is, act as in diſlike to ſuch his Actions, and in Counteraction.

Reflect, Vid. *Jeer* ſupra.

Refuſe to eat, that is, accept of a Profit offer'd.

Of his dead Father with his Brothers, ſhew'd *A.* dying before his Father, and not inheriting with them.

A Prodigal's Offer, act as in contradiction to his Courſes.

To ſalute you ſee a Woman, find of a beneficial Fortune waving you.

A. refuſes you, he acts to thwart you, as *&c.*

Repetition mock'd in Prayer by a Ghoſt, cheated in your hotteſt Deſires.

Affirm twice, vid. *Affirm* ſupra.

Vid. *Tautology* infra.

Reply, Vid. *Demand* ſupra.

Reports of Cenſure ſhew of Actions done toward them.

In general ſhew of publick ſlight Appearances, and ſuch as might occaſion them.

Reports

Reports in general. *A.* heard said his Anceftor was dead but believ'd it not, he flighted not Induftry for the Expectation of Inheritance.

That Mrs. *E.* was brought to Bed, fhe was not, but a Nurfe came to her as if therefore.

That the King was at *Nottingham* raifing an Army, and that *London* was preparing againft him, that according to common Opinion, that is, that it was to have been fuppos'd fo.

Reprove, vid. *Rebuke* fupra.

Said, that is, in Circumftances might make you deem'd fo.

Said, Vid. *Report* fupra.

Saluting a Friend gives you good News.

Neighbours feen, fhews of diftant Hopes, and bids beware of Tricks.

Enemies feen, fhews of Reconciliations.

Satisfied he fays he is, that is, in fact you will find you have left him in no doubt.

Saucy in Words, that is, vexing with Scorn in Actions.

Scandal another and part on it, find he treats you fo ill as to provoke it.

Vid. *Rail* fupra, and *Slander* infra.

Scolding hearing your Wife, threats you with great Torments.

Slandering another fhews you Victor, *& e con.*   Vid. *Saucy* fupra.

'd by one unknown as mad, fhew'd *A.* angry at himfelf as carelefs.

Slander another, act to them as fuppofing fuch Slander true.

Conclude to fay no more, that is, now act otherwife.

Sleep thy Father does, but is not dead, faid one, this fhew'd him blind.

Snap up, Vid. *Mutter* fupra.   Vid. *Interrupt* in *Action.*

Song finging of a Bride, fhew'd *A.* of a new long Contract Joy.

Now Foes gone, *&c.* fhew'd *A.* of happy Times approaching.

An Averfion, fhew'd of the like again at hand.

Vid. *Verfes* infra.

Story tell to a rich Man, that is, find out a Project ufeful for him.

Telling forty in an Hour, fhew'd *A.* of acting inconfiftently.

Reacted fee in an Houfe, find the like, as *&c.*

Vid. *Plays* in *Diverfion,* &c.

Summon fhews to fummon.

Swearing in a matter, acting in defiance therein thro your Truft in G O D.

To others Actions refolute and fierce fo.

Talk of doing fomewhat, act as if fo defigning or poffible to be deem'd fo.

Tautology, thrice *Gladius* read, that is, your Refentment found moft firmly fettled.

Tell,

Tell, vid. *Acquaint* ſupra.

Thanks receive, do Benefits requiring.

That ſhews That.

The ſhews The.

There, that is, in Circumſtance as is the Place.

They ſhews They.

Thought, that is, matters iſſue ſo as to require ſuch Thought.

Threatned by G O D, ſhews of grievous Ills and Dangers.

     Falſe ones is very bad alſo in their ſeveral Juriſdictions.

     Spirits. Devils, threats with Conſpiracies and great Troubles of Mind and Deſpairs.

     Dead Enemies ſhews of Hindrance.

     Tyrants by Robberies.

     If Miſchief follow on it, 'tis irretrievable.

     Vid. *Dead.*   Vid. *Demand* and *Rebuke* ſupra.

     Perſons. Another, ſhews he acts as if deſigning you Damage.

     Parents, ſhews of their Vices hurting us.

     Father, Family Cares oppreſſing.

     Mother in Law, ſhews of hard ſlaviſh Dangers.

     Kings may reach Life, Prieſts not.

     A Goaler, be in danger of Debt and Ruin by it.

     By one, to ſome Danger thro their like Circumſtances.

     A Prodigal, thro Prodigality, &c.

     Your Tenant naked, your ſelf be put hard to it in your Farming, &c.

     Beaſts. The Dragon is ill to all, and to the Sick Death.

     An Eagle, the Efforts of ſome great ambitious Man's Anger.

-ning another, ſhews of your having him at command to do him the Hurt.

     To acquaint another, that is, giving a conceal'd Awe according.

     His Mother in Law and ſparing his Debtor, ſhew'd *A.* thriving to pay his Debts and ſcorn his Enemies.

     A. ſeeing a Soldier he cried Murder on it, *A.* fortified againſt Robbers that ſurvey'd his Houſe.

I heard your Converſe ſaid an Enemy, that is, he proceeded if your Aim foreknown.

I'l find the Mayor out ſays one, that is, he ſtrives ſecretly to outvote you, or command you ſo, &c.

Told, Vid. *Acquaint, Report* and *Tell* ſupra.

     So, that is, matters are as to common Intendment ſtated ſo as to occaſion ſuch ſpeaking.

erſes, Vid. *Song* ſupra.

Verſes,

Verses, to be understood as other Words, but in a manner more formal.

    Writing, shews of acting most regularly, even to a Nicety as are the Words.

    They shew Actions nice to hair.

    Sung, such Actions deliver'd with artful Cunning.

    Rhime is as Consent in Action.   Vid. *Love* in *Passion.*

Upbraided, vid. *Rebuke* supra.

Waiting shews of matters defer'd answerable.

Warming your Servants to be gone, that is, being in Circumstances too mean to keep them.

Welcome bid, gives you a full Command as is the Welcome.

    The Elector of *Brandenburgh* offering to make *A.* shew'd him that how his own Country Laws menacing him, there seems his only reasonable Refuge.

Want 3 *s.* saying, shew'd *A.* gaming and winning so much.

Wheedling one, threats you in want of Aid as is the Person.

    Another wheedles you, he wants your Aid.

    Vid. *Flatter* supra.

Who shews as who.

Why, Vid. *Demand* supra.

Will shews Will.

Worst shews of the Worst.

C H A P. LIV.

Of Discourse.

IN general, Vid. *Conference* infra, and *Manner.*

    Discourse mutually, be mutually bold to Action with each other.

    Talk with, make to bear, as *&c.*

        Talk unto, suffer.

    Scorn Unknown won't answer, be above an odd Course you cannot bring to Action.

With another, that is, act as relating to him, or in his way of rea-
(1)   soning.

    So be bold to deal with him, *&c.* and act according as is shewn by the Talk.

    A Schoolfellow, acting under the Prejudice of such a Relation.

    A Beggar sitting by him, settledly transact as deeming your self no better.

Angels, gives Joy and Truth in what said as sent of G O D.

With

With Angels. So it ſhews of acting on the foot of preſuming your
(1)   ſelf a Divine Meſſenger, and receiving ſuch Meſſages.
     Aged Perſons, in Teſtimony it gives you Credit.
       In Malice or dotage Matters, 'tis croſs.
     Artiſts, believe them aſſuredly in their way, whether known or
       not.
       It ſhews of things iſſuing to the Perfection of ſuch
       Skill.
       Sons and Prentice Boys ſpeaking, ſhew the ſame, and
       give you Command of their ſecret Expectances.
     Beaſt heard is ſtill true.   Vid. *Beaſt.*
       It ſhews thee thine Enemies will fly before thee.
       As are the Words, ſo will iſſue ſuch matter of Appetite or
       Paſſion, as is the Beaſt or Bird.
     Bird as Beaſt, Vid. *Raven* in *Bird.*
     Brethren, threats you with Actions croſſing you in Intereſt.
       They adviſing beware, 'tis as contrary Intereſt inter-
       fering.   Vid. *Dead* infra.
     Children as innocent and unartful, gives you all Truth.
       They advantage you as twatling of their Parents In-
       tereſts.
     Chriſt, gives you Truth, Joy, and Comfort.
       It ſhews alſo of imitating him in Actions.
     Dead, ſhews us as living among Rogues.
       Generally it promiſes us good, and that a clear De-
       ceit will appear.
       It gives a bold Courage and clear Conſcience.
       And with the greater Perſon, the greater.
     Perſons. Virgin *Mary,* Joy.
       What ſhe ſays alſo proves true.
       Friends, gives you a Proſperity as is the Perſon
       Enemies, prevent Evils of Negligence, &c.
       Brethren directing us, our very Rivals coaſſiſting
       us.
       Conſumptive talking with that turn'd to a Can-
       caſe, ſhew'd *A.* his own Infirmity curing eaſily.
       Would talk with you in a Chamber but you eſ-
       cape, finiſh an Oeconomy where Death
       threated preventing.
       Vid. *Call* ſupra.   Vid. alſo *Dead.*
     Devils, Vid. *Spirits.*
     Diſcreet Perſons, and ſo will your Affairs alſo iſſue.
     Diviners, vid. *Artiſts* ſupra.
     Earth, vid. *E.*
     Enemies, ſhews of acting in Courſes will hurt you.
       To ſome of Banters.
       Telling Wonders heard, ſhews of Ironies.
       But overheard as ſpeaking to their Friends, is all Truth
       and to be believ'd.
                                     Wit

With Fathers, believe them in Reverence, and from their Love so be
(1)   suppos'd.

Friends, shews the Transaction will end as friendly.

G O D, vid. *Spirits.*

    It shews of reaching greatest Purity and Truths.

Great Men, shews of being aw'd or designing in Grandeur, &c.
    to awe, as &c.

Kings are as Great Men, but to be believ'd as G O D S.
    Vid. *King* in *Office.*

    Tyrants, dispose of your Affairs as in terror of Tyranny.

Ladies, vid. *Women* infra.

Lords, shews as Great Men and Kings *supra* in their degree.

Master or Mistress, to some design where under Control.
    To others it gives Gain.

Men young and comely, act in Perfection as are they in their
    nature.

Physician your Friend, take an happy Course for your Health, or
    Remedy, as &c.

    Told *Augustus* he'd be stab'd in his Tent, and lying
    thence he escap'd it.

Priests, believe them as G O D's Ministers.
    To some transact in a religious Course according.

Princes, vid. *King* supra.

Prophets, speak Truth as G O D's Messengers.
    They shew us also of Prophetick Transactions.

Prudent Persons, and so also state your Measures of Action.

Selves, we speak as we shall in Will or Interest after act.
    Sometimes as necessitated.

Son his own threatning him with Danger, shew'd *A.* of his Ex-
    pectation answerable in danger.

Sun to be believ'd as if the King.

Strangers, Vid. *Unknown* in *Grammar.*
    They shew of Transactions odd and unaccountable.

Trade, Vid. *Artists* supra.

Unknown, vid. *Strangers* supra.

Unseen heard speak, shew of Actions issuing on a Presumption
    of an unaccountable Course in Action.

    Dead heard calling, shew'd *A.* Death.

    Unknown calls, the Hazard of unaccountable Courses
    moves your Care in Action.

    Tells you of good, an unaccountable Course
    issues therein.

    Man-Servant hearing, that is, regarding his Advice, tho
    not his interested personal Courses and Drifts.

Wise Men, and will issue your Proceeds.

Women, threats us vers'd in weak and speculative Designs.
    To some Instructions in Arts and Sciences.
    Fair ones, to Batchelors has given Marriage.

With

With. Women ; King's Women, triflingly awing in weak Deſigns.

Manner. Loud Speech, Acts of moſt manifeſt Import according.

   (2)   Tell one he is unruly, ceaſe entruſting him in a Secret as if ſo.
        Literal or Allegorick, vid. *Grammar.*
        Dare not ſpeak to the King in an Houſe, that is, make bol
           with his Authority, &c. in an Officer.
        In general, all Speech ſhews of Facts anſwerable.
        Speak hear one, conform your ſelf to his Actions.
            Anſwer, act afreſh upon it.
        See a Friend won't ſpeak, find of a good Courſe in Diſcourſ
           that you can't ripen to Action.
         2 Lovers meeting could not ſpeak, &c. Parents broke off th
           Match.
        Spoke unto ſuffer, ſpeak unto act.
      Place bleſs'd by unknown in his Barn being, ſhew'd *A.* actin
      religiouſly kind to his Farm-Labourers.
      Conference with a Man in general, ſhews of ſome Matter ſtate
      or Account fixed.
        Of 2 Friends ſeen, ſhew'd *A.* of a good Hit near.
           2 or 3 Enemies ſeen, ſhew'd of a Conſpiracy.
           A great Company of unknown, ſhew'd the like.
           Friend and an old *Jew* ſeen together, ſhew'd m
             of a good Courſe to propheſy in ken.
           Rich Man chiding a Spunger *A.* hearing, ſhew't
             himſelf acting ſo as to ſcorn ſuch doings to *A*
           Covetous Man and 1 unknown ſeen, ſhew'd to *A*
             a good Project of Profit.
           A prudent Friend croſſing *A*'s way ſpoke to him
             a Prudent Courſe as are the Words diverts hi
             Deſigns.

Subject. Buying Silk talk of, be in Circumſtances of Plenty according.

   (3)   Of a 2*d* Wife talking, ſhew'd *A.* trick'd up by young Women
        and as if ſo forebeſpoke.
        Prudent is literal, vid. *Grammar.*
        Death, ſhew'd *A.* taking Phyſick to prevent it.
        Riches talking of, to a King ſhew'd *A.* awing others by Proſpec
         of his Riches.
        Conjugal Love talking of, ſhew'd *A.* agreeing well with his
         Wife.
        Eaſt to a Joiner, projecting a Friendſhip that will end in Sepa·
         ration.
        Of my Dream Skill, ſhew'd me grown current in it, and bold
         to ſhew it.
        Of a Prodigal, Tranſactions of his like State occurring.
        Of a Parſonage, ſhew'd *A.* aw'd in Tranſactions thro ſuch re-
         gard.

Quality. Reports, vid. *Words* ſupra.

   (4)   Idle ; Dr. *H.* ſaid he chriſtened *A.* this ſhew'd *A.* talking of
        things of that date.
                                   Quality.

Quality. Hidden Words are always evil, whether obscure or whisper'd.
  (4)   4 Words, as *Mene Tekel, &c.* an Ill of Council.
         Abracadabra, as unknown 'tis ill, as one 'tis absolute;
             and as of 11 Letters 'tis imperfect ; but as it ends in
             a Reverse to its Beginning, it shews such Ill dwin-
             dles to nothing.
         To all, Anger and Loss.
             Vid. *Unknown* in *Grammar.*
             Friends, care not to speak harsh things.
             Enemies, sometimes fear it.
         Found wrote on a Bed, shew'd *A.* of esteeming horri-
             bly of Laziness.
         Speak such, wilfully induce such Fate on your self.
         Upharsin, shews of a broken Potsheard; as told me in
             a Dream *(Daniel.)*
     Imperfect Speeches, imperfect Efforts of Action.
     Angry Words ceasing, leaving off teasing Actions.
         Hard Words had, *A.* turn'd off his Man; he imploy'd
             him not on it as before.
     Inviting one to discourse, shew'd of proposing him a good
         Bargain.
     Doubtful Rain in 3 Days or not in 3 Weeks said, shew'd of first
         3 Days dry, and then 3 Weeks wet.
     Whispering heard, shews of a secret contrary Tendency, and
         threats of either Evil or Deceit.
     Voice, vid. *Hear* in *Sense.*
Sentence of *Latin* give to *A.* deem him a good Scholar.
  (5)

C H A P. LV.

Of Language.

Words in general, shew to us of Actions as Tokens of Words.
  (1)   Heard are soonest done, but less certain.
             Wrote are more slow, but more certain, as
                 wanting a Mover.
              They declare of Methods of Action
                 most solemn.   Vid. *Write* infra.
             Printed, shew of Proceeds on the most solemn
                 and just weighed Resolves. Vid. *Books, &c.*
     Spoken Words, shew of rasher Actions done pursuant.
         Of Birds or Beasts, vid. *Discourse supra.*
         You speak, you act pursuant.
         Another speaks, they do the like.
                 F f   *Words*

Words. Spoken. You ſpeak they anſwer, their Actions correſpond
(1)   to yours, *&c con.*
            In general, they ſhew of the ſecret Tendency of our
            Actions, as *&c.*
        Examples : *Victor,* that is, *qui victus fui.*
            Philotheus, that is, *Vitâ Impius.*
            Amor Roma.
            Told no Danger of Robbers, that is, to
                common Intendment there appears no
                Fear of erring.
            Eid a Youth to ſhave, that is, exhort him
                to be manly.
            Elood 7 Years the better, that is, you ſo,
                the richer.
            I'le gore him a Cow ſaying to a Calf,
                ſhew'd of a Landlord rooting out his
                Tenant.
            Gladius ſeen thrice in a Letter to a *Ci-
                vilian,* ſhew'd *A.* thrice tempted to
                ill Behaviour.
            A. paſſes thro *Rome* and *France,* and told
                ſo *Cromwel* ; that is, hector them.

Tokens and Signs, ſhew of Words purſuant, and as Words of Actions.
(2)   Brother beckoning *A.* to account, ſhew'd him of a Creditor
            ſending to meaſure his Tut-work.
        Shewing *A.* Tickets of *Sepharvaim,* ſhew'd of his ſhew-
            ing Inſtances of her Arbitrarineſs.
    In hœ Signo vinces, us'd with Succeſs by *Conſtantine.*
    Vid. *Ticket* in *Plays* in *Diverſion.*
    Good near *Veſpaſian* when he meets one drawing a Tooth of
        Nero's, that is, *Nero* ſoon after dying he ſucceeded.
    A. mark'd in Back with Chalk by his Father from Ruin, his
        Father's like Husbandry ſupported him from it.
    Anothers ſee, receive a ſure Notice of his Intentions anſwera-
        ble.

Speaking ſhews of actually performing.
(3)   Loud, vid. *Hear* in *Senſe.*
        Vid. *Diſcourſe* ſupra.
        Eirds or Beaſts heard, vid. *B.* and *Diſcourſe* ſupra.
        Mute Perſons ſeen, ſhew of Liars.
    In a ſtrange Tongue, to a Lover write to his Miſtreſs, or commune
        with her in ſecret.
    Unknown dead hear, to you find the Good or Ill unthought done
        you.
    To God, ſhews of the Beginning of Prophecy.
    Againſt another, receiving Provocation as ſo to do.
    Hear another, perceive of his Acts ſo, but anſwer him, act accord-
        ingly on it.

                                    Speaking

Speaking in a Meeting-House an unknown *A.* hearing, shew'd of him-
　　(3)　　　　　self writing a rash *extempore* Letter.

He soon vanith'd on it, he strait blotted out the
　　　　　　Paſſage on it.

Reading ſhews of acting exact, and on ſolemneſt Grounds, and as ſpeak
　　(4)　　is more raſh.

It is vaſtly more ſolemn than ſpeaking, chiefly if of what is
　　printed.　　　Vid. *Books* infra.

Well, ſhews you purſuing a fix'd model'd Method truly.

Ill is bad, and threats you to laſt Days long or ſhort as
　　it is.

News ſhew'd *A.* of converſing variety of Company.

Letters Foreign *A.* ſeeing he could not read, ſhew'd him of ill
　　Succeſs in Buſineſs.

Proper unable to read, doting in a plain matter.

Epiſtolar, vid. *Letters* infra.

Languages unknown, ſhews of ſearching Difficulties.

Words illegible, Scandal thro Inconſiſtency of Action.

Paper, vid. *Write* infra.

A ridiculous one, ſhew'd *A.* of owning ſeriouſly an ex-
　　ploded Opinion.

Church-reſponſes to the Pſalms in your own Church, having your
　　common Deſires there.

But if your private *Memorandums* in their ſtead,
　　ſeek your own Ends only.

Books peruſing, that is, purſuing thoroly ſome Inſtructions, as is
　　the Book.

Near the End, has ſhewn the Readers Life ſo.

To all, act ſolemnly, as is the Inſtruction in the
　　Book.

Law-Books, relating to Dreams.

Romances and Comedies, give Joy and Comfort.

Joſephus, gives you divine Tranſaction, as is the mat-
　　ter.

Moſes's Words of the promis'd Land, gave *A.* as great
　　Proſperity at hand.

The Curſes all left out, with the greater Aſ-
　　ſurance.

Conjuring ones, ſhew'd *A.* of teaſing Men till Quarrels
　　came on't.

Matter ſerious and ſublime, gives Benediction and
　　Wiſdom.

Truanting in one, ſhew'd *A.* of allowing his
　　Servant in idling.

Whole Duty of Man, ſhew'd *A.* acting ſolemnly pur-
　　ſuant to a good Conſcience.

Learning, to the ignorant good.
　　(5)　　to others, Scandal of Folly and Dotage.

Learning, to the Childleſs, a Son that ſhall learn.
(5) Matter, ſtrange Languages, to the Sick frenzy.
to ſome, Marriage or Travel thither.
What you learn before, ſhews of ſuperfluous idle Care.
By Memory, ſhew'd of gathering up things by Degrees.
I earned as others boaſt your ſelf to be, that is, act as wiſely.
Teaching his Man the Mathematicks, ſhew'd *A.* reproving his Waſte Geometrically.
A Sharper would teach *A.* to ſhoot, but he refus'd ; he thriv'd to ſcorn ſuch Shifts.
Decible Birds, as Parrots, ſeen, are good ; but untaught threat with Fatigue.
Taught by a Philoſopher, that is, commanding a noble Inſtruction.
School your own ſeen flouriſh, ſhews of your Learnings being reſpected.
(6) Anothers being in, that is, in a Couverſe under Rebuke.
Stately enter, admit being diſciplin'd, but with Terms of State.
Diſliking Work-Patterns there, to a Woman ſhew'd her ſlighting ſuch like Monitions.
Busby's ſhew'd of Perfection.
Seeing him handle a Rod as I paſs'd among Scholars, ſhew'd me of this laborious Study, *&c.*
Womans be in, that is, comply to their Methods of Accompliſhment, *&c.*
-Maſter being, gives Magiſtracy, Sedition, or makes a Printer.
Enquiring of one, threats with Dotage.
Advise, that is, inſtruct one that thinks he can better teach you.
's Daughter's Husband robbing *A.* Learning Charges waſting him.
Seeing himſelf teach more advanc'd Scholars, ſhew'd him of his own great ſelf Improvement.
Before you, threats you as doting and wanting a Monitor.
Taking up a Rod, your ſelf being under as great a Rigour.
Vid. *Maſter* in *Grammar.*
Send for as Godfather to your Child, ſend to one to eſpouſe your Notions that will rather correct them.
Kiſſing him, ſhew'd *A.* dealing to a Quarrel with one too maſterleſs.
Skilful, vid. *Quality.*
Tutor walk with Deſign, with Imperfection that will ſubject you to reprimand.
Standing by you ſeen, ſhews of your continuing in ſuch State.

Writing.

Writing-Paper fetch from another, that is, get Inſtructions to act in an
(7)　　　Affair according.

Ask'd by a Lawyer, ſhew'd of his demanding an Eſtate to
be ſettled.

Cut out into Books, ſhew'd *A.* of his Eſtate and Life
idled away.

Quire expect of a Servant, that is, a full Temper fit for
your Orders and Service.

Deliver'd you ſome torn, ſome ſcribled ; he
proves humorſom and contrary.

½ wrote ½ blank, that is, an Inſtruction ½ perfect and ' to
be made out.

An Artiſt give you his Papers, you get a footing to diſcover his Art.

A's Maſter ſpoilt and cut out his Quire in blotting &c,
ſhew'd to *A.* a Clerk of his waſting his Eſtate in learning of the Law.

Hindred finding by Writings, ſhew'd *A.* that his Eſtate
being ſettled he had no other Security to offer.

Blotted or torn, may give of Buſineſs diſpatched if well or-
dered.

Out your Name being tho, is a moſt grievous Portent.
Sorts. Inſcription on a Medal, vid. *M.* in *Ornament.*

Wall, vid. *Wall* in *Houſe-parts.*

Church-Wall ſeen, ſhew'd of a Divines
Reſolutions appearing ſincere thro his
letting his Eſtate.

Door that none enter ſee, find a Method
of Acceſs in a Buſineſs reſtrain'd generally from all.

Tomb forget, diſcover of a Menace of
Death not to be.

Writings or Deeds ſealing, gives us Gains great and worthy of ſuch.

Of the dead fetching, ſhew'd me of endeavouring after God's Spiritual Diſpenſations
on ill Men.

Stuck againſt his Houſe reading, ſhew'd *A.* of Loſs by
thieving.

Scrol wrote on, ſhews you of ſome inevitable Fate attending you ſure, even as a Proverb.

So it ſhews of Matters conceal'd a little, as
wrap'd up.

Memorandum Paper *A's* deliver'd him torn, ſhew'd him of
his Neglect therein retriev'd.

Seen in general, ſhews of your Affairs
manag'd by it.

F f 3　　　　　　*Writing.*

Writing. Sorts. Bill in Equity ſee carried croſs you to the left, find good
(7)　　　Conſcience obſtructing your profitable Methods pro-
pos'd.

Write in general is more ſlow, but more certain than ſpeak;
it ſhews of cool Determinations, but wants
a Mover.

Words unknow, vid. *Diſcourſe.*

Vid. *Unknow* in *Grammar.*

Letters learn, to attain to a Spiritual Freedom.
And ſo alſo, copy a ſure Form.

Epiſtles, uſe Endeavours for Friendſhip.

Verſes, ſhew'd as propheſying.

Tranſcribing them, ſhew'd *A.* of acting
by Prophecies by him.

Perſon. Your Writing ſeen in anothers Book, ſhews he pays
you Mony.

To others, it ſhews of their ſolemn Care
of your Concerns.

A Prodigal demands Mony of you by a Bill, but
it proves not to be of your own Hand; that is,
you find Prodigality falſly charged on you,

Manner. With the left Hand ſee another, threats you with
tricking.

You write ſo, you cheat.

Illegible ſeen, threats you with Inconſiſtency in your
Affairs.

In the Church, as to Matters of Religion.

Letters ſhew us of kind Secrets, eſpecially if ſealed.
(8)　　　Vid. *Letters* in *Diſcourſe.*

Anothers, their Friendſhip in cool Determination.

Our own, our Friendſhip,

A. reading her own Letter, ſaid as ſhe had not
ſet her Name to it, ſhe might diſown it if
ſhe pleas'd; this ſhew'd *A.* acting all things
of Friendſhip within Modeſty, to one ſhe
lik'd to be a Sweet-heart.

Quarrelling about, Variance as to the States of Friendſhip.

Reading them, diſpoſes us to the Affairs in them with Friendſhip.

Of a ſingular Perſon, approving with joyful Practice of
his ſingular Methods in Converſe.

Writing, ſhews of Endeavours for ſure Friendſhip.

To a *Civilian,* with Apology of raſh Behaviour, &c.

Seeing only, ſhews of good News preſenting, they give Greet-
ings of Health at leaſt.

Receiving, ſhews of Friends met, or a Friendſhip new made.

To ſome, have a Seaſon to do or receive a Benefit
according as wrote.

Letters

Letters receiving, to some others receive such Letters on their behalf.
(8)   Many, has shewn of many Occasions for them offering.   Vid. *Receive* in *Possess.*

Vid. *Read* supra.

From a Miller, have a friendly Notice about great
Work, *&c.*

Brother-in-law, shew'd of a Friendship offering
from a coaxing Stranger.

Your Father, being friendly to one in Family
regard.

A seal'd one in general, shews of Secrets and a good
Business.

From a Prince, with Dignity.

Your Father, Family Regard engaging
you to a Friendship.

Deliver another let him see you, find him engag'd in a new
Friendship.

Deliver'd you by an Enemy, a Friendship that ends by crossing
an Affair, as *&c.*

Delivering another and telling him the Contents are so, he answers
yes; that is, you treat him as if so, and he acts upon it an-
swerably.

News Letters seeing, shews us of meeting of Friends acquainting us with News.

Diverted in reading them, pleas'd in such Visits.

See writing, act what may occasion such, and by
an Enemy to evil Issue, *&c.*

Foreign ones, act to occasion such.

Offer'd *A.* to buy in a broad way, shew'd *A.* of Reports of Plenty thro Friendship, *&c.*

News, vid. *Reports* in *Words.*

Hear of a fine Stranger dead, find of an unexpected Aid failing us.

Bid go to a Place where to hear good News,
shew'd *A.* of a happy Decree for him there.

CHAP. LVI.

Of Books.

IN general, they shew us of old Affairs and as long, long or short so
(1)   to be our Lives.

To some, of noble Instructions worthy as of
a Book.

With various readings, vid. *Bible* below.

In general. Library fine, an excellent Set of Notions always efforting.
   (1)   Your Fathers, of beſt Uſe to your proper being.
   Sentence *A*'s, his ſet Notion towards ſuch a Method of Action.
      tion.
   Globes ſeen, ſhew of ſolemn Scientifick Schemes relating
      to the whole World.
Property. Meek Man's, that is, his like Methods of Notion.
   Biſhop *F*'s, vid. *Religion.*
   Papiſts, vid. *Common-Prayer* infra.
   Acts. Carried by a Mule ſeen derided, ſhew'd *A.* of his
            pious Intentions hinder'd.
                  In Pocket a Book or Inſtruction, in perpetual
                     Care.
            .Deſtroy or deſpiſe a Book, that is, ſlight the Method
               to attain ſuch a Book or Inſtruction.
            Diſtinguiſh into Sorts, do the ſame as to ſolemn Notions.
               tions.
            Eating them, to Scholars and Bookſellers good, to
               others ſudden Death.
            Finding, that is, ſome good and weighty Inſtruction
                  worthy of being in one.
                  A Dream-Book, that is, diſcovering a true
                     Inſtruction about Dreams.
                  Gold in one, that is, attaining a Profit thro
                     a well thought Management.
                  A Common-Prayer-Book large, getting a way
                     to attain our publick Wiſhes to the full.
            Get away a Papiſt's Pſalms-Book, defeat all the Joys
               of Popery.
            Given you, ſome noble Inſtruction attain'd thro
                     Hopes according.
                  By a Perſon meeting you, that is, thro
                     a Courſe ſtopping your former Methods,
                        thods,
                  In a flying Chariot of Ropes, thro your
                     projective Courſe of Reaſoning.
         Printing your Book deſiring one, threats of your
               Notions exploded.
                  Printed Paper carrying, ſhew'd of ſuing out
                     a Writ.
                  Read, that is, act moſt ſolemnly as you read.
                  A Printer ſeen, to another ſhews ſomewhat
                     of his Book remembred.
                  Shews of Matters more ſolemn and publick
                     than what's wrote.
                  Vid. *Pamphlets* in *Books-ſorts* infra.
         Reading renders us perfect and invincible in what is
               read, to give it Iſſue.

                                                            Ip

In general. **Acts.** Reading near the End, threats your Life so chiefly if
  (1)   Manuscript.

                 It shews acting pursuant to the prudentest
                 Schemes as is the Book.

                 Peruse, that is, thorowly examine into some
                 set Notion offering.

               Vid. *Read* supra in *Language.*

          Seal'd having, shew'd of an Instruction enigmati-
            cally conceal'd.

Book-seller seen,   shew'd of a good Onirocritick.
  (2)

          Offering a Book, shew'd of a Friend's recommend-
          ing one,

      's Shop seen in an Ironmonger's, shew'd *A.* of an Instruc-
      tion Course of force thro Labour.

      Sending *A.* a Bill for Books, shew'd him in Circumstances
      would occasion buying such.

Sorts in general. A 12*d.* Book, an Instruction not tending to Riches.
  (3)

      New having, has shewn having a new House or re-
      moving to such, &c.

      Broken, vid. *Broke* in *Action.*

      A little Book, a Life or Course of Action trifling to
      appearance.

      Close printed, of more weight and variety and notion
      than at first imaginable.

      Unknown unaccountable every way, vid. *Grammar.*

      Known, of Energy estimate according.

      Paper Gold Letters black best, it gives of Notions
      worthy to be wrote on Gold.

      Language ∴ *English* ∴ unintelligible, that is, ∴ Words
      ∴ Signs in Dreams.

      Written shew of Futurities and great Instructions,
      but more private.

           Your own desiring to be printed, threats
           of your Notions exploded.

           Account-Book of another's see your Hand
               in, find he pays you Money.

               Of a good Husband with
               Debts blotted out having,
               shew'd *A.* of command-
               ing his like Methods to
               Profit.

     Pamphlets, to some have shewn of poor Children.

        To others of lighter Instructions, but
        worthy of Regard.

        A torn piece of one only found, a slight
        Instruction from Slights, &c. or an In-
        struction rais'd from a Notion in part
        despis'd.

                            Sorts

Sorts. Almanack wrote on, ſhew'd of a Diary as of Dreams, *&c.*
(3)   Such given you, that is, ſome ſolemn Advice about
            ſome Diary Work, *&c.*
    Bible refuſe to carry further, ceaſe to give it reſpect anſwerable.
      Broken pieces of it ſeen, ſhew'd of reputed Inconſiſtencies
        therein.
      See one with various Readings, find of a new way to in-
        terpret it.
           Pictures in it, ſhew'd of Projects and
            Hieroglyphick to be rais'd thereon.
   Prayers ſeen alter'd there, threats you croſs'd in hotteſt
     publick Piety Deſires.
   Curſes ſeen left out on't, gives all ſuch Bleſſings in abun-
     dance.
  Caſuiſm Books, ſhew'd *A.* of the Accidents of his Life.
       Reading in't of the Prophet *Jonas,* ſhew'd *A.* of his like
        Fate, *&c.*
  Comedies reading, gives Joy or other Fate as is their Drift.
  Comment againſt Dotards reading, ſhew'd *A.* of a rigorous Cen-
   ſure of mad men.
  Common Prayer Book read, attain with fulleſt Aſſurance to com-
   paſs of our perfecteſt religious Deſires.
  Conjuring, Vid. *Spirits.*
  Dream-Book, ſhew'd me of a blank Book to transcribe them in.
      Find in a Place, that is, thro ſuch means you may attain
       their Skill.
      Hiſtory of them ſeeing, ſhew'd me of finding Reflexions
       worthy of ſuch Hiſtory.
  Law-Book ſhew'd me of a Dream-Book.
     Vid. *Books* in *Law.*
  Martyr-Book read ſomewhat in, that is, make ſuch matter ap-
   pear even thro Martyrdom.
  Prodigy-Book ſeen in a Cupboard, ſhew'd *A.* of abhorring and
   revoking as abominable ſome Dealings he had about ſome Cup-
   board Goods.
  Picture Books ſeen, have ſhewn of Dream Hieroglyphicks.
      To others of Methods projective and not fix'd, as what
       is read.
  Pſalm-Book getting his from a Papiſt, attaining to command
   the Glory of Popery.
  Shrewd as *Selden*'s Table-talk read, that is, act to the ſharpeſt
   turn of Wit.
  Romances read, purſue Tranſactions pleaſant, *&c.* as anſwerable.
  Whole Duty of Man read, act to all Perfection of a religious
   Life.
Subiect. Fables. Baſilisk, Vid. *Poyſonous Creatures.*
(4)   *Cerberus* letting in a doors, ſhew'd to *A.* Death.
        Seen only has ſhewn Sin, or Arreſts by Bailiffs.
            Subiect.

Subject. Fables. *Elyzian* Shades, Vid. *Hell* in *Spirits.*

  (4)

    Don *Quixot* walk with, act in his-like extravagant Methods.

    Harpies or Furies ½ Women and ½ Serpents seen, shew Mischief or Treachery, and that greatly from the Envious seeking our Shame, Ruin or Death.

    Fortune seen, foreshews of some changeable State according.

    Pantaglio how brave against, that is, how resolute against fancied Evils.

    Philosopher's Stone, Vid. *P.* in *Arts.*

    Romantick Princess travel with, design with a publick Vainglory answerable.

Verses, vid. *Words-sorts.*

Creed, Vid. *Religion.*

History, a Remembrance of the old Patriarchs occurs, shew'd me of their like Visions renewed.

    That she had finished the Works of *Hercules*, foreshew'd a Woman burning.

    David and *Nabal* hearing of, foreshew'd to *A.* of such another like Transaction.

Another's Death read of in one, find of the inevitable Course to his Death.

Shrewd as *Selden's* Table-talk read, act pursuant to the sharpest Rules of reasoning.

Language. *Greek* Criticisms one busy in seen, shew'd of transacting with a Schoolmaster.

    Latin knowing, shew'd of knowing and keeping good Mony.

    Sentence give one, deem him a competent Scholar.

    Unknown reading shews of searching Difficulties. Vid. *Books-sorts general* supra.

Declaring *extempore*, paying Mony without Aid.

Foreign Learning, shew'd of tedious Labour in searching Difficulties.

    To some marry or have Business there, &c.

CHAP.

CHAP. LVII.
Of Arts and Sciences.

IN general having them, ſhews of our Deſires of them.

Acting in them, gives us ſome Perfection according
Skilful, vid. *Ability* in *Quality*, &c.

Philoſopher ſeen inſtruct you, promiſes you of ſome Wiſdom of Weight.

Diſputing with, gives you good Management,
Profit and Gain.

's Coach ride in with a Divine, ſtudy to your
utmoſt Divine Philoſophy.

On foot out travels you hors'd, ſail thro E-
ſtate Care in your philoſophical Attempts.

's Stone have changing 1 to 10, that is, a
Courſe of Gain to ſuch Profit.

Handling Gobbets of Silver at a Reverſion
Friend's Houſe by it, concluding of Expence
&c. *in futuro.*

Arithmetick ſhews of Children and Debts to be car'd for.

To the Rich Poverty ; to the Poor Riches.

To Nobles Treaſuries.

To ſome being Bankers, &c.

Vid. *Quantity* and *Numbers* ibid.

A bad Accountant being, that is, backward in Payments.

Aſtronomy in general, vid. *Stars* in *Heaven.*

Skil'd in't, to the Poor and Wicked, Galleys or a Shep-
herd's Life.

to the Rich, Soldiery and Divinity.

to ſome, Navigation and Geography.

to ſome, Flight. Hunting, and dwelling on Hills.

Civil Law skilling, promiſes of Magiſtracy and good manners.

To ill Men it threats Deceits and Enormities.

To a Civilian writing a Letter, that is, being ſettledly fix'd for good Manners.

Officer choſe, ſhew'd *A.* fatally confin'd to the Plague of
regulating ill Manners.

Papers before one the more ſolemn.

C. and *D.* therewith, you in their like Circumſtances, &c.

Divination in general, vid. *Spirits.*

Ethicks foreſhew of Prieſthood, Magiſtracy, Slavery, or monaſtick Life.

To Villains it threats Priſons; and if bound, Condemnation.   Geometry,

Geometry, vid. *Mathematicks* infra.

Gives to the Poor Riches thro Husbandry or Taylouring,
to the Rich Purchases.
to others Contemplation, Architecture, or Painting.
Weights shew of Arbitration or Merchandize.

Geography shews of sailing Journies or Soldiery.
To Princes it gives Astronomy and Imploys.

Grammar learning, to a Scholar Dotage with Scorn.
to some it renews the Toils and Miseries of Youth.
to some it shews the learning other Languages.
to others great Cares about Trifles.

Heraldry publick shews always of War, as of use in Shields.
Red Cross, *England.*
3 Flower de Luces, *France.*
Pyed Bull, *Ireland,* &c.

Private. Fetch a Genealogy from a Painter, chuse an Apothecary to blazon your Credit.
Passing by him to the right *A.* seeing a Bull with a torn Coat on, shew'd him of one of that Crest acting ill.
Made up towards another (Crests) shew'd *A.* of a Family Invitation.

Illegible Words seen in the place of the Coat, shew'd of Scandal for Atchievement.

Logick skilling shews of Study with wrangling.

Mathematicks skilling, shew'd *A.* of Ability to finish a Building.
Measuring Rod dropping, shew'd *A.* of delaying Building.
Teach it to your Man, reprove his Waste Geometrically.
Pass by a Moot of imagin'd measure to the left, excel in measurings, &c.
Unknown would measure *A.* for a Coffin, an unthought Occurrence threats his Death.
A known Friend does the same, an Issue and Monition more friendly.
Overmeasure gain by, that is, gain by the Advantage of good Measure.

Sorts, vid. *Geography* and *Geometry* supra.
Vid. *Quantity.*

Figures, vid. *Figure* in *Quality.*
Round is capacious and secure, but inconstant.
A Sphere of Gold or Lead is bad, as unstable and heavy.
A Circle of Drums before you, a compleat Congratulation near.

Mathe

Mathematicks. Figures. Cylinder very bad alſo, but not ſo bad as round.
Triangles threat of Grief and Want.
Squares ſhew of Stability.

A 20 headed Engine having, ſhew'd me of buying 20 Buſhels of Seed-corn.

Diſorderly ſhew of fooliſh Operations, and are every way evil.

Oblong as Tables ſhew us of ſlow Affairs.

Muſick in general ſhews of Grief with Eaſe.

As ſpeaking greatly, but with vehement Paſſion.
Fine, to ſome noble Truth.

Hearing, to a Prince Death.

to a private Man Health and beſt News.

Things touch'd making ſuch, have ſhewn of Revenge and Enemies oppreſs'd.

Confus'd Pſalms ſinging, ſhew'd of violent Religious Diſputes.

Learning ſhews of empty Studies, as Chymiſtry, Necromancy.

To ſome make Plots and Ornaments, and then diſcover them.

Inſtruments kept for others, harmonious Reaſonings for them, &c.

Tunes ſhew us as are their Words, Air, and Compoſure.

Sung heard, ſhew'd me of this Skill prov'd by Examples.

Wrote on a Wall, Protection from the Monition of harmonious Dreams, &c.

String ill play'd on, threats the Gout or Illneſs in the Nerves.
Fiddle pleaſant heard, ſhew'd of fine Country Diverſions.
Lute playing on, gives Succeſs to Lovers.
Harp, ſhews of Harmony with Friends.

Seen with a Stag, threated Deſtruction.

Baſe Viol carrying to be mended, ſhew'd A. reprov'd for Grumneſs.

Virginal or Claricord playing on, threats with Death of Relations.

To ſome, pure harmonious Truth a Nomine.

Wind well play'd on at Weddings, is good.

Playing on, to Lovers Ill.

Ill plaid on, ſhew'd of ſullen hold Breath-Quarrels.

Reed,
Bagpipe, } Play'd on is good to all.

Player ſeen play on the oppoſite Shore, ſhew'd to Julius Cæſar Conqueſt.

Horn heard winding, forbids Law Suits.

Muſick

Mufick. Wind. Bafe Flute, shew'd of a Carriage civil, but grum and fullen.

Pipe untunable given *A.* shew'd him of his Affairs ill reprefented.

Heard found, has shewn of Variances.

Organs playing on, shew'd of finging and dancing with kiffing.

Hearing, gives Joy.

Difordered feen, shew'd of Trees infamoufly Thief shrouded.

Trumpets, to Soldiers and Enquirers after Secrets good.

to fome, it gives good Tydings.

to fome, it reveals Secrets.

to the Sick, Death.

to Servants, it gives Liberty.

Singing hearing, forefhews Deceit.

To fome, Affliction and weeping.

Vid. *Pfalms* in *Religion.*

Hear a Swan, threats your Death.

Crow, is of worft *Omen.*

Maid, shews of weeping.

Bird, promifes you of Joy, Love and Delight.

Your felf, you deceive or fpunge.

And in meafure is good, but to Muficians moft.

In Confort, gives Confolation and Recovery to the Sick, *&c.*

Unskilfully, threats you with Scorn or Sadnefs.

Without Harmony, threats you Poverty and crofs Affairs.

As you travel, shews you of living honeftly and merily.

Publick in Market, to the Rich, Shame, Difhonefty or Derifion.

to the Poor, Folly, be peevifh or dote.

At the *Bath,* has shewn of Lofs of Voice.

A new Song, have a new Occafion of Joy.

Pfalms in publick, become a Monk, or fingularly religious.

To others 'thas shewn hindrance of Bufinefs. Vid. *Religion.*

Natural Philofophy, shews of ftrange Cuftoms.

To others, of foolifh Operations.

Supernatural, has shewn of Religion, Aftrology, Singularity and Madnefs.

Opticks, to fome shews of very curious Studies.

Opticks,

Opticks, to ſome of Deceits and Wonders: Vid. *Mathemat.* ſupra
Poetry, vid. *Verſes in Words.*
     Rhime is as Conſent in an Action to a nick.
Rhetorick ſhews of it ſelf, as alſo long contentious Studies.
    Declare *extempore,* that is, pay in ready Mony.

CHAP. LVIII.

Of Religion.

Things. **Altar** ſeeing a Spaniel on, reproves your Conſcience as
(1)   ſneaking.

Receive an Alms thence, have an unexpected Benefit.
Diſcover or uncover, ſhews Joy.
Breaking down, threats of Death to follow.
Building, foreſhews one in Family made a Prieſt.
Bells in general paſſing, vid. *Dead.*
     's Clapper ſeen flung to *A.* to the left, ſhew'd him
     of the Pariſh Clerk at his Command.
Chime neatly, ſettle ſome Church Diſpute well.
     Whoſe Son chimes with you, is benefited by it.
Playing Tunes on them, ſhew'd of Diſcord between
     Servants.
Hearing them is paſſive from others, and as ringing
     your ſelf is active.
     To ſome, it threats of Trouble and
     Diſgrace.
     To ſome, Sickneſs.
For your ſelf as dead, if ſick die on it.
     Another, by your Help he recovers.
Ring in general, to ſome Power with the People.
     to ſome, want of publick Aid.
     to ſome, Diſgrace, Trouble, Tumult
     and Oſtentation.
     to ſome, Summons to Pariſh Buſineſs
     and true Devotion.
Hinder'd by a Spirit, is as Fruſtration and Loſs in
     Deſigns.
     To a Miniſter, it ſhews him not profiting
     his Auditory.
     Rope drawn and it not ſounding, ſhew'd the
     Sick Health.
Flying in the Air pulling down, ſhew'd *A.* command-
ing a reigning Fever.

Things. Chappel, fhews of a private religious Oeconomy anfwerable
(1)   in oppofition to a Church more publick.

King's burnt down feen, fhew'd his Death.

Nobles, vid. *N.*

Going to, fhew'd *A.* of going to an Houfe Chriftening then expectant.

Paffing by one to the left, fhew'd *A.* of flighting a Chappel Warden.

A. feeing a Minifter alone there, fhew'd of his own Neglect of Family Prayers.

Window fee yours ftop'd up to play at Ball at, find pour private Piety ftop'd by religious Difputes.

Church own, vid. *Grammar.*

Anothers, vid. *Brother in Grammar.*

Declares of Minifters.

To fome it fhews of publick Opportunities of Joy and Comfort.

Note in general; As the common Field and Houfe fhew of the common Human Difputes and Oeconomies, fo do the Church and Church-yard fhew of divine and holy Difputes and Oeconomies; but then this in Allegory, and as in Circumftance.

Going to, that is, being in a Courfe to have your publick Defires anfwer'd.

Building one, making one of your Family a Prieft.

Sort. Cathedral fhutting feen, fhew'd of an huffy Prebend.

Hear Prayers there, be anfwer'd in moft publick and popular religious Defires.

Weftminfter and *Pauls,* are moft grand as more National.

Chappel Walls feen down, and Stones by to repair it, fhew'd my prefent Skill.

London Church, a beft ftated Religious Oeconomy.

Temple, Church there, vid. *Law.*

Unknown Church be haunted from by a Ghoft as you enter, find your perfonal Courfes will not be born in the Church.

A Dream Temple, a divine, publick, religious Oeconomy relating to Dreams.

Brother, vid. *Grammar.*

A plain Church, has fhewn of an ordinary Minifter.

A fair one feen, promifes of greateft Profperity and Joy.

Things. **Church.** Sort a fair one, and ſometimes it has ſhewn of an adorned Miniſter.

    Perſon's. Man ſeen, ſhews of ſome Church Authority.
    Woman, ſhews of ſome Church Opinion.
        Bride of Chriſt, pure.
        Whore of *Babylon*, corrupt.

    Parts. Tower in general, ſhews of the King and God.
    School adorn'd with ſuch ſeen, ſhew'd of
      ſtately Diſcipline, *&c.*
    Remove thither from the Church, turn
      from Man to God.
    Steeple *Sarum* ſo high climbing to a Miniſter,
      ſhew'd him ſo far prefer'd in that Dioceſs.
    Walls ſeen wrote on, ſhew'd of a Miniſter's Re-
      ſolutions appearing thro his letting his Eſtate.
    Windows, Proſpects from ſuch religious Oeco-
      nomy State.
    Make, examine into others religiou
      Converſations.
      Seeing my Neighbour Joine
        break Holes for ſuch (thi
        ſtudy, *&c.*)
    Fair ones, to a Church a religious Oe
      conomy of good Proſpect Com
      mand, *&c.*
    A. has a great one for his Daughter'
      Portion by ſuch State, *&c.* he ad
      vances her.

Pew Cavils, publick Pariſh Brawls.
    Seat you in your Chancel, take you
      Tithe in kind.
    You ſee another ſeated there
      him you except, *&c.*
    A Seat others have withi
      yours, a Right ou
      of your Power.
    He ſtanding in
      leans over you
      he uſes it to ve
      you.

Own, vid. *Grammar.*
    Stately one have, demean you wit
      Grandeur in your publick Pariſ
      Tranſactions.
    Door own a Grave dug at, a Del
      charged on you.
    New find, vid. *Own* in *Gra*
      mar.

                         Thing

Things. Church. Parts. Pew, Ministers, a ruffled feather'd Swan seen in, shew'd of a contemn'd Philosopher officiating.

Angry *A.* seem'd, seeing his Friend minister in Pew, but a Souldier in Pulpit ; this shew'd of such a Minister remov'd by Force from preaching.

Porch own like to fall on him, to a Minister shew'd his Learning questioned.

Sit up with one on a Challenge there, dare venture your Life as long as his.

Rise from lying on a Bier there, narrowly escape Death.

The Walls, beset with Ivy on a lingring Disease.

Top over the Minister untile, cease to act as his Favourer or Benefactor.

Isle, vid. *Tomb* in *Dead.*

House, vid. *House-sort.*

Acts. Bearing little Devils holding him there, shew'd *A.* of overcoming Antichurch Conspirators.

Held there, impeded as to publick religious Actions.

Turn a Papist near out of Church, act near to unchristianise Popery.

Going to, to some has shewn a Minister coming into their Company.

To hear Divine Service, gives you Honour and Joy, and happiest publick Business.

Towards his own walking, to the Sick is as Danger of Death escaping.

Coming thence, shews you of publick religious Hopes compleat, over or in Despair.

Out of a known Minister's Church without hearing Prayers, shews you of having Offence at him, *&c.*

Pass by a Church to the right in a Market Town, deal to gain with a Minister.

Meet singing Men coming out of Church, that is, by benefiting a Minister lose your own Time and Good, *&c.*

Being at and praying devoutly, all that is ask'd is granted.

To some, enjoy all publick Blessings.

Lingua Terſancta.

Being at and praying devoutly at Brother's, even where thwarted in Intereſt.

Sitting, ⎱ Has ſhewn of Change
Lying there, ⎰ of Apparel.

Writing there, forming Notions of Divinity.

Singing confus'd there, ſhews of religious Diſputes.

Idle Talk or vain Thought there, threat with Envy or Sin.

Make Love there, ſeek Temporal Intereſts Sundays.

Playing there, promiſes greateſt Proſperity.

Naked being there, threats you with Madneſs, or as bad.

Shiting there, threats you with impious Shame and Diſcovery.

Precipice being on there, vid. *P.* in Earth, in a Difficulty as to ſome Miniſter, &c.

Company. Drinking ſweet Wine there, gave me fine Muſick at a Miniſters.

Eating there as in an Houſe, ſhew'd *A.* doubling his Family by boarding a Miniſter.

To ſome, has ſhewn of Holy-day Feaſts, as Shrovetide, &c.

A Witch ſeen alone in it, ſhew'd of a Miniſter boarding abroad, as his Family, proving melancholy to him.

Many fine and chearful ſeen in a Church, gave an happy Marriage, &c.

Things.

Things. Church. Acts. Being at. Company many ugly and sad seen there,
(1)   and his Friends apart,
                                         shew'd to *A.* Death.

Seen strutting in a Gal-
lery, *A.* sneaking in
a Pew below (Cloaths
Censure.)

Candle lighted in a Gallery, a Sermon
read to Servants at Home.

Many seen there with Laughter,
shew'd *A.* bury a Wife and
marry a 2*d.*

One seen only lighted there,
shew'd Death.

Going out there as
you carry it, your
religious reason-
ing failing.

Standing there I saw the Sun rise bright, thro
true Religion all things prosper-
ed to me.

A. saw her Head dress'd white, tho
her Body black; her Actions
are censured ill, tho well meant.

Church-yard known, shews of some known Business, or Dispute
with some Minister.

To others, the State of religious
Disputes, as &c.

Unknown, vid. *Grammar.*

Tombs there, vid. *Dead.*

Way there seen worn down, shew'd of
the Ministers Journy stop'd.

Repairing it for him, helping
him therein by some Expe-
dient.

Pav'd thence from his Orchard
seeing, shew'd to *A.* reaching his Studies to Divinity.

Wall seen down, threats you as unconse-
crating it if your own.

Firm seen, secures to you your Right
in holy Disputes, &c.

Acts. Fighting there, Controversy about some Ministers right.

Walking alone there, has shewn of sullen Melancholy.

Sleeping there, to the Sick Death.

Things. Church-yard. Acts. Purſued there, uuder Expectation with
(1)   Fear as to ſome Miniſter.

          Sliding fearing there, that is, being baffled
            at ſome Miniſters.

          Seeing it only, to many is Melancholy or
            Sickneſs; but green ſo is beſt.

Croſſes drive away Ghoſts by, that is, ſhun Errors ſuperſtitiouſly.

Day holy, vid. *Time.*

Eccleſiaſtick Houſe, vid. *Religion* infra.

Holy Ground walking on, is a good Sign.

Incenſe ſeen ſmoke, ſhew'd of efficacious Prayer.

Meeting-Houſe come to where are fine Lords, treſpaſs Church
Laws as uſual with them.   Vid. *Puritan* infra.

Mitẽr ſeen chain'd to a Poſt, ſhew'd of ſuch an Eccleſiaſtick
State under Confinement.

Primitive, vid. *Former* in *Time.*

Pulpit, vid. *Preach* infra in *Acts Religious.*

      Vid. *Pew* ſupra in *Church Part.*

Religious Houſe, give all to ſacrifice all your Intereſts to Piety.

          Enter, die if you profeſs on it, or elſe ſicken
            only.

          Vid. *Monaſtery* in *Houſe-ſorts.*

          With a cripling Door for thoſe are out at
            Night, with a hard Reſtraint againſt Evil.

          Monks ſeen, have ſhewn of preſent Death and
            Calamity.

Temples, ſhew Prieſts.   Vid. *Church* ſupra.

Tythes ſeen in Water, ſhew'd to *A.* of Sharers in Contention
about their Parts.

Perſons. Apoſtle be choſe, that is, be ſeemingly inſpir'd as for a Purpoſe.
(2)   Preſcribing a Cure, ſhew'd of a Divine Remedy accord-
          ingly enſuing.

          Read 2 Forms of Prayers us'd by them, diſcover of
          their Powers, *&c.*

Chaplain, vid. *Chappel* ſupra.   Vid. *Miniſter* infra.

Chriſt ſeeing and preferring *A.* ſhew'd him of his Miniſter doing ſo.

      's Nurſe give i s.to, ſacrifice all to be pious to the higheſt.

      Bleſſing *A*'s Bread, gave him exceeding Plenty.

      Thron'd in Light amidſt Darkneſs ſpeaking to *A.* gave
        him Revelations next to Miracles.

      Offers you one of 2 Evils, what is accepted ſurely be-
        falls you.

      Hearing him ſpeak, ſhews your Obedience to him with
        Gladneſs.

      Diſcourſing him, is more grand than hear.

      Walk with, deſign in his like Courſes.

      Adoring him, gives Joy.

Persons. Chrift and the Virgin *Mary* meeting appearing little and met,
(2)　　　　ſhew'd me of converſing a Papiſt.

　　　　　's Hoſpital Governor inviting *A.* to a Feaſt, ſhew'd him
　　　　　profited by a Miniſter.

Clerk your Friend being, gives you Command in your publick
Deſires anſwerable.

Biſhops ſeen, ſhew of great religious Awe and Reverence.
　　　　　Vid. *Popery* infra.

　　　　You free with one, you awe others *& e con.*

　　　　Being one, is good to all but the Secret.

　　　　In Orders ſeen ſet on their Heads in Ornaments, ſhew'd
　　　　of that Order expos'd a while.

　　　　Dead ſeen ſtrike the Ground thrice, gave Victory to
　　　　the Warrior ſeeing it.

　　　　I have a Book of Biſhop *F's* deliver'd me, which I pe-
　　　　ruſe; I ſtood as a Godfather.

Godfather ſend for your Schoolmaſter to be, try to get one to
eſpouſe your Actions that will rather correct them.

Jew ſee in your Chamber, examine into the State of that People.

　　　　One that flouted I hector'd down Stairs, my Skill
　　　　fruſtrates their Perfection.

　　　　3 looking modeſt I ſuffer'd there, I allow'd of their
　　　　modeſt Eſtabliſhment.

　　　　Jewess I refus'd to whore with, that is, corrupt me
　　　　with their Ceremonies.

Immodeſt Women ſeen, ſcandal you with Impudence if unpleaſant.

　　　　But pleaſant, Whoriſh Joy.　　　Vid. *Whore* in *Perſon.*

Miniſters ſeen in general, ſhew us of good Actions, but unhappy.

　　　　　　Publick State, Conſci-
　　　　　　ence Courſes anſwe-
　　　　　　rable.

　　　　　's Houſe live in, tranſact with Conſcience conforma-
　　　　ble to the State.

　　　　　　In your Brothers, in a Conſcience Oeconomy
　　　　　　ſo againſt your Intereſt.

　　　　　　Own, is abſolute.

Say Prayers your ſelf as ſuch in a publick Cathedral,
get ſome popular End according.

　　　　　's inner Room ſpeaking to God in, ſhew'd *A.* thro
pure Life propheſying.

Pleas'd ſeen, ſhews you anſwer a good Conſcience.

Adviſing, that is, ſuch Conſcience prompting.

Fly before one over Pales, be too large in your Caſuiſm.

G g 4　　　　　　　　　　　　　　　*Perſons.*

Perſons.
(a)

Miniſters own call on, fly to the Aid of your publick Conſcience, &c.

's Daughter feen, ſhew'd of caſuiſtick Diſputes.

King's Chaplain be and pray as ſuch, get your Aims
by Awe, &c. Divine.

Digging in your Court or Garden, your Scheme of
Conſcience accordingly altering.

That married you feen, declares of your Marriage or
ſome Contract.

Dead talk with of a religious Controverſy, be potent
therein beyond all Prieſtcraft.

Helping order many Books of his of the ſame ſort,
diſpoſing of your religious Studies orderly.

Monk, vid. *Religious Houſe* ſupra.

Nun, vid. *Ibid.*

Popery, vid. *Grammar.*

Seen ſet up, has ſhewn of a conſpiring and ſlaving
Knavery as bad.

To others, of ſuch Conſcience Impoſitions mena-
cing.

Papiſt viſiting, ſhew'd *A.* Diſcourſes of ſuperſtitious
Obedience.

's Name know, command the whole Drift of
the Sect.

Fair Maid feen, ſhew'd of a new and delight-
ful, but withal impoſing Scheme,
&c.

Offering to be lain with, proving at
your full Command, &c.

School feen, ſhew'd *A.* of ſome Poor forcing
themſelves on him for Work.

's Houſe, vid. *Grammar.*

Railing heard, ſhew'd of unreaſonable Impoſitions obſtructing.

Religious Houſe, vid. *Things* ſupra.

Trinkets firing, expoſing their Tenets.

Crucifix in Glaſs finding, ſhew'd me of Dr. *O.*
againſt *K. James* lent me.

Proceſſion, vid. *infra* in *Relig. Action.*

Rome, vid. *Country Foreign* in *Earth.*

Pope accompany, be aw'd out of your Intereſt.

Boaſtingly, your ſelf awe others ſo as he
does.

Walking with in *Italy,* and calling Majeſty, and
feeing alſo Wood cut down behind me there,
ſhew'd me of paying anothers Debt.

Images, threat Papiſts and Heathens near as bad as the
Gods themſelves,

Perſons. Popery. Images threat Picture is near the ſame, but leſs.
(2)   Carried to Places unknown ſeen, ſhews of
       Change of Worſhip, *&c.*
      To others, new Ceremonies, *&c.*
   Statues, vid. *Trade.*
   Saints falling on *A.* foreſhew'd him Hurt from
    his Prieſt.
   Vid. *God* and *Dead.*
  Pew-keeper, vid. *Pew* ſupra in *Church.*
  Prieſt, vid. *Relig. Houſe* in *Things* ſupra.
   Seen go rob'd to deſolate Places, threats Ruin to their
    Orders.
   Once 3 now 1, a *Unitarian,* &c.
   High Prieſt ſee ſtand by you, act purſuant to the ex-
    acteſt Rules of Bodily Purity.
  Prophets ſeen, ſhew of their like Methods to Prophecy pre-
   ſenting.
   See *Noah*'s Ark, be as ſingularly pious.
   Eat Bread with *Elijah,* be as ſpiritually ſingular.
   Prophecy publick ſeen, ſhew'd of a publick Account
    of News.
   Foreſee you are to have many Children, become rich
    and as if able to maintain them.
  Puritan Meeting-Houſe be in, that is, be ſingular in Conſcience,
      but truly zealous.
     Vid. *Meeting-Houſe* ſupra.
      Go to with great Lords, break ſome
       Church Diſcipline modiſhly.
    A bold Man ſpeaking in't *A.* after ſaw ſneak a-
     way ; this ſhew'd *A.* blotting out a raſh Pe-
     riod in a Letter upon Conſideration to a Pres-
     byterian.
  Quaker Tavern being at, *A.* engag'd in a Tythe ſquabble.
   Cravat put on, be ſubject to his like Repute.
Acts in general. Omiſſions religious, threat of greateſt Heavineſs to
 (3)   follow.
   Contemning Religion, threats of horrid Misfortunes.
  Anointed, to ſome the Crown ; and to others Prieſthood, as in
    Capacity.
   to ſome, Gain.
   to the Wicked, Torments and Shame.
   to ſome, heavy Diſeaſes.
   to Women, Painters and Chirurgeons good.
  Seeing your ſick Friend, promiſes him his Recovery.
    Manner, firſt the Feet high as the Shoos, and then
     the Locks from the Crown all downwards ; ſo
     ſeen in Dream it recover'd the Sick.
  Ointment Veſſels keeping, it ſhews wiſe Men.

              Acts.

Acts. Anointed Ointment making, threats with Vexation and Trouble.
(3)   Oil anointing our Locks, is beſt.

         Smelling well, gives good Repute; but ill, threats Infamy and Anger.

Bleſſing Bread Chriſt ſeen, multiplied Plenty to *A.* exceedingly. vid. *Words.*

Catechiz'd be by a Schoolmaſter, that is, as ſneakingly approve your religious Principles to ſome others Examination.

Confirm'd being by the Biſhop, ſhew'd to *A.* of happieſt News confirm'd.

Conſecrations to the dead, ſhews of Knaviſh Profits neither good to give nor take.   Vid. *Dedicate* infra.

Conſcience often ſhews of Conſcience.

Contemning Religion, vid. *ſupra* in general.

Creed repeat, act as a moſt true Chriſtian.

Croſſes, &c. vid. *infra* in Law.

        Drive away Ghoſts by them, avoid Cheats ſuperſtitiouſly.

Curſe God, vid. *G.*

Damnation, ⎫
Deſpair,   ⎬ ſhew of horrid Events and Expectations.

        In fear of for ill Acts, too oft literal.

Dedicated a Serpent ſeeh to *Eſculapius,* gave *A.* Health.

Devotion, ſhew of doing religious Acts favouring thereof.

Divorce, vid. *Wife* in *Grammar.*

        Of ones Siſter made by his Father, ſhew'd him Death; God is our Father, and our Soul and Body Brother and Siſter, and the Divorce Death.

        Quarrel one for divorcing your Siſter and marrying another, for breaking your Neighbours Contract.

Faſting, ſhews of doing other things religiouſly, as abſtemious and acceptable.

Funeral Service to the Burial of one dead unable to find, ſhew'd a Miniſter unable to order a Rogue.   Vid. *Dead.*

Grace ſay, eat to Health and Benefit.

        At Pleaſure, at Pleaſure.

Honeſty ſhews of Honeſty.

        An honeſt Man unknown giving *A.* ſomewhat, ſhew'd of his forbearing a Gain in Honeſty.

Judgment, vid. *Damnation* ſupra.

Juſtly or fairly acting, ſhews of really doing ſo.

        Unjuſt Actions ſeen, threat with Grief and Sorrow.

Lent, vid. *Own Church* in *Grammar.*

Marriage in general, vid. *Wife* in *Grammar.*

        Shews of Contracts with as laſting a Care and Damage, the Criterion a durable Contract.

        To ſome, of entering into Religion.

        To Monks, old Men, and the Sick Death.

        To the married, a good Bargain or Divorce.

Acts. Marriage, shews to some the Marriage of their Children.
(3)　　Great seen, shews of some Friendship extraordinary.
　　　　Celebrating, necessitated to a Friends Aid.
　　　　Serving at Table, to their Loss.
　　　　Musick present, Sighing and Tears.
　　　　Sweet Wine given there, great Comfort and Aid
　　　　　thereby.
　　　　Dancing at it, Sickness.
　　　　With Lights, shews of some Funeral or Magi-
　　　　　stracy.
　　　　Inviting Guests, benefiting many.
　　　　Sweet Ointments there, of good Fame for
　　　　　Kindness.
Degrees. Seeming about to marry another in Circum-
　　　　stance proper, to the married Danger of
　　　　Widowhood.
　　　　At my furthest West Market Town to see a
　　　　　Wedding with *A.* I indulge him in a Bar-
　　　　　gain to my Loss.
　　　　Married to *A.* seem, that is, find your Hus-
　　　　　band or Wife proves as *A.*　Vid. *Grammar.*
　　　　Proxy married by, consummate a Friendship
　　　　　contracted.
　　　　Unmarried seeming, shew'd *A.* in a courting
　　　　　State again as when so.
　　　　Seeing a Papist going to marry his Sister, find
　　　　　of an unreasonable Bargain offering.
　　　　Seem already to a Maid, shew'd her acting in
　　　　　scorn of its Expectance.
　　To a Woman deform'd, threats you Death or Discon-
　　　　tent.
　　　　Handsome, gives you Joy and Profit.
　　　　　And lying with her on it tho,
　　　　　　threated Peril of Death next
　　　　　　day.
　　　　Maid, to the Sick Death.
　　　　　to the Enterprizer, Success.
　　　　Girl, shew'd a Man resolv'd to a new
　　　　　Opiniative Course according.
　　　　She fumbling finding his M———
　　　　　lank, shew'd of his Resolution
　　　　　failing therein.
　　　　Widow, compass an old Business.
　　　　Old has shewn of old Affairs, pursued
　　　　　to Profit.
　　　　Sister, has shewn Danger.
　　　　　To others, has shewn dying Ba-
　　　　　chelors.

Acts.

Aſts. Marriage, to a Woman, Wife anothers, contract a Friendſhip with
(3)   her.

Yours married to another ſee, find
they Friendſhip ſo.
With Child on it, to
full Iſſue.

To ſome, Change of Af-
fairs and Separation.

To ſome, their Marriage
State alters, as is the
Perſon.

Sweetheart forſook, threats you with vain
Attempts again.

Turk, ſhew'd *A.* of being reſolv'd againſt
Chriſtnings.

Anothers Whore Daughter, cheated in a
Sale to a bad Debt.

To a Perſon dead, threats of breaking of Contracts.

Covetous Perſons, fix your ſelf to their
like Methods.

Courtier, ſhews of your becoming lazy
and ſtately.

To a Devil, Fury or Serpent, threats you Death with
Horror.

Image of Chriſt crucified, foreſhews ones being
a Nun.

To a Man by a Man, ſhew'd of a Friendſhip contracted,
as is the Man.

Great Man to a Wife, ſhew'd of her Husband
taking much upon him.

King the ſame, but more grand and juſt.

Mean Man to a Woman, ſhew'd her about an
homely Friendſhip, *&c.*

Bride Garters look'd for it on't, that is,
Symptoms of it.

Her Husband ſeeing another, ſhew'd a Wife of
his new Contract alſo.

To ſome, it has ſhewn alſo of a Son to
be married.

Martyrdom talk of, that is, tranſact with pious ſelf-deſtructive
Reſolutions.

Die as a Martyr, that is, be famous here and bleſt hereafter.

Omiſſions, vid. *Aſts* in general *ſupra.*

Prayers to God, to ſome obtaining of the King.

to others, obtain of God ; but to all Succeſs.

Altering, changing your main Deſires.

Hearing the Poor pray, gives you aſſured Relief
in Neceſſities.   *Aſts.*

As. Prayer. Sorts. Publick feen at a Minifters Desk, shew'd of a pub-
(3)　　　　lick Parish Eafe.

Say as a Minifter your felf, fatisfy your felf
and others in your publick Defires anfwerable.

Printed carrying, shew'd *A.* of fuing forth a Writ.

Long and with Additions faying, shew'd *A.* of obtaining beyond Expectation.

The more general or particular, and fo
your Bleffings.

Us'd by the Apoftles faying, attaining to fome of
their Graces.

What faid in them, is ftill obtain'd to a Tittle.

Pfalm refponfes reading in Anfwer to his Minifter
in his Parifh Church, to *A.* shew'd of having his
Defires anfwer'd in common with his Neighbors.

At Prayers being, that is, in Torture and Extremity, but
near its end.

One feen there you fuffer not to kneel by you, that
is, he proves of no Aid to your Wants.

As a King's Chaplain, awing others as by refpect to
your Defires.

Saying them in general, shews you them heard and
granted.

You never neglecting them, bleffes you in all
things.

½ way to one, shew'd him of things wanted
offer'd him, but himfelf wanting more.

All Night, shew'd *A.* in a Bufinefs unfi-
nifh'd next day.

Effects kill a Witch by it, have your Defires fo full as to
cure your crofs Fortune.

For the dead, shews of Petitions not to be granted.

Againft Ghofts hurting, that is, Cheats confounding you.

Interrupted by the Devil, threats lofing a Son, or having fome great Hurt.

A. could not fay on Trial, he found himfelf
in Scruples about them.

Mock'd in faying them by an Apparition, fool'd
by a Cheat therein.

Preach, vid. *Sermon* infra.

Pfalm fing, vid. *Mufick* in *Parts.*

Vid. *Prayers forts* fupra.

Sing, be in Senfe of a publick Joy or Mifery, as are the
Words.

Confus'd heard, shew'd of Religious Difputes.

In publick, become a Monk, or act in fcorn to
Human things.　　　　　　　　　　*As.*

Acts.
(3) Procession Popish fee, that is, conceive of some Mental Abomination carrying on.

Resurrection discours'd of, shew'd A. of Care about curing Consumption.

To others, Endeavours of re-establishing some erring States of Affairs.

In Circumstance proper, has shewn of Death near.

So seen in a Picture also.

It turns Ill to Good, and Good to Ill, &c.

Vid. *Revive* in *Dead.*

The World at an end seen, and the last Trumpet heard, shew'd A. of Death coming.

Sacrament seeing, shews Honour,

To others, it has imparted Divine Secrets, and the Beginning of Prophecy.

Sacrifices from God to God seen, shew'd of great Heresy and Change.

Perfumed Fire worshipping, to a Prince give Victory.

Smelling Ill, e con, Ruin.

Sacrilege, vid. *Robbers* in *Grammar.*

Scripture interpreting, shew'd to A. of receiving Tithes.

Sermon disturb'd in, to a Minister shew'd him in a Quarrel with his Parishioners.

Minister yours see in his Pulpit, act according to the exactest religious Rules, &c.

Unknown preaching against my *New Jerusalem,* I as bad drest sate away; but he quarrelling, fought with one in the opposite Pew, and so became forsook of all; and while I approaching, took my Stick lying down there, and going on it to look for my Wife there, found her lock'd up. This Notice was to shew the Address and Prevalence of my Skill.

Funeral making to a Minister as Literal, has shewn of a Benefit as by such.

to others, has shewn claiming a dead Right.

On the King's Death hear of one to be, learn from your own Folly disappointed.

Making one ready in his own Church, but waking e'er he begun it, to a Minister preach one as expected.

Attorny calling A. to read one, shew'd A. as forc'd to Patience in a Brawl.

Preach against you see another, that is, find him prove contrary in his Actions.

Actions.

Actions. Sermon preach againſt you e'ery where ſee your pitying Friend,
(3)   be at a great loſs to occaſion it.

See one unknown, be in check to
an odd Courſe according.

Hearing is as flying to Piety to juſtify your Doings.

Tempted ſhews of being tempted.

Of an Enemy, admitting a Luſt you repent of.

Thankſgiving make, receive Bleſſings as to merit it.

Virtue and Vice. Gluttony delight in, to a Glutton find the ill
Effects on't.

Paſſions, vid. *P.*   Vid. *Fondle* ibid.

Bawdy write to a Woman, that is, write
with a Freedom near as bad.

A. in Bed with a Domeſtick ſlap'd her Privities, he talk'd Bawdy to her.

Vid. *Lying* in *Bodily Action.*

Worſhip the King, that is, God and Religion.

A perfum'd Fire, to a Prince gave Victory. Sacrifice.

God, gives greateſt Joy.

Change it, vid. *God* in *Spirits.*

A Tomb, ſhews of burying ſome Anceſtor.

'd being by the Sun, Moon, and Stars, *Joſeph.*

CHAP. LIX.

Of Physick.

IN general Diſeaſes ſhew to us of Miſchiefs coming on us of them-
(1)   ſelves.

And as Wounds from others.

To ſome Faults of the Mind.

Dying of, Vid. *Dead.*

Life found lead, keep to your firſt Inſtitution
of Life.

Infirm leading, threats you with Travel,
Change, or ſecret Study.

Sick being, to ſome has ſhewn Want of Buſineſs and Accuſation on it.

to ſome it gives Eſteem.

to ſome being out of humour, as is the Time
and Place.

to the Sick recover, or be worſe.

to the Poor and Captives, Good.

to ſome Idleneſs and Poverty.

to ſome it has ſhewn Impriſonment.

In general. Sick. Others comfort or preſcribe Remedies for, gives joy
(1)　　　　　　　and Comfort.

Brother ſeen put to bed and ſick, ſhew'd *A.* of
his contrary Intereſt fail'd for a while.

Viſit one ſick, he's out of humour, and not the
Dreamer.

Ones Servant ſeen ſo, ſhew'd *A.* himſelf ſo;
the Body is Servant to the Soul.

A's Children ſeen ſo, threated *A.* himſelf with
ſore Eyes.

Fellow-Tradeſman hearing of as ſo, ſhew'd of
A. himſelf as without Buſineſs.

's Father ſeen, ſhew'd *A.* ſick of the Head-ach.

Fearing to diſturb one ſick in a Chamber near
his Barn, ſhew'd *A.* fearing to diſhumour his
Servant in his Work-Methods.

Remedies, call for Burnt Claret, be in fear of a Looſeneſs.

Dreſſing or uſing, being indiſpos'd according.

Drink an Egg in Sack, be ask'd next day to ſing.

Medicines ſeeing, is ill to all.

Blooded, vid. *B.* in *Human Body.*

Cordial Alkermes taſting, ſhew'd *A.* of paying
a Phyſick Bill.

Diſſection, vid. *Body* in *Dead.*

Laxative Herbs eating, good to thoſe who are in
debt.

Ointment making, ſhew'd of grievous Perplexity
of Mind.　　　Vid. *Religion.*

Phyſick-Apples, vid. *A.* in *Fruit.*

Purge take, pay a Debt you were before engag'd
for.

Giving or taking threats with Poverty.

A Lask following it, Prodigality to the
higheſt.

Take at a rich Man's, merchantly try to
live as he does.

Works ill, the Means proves with
troubleſom Iſſue.

Sudatory taking ſhew'd *A.* uſing a Courſe as effectual.

Sweat, vid. *Bodily Action.*

Vomiting, ſhews of Repentance with Reſtitution.

Much and well-coloured, to the Poor
Riches.

to the Rich Hurt, but Humours
better than Blood.

to others Children and Return of
Friends.

In general. Medicines. Vomiting Sirreverence, shew'd *A.* prodigally di-
(1)　　　　　　　　　　　　verting his Expence Mony.

Blood corrupt, threats Sickness to all.
　　　Much and good-colour'd, to the
　　　Poor Riches.
　　　　　to the Traveller, and the Child-
　　　　　less, Return and Issue.
Flegm of all sorts, shews of an end of
　　　Evils.
Meat shews of hurt, and loss of Profits.
　　　Unusual Meat you have eaten, re-
　　　store unlawful Gain.
　　　　　Vid. *Bodies* in *Carcase Human.*
Worms, discover private Enemies and
　　　avoid them. Vid *Insects.*
Bowels, threats with Death of Children,
　　　　　to the Sick, Death.
　　　　　to the Childless, Loss
　　　　　of best Goods.
Bird seen, shew'd of Loss.

Physician, vid. *Grammar.*

Sort. Doctor giving a Glyster seeming, crosses his
　　　Expectation as mean.
Drinking with his Doctor, shew'd *A.*
　　　drinking in full Security of Health.
Own leaving *A.* as talking about Bills
　　　of Exchange, shew'd *A.* of his
　　　Return failing.
Seen prescribe Physick, shew'd
　　　A. of taking some happily
　　　next day.
Esculapius bidding a Doctor Farewel
　　　at a City Gate, shew'd a Doctor of
　　　his Practice failing.
Oculist visiting *A.* shew'd him of a Business
　　　of Search or View imploying him.
Chirurgeon shews as the Apothecary, but
　　　more desperately.
Apothecary's Shop seen to *A.* shew'd him
　　　of his own Closet Medicines.
　　　Changing somewhat there,
　　　seeking to remedy some ill,
　　　as *&c.*
　　　Own seen in distress, shew'd *A.*
　　　vex'd, as that his Wife being
　　　with Child, she could not
　　　take Physick.

In general. Physician. Sort. Apothecary's Brother unknown in a Market Town A. viſiting, ſhew'd of his parting with a good Bargain as unjuſt.

(1)

Seen, to the Sick good, and promiſes a Cure.
to the Well, Misfortune remedied.
to all Trouble, but with Remedy at laſt.

His Horſe travel on, uſe an Art that will want Remedy.

Houſe impriſon'd in, ſhew'd A. in continual Care of Health, but with ſure Remedy.

Wife be with, uſe Remedies your ſelf.
Viſit with, forbear Viſits in Reſentment.

Acts. Arreſted by his A. ſeeming, ſhew'd A. wanting Phyſick, when A. had his Preſcription only.

Beating A. ſhew'd him taking his Phyſick.

Becoming one your ſelf, gives you Security of Health and Cheerfulneſs.

Diſcourſing one, wrangling about Diſorders.
To one in Law, he ſhews of his Lawyer.
A good known one, ſhews you deſigning happily for your Health,

Departing ſeen, to the Healthy Sickneſs.
to the Sick Death.

Leading A's Horſe out of Town, ſhew'd A. that the firſt ſtep in his Buſineſs wanted Remedy.

Quarrelling him, to the Healthy is danger of Sickneſs.

Send for him, ſeek for Remedies.

Travelling from him, threats you Sickneſs.

Walk in your Pariſh Streets with, ſeek a more neighbourly Correſpondence.

With Houſes and Lands ſeen, ſhew'd of their being mortgag'd in Remedy.

(2)

Arm right bliſter'd, ſhew'd to A. his Wife troubled with a Swelling.
To others it has ſhewn Brethren in danger.

Artery cut, to the Rich Contempt.
to the Poor worſe Poverty.

Belly pain or Sickneſs there, Poverty or Sickneſs indeed, as &c.

Blind man ſeen, ſhews of a Fool or Contemner of thee.
Squint-eyed, perfidious.
Glaſs Eye removing A. ſaw well, Awe laid by, he commanded his Affairs truly.
Vid. *Eye* in *Body.*

Breaſt, vid. *Body.*

Cancer

Cancer shews of great Grief with hidden Riches daily increasing.
Cough extreme having, to a Maid threats her Virginity;
        to some publick Vexations of Conscience for
        ill Gains.
        to some Diseases.   Vid. Bodily Action.
Cripple, vid. Lame infra.
        Seeing, that is, a Reasoning full of Error and Imperfection.
        Lame shews of one slow, or a great Deceiver.
        Crutches shew to Malefactors Prisons and Chains.
        to others Sickness or Vagabondry.
Crooked Persons shew of Persons and Courses tricking and perverse.
        Rod seen, shews of vicious and lazy Delays.
Cut, vid. Action.   Vid. Nose in Body.   Vid. Wound infra.
Deaf being, that is, inexorable or a Liar.
Deform'd Men, Reasonings of Corruption and Error.
        Entering A's Hall, shew'd him of a Tenant offering
        unreasonable Proposals.
Dropsys shew us Riches, and sometimes Debts.
Dumb being, shew'd A. of sudden Gladness.
Eye, vid. Blind supra.
Excrescence a golden Bunch seen in A's Neck, promis'd of a sweet
    Futurity on his Death.
Fevers shew of unjust Gain with Passion and Calumny.
        Vid. Dying.
Fire seeming all over, shew'd A. of a burning Ague.
Gelt being, threats Barrenness, Loss of Children, and best Goods and
    Pleasures.
        To some it has shewn Heartlesness and Sickness.
Genitals of Stone having, to some has foreshewn a Rupture.
        to some has threatned of their Son.
Gout see one sick of, live your self in Luxury and Ease.
Hare-lip, vid. Lip in Body.
Head hurt, threats your Father.
Heart hurt, &c. threats you Son, &c.
Hectick your Hands feeling, threats you someway indisposed for
    Action.
Humours, Choler, and Melancholy shew of Mony and rich Wives.
Jaw-bone swell'd, shew'd A. of a Family increas'd to Loss.
Issue Plaister chang'd, Tax Mony chang'd.
        Earth among it, that is, ill Mony.   Vid. Grammar.
Itch foreshews of Love or Injury.
King's Evil, Angel Piece of Gold given A. shew'd him acquiring an
    Opinion securing him against Penal Laws established by the Govern-
    ment.
Lameness threats with Deceit, and Impotence with Slowness.
        To the Rich Loss by Fire.
        To a Prisoner Punishment.
        See your Acquaintance so, discover him a Cheat, &c.
        H h 3.   Leprosy

Leproſy having, threats Miſery and Contempt with popular Hatred.
> To ſome it has ſhewn envied Riches, and Riches thro Gifts.

Looſeneſs ſhews of Idleneſs with Impotence, and Authority loſt.
> To ſome preſent great Expences threatning.
> Vid. *Purge* ſupra in *Remedies*.
> Vid. *Shite* in *Bodily Action*.

Madneſs in general ſhews of a careleſs and ſlighting Negligence.
> Seeming, threats you in Law, Condemnation, &c.
> Being and acting as mad in publick, to ſome long Life.
>> to ſome Favour from the Prince, and Profit from the People.
>> to ſuch as are in Chains it gives Liberty.

Things. Apples, vid. *A*.
> Dog ſeen, ſhew'd of a Man violent and pernicious, but not laſting.

Place. *Bedlam* and its Doctor ſeeing, threats your Methods cenſurable as frantick.
> Croſt in your way by a mad Man, his like Raſhneſs ſtopping your Courſe.

Perſon bear, exceed his Madneſs.
> Bite off his right Ear, be more deſperate in good things than he, Folly.
> Diſcourſe one mad, tranſact your ſelf as if worthy ſuch Character.
> In Bed with a mad Woman being, to a Woman big ſhew'd her Delivery.
>> And trying to lie with her, to others is horrid.
> Another ſee diſtracted and raving, ſhew'd *A.* hearing of his near Friend's Death.
>> 's Friend ſeeing mad, ſhew'd to *A.* of his acting unaccountably and without regard to him.

Bonfires ſeen made near a mad Man's Houſe, ſhew'd *A.* of unjuſt and extravagant Joys.

A. going on in a way near up to a Woman raving, ſhew'd him purſuing a Method near to Madneſs.

Member, vid. *Genitals* ſupra.

Mute ſhews a Liar.

Navel, vid. *Body*.   Noſe, vid. *Body*.

Pain in general threats with great Anxiety of Mind.
> to others Danger or Wickedneſs, as is the Part.
> Drunk and pain'd at Heart or inwardly ſeeming, ſhew'd *A.* rob'd privately by his Servants.
> In the Heart, to ſome threats with ſome dangerous Diſeaſe coming.
>> To others Trouble from ſome grievous Wife, &c.   Pain

Pain in general, in the Belly, Sickness or Poverty indeed.

Phlegm, vid. *Vomit* supra.

Plague, threats with Herefy or Jealoufy fatal.

Sick on't, shew'd *A.* Death-fick in 3 Days.

To some, has shewn *Anathema*, Want and Flight.

A's Sister fick on't, infected her Father and Mother ; this shew'd *A.* Servants loosing her Master and Mistress thro Jealoufy.

Pocky Person see, that is, perceive of some corrupt or wicked Course.

And rotten Thigh having, to a Woman shew'd of her Sinfulness making her Friends to hate her.   Vid. *Rotten* infra.

Poison, vid. *Poisonous Creatures.*

Rotten, vid. *Jaws* in *Body*, and *Mouth* ibid.

Black or mortified Legs have, that is, thro Sin be mortified to ones best Relations.

Breast right, as to ones Son.

Thigh right, as to ones Brother.

Rugged or a rough Man seen, shew'd *A.* of a Dun for Mony.

Rupture, a Care about some ill Matter.

Scabby, leprous or meafled Persons seeing, threats you with Trouble.

Your self seeming so, gives you envied Gifts ; but withal, reveals Secrets.

To many, Riches with Infamy.

Legs having, has shewn of fruitless Perplexities.

Slain Men, vid. *Dead.*

Small-Pox having, gives Riches with Infamy.

Your Son having it, your Expectation like to be so crown'd. Vid. *Pox* supra.

Sores raw seen, have shew'd of Plaisters.

Sore Feet walking with, shew'd *A.* fasting.

Breast having, has shewn of Sickness to come.

To some, it has shewn Uneasiness of Mind.

Eyes having, has shewn to Parents their Children sick.

Stone having, shew'd of a great Family with little Riches, and they hid.

Swell'd in general, vid. *Scabby* supra.

Tongue, shews of boasting idle Speech,

Belly have, be rich in Esteem, tho you are really poor.

Cheeks, manifest of some Injury.

Jaw-Bone by Disease have, that is, a Family encreas'd to Less.

Impostumes, Warts and Pusthules, shew of great Rents.

Knees having, shews of Sickness or Business hinder'd.

Leprous, meafled or small-pox'd being, shews being rich with Infamy.

Members, great Cares for Sons, or a Wife troublesom.

Ulcer, vid. *Arms* in *Body.*   Vid. *Scabby, Sore* and *Swell'd* supra.

Worms knawing inwardly, have shewn of false Servants.

Rid you of them, deliver you of such.

Vid. *Worms* in *Insects.*

Wounds in general, vid. *Sword* in *War*.

    Shew to many of Labour and Grief..

        to all, of Changes by Violence, as Diſeaſes of Growth in it ſelf.

    Hear Men wounded by Robbers groan, that is, be zealous at others dangerous Errors.

Parts. Arms and Legs ſhot off by Robbers, you fight Errors you would oppoſe, ſtop your Endeavours quite.

    Bowels going out on't, reveals Secrets of Riches.

    Brains going out on't, reveals Secrets of Honour.

    Hand wounded, Hurt from ſome writing.

        Right, by Debt or War.

        Stab'd in it, prevented in the Aid of ſome Service.

        Shot off, vid. *Arm* ſupra.

    Heart wounded, hurt as to Life.

        To the young, Love ; to the old, Grief.

    Feet wounded very bad, greateſt and general Impediments.

        To ſome, it menaces Domeſticks.

        Leg cut off with an Hatchet ſeen, to one Gouty gave him Recovery.

        Vid. *Arm* ſupra.

    Liver wounded, threats Poverty.

    Thigh wounded, has ſhewn Diſturbance by Relations.

    Tongue wounded, hurt by ſome raſh Speech.

State dry, threats with Want of Neceſſaries.

    Scars or Cures ſeen, ſhews of the End of all Evils.

    Wounds heal'd, ſhew of the Boaſts of Valour.

    The Hole dry after a Wound by a raſh Man, ſhew'd his like Raſhneſs Miſchief in *A*. perpetual.

Out on it Brains, reveals Secrets of Honour.

    Bowels, reveals Secrets of Riches.

    Heart, reveals Secrets as to Life.

    Teeth, loſes your Friends.

To Bloodſhed, threats with Loſs of Labour and Materials.

    But powred on the Clothes, not the Earth, Gain.   Vid. *Blood* in *Body*.

Manner. Perſons conjoint Aid in't, ſhew'd of conjoint Aid.

    By a Fidler, ſhew'd *A*. of having much Muſick.

    Souldier, become of his like deſperate Fortune.

    Raſh Perſon, Hurt thro his like raſh Courſes.

    Leaving an Hole dry after it, creating an Habit perpetual. Wounds.

Wounds. Manner. Inftrument cut, vid. *Action.*

Knife or Sword ftruck with by a mean Perfon as ftanding, to a Prince fhews Danger of Death or Slavery.

By a Dart, thro Court pleading and a laid Aim.

Falling from Heaven on his Foot, fhew'd *A.* Death, Snake-ftung there.

Stone, that is, a Chance Calumny. Sword, is for Honour or Safety.

To Blood, has fhewn fome of greatKind-neſs.

No Blood iffu-ing,the Kind-neſs the leſs.

Acts. Bit by a Serpent, damag'd by a mean Enemy lying in wait.

Bite off a Madman's Ear, be reputed in Fame more defperate than he.

Fighting wounded in, threats with Shame and Difhonour.

But to Butchers, Cooks and Chirurgeons, 'tis good.

C H A P. LX.

Of Quantity.

IN general, vid. *Quality.*   Vid. *Mathematicks* in *Arts.*
     Broad, vid. *Narrow* infra.
Diftance things feen at, are fo in time.

In a Goal Court be, but far from the Goaler, that is, in Circumftance of future Debt and Ruin, but with-out Danger.

Next Market-Town go to, that is, buy or fell immediately.

Chamber to a Mifer's be in, that is, act near as hardly.

Woman's be in, act near as effeminately.

Market-Town to you fee flourifh, that is, command all Mony for Bargains at your Wifh.

Far from another fit and out of hearing, be fixed to have no Tranfaction with them according.

Near in general, vid. *Pofture.*

Diſtance.Near.Nearer coming to you, that is, nearer approaching in time.

A Friend ſeen, ſhew'd of an Aid anſwering his Temper more at Command.

Further remov'd, *e con.*

Things change on View, their Expectation fails on Examination.

Far from Home find your ſelf, threats you in Affairs hard to accompliſh.

You ſee Beggars, that is, be in Terror at diſtant Wants in Futurity.

Have reſpect for fair Women, but keep at diſtance from them, gives you their Love.

Home in a Market Town, at a difficulty in a Buſineſs of bargaining.

In a little travelling Road, ſhew'd A. ſtreſs'd in Tackle only.

At a Smiths Shop there, about Iron Work.

Miles 3 off, a Matter of greateſt Difficulty in Command.

4 Miles off diſtant, a Diſtance of Council.

Encreas'd, vid. *Fleſh* in *Body.*

In Courage ſeem, that is, act with greater Vigor.

A Spring to a Brook ſeen, gave great Riches.

Enlarg'd Houſe having, gives an Increaſe in Eſtate, Power or Family.

Equal ſized Stones build with, uſe juſt Reaſonings in Deſigns.

Match an Horſe to the worſe, diſparage him in his Uſe.

Exceeding, vid. *Honour.*

Great in general, anſwers to the Greatneſs of Effects, as *&c.*

To great Men, 'tis good to ſee great things; to others it ſhews vain Hopes.

Vid. *Little* infra.   Vid. *Overgreat* infra.

Angel or Devil, vid. *Spirits.*

Creatures. Birds ſeen, to the Rich good, *& e con.*

Beaſts, mighty Powers or Kingdoms.

And gentle, ſhew of Terror without Hurt.

Oxen ſeen ſo, ſhew'd of good Farming and Rents.

Mouſe ſeen that would not enter his Hole, ſhew'd A. of a proud Houſe-Mate that would not ſtoop.

Serpent, an Enemy your Superior.

Little one, your Inferior.

Dragon help'd by little ones, ſhew'd of a Popiſh King help'd by Papiſts.

Fiſh ſeen in the Sea is ill to all, the Dolphin excepted.

Eating is good, except in Defluxions and Melancholy.

G reat

Great Creatures. Fish eating little ones, threats with Enmity among Friends, from their little Bones.

Weeds seen trod down, shew'd A. of mighty Pretenders baffled.

Thistle seen in a Pasture, shew'd A. of a great Waste rectifiable there.

Persons. Self overbig seeming, shew'd A. Death.

Great as another seem, that is, of equal Power or Merit.

Son A. seeing his overbig, foreshew'd his Death.

Creditor seen overbig, shew'd A. of an excessive Debt demanded.

Daughter tall as your self, a Debt to your whole Value. Vid. *Change* in *Sense.*

Giants seen, generally shew good.

To most they shew of Stately Actions according.

Overgreat seen, have shewn of some taking too much on them.

Thrusting into your Parlour, presuming to command your best Converse.

Parts. Breast, vid. *Body.*

Beard, vid. *Body.*

Head, vid. *Body.*

Nose great have, be of subtle Sense and great Acquaintance.

To Deformity, live in Plenty, but with Popular Hate.

Privities, that is, a Son scandalous and troublesom.

Teeth have, that is, be of extraordinary Power against Enemies.

Things shew of great or stately Actions according.

Books great and long, shew of long Life according, or mighty Instructions.

Business of great Concern managing, threats with Obstructions.

Cut of Bread seen cut by a Woman in an House, gave A. a bare Plenty near.

Ease, to the Sick Death.

House, shews of a noble Converse or Oeconomy.

Chamber so, a private Managery so, &c.

Mony Sums have, that is, do what will want and require such.

Rain see on a Road, be in great Trouble, but to good Hopes.

Greater is as more Grand or Glorious.

Overgreat Hearth, Fire in House, is Danger.

Moderate, plenty.

Light, threats with Blindness.

Great. Overgreat Light Moderate, gives Truth and a good Underſtanding.

     Sun or Moon ſeeming, gives Proſperity.

     Leſs, ſhews Decay.

     A's Church ſeeming Cathedral-like to him, ſhew'd A. monopolizing to himſelf full and true Chriſtianity

High, vid. *Poſture*.

     Tall unknown Farmer, and odd prudent Courſe of farming.

     Taller Husband ſeem to have, ſhew'd to A. her own proving of unexpected Power and Prudence.

     Seeming than he was, ſhew'd A. of proving after very ſick

Hollow Ring ſeen, ſhew'd A. of greater Hopes than Profit.

     Swell'd Belly have, that is, be rich in Eſteem when you are really Poor.

     And curl'd Roots eating, ſhew'd A. of vain Hopes, and Supper weaker than thought for.

Little in general, vid. *Great* ſupra.

     It ſhews of things rough and ſlovenly.

     Seeming, ſhew'd of Anger and Emulation.

     And growing bigger, ſhew'd of Increaſe in Might and Power.

     Angel in Glory, a meaner State of Divine Meſſage Conſideration

     Perſon unknown ſeeing alone, threats of your Methods as contemptible as ſuch is your Company.

     A ſhort Man, a Courſe of mean Power and Foreſight.

     A little Virgin *Mary* and Chriſt Jeſus, vid. *Saints* in *Dead*

Action. Enter a Room a little way, in part proceed in an Oeconomy, *&c.*

     A. ſeeming drunk at an Alehouſe, and to pay but 3 d the Bar-keeper on it wondred it was ſo little ; this ſhew'd A. in danger of a Cheat Cenſure in his Gain.

Creatures Fleſh eating, threats with Imbecillity.

     Poiſonous little Creatures, contemptible Perſons of dangerous Facts.

     Birds Eggs having in Pocket, ſhew'd of loitering.

     Fiſh catching, ſhew'd A. of Grief for Gain.   (The Fiſhermans Loſs.)

     Salted, ſhew Waſte.

     Pickled, ſhew Delicacy.

Things, hollow Rings ſeen, ſhew of greater Hopes than Profits.

     Mony in Pocket, promiſes of your Affairs orderly.

     Rob'd of, ſhew'd A. of Store approaching.

     Court having, ſhew'd A. of being ill dreſs'd for Receptions.

     Bed lying on Bolſter ſize, ſhew'd A. lazy in Poverty.

     Rooms, of ſmall Reſort.

     The Handle of a Sword ſeen on handling, ſhew'd of Value difference on buying.

                        Lor

Long in general, vid. *Short* infra.

   Longer than ordinary one Tooth have, that is, a factious Kindred or Family.

   Lengthen anothers Bed, make Excuses for his Delay.

Book or great seen, promises of a long Life according.

Coat wear, be in a reputable but troublesom State.

Hair, vid. *H.* in *Body.*

Market-Town pass, that is, finish a Bargain long in making.

Mony having, shew'd A. of having some defer'd longer in his keeping.

-liv'd Trees, as the Oak, *&c.* seen, give of long Life according.

Passage below in an House, that is, a long publick Family Transaction.

Pursuit, shew'd of a long Expectation of Menace.

Road pav'd seen, shew'd A. of old and long Variances reconcil'd.

Staff doing somewhat with, shew'd A. of doing somewhat by the Help of a tall Man.

Sword having, gives a Life long according.

Table, a large Converse or Oeconomy in Time, or Extent, *&c.*

Teas'd by a Devil, under numerous Efforts of Despair.

Voyage going asleep, shew'd to A. of anothers hazardous Labour advancing his good.

Match, vid. *Equal* supra.

Narrow things confine in time, *& e con,* broad. Vid. *Wide* infra.

  Iron Frame stand in, be confin'd in some resolute Project.

  Your Court, debar Approaches to you.

  -mouth'd Glass seen broke, shew'd A. of an end of all Evils.

  -footed seeming, go not about your Journy.

   Broad being, threats you with great Evils and Hardships.

  Ways going, threats you with great Difficulties and Hardships in executing things.

   Not pass'd thro, shews you'l neglect such Course for its Difficulty.

  Street seen in a Market Town, shew'd A. of a Bargain failing for Difficulty.

  Chamber being in, that is, strait circumstanc'd in your Manageries.

  Streams seen, shew of Courses of difficult Pursuit in Volition.

Near, } Vid. *Distance* supra, and *Posture.* Vid. also *Done* in *Action general.*
Next, }

None, vid. *Nothing* in *Part.*

Plentiful Provisions, have shewn of great Gains, but then of Subsistence ; not to Encrease of Estate, as Deeds shew.

Short in general, vid. *Long* supra.

  Things, shew of Time short.

  Letter, a Friendship of no great Duration.

  A Grave proving shorter than expected, shew'd A. of a Debt proving so.

               Short

Short Play ſeen acting, ſhew'd of a Child's dying.

Spreading a Tree ſeen over the Earth, *Nebuchadnezzar's* Dream.

Store of Goods, ſhews Profit.

Superfluity, fighting an Hog with Stags Horns, ſhew'd *A.* diſputing one would reſiſt with Force.

Have an odd Gold Button ſet on your beſt Clothes by the King Officer, ſhew'd *A.* in great Defect in's publick Credit.

Tall, vid. *High* ſupra.

Thick and hard-bark'd Trees ſeen, ſhew mighty Men,

Stinking Mifts, have ſhewn of palpable Errors,

Thin cloth'd, to a Prince Eaſe of Care.

Fiſh eat, get but the Appearance of Profit and with Trouble.

Corn ſeeming growing, ſhew'd to a Farmer of its Price falling.

Wide Steps or Strides, full or large Efforts in Reaſoning.

Mouth, vid. *M.* in *Body.*

Widen a Way, give more Variety and Freedom to a Method, &c

Vid. *Narrow* ſupra.

CHAP. LXI.

Of Part.

IN general. Part took away, is often Literal,

Some left, is ſo too.

Before you, gives you Gain according.

Vid. *Half* and *Piece* infra.

A 3d Part of the Sun dark, a 3d Part of the Empire loſt

Near all the Rooms of a Palace paſs, compaſs near all it State.

undreſt being, that is, of a careleſs imperfect Repute.

Almoſt ſhews almoſt.

All ſhews all.

Border, vid. *Statuary* in *Trade.*

Bottom of a new Oat Barn having Logs at, ſhew'd *A.* of ſelling unexpectedly ſome Oats by the Great.

A Barn finding Deeds in, ſhew'd *A.* getting Riches worth of Deeds by farming.

A Coffin ſeeing, ſhew'd *A.* avoiding the worſt of a Sickneſs

Degrees. Gather up things by Degrees, learn by Memory.

Firſt exhorted to be gone, then puſh'd away, and after ſtruck in the Forehead with a Stone ; ſhew'd *A.* on ſeeking his Fortune in a Temple, of dying by a Stone in War.

Vid. *Dead* in general.

Degrees

Degrees. Hell feeing, threats Sadnefs.

Living in't, fhew'd Wickednefs.

Suffering in't, fhew'd Difcovery of Wickednefs.

Divifion or Field his own a black Horfe coming to *A.* in, fhew'd *A.* of his as freely commanding an Horfe to fpare from other Occafions.

Rooms feeing having, fhew'd of Oecconomies diftinguifhed into Capacities, as *&c.*

With Tapeftry, by a fair Appearance of Reafon only.

End of a Book reading, fhew'd *A.* of his Life near an end alfo.

Room, fhews of the Extremity of an Oeconomy or Converfe, *&c.*

Drive one thither, put him to fuch Extremities.

Finifhing the Works of *Hercules,* forefhew'd a Woman being burnt.

Endlefs Rooms pafs, find an Oeconomy State of that Variety that you can't avoid, ftate it as you will.

Of your Journy, come to finifh your defigned Purpofe.

A Walk go to, purfue a Method to its Conclufion.

An Hunting Match fee, attain to your propos'd Purpofe againft others.

Every fhews every.

Where fhews every where.

Room be with one in, agree with them in all forts of Oeconomy States.

Full in general, declares of Fulnefs.

Vid. *Tomb* in *Dead.*

His Paffage being below with Men that he could not ftir, fhew'd *A.* encumbred by Workmen.

Your Breaft feeming of Milk, gives you Profit.

Empty of Water a Well found, fhew'd *A.* of a reftlefs Defire in him unfatisfied.

A full-fhap'd Child feeling in her, to a Woman big fhew'd her of Symptoms of her time near.

Of Corn, gives Plenty of Neceffaries.

Scarlet Clothes drive a Waggon, as laborioufly compafs a Courfe to great Honour.

Goods a Ship feen, gave Profperity.

Serpents a Tomb feen, vid. *Tomb* in *Dead.*

Darknefs, that is, Ignorance, Impotence and Defpair.

Beans *A*'s Clothes feen, fhew'd *A.* as fcandal'd by his Hogs trefpaffing others Beans.

General Flood feen, threats with Herefy, Plague, Famine or War.

Half, vid. *Ability* in *Quality.*

Vid. *Piece* infra.

Vid. 2 in *Numbers.*

Beheaded, vid. *Head* in *Body.*

Half-bearded, to a Wife ſhew'd Divorce.

Daughters unknown his *A.* ſeeing reviv'd, ſhew'd him of a Debt paid return'd as bad Mony.

Angel ſee ſtand in your way, find of a pretended Divine Meſſage that would obſtruct you.

An Hill climb and wake e'er on top, fails you in your ambitious Aims.

-Way ſay your Prayers, ſhews to ſome have good Offers, but want Mony.

Sheer your Sheep and wake, fruſtrates your profitable Hopes.

His Study falling, ſhew'd *A.* of his Fellow Student's leaving him.

Of him took away, ſhew'd *A.* loſing ½ his Eſtate and Life too.

Undreſt Woman, that is, of careleſs impeiſect Repute.

Heaps of Stones, ſhew of great Hardſhips.

Seen to a Woman big, ſhew'd of her Delivery near.

Dung put on ones Head by the Rich, great Gifts.

By the Poor, Contempt.

Of Salt ſeen, ſhew'd of an Aſſembly of ill wiſe Men.

To others, it has ſhewn Grief, and a dangerous Commodity as melting.

Higher, vid, *Quantity* ſupra.

End of a Table ſit at, command in chief in ſome Oeconomy or Converſe State.

Imperfect, vid. *Half* ſupra.   Vid. *Want* in *Paſſion.*

Your Head or Neck being, threats you with Sickneſs.

Return from a Place e'er your Deſires are finiſh'd, have vain Expectations.

A. hearing of a Merchant lying ſhort of a Market, ſhew'd of himſelf miſſing of a good Bargain.

Awake at a Market-Towns Entrance, leave a Bargain e'er made.

Your Throat cut and you not dead, gives you Hopes with good Succeſs.

Got to *Sarum* toward *London,* finiſh a fair Deſign in part, but perfect it not.

Knob Golden one ſeen in *A.*'s Neck, promis'd him of happy times on his Death.

Laſt ſhews of the laſt.

Middle ſhews of the middle, either in Time or Place.

Of a Walk in your Garden, of your Methods in your Eſtate, plenty Managery.

More, vid. *Fine Company* in *Company.*

Nothing found, diſappointed with nothing.

No further Way found on Travel, no other reaſonable Method offering him in Proceed.

Parings of Cheeſe large given to Dogs, ſhew'd of cheated Liberality Vails to ill Men.

Gold, comprehenſive Items of good Notions.

Of Apples, amidſt Contentions.

Particular

Particular, none but Serjeants admitted to such Feasts, to a Council shew'd
    him barr'd of such Advantages.

    Letters and Books to *J. F.* but none to *A.* good Tidings,
        but in his like Courses only.

    Give 1 *l.* but not your Gold Watch, to a Beggar ; find your
        grand Plenty, but not your Finery subsisting beggarly.

Pieces a Door broke into, shew'd of Resolutions obstructive destroy'd.
                    The Boards only and not the Rails, in Appearance
                    only.

    A Piece of Cake given *A.* at a Funeral, shew'd *A.* of
        Bread given in its stead.

    A Piece of Funeral Cake given *A.* no Funeral seen, shew'd
        of the Person's Recovery where, &c.

Scatter'd Salt seen in an House, threats its Desolation.

    Corn pick up, retrieve trifling Losses.

Several shews several.

Sever'd Husband's Privities taking care of, to a Wife shew'd breeding
    his Son well on his Death.

Top of a Wheel sit on, that is, decay in Fortune, &c e con.

    Sword break, abate or avert the present Force of some Re-
        sentment.

    An House walk on, that is, live in Straits and Extremities.

            Ornaments falling, shew'd to *A.* of Instruments and
            Goods of House Plenty failing.   Vid. *House-parts.*

C H A P. LXII.

Of Numbers.

I*N general.* Double being, to the well gives a dear Friend or Mistriss.
(1)   Vid. 2 *infra.*   Vid. *Affirm* in *Words.*

    To the Sick, Death.

    To the Dealer, Deceit, double Counsel and Tricks.

    To some, has shewn one of their Name like to
        benefit them.

    Seem in a Looking Glass, gives you a Friend or Son
        like you.

    House live in, that is, by Estate and Practice too.

    Plow seen work, to a Farmer shew'd his own over-
        work'd.

Many things reduc'd to one, shew'd *A.* of Aid wanting.
                            To some, the Multitude
                            conspiring.

    Few Eggs, Gain and handy Profit.

            Many shew of Care and Pains with
            Noise and Law-Suits.   *In*

In general. Many Beaſts. A 3-horn'd Ox, a Dominion eaſy of Conqueſt.
(1)
　　　　　　　Many Horſes ſeen walk, ſhew'd of good Hopes,
　　　　　　　　and Gains to follow.
　　　　　　　But confuſedly, has ſhewn of Trou-
　　　　　　　　ble of Mind.
　　　Birds ſeen in Flight, ſhew'd *A.* of Law-Suits.
　　　　　　Storks ſeen together, ſhew of Thieves, Tem-
　　　　　　　peſt or Draught.
　　　　　　One ſeen alone, has ſhewn a Return to
　　　　　　　Travellers.
　　Candles ſeen in's Parlour, preſented *A.* with great
　　　Joy and Mirth.　　　　Vid. *Church* in *Religion.*
　　Jewels, to a Prince Children.
　　Lice, vid. *L.* in *Inſects.*
　　Moons, &c. vid. *Stars.*
　　Perſons. Men, to many great things are ſeldom good.
　　　　　　　Ill, as the Plague often.
　　　　　　Friends ſeen, threats you Miſery,
　　　　　　　as wanting their Aid.
　　　　　　One alone tho, promiſes
　　　　　　　you well, and as is his
　　　　　　　Diſpoſition.
　　　　　　Enemies many ſeen, *e con,* ſhews
　　　　　　　you good as you are their
　　　　　　　Envy.
　　　　　　One is Ill, and as he is you
　　　　　　　are ſpited.
　　　　Women, vid. *Company.*
　　　　　Wives, vid. *Grammar.*
　　　State ſeen with you in a fatal Place, ſhews
　　　　　you dying with them in War or
　　　　　Plague.
　　　　　Fathers Kin ſeen with *A.* ſhew'd of
　　　　　his Mothers Kin leaving him.
　　　Parts. Breaſts having many, to a Woman
　　　　　ſhew'd follow whoring.
　　　　　Ears, ⎫ Head, ⎫ Vid. *Body.*
　　　　　Eyes, ⎬ Noſe, ⎬ Vid. *Members in ge-*
　　　　　Feet, ⎭ Privity. ⎭ *neral,* ibid.
　　　　　3 Eyes having, ſhew'd *A.* loſing a Son.
　　Peaſe *A.* having in his Iſſue, ſhew'd of his finding
　　　ways to vent many Humours.
　　Suns, vid. *Stars.*
　　Ways ſeen, ſhew'd of Variety of Methods preſenting.
　　Windows having, diſcovers of Family Secrets, &c.
Multiplied is greatly, as many *ſupra.*
　　　Members having, gives of great Aid or Confuſion.

Fi

Multiplied, vid. *Company* and *Many* supra.

Rabble pursuing you, threats you with publick Slander.

Killing one, gives you some Victory in the Dispute.

Hasting by *A.* seen, shew'd him of a Neglect thro Hurry.

Thronging thro them, shews you Victor in a Faction.

Creeping things seen, shew of Conspiracies of little Enemies.

Fish seen, has shewn of Business inextricable.

Locusts seen, shew of Tempests.

Particular, vid. *Arithmetick* in *Language*.

None shews of none.   Vid. *Want* in *Passion*.

Vid. *Members* in *Body*.

20 Ships sailing in cross the *Italian* Seas, shew'd a *Roman* Emperor so long reigning.

Odd Numbers shews of the Male.

Even of the Female.

1. One in general, vid. *Company*.

One is perfect in its own Nature, as 3 thro Order and Endeavour.

So it shews of Singularity, Absoluteness, and a Desert.

1 s. give, be absolutely liberal, as to a Purpose in a meaner way.   Vid. *Mony*.

1 Goslin I saw at Mr. *F's* lusty, that is, I found all his to thrive well.

Weak, but the rest lusty; they promis'd well, but fail'd all.

1 above a perfect Number, shews a Defect thro Error of overdoing.

Under such a Number, shews of a Defect thro Want or Imbecillity.

2. In general, shews of Confusion and Repugnance.

Vid. *Company*.   Vid. *Double* supra.

Twice spoke, vid. *Tautology* in *Words*.

1 and 2 is 3, therefore 2 is 3.

2 and an half shews a possible Perfection, as the middle between 2 and 3, the great Opposites.

Twice dreaming of a Matter, gives a most material Notice.

Pharaoh, in Corn and Beasts.

Joseph, in the Sun, &c. and Sheaves.

Nebuchadnezzar, in a Tree and Image.

Endeavouring tho, is vain, and shews as if that you ought to try a 2d time.

Nullifies to all their first Attempts.

On 2d View, that is, on further Orders Matters may do well, but not as new.

2. Two Boars have your own and 1 unknown, that is, find your own become troubleſome.

     Caps wearing, ſhew'd *A.* hiding one ill Repute by a Crime in another.

     Coaches ſeeing his own and another, ſhew'd *A.* of his own proving uſeleſs.

     Doors off, ſhew'd of a Matter 2 Days off.

     Friends only ſeen with you, ſhews you your Aid expected will fail you.

         They going off too, all further Hopes vaniſhing on that Score.

     Chicken her Hen having *A.* handed it, ſhew'd her deferring hatching a while.

     Heads have, ſhew of Company, Society, Imitation, &c.

     Notes having, has ſhewn Confuſion in Family.

     Ovens having in Houſe, ſhew'd of the Maſter and Boarder at Variance, &c.

3. In general is every way the moſt perfect, but then not in Nature as is one, but thro Order or Endeavour, &c.   Vid. *Company.*

     Thrice eſſaying, aſſures all Actions of Endeavour.

         Sacrificing, *Apollo* required.

         Failing, that is, failing on utmoſt Endeavour.

         Struck at, that is, notoriouſly deſign'd againſt mentally.

         Call'd by the Dead, ſhew'd *A.* the ſureſt deadly Symptoms approaching him, but he refuſing died not for all.

     1, 2, and 3 is 6. therefore 3 is 6.

     3 robbing you, threats you perfectly hurt by Waſters.

         Give Chocolate to, that is, be abſolutely liberal in fine Entertainments.

         Blows ſtruck, 3 Days off, &c.

         Neighbour Enemies ſeen on Apple Trees, prevented *A.* quite thro Unneighbourlineſs in a Farm Profit.

         Baskets and 3 Vine Branches, 3 Days time *Joſeph*; and in anſwering as the Crown of Endeavours.

         3 Ravens flying round *A.* thrice, threated him Death in 9 Days, one ſpeaking as to his Life.

4. Four ſhews of things perfect thro Counſel.

         Decent and agreeable and firm as a Square tho, poſſible of Imperfection.   Vid. *Company.*

     Sheep up to you coming kill, that is, deſtroy a well-counſel'd Profit offering.

     Conies the ſame, as to a leſſer ſecret Profit.

     Fight with, that is, contend againſt a Conſpiracy.

     1, 2, 3, and 4 is 10. and therefore 4 is 10.

5. Hurts by Surpluſage, as one beyond the Number of Counſel.

6. Six ſhews of a competent Perfection for a while, but what will fail in the end.

6.

Six is bad as but ½ of 12. the real competent Perfection.

Times kiss your sick Friend imperfectly, give her Hopes of Recovery which will fail at last.

Seven is Motherly, and shews a Perfection of Commencement between Counsel and Endeavour, but not absolute as 1 and 3.

A. saw her Hen have 7 Chickens, that is, she begun that Day to hatch and no more.

8. Eight shews of Stability and Firmness in Instability, as it makes A. solid of 2.

9. Nine for the same Cause makes a perfect Neatness as the Square of 3. It is as the Crown of full Endeavours upon full Endeavours.

10. Ten as the end out of which all other Numbers are compounded, shews of the Masterpiece of Action.

20, 30, 40, &c. the several States of simple numerous Efforts.

35 in such Case is as a middle between Endeavour and Counsel Efforts, &c.

11. Eleven renders great Works imperfect, thro Surplusage of Endeavours.

12. A Dozen gives a sort of Perfection, but not great. It shews of a present competent Establishment, till a further greater be fix'd.

13. As its Surplusage is very imperfect.

14. Is tolerable, but bad. 'Tis imperfect, as doubling the Mother Number 7. Teeth out with Pieces on his right side, shew'd to A. of all his own Corn as too bad to eat.

15. Shews Defect to a great or full Perfection nearly aim'd at.

16. Shews the Perfection of Counsel upon Counsel, as 10 of Action. 16 *l.* Gold expecting of the Spirit, that is, the Perfection of Grace of him.

17. As it writes *vixi,* threats Death. 'Tis in all Cases ill as greatest things overdone by one, that is, absolute Perfection.

18. Is the Imperfection of 16 corrigible on 2d Trial, as 2 above 16.

19 *s.* give to Religious Uses, that is, nothing or all but the Perfection 1 *l.*

20. as 10 *supra.*

24. gives the Repugnancy of a numerous Perfection as the Double of 12.

25. gives a new Perfection from its Inconvenience.

27. gives perfect Security in stable as 8. in instable, as the Cube of the Square 9.

28. shews of the Perfection of Motherly Actions thro Counsel, as the Square of 7.

30, vid. 10. *supra.*

35, vid. 10. *supra.*

40, vid. 10, &c.

100*ds* and 1000*ds* shew as the L. but with greater Grandeur.

Rules.
{
   o. at the end, shews of great Effects from little Force.
        The more os after a Number, the greater.
   2997. bad, as 3 wanting of 3000.
   To an 100*d* shews Years to 30 Days, to 24 Hours, and to 12
     Months, as *&c.*
   100*ds*, 1000*ds* are as the first Number 1, 2, 3, *&c.*
}

C H A P. LXIII.

Of Time.

IN general. Things seen distant as in Heaven, *&c.* shew of things to
(1)   come at distance.

         Short and narrow, shew soon.

         Long and broad, so in time.

         7 Ears of Corn and 7 Oxen, *Joseph* ; 7 Ears
         as *Annuatim Renovantia.*

         3 Baskets, 3 Cups, 3 Days, *Joseph.*

         Scithe seen, has shewn of ½ a Year from its
         Figure.

         Ring, a Year.

         ☽, a Months Space.

         An Oak and an Elephent, shew of things slow
             but durable, as is their Growth.

             Hogs, Akeles, Plants, *&c.* quick and
             fading.

         Man's Image, has shewn the Head first, and so
         downwards in time, *Nebuchadnezzar.*

     Actions, Times and Laws change, that is, Customs and
         Manners.

         Outlive a Misfortune be told, shew'd *A.* of its
         going off that Day.

         From the Creation, that is, the first of your E-
         state.

         Duration of Vision, Continuance of Time.

             Long teas'd by the Devil, that is, under
             divers Solicitations to Despair.

         Daily, vid. *Day* infra.

         Having a dead fat Ox ready to be cut up, shew'd
         A. of having some to sell ill to keep longer.

         Appointed Time as Monday Fortnight do so, *&c.*
         in literal Dreams is literal.

Age in general. Our several Ages seeing in Succession, gives a Life free
(2)   of Cares.

         Purely seen so tho, threats with want of
         Children.
                             Age

Age in general our several. But seeing several Plants there, is as Poste-
(2) rity in Quality, as *&c.*

> Books and Weapons, shew of our Lives long or short,
> as we see them.
> Full grown, vid. *Grow* in *Bodily Action.*
> Vid. *Change* and *Man* in *Grammar.*
> Vid. *Son and Sister* in *Family* in *Grammar.*

Young, vid. *Beasts general.*

> Bear seen, amends your Affairs for the better.
> Birds seeing is ill and Trouble to all, it shews of imper-
> fect Projects.
> Woman, a new Fortune presenting.
> Ones having by a Camel, shew'd *A.* of having deform'd
> Children by as deform'd a Wife.
> Younger than our selves our Parents seeming, if Dead gives
> us Success.
> > If alive, threats of our Children
> > ruling us.

Old Age seen in general, threats with Care, Fear and Despair.

> With Grey Hairs, gives Honour and Wisdom, but
> with Sickliness.
> Doting, threats with Grudges and Blunders.
> Man's Ghost frighting *A.* shew'd *A.* in fear of Delusion
> thro Dotage, *&c.*
> Decayed much, threats with Impotence.
> > But for Witness and Surety, 'tis good.
> > In Malice seen is very bad.
> Woman stout seen, repeats to you your good old Fortune.
> > Courting *A.* shew'd him Riches by Marriage, but
> > with Discontent.

> > To others, a good Bargain of-
> > fering, but disgraceful.
> Servant you have see do admirably, prefer such before
> new ones.

Middle-ag'd and active Men hear advise, follow discreet and active
Courses according.

Seeming ag'd, threats to a Youth Cares, but to a Child Death.

> To a Man it gives Wisdom and Authority.
> Cradled again, to a Youth Death.
> > To an elderly Person it shews exceeding Feebleness.
> > In a Kitchin Passage, to the Obstruction
> > of Housekeeping.
> Bed your Wife cradled, lie with her when infirm.
> > An Apothecaries Wife angry on it a-
> > gainst all Physick Rules.
> In your Mother's Womb again, die. Enter another World
> again as then.
> Long-liv'd, threats you with heavy Labour and Grief.

Age. Seeming found-liv'd, that is, keeping to your firft Inftitution.

(2)   Infirm, threats you with Travel, Change and fecret Study.

       Swadled, to the Artificer and the Rich fhews Weaknefs and Impediment.

         To the Poor good, and care according for them.

     Too forward bearded your Son feen, fhews him Pragmatically offending.

     Young again, threats Danger, Labour and a violent Death.

(3)   To an old Man is the fame as *Rejuvenifcence.*

fore, vid. *Former* infra.

Continuance in Place. anfwers to ftay in Time.

     For a while, that is, for a while.

     In Fear, Delay in Safety, but with Danger.

Day of Judgment feen, premis'd *A.* of Juftice in the Place where feen.

       To fome, has fhewn their Death.

Dark feen, has fhewn of an unhappy State.

Sleep at Noon, die in prime, or neglect Bufinefs.

Sunday keeping, fhew'd *A.* that his Servant leaving him his Work ceas'd.

Not quite dreft, that is, juft about Sun-fet.

Holy-Days, to thofe would marry are good.

     to the Poor and Fearful, Happinefs.

     to the Rich and Debauchee, Trouble and Secrets reveal'd.

     Of Humiliation keep, attain to fome great popular Good, as *&c.*

     Gunpowder-Treafon-Day, has fhewn of Joy for Delivery from flavifh Impofitions.

Daily be at 10 *s.* Repair, that is, lay out 5 *l. per Ann.* on Repairs.

Early in the Morn, has fhewn of late at Night.

     To fome, it has fhewn of full Command of Time anfwerable.

Late at Night and with a Lanthorn, early next Morning.

     Too late to fee, very late in the Evening.

     Defign a Journy, begin a Bufinefs will be deferr'd.

Forenoon Hours in a Clock told is beft, it fhews of commanding good Opportunity.

Darkifh, fhew'd of an Hour or two before Sun-fet.

Hour and an $\frac{1}{2}$, to fome a Day and an $\frac{1}{2}$, to fome a Year and an half.

erring for a Day, incapacitating for a Year.

     Told a Matter is preparing, threats with Delay.

     Invited being to a roafted Pig, fhew'd *A.* of a Rent deferr'd receiving.

an Houfe having, fhew'd of Mony borrow'd at Intereft.

Seen on a Razor to be mended, fhew'd *A.* in Treaty of encreafing a Sum at Intereft.

                                 Early,

vid. *Day supra.*

things repeated, forefhew of the like again in Circumftance.

A Primitive Building ftand on, act in Piety with a
Oeconomy.

Apparel, vid. *A.*

Building fee ftand, ideally renew an Oeconomy Rule
old, not now to be.

Fears having, fhews of their Occafions again repeated.

Order. Firft things prefented anfwer in time according.

Succeeding Perfons, fucceeding Courfes.

Before unable, fhew'd of one before unable.

Taught by one to fing as before, fhew'd *A.*
that Teacher vifiting him.

Late coming to Church Prayers, defers of having one
publick Defires.

State feem in, expect the fame Treatment as when in it.

To fome, it has fhewn of Confiderations of the
State, &c.

Bad talk of how curft 'twas, be happy at prefent above it.

See your Friend in fuch, and him behave himfelf again
as then to you.

Live as of old with her Parents and talk of Sweethearts,
fhew'd to a Wife her Husband fick.

Die again, fee *A.* talk again of things in Tranfaction at
that time.

Mony have again to buy Goods as before Marriage, fhew'd
to *A.* fuch Gifts renewed.

Poverty former being in, fhews it in Circumftance at leaft
returning.

Unhappy that was rectified to good being in, fhew'd *A.*
of the like curable Mifery returning again.

Dr. *H.* faid he chriftned *A.* this fhew'd *A.* talking of things
of that Date.

Perfon. Servant feen come again, threats of your prefent like
to leave you.

Lord Chancellor's Houfe pafs by, act what tho once was
Equity, yet now exceeds all Thoughts on't.

King deceas'd fee, feel on you an helplefs Injuftice.

Give him way to pafs, admit of an Authority extinct.

Dead, vid. *D.*

Enemy once vanquifh'd quarrel, that is, conquer another again as you did him.

Of *A.* quarrel, that is, differ with *A.* as he did
with that Enemy.

Miftrefs feen pafs you, threats you baulk'd in your hot-
teft Defires.

Future State delighting in, fhews you uneafy at the prefent.

Future

Future State being in, ſhews of Deſigns reſolv'd on, as is ſuch Futurity.
      Good ſeen come, ſhew'd A. of ſome of its Benefits already approaching.
      Vid. Reſurrection in Religion.
  Things to be done, ſhew of things to be done.
      to be buried have a Corps in your Paſſage, that is, a Buſineſs to be done e'er you act.
  Viſit your Children in A's Houſe, be near Death if he is their next Guardian.
  Promis'd only to be at a Feaſt, deſerr'd to A. a Mony Receipt.
  A Crown of white Flowers falling from Heaven to be put on, ſhew'd to A. Death near.
  His Rival ſeen come, and he to be gone, ſhew'd ſuch Rival commended before A.
Holyday, vid. Day ſupra.
Laſt, vid. Firſt in Former ſupra.
Late, vid. Former ſupra.   Vid. Day ſupra.
Long Fight be in, contend with Variety of Efforts.
  -liv'd ſeeming, threated with Labour and Sadneſs.
  Vid. Age ſupra.
Never. In an old painted Room of my Father's never in before, ſhew'd me as vers'd with ſome of his old and deceitful Acquaintance, &c.
New things in general ſeen, are bad to thoſe who deſire Change.
      Vid. Old intra.   Vid. Condition in Apparel.
  Barn of Oats having with Logs at the bottom, ſhew'd A. of ſelling out all his Oats, as by Wholeſale unthought.
  Buildings loſt among in his Native City, ſhew'd A. of hearing of Friends Death there.
  Clothes and faſhionable having, gives Honour.   Vid. Apparel.
  Door to the Houſe ſeen, threats the Maſter's Death.
      To others, has ſhewn Affairs order'd contrary to their Will.
      Shut within too, ruins the Family by it.
  To a new Building, the ſame to a new Managery or Oeconomy.
  Gate of a City ſeen ſet up, ſhew'd A. of a new Rule of Permiſſion and Prohibition fix'd in publick Tranſaction States.
  Head buy at Exchange, to a Wife ſhew'd her Husband in an unexpected Plenty.
  Houſe, that is, a new State of Oeconomy.
      A new Building added to your old one, an Additional State to your former Oeconomy.
  Market-Town and ſtrange paſs, that is, diſcover an ill Trade robbing you.
  Mony find, that is, a new Profit, &c.
  Room, vid. Houſe ſupra.
  Sheets waſh'd hang'd to dry having, ſhew'd A. inviting a new Boarder to live with him.

New Shelf to hold Mony finding, shew'd *A.* discovering a new way to save it.

Shoos, vid. *Apparel.*

Song, shew'd of a new Occasion of Joy.

Stockings and Shoos having, shews you as in thriving Case, *&c.*

Vessel seen, shews of some young Person.

Night in general, vid. *Watch* in *Action.* Vid. *Day supra.*

Vid. *Appear* and *Darkness* in *Sense.*

Vid. *Candles* in *Fire.* Vid. *Stars.*

State without Star seen, threats you with a Life full of terrible Occurrences.

With Stars seen, has shewn of a continued Confusion between Hopes and Fears.

Walking in it, has shewn of Trouble and Melancholy.

To some, designing in worst of Necessities.

To most, Obstruction of Business thro unknown Causes.

Clothes see one drest in, that is, rude to you.

Friend bringing in a Candle, a Settlement and Ease on it.

Creatures, shew oft of Thieves and Adulterers.

Old in general, vid. *Condition* in *Apparel.* Vid. *New supra.*

Bread, vid. *B.* in *Victuals.*

Clothes losing, gives Preferment.

Girdle wearing, threats with Labour and Pains.

New wearing, gives Honour.

Worn much having, has shewn Damage.

House die out of, attain a better Oeconomy.

Continue in, pursue your old Oeconomy Condition.

In an old unknown painted Room of my Father's, in a deceitful Neighbourhood of his.

Shoos seeing only, threats with Loss and Sadness.

Torn and falling off, threats with greatest Poverty and Distress.

Cutting to Pieces, mastering Inconveniencies.

Vid. *Apparel.*

Stockings, vid. *Apparel.*

Trees seeing, gives Assurance in Doubts.

With Branches at Root, has given Children in old Age.

Woman stout one seen, renew'd to *A.* his good old Fortune.

With a new Pair of Shoos, shew'd a Servant of removing Service, as of old she was accustomed.

Opportunity; a Man seen with an Hat having no Brim before, shew'd him of Opportunity in Prevention, *&c.*

Out-live a Misfortune said, shew'd *A.* of its that Day ceasing.

Past, vid. *Former supra.*

Predecessors expell'd seen good, it renews to you the like Benefits as by their Removal.

Primitive, vid. *Former supra.*

Seasonable

Seaſonable things, ſhew of happy Iſſue and good Luck.
               Vid. *Unſeaſonable* infra.
          Rain, Riches.
          Flowers ſeen are generally good, as giving of Joy
            and Eaſe.
       Seen out of Seaſon, ſhew of Ill out of Good.
              Unſeaſonable ſeen in Seaſon, is Good out of Ill.
                 Seaſonable in Seaſon, Perfection, *& e contra.*
       For a ſeaſon or a while ſtaying, ſhew'd literally.
Staying ſomewhere, that is, reſolving according, and having your Af-
   fairs ſo, *&c.* in Circumſtance.
     At an Inn, being in a Delay in the midſt of Buſineſs.
      A Place in general, anſwers according with a Continuance in
       Time.
Succeed, vid. *Former* ſupra.
Quickly ſhews quickly.
Summer-Houſe, vid. *Out-houſes*, &c.
       Apples, ſhews of Joy and a good Time.
       Birds as Nightingals and Swallows, ſhew of Joy, but for a
        time only.
       Stars ſeen, cauſe Good from Ill, *& e con.*
Unſeaſonable Fruit, to ſome Calumny and Detraction.
             Vid. *Seaſonable* ſupra.
             to ſome, defers their Work till then.
Until, vid. *Wait* in *Company.*
Waiting, vid. *Company.*
       By you ſee another, that is, force their Patience to your
        Neglects.
Years 6 ago you ſaid ſo, literally you acted or wrote then as if you
   thought ſo.

CHAP. LXIV.

Of Government.

King in general, ſhews of God, the Law, the Soul, and publick
  (1)   Cuſtom and Mony.
           Of the Mind, when in true Command and
              with publick Nobleſs.
              And ſo the more ſtately the bet-
               ter.
           To ſome, Tranſactions under an Awe anſwe-
             rable.
           Running from King or Queen, a-
             voiding an Awe anſwerable.
   's Houſe, vid. *Known* in *Grammar.*   *King*

King acting weakly, shews of the Mind.
(1) Violent Custom, or a Prince doing so.
 Familiar the King himself, if in Circumstance, &c.
 Ruling, the Law.
 Blessing, &c. God.
 If great seen, has shewn of a Governor.
  Little, a Tax-Gatherer.
 Foreign, vid. F. in *Earth.*
Being one, to the Sick Death, no Subjects there.
 to the Healthy, Loss of Friends, Kings have no Companions.
 to Malefactors, Surprizal; Kings are known of all.
 to Servants, Liberty.
 to Philosophers, Renown.
 to the Poor, good Deeds and Honour without Profit.
 to the Mony Borrower, Denial; none care to lend Kings who are unaccountable near.
 to Players, Good, it has shewn of acting to the Life.
 to some, with ill Dress, publick Punishment to Death, &c.
 Royal Ornaments having on, shews the same as being King.
Queen and Kings Women, shew of the Law, Soul, Mony, Custom, Wisdom and Religion, as, &c.
 's Company be in, expect your stately trifling to be heeded.
  Dead Queen, where your Authority is stifled.
   Vid. *Dead.*
 Seeming to be, shews of a Deceit according.
Tyrants, shew of our Hopes and Fears, as also of our Lusts and Women.
 Seen only, threat with violent and powerful Enemies.
  To some, Trouble, Fear, Slavery, Prison, Sickness and Poverty.
  Threatning, has shewn of all the Plagues of their Power offering.
  Sneaking, shews of your Terrors repeal'd.
 Beating, overcoming unruly Passions.
 Watching, secures you from such like Ills.
 Angry be at, refuse to obey some Lust.
 Dead threatning *A.* shew'd him of Robbers menacing him, and who would command as arbitrary.
Accompanying, threats you Awe and Servitude.
 In House being with a mean King, shew'd *A.* of paying a King's Officer a Tax.
  Dare not speak to him for fear, that is, use any Liberty in the Matter.
Acting seen, shews the same of your Mind, and that well or ill, as &c. but in Glory best.
Adoring him, that is, God and Religion.
Angry seen, is ill to all.
          King.

King. Barber Chirurgeons ſeeing, that is, conſidering of his Hangmen.

(1) Bribing for Court Intereſt, ſhew'd *A.* of acting to merit of God.

Buſineſs having with him, gives you Advancement.

Candles many ſeeing lighted in his Palace, ſhew'd of his chuſing wiſe Servants.

Centurion ſeen make one, ſhew'd *A.* of receiving an 100*d* Epiſtles.

Chaplain pray as ſuch, that is, get your Wiſhes by Awe of Reſpect.

Cloak Royal, has ſhewn the Queen.

Cloth'd thin, to a Prince gives him Eaſe of Care.
　　Vid. *State* infra.

Clouds ſitting on, threats him of haſty Ruin to follow.

Condemn'd by him, to moſt is but popular Scandal.

Contending with the King or Magiſtrate and overcoming them, is good to all.

Crown new having, gives him a Son and Heir.
　　His Wife to a King, ſhew'd him recovering a Dominion her Right.

Dead ſeen in Obſcurity, threats our Minds with Madneſs or Folly.
　　To ſome, loſe ſome Safeguard.
　　To a Maſter, threats his Family diſordered.
　　Vid. *Dead.*
　　Give way to a dead King paſſing by you, act by an Authority extinct.

Dying ſeen, threats us as diſtreſs'd in our greateſt Safeguard.

Diſcourſing him, gives Honour in Abſence thro a Preſence demanding Reſpect.
　　Hear him reprove your Clothes, find your Condition unapt for ſuch Pretence.

Doing, vid. *Act* ſupra.

Drinking Poiſon, loſes his Hair on't, and yet recovers; gives him Victory over his Enemies.
　　A Fiſh ſeen brought home poiſon'd with what was deſign'd for him, ſhew'd *A.* of his fatal Error clear'd.

Dwelling with him, gives Joy and Advancement.

Dying, vid. *Dead* ſupra.

Falling off his Throne, and unable to get in again on it, ſhew'd him dethron'd.

Familiar ſeen, ſhew'd of a great Mans being ſo.

Flung from his Throne ſeen, ſhew'd of a Cuſtom deſtroy'd.
　　Down by a Ram ſeeming to himſelf, ſhew'd him as overcome by a weak Enemy.

Gifts from the King are good, and ſhew great Joy.

Governing ſeen, promiſes you all Security.

Houſe, vid. *Accompany* ſupra.　　Vid. *Palace* in *Building.*
　　Vid. *Known* in *Grammar.*

Kiſs'd by him, gives Gain and Joy.

King. Live with him, vid. *Dwell* supra.

(1) Lean'd on by the King a Board *A.* carried thro *Westminster-Hall*, he gloried in the Pillory.

Meat, vid. *Serve infra.*

Mouth taking out of 2 of *A's* Teeth, shew'd *A.* preferr'd by him.

Musick fine he hearing, threats him with Death.

Negligent seen, threats your Mind accordingly faulty.

Palace Royal, vid. *House-fort.*

Perfumes great he smelling, threats him Death.

Pomp notable he seeing, threats him Death if sick.

Poison, vid. *Drink* supra.

Proclamation, vid. *Words.*

Presenting Jewels seen, shew'd *A.* of a great Man as generous in Offers.

Receive of him, vid. *Gift* supra.

Rings, as many as seen on his Fingers, so many Children.

Reported at *Nottingham* with an Army, the City raising another; that is, to be suppos'd at Variance, and as if so.

But the King appears with a Party at *London*, that is, at last they voluntarily sought *Cha.* 2d.

Robes going with into an obscure Place, shew'd him of Ruin to his Dominions.

Seen, to poor Men has threated them of a publick Death.

Speaking fine and then chose King, tortur'd to confess and then executed.

King and Queen, to some has shewn of great Honour and Joy.

In a great Hall or Chamber, the more set Oeconomick Renown.

's Presence being in, threats you awing or aw'd according from Freedom.

Sitting, vid. *Clouds* supra.

Speaking in general, shews of Truth, as is the Matter.

So it gives Gain with Joy.

With the Earth, promises him Victory.

State seen in Glory, ennobles our Mind according.

Sackcloth, in Humiliation, &c.

Sun having in his Hand, gives him some captive Prince.

Taken or dead seen in Obscurity, threats us with Madness to our Mind.

Tapestry fair and open seen to him, gives him good News.

Torn, threats him with short Life.

Old seen tho, has given a good end to Matters hop'd for.

Trees rooting up, destroying his Nobles.

Falling seen, such dying.

Slips seen grow from their Roots, to a Prince has shewn Increase of People.

Two seen, relate to our Eyes.

King.

King. Victorious ſeen, ſhews of ſome glorious Profit.
(1) Way or Walk Royal, vid. *Travel*.
    Worſhip him, that is, God and Religion.
Great Men deny you ſomewhat, ambitious Courſes of Grandeur fail
(2)   you.
    's Table ſitting at, ſhews you of Joy and Gladneſs.
    Buſineſs having with them, gives Advancement.
    Seeing, to ſome has ſhewn of dealing with Men ſtately and
      proud.
  Princes Foreign, vid. *F.* in *Earth.*
     Deal with, that is Men arbitrary and ſtately.
     Dead merry ſeen, has ſhewn of vain Hopes to follow.'
     Prince and Princeſs of *Denmark* ſeen in *A*'s Hall ſeem'd
      as Beggars. Heirs ſcorn'd in that Family.
  Lord travel with, deſign in Grandeur and Honour.
    Viſit ſeem a while, in Proſpect of Grandeur.
    's Chappel ſeeming at, ſhew'd *A.* beſtowing a Charity with
     Grandeur.
    Diſcourſe with, have ſtately Tranſactions.
        Your own, gives you Joy as able in Fidelity.
    's Garden be in, that is, in an Eſtate Circumſtance of Gran-
     deur according.
    's Houſe, vid. *Grammar.*
    Dead, vid. *D.* and vid. *Grammar.*
  Lady's Houſe be in, that is, in a ſtately Oeconomy in Theory, *&c.*
    Of vaſt Stature kiſſing, ſhew'd *A.* of allowing great Pow-
     er in a Woman for a turn.
        Paſſing by the Lord to the left, to the Neglect of
        your own Regard.
  Knighthood ſeen confer'd by the King, ſhew'd *A.* of God ho-
    nouring him.
  Gentleman, vid. *Grammar.*
Rule in general as Mayor or Bailiff, is Trouble to all with Anger or
(3)   Scandal.
    To Phyſicians, it gives Practice with Succeſs.
    Governing in a Ship, that is, in ſome anxious Hazard State.
      Well, gives Succeſs in it.
      The King ſeen, gives Security.
    Rebellious your Family and Steward being, threats your Af-
     fairs neceſſitous.
      Threatning them Puniſhment therefore, gives its
      Amendment.
    Unruly his Wife ſeeming, ſhew'd to *A.* of an Hireling being
     ſo.
    Horſe, ſhews of a Wife, Friend or Servant ſo.
    Tenant ſeen, threats of your Eſtate in ill Condition.
    Servant, that is, one not fit to be truſted in a Matter.

Office in general. Dreams of us as Magistrates are all fatal.

(4)　　　　　　　Abfurd, threats us often with Ill and Misfortunes.

Being in, fhews of a fatal Change of Life in Perfon or Manners, as &c. and that for Life or not, as is that Office.

If for a Year, for a Year only.

To the Rich, good Bufinefs and Succefs, if the Office good.

To the Poor, great Charge and Lofs.

To the Wicked, publick Death, if with Apparel. And fo for Banifhment or any other Punifhment.

To the Miferable, Delivery from Ill, or greater coming.

Chufing unto, fhews of preferring fatally in Tranfactions.

Fearing Management, diftrufting your Friends Fidelity.

Chofe Pew-keeper, to a lying-in-Woman allow'd her Command in goffipping.

Change. Changing Garments for it, **Death.**

With Gold or Purple, fure Death to the Sick.

Your Friend fee rejected in't, that is, find your felf flighted in what he efteems you for.

Depos'd from it is ill to all, and to the Sick Death.

Depriv'd of Gifts and Salaries too is very bad.

Executing it, to fome do fuch Actions.

to others, what anfwers the Name, as *Oedile* Building.

Magiftrates feen, threats us Danger and Peril with Anxiety.

Sorts yearly as Proctor *Oxon*, a Fate of Durance according.

Vid. *War.*　Vid. *Law.*　Vid. *Religion.*

Beating you, threats you fentenc'd to Infamy.

With a Mace, in all Formality.

Being one, to the Good and Prudent happy Employ.

to the Miferable great Ill.

Deliver'd by one, avoiding a Danger by fome formal Courfe.

Enquiring for, taking Meafures to rectify Diforders.

Fighting, that is, running againft Swords.

Overcoming them tho thereon, is excellent.

Hector another by Officers in the Kings Name, find him yield in Confcience.

Seizing you, a formal Reafoning affecting you.

Slighted by Men in Office, contemn'd in all Form and Pomp.

Mace beat with, fentenc'd to Infamy in all Formality.

Ambaffadors yours threatned to be ftop'd, your Correfpondence with one near loft.

Attorny General pafs by to the right, being in a Coach with 2 black Horfes, as he on Foot, on an high Cawfy by Houfes; fhew'd A is profecuted by him for fine Books.

Offic.

Office.
(4)

Clerk Female one ſeen, to a Wife ſhew'd of her reading in Family, her Husband after praying.
     Vid. *Town-Clerk* infra.

Civil Law, vid. *Arts,* &c.

Crier ſeen, to the Loſer Good.
     to the Secret, Ill.
     to the Sick, Death.

Judg being to one not like to be ſo, has ſhewn Poverty, Trouble of Enemies, and Danger of Robbers.

Juſtice of Peace ſeen, has ſhewn of Ills requiring his Preſence.
     Vid. *infra* in *Law Perſons.*
     Forcing Diſorders before him, ſhew'd *A.* of trying to unite them.
     Travelling unto, deſigning for ſome Courſe or Aid from him.

Lord-Keeper fidling before, ſhew'd *A.* doing an equitable Offence.
     Vid. *Law-Officer.*
     Having your Letters in his Hand, threats you at his Mercy thro ſome Writing.
     Seen view from on far, ſhew'd *A.* of an equitable Relief near.

Mayor being, threats with greateſt Cares ; and to ſome, with Danger of Puniſhment.
     Appeal to, that is, mentally conteſt the orderly Authority of ſome Affair.
     Threat to have one before, that is, Force for better Orders in ſome Affair.
     's Houſe break into, act preſumptuouſly on his like Authority.

Meſſengers ſeen, ſhew of the like you are to ſend or expect.
     Young Man ſent from *Jupiter* to *Hannibal,* ſhew'd his Captainſhip.
     Friend Divine gives *A.* ſomewhat from the Spirit, a familiar Divine Courſe gave a Converſe to *A.* from the Spirit.

Over a Jakes made, ſhew'd *A.* of a continual Care in Regulation of Expence to get Neceſſaries.
     A Trouble without Profit, ſhews of a Trouble without Gain.

Pew-Keeper, vid. *Religion.*

Prefect of a Silver Temple made, ſhew'd *A.* prefer'd in a King's Treaſury.
     Over harveſting, ſhews of ſtudying Phyſick, or being a Prieſt.   Vid. *Over* ſupra.

Preſident be, that is, a Schoolmaſter, a publick Treaſurer, or Cook.

Senator, ſhew'd to one being a Singer.

Sheriffs Coach ride in, that is, be in a Buſineſs of ſure Execution.

Office. Sheriff being chose, that is, self-profitlefsly active in others Bu-
(4)   finefs.

Souldier, vid. *War.*

Town-Clerk being, fhews you of doing others Work without
Profit.

To the Servant, good Succefs.

To the Sick, Death.

Under Treafurer, vid. *Temple* in *Law.*

Honour in general defiring, has fhewn of being in want of an Horfe.
(5)   Having, to the Poor Mifery.

to the Rich, good Actions and Mifery.

From a Perfon, that is, by a Courfe anfwerable.

Give to your Goaler, that is, glory in your Confinement as me-
ritorious.

Serv'd at Table be laft, that is, humour others in Profit.

Turn'd from Table being, threats of Offence and Scandal
at you.

All rife to you and nothing is done without you, you are in
chief, *&c.*

Have from a King of a Defart, be aw'd into a Cheat.

Advanc'd to, threats Poverty.

Applaufe publick, threats with publick Cenfure and Condemnation
of Juftice.

Adorning the Temple of *Venus* with Spoils, forefhew'd
Pompey's Overthrow.   Vid. alfo *Comfort* in *Paffion.*

Chief of a publick Meeting being, threats Pain and Anger, and
often Hurt.

Officer delivered by, that is, reliev'd in all Honour.

Chofen, vid. in *Officer* fupra.

O'er Jakes, chofe an Officer fatally chain'd to regulate Expences.

Exceeding, you plow with 6 Beafts where your Anceftors uf'd 9;
that is, you farm better.

A 3 horn'd Bull feen, fhew'd of a Dominion ready for
Conqueft.

Excel Spungers, that is, get the fame Benefits as they, but more
cleverly.

Pomp, fhews publick Dangers to all, tho with Priefts.

Seen by a King with Odours and Mufick, threats his Funeral
if fick.

To a private Perfon, it gives Health.

Popularity; fhe fees her Husband angry and all taking her part, fhe
ceafes offending him.

Prefer your Keeper, that is, glory in your Imprifonment.

Reputed, vid. *Paffion.*

Refpect; waiting at Meat till others ferv'd, humouring them in Profit.

Honour'd before others, entertain'd kindly in your Motions.

Kk

Honour. Refpect have great for fair Women, but keep at diftance, gives
(5)   their Love.

        Stay till others pafs, defers your Defigns till fuch Courfe
        have Iffue.

        Run thro Company, proceed with flight to others Over-
        tures.

     Reverence anothers walk with Fear, approach the Ufe of his
     Courfes.

     Worfhip'd *Jofeph's* Sheave by his Brethren, his Grandeur.
        Sun, Moon and Eleven Stars, the fame.

Tax, vid. *Grammar.*

(6) Forc'd to pay at a Nobles Chappel, fhew'd *A.* nobly generous in
    Charity.

C H A P. LXV.

Of Law.

PErfons. Attornies feen, threat us Delay with Controverfy.
(1)

        Standing in his Court, fhew'd to *A.* of Suits
        threatning to obftruct Dealings
        with aim.

         London Attorny, *London* Suits, or
         the beft manag'd.

    Acting, Courfes of vexatious Controverfy in Tranf-
    action.

        With one, endeavouring to force a Right by
        wrangling.

    Vifiting, fhew'd *A.* of being awhile in a teafing
    Erangle.

    's Feaft feeing, fhew'd *A.* of entering into a Law-
    Suit.

    With a Wax-Candle feen, to a Council fhew'd of a
    good Chamber-Practice in Offer.

    's Houfe feen thrive to the left in a Market-Town,
    fhew'd *A.* at a Lofs in a Bargain thro Controverfy.

    Seeing carry a Bill of Equity crofs a Market-Street,
    fhew'd *A.* of relinquifhing a Bargain for Confci-
    ence.

   Bayliffs arrefted by 2, fhew'd *A.* accufed by 2 Cenfures of
   a Bifhop.

   Keeper feen take *A.* into Cuftody, fhew'd of his entering an hard Study.

  Conftable, vid. *Arreft* infra.

    Act with, that is, in a Courfe moft furely warran-
    table.
                   Perfons.

Persons. Council seen to all, threats them with Delay and Controversy.
(1)   's Wife see wrong you, if a Friend, be in a Wrangle
          will end happily.
          In ill Business seeming, shew'd to him of his Advice
          ask'd without a Fee.
          Sometimes also, has shewn me of this Allegorick Skill
          Course.
          Brother Council seeing boast of his Fees and Motion,
          shew'd A. of a Brother Controvertist vaunting of
          his Performances.
          Inventorying Goods A. seeing an Attorny, shew'd him
          of a Council examining into his Estate.
Ecclesiastick Judg hear chide, do things worthy of his Repri-
      mand.
Executioners seen with a bloody Sword, threated to a Nation
      War.
Hangmen seen, threat of Captivity or Heaviness.
                To Malefactors, Discovery.
Judg pleas'd seen, shews of your Affairs going easy.
          Favouring another against you, threats you losing your
          Aim.
          Your self being, shews your Suit obtain'd, and gives you
          your Princes Favour.
          Dispute and parly too, threats you overcome in Contro-
          versy.
          Seen to go a Journy, shew'd A. of consulting Historians
          to a purpose.
          Seeing try a Cause no Record made up, shew'd A. of his
          Creditors paying him at his own time.
          Being, to some has shewn them wrong from Robbers and
          Enemies.
          Leave and go from him, that is, act illegally and to Con-
          troversy.
          Wounding him is as favouring the Rich.
          Judging right, gives the Princes Favour and Peoples Hate.
          Judgment Day, promises of Judgment in the Place
          where seen.
Justice of the Peace, vid. *Officer* in *Government.*
          Jeer one, be in scorn of the Terrors of his Authority.
          Leave his House, cease of using his Methods.
Lord Chief Justice of the Common Pleas made, troubled to
          controul others Actions as well as your own.
          Seen to chuse one to Office, shew'd to A. of the
          Parliament's honouring such an one.
Lord Chancellor, shews of an equitable Relief under some
          Oppression.   Vid. in *Government.*
          His House pass, that is, be more equitable, even
          than Equity it self, in your Oeconomy.
                    K k 2   Persons

Perſons. Lord Chancellor. Late Lord, vid. *Former* in *Time.*

(1)   Having your Letters ſeen, threats you acting what you are accountable to him for.

Parliament, vid. *Company.*

Philizars Chamber be in, that is, only threatned with Arreſts.

l.   Offer'd you to manage or buy, that is, not maliciouſly, but you may compound in't if you will.

Prothonerary and his Office, have ſhewn me of my long and laborious ſhort Notes to this Skill.

Serjeant ſeen as Hangman *ſupra.*

Witneſs none to a Fact, that is, a Matter wherein Witneſs avails not.

Sheriff, vid. *Government* ſupra.

Place. Courts ſeen, threats with Attendance, Anger and Charge.

(2)   Empty, ſhew'd A. of his Suit gone without an Anſwer good or bad.

Fly over one to a Seat in a Room beyond one, ſhew'd A. of buying a Court-Office.

Pleading there, ſhews of brawling and revealing of Secrets.

Suit obtain there, if ſick you live, if not you die.

Fine A. ſaw with his Taylor among the Judges, doubting whether he ought to pull off his Hat or no; A. went next Day to attend a Mercer in ſomething like a judicial Power, that acted to his Will.

Crowded there by the Dead, pining near away thro the Care of it.

Judg of the Court, is as the Maſter of the Aſſembly. Matters end well or ill, as is the Judg.

None ſeen there, ſhews of an Hub-bub as a Court, and without a Reconciler as no Judg there.

Be paid in by a Debtor, that is, after great wrangling.

Gallows going by, ſhews of doing ill or ſcandalous Actions. Vid. *Hung* in *Condemn* infra.

Guild-hall London ſeen to a Pariſh Villager, ſhew'd of his Pound.

Waſte Timber of Repairs, ſhew'd of the Bailiffs Fees.

New Inn being in, to a Council threats Diſparagement.

Seeing my ſelf there with a famous Council, ſhew'd me advanc'd in Skill to ſtate my ſelf in fairer Methods.

Lincolns-Inn, vid. *London.*

It ſhews the Imperfection of Dream Skill, as an Inn in oppoſition to the Temple, but it is better than the Inns of Chancery, &c. as an Inn for Council, &c.

Scorning an unknown Schoolmaſter chiding me for not eating his Meat there, ſhew'd my Allegorick Skill advancing to Perfection.

Place.

Place. Pound near unto, that is, near a legal Confine-
(?)   ment according.

Serjeants-Inn, vid. *Lon-*
don.

Leaving my Wife at *Lincolns-Inn*
Gate, crying with her Brother, I
went and boarded at a Farthing-Pye-
House. My Skill suppos'd Estate
careless.

It shews of the Perfection of Dream-Skill, but in imperfect Advance or Effort as an Inn, *&c.*

Turn a *Jew* out of a Chamber there, discard Judaism
of Power according, *&c.*

Temple-Bar, vid. *London.*

In general, shews of a more poofperous and prudent
State of Dream-Study.

Inner Temple, a more secret Course and
happy, both as *a nomine* and East.

Chamber buy in't, to a Council act to merit Practice there.

Common for all to shite in, that is, by
doing Business *gratis.*

Firm where not so literal, a sure Managery in
Dream-Skill.

Fine having in a Court, gave a glorious Master-
dom in Dreams.

Transactions seen there, are Futurities foreknown by Dream-Skill.

Put on a Knaves Coat there, find you'l
hereafter be deem'd a Cheat in Repute, as *&c.*

See a Woman's Stockings pull'd off
there to bed her Lover, occasion
their marrying.

Lanes and Courts pass, be in a more publick Consideration of Dreams.

Inner Temple, the more secret.

Horses seen there, have shewn of Transactions laborious to the Employment of Estate therein.

Walking down the Inner Temple Lane, and seeing
Books titled up there ; shew'd me of taking
Resolutions of printing about Dreams.

Courts there, mutual Intercourses betwixt Oeconomy Manageries, as Lanes direct Proceeds.

Rising from a Precipice I lay on o'er an Arch-Wall
in *Elm-Court* Passage to the Inner Temple, shew'd
me with Difficulty proceeding to print this Art,
as Friends unbelieving.

A Tumult being in the Temple Courts, and I fearing
being stab'd, wak'd for Joy, finding the King ruling and my Head between 2 Divines there. Pro-
phetick on my Wife's inventorying my Goods that
my Studies thus should not destroy me.

Place. Temple Lane. Paſſing *Eſſex-Street* to the Temple, Baron *Wallop*
(2) meeting me ſaid, I was choſen Reader thereof,
and was to have 300 *l. per Ann.* I read alſo
News of a Lottery there, and after fetch'd my
Whip and Hat from my Mother-in-law in Bed
there. My Skill to be of Force, but long firſt.

Going toward the Temple by a Coffee-Houſe thro
White-Friers, and calling for Coffee there, on my
not finding a Way I wake, ſeeing Counſellor *Dod*
as ſlighting me there. Reading News no Impediment to a Divine Frame of Spirit, for
Dream's a Diverſion from it indeed.

Go from Chamber to the Court, paſs from private
to publick Tranſaction.

Court fair with noble Rooms belonging to me, I ſaw in
the Temple, at firſt I imagin'd to have it private, but at laſt I ſaw it muſt be publick, and
it ſeem'd deſign'd as a fair Building, and Ma-
ſons ſtood at him there, among the reſt a fine
Youth with excellent Sample, Brick and Mortar. My future Skill.

Chamber there I left walking with a Man-Midwife
below, and who ſaid this Dream interpreted
was bad ; and tho others above talk'd, it ſhew'd
a Friend in Expectancies Death.

Garden, the more plentiful and noble State of Dream
Skill.

Hall feaſting in, ſhew'd me of a Profit in Futurity, &c.

Church I ſeeming dead in, reviv'd to carry out an unknown Corpſe thence ; getting to better Prophecy.

Seeming nobly gilt, I paſs'd the Under-Treaſurer
there, who ſpoke not to me, as leaving it ; but
ſeeing a Golden Cherub's Head o'er the Door,
it ſtop'd me, and I wak'd. I keep to my Art, as
God is near in't.

Reader choſe there, deſtin'd by God the publick Allegorizet.

Walking confuſedly there, maz'd in Deſigns according.

Butler attended by, ſhew'd me of Services in a Pro-
phetick Monitory Scheme.

Bringing me Letters of Dreams, ſhew'd of my
Skill procuring me Friendſhip.

Law. Leaving the Judges at the Temple-Hall, and paſſing with my Tutor Eaſt ; after I left him to ſee the
Bookſellers, and where refuſing to buy, as I paſs'd
back thro *Pomp-Court*, I ſaw a Friend Council known
and

Place. Temple.
(2)

and 2 unknown at Cards to the left there, and whom I pass'd by West also in Chamber there, also one told me I rob'd him of his Hat. Thro my Law-Skill I avoid a Cheat offering.

Westminster-Hall, Sheep pursued there A. saw vanish, he lost a Profit in a Wrangle.

Carrying a Board thro it that the King lean'd on, shew'd A. glorying in the Pillory.

Leaving to a Council, shew'd of his ceasing to practise the Law.

So it shews also of fatal Predictions, as the Temple above of more ordinary ones.

Passing by a Book on Ground there, and coming to a Picture Shop, I seem'd offer'd 2 to buy there, one of *Michael Angelo,* of the Day of Judgment, with himself plac'd in a good Corner of it, and the other of *Italy* as in a Map. This before my Leg broke.

Things.
(3)

Administration an Enemy gave me, he seem'd as in hopes of my Death.

Bill own, vid. *Writing.*

Bond entering into, shew'd of becoming engag'd in Conscience.

Books buying, shew'd me thro great Pains of attaining to interpret Dreams.

Littleton has shewn me of the most judicious Dream-Reflections with the best Courses therein.

Bracton and old Law-Books, have shewn of the obsolete Notions of Visions.

Read Cases in *Siderfin,* discover of Dream Variety Cases like, *&c.*

Some about *Abraham,* some about Immorality in Variety, as *&c.* Vid. *Literature.*

Debt in general, vid. *Debtor* and *Creditor* in *Grammar.*

To the well, it has shewn ill Life, and Reformation requir'd.

To the Sick, it shews Life in Hazard.

To the Skilful, it gives a just Performance of their Art on demand.

Mony for Corn ask'd, that is, a just Instruction on a *Thesis.*

Scores, vid. *Alehouse* ; and *Inn* in *House-sorts.*

Deeds fight for, contend about Estates.

Find, that is, discover a Profit worthy to be put in them.

Condition treating about, shew'd of the examining of the Ability of Estate, *&c.*

Gown Bar being in, to a Council shew'd of having Good by his Profession.

Inventory taken by an Attorny seen, shew'd A. of his Estate examin'd into by Council.

Things. Legacies contriving as on ſome ones Death, ordering of Pa
(3)   ments before you have Mony.

     Proclamation, vid. *Words.*

     Will making, to the Rich, confeſs Secrets and be in Torture.
             to the Poor, great Riches.
             to ſome, it threats of Diſſenſion.
             to Slaves, it gives Liberty.
        In general, it threats with long Journies and great Sic
        neſs.

     Writings, vid. *Deeds* ſupra.

Proceedings. Acting againſt Law, threats with Infamy.
(4)   by Law, buried in Foreknowledg doom'd to Deat
             Killing a Man, compaſſing a full method of Skill
                 Hal'd by Officers to be hang'd for't, call
                 in Glory to uſe it.
             Wrong done you by a Friend, ſhews of Injur
             will tend to your good.
     Arreſted by 2 *Wells* Bailiffs, cenſured doubly by a Biſhop the
             A Couſin as riding in a Coach, fool'd into De
             by a ſtately Prodigality.
             A Conſtable, love Fidlers, &c. and want Wit.
             Souldiers, be under violent Suſpicion of Gui
             as &c.
             Men winking you off in a Coffee-Houſe, ſu
             mon'd to a Payment as if ſo.
             A Taylor ſee your Friend, find he wants Mony
             Building.
             His Apothecary ſhew'd to *A.* being ſick, and th
             Apothecary having his Preſcriptions.
        Arreſt a Miniſters Wife for your Siſter, accuſe o
             to Diſcord in Caſuiſm.
                Your Mother-in-law, confound a ſelf-end
                Commander.
     Collection on the Hundred on a Robbery, ſhew'd of a gent
        begging, &c.
     Judgment oppreſs one in, get ſome Power or Right agai
        him.
     Forgiven by God, pardoned by the King or State.
     Forfeiting an 100 *l.* if abſent ſeeing Men bound to, ſhew
        of their being zealouſly preſent at ſomewhat.
     Bill in Equity ſeen carried croſs *A*'s way' to the left, ſhew
        him of an Equity hindring in Conſcience his Methods,
        is the way.
     Diſtraining your Tenant, ſhews you as forc'd to ſell your Sto
     Papers of Juſtification loſt to one accus'd, ſhew'd him acqu
        ted next Day.
     Proclamation, vid. *Words.*

Proceedings. Refer a Matter to another, be in Distress according.
(4)　　　　　Be refer'd to, e con.

Try a Cause see a Judg no Record made up, be settled in
your Controversy just at the Pleasure of your Adversary.
Warrant seeing, that is, wanting the like.

Condemn'd in general, shews of Death or great Oppression; to some,
(5)　　　　　have the Reward of a happy Villany without
the Punishment, &c.

Shews the Affection.

Punishment on it, the Action begun thereon.

A condemning one to hanging, shew'd him of exalting
one who would after abuse him for it.

Of God, that is, the King.

The King only, threats with Scandal.

Deliver'd at Stake, threats Restitution with Disgrace.

Coming down to the Gibbets Bottom on it, greatest Disgrace.

Seeing Men or Women executed, being under Importunity thro others Disgrace.

To some, be ot clear Conscience and
bold Courage.

Banishment, vid. *Exile* infra.

Beheaded. vid. *Head* in *Human Body.*

Boar'd thro the Cheek, that is, in danger of Blasphemy Accusa-
tion.

Buried alive, overwhelmed in vast Treasures.

Burnt, that is, blazed in Fame, and Riches, and Honour.

Consum'd quite tho, is as destroy'd in the End.

Seeing another in publick, threats you Loss in Merchandize or Sickness.

Cross, threats with great Evils.

Seen carried along, has threated with Sadness.

Bloody in the Moon, shew'd of a persecuting Church
menacing.

Death in general seen, threats you as casually near it.

By Wolves and Vultures, destroy'd by cruel E-
nemies.

Kill'd by Justice, vid. *Dead.*

Disgrac'd, foreshew'd of Honour and Magistracy.

Bound and apparelled for it, that is, with greater
Grandeur and Ceremony.

Exile, shews Death, Loss of Friends or City.

Seem a banish'd Man, do some great Offence after.

To some, a ruin'd House, a Prison and *Anathema.*

To some, a Foreign Wife or City.

Gallies, shew of sailing long Journies, Fishing and Merchandize.

To some, continual Labours or the Gout.

Condemn'd.

Condemn'd. Hang'd, ſhews of enjoying Praiſe and Dignity with Envy.

(5)   The higher the Gallows, the greater the Glory, but the worſe the Anxiety.

To the Sick, Health with Content.

To moſt, doubtful Gain as to Right with rivalling.

To ſome, it threats Exile or the Gallies.

On a Gibbet ſeeing a Man, threats Damage with great Affliction.

Purſued by ſome would hang you, be in danger of being charg'd as a Thief.

Your ſelf or Acquaintance being, defers to you ſome Buſineſs in hand.

         To all, deſperate Trouble and Sorrow.

         One unknown, a Stranger for whom concern'd.

         Vid. *Hang* in *Poſture.*

By Sentence of Law, the Riches or Honour the greater.

On a Bough in the Sea, ſhew'd *A.* of an exceeding Popular Deſpair.

Man's Fleſh eating, enrich'd by foul Practice.

Unknown Perſon with a Sword taking off the Rope, to a Malefactor ſhew'd him unexpected Delivery by Force from hanging.

Member loſe. Ears cut off, Infamy and Obſtructions of Study.

Eye, your Son goes away or dies.

Beard loſe in Gallies, Prieſthood or Magiſtracy.

Foot, threats you loſing your beſt Confidence.

Hand, threats your Son or Brother dies, or that you loſe your Art.

Face mark'd, ſcandal'd before all.

Head, loſs of Power, Liberty and Dignity.

         Vid. *Head* in *Body.*

Noſe, the greateſt Misfortune next Life, Solitarineſs.

Stones, Loſs of Pleaſure and Authority till Death.

Tongue, Loſs in Strife or Authority.

Mines, threats Death, or Inheritance thro Friends.

         So Chymiſtry and the Enquiry of Secrets.

         Chain'd there, has ſhewn of Lechery and Luxury.

Pecuniary, ſhews of Freedom from Care.

Priſon, to ſome Diſeaſes and Quiet from Buſineſs.

                                  Condemn'd.

Condemn'd. Prifon, to fome the Death of Friends.
 (s)   to fome, Magiftracy, as keeping Towers, Ships, &c.
      Perpetual Death, or folitary Life and Study.
      Seeing an Adulterefs for a time in one, fhew'd *A.*
       delaying to do a right, &c.
   Quarters hang'd up Family famous Sons every where, the
    Reward of the Punifhment got, but the Punifhment a-
    voided.
   Scourg'd, vid. *Whip'd* infra.
   Strangled in Prifon, gives Magiftracy, or being a Privy
      Counfellor Royal.
      Your felf, is as hang your felf above.
   Tortur'd, enrich'd by Law-Suits or Strife.
      Wheel tortur'd in, exalted with great Attendance.
   Whip'd of a Magiftrate, and not Beadle or Officer with-
   out Crime, threats the Sentence of Law againft you.

C H A P. LXVI.

Of War.

*I*N *general.* It fhews of Trouble and Anger to all but Soldiers.
 (1)   Vid. *Soldiers* infra.
   Fight, that is, perfecute or be fick.
   Lifting Soldiers, to the Sick Death.
       to fome, Anger.
       to fome, Trouble, Flight or Voyages.
       to the Poor and Idle, Honour and
        Profit.
       to Servants, Honour.
   Battel being in, fhews of your Affairs in a defperate
     State, &c.
    A Friend ftab'd befides you in't, an aiding Courfe
     expefted failing.
    Between *French* and *Germans* feen in *A's* Court,
     fhew'd *A.* hearing of defperate Fewds of o-
     thers on his account.
   Difciplining arm'd Men feen, has fhewn of merry Meet-
    ings terminating in Quarrels.
   Flag, vid. *Banner* in *Ornaments.*   Vid. *Heraldry.*
    Carrying the Flower de Luce, fhew'd of the
     French Army.
    Mourning treading on, fhew'd *A.* triumphing o'er
     the Terrors of Death.
    Seen in general, threats you oppreft with fome
     great Crimes near Rebellion, &c.   *Army*

Arms in general, Defenſive, ſhew of Prudence and Security.

(2)   Helmet having, declares of Security.

Breaſtplate of Iron, ſhew'd of Cruelty and Perverſeneſs.

Buckler, ſhews of Safety, as alſo the Wife.

Shield very fine having, gives Honour and Nobleſs (Heraldry.)

To others, Conteſts with noble Operations.

Armor carrying, ſhews of Safeguard or Honour.

Loſing or breaking, threats Damage.

Offenſive held in Hand as Swords, ſhews of Servants, Strength of Body, and Riches.

Flung as Darts, Aiders and Words.

Arrows, ſhew of Speed with Contrivance of Sedition.

Arrows in general, ſhew of Speed with Contrivance of Sedition.

Gather many together, intend of ſuch Acts againſt ſome one.

Artillery manag'd by Boys, miſcarriage thro Negligence in Deſigns to the good of others Expectations.

Bows finding, ſhew'd *A*. about a Journy.

Bending, to ſome, Sorrow and Labour.

Carrying one, ſhews of Deſire or Torment.

Breaking or loſing one, ſhews Honour.

Shooting in, gives Honour and Comfort.

But formerly, it threated with Sorrow and Labour.

Breaſtplate,   } Vid. *Defenſive* ſupra.
Buckler,   }

Dart falling from Heaven wounding *A*. in the Foot, ſhew'd *A*. dying Snake-ſtung there.

Drums a Circle of them ſeen in the Air before you, gives you Glory, but on bold Acts.

Flags, vid. *War in general* ſupra.

Gun *Wiltſhire* fine one ſeeing, ſhew'd *A*. in want of a good Courſe uſed there.

Cannon ſeen ſet defending his Garden, ſhew'd *A*. of Debts, &c.

Shooting with, threats of Deceit, Grief and Anger.

Taught by a Sharper, learning his Tricks.

Aiming at ſomewhat, Good or Ill, as &c.

At Summer-Apples, gave Benefit.

Flint not ſtriking Fire, threats with Inability in Deſigns.

At Fowl in general, aiming at Projects.

A Raven flying, vanquiſhing ſome croſs Affair.

Another flying, anſwering them in their projected Glory.   *Arms.*

Arms. Gun. Shot backward and forward, shew'd of Censures nearly
    turn'd.

(2)   Fear being, that is, in danger of Censure.

By a Bow, affaulted by a cunning Plot.

Mankind feen by Death, shew'd of a great Mortality.

Arms and Legs to the Stumps by Robbers he fought,
    shew'd *A.* that the Errors he oppos'd would dif-
    arm his further Attacks.

Seeing a Raven to the left, shew'd *A.* of his ill Luck
    prevented.

    A Bittern by his next Neighbour as croffing
    his Court, shew'd *A.* that next Day he
    would defeat anothers Clamours before.

Planted, Defigns laid.

Inftruments of War, artificial Methods to Victory, *&c.*

Knife, } Vid. *Goods.*
Penknife, }

Pike, shews of Debate and Sedition.

Shield, vid. *Defence fupra.*

Shoot, vid. *Gun fupra.*

Speer, shews of War and Valour.

    Darted, shews of our Words and Aims.

Sword in general, shews of our Force and Arms, and if bound
    on atchiev'd.

    To Travellers, Journies.

    To moft, of Contention and Quarrels.

Sorts long being, shews of long Life, Power and Re-
    fentment.

    Short, *e còn.*

    Two-edged from the Mouth, Truth spoke irre-
    fiftible.

    Hand, the fame by writing.

Player, vid. *Fencing-Mafter* in *Fight.*

State, bloody feen in an Executioners Hand, shew'd a
    Nation War.

    Leaden feen, powerlefs in Refentment, as *&c.*

    Naked receive, threats your Wife fickens.

    With the Sheath, she recovers.

    Bright, gives Affurance in Refentment.

    Tip broken, the Sharpnefs of Refentment gone.

    Frozen, your Refentment cool and ftiff.

    Lying toward you, a Refentment you may feel
    on Occafion.

    Spoil'd, the Force of your Controverfy failing.

    Broke mutually, Cavils as by Confent laid afide.

    :ceive, vid. *Naked* fupra in *State.*

    Linding about himfelf, is Dignity to one not
    us'd to wear one.

                        Arms.

Arms. Sword. Uſe. Held in Hand, ſhews of War for Honour or Safety.
(2)   Wanting it, ſhews your Reſentment fails.

Forcing another with it, your Virtue prevailing a-
gainſt him.

Drawing againſt one, is as Defidnce in Quarrel or
Diſpute.

Running one thro with it, gives you your full Reſentment, as *&c.*

Stabbing Men unknown, deſtroying unaccountable
Courſes.

In vain, deſperate Reſentments in
vain.

You can't kill, reſenting Courſes
you can't remedy.

Stabbing Enemies, threats of long
and deſperate Quarrels.

Wild Beaſts, ſhews as does overcoming of
Enemies.

Stab'd by a Soldier, ſeeming beware of his
like deſperate Fortune occurring.

Wounded by the King with it, honoured to the
Extremity of the Wound.

To a Woman, it gives a Male Child,
and Delivery to Honour.

Another's having, commanding him in your Reſentment.
bloody, but not to your full Pleaſure.

Breaking, deſtroying his Power.

Bad ſeeming, ſhews he miſtakes the Force of
his Quarrels.

Help'd by unknown with one, ſhew'd *A.* of an
unexpected Aid by Force.

Wounded by one with it, great Benefit.

Blood coming on it, beſt.

So the more Wounds the better.

Trumpet, vid. *Muſick* in *Arts,* &c.

Perſons. Armed Men ſeen, give Strength and Succeſs in Affairs if for you.
(3)   Diſciplining, has ſhewn of Chriſtnings and merry
Meetings, but tending to Quarrels.

Flying ſeen, gives you Victory.

Coming againſt, threats Sadneſs and Cares too mighty.

Being and yet ſmote by one, threats you oppreſt by ſome
great Enemy.

Diſarm'd the Saints ſeen, threats you greateſt Miſery.

Armies 2 ſeen in Battalia, in publick Prophecy ſhew'd of a
ſolemn War.

In private Dreams, it ſhews of great and Popular Diſputes.

One routed and the Men ſlain, ſuch Reaſonings brought
to a Concluſion.   *Perſons.*

Perfons. Armies. Burning one feen march, fhew'd of *Alexander's* in-
(3)   vincible one.

Captain being, to all but the Poor good, to them Defamation.
        to a Servant, Liberty.

        Shews of prudent Command amidft perplexing
           Methods.

        With all his Troops aids you, that is, with all his
           Power and Might.

        Chofe by others Boys, happily controul others
           Ends to your Purpofes.

Guard Royal accofting me, initiated me in this Study.

        His Musket broke and another called, fhew'd me
           of Change of Method.

Officers, vid. *Hat* in *Apparel*.   Vid. *Captain* fupra.

        A Major feen threatning, fhew'd *A.* of Law and daring
           Attempts.

Souldier being, threats you Contention, Exile, and leaving
           your Calling.

        's Bed like a Carpet lying on, fhew'd me of
           my broken Leg.

        Heading a Troop your felf, barefacedly dared
           to a Quarrel.

        Deferting his Arms, fhew'd *A.* forfaking his
           Religion.

Seeing in general, as armed Men *fupra.*

              To fome literal, as *&c.*

              To many, Difquiet.

        Whofe Flag is the Flower de Luce, that is,
           the *French* Army.

        Threatning him, and he crying Murder on't,
           fhew'd *A.* fortifying againft Robbers.

        In the Pulpit the Minifter out, fhew'd of that
           Minifters Remove by Force.

        Come from lying with Women whilft he fe-
           cur'd his Wife, fhew'd *A.* of preferving his
           Confcience from Violence.

Afting. Would lie with his Wife, threated *A.* as tempt-
           ed to opprefs.

        And would pufh you down Stairs, in
           flight to your Managery.

        Acquainted be with fuch, threats you in Cir-
           cumftance near to become fuch.

        Arrefted by them, that is, under violent Suf-
           picion of Guilt, as *&c.*

        Purfued by them, to many has fhewn them
           Danger from the Government.

        Affaulting you, fome reafoning of Violence of-
           fering.

Perfons.

Serpent. Souldier. Acting. Assaulting you, to some the Menace of Robbers.

(3)

Troops a Captain seen with, shews him in his utmost Glory and Power.

Barrel. Going into, declares of grievous Sorrow.

Leffened City being in, that is, under the preffingeft Straits in your publickeft Tranfactions.

CHAP. LXVII.

Of Fighting.

IN general, vid. *Fight* in the *Alphabet* infra.

Affault another, that is, defign as relating to him mentally.

At a Window, in fome Hope or Prospect as to Converse or Oeconomy.

Vid. *Kill* in *Dead*, and *Sword* in *War*.

Upon an Angel by me, shew'd of my Divine Presumption censured and profecuted.

My self after, my Personal Interest menac'd also.

By the Devil as a Man, State Bailiff menacing.

Woman, Church-Profecutions menacing.

Another, shews you of Defigns from him, as to you so express'd.

A Souldiers, vid. *Souldier*.

Death in vain, and leaving a green Bough behind him; shew'd A. by such Bough escaping Death.

Beasts like Lions in her Son's Palace, his Chappel burnt down on it, and she getting her Saints Reliques together; shew'd to a Queen how inteftine War would kill her Son, her self hardly escaping.

Stags, at great danger of Loss thro Merchandize.

Snakes, in danger of Temptations or Enemies, as is the Place where.

A Bull gently and he feeming another (Crefts fo) Family Invitation.

Beaten in general, in Conteft for Inheritance, shews Victory.

In fighting, threats with Mockery or Sickness.

To a Criminal if by a Friend, it shews he escapes Punifhment.

By God, Heaven or the Stars being, threats Death.

Perfons unknown, oppreft thro falfe Counfels.

Beaten

Beaten by Persons unknown at the Ear, offering to teafe your hearing.

Known, gives you Methods of Aid as is the Perfon.

It in literal Dreams, offend to require it, but efcape.

To others, receive an Aid as an Acquaintance not a Friend.

King's Scepter, benefited by the King.

Officers, but feeming light, have an Infamy formal but trifling.

Magiftrates in general, be fentenc'd to Infamy.

Phyficians, fhews of taking Phyfick.

Sticking up Bills on a Poft, a Quack.

Friends, fhews of Admonitions and with Blows to Benefit.

To a Criminal, efcape Death on it.

To a condemn'd Perfon, Exile.

7 Sons by a Father, fhew'd of his dying and leaving them well.

Parents in general, threats of Slander or Impediment.

Enemies, Difgrace, and with Blows to Damage.

With Pain, threats with greateft Anxiety.

Beating one, vid *Fight* infra.

Shews of fulfilling your Will and Refentment.

To fome, confuting one in Difpute.

If one you love, arrive to enjoy her.

Unknown Perfons down, rejecting falfe Counfels.

To cloth, make odd Courfes to be of Ufe.

A Tyrant, overcoming fome unruly Paffion.

Your Rival, being more profperous, as &c.

A Beggar maundring you, rectifying your own Beggarlinefs.

Your Wife in a Market-Road, turning your Art to the worft in a Bargain.

Her Husband, to a Woman threats her in Fear.

Gallant, to a Woman fhews her of fuch Lover in Trouble.

A defpairing Man, being worfe your felf.

An Oppreffor with a Knife, being your felf worfe than he.

Correcting Inferiors, fhews of their becoming orderly to you.

To others, attain to a Power to make them fo.

Vid. *Son* in *Grammar*, &c.

Beaten. Beating. With Fist beating one, shew'd of Peace betwixt Man and Wife.

To the unmarried, it shew'd Marriage near.

To some, the Vanquishment of Enemies.

Frogs, gave *A.* Authority over Servants.

With Feet or kicking, is as other beating, but with Contempt.

With a Stick, gives Command, Profit and Manumission.

Mallet and dying on't, shew'd *A.* of Oppression to Idleness.

Whip'd with the Hand or Rods, Profit.

Leather, Reeds or Cudgels, is Ill to all, as not Filial.

Leather, forc'd supple to another, as is that Leather.

By Inferiors, is Ill as not for our good.

The Gods or the Dead, the like, *&c.*

God, be sick, but departing smiling on't with Recovery.

A Woman Traveller with an Horse-whip, shew'd me making Apology to such an one for not returning her Visit.

Boxing is as using all ordinary personal Endeavours to each others Hurt.

Buffeted by a Giant, overpowered in Opinion by one thro Respect and Grandeur.

Challenging to fight, threats Law with the Person challenged.

Not accepted, no Law Issues altho offer'd.

By one in Street you in House, by one in publick Transaction, you as yet not.

At large and with Insolence, has shewn triumphing o'er Inferiors.

Any to hop, stride and jump, that is, to notable Feats, *&c.*

Going to fight, who is foremost is vanquish'd.

Daring shews of daring.

Refuse, refuse a Law-Suit.

Forbearing on't, is as refuse.

Contention with Kings and Magistrates, is excellent if to overcome them.

Cut, vid. *Action.*

Dare not is as dare not.

An Enemy, be in Circumstances to scorn his Efforts.

Vid. *Challenge* supra.

Defence shews of Defence.

Vid. *Preserve* in *Action.*

Lay aside Stones therefore, have a Mishap may require the Aid of Many.

Defence.

Defence. Defended by an Angel, the Presumption of a Divine Message supporting.

Fencing, to a Chirurgeon Business, to others Ill.

Gladiator being, foreshews ones being a Jugler or an Almoner.

Master seen fight, shew'd of Quarrels between Artists at them in Disputes, &c.

Eeing, threats you of greatest Evils to follow.

Fighting in general, threats with Shame and Hurt, but thro Word and mental Controversy.

To some, Sickness.

To most, Contention or mental Fighting.

To Wounds, to Disgrace.

Preparing for it, that is, some long Dispute.

To some, jesting Bouts, but Controversal.

In general. Being in, to some Law Cavils and Strife.

Wake fighting, end in a drawn Battel, Suit or Dispute.

Trying for Help, seeking for Aid as worsted.

Back near a Corner, near to Despair.

Overcoming, avoiding some Danger.

Wounds, scandaling Efforts.

Sores, old Faults teas'd at in us.

Seeing 2 and parting weary, shew'd me as hearing of a Wrangle then over, but on my account.

Their Blows falling on you, their Strife to your Loss.

One dead and 1 alive together, shew'd of a negative Dispute.

Birds, threats you with Grief and Loss.

Owls, a more melancholy Grief.

Mountains fighting, that is, great Men contending.

Saints fighting, threats of War between Kingdoms.

3, or 4 challenge, contend with many Enemies.

Singly, shews Law-Suits and the Aggressor Plantiff.

And prevail, that is, persecute.

Being beat in't, threats with Mockery and Sickness.

To the Sick, being senseless.

Batchelor, Marriage.

Enemy young and neatly arm'd, a fair Wife.

Horsemen one rich and generous, but foolish.

In the dark, shew'd of Quarrels in sullen Reserve.

Box one boxing before, be in Law with one in Law before.

Fighting. Singly. Mumble a Man to a Skin, thro confus'd Eſſays confound a Courſe to all but Appearance.

   With a Penknife, in ſome cloſe and deſperate, but
ſhort Diſpute.

    Knife, in a Diſpute leſs quick and deſperate.

    Stick, lay Wagers, &c.

Quarter, Q. infra.

With a Devil, threats with greateſt Troubles of Mind.

   Beaſts in general, vid. *Beaſts* in *Creatures*.

    To the Rich, it ſhews railing and ſlander.

    To the Poor, it gives Support.

   Vid. *Eagle* in *Birds*.

   Great ones, as Bulls, Lions, Elephants, &c. unequal Matches.

   A Lion, a bold, brave and ſtrong Adverſary ; and
as you are Victor ſo you ſucceed.

   Serpents and Adders, the Overthrow of mean
and ſubtle Enemies.

   Vid. *Poiſonous Creatures*.

Perſons. Acquaintance, to the Sick Diſtraction.

   Another, vid. *Beat* ſupra.

    An Enemy of anothers, quarrel them
as they do that Enemy.

    A deſpairing Man's right Ear bite off, be found
more deſperate but good.

    He drawing his Penknife, exceeding
you otherwiſe.

    Calling on your Miniſter wake, be
excus'd therein thro Conſcience.

   Children, vid. *Grammar*.

    And throwing them, threats their
Death.

    Others Boys, ſhew'd *A.* of Debts
encumbring him.

    Beat by you, commanded to
your Eaſe.

    See a Child wreſtle, a Man is good,
it ſhews he'l be forward.

    Your Sons fight, threats
you in Straits inextrica-
ble.

   Enemies turning to Children, contend and get
your Intereſt in't.

   Horſemen, Enemies rich and generous but
fooliſh.

    His Arms ſhew his Condition.

Fighting

Fighting with Perfons impertinent, be plagu'd by fuch like Courfes.

    Magiftrates, threats you Shame and Hurt, the Means are in their Hands.

    Prodigals, be in Difficulty to avoid their Courfes.

    Spaniard to kill him, try to remove fome jealous Courfe.

    Tutor, withftand fome Method would teach you offering.

    Unknown Throngs and kill them, difmifs fome odd unaccountable Courfes.

        In the *Strand London,* vid. *London* in *City.*

    Woman as in Circumftance, contend with a Woman in Words.

Hector, vid. *Huff* in *Paffion.*

Kick, vid. *Bodily Action.*

Kill, vid. *Dead.*   Vid. *Butcher* in *Trade.*

Maim, vid. *Phyfick.*

Overcome, vid. *Victory* infra.   Vid. *Beat* fupra.

Pufh, vid. *Action.*

Quarrelling, to Lovers fhews of a Conftancy in their Affections.

    Your Sifter, being in Circumftances to outbrave her.

    With an once vanquifh'd Enemy, gives you the like Advantage over fome other.

    Your Mother-in-law, be in Circumftances to oppofe all felf-ended Commanders.

Quarter beg'd and given, is as Vanquifhment in Defigns, and Difgrace palliated.

    Crying for Aid is as bad.

Reconcil'd fhews being reconcil'd.

    Rejoice to fee your Enemy, be in Circumftances to fcorn his Injuries.

    To your Friend feem, threats you with vain Hopes and Flattery.

Stab, vid. *Sword* in *War,* and *Wound* in *Phyfick.*

    Vid. *Butcher* in *Trade.*

Striking, vid. *Breaft* in *Body.*

    A Blow, making a deftructive Refolution.

        With a Butcher's Cleaver, a moft defperate one.

    Mifs your Blow at an Enemy, fuch an Ill efcapes and is not overcome.

    Unknown ftriking my Horfe under me, but he not falling, fhew'd my Wife fickning but with Recovery.

    A Ball to the Parifh Tower, levelling a Difpute to God.

    In general, fhews of mentally aiming in fome Defign.

    Vid. *Thunder* in *Air,* and *Wound* in *Phyfick.*

Stroke bearing, mentally baffled, as *&c.*

Striking. Stroke. Receiving an hard Blow in the Neck, to a Combatant
  ſhew'd Vanquiſhment.
Victory fighting and overcoming, ſhews of avoiding ſome danger.
                    The King or a Magiſtrate, as to the Law,
                              &c.
        Ceaſe fighting, yield in a Diſpute.
    Overcome by Robbers you fight, at the Mercy of Errors you
              reprove.
              Wheat ſee anothers by Oats, find his good Notions
                ſpoil'd by Fancies.
              Wild Beaſts, vanquiſh Enemies or Diſeaſes, as &c.
    Victorious ſeeing a King, gives you ſome glorious Profit.
    Force from the Dead haling you, recover from Sickneſs.
        Overcome by them, Death.
    Your once vanquiſh'd Enemy quarrelling, gives you the like
        Good again.
Wound, vid. Phyſick.   Vid. Cut in Action.
Wreſtling in general, threats with great Grief and Death.
              Beaten at it, beſt in Strife for Inheritance.
                  Overcoming elſe ſtill is beſt.
    A Child, burying ſome Body.
              Seeing with a Man, gives things beyond Expecta-
                tion.
    With a Stranger, Sickneſs.
              Rival good, and gives Performance and Succeſs anſwe-
                rable as is the Place, &c.
              Dead Perſons, ſhews Sickneſs or Conteſts with Heirs.
              One known, Strife with the ſame Perſon and the
                ſtrongeſt Victor.
              The Devil, contending with Conſpirators or Deſpair.
              Death, as Dead ſupra.

C H A P. LXVIII.

Of Trade.

IN general. Perſons. Apprentice be to a Seaman, with great Pains
  (1)   learn a gainful Hazard on it.
              Bankrupt's dead Body ſeeing cut up, threats your
                Eſtate expos'd as his.
              Fellow-Trader ſeen ſick, threats the Dreamer
                  Loſs of Buſineſs.
                  Dead, remov'd the Dream-
                  er away.

                                                          In

In general. Perfons. Tradefman go to, that is, be in want of his Aid.
(1) He not at Home, be fail'd in your Supplies.
Offering things at your Door, fhews you do the like at anothers.
Neighbours, vid. *Grammar.*
Mutual Phyficians and a Cobler, fhew each other mutually.
So alfo a Counfellor.
Painters Shop, fhew'd of an Apothecaries.
Taylor, fhew'd of a Carpenter.
Thatcher, fhew'd of an Hatter.

Actions. Learning a Trade, threats with great Trouble and Difgrace.
Fruftrate in it, doing well with bad Iffue.
Exercifing, gives Pleafure and Gain.
Doing things untaught, gives Succefs beyond Reafon.
Teaching, gives great Trouble with Honour.
Knowing it, affimilates your Affairs to it.
Credited alone in a Painters fidling, fhew'd *A.* trufted by an Apothecary.
No longer, fhew'd *A.* of wearing ill Clothes.

Works. Patterns diflike at a School, flight a Reproof, as *&c.*
Crane fet up in his Garret, fhew'd *A.* of multiplying his Stock.
Making Candles, fhews rejoicing.
Tombs many, doing many worthy-Acts.
Bricks feeing his Hireling, fhew'd *A.* of his Servant buying and fetching fome.
Statues, to the married, Children.
to Teachers, Succefs.
Perfumes, and prefenting them to ones Friends, difcovering Secrets beneficial to your felf and them.
Vid. *Judg* in *Law.*
Made a Mountain of Snow or Sand, a great Power of little ftay.

Bakers, fhew us perpetual Labours, but neceffary and pleafant.
Bread feen ready to bake, to the Sick a Fever and then recover.
Go to a publick Bakehoufe, feek for a new Fortune of Subfiftence.
See Meal there, find not all things ready to anfwer your Defires.
Baking at a Neighbours, ftaying abroad in vifiting a while.
A Child in a Pie there, carrying abroad anothers Child too there.

Banker. Bankers rich, are good to be feen on wanting to borrow Mony.
Barber in general, vid. *Hair* in *Body.*

Barber's

Barber's Cloth deliver one, rebuke their Sluttiſhneſs.
    Surgeons the Kings, has ſhewn of Hangmen.
    's Looking-Glaſs, vid. *Goods.*
    's Comb, gives Eaſe under preſent Preſſures.
        If broke under Proſpect of Eaſe, greater Trouble.
        Combing your ſelf, delivers you of ill Times and bad
            Affairs.
            To ſome, it ſhews trifling away time.
            Hair tangled that the Comb can't paſs,
              Trouble and Law-Suit.
        Comb'd by one unknown, ſhews your Affairs ripening
            by an unaccountable Courſe,
            Dandriff in abundance, Vexation and Incum-
            brances.
    Razor ſeen with a Dial on it, ſhew'd of Mony at Intereſt.
        Have to ſhave another, want Mony of him.
        Made larger, the Sum at Intereſt increas'd.
    Cut anothers Hair, benefit him to your own Loſs, or be at the
        Trouble to order his Affairs, *&c.*
Bookſellers-Shop ſee, that is, be in preſent want of ſome Inſtruction
    according.
    Want Directions to it, be at a Fault therein.
Brewer careſs, that is, glory in your Drink Entertainments.
Butcher ſeen, ſhews of Impudence and Cruelty without Grief.
        To ſome, Actions unnatural and Innocence wrong'd.
        To all Danger or Hurt, except to Bondmen
            Freedom.
        To the doubtful, greater Doubt.
        To the Sick, an hard Death.
    Neighbour ſtabbing *A*'s Calf whilſt an unknown, kill'd him quite,
    ſhew'd *A.* uſing his firſt Farm Profits oddly.
    Vid. *Fleſh* in *Victuals.*
    With ſuſpicious Beef to ſell, ſhew'd of deſperate and con-
        ceal'd Remedies in Farm Profits.
        Mangled Meat, ſhew'd of Farm Profits order'd againſt all
        Diſcretion.
    Fighting, ſhews of doubtful and deſperate Quarrels.
    Cutting a Bit of Fleſh from the Belly, as ſpaying, *&c.*
    Kill his Wife and ſell her Fleſh at Shambles, proſtitute her for
    Gain.
Carpenter being, ſhews of hard Labour with niceneſs.
    Vid. alſo *Joiner* infra.
Carver, vid. *Graver* infra.
Chirurgeon Bone-ſetters Houſe paſs by, be Friends with Relations be-
    yond meer Reconciliations.
Clothier his own ſeen mean ſhop'd, reflected on *A.* himſelf as bad ap-
    parel'd.
    Cloth beat one to, force a Courſe to a good and reaſonable
    State.   Cooks,

Cooks, fhew of the Decency of our Actions, as alfo of Feafts.
>To fome, their Eftates, their Feafts and Rents.
>To fome, Tears, and revealing of Secrets.
>To a Marriage, Joy.
>To the Poor, Plenty.
>To the Sick, Inflammation.
>Vid. *Servant* in *Family*.

Bringing in Dinner quite raw, fhew'd of his going abroad and not dreffing it.

Having an Ox in Houfe fat and ready to be cut up, fhew'd *A.* as having 2 to fell, ill to keep longer.

Victuallers feen, fhew us of Fraud for Manners, and good Words for Gain.
>To others, the Approach of Guefts or Travel.

Drugfters fhew us of heavy Difeafes, as alfo Deceit and Pleafure.
>So alfo fine Women from their Paints.

Dyer, dying Colours reveals Secrets, and is Ill to all.
>To fome, it gives Joy without Profit.
>Leather, dying is Ill to all.

Farmer, vid. *Husbandry.* — Vid. *Perfon* in *Grammar.*
Fuller being, gives Deceit for Gain.
>To fome it gives Death, Corps are wafh'd.

Gardner, vid. *Houfe-range.*
Goldfmiths feen, threat with Danger from the Poifons they deal in.
>Vid. *Banker* fupra.

Graver or Carver being, is good for Cheats.   Graving fhews of lafting Motto Powers attain'd, as &c.
>Engraving fhews concealing, as Carving Manifeftation.
>>Of Futurities, as carving of Matters prefent.
>>Pictures differ, as of fhorter Date.
>>Carving is moft noble, as moft durable.
>Words, *Amor Roma,* } Impreffion contrary.
> *Gaudium triftitia,* }
>2 Hawks, fhew'd of a Marriage with wonderful Profperity.
>*Spanifh* Fly, an ungovernable barren Buggerer.
>Members privy in Hand, Chaftity.
>Hand Left fhut, Covetoufnefs.
>>Right open, Liberality.   Other Engravements as in other Dreams.

Hatter, vid. *Hat* in *Apparel.*
Huckfter pafs by, that is, deal harder than he.
>Scorning you feen, fhews of your wanting Mony to deal as he.
Jewels polifhing feen, fhew'd of Oratory and fine Speeches.
>Vid. *Jewels* in *Ornaments.*
Joiners Tools remove, lay by the Care of Friendfhip in fome Matter.
>Confult, defign in Matters of Friendfhip.
>Vid. *Carpenter* fupra.   Ironmongers

Ironmongers-Shop ſeen turn'd to a Bookſellers, ſhew'd *A.* of an In-
    ſtruction of vaſt Force offering.   Vid. *Iron* in *Commodities.*
    Paſs by, be more laborious but mentally than they of that Trade.
    Like the Royal Armory, to Prodigy and Wonder.
Maſon-like building an Houſe your ſelf, threats you Trouble, Loſs,
    Sickneſs or Death.
    's fair ſeen, ſhew'd of excellent building Notions of Wiſdom
        preſenting.
        With beſt Morter, trueſt cementing Reaſonings.
        With Stones great and true-ſquared, ſhew'd of Notions
        worthy and adapt.
    Vid. *Build in general.*   Vid. my *New Jeruſalem.*
Merchant lying ſhort of a Town hearing of, ſhew'd *A.* himſelf ſailing
    of a deſign'd Bargain.
Midwife in general, to a deliver'd Woman is as her Phyſician.
    Gives you ſomewhat, that is, you have a means to aid your
        Arts Production.
    Seen, to the Sick Death.
        to the Priſoner, Relief.
        to moſt, Aid wanting in Difficulties out of their own
        Power.
        to Women not with Child, Sickneſs.
        to others, Diſcovery of Secrets.
    's Stoles ſeen ſwim in the Sea, foreſhew'd a Woman Children
        that liv'd not.
Millers ſhew great and perpetual Labours, but uſeful.
        Helping you, great and continual Labours aſſiſting you.
    Mill be in, be in a Concern of great and various Cares in Oe-
        conomy.
        It ſhews of much Work, and going well with Succeſs.
        Water holding, threats with greateſt Trouble in Perfor-
        mances.
    Milſtone, ſhews the end of difficult and angry matters.
             To others, an able and extraordinary Servant.
             To ſome, gaming, as playing at Cards, *&c.*
    Mill-dam holding back Water, threated *A.* with the Stone.
Painters ſeen, threat with Cozenage and Cheats.
    Seeming to be, good to Cheats.
        Vid. *Image* in *Popery.*   Vid. *Statuary* infra.
        Vid. *Herald* in *Arts* and *Sciences.*   Vid. *Engrave* ſupra.
    Picture-Shop come into, be in proſpect of Projects.
        Offer'd to be bought, in Power to be merited.
        Of the Reſurrection, to Death.
        Of *Italy,* to Slavery and Miſery.
    Painting, ſhews Shame to all but Painters and Women.
    In Tables, has ſhewn long Life.
        Fine Foreign ſeeing, conſidering the excellent No-
        tions of others.

                                         Painter

Painter. Painting feen in a Room, fhew'd of idle projective Hopes according.

Women feen, threats with Deceit and ill Fortune.

Pictures feen, threats with Treachery and Deceit.

In an Houfe, fhew'd of projective Oeconomies, as is the Room and Picture.

Drawing your felf, gives you Joy without profit.

Your own feen well drawn, promifes you long Life, protracts your Life Actions to be a fit Project for others.

Fine of God feen, fhew'd of Examples of his Vengeance heard of.

Of a fair Woman naked feen, good Luck.

King crown'd feen, forefhew'd him to be fo.

Images feen move in them, fhew'd of Enchantment and deceiving Projects.

Books feen explain'd, fhew'd of a Dream interpreted.

Friends feen fair, fhew'd of his Imitation offering beneficially.

Man's Head well drawn, a good active Project prefenting.

Offer'd to Sale, Propofals on it to others in Gain.

Potter being is good to Cheats, it fhews a Counterfeit with Violence as by Fire.

Scriveners with News feeing, threats you with their like Trouble, as in writing long Letters, &c.

Semftrefies feen fow, threats with Slander and Deceit.

Sowing Clothes, the Coherence of Reputation, as &c.

Shoemaker feen at work, fhew'd of the Reconciliation of Enemies.

Make Shoos as fuch, to the Rich Decay.

to Artifts, Profperity.

Smith being, threats with hard Actions, and chofe with Strife and Trouble.

Sell fomewhat to one, omit a Gain according for its hard Labour.

Blow the Bellows, get a Wife.

To an Houfe he fhews Sedition and Law-Suits from his hammerings.

Statuary, vid. *Images* in *Pofery,* and *Looking-Glafs* in *Goods.*

Vid. *Painters* fupra.   Vid. *Cherub* in *Spirit.*

Statues fhew Magiftrates greatly, and what they fay befals them.

So fubftantial Projects in Oppofitions to Pictures lefs real ones.

Brazen great ones feen move, fhew'd of great Riches.

Monftrous feen, have fhewn of Perils and great Dangers.

Coloffus, has fhewn of fome great learned Man.

Broken, his Death.

Statuary.

Statuary. Statues. *Coloſſus.* Pieces, his Scholers.

         Anceſtors ſeeing, promiſes you of great and laſting Fame.

Baby dreſs for one, give him Clothes for Children.

Image of a Man in Scripture, Government.

        His Looks, his Qualities.

         Seeing, declares of new model'd Mutations.

           To ſome, has ſhewn of Hatred.

      Own its Border looſe ſeen, foreſhew'd the Perſon lame in both Feet, as outward Parts.

        And fine Clothes got away by a Servant, to a Wife ſhew'd that Servant ſeparating her from her Husband.

King, Projects of Royal Power, &c.

Head firſt in time, and ſo downwards (*Nebuchad.*)

Of Gold, good but feeble.

     Iron hard, but laſting and firm.

     ¼ of Clay, that is, contemptible and of ſeeming Force only.

Seen in the Sun or Moon Children, to Men Sons, & è con.

        3 in the Moon, to a Woman deliver'd of 3 Girls dying in a Month.

Of God falling on one, threated him Hurt by the High Prieſt.

Grim of anothers ſee with Delight, uſe with Pleaſure his ſurly Projects.

Making, to the Married, Children like them.

       to Teachers, Succeſs.

     The ſounder, the better.

     What befals them befals the Children alſo.

Tanners ſhew to us mean Actions, with the Diſcovery of Secrets.

Tapeſtry making, gives Joy with Profit.

Tailor ſeen, ſhew'd of a Carpenter.

     Arreſted by him, ſhew'd A. in want of Mony for building.

     Meaſured by him for Clothes, a new Repute on foot to you.

Thatcher ſhew'd of an Hatter.

Tooth-Drawer that eas'd you ſeen, gives you ſome ſuch like Relief again.

Turner being, is good for Cheats and Painters.

Victualler, vid. *Cook* ſupra.

Vintner ſee retir'd to his Country Houſe and live on Milk, be your ſelf in want amidſt Plenty.

Weavers ſeen, ſhew of Deceit with Secrecy and Intricacy.

     Weaving, to ſome has ſhewn good Tidings and Joy.

Wire-Drawers ſeen work, threats you with their great and continued Labours.

                            C H A P.

CHAP. LXIX.

Of Tools and Commodities.

TOols in general, shew of our Friends, Children and Parents.
Lost to a Farmer, shew'd Loss of Labour and ill
Harvest Weather.
Kind breaking, threats with Discord and Hurt.
Compassing, reveals Secrets.
Directing, reveals Secrets, or helps in Despair.
Dividing, threats with Sedition.
Golden, efficacious as if Mony.
Joiners remove, lay by Friendship in some Proceed.
Polishing shews of Reconciliations.
Sowing and smoothing, appease Strife.
Uniting and bending in Marriage and Friendship, good.
To Voyagers and Travellers, Hindrance.
Besom shew'd of a Washerwoman.
Carts shew'd of a Farmer.   Vid. *Goods.*
Chocolate give to 3, be nicely hospitable beyond all Bounds.
Cakes given *A.* by a kind look'd Man, a good Course he fol-
lows blesses him even to such Delicacy according.
Cloth, vid. *Clothier* in *Trade.*   Vid. *Weaver* ibid.
Cotton dealing in, gives Profit, but not so much as Wool.
Engines in general, shew of active Models.
Exploded, shew of Cheats and Forgeries.
Casting away, rejecting.
Iron escape from, free you from such State of Hardship.
Flying in one projecting, aided by such Model.
Removing, mighty Rocks of Force irresistible.
Wooden, feebler Models.
Heavenly, relating to Government.
Decayed, mutable, erroneous and reprehensible.
Arch-wise, fram'd by Policy and Society Rules.
High and large, stately and extensive.
Crane, *&c.* seen set up in his Garret, to a Farmer shew'd In-
crease of Stock.
20 headed square seen hanging on Strings, shew'd of
my buying 20 Bushels of Seed Wheat.
Flax shews of Benefit, but with Deceit and Intricacy.
Flail cutting, to a Servant shew'd of his threshing next Day.
Glass broke seen, shew'd a Shipwreck.
Handling, threats with Perplexities of Mind, your Affairs will
be as ticklish.
Glass

Glaſs Door, vid. *Gate* in *Houſe-parts.*

Eye remov'd ſee better without it, Awe remov'd command your Affairs better.

Teeth of it, have ſhewn violent Death.

Narrow-mouth'd broke, an end of Evils.

Shoulders of it, have ſhewn of Loſs of Authority.

Veſſels of it, ſhew of our frail, open and uncertain Actions.

Incloſ'd in it, that is, involv'd in a neat but brittle Fate.

Broke the Water unſpilt, your Wife dies, your Child alive, & e con.

Goats Hair, gives great Labour but with little Profit.

Hogs Hair, threats with vain Expectations.

Trading in it, ſhew'd of Sickneſs.

Horſe Tails give great ſhew with little Gains.

Inſtruments of War, artificial Methods to Victory.

Iron, vid. *Metal* infra.

Ivory, ſhews of Grandeur from its Uſe.

Deaths Head ſee, diſcover a Death of Nobleſs.

Shoulders of it, ſhew'd of Power obtain'd by Virtue, *Antoninus Pius*'s Dream.

Leather ſowing, good to ſecure Marriage and Friendſhip.

Apparel, rich Dignity.

Mean, Poverty.

Dying, is evil to all.

Scraps ſeen, exhort us to Care, and avoiding Looſeneſs.

Linen gives a more glorious Gain, but not ſo firm as Woolen.

Vid. *Apparel.*

Metal. Braſs in general, ſhews of War and Religion (Bells and Cannons of it.)

Much ſeen, ſhews of Affairs of Impudence and Strife.

Working in it, threats with noiſy Strife.

To ſome, Wounds and Stripes with Grief.

To ſome, Blows and Wounds with Diſcovery of Secrets.

Mony ſeen, threats with brawling and Diſcord, as in Change.

Pocket Mony found turn'd to it, ſhew'd *A.* of his Plenty diverted.

Mix'd, ſhews of Deceit, but with leſs Hurt.

Cyprian, as mix'd.

Statues, vid. *Statuary* in *Trade.*

Copper working in, ſhews of Strife with Noiſe and Deceit, and ſo of empty Deceivers.

Gold, vid. *Riches.*

Latin, ſhews us of empty and vain glorious Cheats.

Iron, vid. *Trade* ſupra.

Seeing it, to Men in doubts Surety.

to ſome, horrid Difficulties.

Dealing in't, threats with Loſs and Misfortunes.

Metals.

Metals. Iron. Eating it, gave long Life, Strength and Victory.

    Cut with it, vid. *Action.*

    Embracing it, shews of Imprisonment or teaching fencing.

    Bright, gives firm Assurance with Chearfulness.

        Rusty, threats with Diffidence and Jealousy.

    Cast Iron seen, shew'd of Iron Work broke as brittle.

    Drop'd down Stairs, hard Gains lost at Cards.

    Hurt with it, Damage.

    Limbs of it, that is, of uncontrolable Force.

        Privities of it, shew'd of a Son that kill'd his Father.

        Tongue, that is, sharp and piercing.

    Things. Frame crumpled in, that is, straitned by some hard Model.

        Rings of it, shew of Goods thro Labour with Security.

        Window-Bar stops, your firmest Resolutions obstruct you.

        Gate stops your Entrance, that is, invincible Denial obstructs it.

Lead, shews us of Impediments, Difficulties and Despair.

    To some, Burden and Labours.

    Trading in't, threats Sickness.

    Teeth of it, Shame and Dishonour from Speech.

    Sword, a Resentment powerless.

    Mony, that is, what is bad and to go at Loss.

    White, shews Diseases with Grief.

    Black, shews of Envy.

        To others, mortal Diseases without Pain.

    Crown, vid. *C.* in *Ornaments.*

Silver, vid. *Riches.*

Instruments, shew of the Constancy of our Life.

    Pickax of Iron, an all-confounding Force, as *&c.*

    Bar and Wedg of Iron, a Power of irresistible Confusion.

    Nails, shew of Obstructions absolute, as Locks, Keys, Doors conditional.

        Having in Hand, bids beware of Enemies.

        Rusty, the same with Diffidence and Jealousy.

Millstone, vid. *Miller* in *Trade.*

Minerals, *Auripigmentum* shews of Grief, Cheat and Diseases.

Ladder in general, shews of our Designs of Profit and Glory, but somewhat deceitful.

    To others, the Designs of Travel, and the Steps hazard.

    Going down, threats Poverty and cross Affairs.

Ladder in general, aſcending, gives Succeſs and Honour.

>   To Heaven with Angels on it God on Top
>   *Jacob's* Revel.

> Call for to deſcend a Precipice, ſeek for Aid in
> Difficulty.

Nutmegs ſeen, give Profit from Strangers eat or not.

Oil, vid. *Religion.*

> Seen, promiſes of Deliverance.

> Anointing the Locks is beſt.

Pitch ſcalding flung into, ſhew'd *A.* of vomiting Choler.

Plow ſeen, ſhew'd of an Hind.   Vid. *Domeſtick Acts* infra.

Quickſilver, ſhews of Sickneſs, and moſtly weakneſs.

> In dealings, it threats with Snares and Deceits of great Men.
> To ſome, ſtrange Change of Fortune.

Ropes, ſhew to us of Arguments and Reaſonings.

> Tie up a broken Chriſtal, retrieve an endamag'd ſelf-evident
> fine Truth.

> Engines of them, Models artificially compil'd.

>> High in the Air, loftily projective.

>> Sliding forwards, progreſſive withal.

> I make whole my Cutskein of Thred, I live ſteady from Sur-
> feits.

> String an Egg ſeen hang by, ſhew'd of Treaſure under it, as
> where ſeen.

>> 3 Strings, a perfect Endeavour of reaſoning, &c.

> Vid. *Muſick* in *Arts,* and *Thred* infra.

Ruler ſtanding on, to St. *Auſtin's* Mother ſhew'd of his living Chriſtianly.

> Ruled by a Serpent, become full of Malice and Deceit.

> Yours flung at another is return'd, he obeys your Orders.

Saltpeter, vid. *Sulphur* infra.

Saw ſeen, ſhews of the Woman and her Profit.

> Cutting of Elm Boards, ſhew'd of burying a Friend.

Scales, vid. *Weight* infra.

Scythes ſeen threat Hurt, they cut all.

> They ſhew alſo half a Year from their Figure.

Silk gives a more glorious Gain than Wool, but not ſo firm.

Skins of Beaſts, ſhew of ſordid Gains with Labour.

>   Vid. *Body Human.*   Vid. *Leather* ſupra.

> Fleaing his Son for a Bag, foreſhew'd to a Father of his Son
> drown'd next day.

String, vid. *Rope* ſupra.

Sulphur, threats Infamy with the Cauſe of all Strife, as making Gun-
powder.

> To ſome, it ſhews wicked Men.

Thred as Ropes *ſupra.*

Wax ſeen, threats us with great Sickneſs or Death.

> Handling to ſome tho, is good.

Wa

Wax have for sealing Letters, have occasion to write such.
   Candle seen, gave Chamber Practice to a Lawyer.
       Vid. *Fire.*
   Vid. *Crown* in *Ornaments.*
Weight. *Claudius* and *Nero* equal to *Vespasian* and his Son, they reigned
     alike in time.
   Light Mony, shews of defective Actions or Notions.
   On *A*'s Back a Load lying, shew'd him charg'd with Guilt.
   Scales want to weigh Plate, be at a Loss to value a Bargain as
     sure in Profit.   Vid. *Feel* in *Sense.*
Wheel seen, threats with some great Change of Affairs.
   Sitting at Bottom on't, gives Increase.
       Top, threats with Decrease of Affairs.
   Approaching or push'd back, and so such Change treated.
   Sitting expecting thereon, settledly compos'd to await the
     Chance of a matter.
Wool having, gives a Gain great and continued.
     For Hair, threats with Sickness and the Itch.
Yoke seen is good, but not to Servants, except broke.
Yard, vid. *Thred* in *Rope* supra.

CHAP. LXX.

Of Domestick Actions.

IN *general.* Let or hinder'd, threat with Mockery to Anger.
 (1)   Proceeding abruptly, Loss thro Negligence.
        Orderly, shews lazily neglecting, *&c.*
   Doing out of season, defers your Works till then.
     On a Precipice, assaying things of Difficulty.
   Fidling, crack Nuts, roast Apples by Fire side, live idle
     and hated of all.
   Set Boys about it, neglect it to your Hurt.
   Managing of great Concerns in general, threats with
     Obstructions.
   Your Plow runs too deep, you undertake too much
     Husbandry.
Persons, the dead seen make all *A*'s Beds, shew'd to him
    and his Guests Sickness.
   Idle Persons seen, threats you like them.
       His Fellow Servant seen he only serv-
       ing the Guests, shew'd *A.* only re-
       warded by such Guests, and not such
       Servant.

In general. Perſons. Loitering Perſons ſeen, interrupt your Affairs with
(1)　　　　　Excuſe.

Officious your Friend ſeeming, threats you with
vain Hopes or Flattery.

Succeſsfully carried in your Cart, happy in your
Country Affairs.

A Beggar ſeen do all the Work in *A*'s Houſe,
ſhew'd of his even ſubſiſting by Shifts.

Farmer ſeeing begin his plowing, ſhew'd *A.* of its
being juſt then in Seaſon.

For your Brother act, be in a Buſineſs will croſs
you in Intereſt.

Siſter, in a Buſineſs will end in Separation and Diſcord.

Buſineſs have with an Emperor, King or Judg, *&c.* gives you Advance.

Burnbreaking ſeen, ſhews of ſome Profit extraordinary offering.

Digging ſhews of hard Labour with ſlender Hopes.

To others of going to the worſe, as building ſhews of
Advance.

Molehills, enquiring into dark Prophecies.

Turnips, diſcloſing obſcure ſlender Secrets.

Dirt wherein you are faſtned, removing Diſgrace and Trouble
obſtructing you.

In a way, ſtops Journies.

Going in ſuch, the worſe.

A Grave found at *A*'s Pew-Door, ſhew'd of a Neighbour requiring a Debt of him.

For Water and finding none, acting with Rogues and being
puniſh'd.

It, fortunates you.

Your ſelf a Pit, build you an Houſe.

Caſting one alive into ſuch an one, Impriſonment.

To others, Hindrance in Buſineſs.

A Hole in a Court ſeeing a Miniſter, ſhew'd of a publick Conſcience State obſtructing an Oeconomy Approach.

Baking and ⎫ A Match forwarded by Father and Mother.
Brewing too, ⎰

Blow the Fire, ⎫ To the Rich, Servitude.
Buck Linen, ⎰ To the Poor, Profit.

Brew, vid. *Furnace* in *Houſe-parts.*

By an unknown Furnace in his Hall, ſhew'd *A.* of buying in
Grains for his Hogs.

Carry Wood, as blow the Fire *ſupra.*

Drawing Drink in Cellar, to a Maid ſhew'd a falſe Sweetheart.　　(Tap-
love.)-

Eggs ſetting, ſhew'd of Oppreſſion thro projective Cares and Fears.

Young coming on it, ſome near Perfection.　Vid. *Birds.*
Feeding

Feeding Cattel, vid. *Keep* infra.
Husbandry in general, the Ground the Wife.
The Seeds and Plants, the Children.
Wheat, Males.
Barly, Abortives and Females.
Medow, Riches without Labour.
Corn, Riches with Labour.
Oxen, vid. *Beaſts* and *Keep* infra.
Vid. *Plowing* infra.
Ironing Clothes, ſhew'd of taking them out to Air in a literal Dream.
Keeping Beaſts, to the Rich Diſgrace.
to the Poor, Dignity.
Feeding in a pleaſant good Paſture, Abundance with a quiet
Mind.
Change of Place, unconſtant Gain.
Oxen, as to more Grand Profits.
Sheep leſſer, and Gain with Sorrow.
Aſſes, as to Servile Labour.
Sows, with Fruitfulneſs.
By another, gain ſo by a Foreign means.
Feeding ⎰
Breeding ⎱ Beaſts, vid. *Action.*
Conies in his Orchard that hid, following Studies he will
aſham'd to own.
Turkies, living delicately and plentifully, but projectively.
Linen mend and ſort, prepare for a Waſhing.
Burning Rags, foreſhew'd of mending Linen.
Load tying upon ones Back, charging him with Guilt.
Mowing Medow, vid. *Husbandry* ſupra.   Vid. *Eſtate* in *Earth.*
Down Flower de Luces, deſtroying *French* Men.
Gathering up Corn newly mow'd, gives you Joy and Profit.
Haymaker, vid. *Perſon* in *Grammar.*
Oxen fat ſeen, ſhew'd *A.* of a good Tenant offering.
Yok'd ſeen, ſhew'd *A.* of going to plow next Day happily.
Vid. *Oxen* in *Keep* ſupra, and in *Beaſt.*
Yok'd as an Ox ſeeming, and forc'd to draw with his dead Bro-
ther by his Mother, ſhew'd *A.* Death.
Plowing and ſowing, to the Husbandman Good, but with Delay (Crop.)
to moſt, generally Abundance with Labour.
to the Retir'd, Melancholy.
to the Sick, Death.
to the Batchelor, a Wife and Children.
Vid. *Husbandry* ſupra.
to ſome, Anger and Sickneſs, and Return of Family.
Wheat, ſhew'd to one the Return of his travell'd
Wife and Children.

M m 2   Plowing

Plowing in general, vid. *Carts* in *Goods*.   Vid. *Corn* in *Vegetables*.
           Vid. *Riches* and *Eſtate* in *Earth*.
     Vid. alſo *Grammar* for Literals.
     In a dear time Plenty, *&c con.*
     Plow ſtopping for anothers croſſing his way, ſhew'd *A.* of
         lending out his Cattel.
         Seeing run about his Hall, ſhew'd *A.* of his Gueſts riding
           out in his Waggon.
         Seeing his Man plow in the High Way, ſhew'd *A.* of
           letting him work at Hire.
         4 Men drawing it made ill Work, by working for 3 he
           neglected his own.
Reaping ſeen, defers your Work till that Seaſon.
Sheering griſled Sheep, ſhew'd *A.* of killing young Pigeons.
         Hogs, ſhews Damage.   Vid. *Sheep* in *Beaſt*.
Servants work doing to a Maſter, ſhew'd of ſuch Servants going away.
         Seen better done on a new Servant's coming, promis'd of
          his proving happily.
         Doing, to ſome has ſhewn ſneaking to ſuch Servant.
     Serve a King at Meat, have a Benefit as is the Meat.
     Literal, vid. *Grammar*.
     Work doing in odd Circumſtances, ſhew'd *A.* owning how he
         had once been a Servant.
Skim Milk Bowls, to Maids gives them their Deſires.
     Vid. *Drink*.
Sowing, vid. *Plow* ſupra.   Vid. *Apparel* and *Semſtreſs* in *Trade*.
Spinning, ſhews of Superſtition and Perſeverance.
     Wool, ſhew'd Journies.
     Flax or Cotton, Ignominy.
     Thred cut, ſhew'd Death.
Sipping, ſhew'd of paying Mony little by little.
     Brandy, ſhews of the refinedſt Speculations not eaſily father'd.
         Vid. *Strong Water* in *Drink-ſort*.
Sweeping anothers Houſe, gives you Gain.
     Your Houſe ſeen, threats you Loſs.
     Swept the Duſt all on *A.* the Houſe Trouble laid all to his Ac-
         count.
Threſh'd his Corn ſeen, ſhew'd *A.* of its Price riſing to move him to it.
     Winnowing Corn, ſhew'd of having occaſion to ſpend it.
Turn the Spit as blow the Fire ſupra.
Waſhing, vid. *Water*.
Winnowing, vid. *Threſh* ſupra.

Deo Gloria.

The

The General Table.

Bility, *vid.* Quality.
Abjure, *vid.* Difcourfe.
Above, *vid.* High in Pofture.
About, *vid.* Pofture.
    vid. Earth.
    vid. Place in Travel.
    vid. Concerning in Words.
Abroad, *vid.* Home in Houfe-ftate.
Abrupt, *vid.* Soul.
Abfent, *vid.* Want in Paffion.
Abfurdity, *vid.* Soul.
Abufe, *vid.* Action.
Accept, *vid.* Soul.
Accidental, *vid.* Soul.
Acompany, *vid.* Company.
Account, *vid.* Arts and Sciences.
    vid. Number.
    vid. Difcourfe.
Accufation, *vid.* Law.
    vid. Difcourfe.
Acquaint, *vid.* Difcourfe.
Acquainted, *vid.* Company.
ACTION. ACTION BODILY.
Adjuration, *vid.* Conjure in Spirit.
Adminiftration, *vid.* Law.
Admiration, *vid.* Paffion.
Admitted, *vid.* Action in Company.
Adorned, *vid.* Ornaments.
Advance, *vid.* Honour in Govern-
ment.
Adultery, *vid.* Lie in Bodily Ac-
tion.
Affection, *vid.* Paffion.
Affirm, *vid.* Difcourfe.
Afflicted, *vid.* Paffion.
    vid. Action.
Afraid, *vid.* Fear in Paffion.
After, *vid.* Follow in Travel.

Againft, *vid.* Pofture.
    vid. Contrary in Quality.
Age, *vid.* Time.
Agats, *vid.* Stones in Riches and
    Ornaments.
    vid. Stones in Earth.
Agility, *vid.* Quality.
Agreeable, *vid.* Seafonable in
    Quality and in Time.
Agree, *vid.* Soul.
Aid, *vid.* Help in Action.
    vid. Hurt in Action.
Aim, *vid.* War.
    vid. Fight.
    vid. Difcourfe.
AIR.
Ale, *vid.* Drink.
Alehoufe, *vid.* Houfe-fore.
Alive, *vid.* Dead.
All, *vid.* Part.
Ally, *vid.* Street in Habitation and
    London.
Almoft, *vid.* Part.
Alms, *vid.* Beggar in Grammar.
Alone, *vid.* Company.
Altar, *vid.* Religion.
Alter, *vid.* Change in Sight in
    Senfe.
Amaranthus, vid. Crown in Orna-
ments.
Amber, *vid.* Rings in Ornaments.
Amendment, *vid.* Action.
Amethift, *vid.* Jewel in Riches.
Among, *vid.* Company and Pofture.
Anceftor, *vid.* Dead and Perfon
    in Grammar.
Andirons, *vid.* Goods.
Angels, *vid.* Spirit.

M m 3   Anger,

Anger, *vid.* Paſſion.
Anointed, *vid.* Religion.
ANOTHER and SELF.
Ants, *vid.* Inſects.
Ape, *vid.* Beaſts.
Apology, *vid.* Diſcourſe.
Apothecary, *vid.* Phyſick.
APPAREL.
Appeal, *vid.* Words.
Apparition, *vid.* Spirits.
Appear, *vid.* Sight in Senſe.
Applauſe, *vid.* Honour in Govern-
ment.
Apples, *vid.* Vegetables.
    -Loſt, *vid.* Houſe.
    -Pies, *vid.* Victuals.
Apprentice, *vid.* Trade.
Approach, *vid.* Travel.
Apron, *vid.* Apparel.
Arbour, *vid.* Houſe-range.
Arch, *vid.* Houſe-parts.
Argument, *vid.* Diſcourſe.
Arithmetick, *vid.* Arts, &c.
    vid. Numbers.
Armholes, *vid.* Body.
Arms, *vid.* Body.
    vid. War.
Armies, *vid.* War.
Arreſted, *vid.* Law.
Arrogant, *vid.* Paſſion.
Arrows, *vid.* War.
Arſe, *vid.* Body.
    vid. Dung in Earth.
Arteries, *vid.* Body.
    vid. Phyſick.
Artificial, *vid.* Quality.
    vid. Arts and Sciences.
Artillery, *vid.* War.
ARTS and SCIENCES.
    vid. alſo Trade.
As, *vid.* Appearance in Senſe.
    vid. Like in Senſe.
Aſcend, *vid.* Travel.
Aſham'd, *vid.* Shame in Paſſion.
Ask, *vid.* Queſtion in Diſcourſe.
Askew, *vid.* Looks in Senſe.
Aſſault, *vid.* Fight.
Aſſes, *vid.* Beaſts.

Aſſes, *vid.* Travel.
Aſſiſtance, *vid.* Help in Action.
Aſtrology, *vid.* Arts and Sciences.
Aſtronomy, *vid.* ibid.
Attorny, *vid.* Law.
Avoid, *vid.* Travel.
Auſpicium, *vid.* Divination in Spi-
    rits.
Authority, *vid.* Office in Govern-
    ments.
Awake, *vid.* Bodily Action.
Away, *vid.* Depart in Travel.
    vid. Take in Poſſeſs.
    vid. Force in Action.
Aukward, *vid.* Quality.

B.

Baby, *vid.* Statue in Trade.
Back, *vid.* Body.
    vid. Poſture.
Backſide, *vid.* Houſe-range.
Bacon, *vid.* Victuals.
Badger, *vid.* Beaſt.
Baiting, *vid.* Bull in Beaſt.
    vid. Bear ibid.
Baking, *vid.* Baker in Trade.
Balcony, *vid.* Houſe-rooms.
Bald, *vid.* Hair in Body.
Ball, *vid.* Diverſion.
Ballance, *vid.* Weight in Tools.
Baniſhment, *vid.* Exile in Law.
Banker, *vid.* Trade.
Bankrupt, *vid.* Trade.
Banner, *vid.* Ornament.
    vid. Heraldry in Arts.
Banter, *vid.* Trick in Diverſion.
    vid. Words.
Barber, *vid.* Hair in Body.
    vid. Trade.
Bark, *vid.* Dog in Beaſt.
Early, *vid.* Corn in Vegetables.
    vid. Bread in Victuals.
Barm, *vid.* Eaſt in Drink.
Barn, *vid.* Out-houſes.
Bar, *vid.* Door in Houſe-parts.
    vid. Tavern in Houſe-ſorts.
Baſon, *vid.* Goods.
Baſiliſk, *vid.* Poiſonous Creatures.
                                    Bat,

Eat, *vid.* Bird.
Bath, *vid.* Water.
Bathing, *vid.* Water.
Battel, *vid.* War.
Bawdy, *vid.* Whore in Grammar.
  vid. House in House-fort.
  vid. Religion.
Bay-Tree, *vid.* Tree.
Beam, *vid.* House-parts.
Beans, *vid.* Corn in Vegetable.
Bear, *vid.* Beast.
  vid. Carry in Travel.
Beard, *vid.* Body.
Bearers, *vid.* Dead.
BEAST.
Beat, *vid.* Fight.
Beauty, *vid.* Fair in Quality.
Beckon, *vid.* Token in Language.
Become, *vid.* Change in Appear in Sense.
Bed, *vid.* Goods.
  vid. Lie down in Posture.
Bedlam, *vid.* Physick and House-forts.
Beech, *vid.* Tree.
Beef, *vid.* Victuals.
Beer, *vid.* Drink.
Bees, *vid.* Insects.
Beetles, *vid.* Insects.
Before, *vid.* Posture.
  vid. Time.
Begin, *vid.* Action.
Behind, *vid.* Back in Posture.
Beheaded, *vid.* Head in Body.
Belching, *vid.* Bodily Action.
Believe, *vid.* Soul.
  vid. Discourse.
Bells, *vid.* Religion.
Belly, *vid.* Body.
Below, *vid.* High in Posture.
Bend, *vid.* Quality.
Besieg'd, *vid.* War.
Best, *vid.* Quality.
Better, *vid.* Quality.
Between, *vid.* Posture.
Beyond, *vid.* Travel.
  vid. Posture.
Bible, *vid.* Book.

Big, *vid.* Quantity.
  vid. Quality.
  vid. Child in Grammar.
Bill, *vid.* Inn in House-forts.
Bind, *vid.* Action.
BIRDS.
Birth, *vid.* Bodily Action.
Bishop, *vid.* Religion.
Bite, *vid.* Bodily Action.
Bitter, *vid.* Taste in Sense.
Black, *vid.* Sight in Sense.
Blackberys, *vid.* Fruit in Vegetable.
Blame, *vid.* Accuse in Discourse.
  vid. Chide *ibid.*
Blankets, *vid.* Goods.
Blasphemy, *vid.* Curse in God.
Bleeding, *vid.* Blood in Human Body.
Blessing, *vid.* Discourse.
Blind, *vid.* Eyes in Body.
  vid. Sight in Sense.
  vid. Physick.
Blister, *vid.* Physick.
Blood, *vid.* Human Body.
  vid. Drink.
  vid. Beasts.
Bloody, *vid.* Sword in War.
Blossom, *vid.* Vegetable.
Blotted, *vid.* Language.
Blow, *vid.* Fight.
  vid. Air.
  vid. Wound in Physick.
Blustering, *vid.* Passion.
Boar, *vid.* Beast.
Boast, *vid.* Discourse.
Boat, *vid.* Sail in Water.
BODY HUMAN.
BODILY ACTION.
Bold, *vid.* Passion.
Bolt, *vid.* Door in House-parts.
Bond, *vid.* Law.
Bones, *vid.* Body.
  vid. Dead.
Bonfire, *vid.* Joy in Passion.
BOOK.
Bookseller, *vid.* Trade.
Boots, *vid.* Apparel.

M m 4   Border,

Border, *vid.* Statuary in Trade.
Born, *vid.* Bodily Action.
    vid. Bear in Action.
    vid. Carry in Travel.
Borrow, *vid.* Possession.
Boughs, *vid.* Trees.
Bounds, *vid.* Fence in Earth.
Bow, *vid.* War.
Bowels, *vid.* Body Human.
    vid. Lion in Beast.
Box, *vid.* Trees.
    vid. Goods and Trunk *ibid.*
    vid. Fighting.
Boiling, *vid.* Water Action.
Boys, *vid.* Age in Time.
    vid. Person in Grammar.
Brain, *vid.* Body.
Brawl, *vid.* Action.
Brandy, *vid.* Drink.
    vid. Still in Domestick Action.
Brass, *vid.* Metal in Commodity.
Bread, *vid.* Victuals.
Break, *vid.* Action.
Breast, *vid.* Body Human.
Breastplate, *vid.* War.
Breathing, *vid.* Bodily Action.
Breeches, *vid.* Apparel.
Breeding, *vid.* Action.
    vid. Child ⎱ in Gram-
    vid. Woman ⎰ mar.
Bribe, *vid.* Action.
Brick, *vid.* House-state.
Bridg, *vid.* Building, &c.
Briers, *vid.* Vegetables.
Bright, *vid.* Appear in Sense.
    vid. Sun in Stars.
Brimstone, *vid.* Crown in Orna-
    ments.
Bring, *vid.* Travel.
    Forth, *vid.* Bodily Action.
Briskness, *vid.* Quality.
    vid. Passion.
Brittle, *vid.* Quality.
Broad, *vid.* Quantity.
Broke, *vid.* Action.
Brook, *vid.* Water.
Broom, *vid.* Besom in Goods.

Broth, *vid.* Porridg in Victuals.
    vid. Grewel *ibid.*
Brow, *vid.* Body.
Brew, *vid.* Action.
    vid. Drink.
Brush, *vid.* Elementary Fire in F.
Bubling, *vid.* Water Action.
Buckler, *vid.* War.
BUILDING.
Buffeted, *vid.* Fight.
Bull, *vid.* Beast.
Bunch, *vid.* Knob in Quantity.
Bundle, *vid.* Parcel in Goods.
Burden, *vid.* Action.
    vid. Carry in Travel.
    vid. Domestick Work.
Buried, *vid.* Dead.
Burning, *vid.* Fire.
Bursting, *vid.* Action.
Business, *vid.* Action. *vid.* Trade.
    vid. Domestick Action.
Bustling, *vid.* Passion.
Busy, *vid.* Action.
Butcher, *vid.* Trade.
Butler, *vid.* Servant in Family
    Grammar.
Butter, *vid.* Victuals.
    Flies, *vid.* Insects.
Buttery, *vid.* House-rooms.
Buttocks, *vid.* Body.
Buy, *vid.* Possess.
By, *vid.* Near in Posture.
    vid. Sit in Posture.
    vid. Pass in Travel.
    vid. Means in Action.

C.

Caballing, *vid.* Company.
Cabbage, *vid.* Victuals.
Cabinet, *vid.* Goods.
Cage, *vid.* Birds.
Cake, *vid.* Victuals.
Calf, *vid.* Ox in Beast.
Call'd, *vid.* Words.
Calumny, *vid.* Slander in Words.
Camel, *vid.* Beast.
Cameleon, *vid.* Beast.
Can, *vid.* Ability in Quality.
                   Cancer,

Cancer, *vid.* Physick.

Candle, *vid.* Fire.

Candlestick, *vid.* Goods.

Cane, *vid.* Vegetables and Stick in Goods.

Canker, *vid.* Tomb in Dead.

Cantharides, *vid.* Insects.

Capers, *vid.* Victuals.

Caps, *vid.* Apparel and Night-caps *ibid.*

Captain, *vid.* War.

Carbuncle, *vid.* Jewel in Riches.

Carcase, *vid.* Dead.

Cards, *vid.* Diversion.

Care, *vid.* Soul.

Carpenter, *vid.* Trade.

Carrion, *vid.* Dead.

   vid. Flesh in Victuals.

Carrot, *vid.* Vegetable.

Carry, *vid.* Travel.

Cart, *vid.* Goods.

Carving, *vid.* Trade.

Cast, *vid.* Action.

Castle, *vid.* House-fort.

Catch, *vid.* Action.

   vid. Surprise in Passion.

   Birds, *vid.* Diversion.

   vid. Birds.

Caterpiller, *vid.* Insect.

Cathedral, *vid.* Religion.

Cat, *vid.* Beast.

Cave, *vid.* Hole in Earth.

Cause, *vid.* Action.

   vid. Weep in Passion.

Cawsy, *vid.* Travel.

Caution, *vid.* Soul.

Cease, *vid.* Leave in Action.

Cedar, *vid.* Tree.

Ceiling, *vid.* House-parts.

Cellar, *vid.* House-room.

   vid. Shop in Habitation.

Censure, *vid.* Soul.

Cerberus, *vid.* Fable in Literature.

Chaff, *vid.* Corn in Vegetables.

Chain, *vid.* Goods.

   vid. Prison in House-forts.

Challenge, *vid.* Fight.

Chamber, *vid.* House-rooms.

Chancel, *vid.* Religion.

Change, *vid.* Sight in Sense.

Channel, *vid.* Street in Habitation.

Chappel, *vid.* Religion.

Chariot, *vid.* Goods.

Charm, *vid.* Discourse.

Catechis'd, *vid.* Religion.

Chattering, *vid.* Birds.

Cheap, *vid.* Buy in Possess.

   vid. Value in Riches.

Cheat, *vid.* Trick in Diversion.

Cheeks, *vid.* Body.

Cheerful, *vid.* Passion.

Cheese, *vid.* Victuals.

Chief, *vid.* Honour in Government.

Cherubims, *vid.* Spirits.

Chess, *vid.* Diversion.

Chew, *vid.* Bite in Bodily Action.

Chide, *vid.* Discourse.

Child, *vid.* Age in Time.

   vid. Grammar.

Chimera, *vid.* Monster in Creature.

   vid. Fable in Literature.

Chimny, *vid.* Fire.

   vid. Hearth in House-parts.

Chin, *vid.* Body.

China Cups, *vid.* Goods.

Chirping, *vid.* Birds.

Chirurgeon, *vid.* Physick.

Chocolate, *vid.* Commodities.

Chuse, *vid.* Honour and Office in Government.

Christ, *vid.* Religion.

Christal, *vid.* Riches.

Church, *vid.* Religion.

Chyromancy, *v.* Divinist in Spirits.

Ciclops, *vid.* Fable in Literature.

Cinnamon, *vid.* Victuals.

   vid. Tree in Vegetable.

Cipress, *vid.* Crown in Ornaments.

   vid. Tree.

Circle, *vid.* Mathematicks in Arts and Sciences.

   vid. Figure in Quality.

Circumstance, *vid.* Soul.

   vid. Grammar.

Cistern, *vid.* Water.

Citizen, *vid.* Habitation.

CITT. Civility,

Civility, *vid.* Paſſion.
    vid. Words.
Civil Law, *vid.* Arts and Sciences.
Civit Cat, *vid.* Beaſt.
Claim, *vid.* Demand in Diſcourſe.
Clerk, *vid.* Office in Government.
    vid. Religion.
Claws, *vid.* Beaſt.
    vid. Lion in Beaſt.
Clay, *vid.* Earth.
Clean, *vid.* Quality.
Clear, *vid.* Quality.
    vid. Air.
Cleave, *vid.* Trees.
Cleft, *vid.* Trees.
Climb, *vid.* Aſcend in Travel.
Clip, *vid.* Action.
Cloke, *vid.* Apparel.
Clock, *vid.* Goods.
Cloſe, *vid.* Earth.
Cloſet, *vid.* Houſe-rooms.
Clothes, *vid.* Apparel.
    vid. Trade.
Cloud, *vid.* Air.
Clown-all-heal, *vid.* Vegetable.
Coach, *vid.* Chariot in Goods.
Coals, *vid.* Fire.
Coat, *vid.* Apparel.
Cock, *vid.* Bird.
Cockatrice, *vid.* Baſilisk in Poiſo-
    nous Creatures.
Cockle, *vid.* Corn.
Codpiece, *vid.* Apparel.
Coffee-Houſe, *vid.* Habitation and
    Houſe-fort.
Coffer, *vid.* Goods.
Coffin, *vid.* Dead.
Coining, *vid.* Gold in Riches.
Cold, *vid.* Air.
    vid. Senſe.
    vid. Physick.
Collection, *vid.* Law Proceeding.
College, *vid.* Univerſity in Habi-
    tations.
Coloſſus, *vid.* Statue in Trade.
Colour, *vid.* Senſe.
    vid. Apparel.
Colours, *vid.* Enſign in War.

Comb, *vid.* Barber in Trade.
Comedy, *vid.* Diverſion.
Comely, *vid.* Fair in Quality.
Comets, *vid.* Stars.
Comfort, *vid.* Paſſion.
Coming, *vid.* Travel.
    vid. Cauſe in Action.
Command, *vid.* Diſcourſe.
Commend, *vid.* Praiſe in Diſcourſe.
Commodities, *vid.* Tools.
Common, *vid.* Earth.
COMPANY.
COMPANY NUMBER.
Compariſon, *vid.* Diſcourſe.
Compell'd, *vid.* Willing in Soul.
    vid. Force in Action.
Complaint, *vid.* Diſcourſe.
Complection, *vid.* Face in Body.
    vid. Appearance in Senſe.
Conceal, *vid.* Hide in Action, &c.
Concern, *vid.* Paſſion.
Concerning, *vid.* Diſcourſe.
Conclude, *vid.* Reſolve in Soul.
Condemn'd, *vid.* Law.
Confeſs, *vid.* Words.
Confus'd, *vid.* Soul.
Confirm, *vid.* Religion.
    vid. Repetition in Diſ-
    courſe.
Conjoint, *vid.* Conſpiracy in Com-
    pany.
Conjuring, *vid.* Spirits.
Conſcience, *vid.* Religion.
Conſecration, *vid.* Religion.
Conſent, *vid.* Will in Soul.
Conſpiracy, *vid.* Company.
Conſtable, *vid.* Officer in Law.
Conſtantinople, *vid.* Country.
    vid. Habitations.
Conſum'd, *vid.* Action.
    vid. Fire.
Contemplation, *vid.* Univerſity.
Contempt, *vid.* Paſſion.
Content, *vid.* Paſſion.
Contention, *vid.* War.
    vid. Fight.
Continuance, *vid.* Time.
Contrary, *vid.* Quality.
                 Contrivance

Contrivance, *vid.* Design in Soul.
Converse, *vid.* Discourse.
Cook, *vid.* Trade.
    vid. Victuals.
Copper, *vid.* Metals in Commo-
    dities.
Copse, *vid.* Wood in Estate.
Cordial, *vid.* Hearty in Passion.
    vid. Physick.
Cormorant, *vid.* Bird.
Corn, *vid.* Vegetable.
Corner, *vid.* Posture.
Coral, *vid.* Stones in Earth.
Correction, *vid.* Fight.
Cottage, *vid.* House-sort.
Cotton, *vid.* Trees.
    vid. Commodities.
Couch, *vid.* Goods.
Cover'd, *vid.* Action.
Coughing, *vid.* Bodily Action.
    vid. Physick.
Council, *vid.* Law.
    vid. Advise in Discourse.
Countenance, *vid.* Face in Body.
    vid. Appear in Sense.
    vid. Favour in Passion.
Counterfeit, *vid.* Quality.
Counters, *vid.* Goods.
Countess, *vid.* Government.
Counting-House, *vid.* House-sort.
COUNTRY.
Courageous, *vid.* Passion.
Course, *vid.* Mean in Quality.
Court, *vid.* House-range.
    vid. Passion.
    vid. Law.
Courtier, *vid.* Government.
Coy, *vid.* Passion.
Cradle, *vid.* Age.
Crane, *vid.* Bird.
Crave, *vid.* Ask in Discourse.
Cream, *vid.* Victuals.
    vid. Milk in Body.
CREATURES.
Credit, *vid.* Trade.
Creed, *vid.* Religion.
Creeping things, *vid.* Insects.
    vid. Travel.

Cricket, *vid.* Insects.
Crier, *vid.* Office in Government.
Crying, *vid.* Passion.
Cripple, *vid.* Physick.
Crocodile, *vid.* Beast.
Crooked, *vid.* Quality.
    vid. Physick.
    vid. Upright in Posture.
Cross, *vid.* Passion.
    vid. Religion.
    vid. Law.
    vid. Posture.
    vid. Travel.
Crowd, *vid.* Company.
    vid. Quantity.
Crow, *vid.* Bird.
Crown, *vid.* Ornament.
    vid. King in Government.
Crown'd, *vid.* Ornament.
Crucified, *vid.* Dead.
    vid. Condemn in Law.
Crucifix, *vid.* Religion.
Cruel, *vid.* Passion.
Crutches, *vid.* Physick.
Crying, *vid.* Passion.
Cucumbers, *vid.* Vegetables.
    vid. Victuals.
Cup, *vid.* Goods.
Curious, *vid.* Quality.
Curl, *vid.* Hair in Body.
    vid. Figure in Quality.
Curse, *vid.* Discourse.
Curtain, *vid.* Play in Diversion.
    vid. Bed in Goods.
Cushion, *vid.* Goods.
Custard, *vid.* Milk in Body.
    vid. Drink and Victuals.
Custom, *vid.* Quality.
Cut, *vid.* Action.

D.
Daffodil, *vid.* Vegetables.
    vid. Crown in Ornaments.
Dainties, *vid.* Victuals.
Dairy, *vid.* House-rooms.
Damage, *vid.* Hurt in Action.
Dancing, *vid.* Diversion.
Danger, *vid.* Hurt in Passion.

Danger, *vid.* Fear in Paſſion.

Dare, *vid.* Fight.

Darkneſs, *vid.* Sight in Senſe,
     vid. Night in Time.

Darnel, *vid.* Cockle in Corn.

Dart, *vid.* War.

Daughter, *vid.* Family in Grammar.

Day, *vid.* Time,
    Holy, *ibid.*

D E A D.

Deaf, *vid.* Phyſick.

Dear, *vid.* Value in Riches.
    vid. Buy in Poſſeſs.

Death, *vid.* Dead.
    Watch *ibid.* in Dead.

Debauch, *vid.* Perſon in Grammar.

Debt, *vid.* Law.

Decay'd, *vid.* Quality.

Decent, *vid.* Agreeable in Quality.

Deep, *vid.* Earth.
    vid. Precipice and Hole *ibid.*
    vid. Fall in Action.

Dedicated, *vid.* Religion.

Deer, *vid.* Beaſt.

Defence, *vid.* Fight.

Defer, *vid.* Time.

Defy, *vid.* Diſcourſe.

Deform'd, *vid.* Quality.

Degenerate, *vid.* Quality.

Degrees, *vid.* Part.

Delay, *vid.* Time.

Delight, *vid.* Paſſion.

Deliver, *vid.* Give in Poſſeſſion.
    vid. Action.
    Of a Child, *vid.* C. in
      Grammar.

Demand, *vid.* Diſcourſe.

Deny, *vid.* Forbid in Diſcourſe.
    vid. Refuſe *ibid.*

Departure, *vid.* Travel.

Depoſe, *vid.* Office in Government.

Deſcend, *vid.* Travel.

Deſert, *vid.* Earth.

Deſerter, *vid.* Souldier in War.

Deſign, *vid.* Soul.

Deſire, *vid.* Paſſion.

Deſolate, *vid.* Deſert in Earth,
    vid. Company.

Deſpair, *vid.* Hope in Paſſion.

Deſpiſe, *vid.* Paſſion.

Deſtroy, *vid.* Action.
    vid. Ruin in Action.

Devil, *vid.* Spirits.

Devotion, *vid.* Religion.

Devour, *vid.* Eat in Victuals.
    vid. Bodily Action.

Diadem, *vid.* Ornament.

Dial, *vid.* Time.

Diamond, *vid.* Riches.

Dice, *vid.* Diverſion.

Differ, *vid.* Paſſion.
    vid. Quarrel in Fight.

Different, *vid.* Quality.

Difficult, *vid.* Quality.

Digging, *vid.* Domeſtick Work.

Digeſtion, *vid.* Eat in Bodily Action.

Dinner, *vid.* Eat in Bodily Action.

Dip, *vid.* Water.
    vid. Action.

Direct, *vid.* Action.
    vid. Words.

Dirt, *vid.* Earth.

Dirty, *vid.* Travel.
    vid. Clean in Quality.

Diſappear, *vid.* See in Senſe.

Diſappoint, *vid.* Company.

Diſarm, *vid.* War.

Diſcipline, *vid.* Company and War.

Diſcontent, *vid.* Content in Paſſion.

Diſcover, *vid.* Find in Poſſeſs.

D I S C O U R S E.

Diſcreet, *vid.* Soul.

Diſeaſe, *vid.* Phyſick.

Diſgrace, *vid.* Condemn in Law.

Diſh, *vid.* Goods.

Diſown, *vid.* Diſcourſe.

Diſpleaſe, *vid.* Satisfaction in Paſſion.

Diſpute, *vid.* Diſcourſe.

Diſtant, *vid.* Quantity.

Diſtinguiſh, *vid.* Chuſe in Soul.

Diſtracted, *vid.* Mad in Phyſick.
               Diſtracted,

Diftracted, *vid.* Paffion.
Diftrain, *vid.* Law.
Diftrefs, *vid.* Misfortune in Action.
Difturb, *vid.* Action.
Ditch, *vid.* Eftate in Earth.
Divers, *vid.* Quality.
D I V E R S I O N.
    vid. Paffion.
Divination, *vid.* Spirits.
Divine, *vid.* Religion.
Divifion, *vid.* Part.
Divorce, *vid.* Religion.
Dizzy, *vid.* Soul.
Dogs, *vid.* Beaft.
Doing, *vid.* Action.
Dolphin, *vid.* Victuals.
    vid. Fifh.
D O M E S T I C K A C T I O N.
Doting, *vid.* Soul.
Double, *vid.* Quantity.
    vid. Words.
    vid. Numbers.
Doubting, *vid.* Soul.
Doubtful, *vid.* ibid.
Dove, *vid.* Pigeon in Bird.
Down, *vid.* Pofture.
    vid. Fling in Action.
    vid. Fly in Air.
Dragon, *vid.* Poifonous Creature.
    vid. Travel.
    vid. Tomb in Dead.
Drain, *vid.* Office in Houfe-parts.
Drawing, *vid.* Travel.
    vid. Action.
Dream, *vid.* Divination in Spirit.
    vid. Direct in Action.
    vid. Sleep in Bodily Action.
Dreffing, *vid.* Apparel.
    vid. Victuals.
Drinefs, *vid.* Quality.
D R I N K.
Driving, *vid.* Travel.
Droll, *vid.* Difcourfe.
Drop, *vid.* Action.
Dropfy, *vid.* Die in Dead.
    vid. Difeafe in Phyfick.
Drown'd, *vid.* Dead.

Drum, *vid.* War.
Drunk, *vid.* Drink.
Dry, *vid.* Quality.
Dublin, *vid.* City in Habitation.
Duck, *vid.* Bird.
    vid. Travel.
Due, *vid.* Air.
Dumb, *vid.* Phyfick.
Dung, *vid.* Earth.
Dungeon, *vid.* Houfe-forts.
Durable, *vid.* Laft in Quality.
Duft, *vid.* Wind in Air.
Dufty, *vid.* ibid. and Sweep in Domeftick.
Dwelling, Houfe State and Occurrences.
    vid. Grammar.
Dying, *vid.* Dead.
    vid. Law.
    vid. Phyfick.
    vid. Trade.

E.

Eagle, *vid.* Bird.
Ear, *vid.* Body.
    vid. Jewels in Ornaments.
    in Riches.
Early, *vid.* Time.
E A R T H.
Eafe, *vid.* Action.
Eaft, *vid.* Pofture.
    vid. Travel.
    vid. Stars.
    vid. Drink.
Eat, *vid.* Bodily Action.
    vid. Victuals.
Ecclefiaftick, *vid.* Religion.
    Judg, *vid.* Law.
Eclipfe, *vid.* Sun in Stars.
Eels, *vid.* Fifh.
Eggs, *vid.* Victuals.
    vid. Birds.
Elbow, *vid.* Arm in Body.
Element, *vid.* Sky in Air.
Elephant, *vid.* Beaft.
    vid. Travel.
Elm, *vid.* Tree.
Elyfian Shades, *vid.* Hell in Spirits.
    Embalment.

Embalment, *vid.* Dead.
Embrace, *vid.* Company.
　　vid. Passion.
Emerald, *vid.* Riches.
Emperor, *vid.* King in Government.
　　vid. Country.
Employ, *vid.* Action.
　　vid. Trade.
　　vid. Domestick Action.
Empty, *vid.* Full in Quantity.
Enchantment, *vid.* Spirits.
Encompass, *vid.* Incompass in Posture.
Encourage, *vid.* Passion.
Encrease, *vid.* Quantity.
Encroach, *vid.* Wrong in Action.
End, *vid.* Part.
　　vid. Done in Action.
Endless, *vid.* End in Part.
Endeavour, *vid.* Action.
Engines, *vid.* Tools.
Engrave, *vid.* Trade.
Enlarge, *vid.* Quantity.
Enquire, *vid.* Discourse.
Ensign, *vid.* War.
　　vid. Sign in City.
　　vid. Heraldry in Arts.
Enter, *vid.* Go in Travel.
Entertain'd, *vid.* Company.
　　vid. Discourse.
　　vid. Welcome in Discourse.
Entreat, *vid.* Discourse.
Entry, *vid.* House-rooms.
Envy, *vid.* Passion.
Equal, *vid.* Quantity.
Errand, *vid.* Fetch in Travel.
Escape, *vid.* Travel.
Estate, *vid.* Riches.
　　vid. Earth.
Esteem, *vid.* Honour in Government.
Ethicks, *vid.* Arts and Sciences.
Evergreens, *vid.* Trees.
Every, *vid.* Common in Earth.
　　vid. Part.
Evil, *vid.* Good in Quality.

Examine, *vid.* Soul.
　　vid. Seek in Action.
Exceed, *vid.* Honour in Government.
　　vid. Many in Numbers.
　　vid. Extreme in Quality.
Excel, *vid.* Honour in Government.
Exception, *vid.* Particular in Part.
Exchange, *vid.* London.
Exclamation, *vid.* Discourse.
Excuse, *vid.* Discourse.
Executioner, *vid.* Law.
Exercise, *vid.* Diversion.
Exhort, *vid.* Advise in Discourse.
Exile, *vid.* Condemn'd in Law.
Expect, *vid.* Soul.
　　vid. Reversion in Heir Grammar.
Expedient, *vid.* Soul.
Expose, *vid.* Discourse.
　　vid. Contemn in Passion.
Extempore, *vid.* Discourse.
Extraordinary, *vid.* Ordinary in Quality.
Extravagant, *vid.* Soul.
Extreme, *vid.* Quality.
Eye, *vid.* Body.

F.

Fable, *vid.* Literature in Books.
Face, *vid.* Body.
Faction, *vid.* Company.
Faggots, *vid.* Wood.
Fair, *vid.* Quality.
　　vid. Market in Habitations.
Fairly, *vid.* Honest in Religion.
Fail, *vid.* Want in Passion.
　　vid. Ability in Quality.
Fairies, *vid.* Spirits.
Faithfulness, *vid.* Passion.
Falcon, *vid.* Bird.
Fall, *vid.* Action.
Follow, *vid.* Field in Estate.
Falshood, *vid.* Truth in Soul.
　　vid. Lie in Discourse.
Familiar, *vid.* Passion.
Fan, *vid.* Apparel.
Far, *vid.* Further in Travel.
　　　　　　　　　　　Farewel,

Farewel, *vid.* Discourse.
Farm, *vid.* Domestick Action.
    vid. Estate in Earth.
Farthing, *vid.* Mony in Riches.
Farting, *vid.* Bodily Action.
Fashion, *vid.* Fair in Quality.
Fast, *vid.* Swift in Quality.
    vid. Religion.
Fasten, *vid.* Action.
    vid. Bind in Action.
Fat, *vid.* Quality.
    vid. Flesh in Victuals.
Fatal, *vid.* Place in Travel.
Fault, *vid.* Accuse in Law.
                in Words.
    vid. Chide in Words.
Favour, *vid.* Passion.
Fawn, *vid.* Passion.
Fear, *vid.* Passion.
Feasting, *vid.* Diversion.
Feathers, *vid.* Birds.
Fever, *vid.* Physick.
    vid. Hectick in Physick.
    vid. Dying in Dead.
Feeding, *vid.* Action.
Feeling, *vid.* Touch in Sense.
Feet, *vid.* Body.
Feigned, *vid.* Perfect,
    vid. Artificial, } in Quality.
    vid. Counterfeit, }
    vid. Soul in Man.
    vid. Lie in Discourse.
Field, *vid.* Country.
Felling, *vid.* Trees.
Female, *vid.* Apparel.
    vid. Sex in Beast.
Fences, *vid.* Country.
Fencing, *vid.* Fight.
Ferret, *vid.* Beast.
Ferryman, *vid.* Person in Grammar.
Fetch, *vid.* Travel.
Fetters, *vid.* Prison in House-sorts.
Few, *vid.* Quantity.
Fewel, *vid.* Wood.
Fidling, *vid.* Action.
Fig, *vid.* Tree.
    vid. Fruit.

Figure, *vid.* Sense.
    vid. Quality.
    vid. Mathematicks in Arts.
FIGHT.
Filbert, *vid.* Nut in Fruit Vegetable.
Filthy, *vid.* Nasty in Quality.
Find, *vid.* Possess.
Fine, *vid.* Ornaments.
    vid. Apparel.
    vid. Fair in Quality.
Fingers, *vid.* Body.
Finish'd, *vid.* Done in Action.
    vid. End in Part.
FIRE.
Fiery, *vid.* ibid.
Firm, *vid.* Sound in Quality.
First, *vid.* Quantity.
    vid. Time and Numbers.
FISH.
Fist, *vid.* Hand in Body.
Fit, *vid.* Agreeable in Quality.
Fix'd, *vid.* Fastned in Action.
    vid. Nails in Commodities.
Flags, *vid.* War.
Flame, *vid.* Fire.
Flashes, *vid.* Fire.
Flat, *vid.* Thin in Quantity.
    vid. Prostrate in Posture.
Flattery, *vid.* Discourse and Passion.
Flails, *vid.* Tools.
Flax, *vid.* Commodities.
Flea, *vid.* Skin in Commodity.
Fleas, *vid.* Insects.
Fleering, *vid.* Contempt in Passion.
Flesh, *vid.* Victuals.
    vid. Body.
Flesh, *vid.* Beast.
Flight, *vid.* Fly in Air.
    vid. Birds.
Fling, *vid.* Action.
Flock, *vid.* Many in Quantity.
Flood, *vid.* Water.
Flounder, *vid.* Victuals.
    vid. Fish.
Flourishing, *vid.* Quality.
                    Flower,

Flower, *vid.* Vegetable.
    vid. Crown in Ornaments.
    vid. Woman in Grammar.
Flung, *vid.* Fling in Action.
Flux, *vid.* Dying in Dead.
Flies, *vid.* Insects.
Flying, *vid.* Air.
    vid. Birds.
    vid. Escape in Travel.
Follow, *vid.* Travel.
Fondle, *vid.* Passion.
Fool, *vid.* Trick in Diversion.
For, *vid.* Come in Travel.
    vid. Another in Person.
Forbear, *vid.* Soul.
    vid. Refuse in Discourse.
    vid. Leave in Action.
Forbid, *vid.* Discourse.
Force, *vid.* Action.
    vid. Victory in Fight.
Forehead, *vid.* Body.
Foreign, *vid.* Earth.
Foresee, *vid.* Prophecy in Relig.
Forfeit, *vid.* Law.
Forget, *vid.* Soul.
Forgive, *vid.* Law.
Formal, *vid.* Quality.
Force, *vid.* Quality.
Former, *vid.* Time.
Forest, *vid.* Earth.
Forsake, *vid.* Soul.
    vid. Lover in Person in
    Grammar.
    vid. Leave in Travel.
Fortune, *vid.* Fable in Literature.
Forward, *vid.* Posture.
    vid. Free in Passion.
    vid. Rash in Passion.
Foul, *vid.* Nasty, } in Quality.
    vid. Clean, }
Fox, *vid.* Beast.
    vid. Hurt in Diversion.
Free, *vid.* Passion.
    vid. Bind in Action.
    vid. Fasten in Action.
Freely, *vid.* Quality.
Freeman, } *vid.* Grammar.
Friend, }

French, *vid.* Foreign in Country.
Grass, *vid.* Herbage in Field
    Earth.
Frequent, *vid.* Haunt in Company.
Fright, *vid.* Action.
Frize, *vid.* Woolen in Apparel.
Frog, *vid.* Poisonous Creatures.
Frolick, *vid.* Diversion.
From, *vid.* Posture.
    vid. Prospect in Sense.
    vid. Fly in Air.
    vid. Travel.
    vid. Messenger in Govern-
    ment.
Front, *vid.* House-parts.
FROST.
Fruit, *vid.* Vegetables.
    ful, *vid.* ibid.
Fryingpan, *vid.* Goods.
Fuller, *vid.* Trade.
Fulness, *vid.* Part.
Funeral, *vid.* Dead.
    Service, *vid.* Religion.
Furnace, *vid.* Goods.
Further, *vid.* Travel.
Furies, *vid.* Fable in Literature.
Future, *vid.* Time.

G.

Gain, *vid.* Play in Diversion.
    vid. Increase in Quantity.
    vid. Riches.
Gall, *vid.* Body.
Gallery, *vid.* House-rooms.
Gallies, *vid.* Condemn'd in Law.
Gallows, *vid.* Law.
Gaming, *vid.* Diversion.
Garden, *vid.* House-range.
Garland, *vid.* Ornaments.
Garlick, *vid.* Victuals.
Garret, *vid.* House-rooms.
Gate, *vid.* House-parts.
Gathering, *vid.* Action.
Gilt, *vid.* Physick.
    vid. Horse in Beast.
    vid. Privities in Beast.
General, *vid.* Part.
Genius, *vid.* Spirit.

Gentle,

Gentle, *vid.* Paffion.

   vid. Violent in Action.

Geography, } *vid.* Arts, *&c.*
Geometry, }

Getting, *vid.* Poffefs.

Gueft, *vid.* Entertain in Company.

Ghoft, *vid.* Spirit.

   vid. Dead.

Giant, *vid.* Great in Quantity.

Gibbet, *vid.* Condemn in Law.

Giddy, *vid.* Soul.

Gins, *vid.* Diverfion.

Girdle, *vid.* Apparel.

Gives, *vid.* Prifon in Houfe-forts.

Give, *vid.* Poffefs.

Glad, *vid.* Joy in Paffion.

Glafs, *vid.* Commodity.

   vid. Cupboard in Goods.

Globes, *vid.* Books.

Glory, *vid.* Spirit.

Gloves, *vid.* Apparel.

Gloworm, *vid.* Tomb in Dead.

Gnaſhing the Teeth, *vid.* Teeth in Body.

Gnat, *vid.* Infect.

Gnaw, *vid.* Bite in Bodily Action.

Go, *vid.* Travel.

Goal, } *vid.* Prifon in Houfe-
Goaler, } forts.

Goat, *vid.* Beaft.

   Victuals.

Goats Hair, *vid.* Commodities.

God, *vid.* Spirits.

Godfather, *vid.* Religion.

Gold, *vid.* Riches.

Good, *vid.* Quality.

   Religion.

G O O D S.

Goofe, *vid.* Birds.

   Travel.

G O V E R N M E N T.

Gourds, *vid.* Vegetables and Victuals.

Gout, *vid.* Phyfick.

Gown, *vid.* Apparel.

Grace, *vid.* Religion.

Grammar, *vid.* Arts, *&c.*

Grapes, *vid.* Fruit in Vegetables.

Graſhopper, *vid.* Infect.

Graſp, *vid.* Action.

Gratis, *vid.* Freely in Quality.

Gravel, *vid.* Earth.

Grave, *vid.* Dead.

Great, *vid.* Quantity.

Graver, *vid.* Trade.

Greedy, *vid.* Victuals.

   Eat in Bodily Action.

Green, *vid.* Vegetable.

   Quality.

   Sight in Senfe.

Grieve, *vid.* Paffion.

Grievoufly, *vid.* Paffion.

Greyhound, *vid.* Dog in Beaft.

Griffin, *vid.* Travel.

Gripe, *vid.* Bird.

Groans and Sighs, *vid.* Bodily Action.

Ground, *vid.* Earth.

   Domeftick Action.

Grown, *vid.* Bodily Action.

   Age in Time.

Grewel, *vid.* Victuals.

Grumble, *vid.* Mutter in Difcourfe.

Guard, *vid.* War.

Guilt, *vid.* Accufe in Law.

Guineas, *vid.* Mony in Riches.

Gulf, *vid.* Earth.

Gun, *vid.* War.

Gutter, *vid.* Earth.

   Channel in City.

Guts, *vid.* Body.

H.

Habit, *vid.* Apparel.

H A B I T A T I O N S.

Hackney, *vid.* Hire in Poffefs.

Hagrid, *vid.* Nightmare in Sleep.

Hail, *vid.* Froft.

Hair, *vid.* Body.

   Beaft.

   Wig in Apparel.

Half, *vid.* Part.

Hall, *vid.* Houfe-rooms.

Hal'd, *vid.* Dead Acting.

   Force in Action.

Hand, *vid.* Body.

N n   Hand

Handkerchief, *vid.* Apparel.
Handling, *vid.* Possess.
Handsom, *vid.* Quality.
Hang'd, *vid.* Posture.
    Condemn in Law.
Hangings, *vid.* Goods.
Hangman, *vid.* Person in Law.
Hard, *vid.* Quality.
    Difficult in Quality.
    Words in Discourse.
Hare, *vid.* Beast.
    Hunt in Diversion.
Harelip, *vid.* Lip in Body.
Harness, *vid.* Goods and Horse in Beast.
Harp, *vid.* Musick in Arts and Sciences.
Harpys, *vid.* Fable in Literature.
Harsh, *vid.* Taste in Sense.
Harvest-Work, *vid.* Domestick Action.
Haste, *vid.* Action.
Hatred, *vid.* Passion.
Hat, *vid.* Apparel.
Having, *vid.* Possess.
Haunted, *vid.* Spirit.
    Enchantment in Spirit.
    Dead.
    Company.
Hawking, *vid.* Diversion.
    Bird.
Hay, *vid.* Crown in Ornaments.
    Vegetables.
 -Tallaught, ⎫
 -Stable, ⎬ *vid.* House-range.
Hail, *vid.* Frost.
Hazard, *vid.* Danger in Fear in Passion.
Head, *vid.* Body and Beast.
Heap, *vid.* Quantity.
Hear, *vid.* Sense.
Heart, *vid.* Body.
    Beast.
Hearth, *vid.* Fire and House-parts.
Heartily, *vid.* Passion.
Heat, *vid.* Quality.
    Fire.

Heath, *vid.* Country.
Heave, *vid.* Heavy in Quality.
    Bear in Travel.
Heaven, *vid.* Air.
Hettick, *vid.* Physick.
Hectoring, *vid.* Huff in Passion.
Hedg, *vid.* Earth.
Hedg-Hog, *vid.* Beast.
    Victuals.
Held, *vid.* Hold in Action.
Hell, *vid.* Spirits.
Helmet, *vid.* War.
Help, *vid.* Action.
Hen, *vid.* Cock in Birds.
Heraldry, *vid.* Arts, &c.
Herbage, *vid.* Earth.
    Vegetables.
    Domestick Action.
    Crown.
    Victuals.
Hermaphrodite, *vid.* Grammar.
Heron, *vid.* Bird.
Hiccough, *vid.* Bodily Action.
Hidden, *vid.* Words in Discourse.
Hiding, *vid.* Action.
    Private in Company.
    Peep in Sight in Sense.
Hidra, *vid.* Fable in Literature.
High, *vid.* Posture.
    Fly in Air.
    Precipice in Place.
 -Priest, *vid.* Religion.
 -Way, *vid.* Travel.
Hills, *vid.* Earth.
Hinder, *vid.* Action.
Hinges, *vid.* Door in House-parts.
Hir'd, *vid.* Possess.
Hiss'd at, *vid.* Contempt in Passion.
History, *vid.* Books.
Hog, *vid.* Beast.
    Victuals.
Holding, *vid.* Action.
Hole, *vid.* Earth.
Hollow, *vid.* Quantity.
Holly, *vid.* Trees.
Holy, *vid.* Religion.
 -Day, *vid.* Time.

Home, *vid.* House-ftate and Grammar.

Honefty, *vid.* Religion.

Hony, *vid.* Victuals.

Honour, *vid.* Government,

Hood, *vid.* Apparel.

Hope, *vid.* Paffion.
 Difcourfe.

Horns, *vid.* Beaft.

Hornet, *vid.* Infect.

Horfe, *vid.* Beaft.

Horfelitter as the Chariot, *vid.* Goods.

Hofpital, *vid.* Houfe-fort.

Hoft, *vid.* Heaven in Air.

Hoftefs, *vid.* Inn in Houfe-fort.

Hot, *vid.* Quality.

Hound, *vid.* Dog in Beaft.

Hour-Glafs, *vid.* Goods.

Hours, *vid.* Time.

HOUSE.

Houfeholdftuff, *vid.* Goods.

Houfe-keeping, *vid.* Houfe-ftate and Occurrences.

Howling, *vid.* Hear in Senfe.
 Dog in Beaft.
 Cry in Paffion.

Huckfter, *vid.* Trade.

Huffing, *vid.* Paffion.

HUMANE BODY.

Humours, *vid.* Phyfick.

Hundred, *vid.* Collection in Law.

Hungry, *vid.* Bodily Action.
 Victuals.

Hunting, *vid.* Dog in Beaft.
 Stag,⎫
 Deer, ⎬ in Beaft.
 Hare, ⎭
 Diverfion.

Hurried, *vid.* Forc'd in Action.

Husbandry, *vid.* Earth.
 Domeftick Action.

Hurt, *vid.* Action.

I.

Jacinth, *vid.* Jewels in Riches.

Jaw, *vid.* Body.

Jay, *vid.* Bird.

Idle, *vid.* Action.
 Perfon in Grammar.
 Domeftick Action.

Ice, *vid.* Froft.

Jakes, *vid.* Dung in Earth.
 Houfe-range.

Jealous, *vid.* Paffion.

Jeering, *vid.* Difcourfe.

Jefting, *vid.* Difcourfe.
 Diverfion.

Jew, vid. Religion.
 Country in Earth.

Jewel, *vid.* Riches.
 Stones in Earth.

Jeweller, *vid.* Trade.

Ill-favour'd, *vid.* Ridiculous in Soul.
 Form in Quality.

Ill, *vid.* Misfortune in Action.
 Good in Quality.

Image, *vid.* Statuary in Trade.

Imaginary, *vid.* Country.
 Unknown in Soul.
 Feign in Quality.
 Fable in Literature.

Imagination, *vid.* Soul.

Imitate, *vid.* Action.
 Company.

Immodeft, *vid.* Religion.

Imperfect, *vid.* Part.

Imploy, *vid.* Trade.

Impoffible, *vid.* Abfurd in Soul.

Impofthume, *vid.* Swell in Phyfick.

Impotent, *vid.* Quality.

Imprifoned, *vid.* Prifon in Houfe-forts.

Improper, *vid.* Soul.

Imps, *vid.* Witch in Spirits.

In, *vid.* Pofture.
 Place.

Inn, *vid.* Houfe-fores.

Incenfe, *vid.* Religion.

Inceft, *vid.* Lying in in Bodily Action.

Inchantment, *vid.* Spirit.

Inclofe, *vid.* Action.
 Fence in Earth.

Incoherent, *vid.* Abfurd in Soul.

Incompaft, *vid.* Pofture.
Inconftant, *vid.* Appear in Senfe.
Increafe, *vid.* Encreafe in Quan-
tity.
Incroachment, *vid.* Action.
Indifferent, *vid.* Quality.
Indulgent, *vid.* Fond in Paffion.
       Perfon in Grammar.
Inferior, *vid.* Beat in Fight.
Infirmity, *vid.* Quality.
       Phyfick.
Innkeeper, *vid.* Inn in Houfe-forts.
Inner, *vid.* Pofture.
Inquire, *vid.* Difcourfe.
Infcription, *vid.* Write in Lan-
guage.
INSECTS.
Infenfible, *vid.* Action.
       Earth.
Infolence, *vid.* Paffion.
Infolvent, *vid.* Pay in Mony.
Infpire, *vid.* Encourage in Paffion.
Inftead, *vid.* Honour in Govern-
ment.
Inftrument, *vid.* Mufick in Arts.
       Tools in Trade.
Intelligible, *vid.* Known in Soul,
       and Grammar.
       Underftand *ibid.*
Intending, *vid.* Soul.
       Difcourfe.
Interpofe, *vid.* Action.
       Reconcile in Fight.
Interpret, *vid.* Difcourfe.
Interpreter, *vid.* Divination in
Spirit.
Interrupt, *vid.* Action.
Into, *vid.* In *fupra.*
       Break in Action.
Introduce, *vid.* Company.
Inventory, *vid.* Law.
Invifible, *vid.* Spirit.
Inward, *vid.* Pofture.
Inwards, *vid.* Body.
Joints, *vid.* Body.
       Mafon in Trade.
Joint-Stool, *vid.* Goods.
Journy, *vid.* Travel.

Joy, *vid.* Paffion.
Iron, *vid.* Commodity.
Ifland, *vid.* Earth.
Iffue, } *vid.* Phyfick.
Itch, }
Judg, *vid.* Law.
Jump, *vid.* Action.
Ivory, *vid.* Commodity.
Juft, *vid.* Religion.
Juftice of the Peace, *vid.* Law.
Juftly, *vid.* Honeft in Religion.
Ivy, *vid.* Trees.

K.

Keep, *vid.* Hinder in Action.
       Breed in Action.
       Domeftick Action.
Keeper, *vid.* Law.
       Prifon in Houfe-fort.
Kennel, *vid.* Street in City.
Key, *vid.* Goods.
Kick, *vid.* Bodily Action.
Kid, *vid.* Lamb in Beaft.
       Goat in Beaft.
Kidney, *vid.* Body.
Kill, *vid.* Dead.
       Fight.
Kind, *vid.* Paffion.
       Variety in Quality.
Kindred, *vid.* Grammar.
King, *vid.* Foreign in Earth.
       Government.
Kifs, *vid.* Bodily Action.
Kitchin, *vid.* Houfe-rooms.
Kite, *vid.* Bird.
       Diverfion.
Kneel, *vid.* Knees in Body.
Knees, *vid.* Body.
Knife, *vid.* Goods.
       Fight.
Knighthood, *vid.* Government.
Knob, *vid.* Part.
Knocking, *vid.* Action.
Knot, *vid.* Thred in Commodity.
Known, *vid.* Soul.
       Grammar.
Knowing, *vid.* Soul.

I

L.

Labyrinth, *vid.* House-range.
Labour, *vid.* Action.
   Trade.
   Domestick Action.
Ladder, *vid.* Tools.
Lading, *vid.* Carry in Travel.
   Cart in Goods.
Laid, *vid.* Posture.
Lake, *vid.* Water.
Lamb, *vid.* Sheep in Beast.
Lame, *vid.* Physick.
Lamentation, *vid.* Passion.
Lamp, *vid.* Candle in Fire.
Lane, *vid.* Travel.
L A N G U A G E.
Lanthorn, *vid.* Candle in Fire.
Lap, *vid.* Body.
Large, *vid.* Quantity.
Lark, *vid.* Bird.
Last, *vid.* Part.
Lasting, *vid.* Quality.
Late, *vid.* Time.
Latin, *vid.* Language in Literature.
Laughing, *vid.* Passion.
Lawrel, *vid.* Tree.
L A W.
Lechery, *vid.* Bodily Action.
Lead, *vid.* Commodity.
Lead, *vid.* Travel.
Lean, *vid.* Fat in Quality.
Leaning, *vid.* Posture.
Leaping, *vid.* Bodily Action.
Learning, *vid.* Literature.
   Arts and Sciences.
Lease, *vid.* Riches.
   Estate *ibid.* and in
   Earth.
Leather, *vid.* Commodity.
Leave, *vid.* Willing in Soul.
   Action.
   Travel.
   Farewel in Discourse.
Leeches, *vid.* Insects.
Left, *vid.* Posture.
Legacies, *vid.* Law-things.
Legs, *vid.* Body.

Lend, *vid.* Possess.
Lengthen, *vid.* Quantity.
Leopard, *vid.* Beast.
Leprosy, *vid.* Physick.
Letters, *vid.* Literature.
   Discourse.
Lettice, *vid.* Vegetable.
Lewd, *vid.* Religion.
Liar, *vid.* Lying infra.
Liberty, *vid.* Quality and Prison
  in House-sorts.
Library, *vid.* Books.
Lice, *vid.* Insects.
Lie down, lying *infra*, and in Pos-
 ture, &c.
Lift, *vid.* Heavy in Quality.
   Bear in Travel.
Light, *vid.* Quality.
   Appear in Sense.
   Fire.
Lights, *vid.* Body.
Lightning, *vid.* Air.
Like, *vid.* Appear in Sense.
   Soul.
Lilly, *vid.* Crown in Ornaments.
Line, *vid.* String and Rope in Tools.
Lining, *vid.* Apparel.
Linen, *vid.* Apparel.
Linnet, *vid.* Bird.
Lion, *vid.* Beast.
   Travel.
Lips, *vid.* Body.
Little, *vid.* Quantity.
Live, *vid.* Dwell in House-state.
Liver, *vid.* Body.
Lizard, *vid.* Tomb in Dead.
Load, *vid.* Action.
   Domestick Action.
Lock, *vid.* Door in House-parts.
   Key in Goods.
Locust, *vid.* Insect.
Lodger, &c. *vid.* Grammar.
Logick, *vid.* Arts, &c.
Loitering, *vid.* Idle supra.
   Domestick Action.
Long, *vid.* Quantity.
L O N D O N.
Long-liv'd, *vid.* Time.

Looks, *vid.* Face in Body.
   Appear in Sense.
   Seeing in Sense.
Looking-Glass, *vid.* Goods.
   vid. Barber in Trade.
Loose, *vid.* Bind.
   Fasten in Action.
Looseness, *vid.* Shite in Bodily
   Action.
   Physick.
Loss, *vid.* Possess. *vid.* Gain *supra.*
Lord, *vid.* Government.
   Chancellor, *vid.* Law Per-
   sons.
   Chief Justice, *vid.* ibid.
Lote-Tree, *vid.* Trees.
Lots, *vid.* Diversion.
Loud, *vid.* Hear in Sense.
Love, *vid.* Passion.
Lover, *vid.* Grammar.
Louse, *vid.* Insect.
Lower, *vid.* High *supra.*
Lungs, *vid.* Body.
Lust, *vid.* Lying in Bodily Action.
Lying, *vid.* Discourse.
   Down, *vid.* Posture.
   Carnally, *vid.* Bodily Action.
   vid. Liar in Grammar.
   Bed in Goods.

M.

Mace, *vid.* Government.
Mad, *vid.* Physick.
Made, *vid.* Trade.
   Action.
   Domestick Action.
Magick, *vid.* Spirit.
Magistrate, *vid.* Government.
Magpy, *vid.* Bird.
Maids, *vid.* Grammar.
Maiden Hair, *vid.* Vegetables.
Maim'd, *vid.* Physick.
Major, *vid.* War.
Make, *vid.* Made *supra.*
Male, *vid.* Sex in Beast.
   Mankind.
Malice, *vid.* Passion.
Mallows, *vid.* Vegetables.

Management, *vid.* Action.
   vid. Trade.
   Domestick Action.
Mangled, *vid.* Action.
Manteager, *vid.* Beast.
Many, *vid.* Quantity.
Marble, *vid.* Stone in Earth.
Mark, *vid.* Seal in Ornament.
   Possess.
   Token in Discourse.
Market, *vid.* Habitations.
Marriage, *vid.* Religion.
Marshes, *vid.* Earth.
Martyrdom, *vid.* Religion.
Master, *vid.* Grammar.
Mastiff, *vid.* Dog in Beast.
Match, *vid.* Marriage *supra.*
   Quantity.
Mathematicks, *vid.* Arts, &c.
Maundy, *vid.* Civil in Passion.
   Discourse.
Maypole, *vid.* Diversion.
Maze, *vid.* Labyrinth in House-
  range.
Meal, *vid.* Eat in Bodily Action,
   and Victuals.
   Wheat in Vegetables.
Mean, *vid.* Quality.
Means, *vid.* Action.
Measled, *vid.* Scabby in Physick.
Measuring Rod, *vid.* Mathematicks
  in Arts.
Meat, *vid.* Eat in Bodily Action.
   Victuals.
Medal, *vid.* Ornament.
   Gold in Riches.
Medicine, *vid.* Physick.
Meeting, *vid.* Travel.
   House, *vid.* Religion.
Melt, *vid.* Action.
Members, *vid.* Body.
   Condemn in Law.
Memory, *vid.* Soul.
Mend, *vid.* Action.
Merchant, *vid.* Trade.
Merry, *vid.* Passion.
   Bouts, *vid.* Diversion.

Messenger,

Messenger, *vid.* Office in Government.
Metoposcopy, *vid.* Arts, &c.
Meteor, *vid.* Air.
Metal, *vid.* Commodity.
Mice, *vid.* Beast,
Tomb in Dead.
Middle, *vid.* Part.
Ag'd, *vid.* Age in Time.
Midwife, *vid.* Trade.
Mile, *vid.* Distance in Quantity.
Milk, *vid.* Breast in Body.
Drink.
Milkhouse, *vid.* House-rooms.
Miller, *vid.* Trade.
Stone, *vid.* ibid.
Milt, *vid.* Body.
Minerals, *vid.* Commodity.
Mines, *vid.* Condemn in Law.
Minister, *vid.* Religion.
Mired, *vid.* Stock in Travel.
Dirt in Earth.
Mirrhe, *vid.* Crown in Ornaments.
Mirth, *vid.* Merry *supra.*
Miscarriage, *vid.* Bodily Action.
Misery, *vid.* Misfortune in Action.
Mislaid, *vid.* Place.
Miss, *vid.* Possess.
Mistake, *vid.* Soul.
Mist, *vid.* Air.
Mistriss, *vid.* Grammar.
Mitre, *vid.* Religion.
Mix'd, *vid.* Quality.
Moan, *vid.* Grief in Passion.
Mock, *vid.* Discourse.
Model, *vid.* Platform in Action.
Modest, *vid.* Lying in Bodily Action.
Moderate, *vid.* Quality.
Moist, *vid.* Quality.
Mole, *vid.* Beast.
Monastery, *vid.* House-sorts.
vid. Relig-House in Religion.
Mony, *vid.* Riches.
Monk, *vid.* Relig. House in Religion.
Monky, *vid.* Ape in Beast.
Monster, *vid.* Creature in general.

Monument, *vid.* Tomb in Dead.
Moon, *vid.* Stars.
More, *vid.* Quantity.
Morter, *vid.* Buildings and House-parts.
Moss, *vid.* Victuals.
Mote, *vid.* Water.
Mother, *vid.* Grammar.
Motion, } *vid.* Action.
Moving, }
Mouldering, *vid.* Ruin in Action.
Mountain, *vid.* Earth.
Mounted, *vid.* Posture.
Mounteer, *vid.* Hat in Apparel.
Mounting, *vid.* Ascend in Travel.
Mourning, *vid.* Passion,
Apparel.
Dead.
Mouse, *vid.* Beast.
Tomb in Dead.
Mowe, *vid.* Vegetables.
Domestick Action.
Mulberry, *vid.* Fruit.
Tree.
Mule, *vid.* Beast.
Multiplied, *vid.* Quantity.
Multitude, *vid.* Quantity.
Company.
Mumble, *vid.* Fight.
Murder, *vid.* Kill in Dead.
Murderer, *vid.* Grammar.
Muscles, *vid.* Body.
Mushroom, *vid.* Victuals.
Musick, *vid.* Arts.
Mustard, *vid.* Vegetable and Victuals.
Muttering, *vid.* Discourse.
Mutton, *vid.* Victuals.
Mutual, *vid.* Company.

N.

Nails, Fingers, *vid.* Body.
vid. Commodities.
Naked, *vid.* Posture.
Apparel.
Name, *vid.* Discourse and Words.
Narrow, *vid.* Quantity.
Nasty, *vid.* Quality.

Nation, *vid.* Earth.
Natural, *vid.* Soul.
   Philosophy, *vid.* Arts, &c.
   vid. Artificial in Quality.
Navel, *vid.* Body.
Nail, *vid.* Nails *supra.*
Near, *vid.* Posture.
   Distance in Quantity.
Neat, *vid.* Quality.
Necessary, *vid.* Action.
   House, *vid.* Outhouses,
  &c.
Neck, *vid.* Body.
Neglect, *vid.* Action.
Neighbour, *vid.* Grammar.
Nerves, *vid.* Body.
Nest, *vid.* Bird.
Nettle, *vid.* Vegetable.
Never, *vid.* Time.
New, *vid.* Time.
News, *vid.* Letters in Language.
Next, *vid.* Near in Posture.
   Distance in Quantity.
Nice, *vid.* Passion.
Night, *vid.* Time.
Nightingale, *vid.* Bird.
Nightmare, *vid.* Sleep in Bodily
 Action.
Nimble, *vid.* Agility in Quality.
Noble, *vid.* Ornaments.
   Fine in Quality.
   Great in Quantity.
Noise, *vid.* Hear in Sense.
None, *vid.* Want in Passion.
   Quantity.
Nonsense, *vid.* Soul.
Noon, *vid.* Time.
North, *vid.* Travel.
   Posture.
Nose, *vid.* Body.
Nostril, *vid.* Body.
Nothing, *vid.* Part.
Nourishing, *vid.* Breed in Action.
   And in Domestick Action.
Nourishment, *vid.* Victuals.
Noisy, *vid.* Birds.
   Hear in Sense.
NUMBERS.

Numbers, *vid.* Company Num-
 bers.
Numfish, *vid.* Fish.
Nunnery, *vid.* Relig. House in Re-
 ligion.
Nurse, *vid.* Grammar.
Nursery, *vid.* Trees.
Nutmeg, *vid.* Commodities.
Nuts, *vid.* Trees.

O.

Oak, *vid.* Crown in Ornaments.
   Tree.
Obscure, *vid.* Appear in Sense.
Observe, *vid.* Day in Time.
Of, *vid.* From in Posture.
   Travel.
   Fall in Action.
   Pull in Action.
Oculist, *vid.* Physician.
Offend, *vid.* Action.
Offer, *vid.* Possess.
   Discourse.
Officer, *vid.* Government.
Officious, *vid.* Action.
Oil, *vid.* Trade.
Ointment, *vid.* Physick.
   Anoint in Religion.
Old, *vid.* Time.
Olive, *vid.* Tree.
Omit, *vid.* Leave in Action.
   Travel.
   Neglect in Passion.
Onions, *vid.* Vegetables.
   Victuals.
   Crown in Ornaments.
Open, *vid.* Action.
Opinion, *vid.* Soul.
Opportunity, *vid.* Time.
Oppose, *vid.* Action.
Opposite, *vid.* Against in Posture.
Opprest, *vid.* Action.
Oppressor, *vid.* Grammar.
Opticks, *vid.* Arts, &c.
Orchard, *vid.* House-range.
Order, *vid.* Soul.
   Command in Words.
Organs, *vid.* Musick in Arts, &c.
      ORNA-

ORNAMENTS.
Oftrich, *vid.* Birds.
Others, *vid.* Self and Another.
Grammar.
Oven, *vid.* House-parts.
Over, *vid.* Posture.
Upon in Posture.
Fly in Air.
Come, *vid.* War and Fight.
Flowing, *vid.* Water.
Heard, *vid.* Hear in Sense.
Great, *vid.* G. in Quantity.
Look'd, *vid.* See in Sense.
Powr'd, *vid.* Overcome *supra.*
Run, *vid.* Travel.
Take, *vid.* Travel.
Turn, *vid.* Wind in Air.
Out, *vid.* Travel.
Live, *vid.* Time.
Outward, *vid.* Posture.
Furnace in House.
Owl, *vid.* Bird.
Tomb in Dead.
Own, *vid.* Self and Another.
Possess.
Oxen, *vid.* Beasts.

P.

Pacing, *vid.* Horse in Beast.
Packhorse, *vid.* ibid.
Packing, *vid.* Stuff in Goods.
Pain, *vid.* Physick.
Payment, *vid.* Mony in Riches.
Painting, *vid.* Trade.
Palace, *vid.* House-state and Sort.
Palat, *vid.* Body.
Pale, *vid.* Colour in Quality.
Sight in Sense.
Palm, *vid.* Crown in Ornaments.
Pantry, *vid.* Kitchin in House-rooms.
Paper, *vid.* Literature Language.
Papist, *vid.* Religion.
Paps, *vid.* Breast in Body.
Paradise, *vid.* Spirits.
Parcels, *vid.* Goods.
Parelio's, *vid.* Meteor in Air.
Parents, *vid.* Grammar.

Paring, *vid.* Part.
Paris, *vid.* City in Habitations.
Parish, *vid.* Village in Habitations.
Park, *vid.* House-range.
Parliament, *vid.* Company.
Parlour, *vid.* Room-sort.
PART.
vid. Travel.
Particular, *vid.* Part.
Passage, *vid.* House.
Pass, *vid.* Travel.
PASSIONS.
Past, *vid.* Former in Time.
Patches, *vid.* Ornaments.
Path, *vid.* Travel.
Place.
Partridges, *vid.* Birds.
Patterns, *vid.* Trade.
Paving, *vid.* House-parts.
Way in Travel.
Pay, *vid.* Mony in Riches.
Peach, *vid.* Fruit in Vegetable.
Tree.
Peacock, *vid.* Bird.
Pear, *vid.* Vegetable.
Tree.
Pearl, *vid.* Jewel in Riches.
Pease, *vid.* Corn in Vegetable.]
Peep, *vid.* See in Sense.
Hide in Action.
Pert, *vid.* Brisk in Action.
Pieces, *vid.* Part.
Pepper, *vid.* Victuals.
Perfect, *vid.* Imperfect in Part.
Done in Action.
Perform'd, *vid.* Done in Action.
Perfum'd, *vid.* Ornament.
Smell in Sense.
Periwig, *vid.* Apparel.
Permit, *vid.* Suffer in Action.
Persecute, *vid.* Action.
Person, *vid.* Grammar.
Perswade, *vid.* Discourse.
Pert, *vid.* Brisk in Action.
Peruse, *vid.* Read in Language.
Pestle, *vid.* Goods.
Pew, *vid.* Religion.
Pheasant, *vid.* Bird.

Phenix,

Phenix, *vid.* Bird.
Philosopher, *vid.* Arts, &c.
        Stone, *ibid.*
Phlegm, *vid.* Physick.
PHYSICK.
Physiognomy, *vid.* Divination in Spirits.
Picking, *vid.* Actions.
Pickle, *vid.* Victuals.
Pickpocket, *vid.* Rogue in Person Grammar.
Picture, *vid.* Trade.
Pigeon, *vid.* Bird.
        Travel.
        House, *vid.* Outhouses.
Pike, *vid.* War.
Pillar, *vid.* Build and House-parts.
Pillow, *vid.* Goods.
Pimp, *vid.* Lie in Bodily Action.
Pine, *vid.* Tree.
Pinch, *vid.* Bodily Action.
Pins, *vid.* Apparel.
Pipe, *vid.* Musick in Arts, &c.
Piss, *vid.* Bodily Action.
Pit, *vid.* Earth.
Pitch, *vid.* Commodities.
Pitching, *vid.* Way in Travel.
Pity, *vid.* Passion.
Plac'd, *vid.* Laid in Action.
        Posture.
PLACE.
Plague, *vid.* Physick.
Plain, *vid.* Quality.
        Earth.
Plaister, *vid.* Issue in Physick.
Plane Tree, *vid.* Tree.
Planets, *vid.* Stars.
Plant, *vid.* Vegetable.
        Tree.
Plantation, *vid.* Earth.
Platform, *vid.* Actions.
Plate, *vid.* Goods.
Platters, *vid.* Goods.
Play, *vid.* Diversion.
Pleasant, *vid.* Looks in Sense.
Pleasure, *vid.* Diversion.
        Delight in Passion.
        Satisfaction in Passion.

Pleasure, *vid.* Voice in Sense hearing.
Pleat, *vid.* Apparel.
Plentiful, *vid.* Quantity.
        Quality.
        Want in Passion.
Plowing, *vid.* Earth.
        Domestick Work.
Pluck, *vid.* Pull in Action.
Plumb, *vid.* Fruit in Vegetable.
Plume, *vid.* Feather in Bird.
Plunging, *vid.* Water.
Pocket, *vid.* Apparel.
Pocky, *vid.* Disease in Physick.
Point, *vid.* Apparel.
Pole, *vid.* Goods.
Polipus, *vid.* Fish.
Polish, *vid.* Tools.
Pomegranat, *vid.* Vegetable.
Pomp, *vid.* Honour in Government.
Pompion, *vid.* Victuals.
        Vegetables.
Pond, *vid.* Water.
Poor, *vid.* Grammar.
Popery, *vid.* Religion.
Poppy, *vid.* Vegetable.
Popular, *vid.* Honour in Government.
Porch, *vid.* Church in Religion.
Porridg, *vid.* Victuals.
Portion, *vid.* Daughter in Grammar.
POSSESS,
Postilion, *vid.* Coach in Goods.
POSTURE.
Potter, *vid.* Trade.
Potherbs, *vid.* Victuals.
Pots, *vid.* Goods.
Poverty, *vid.* Poor in Riches.
        Beggar in Person Grammar.
Pound, *vid.* Law.
Power, *vid.* Ability in Quality.
        Force in Action.
Pox, *vid.* Physick.
Poison, *vid.* Poisonous Creatures.
POISONOUS CREATURES.
        Prayer,

Prayer, *vid.* Religion.

Praise, *vid.* Discourse.

Preach, *vid.* Religion.

Precious, *vid.* Riches,

Precipice, *vid.* Place in Earth.

Fall in Action.

Predeceffor, *vid.* Time.

Person in Grammar.

Prefer, *vid.* Honour in Government.

Priest, *vid.* Religion.

Prepar'd, *vid.* Quality.

Presence, *vid.* Company.

Present, *vid.* Want in Paffion.

Presenting, *vid.* Poffefs.

Preserve, *vid.* Action.

Prefs, *vid.* Action.

Pretend, *vid.* Soul.

Prevent, *vid.* Action.

Price, *vid.* Value in Riches.

Buy in Poffefs.

Primitive, *vid.* Former in Time.

Prince, *vid.* King in Government.

Printed, *vid.* Language and Books.

Prifon, *vid.* Houfe-fort.

Condemn'd in Law.

Privacy, *vid.* Company.

Privateer, *vid.* Sail in Water.

Privities, *vid.* Body.

Proceeding, *vid.* Travel.

Proclamation, *vid.* Difcourfe.

Procurer, *vid.* Servant in Grammar.

Prodigal, *vid.* Riches.

Prodigy, *vid.* Spirits.

Profeffion, *vid.* Trade.

Arts, &c.

Domeftick Action.

Proffer, *vid.* Offer in Poffefs.

Profit, *vid.* Riches.

Promife, *vid.* Difcourfe.

Proper, *vid.* Abfurd in Soul.

Property, *vid.* Riches.

Grammar.

Poffefs.

Self and Another.

Prophet, *vid.* Religion.

Profpect, *vid.* See in Senfe,

Profperous, *vid.* Quality.

Proftrate, *vid.* Pofture.

Protector, *vid.* Tutelar in God, &c.

Proteft, *vid.* Affirm in Difcourfe.

Prothonotary, *vid.* Law.

Provifion, *vid.* Victuals.

Proxy, *vid.* Marriage in Religion.

Prudent, *vid.* Soul.

Pfalm, *vid.* Religion.

Mufick in Arts, &c.

Publick, *vid.* Company.

Puddle, *vid.* Water,

Puff, *vid.* Victuals.

Pull, *vid.* Action.

Apparel.

Pulpit, *vid.* Religion.

Pulfe, *vid.* Victuals.

Bodily Action.

Punifhment, *vid.* Action.

Condemn'd in Law.

Puppet, *vid.* Diverfion.

Purchafe, *vid.* Eftate in Riches.

Purge, *vid.* Phyfick.

Purfe, *vid.* Riches.

Goods.

Purfued, *vid.* Travel.

Pufh, *vid.* Action.

Put, *vid.* Laid in Pofture.

Action.

On, *vid.* Drefs in Apparel.

Q.

Quails, *vid.* Bird.

Quaker, *vid.* Religion.

QUALITIES, QUANTITY.

Quarrel, *vid.* Fight.

Quarter, *vid.* Pofture.

Quarter'd, *vid.* Condemn'd in Law.

Queen, *vid.* King in Government.

Queftion, *vid.* Difcourfe.

Quickly, *vid.* Time.

Quickfand, *vid.* Earth.

Quickfilver, *vid.* Commodity.

Quiet, *vid.* Action.

Quills, *vid.* Birds.

Quinces, *vid.* Vegetables.

R.

Rabbits, *vid.* Beasts.

Rabble, *vid.* Company.

Race, *vid.* Travel.

Racket, *vid.* Buftle in Paffion.

Radish, *vid.* Victuals.

Raging, *vid.* Action.

Railing, *vid.* Difcourfe and Words.

Rain, *vid.* Air.

Rainbow, *vid.* Air.

Raife, *vid.* Rife in Action, Spirit.

Ram, *vid.* Sheep in Beaft.

Rank, *vid.* Feet in Body.

Rape, *vid.* Ravifh in Bodily Action.

Rarities, *vid.* Victuals.

Rafh, *vid.* Paffion.

Rattles, *vid.* Dying in Death.

Rats, *vid.* Beafts.

Raven, *vid.* Bird.

Ravenous, *vid.* Beaft and Bird. Devour *fupra.*

Raving, *vid.* Paffion.

Ravifh, *vid.* Bodily Action.

Raw, *vid.* Victuals.

Rays, *vid.* Spirit.

Rayfins, *vid.* Vegetables.

Razor, *vid.* Barber in Trade.

Reach, *vid.* High in Pofture.

Reading, *vid.* Language.

Ready, *vid.* Quality. Prepar'd in Victuals. In Apparel.

Reap, *vid.* Domeftick Work.

Reafon, *vid.* Soul.

Reafonable, *vid.* Soul. *vid.* Moderate in Quality.

Rebellious, *vid.* Government.

Rebuke, *vid.* Forbid in Words. Chide in Difcourfe.

Receive, *vid.* Poffefs. Welcome in Words. Take in Action.

Reckoning, *vid.* Inn in Houfe-forts.

Reconcil'd, *vid.* Fight.

Reconcil'd, *vid.* Friend, ⎫ in Gram-
Enemy, ⎭ mar.

Recover, *vid.* Handle in Poffeff.

Recreation, *vid.* Diverfion.

Red, *vid.* Colour in Quality. See in Senfe.

Reed, *vid.* Vegetables.

Reeks, *vid.* Corn in Vegetables.

Reenter, *vid.* Born in Bodily Action. Return in Travel.

Refer, *vid.* Law.

Reflection, *vid.* Looking Glafs in Goods. Image in Trade. Jeer in Difcourfe.

Refrain, *vid.* Forbear in Soul.

Refuge, *vid.* Efcape in Travel.

Refufe, *vid.* Difcourfe. Soul.

Regard, *vid.* Neglect in Paffion. Honour in Government.

Reins, *vid.* Body.

Rejoice, *vid.* Joy in Paffion.

Relation, *vid.* Family in Grammar.

R E L I G I O N.

Remedy, *vid.* Phyfick. Help in Action.

Remember, *vid.* Memory in Soul.

Remove, *vid.* Travel.

Rent, *vid.* Riches and Eftate in Earth.

Repair, *vid.* Action. Build.

Repent, *vid.* Paffion.

Reply, *vid.* Words.

Repetition, *vid.* Action. Difcourfe.

Report, *vid.* Difcourfe.

Reprove, *vid.* Rebuke *fupra.*

Repute, *vid.* Paffion.

Require, *vid.* Demand in Words.

Refcue, *vid.* Deliver in Action.

Refift, *vid.* Oppofe in Action.

Refolve, *vid.* Soul.

Refpect,

Respect, *vid.* Honour in Government.

Resting, *vid.* Knees in Body.
   Stay in Time.
   Night in Time.

Restoration, *vid.* Possess.

Resurrection, *vid.* Religion.

Retiring, *vid.* Company.

Retreat, *vid.* Travel.

Return, *vid.* ibid.

Reverence, *vid.* Honour in Government.

Reversion, *vid.* Heir in Family.

Revive, *vid.* Dead.

Rhetorick, *vid.* Arts, &c.

Rhime, *vid.* Poetry in Arts.
   Verse in Words.

Ribbon, *vid.* Ornaments.

Ribs, *vid.* Body.

Rich, *vid.* Ornament.
   Apparel.

R I C H E S.

Ricks, *vid.* Corn.

Ridiculous, *vid.* Soul.

Riding, *vid.* Travel.
   Horse in Beast.
   Hood, *vid.* Apparel.

Right, *vid.* Posture.

Ring, *vid.* Riches.

Ringing, *vid.* Bells in Religion.

Rioters, *vid.* Grammar.

Rise, *vid.* Action.

River, *vid.* Water.

Roasted, *vid.* Victuals.

Robbers,
Robb'd, } *vid.* R. in Grammar.
Robbing,

Robes, *vid.* Apparel.
   Crown in Ornaments.

Rock, *vid.* Earth.

Rod, *vid.* Goods.

Rogues, *vid.* Grammar.

Romance, *vid.* Fable in Literature.
   Books.

Rome, *vid.* City in Habitations.

Roof,
Room, } *vid.* House-parts.

Roots, *vid.* Vegetable.

Roots, *vid.* Victuals.

Ropes, *vid.* Tools.

Roses, *vid.* Vegetables.

Rotten, *vid.* Quality.

Rough, *vid.* Quality.

Round, *vid.* Quality.
   About in Posture.
   Mathematick in Arts,
   &c.

Rowe, *vid.* Order in Soul.

Rub,
Ruffle, } *vid.* Action.
Ruin,

Rude, *vid.* Quality.
   Civil in Passion.

Rug, *vid.* Blanket in Goods.

Rule, *vid.* Tools.

Run, *vid.* Travel.

Rupture, *vid.* Physick.

Rusty, *vid.* Quality.

S.

Sackcloth, *vid.* Apparel.

Sack-Posset, *vid.* Victuals.

Sacrament, *vid.* Religion.

Sacrifice, *vid.* Religion.

Sacrilege, *vid.* Robber in Grammar.

Sad, *vid.* Passion.
   Colour in Sense.

Saddle, *vid.* Horse in Beast.

Safe, *vid.* Quality.

Safron, *vid.* Vegetable.

Sail, *vid.* Ship in Water.

Sails, *vid.* ibid.

Saints, *vid.* Dead.

Sake, *vid.* Self and Another.

Salted, *vid.* Victuals.
   Vegetables.

Salt, *vid.* Victuals.
   Crown in Ornaments.

Saltpeter, *vid.* Sulphur in Commodity.

Salute, *vid.* Discourse.

Sand, *vid.* Earth.

Sap, *vid.* Vegetable.

Saphir, *vid.* Jewel in Riches.

Satyr, *vid.* Beast.

Satis-

Satisfaction, *vid.* Passion.
Satisfied, *vid.* Quality and Words.
Savages, *vid.* Person in Grammar.
Sauce, *vid.* Victuals.
Saucy, *vid.* Discourse.
   Civil in Passion.
Save, *vid.* Preserve in Action.
Saw, *vid.* Tools.
Sailing, *vid.* Water Actions.
Scabby, *vid.* Physick.
Scaffold, *vid.* Building.
Scalding, *vid.* Water Action.
Scales, *vid.* Fish.
   Weight in Commodity.
Scandalize, *vid.* Discourse in Words.
Scandalous, *vid.* Quality.
Scar, *vid.* Wound in Physick.
Scattered, *vid.* Part.
Search, *vid.* Examine in Soul.
Searchers, *vid.* Dead.
Skeleton, *vid.* Dead.
Scepters, *vid.* Ornaments.
Sceptick, *vid.* Doubt in Soul.
Scholers, *vid.* University in City.
School, *vid.* Language.
  Master, *vid.* ibid.
  vid. Grammar.
Scithe, *vid.* Tools.
Scold, *vid.* Discourse in Words.
   Wife in Grammar.
Score, *vid.* Debt in Law.
Scorch, *vid.* Quality.
Scorn, *vid.* Contemn in Passion.
Scorpion, *vid.* Poisonous Creatures.
Scrape, } *vid.* Action.
Scratch, }
Screen, *vid.* Goods.
Scripture, *vid.* Religion.
Scroll, *vid.* Writings in Language.
Scruple, *vid.* Doubt in Soul.
Skullery, *vid.* Kitchin in House-rooms.
Sea, *vid.* Water.
  Fowl, *vid.* Bird.
Seal, *vid.* Ornament.
Seaman, *vid.* Grammar.
Seasonable, *vid.* Time.

Seat, *vid.* Sit in Posture.
Second Sight, *vid.* Divination in Spirit.
Secret, *vid.* Company.
Secure, *vid.* Safe in Quality.
Sedan, *vid* Chariot in Goods.
See, *vid.* Sense.
Seed, *vid.* Vegetable.
Seek, *vid.* Action.
Seeming, *vid.* Sight in Sense.
Seize, *vid.* Action.
Sell, *vid.* Possess.
SELF and ANOTHER.
Self-Murderer, *vid.* M. in Grammar.
Semstress, *vid.* Trade.
SENSE.
Sent, *vid.* Travel.
   Present in Give.
Sentence, *vid.* Discourse.
Separate, *vid.* Sever in Part.
Sepulcher, *vid.* Tomb in Dead.
Serjeant, *vid.* Person in Law.
Sermon, *vid.* Religion.
Serpent, *vid.* Travel.
   Crown in Ornaments.
   Tomb in Dead.
   Poisonous Creatures.
Servant, *vid.* Grammar.
Serve, *vid.* Domestick Action.
Set aside, *vid.* Side in Posture.
Setter, *vid.* Dog in Creature.
Settle, *vid.* Sit in Posture.
Several, *vid.* Part.
Sever, *vid.* Passion.
Sever'd, *vid.* Part.
Sex, *vid.* Creatures in general.
Shadow, *vid.* See in Sense.
   Apparition in Spirit.
Shaking, *vid.* Hear in Sense.
Shallow, *vid.* Deep in Earth.
   Swim in Water.
Shambles, *vid.* Butcher in Trade.
Shame, *vid.* Passion.
Shape, *vid.* Form in Quality.
Sharp, *vid.* Quality.
   Sense.
Sharper, *vid.* Grammar.
Sheaf, *vid.* Corn in Vegetable.
      Shed,

Shed, *vid.* Fall in Action.
Sheep, *vid.* Beast.
Sheering, *vid.* Domestick Acts.
Sheet, *vid.* Goods.
  Winding, *vid.* Dead.
Shield, *vid.* War.
Shelt, *vid.* Goods.
Shelnih, *vid.* Fish.
Sheltred, *vid.* Action.
Sheriff, *vid.* Law.
Shew, *vid.* Sight in Sense. —
Shewing, *vid.* Action.
Shifting, *vid.* Action.
  Apparel.
Shining, *vid.* Quality.
  Appear in Sense.
Ship   ⎫
 -Wreck, ⎬ *vid.* Sail in Water.
    ⎭
Shirt, *vid.* Apparel.
Shite, *vid.* Fart in Bodily Action.
  . Dung in Earth.
Shittlecock, *vid.* Diversion.
Shoomaker, *vid.* Trade.
Shop, *vid.* House-rooms.
Shoos, *vid.* Apparel.
Short, *vid.* Quantity.
Shortly, *vid.* Time.
Shoulders, *vid.* Body.
Shrewd, *vid.* Man in Grammar.
Shrine, *vid.* Tomb in Dead.
Shrowd, *vid.* Dead.
Shutting, *vid.* Action.
  Door in House.
Shy, *vid.* Passion.
Sick, *vid.* Physick.
Side, *vid.* Posture.
Sighing, *vid.* Bodily Action.
Sight, *vid.* Sense.
  Shew in Sight in Sense.
  Diversion.
Sign, *vid.* Stars.
  Token in Language.
  Ornament.
  Habitations and *London.*
Silent, *vid.* Discourse.
Silk, *vid.* Commodity.
  Apparel.
Silkworm, *vid.* Insect.

Silver, *vid.* Riches.
Sing, *vid.* Musick in Arts, &c.
Single, *vid.* Company.
Singular, *vid.* Persons-sorts in
  Grammar.
Sister, *vid.* Family in Grammar.
Sitting, *vid.* Posture.
Skilful, *vid.* Quality.
Skin, *vid.* Body.
  Beast.
  Commodity.
Sky, *vid.* Air.
Slain, *vid.* Kill'd in Dead.
Slander, *vid.* Discourse and Words.
Sleep, *vid.* Bodily Action.
  Words.
Sleep, *vid.* Apparel.
Sliding, *vid.* Action.
Slight, *vid.* Weak in Quality.
Slighting, *vid.* Passion.
Slipper, *vid.* Apparel.
Slow, *vid.* Quality.
Slut, *vid.* Grammar.
Small, *vid.* Little in Quantity.
Smallage, *vid.* Victuals.
Smartly, *vid.* Quality.
Smell, *vid.* Sense.
Smile, *vid.* Look in Sight in Sense.
Smith, *vid.* Trade.
Smock, *vid.* Apparel.
Smoke, *vid.* Fire.
Smoothness, *vid.* Quality.
Smother, *vid.* Dying in Dead.
Snake, *vid.* Poisonous Creatures.
Snap up, *vid.* Interrupt in Action.
Snatch, *vid.* Take in Possess.
Sneaking, *vid.* Passion.
  Mean in Quality.
Sneering, *vid.* Contemn in Passion.
Sneezing, ⎫
Snorting, ⎬ *vid.* Bodily Action.
Snot, *vid.* Nose in Body.
  Blow in Action.
Snow, *vid.* Frost.
Sober, *vid.* Passion.
Society, *vid.* Company.
Sock, *vid.* Apparel.
Soft, *vid.* Quality.

       Sold,

Sold, *vid.* Poffefs.
Soles, *vid.* Victuals.
Soliciting, *vid.* Company.
Solitude, *vid.* Company.
Somewhat, *vid.* Uncertain in Soul.
Son, *vid.* Grammar.
Song, *vid.* Words.
      Mufick in Arts, &c.
Soon, *vid.* Quickly in Time.
Soot, *vid.* Chimny in Houfe-parts.
Sophifticate, *vid.* Counterfeit in Quality.
Sorely, *vid.* Grievoufly in Paffion.
Sores, *vid.* Phyfick.
Sorry, *vid.* Grief in Paffion.
Sort, *vid.* Variety in Quality.
S O U L
Souldier, *vid.* War.
Sound, *vid.* Hear in Senfe.
      Quality.
South, *vid.* Travel.
      Pofture.
Sowing, *vid.* Apparel.
      Semftrefs in Trade.
      Shoomaker, *ibid.*
      Domeftick Action.
Sour, *vid.* Quality.
Spaying, *vid.* Cut in Action.
Spaniel, *vid.* Dog in Beaft.
Sparrow, *vid.* Bird.
Speak, *vid.* Difcourfe.
Speckled, *vid.* Divers colour'd in Senfe.
Spectacles, *vid.* Goods.
Speer, *vid.* War.
Spew, *vid.* Drunk.
Spice, *vid.* Victuals.
Spider, *vid.* Poifonous Creatures.
Spill, *vid.* Water.
      Fall in Action.
Spinning, *vid.* Domeftick Action.
S P I R I T S.
Spitting, *vid.* Bodily Action.
Spleen, *vid.* Body.
Sports, *vid.* Diverfion.
Spotty, *vid.* Quality.
Spoil, *vid.* Action.
      Wafte, *ibid.*

Spread, *vid.* Quantity.
Spunger, *vid.* Grammar.
Spur, *vid.* Action.
Squint-ey'd, *vid.* Eye in Phyfick.
      Eye in Body.
Squirrel, *vid.* Beaft.
Stab, *vid.* Sword in War.
      Wound in Phyfick.
Stable, *vid.* Houfe-range.
Staff, *vid.* Staves in Goods.
Stag, *vid.* Victuals.
      Beaft.
      Hunt in Diverfion.
Staying, *vid.* Staying *infra.*
Stairs, *vid.* Houfe-parts.
Standing, *vid.* Pofture.
Staring, *vid.* Hairs in Body.
S T A R S.
Starting, *vid.* Bodily Action.
State, *vid.* Quality.
Stately, *vid.* Ornament.
      Quality.
Statue, *vid.* Trade.
Stature, *vid.* Tall in Quality.
      Quantity.
Staves, *vid.* Goods.
Stay, *vid.* Time.
      Stop in Travel.
Stead, *vid.* Place.
Steddy, *vid.* Pofture.
Steal, *vid.* Poffefs.
      Robber in Grammar.
Steep, *vid.* Place in Earth.
      Precipice and Hole *ibid.*
Stepping, *vid.* Action.
Stern, *vid.* Severe in Paffion.
Steward, *vid.* Servant in Grammar.
Stick, *vid.* Goods.
Stiff, *vid.* Quality.
Stifled, *vid.* Smother'd in Dead.
Stiles, *vid.* Fence in Earth.
Stilling, *vid.* Action.
Sting, *vid.* Snake in Poifonous Creatures.
      Bees in Infects.
Stinking, *vid.* Smell in Senfe.
Stock'd, *vid.* Travel.

Stockin, *vid.* Apparel.
Stomach, *vid.* Body.
Stones, *vid.* Earth.
  Jewels in Riches.
  Physick and Privities
  in Body.
Stool, *vid.* Chair in Goods.
  Sit in Posture.
Stop'd, *vid.* Action.
  Way in Travel.
Store, *vid.* Quantity.
Stork, *vid.* Bird.
Storms, *vid.* Air.
Story, *vid.* Discourse.
Stout, *vid.* Quality.
Strange, *vid.* Place in Earth.
  Soul.
  Unknown in Grammar.
Strangled, *vid.* Dead.
  Condemn in Law.
Strawberry, *vid.* Vegetable.
Street, *vid.* Habitation.
Streight, *vid.* Quality.
Strengthen, *vid.* Action.
  Strong in Quality.
Stride, *vid.* Step in Action.
Strike, *vid.* Hurt in Action.
  Fight.
  Thunder in Air.
String, *vid.* Musick in Arts.
  Ropes in Commodities.
Stripes, *vid.* Fight.
Strive, *vid.* Struggle in Action.
  Fight.
Stroke, *vid.* Action.
Strong, *vid.* Quality.
  Waters, *vid.* Drink.
Strugle, *vid.* Action.
  Fight.
Strutting, *vid.* Posture.
Stubborn, *vid.* Correct in Fight.
  vid. Person in Grammar.
Student, *vid.* University in Habitation.
Studying, *ibid.*
Stuff, *vid.* Goods.
Stumbling, *vid.* Quality.

Sturdy, *vid.* Stout in Quality.
Successful, *vid.* Trade.
Successor, *vid.* Former in Time.
  Grammar.
Suffer, *vid.* Hurt in Action.
Sugar, *vid.* Victuals.
Suit, *vid.* Law.
Suiting, *vid.* Like in Sight in Sense.
Sulphur, *vid.* Commodity.
Summer, *vid.* Time.
Sums, *vid.* Mony in Riches.
Summon, *vid.* Send in Travel.
  Discourse in Words.
Sun, *vid.* Stars.
Sup, *vid.* Victuals.
  Eat in Bodily Action.
Superfluity, *vid.* Quantity.
Support, *vid.* Ability in Quality.
  Carry in Travel.
Surprize, *vid.* Passion.
Surrender, *vid.* Possess.
Surround, *vid.* Company.
  vid. Incompass in Posture.
Suspence, *vid.* Expectation in Soul.
Swallow, *vid.* Bird.
Swan, *vid.* Bird.
Swarm, *vid.* Many in Quantity.
  Flies in Insects.
Swarthy, *vid.* Face in Body.
Swear, *vid.* Words.
Sweat, *vid.* Bodily Action.
Sweep, *vid.* Domestick Action.
Sweet, *vid.* Taste in Sense.
  Meat, *vid.* ibid.
  Victuals.
  Heart, *vid.* Lover in Grammar.
Swell'd, *vid.* Physick.
Swiftly, *vid.* Quality.
Swimming, *vid.* Water.
Sword, *vid.* War.

T.

Tables, *vid.* Goods.
  Diversion.
Tail, *vid.* Beast.
Take, *vid.* Possess.
  Snatch in Apparel.
  Esteem in Government.
Q o   Talk,

Talk, *vid.* Difcourfe.
Tall, *vid.* High in Quantity.
Tame, *vid.* Beaft.
Tanner, *vid.* Trade.
Tapeftry, *vid.* Goods.
Tafte, *vid.* Senfe.
Tavern, *vid.* Travel.
  Houfe-forts.
Tax, *vid.* Government.
Teach, *vid.* Literature.
Teaboxes, *vid.* Goods.
Tear, *vid.* Action.
Teafe, *vid.* Vex in Paffion.
Teeth, *vid.* Body.
Tell, *vid.* Acquaint in Words.
  Report in Words.
Tempeft, *vid.* Air.
Temple, *vid.* Religion.
  Body.
  Lawyer.
Tempted, *vid.* Religion.
Tenant, *vid.* Grammar.
  Eftate in Earth.
  Domeftick Action.
Tennis, *vid.* Ball in Diverfion.
Terrible, *vid.* Fear in Paffion.
  Fright in Beaft.
  Threaten in Words.
Terrify, *vid.* Action.
Thanks, *vid.* Words.
Thankfgiving, *vid.* Religion.
Thatch, *vid.* Houfe-fort.
Thieves, *vid.* Grammar.
  Steal in Poffefs.
Thick, *vid.* Quantity.
Thigh, *vid.* Body.
Thin, *vid.* Quantity.
Things, *vid.* Change in Senfe.
  Infenfibles in Action.
Thinking, *vid.* Soul.
Thirft, *vid.* Drink.
Thiftle, *vid.* Vegetable.
Thorn, *vid.* Tree.
Thought, *vid.* Soul.
Thoroffare, *vid.* Travel.
Thred, *vid.* Commodity.
Threaten, *vid.* Difcourfe.
  Hurt in Action.

Thrive, *vid.* Poffefs.
Throat, *vid.* Body.
Throne, *vid.* King in Government.
Throng'd, *vid.* Thruft infra.
Thruft, *vid.* Againft in Pofture.
  Pufh in Action.
Thro, *vid.* Place in Earth.
  Place in Travel.
Throw, *vid.* Fling in Action.
Thunder, *vid.* Air.
Tickets, *vid.* Token in Difcourfe.
  Play in Diverfion.
Tickling, *vid.* Bodily Action.
Tied, *vid.* Bound in Action.
Tiles, *vid.* Top in Houfe-parts.
Tiger, *vid.* Beaft.
Timber, *vid.* Trees.
TIME.
Tired, *vid.* Quality.
Tythes, *vid.* Religion.
To, *vid.* Travel.
  Aim in War.
Toad, *vid.* Poifonous Creatures.
Tobacco, *vid.* Vegetable.
  Stopper, *vid.* Goods.
  Pipe, *vid.* ibid.
Toes, *vid.* Body.
Token, *vid.* Ticket *fupra.*
  Language.
Tolerable, *vid.* Good in Quality.
Told, *vid.* Report in Difcourfe.
Tomb, *vid.* Dead.
Tongue, *vid.* Body.
TOOLS and *COMMODITIES.*
Toothdrawer, *vid.* Trade.
Top, *vid.* Diverfion.
  Part.
  Houfe-parts.
Torches, *vid.* Fire.
Torment, *vid.* Action.
Torn, *vid.* Tear in Action.
Touching, *vid.* Senfe.
Towards, *vid.* Pofture.
  Travel.
Tower, *vid.* Religion.
Town, *vid.* Habitation.
  Clark, *vid.* Officer in Government.
        TRADE.

TRADE.
Tragedy, *vid.* Play in Diverſion.
Trample, *vid.* Tread in Action.
Tranſcribe, *vid.* Write in Litera-
ture.
Tranſparent, *vid.* Quality.
Traps, *vid.* Nets in Diverſion.
TRAVEL.
Treading, *vid.* Action.
Treaſure, *vid.* Riches.
Treated, *vid.* Victuals.
       Feaſt in Diverſion.
TREES.
Trembling, *vid.* Bodily Action.
Treſſel, *vid.* Goods.
Trial, *vid.* Law.
       Stone in Earth.
Trick, *vid.* Diverſion.
       Sharper in Grammar.
Trifle, *vid.* Diverſion.
Troops, *vid.* Souldiers in War.
Trouble, *vid.* Quality.
       Paſſion.
       Tempeſt in Air.
Trumpets, *vid.* Muſick in Arts,
    &c.
Trunk, *vid.* Goods.
Truſt, *vid.* Credit in Trade.
       God in Spirit.
Truth, *vid.* Soul.
Trying, *vid.* Action.
Tub, *vid.* Goods.
Tumbled, *vid.* Action.
Turbant, *vid.* Ornament.
Turf, *vid.* Field in Earth.
Turk, *vid.* Earth.
Turn, *vid.* Action.
       Travel.
       Side in Poſture.
Turner, *vid.* Trade.
Turtle, *vid.* Bird.
Tutelar, *vid.* Perſon and God.
Tutor, *vid.* Literature.
Twice, ⎱ *vid.* Numbers.
Two, ⎰
Tired, *vid.* Quality.
Tie, *vid.* Thred in Commodity.

V.
Vail, *vid.* Cover in Act.
Vain, *vid.* Quality.
Vain Glory, *vid.* Paſſion.
Vale, *vid.* Earth.
Valiant, *vid.* Courageous in Paſ-
ſion.
Value, *vid.* Riches.
Vaniſh, *vid.* Appear in Senſe.
Vanquiſh, *vid.* Overcome in Fight
and in Death.
Various, *vid.* Divers in Quality.
       Colour in Senſe.
Vault, *vid.* Cave in Earth.
       Cellar in Houſe-rooms.
Vear, *vid.* Beaſt.
VEGETABLES.
Veins, *vid.* Body.
View, *vid.* Proſpect in Senſe.
       See in Senſe.
Velvet, *vid.* Apparel.
Veniſon, *vid.* Victual.
Venture, *vid.* Action.
       Bold in Paſſion.
Vermin, *vid.* Creatures.
Verſes, *vid.* Literature.
       Words.
Veſſels, *vid.* Goods.
Vexing, *vid.* Paſſion.
Ugly, *vid.* Fair in Quality.
Vials, *vid.* Veſſels in Goods.
Vice, *vid.* Virtue in Religion.
Victory, *vid.* Fight.
VICTUALS.
Village, *vid.* Habitation.
Vine, *vid.* Tree.
Vinegar, *vid.* Victuals.
Vintner, *vid.* Habitation.
       Tavern in Houſe-
       ſort.
Violent, *vid.* Action.
Violet, *vid.* Vegetable.
       Crown in Ornament.
Vipers, *vid.* Victuals.
       Creatures.
Virtue, *vid.* Religion.
Viſible, *vid.* Appear in Senſe.

Visions, *vid.* Apparitions in Spirits.
Visit, *vid.* Company.
Ulcer, *vid.* Physick.
Unaccustomed, *vid.* Unusual infra.
Uncertain, *vid.* Soul.
Uncle, *vid.* Grammar.
Unclothe, *vid.* Apparel.
Undecent, *vid.* Soul.
Under, *vid.* Posture.
　　Tread in Action.
Understanding, *vid.* Soul.
Under-Treasurer, *vid.* Temple in Law.
Undo, *vid.* Hurt in Action.
Undress, *vid.* Dress in Apparel.
Uneven, *vid.* Quality.
　　Equal in Quantity.
Unexpected, *vid.* Expected in Soul.
Unfurnished, *vid.* Goods.
　　House-state.
Ungovernable, *vid.* Government.
United, *vid.* Conspiracy in Company.
Universal, *vid.* Flood in Water.
　　General in Quantity.
University, *vid.* London.
Unjust, *vid.* Just in Religion.
Unkind, *vid.* Cross in Passion.
Unknown, *vid.* Grammar.
　　Discourse.
　　Soul.
Unmarried, *vid.* Married in Religion.
Unnatural, *vid.* Absurd in Soul.
Unnecessary, *vid.* Necessary in Action.
　　Use in Action.
Unpleasant, *vid.* Pleasant in Diversion.
　　Looks in Sense.
Unprofitable, *vid.* Profitable in Riches.
Unreasonable, *vid.* Soul.
Unruly, *vid.* Office in Government.

Unsatisfied, *vid.* Satisfied in Quality.
Unseasonable, *vid.* Time.
Unseen, *vid.* Sense.
　　Discourse.
Unsettled, *vid.* Quality.
Until, *vid.* Wait in Company.
Unto, *vid.* Travel.
　　Aim in War.
Untoward, *vid.* Aukward in Quality.
Unusual, *vid.* Quality.
Unwilling, *vid.* Soul.
Voice, *vid.* Hear in Sense.
Vomit, *vid.* Physick.
Upon, *vid.* Posture.
　　Travel.
　　Over *supra.*
Uppingstock, *vid.* House-range.
Upright, *vid.* Posture.
Urin, *vid.* Piss in Bodily Action.
　　Beast.
Use, *vid.* Sword in War.
Useful, *vid.* Action.
　　Quality.
Vulture, *vid.* Bird.

W.
Wager, *vid.* Diversion.
Waggon, *vid.* Cart in Goods.
Wainscot, *vid.* House-parts.
Wait, *vid.* Time.
　　Company.
Waking, *vid.* Bodily Action.
Walk, *vid.* Travel.
Wall, *vid.* House-parts.
Walnut, *vid.* Tree.
　　Vegetable.
Wandring, *vid.* Travel.
Wanting, *vid.* Passion.
Wardrobe, *vid.* Apparel.
Warm, *vid.* Cold in Sense.
WAR.
Wary, *vid.* Cautious in Soul.
Washing, *vid.* Water.
Wasps, *vid.* Insects.
Wastecoat, *vid.* Apparel.
Waste, *vid.* Action.
　　　　　　Watch,

Watch, *vid.* Goods.
  -Death, *vid.* D. in Dead.
Watching, *vid.* Action.
    Passion.

WATER.
Waves, *vid.* Sea in Water.
Wax, *vid.* Commodity.
Way, *vid.* Travel.
Weakness, *vid.* Quality.
Weapon, *vid.* War.
Wearing, } *vid.* Quality.
Weary, }
Weather, *vid.* Air.
    Glass, *vid.* Goods.
Weaver, *vid.* Trade.
Weed, *vid.* Vegetable.
Weep, *vid.* Passion.
Weesel, *vid.* Beast.
Weight, *vid.* Heavy in Sense.
    Tools in Trade.
Welcome, *vid.* Words.
    Accept in Soul.
Well, *vid.* Water.
    Quality.
West, *vid.* Sun in Stars.
    Posture.
    Travel.
Wheat, *vid.* Vegetable.
Wheel, *vid.* Tool.
Whelp, *vid.* Beast.
Whip, *vid.* Fight.
    Arse in Body.
    Condemn in Law.
    Diversion.
Whirlpool, *vid.* Water.
    Wind, *vid.* Air.
Whisper, *vid.* Discourse and Words.
White, *vid.* Sight in Sense.
Whole, *vid.* Part.
Whore, *vid.* Grammar.
Wisdom, *vid.* Soul.
Wide, *vid.* Mouth in Body.
    Quantity.
Wife, *vid.* Grammar.
Wig, *vid.* Apparel.
    Hair in Body.
Wild, *vid.* Quality.

Wilderness, *vid.* Earth.
Will, *vid.* Law.
    Soul.
Willing, *vid.* Soul.
Win, *vid.* Play in Diversion.
Wincing, *vid.* Quality.
    Horse in Beast.
Wind, *vid.* Air.
Winding Sheet, *vid.* Dead.
Window, *vid.* Church.
    House-parts.
Wine, *vid.* Drink.
Wings, *vid.* Birds.
Winking, *vid.* Bodily Action.
Wipe, *vid.* Clean in Quality.
Wise, *vid.* Soul.
Wish, *vid.* Desire in Passion.
Witchcraft, *vid.* Spirit.
With, *vid.* Company.
    Want in Passion.
Withered, *vid.* Quality.
Within, *vid.* Posture.
Withy, *vid.* Tree.
Witness, *vid.* Law.
Wolf, *vid.* Beast.
Woman, *vid.* Grammar.
Womb, *vid.* Body.
Wonder, *vid.* Admire in Passion.
    Words.

WOOD.
Woods, *vid.* Estate.
Wool, *vid.* Apparel.
    Sheep in Beast.
    Commodity.

WORDS.
Work, *vid.* Action.
    Trade.
    Domestick Action.
World, *vid.* Earth.
Worm, *vid.* Insect.
Wormwood, *vid.* Vegetable.
    Drink.
Worn, *vid.* Wear in Quality.
Worship, *vid.* Religion.
Worst, *vid.* Good in Quality.
Would, *vid.* Soul.
    Desire in Passion.

Wound,

Wound, *vid.* Physick. Fight.

Wren, *vid.* Bird.

Wrestle, *vid.* Fight.

Wrinkled, *vid.* Quality.

Writing, *vid.* Language.

Writings, *vid.* Deed in Law.

Wrong, *vid.* Law.

Yarn, *vid.* Thred in Commodities.

Yawning, *vid.* Bodily Action.

Yellow, *vid.* See in Sense.

Yoke, *vid.* Oxen in Domestick Action.

Young, *vid.* Age in Time.

Years, *vid.* Time.

Y.
Yard, *vid.* Backside in House-range.

Z.
Zeal, *vid.* Religion and Passion.

A

A Table of Chapters.

		Page				Page
1.	Of Spirits,	1.	Chap.	32.	Of Sense,	226.
2.	Of Death Literal,	10.		33.	Of Bodily Action,	241.
3.	Of Death Allegorical,	16.		34.	Of Posture,	253.
4.	Of the Sun and Stars,	31.		35.	Of the Soul,	268.
5.	Of Heaven and Air,	36.		36.	Of Company,	274.
6.	Of the Fire,	46.		37.	Of Company Number,	279.
7.	Of Frost and Snow, &c.	54.		38.	Of Self,	285.
8.	Of Water Actions,	55.		39.	Of Another,	287.
9.	Of Water,	61.		40.	Of Possession,	290.
10.	Of the Earth,	68.		41.	Of Riches,	302.
11.	Of Country and Place, &c.	75.		42.	Of Ornaments,	307.
12.	Of Building and Bridges,	89.		43.	Of Apparel,	313.
13.	Of House-parts,	90.		44.	Of Apparel-sorts,	320.
14.	Of House-rooms,	95.		45.	Of Goods,	325.
15.	Of Out-houses and House-ranges,	102.		46.	Of Drink,	337.
16.	Of House-state and Occurrences,	105.		47.	Of Victuals,	341.
17.	Of House-sorts,	110.		48.	Of Passion,	350.
18.	Of Habitations,	114.		49.	Of Action,	362.
19.	Of Cities,	118.		50.	Of Diversion,	387.
20.	Of London and the Universities,	123.		51.	Of Travel,	394.
21.	Of Qualities.	131.		52.	Of Travel-Actions,	395.
22.	Of Vegetables,	141.		53.	Of Words-sorts,	416.
23.	Of Wood and Trees,	149.		54.	Of Discourse,	429.
24.	Of Creatures in general,	155.		55.	Of Language,	433.
25.	Of Insects,	158.		56.	Of Books,	439.
26.	Of Poisonous Creatures.	161.		57.	Of Arts and Sciences,	444.
27.	Of Beasts in general,	164.		58.	Of Religion,	448.
28.	Of Beasts-sorts,	170.		59.	Of Physick,	453.
29.	Of Birds,	185.		60.	Of Quantity,	471.
30.	Of Fish,	196.		61.	Of Part,	475.
31.	Of Human Body,	199.		62.	Of Numbers,	479.
				63.	Of Time,	484.
				64.	Of Government,	490.
				65.	Of Law,	498.
				66.	Of War,	507.
				67.	Of Fighting,	512.
				68.	Of Trade,	518.
				69.	Of Tools and Commodities,	525.
				70.	Of Domestick Actions,	529.

FINIS.

ERRATA.

N. B. *Where there is a b with the Figure of the Line, it de-
notes that Line to be reckon'd from the Bottom.*

Pag. Line.

7. 32. dele *Comma,* and r. *there.*
8. 31. r. *Beguilers and Imposers.*
21. 20. r. *away.*
14. 36. r. *recoverable.*
   3.b. r. *Flag.*
15. 5.b. then r. *there.*
22. 8.b. dead r. *wicked.*
28. 9.b. r. *in a Coffee-house.*
38. 1. r. *going out in, return'd back
   on Ice.*
45. 12.b. r. *burning.*
46. 9. *you* r. *them.*
   10.b. *on* r. *an.*
62. ult. *loss* r. *less*
63. 27. *or* r. *an.*
64. 7.b. r. *Henge.*
75. 6. r. *Rose.*
82. 10. r. *were.*
98. 14. *is,* r. *ill*
100. 8. r. *Study.*
103. 10. *Sun,* r. *seen.*
108. 15. b.r. *Row.*
110. 14. r. *but then withal.*
113. 8.b. r. *meaner.*
127. 22. dele *Sick there,* r. *Silk.*
128. 5. b.*Carnal,* r. *Casual.*
129. 7.b. *two,* r. *unto.*
130. 16. r. *Terers.*
   7. b.r. *unknown Person.*
134. 16. r. *his Barns door.*
144. 10.b. r. *Rental.*
152. 2.b. r. *but.*
172. 26. *Ox,* r. *or.*
181. 14. r. *Charge.*
182. 11. r. *Shipwreck.*
187. 8.b.r. *broken seen, &c.*
193. 21. r. *Hiero's.*
195. 4. *Store,* r. *Stare.*
223. 10. r. *his Sons being drown'd.*
   12. *as,* r. *as.*
237. 17. r. *unknown.*
   25. *Death,* r. *Debt.*
240. 22. *in,* r. *and.*
242. r. dele *A's Finger.*

247. 18.b. *C——n,* r. *Cousin.*
250. 27. r. *Trouble and Anguish.*
258. 15.b. *Stick,* r. *Sick.*
259. 1. dele *an Entry.*
   28. r. *Fleet-street.*
277. 30. r. *Cousin.*
290. 1. dele *you're.*
320. 10.b. r. *shew'd ; Reproof, r.
   Repute,*
325. 4. r. *Disorder.*
334. 2. r. *Pillow.*
358. 19. r. *like dangerous State.*
364. 7.b. *Joy,* r. *Ivy.*
365. 15. r. *theirs.*
401. 1. r. *the Devil.*
404. 9. r. *poor and weak good.*
406. 11. r. *her Death.*
411. 7. *Master,* r. *Mistress.*
412. ult. *out,* r. *on it.*
422. 1. r. *demanded.*
   ult. r. *flatter.*
423. 8.b. r. *proceeds on.*
431. 4.b. r. *and so will.*
434. 27. *her,* r. *his.*
440. 7.b. r. *to an Author.*
445. 27. r. *strutting.*
461. 28. *more,* r. *Mony.*
468. 24. r. *in Folly.*
481. ult. *new,* r. *now.*
482. 12. r. *handling them.*
483. 5.b. r. *Square of 7 by 4.*
484. 13, 14. r. *Tears, as &c.*
497. 11. r. *Actions and Magistracy.*
498. 19. *Aim,* r. *him.*
502. 19 *him,* r. *hire.*
   ult. r. *a known.*
505. 20. *Disgrace,* r. *distress'd.*
532. 13.b. *sipping,* r. *stilling.*
   12.b. r. *fathom'd.*
542. 6.b. *follow,* r. *fallow.*
544. 7.b. *hurt,* r. *hunt.*
558. 15.b. *sever,* r. *severe.*
559. 17. *Sleep,* r. *Sleeve.*
560. r. *Stilling, v. Domestick Action.*

5

ritions
ingular, expect
a by all, is no h

RETURN TO: **CIRCULATION DEPARTMENT**
198 Main Stacks

LOAN PERIOD 1 Home Use	2	3
4	5	6

ALL BOOKS MAY BE RECALLED AFTER 7 DAYS.
Renewals and Recharges may be made 4 days prior to the due date.
Books may be renewed by calling 642-3405.

DUE AS STAMPED BELOW.

APR 1 1 2002		

FORM NO. DD6
50M   6-00

UNIVERSITY OF CALIFORNIA, BERKELEY
Berkeley, California 94720–6000

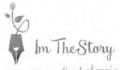